Wash D1083886

Investment Philosophies

Founded in 1807, John Wiley & Sons is the oldest independent publishing company in the United States. With offices in North America, Europe, Australia, and Asia, Wiley is globally committed to developing and marketing print and electronic products and services for our customers' professional and personal knowledge and understanding.

The Wiley Finance series contains books written specifically for finance and investment professionals as well as sophisticated individual investors and their financial advisors. Book topics range from portfolio management to e-commerce, risk management, financial engineering, valuation, and financial instrument analysis, as well as much more.

For a list of available titles, visit our Web site at www.WileyFinance.com.

Investment Philosophies

Successful Strategies and the Investors Who Made Them Work

Second Edition

ASWATH DAMODARAN
www.damodaran.com

John Wiley & Sons, Inc.

Published by John Wiley & Sons, Inc., Hoboken, New Jersey.
First Edition Copyright © 2003 by John Wiley & Sons, Inc. All rights reserved.
Published simultaneously in Canada.

For general information on our other products and services or for technical support, please contact our Customer Care Department within the United States at (800) 762-2974, outside the United States at (317) 572-3993 or fax (317) 572-4002.

Wiley also publishes its books in a variety of electronic formats. Some content that appears in print may not be available in electronic books. For more information about Wiley products, visit our web site at www.wiley.com.

Library of Congress Cataloging-in-Publication Data:

Damodaran, Aswath.
  Investment philosophies : successful strategies and the investors who made them work / Aswath Damodaran.—2nd ed.
    p. cm.—(Wiley finance series)
  Includes index.
  ISBN 978-1-118-01151-5 (cloth); ISBN 978-1-118-22192-1 (ebk);
  ISBN 978-1-118-23561-4 (ebk); ISBN 978-1-118-26049-4 (ebk)
  1. Investment analysis. I. Title.
  HG4529.D36 2012
  332.6—dc23

                                                        2012005823

Printed in the United States of America.

10 9 8 7 6 5 4 3 2 1

Contents

Investment Philosophies

CHAPTER 1

Introduction

Who wants to be an average investor? We all dream of beating the market and being super investors, and we spend an inordinate amount of time and resources in this endeavor. Consequently, we are easy prey for the magic bullets and the secret formulas offered by salespeople pushing their wares. In spite of our best efforts, though, most of us fail in our attempts to be more than average. Nonetheless, we keep trying, hoping that we can be more like the investing legends—another Warren Buffett, George Soros, or Peter Lynch. We read the words written by and about successful investors, hoping to find in them the key to their stock-picking abilities, so that we can replicate them and become like them.

In our search, though, we are whipsawed by contradictions and anomalies. On one corner of the investment town square stands an adviser, yelling to us to buy businesses with solid cash flows and liquid assets because that's what worked for Buffett. On another corner, another investment expert cautions us that this approach worked only in the old world, and that in the new world of technology we have to bet on companies with great growth prospects. On yet another corner stands a silver-tongued salesperson with vivid charts who presents you with evidence of the charts' capacity to get you in and out of markets at exactly the right times. It is not surprising that facing this cacophony of claims and counterclaims we end up more confused than ever.

In this chapter, we present the argument that to be successful with any investment strategy, you have to begin with an investment philosophy that is consistent at its core and matches not only the markets you choose to invest in but your individual characteristics. In other words, the key to success in investing may lie not in knowing what makes others successful but in finding out more about yourself.

WHAT IS AN INVESTMENT PHILOSOPHY?

An investment philosophy is a coherent way of thinking about markets, how they work (and sometimes do not), and the types of mistakes that you believe consistently underlie investor behavior. Why do we need to make assumptions about investor mistakes? As we will argue, most investment strategies are designed to take advantage of errors made by some or all investors in pricing stocks. Those mistakes themselves are driven by far more basic assumptions about human behavior. To provide an illustration, the rational or irrational tendency of human beings to join crowds can result in price momentum: stocks that have gone up the most in the recent past are more likely to go up in the near future. Let us consider, therefore, the ingredients of an investment philosophy.

Human Frailty

Underlying every investment philosophy is a view about human behavior. In fact, one weakness of conventional finance and valuation has been the short shrift given to behavioral quirks. It is not that conventional financial theory assumes that all investors are rational, but that it assumes that irrationalities are random and cancel out. Thus, for every investor who tends to follow the crowd too much (a momentum investor), we assume there is an investor who goes in the opposite direction (a contrarian), and that their push and pull in prices will ultimately result in a rational price. While this may, in fact, be a reasonable assumption for the very long term, it may not be a realistic one for the short term.

Academics and practitioners in finance who have long viewed the rational investor assumption with skepticism have developed a branch of finance called behavioral finance that draws on psychology, sociology, and finance to try to explain both why investors behave the way they do and the consequences for investment strategies. As we go through this book, examining different investment philosophies, we will try at the outset of each philosophy to explore the assumptions about human behavior that represent its base.

Market Efficiency

A closely related second ingredient of an investment philosophy is the view of market efficiency or inefficiency that you need for the philosophy to be a successful one. While all active investment philosophies make the assumption that markets are inefficient, they differ in their views on what parts of the market the inefficiencies are most likely to show up in and how long they will last. Some investment philosophies assume that markets are correct most of the time but that they overreact when new and large pieces of information are released about individual firms: they go up too much on good news and down too much on bad news. Other investment strategies are founded on the belief that markets can make mistakes in the aggregate—the entire market can be undervalued or overvalued—and that some investors (mutual fund managers, for example) are more likely to make these mistakes than others. Still other investment strategies may be based on the assumption that while markets do a good job of pricing stocks where there is a substantial amount of information—financial statements, analyst reports, and financial press coverage—they systematically misprice stocks on which such information is not available.

Tactics and Strategies

Once you have an investment philosophy in place, you develop investment strategies that build on the core philosophy. Consider, for instance, the views on market efficiency expounded in the previous section. The first investor, who believes that markets overreact to news, may develop a strategy of buying stocks after large negative earnings surprises (where the announced earnings come in well below expectations) and selling stocks after positive earnings surprises. The second investor, who believes that markets make mistakes in the aggregate, may look at technical indicators (such as cash held by mutual funds or short selling by investors in the stock) to find out whether the market is overbought or oversold and take a contrary position. The third investor, who believes that market mistakes are more likely when information is absent, may look for stocks that are not followed by analysts or owned by institutional investors.

It is worth noting that the same investment philosophy can spawn multiple investment strategies. Thus, a belief that investors consistently overestimate the value of growth and underestimate the value of existing assets can manifest itself in a number of different strategies ranging from a passive one of buying low price-earnings (P/E) ratio stocks to a more active one of buying cheap companies and attempting to liquidate them for their assets. In other words, the number of investment strategies will vastly surpass the number of investment philosophies.

WHY DO YOU NEED AN INVESTMENT PHILOSOPHY?

Most investors have no investment philosophy, and the same can be said about many money managers and professional investment advisers. They adopt investment strategies that seem to work (for other investors) and abandon them when they do not. Why, you might ask, if this is possible, do you need an investment philosophy? The answer is simple. In the absence of an investment philosophy, you will tend to shift from strategy to strategy simply based on a strong sales pitch from a proponent or perceived recent success. There are three negative consequences for your portfolio:

1. Lacking a rudder or a core set of beliefs, you will be easy prey for charlatans and pretenders, with each one claiming to have found the magic strategy that beats the market.
2. As you switch from strategy to strategy, you will have to change your portfolio, resulting in high transaction costs, and you will pay more in taxes.
3. While there may be strategies that do work for some investors, they may not be appropriate for you, given your objectives, risk aversion, and personal characteristics. In addition to having a portfolio that underperforms the market, you are likely to find yourself with an ulcer or worse.

With a strong sense of core beliefs, you will have far more control over your destiny. Not only will you be able to reject strategies that do not fit your core beliefs about markets, but you will also be able to tailor investment strategies to your needs. In addition, you will be able to get much more of a big picture view of both what it is that is truly different across strategies and what they have in common.

THE BIG PICTURE OF INVESTING

To see where the different investment philosophies fit into investing, let us begin by looking at the process of creating an investment portfolio. Note that this is a process that we all follow—amateur as well as professional investors—though it may be simpler for an individual constructing his or her own portfolio than it is for a pension fund manager with a varied and demanding clientele.

Step 1: Understanding the Client

The process always starts with the investor and understanding his or her needs and preferences. For a portfolio manager, the investor is a client, and the first and often most significant part of the investment process is understanding the client's needs, the client's tax status, and, most importantly, the client's risk preferences. For an individual investor constructing his or her own portfolio, this may seem simpler, but understanding one's own needs and preferences is just as important a first step as it is for the portfolio manager.

Step 2: Portfolio Construction

The next part of the process is the actual construction of the portfolio, which we divide into three subparts.

The first of these is the decision on how to allocate the portfolio across different asset classes, defined broadly as equities, fixed income securities, and real assets (such as real estate, commodities, and other assets). This *asset allocation decision* can also be framed in terms of investments in domestic assets versus foreign assets, and the factors driving this decision.

The second component is the *asset selection decision*, where individual assets are chosen within each asset class to make up the portfolio. In practical terms, this is the step where the stocks that make up the equity component, the bonds that make up the fixed income component, and the real assets that make up the real asset component are selected.

The final component is *execution*, where the portfolio is actually put together. Here investors must weigh the costs of trading against their perceived needs to trade quickly. While the importance of execution will vary across investment strategies, there are many investors who fail at this stage in the process.

Step 3: Evaluate Portfolio Performance

The final part of the process, and often the most painful one for professional money managers, is performance evaluation. Investing is, after all, focused on one objective and one objective alone, which is to make the most money you can, given your particular risk preferences. Investors are not forgiving of failure and are unwilling to accept even the best of excuses, and loyalty to money managers is not a commonly found trait. By the same token, performance evaluation is just as important to the individual investor who constructs his or her own portfolio, since the feedback from it should largely determine how that investor approaches investing in the future.

These parts of the process are summarized in Figure 1.1, and we will return to this figure to emphasize the steps in the process as we consider different investment philosophies. As you will see, while all investment philosophies may have the same end objective of beating the market, each philosophy will emphasize a different component of the overall process and require different skills for success.

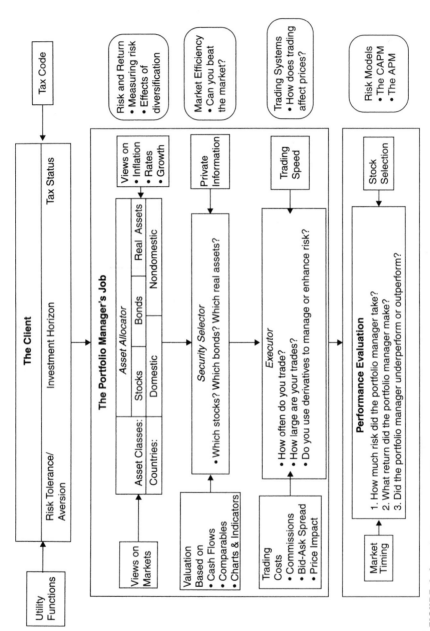

FIGURE 1.1 The Investment Process

CATEGORIZING INVESTMENT PHILOSOPHIES

We present the range of investment philosophies in this section, using the investment process to illustrate each philosophy. While we will leave much of the detail for later chapters, we attempt to present at least the core of each philosophy here.

Market Timing versus Asset Selection

The broadest categorization of investment philosophies is by whether they are based on timing overall markets or finding individual assets that are mispriced. The first set of philosophies can be categorized as *market timing* philosophies, while the second can be viewed as *security selection* philosophies.

Within each, though, are numerous strands that take very different views about markets. Consider market timing. While most of us consider market timing only in the context of the stock market, there are investors who consider market timing to include a much broader range of markets: currency markets, commodities, bond markets, and real estate come to mind. The range of choices among security selection philosophies is even wider and can span charting and technical indicators; fundamentals (earnings, cash flows, or growth); and information (earnings reports, acquisition announcements).

While market timing has allure to all of us (because it pays off so well when you are right), it is difficult to succeed at for exactly that reason. There are all too often too many investors attempting to time markets, and succeeding consistently is very difficult to do. If you decide to pick stocks, how do you choose whether you pick them based on charts, fundamentals, or growth potential? The answer, as we will see in the next section, will depend not only on your views of the market and what works, but also on your personal characteristics.

Activist versus Passive Investing

At a general level, investment philosophies can also be categorized as activist or passive strategies. (Note that activist investing is not the same as active investing.) In a *passive strategy*, you invest in a stock or company and wait for your investment to pay off. Assuming that your strategy is successful, this will come from the market recognizing and correcting a misvaluation. Thus, a portfolio manager who buys stocks with low price-earnings ratios and stable earnings is following a passive strategy. So is an index fund manager, who essentially buys all stocks in the index. In an *activist strategy*, you invest in a company and then try to change the way the company is run to make it more valuable. Venture capitalists can be categorized as activist investors since they not only take positions in promising businesses but also provide significant inputs into how these businesses are run. In recent years, we have seen investors bring this activist philosophy to publicly traded companies, using the clout of large positions to change the way companies are run. We should hasten to draw a contrast between activist investing and active investing. Any investor who tries to beat the market by picking stocks is viewed as an active investor. Thus, active investors can adopt passive strategies or activist strategies. In the popular vernacular, active investing includes any strategy where you try to beat the market by steering your money to either undervalued asset classes or individual stocks/assets.

Time Horizon

Different investment philosophies require different time horizons. A philosophy based on the assumption that markets overreact to new information may generate short-term strategies. For instance, you may buy stocks right after a bad earnings announcement, hold for a few weeks, and then sell (hopefully at a higher price, as the market corrects its overreaction). In contrast, a philosophy of buying neglected companies (stocks that are not followed by analysts or held by institutional investors) may require a much longer time horizon.

One factor that will determine the time horizon of an investment philosophy is the nature of the adjustment that has to occur for you to reap the rewards of a successful strategy. Passive value investors who buy stocks in companies that they believe are undervalued may have to wait years for the market correction to occur, even if they are right. Investors who trade ahead of or after earnings reports, because they believe that markets do not respond correctly to such reports, may hold the stock for only a few days. At the extreme, investors who see the same (or very similar) assets being priced differently in two markets may buy the cheaper one and sell the more expensive one, locking in arbitrage profits in a few minutes.

Coexistence of Contradictory Strategies

One of the most fascinating aspects of investment philosophy is the coexistence of investment philosophies based on contradictory views of the markets. Thus, you can have market timers who trade on *price momentum* (suggesting that investors are slow to learn from information) and market timers who are *contrarians* (which is based on the belief that markets overreact). Among security selectors who use fundamentals, you can have *value investors* who buy value stocks because they believe markets overprice growth, and *growth investors* who buy growth stocks using exactly the opposite justification. The coexistence of these contradictory impulses for investing may strike some as irrational, but it is healthy and may actually be necessary to keep the market in balance. In addition, you can have investors with contradictory philosophies coexisting in the market because of their different time horizons, views on risk, and tax statuses. For instance, tax-exempt investors may find stocks that pay large dividends a bargain, while taxable investors may reject these same stocks because dividends are taxed.

Investment Philosophies in Context

We can consider the differences between investment philosophies in the context of the investment process, described in Figure 1.1. Market timing strategies primarily affect the asset allocation decision. Thus, investors who believe that stocks are undervalued will invest more of their portfolios in stocks than would be justified given their risk preferences. Security selection strategies in all their forms—technical analysis, fundamentals, or private information—center on the security selection component of the portfolio management process. You could argue that strategies that are not based on grand visions of market efficiency but are designed to take advantage of momentary mispricing of assets in markets (such as arbitrage) revolve around the execution segment of portfolio management. It is not surprising that the success of such opportunistic strategies depends on trading quickly to take advantage of pricing errors, and keeping transaction costs low. Figure 1.2 presents the different investment philosophies.

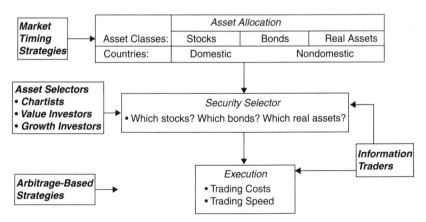

FIGURE 1.2 Investment Philosophies

DEVELOPING AN INVESTMENT PHILOSOPHY

If every investor needs an investment philosophy, what is the process that you go through to come up with such a philosophy? While this entire book is about the process, in this section we can lay out the three steps involved.

Step 1: Understand the Fundamentals of Risk and Valuation

Before you embark on the journey of finding an investment philosophy, you need to get your financial tool kit ready. At the minimum, you should understand:

- How to measure the risk in an investment and relate it to expected returns.
- How to value an asset, whether it is a bond, stock, real estate holding, or business.
- What the ingredients of trading costs are, and the trade-off between the speed of trading and the cost of trading.

We would hasten to add that you do not need to be a mathematical wizard to understand any of these, and we will begin this book with a section dedicated to providing these basic tools.

Step 2: Develop a Point of View about How Markets Work and Where They Might Break Down

Every investment philosophy is grounded in a point of view about human behavior (and irrationality). While personal experience often determines how you view your fellow human beings, before you make your final judgments you should expand this to consider broader evidence from markets on how investors act.

Over the past few decades, it has become easy to test different investment strategies as data becomes more accessible. There now exists a substantial body of research on the investment strategies that have beaten the market over time. For instance, researchers have found convincing evidence that stocks with low price-to-book value ratios have earned significantly higher returns than stocks of equivalent risk but higher price-to-book value ratios. It would be foolhardy not to review this evidence in the process of developing your investment philosophy. At the same time, though, you should keep in mind three caveats about this research:

1. Since they are based on the past, they represent a look in the rearview mirror. Strategies that earned substantial returns in the past may no

longer be viable strategies. In fact, as successful strategies get publicized either directly (in books and articles) or indirectly (by portfolio managers trading on them), you should expect to see them to become less effective.

2. Much of the research is based on constructing hypothetical portfolios, where you buy and sell stocks at historical prices and little or no attention is paid to transaction costs. To the extent that trading can cause prices to move, the actual returns on strategies can be very different from the returns on the hypothetical portfolio.

3. A test of an investment strategy is almost always a joint test of both the strategy and a model for risk. To see why, consider the evidence that stocks with low price-to-book value ratios earn higher returns than stocks with high price-to-book value ratios, with similar risk (at least as measured by the models we use). To the extent that we mismeasure risk or ignore a key component of risk, it is entirely possible that the higher returns are just a reward for the greater risk associated with low price-to-book value stocks.

Since understanding whether a strategy beats the market is such a critical component of investing, we will consider the approaches that are used to test a strategy, some basic rules that need to be followed in doing these tests, and common errors that are made (unintentionally or intentionally) when running such tests. As we look at each investment philosophy, we will review the evidence that is available on strategies that emerge from that philosophy.

Step 3: Find the Philosophy That Provides the Best Fit for You

Once you understand the basics of investing, form your views on human foibles and behavior, and review the evidence accumulated on each of the different investment philosophies, you are ready to make your choice. In our view, there is potential for success with almost every investment philosophy (yes, even charting), but the prerequisites for success can vary. In particular, success may rest on:

- *Your risk aversion.* Some strategies are inherently riskier than others. For instance, venture capital or private equity investing, where you invest your funds in small, private businesses that show promise, is inherently more risky than buying value stocks or equity in large, stable, publicly traded companies. The returns are also likely to be higher. However, more risk-averse investors should avoid the first strategy and focus on the second. Picking an investment philosophy (and strategy) that requires you to take on more risk than you feel comfortable taking on can be hazardous to your health and your portfolio.

- *The size of your portfolio.* Some strategies require larger portfolios for success, whereas others work only on a smaller scale. For instance, it is very difficult to be an activist value investor if you have only $100,000 in your portfolio, since firms are unlikely to listen to your complaints. At the other extreme, a portfolio manager with $100 billion to invest may not be able to adopt a strategy that requires buying small, neglected companies. With such a large portfolio, the portfolio manager would very quickly end up becoming the dominant stockholder in each of the companies and affecting the price every time he or she trades.

- *Your time horizon.* Some investment philosophies are predicated on a long time horizon, whereas others require much shorter time horizons. If you are investing your own funds, your time horizon is determined by your personal characteristics (some of us are more patient than others) and your needs for cash (the greater the need for liquidity, the shorter your time horizon has to be). If you are a professional (an investment adviser or portfolio manager) managing the funds of others, it is your clients' time horizons and cash needs that will drive your choice of investment philosophies and strategies. You are only as long term as your clients allow you to be.

- *Your tax status.* Since such a significant portion of your money ends up going to the tax collectors, taxes have a strong influence on your investment strategies and perhaps even the investment philosophy you adopt. In some cases, you may have to abandon strategies that you find attractive on a pretax basis because of the tax bite that they expose you to.

Thus, the right investment philosophy for you will reflect your particular strengths and weaknesses. It should come as no surprise, then, that investment philosophies that work for some investors do not work for others. Consequently, there can be no one investment philosophy that can be labeled "best" for all investors.

CONCLUSION

An investment philosophy represents a set of core beliefs about how investors behave and how markets work. To be a successful investor, not only do you have to consider the evidence from markets, but you also have to examine your own strengths and weaknesses to come up with an investment philosophy that best fits you. Investors without core beliefs tend to wander from strategy to strategy, drawn by the anecdotal evidence or recent successes, creating transaction costs and incurring losses as a consequence. Investors with clearly defined investment philosophies tend to be more consistent and disciplined in their investment choices, though success is not guaranteed to them, either.

In this chapter, we considered a broad range of investment philosophies from market timing to arbitrage and placed each of them in the broad framework of portfolio management. We also examined the three steps in the path to an investment philosophy, beginning with the understanding of the tools of investing—risk, trading costs, and valuation; continuing with an evaluation of the empirical evidence on whether, when, and how markets break down; and concluding with a self-assessment to find the investment philosophy that best matches your time horizon, risk preferences, and portfolio characteristics.

EXERCISES

1. Get access to a comprehensive database that covers all or most traded companies in the market and has both accounting numbers for these companies and market data (stock prices and market-based risk measures like standard deviation).
   a. If you are interested only in U.S. companies, you have lots of choices, with varying costs. You can always use the free data on Yahoo! Finance or similar sites, but they come with restrictions on data definitions and downloads. I use Value Line's online data (cost of about $1,000 per year in 2011) and have used Morningstar's online data as well (it requires a premium membership costing about $200 in 2011).
   b. If you are interested in global companies, you have to be willing to spend more: Capital IQ and Compustat (both S&P products) and FactSet have information on global companies. The good news is that the choices are proliferating and getting more accessible.
2. It will make your life far easier if you are comfortable using a spreadsheet program. I use Microsoft Excel simply because of its ubiquity and power, but there are cheaper alternatives.
3. Also, check out my website (www.damodaran.com) and click on updated data. You will find sector averages for pricing multiples and accounting ratios, and data on stock returns and risk-free rates.

CHAPTER 2

Upside, Downside: Understanding Risk

Risk is part of investing, and understanding what it is and how it is measured is essential to developing an investment philosophy. In this chapter, we lay the foundations for analyzing risk in investments. We present alternative models for measuring risk and converting these risk measures into expected returns. We also consider ways investors can measure their risk aversion.

We begin with an assessment of conventional risk and return models in finance and present our analysis in three steps. In the first step, we define risk in terms of uncertainty about future returns. The greater this uncertainty, the more risky an investment is perceived to be. The next step, which we believe is the central one, is to decompose this risk into risk that can be diversified away by investors and risk that cannot. In the third step, we look at how different risk and return models in finance attempt to measure this nondiversifiable risk. We compare and contrast the most widely used model, the capital asset pricing model (CAPM), with other models, and explain how and why they diverge in their measures of risk and the implications for expected returns.

We then look at alternative approaches to measuring risk in investments, ranging from balance-sheet-based measures (using book value of assets and equity as a base) to building in a margin of safety (MOS) when investing in assets, and present ways of reconciling and choosing between alternative measures of risk.

In the last part of the chapter, we turn to measuring the risk associated with investing in bonds, where the cash flows are contractually set at the time of the investment. Since the risk in this investment is that the promised cash flows will not be delivered, the default risk has to be assessed and an appropriate default spread charged for it.

WHAT IS RISK?

Risk, for most of us, refers to the likelihood that in life's games of chance, we will receive an outcome that we will not like. For instance, the risk of driving a car too fast is getting a speeding ticket or, worse still, getting into an accident. Webster's dictionary, in fact, defines risk as "exposing to danger or hazard." Thus, risk is perceived almost entirely in negative terms.

In finance, our definition of risk is both different and broader. Risk, as we see it, refers to the likelihood that we will receive a return on an investment that is different from the return we expected to make. Thus, risk includes not only the bad outcomes (i.e., returns that are lower than expected) but also good outcomes (i.e., returns that are higher than expected). In fact, we can refer to the former as downside risk and the latter is upside risk; but we consider both when measuring risk. In fact, the spirit of our definition of risk in finance is captured best by the Chinese symbols for risk, which are reproduced here:

危机

The Chinese Symbol for Risk

The first symbol is the symbol for "hazard" while the second is the symbol for "opportunity," making risk a mix of danger and opportunity. It illustrates very clearly the trade-off that every investor and business has to make between the higher rewards that come with the opportunity and the higher risk that has to be borne as a consequence of the danger.

Much of this chapter can be viewed as an attempt to come up with a model that best measures the "danger" in any investment and then attempts to convert this into the "opportunity" that we would need to compensate for the danger. In financial terms, we term the danger to be *risk* and the opportunity to be the *expected return.*

EQUITY RISK: THEORY-BASED MODELS

To demonstrate how risk is viewed in financial theory, we will present risk analysis in three steps. First, we will define risk as uncertainty about future returns and suggest ways of measuring this uncertainty. Second, we will differentiate between risk that is specific to one or a few investments and risk that affects a much wider cross section of investments. We will argue that in a market where investors are diversified, it is only the latter risk, called market risk, that will be rewarded. Third, we will look at alternative models for measuring this market risk and the expected returns that go with it.

Defining Risk

Investors who buy assets expect to earn returns over the time horizon that they hold the asset. Their actual returns over this holding period may be very different from the expected returns, and it is this difference between actual and expected returns that is the source of risk. For example, assume that you are an investor with a one-year time horizon buying a one-year Treasury bill (or any other default-free one-year bond) with a 5 percent expected return. At the end of the one-year holding period, the actual return on this investment will be 5 percent, which is equal to the expected return. The return distribution for this investment is shown in Figure 2.1. This is a riskless investment.

To provide a contrast to the riskless investment, consider an investor who buys stock in a company like Netflix. This investor, having done her research, may conclude that she can make an expected return of 30 percent on Netflix over her one-year holding period. The actual return over this period will almost certainly not be exactly 30 percent; it might even be much greater or much lower. The distribution of returns on this investment is illustrated in Figure 2.2.

In addition to the expected return, an investor has to note that the actual returns, in this case, are different from the expected return. The spread of

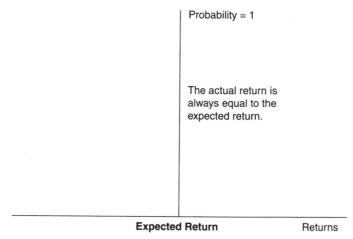

FIGURE 2.1   Probability Distribution for Risk-Free Investment

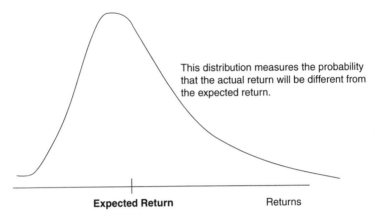

This distribution measures the probability that the actual return will be different from the expected return.

Expected Return   Returns

FIGURE 2.2   Probability Distribution for Risky Investment

the actual returns around the expected return is measured by the *variance or standard deviation of the distribution*; the greater the deviation of the actual returns from expected returns, the greater the variance.

NUMBER WATCH

Most and least volatile sectors: Look at the differences between average annualized standard deviation in stock prices, by sector, for U.S. companies.

One of the limitations of variance is that it considers all variation from the expected return to be risk. Thus, the potential that you will earn a 60 percent return on Netflix (30 percent more than the expected return of 30 percent) affects the variance exactly as much as the potential that you will earn 0 percent (30 percent less than the expected return). In other words, you do not distinguish between downside and upside risk. This view is justified by arguing that risk is symmetric—upside risk must inevitably create the potential for downside risk.[1] If you are bothered by this assumption, you could compute a modified version of the variance, called the *semivariance,* where you consider only the returns that fall below the expected return.

---

[1]In statistical terms, this is the equivalent of assuming that the distribution of returns is close to normal.

It is true that measuring risk with variance or semivariance can provide too limited a view of risk, and there are some investors who use simpler stand-ins (proxies) for risk. For instance, you may consider stocks in some sectors (such as technology) to be riskier than stocks in other sectors (say food processing). Others prefer ranking or categorization systems, where you put firms into risk classes, rather than trying to measure a firm's risk in units. Thus, Value Line ranks firms in five classes based on risk.

There is one final point that needs to be made about how variances and semivariances are estimated for most stocks. Analysts usually look at the past (stock prices over the prior two or five years) to make these estimates. This may be appropriate for firms that have not changed their fundamental characteristics—business or leverage—over the period. For firms that have changed significantly over time, variances from the past can provide a very misleading view of risk in the future.

Diversifiable and Nondiversifiable Risk

Although there are many reasons that actual returns may differ from expected returns, we can group the reasons into two groups: firm-specific and marketwide. The risks that arise from firm-specific actions affect one or a few companies, whereas the risks arising from marketwide actions affect many or all investments. This distinction is critical to the way we assess risk in finance.

The Components of Risk   When an investor buys stock, say in a company like Boeing, he or she is exposed to many risks. Some risk may affect only one or a few firms, and it is this risk that we categorize as *firm-specific risk*. Within this category, we would consider a wide range of risks, starting with the risk that a firm may have misjudged the demand for a product from its customers; we call this *project risk*. For instance, consider the investment by Boeing in the Dreamliner, its newest jet. This investment was based on the assumption that airlines wanted larger, more updated aircraft and would be willing to pay a higher price for them. If Boeing has misjudged this demand, it will clearly have an impact on Boeing's earnings and value, but it should not have a significant effect on other firms in the market.

The risk could also arise from competitors proving to be stronger or weaker than anticipated; we call this *competitive risk*. For instance, assume that Boeing and Airbus are competing for an order from Qantas, the Australian airline. The possibility that Airbus may win the bid is a potential source of risk to Boeing and perhaps a few of its suppliers. But again, only a handful of firms in the market will be affected by it. In fact, we would extend our risk measures to include risks that may affect an entire sector but are restricted to that sector; we call this *sector risk*. For instance, a cut in the defense budget in the United States will adversely affect all firms in the defense business, including Boeing, but there should be no significant impact on other sectors, such as food and apparel. What is common across the three risks described—project, competitive, and sector risk—is that they affect only a small subset of firms.

There is other risk that is much more pervasive and affects many, if not all, investments. For instance, when interest rates increase, all investments, not just Boeing, are negatively affected, albeit to different degrees. Similarly, when the economy weakens, all firms feel the effects, though cyclical firms (such as automobiles, steel, and housing) may feel it more. We term this risk *market risk*.

Finally, there are risks that fall in a gray area, depending on how many assets they affect. For instance, when the dollar strengthens against other currencies, it has a significant impact on the earnings and values of firms with international operations. If most firms in the market have significant international operations, as is the case now, it could well be categorized as market risk. If only a few do, it would be closer to firm-specific risk. Figure 2.3 summarizes the breakdown or spectrum of firm-specific and market risks.

Why Diversification Reduces or Eliminates Firm-Specific Risk: An Intuitive Explanation   As an investor, you could invest your entire wealth in one stock, say Boeing. If you do so, you are exposed to both firm-specific and market risk. If, however, you expand your portfolio to include other assets or

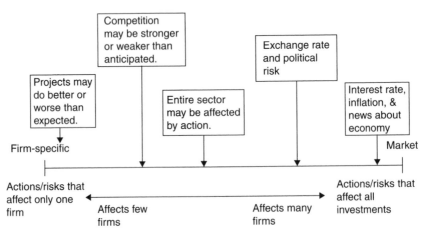

FIGURE 2.3   A Breakdown of Risk

stocks, you are diversifying, and by doing so, you can reduce your exposure to firm-specific risk. There are two reasons why diversification reduces or, at the limit, eliminates firm-specific risk. The first is that each investment in a diversified portfolio is a much smaller percentage of that portfolio than would be the case if you were not diversified. Thus, any action that increases or decreases the value of only that investment or small group of investments will have only a small impact on your overall portfolio, whereas undiversified investors are much more exposed to changes in the values of the investments in their portfolios. The second and stronger reason is that the effects of firm-specific actions on the prices of individual assets in a portfolio can be either positive or negative for each asset in any period. Thus, in very large portfolios, this risk will average out to zero and will not affect the overall value of the portfolio.[2]

NUMBER WATCH

Risk breakdown by sector: Take a look at variations in the proportion of risk explained by the market, broken down by sector for U.S. stocks.

In contrast, the effects of market-wide movements are likely to be in the same direction for most or all investments in a portfolio, though some assets may be affected more than others. For instance, other things being equal, an increase in interest rates will lower the values of most assets in a portfolio. Being more diversified does not eliminate this risk.

One of the simplest ways of measuring how much risk in an investment (either an individual firm or even a portfolio) is firm-specific is to look at the proportion of the price movements that are explained by the market. This is called the *R-squared* and it should range between zero and 1, and can be stated as a percentage; it measures the proportion of the investment's stock price variation that comes from the market. An investment with an R-squared of zero has all firm-specific risk, whereas a firm with an R-squared of 1 (100 percent) has no firm-specific risk.

---

[2]This is the insight that Harry Markowitz had that gave rise to modern portfolio theory. Harry M. Markowitz, "Foundations of Portfolio Theory," *Journal of Finance* 46, no. 2 (1991): 469–478.

WHY IS THE MARGINAL INVESTOR ASSUMED TO BE DIVERSIFIED?

The argument that diversification reduces an investor's exposure to risk is clear both intuitively and statistically, but risk and return models in finance go further. The models look at risk in an investment through the eyes of the investor most likely to be trading on that investment at any point in time (i.e., the marginal investor). They argue that this investor, who sets prices for investments at the margin, is well diversified; thus, the only risk that he or she cares about is the risk added to a diversified portfolio (market risk). This argument can be justified simply. The risk in an investment will always be perceived to be higher for an undiversified investor than for a diversified one, since the latter does not shoulder any firm-specific risk and the former does. If both investors have the same expectations about future earnings and cash flows on an asset, the diversified investor will be willing to pay a higher price for that asset because of his or her perception of lower risk. Consequently, the asset, over time, will end up being held by diversified investors.

This argument is powerful, especially in markets where assets can be traded easily and at low cost. Thus, it works well for a large market cap stock traded in the United States, since investors can become diversified at fairly low cost. In addition, a significant proportion of the trading in U.S. stocks is done by institutional investors, who tend to be well diversified. It becomes a more difficult argument to sustain when assets cannot be easily traded or the costs of trading are high. In these markets, the marginal investor may well be undiversified, and firm-specific risk may therefore continue to matter when looking at individual investments. For instance, real estate in most countries is still held by investors who are undiversified and have the bulk of their wealth tied up in these investments.

Models Measuring Market Risk

While most risk and return models in use in finance agree on the first two steps of the risk analysis process (i.e., that risk comes from the distribution of actual returns around the expected return and that risk should be measured from the perspective of a marginal investor who is well diversified), they part ways when it comes to measuring nondiversifiable or market risk. In this section, we discuss the different models that exist in finance for measuring market risk and why they differ. We will begin with the capital asset pricing model (CAPM), the most widely used model for measuring market risk in finance—at least among practitioners, though academics usually get blamed for its use. We will then discuss the alternatives to this model that have developed over the past two decades. Though we will emphasize the differences, we will also look at what all of these models have in common.

The Capital Asset Pricing Model The risk and return model that has been in use the longest and is still the standard in most real-world analyses is the capital asset pricing model (CAPM). In this section, we will examine the assumptions made by the model and the measures of market risk that emerge from these assumptions.

Assumptions While diversification reduces the exposure of investors to firm-specific risk, most investors limit their diversification to holding only a few assets. Even large mutual funds rarely hold more than a few hundred stocks, and some of them hold as few as 10 to 20. There are two reasons why investors stop diversifying. One is that an investor or mutual fund manager can obtain most of the benefits of diversification from a relatively small portfolio, because the marginal benefits of diversification become smaller as the portfolio gets more diversified. Consequently, these benefits may not cover the marginal costs of diversification, which include transaction and monitoring costs. Another reason for limiting diversification is that many investors (and funds) believe they can find undervalued assets and thus choose not to hold only those assets that they believe are most undervalued.

The capital asset pricing model assumes that there are no transaction costs and that everyone has access to the same information, that this information is already reflected in asset prices and that investors therefore cannot find under- or overvalued assets in the marketplace. Making these assumptions allows investors to keep diversifying without additional cost. At the limit, each investor's portfolio will include every traded asset in the market held in proportion to its market value. The fact that this diversified portfolio includes all traded assets in the market is the reason it is called the *market portfolio*, which should not be a surprising result, given the benefits of diversification and the absence of transaction costs in the capital asset pricing model. If diversification reduces exposure to firm-specific risk and there are no costs associated with adding more assets to the portfolio, the logical limit to diversification is to hold every traded asset in the market, in proportion to its market value. If this seems abstract, consider the market portfolio to be an extremely well-diversified mutual fund (a supreme index fund) that holds all traded financial and real assets, along with a default-free investment (a treasury bill, for instance) as the riskless asset. In the CAPM, all investors will hold combinations of the riskless asset and the market index fund.[3]

Investor Portfolios in the CAPM   If every investor in the market holds the identical market portfolio, how exactly do investors reflect their risk aversion in their investments? In the capital asset pricing model, investors adjust for their risk preferences in their allocation decision, where they decide how much to invest in a riskless asset and how much in the market portfolio. Investors who are risk averse might choose to put much or even all of their wealth in the riskless asset. Investors who want to take more risk will invest the bulk or even all of their wealth in the market portfolio. Investors who invest all their wealth in the market portfolio and are still desirous of taking on more risk would do so by borrowing at the riskless rate and investing more in the same market portfolio as everyone else.

These results are predicated on two additional assumptions. First, there exists a riskless asset whose returns are known with certainty. Second, investors can lend and borrow at the same riskless rate to arrive at their optimal allocations. Lending at the riskless rate can be accomplished fairly simply by buying Treasury bills or bonds, but borrowing at the riskless rate might be more difficult to do for individuals. There are variations of the CAPM that allow these assumptions to be relaxed and still arrive at the conclusions that are consistent with the model.

NUMBER WATCH

Highest and lowest beta sectors: Take a look at the average beta, by sector, for U.S. stocks. The betas are estimated before and after considering leverage.

---

[3]The significance of introducing the riskless asset into the choice mix and the implications for portfolio choice were first noted in Sharpe (1964) and Lintner (1965). Hence, the model is sometimes called the Sharpe-Lintner model. J. Lintner, "The Valuation of Risk Assets and the Selection of Risky Investments in Stock Portfolios and Capital Budgets," *Review of Economics and Statistics* 47 (1965): 13–37; W. F. Sharpe, "Capital Asset Prices: A Theory of Market Equilibrium under Conditions of Risk," *Journal of Finance* 19 (1964): 425–442.

Measuring the Market Risk of an Individual Asset   The risk of any asset to an investor is the risk added by that asset to the investor's overall portfolio. In the CAPM world, where all investors hold the market portfolio, the risk to an investor of an individual asset will be the risk that this asset adds to that portfolio. Intuitively, if an asset moves independently of the market portfolio, it will not add much risk to the market portfolio. In other words, most of the risk in this asset is firm-specific and can be diversified away. In contrast, if an asset tends to move up when the market portfolio moves up and down when it moves down, it will add risk to the market portfolio. This asset has more market risk and less firm-specific risk. Statistically, the risk added to the market portfolio is measured by the *covariance* of the asset with the market portfolio.

The covariance is a percentage value, and it is difficult to pass judgment on the relative risk of an investment by looking at this value. In other words, knowing that the covariance of Boeing with the market portfolio is 55 percent does not provide us a clue as to whether Boeing is riskier or safer than the average asset. We therefore standardize the risk measure by dividing the covariance of each asset with the market portfolio by the variance of the market portfolio. This yields a risk measure called the *beta* of the asset:

$$\text{Beta of an asset} = \frac{\text{Covariance of asset with market portfolio}}{\text{Variance of the market portfolio}}$$

The beta of the market portfolio, and by extension the average asset in it, is 1. Assets that are riskier than average (using this measure of risk) will have betas that are greater than 1, and assets that are less risky than average will have betas that are less than 1. The riskless asset will have a beta of zero.

Getting Expected Returns   Once you accept the assumptions that lead to all investors holding the market portfolio and you measure the risk of an asset with beta, the return you can expect to make can be written as a function of the risk-free rate and the beta of that asset.

Expected return on an investment = Risk-free rate + Beta * Risk premium
for buying the average-risk investment

Consider the three components that go into the expected return.

1. *Riskless rate.* The return that you can make on a risk-free investment becomes the base from which you build expected returns. Essentially, you are assuming that if you can make 5 percent investing in a risk-free asset, you would not settle for less than this as an expected return

for investing in a riskier asset. Generally speaking, we use the interest rate on government securities as the risk-free rate, assuming that such securities have no default risk. This used to be a safe assumption in the United States and other developed markets, but sovereign ratings downgrades and economic woes have raised questions about whether this is still a reasonable premise. If there is default risk in a government, the government bond rate will include a premium for default risk and this premium will have to be removed to arrive at a risk-free rate.[4]

2. *The beta of the investment.* The beta is the only component in this model that varies from investment to investment, with investments that add more risk to the market portfolio having higher betas. But where do betas come from? Since the beta measures the risk added to a market portfolio by an individual stock, it is usually estimated by running a regression of past returns on the stock against returns on a market index. Consider, for instance, Figure 2.4, where we report the regression of returns on Netflix against the S&P 500, using weekly returns from 2009 to 2011.

The slope of the regression captures how sensitive a stock is to market movements and is the beta of the stock. In the regression in Figure 2.4, for instance, the beta of Netflix would be 0.74.[5] Why is it so low? The beta reflects the market risk (or nondiversifiable risk) in Netflix, and this risk is only 5.4 percent (the R-squared) of the overall risk. If the regression numbers hold up, the remaining 94.6 percent of the variation in Netflix stock can be diversified away in a portfolio. Even if you buy into this rationale, there are two problems with regression betas. One is that the beta comes with estimation error—the standard error in the estimate is 0.31. Thus, the true beta for Netflix could be anywhere from 0.12 to 1.36; this range is estimated by adding and subtracting two standard errors to/from the beta estimate. The other is that firms change over time and we are looking backward rather than looking forward. A better way to estimate betas is to look at the average beta for publicly traded firms in the business or businesses Netflix operates in. Though

---

[4]Consider, for example, a government bond issued by the Indian government. Denominated in Indian rupees, this bond has an interest rate of 8 percent. The Indian government is viewed as having default risk on this bond and it's local currency bon is rated Baa3 by Moody's. If we subtract the typical default spread earned by Baa3-rated country bonds (about 2 percent) from 8 percent, we end up with a riskless rate in Indian rupees of 6 percent.

[5]Like most beta estimation services, Bloomberg estimates what it calls an adjusted beta. This number is just the raw (regression) beta moved toward 1 (the average for the market).

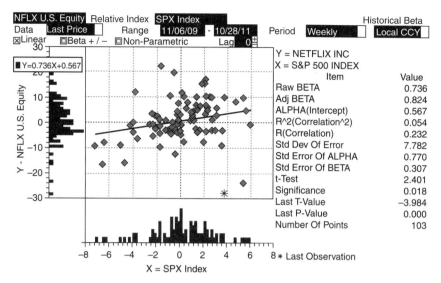

FIGURE 2.4   Beta Regression—Netflix versus S&P 500

these betas come from regressions as well, the average beta is always more precise than any one firm's beta estimate. Thus, you could use the average beta of 1.38 for the entertainment business in the United States in 2011 and adjust for Netflix's low debt-to-equity (D/E) ratio of 2.5% to estimate a beta of 1.40 for Netflix.[6]

NUMBER WATCH

Risk premium for the United States: Take a look at the equity risk premium implied in the U.S. stock market from 1960 through the most recent year.

3. *The risk premium for buying the average-risk investment.* You can view this as the premium you would demand for investing in equities as

---

[6]The beta can be adjusted for financial leverage using the following equation:

$$\text{Levered beta} = \text{Unlevered beta} \, (1 + (1 - \text{tax rate}) \, (D/E))$$

Assuming a 40% tax rate for Netflix and using its debt to equity ratio of 2.5%

$$\text{Levered beta for Netflix} = 1.38 \, (1 + (1 - .40) \, (.025)) = 1.40$$

a class as opposed to the riskless investment. Thus, if you require a return of 9 percent for investing in stocks and the Treasury bond rate is 5 percent, your equity risk premium is 4 percent. There are again two ways in which you can estimate this risk premium. One is to look at the past and calculate the typical premium you would have earned investing in stocks as opposed to a riskless investment. This number is called a historical premium and yields about 4.10 percent for the United States, looking at stock returns relative to returns on Treasury bonds from 1928 to 2011. The other is to look at how stocks are priced today and to estimate the premium that investors must be demanding. This is called an implied premium and yields a value of about 6 percent for U.S. stocks in January 2012.[7]

Bringing it all together, you could use the capital asset pricing model to estimate the expected return on a stock for Netflix, for the future, in January 2012 (using a Treasury bond rate of 2 percent, the sector based beta of 1.40, and a risk premium of 6 percent):

$$\text{Expected return on Netflix} = \text{T-bond rate} + \text{Beta} * \text{Risk premium}$$
$$= 2\% + 1.40 * 6\% = 10.40\%$$

What does this number imply? It does not mean that you will earn 10.4 percent every year, but it does provide a benchmark that you will have to meet and beat if you are considering Netflix as an investment. For Netflix to be a good investment, you would have to expect it to make more than 10.4 percent as an annual return in the future.

In summary, in the capital asset pricing model, all the market risk is captured in the beta, measured relative to a market portfolio, which at least in theory should include all traded assets in the marketplace held in proportion to their market value.

Betas: Myth and Fact   There is perhaps no measure in finance that is more used, misused, and abused than beta. To skeptical investors and practitioners, beta has become the cudgel used not only to beat up theorists but also to discredit any approach that uses beta as an input, including most *discounted*

---

[7]The implied premium for U.S. equities (and equities of other developed markets) was stable and varied between 4 and 5 percent between 2002 and 2008. It spiked sharply to hit 6.5 percent during the banking crisis of 2008, and has been much more volatile since. In 2011, for instance, the premium started the year at about 5 percent and rose to 6 percent by January 2012.

cash flow (DCF) models. There are plenty of legitimate critiques of betas, and we will consider several in the next few pages. Here are five clarifications on what beta tells you and what it does not:

1. *Beta is not a measure of overall risk.* Beta is a measure of a company's exposure to macroeconomic risk and not a measure of overall risk. Thus, it is entirely possible that a very risky company can have a low beta if most of the risk in that company is specific to the company (a biotechnology company, for instance) and is not macroeconomic risk.

2. *Beta is not a statistical measure.* The use of a market regression to get a beta leaves an unfortunate impression with many that it is a statistical measure. We may estimate a beta from a regression, but the beta for a company ultimately comes from its fundamentals and how these fundamentals affect macroeconomic risk exposure. Thus, a company that produces luxury products should have a higher beta than one that produces necessities, since the fate of the former will be much more closely tied to how well the economy and the overall market are doing. By the same token, a company with high fixed costs (operating leverage) and/or high debt (financial leverage) will have higher betas for its equity, since both increase the sensitivity of equity earnings to changes in the top line (revenues). In fact, that is why it is preferable to estimate a beta from sector averages and adjust for operating and financial leverage differences rather than from a single regression.

3. *Beta is a relative (market) risk measure.* Shorn of its theoretical roots, beta is a measure of relative risk, with risk being defined as market risk. Thus, a stock with a beta of 1.20 is 1.20 times more exposed to market risk than the average stock in the market. Thus, the betas for all companies cannot go up or down at the same time; if one sector sees an increase in beta, there has to be another sector where there is a decrease.

4. *Beta is not a fact but an estimate.* This should go without saying, but analysts who obtain their beta estimates from services (and most do) often are provided with a beta for the company that comes from either a regression or a sector average, and both are estimates with error associated with them. That, of course, will be true for any risk measure that you use but it explains why different services may report different estimates of beta for the same company at the same point in time.

5. *Beta is a measure of investment risk, not of investment quality.* The beta of a company is useful insofar as it allows you to estimate the rate of return you need to make when investing in that company; think of it as a hurdle rate. You still have to look at its market size, growth,

and earnings potential to make an assessment of whether it is a good investment. If your analysis leads you to conclude that you can earn a higher return than your hurdle rate, you have a good investment. In other words, a great investment can come with a high beta (because the return that you expect to earn on that investment is much higher than what you would require, given its risk), and awful investments can have low betas.

Alternatives to the Capital Asset Pricing Model   The restrictive assumptions on transaction costs and private information in the capital asset pricing model and the model's dependence on the market portfolio have long been viewed with skepticism by both academics and practitioners. Within the confines of economic theory, there are two alternatives to the CAPM that have been developed over time.

1. *Arbitrage pricing model.* To understand the arbitrage pricing model, we need to begin with a definition of arbitrage. The basic idea is a simple one. Two portfolios or assets with the same exposure to market risk should be priced to earn exactly the same expected returns. If they are not, you could buy the less expensive portfolio, sell the more expensive portfolio, have no risk exposure, and earn a return that exceeds the riskless rate. This is arbitrage. If you assume that arbitrage is not possible and that investors are diversified, you can show that the expected return on an investment should be a function of its exposure to market risk. While this statement mirrors what was stated in the capital asset pricing model, the arbitrage pricing model does not make the restrictive assumptions about transaction costs and private information that lead to the conclusion that one beta can capture an investment's entire exposure to market risk.[8] Instead, in the arbitrage pricing model you can have multiple sources of market risk and different exposures (betas) to each market risk, and your expected return on an investment can be written as:

Expected return = Risk-free rate

+ Beta for factor 1(Risk premium for factor 1)

+ Beta for factor 2(Risk premium for factor 2) ⋯

+ Beta for factor n(Risk premium for factor n)

---

[8]Stephen A. Ross, "The Arbitrage Theory of Capital Asset Pricing," *Journal of Economic Theory* 13, no. 3 (1976): 341–360.

The practical questions then become knowing how many factors there are that determine expected returns and what the betas for each investment are against these factors. The arbitrage pricing model estimates both by scanning past data on stock returns for common patterns (since market risk affects most or all stocks at a given time) and estimating each stock's exposure to these patterns in a process called factor analysis. A factor analysis provides two output measures:

1. It specifies the number of common factors that affected the historical return data.
2. It measures the beta of each investment relative to each of the common factors and provides an estimate of the actual risk premium earned by each factor.

The factor analysis does not, however, identify the factors in economic terms—the factors remain unnamed. In summary, in the arbitrage pricing model, the market risk is measured relative to multiple unspecified macroeconomic variables, with the sensitivity of the investment relative to each factor being measured by a beta. The number of factors, the factor betas, and the factor risk premiums can all be estimated using the factor analysis.

2. *Multifactor models for risk and return.* The arbitrage pricing model's failure to identify the factors specifically in the model may be a statistical strength, but it is an intuitive weakness. The solution seems simple: replace the unidentified statistical factors with specific economic factors, and the resultant model should have an economic basis while still retaining much of the strength of the arbitrage pricing model. That is precisely what multifactor models try to do. Multifactor models generally are built from historical data, rather than economic theory. Once the number of factors has been identified in the arbitrage pricing model, the behavior of these factors over time can be extracted from the data. The behavior of the unnamed factors over time can then be compared to the behavior of macroeconomic variables over that same period to see whether any of the variables are correlated, over time, with the identified factors.

For instance, Chen, Roll, and Ross suggest that the following macroeconomic variables are highly correlated with the factors that come out of factor analysis: industrial production, changes in default premium, shifts in the term structure, unanticipated inflation, and changes in the real rate of return.[9] These variables can then be correlated

---

[9] N. Chen, R. Roll, and S. A. Ross, "Economic Forces and the Stock Market," *Journal of Business* 59 (1986): 383–404.

with returns to come up with a model of expected returns, with firm-specific betas calculated relative to each variable.

$$E(R) = R_f + \beta_{GNP}[E(R_{GNP}) - R_f] + \beta_I[E(R_I) - R_f] + \cdots$$
$$+ \beta_\partial[E(R_\partial) - R_f]$$

where β_{GNP} = Beta relative to changes in industrial production
$E(R_{GNP})$ = Expected return on a portfolio with a beta of 1 on the industrial production factor and zero on all other factors
β_I = Beta relative to changes in inflation
$E(R_I)$ = Expected return on a portfolio with a beta of 1 on the inflation factor and zero on all other factors

The costs of going from the arbitrage pricing model to a macroeconomic multifactor model can be traced directly to the errors that can be made in identifying the factors. The economic factors in the model can change over time, as will the risk premiums associated with each one. For instance, oil price changes were a significant economic factor driving expected returns on stocks in the 1970s but were not significant in subsequent time periods. Using the wrong factor or missing a significant factor in a multifactor model can lead to inferior estimates of expected return.

In summary, multifactor models, like the arbitrage pricing model, assume that market risk can be captured best using multiple macroeconomic factors and estimating betas relative to each. Unlike the arbitrage pricing model, multifactor models do attempt to identify the macroeconomic factors that drive market risk.

ASSESSING CONVENTIONAL RISK AND RETURN MODELS

All the risk and return models developed hitherto in this chapter are built on a common foundation. They all assume that only market risk is rewarded and they derive the expected return as a function of measures of this risk. The capital asset pricing model makes the most restrictive assumptions about how markets work but arrives at the simplest model, with only one factor driving risk and requiring estimation. The arbitrage pricing model makes fewer assumptions but arrives at a more complicated model, at least in terms of the parameters that require estimation. The capital asset pricing model can be considered a special case of the arbitrage pricing model, where there is only one underlying factor and it is completely captured by the market index. In general, the CAPM has the advantage of being a simpler model to estimate and to use, but it will underperform the richer multifactor models when an investment is sensitive to economic factors not well represented in the market index. For instance, oil company stocks, which derive most of their risk from oil price movements, tend to have low CAPM betas and low expected returns. An arbitrage pricing model, where one of the factors may measure oil and other commodity price movements, will yield a better estimate of risk and a higher expected return for these firms.[10]

Notwithstanding the impressive economic underpinnings of these models for risk, key questions remain: Do these models work at measuring what they claim to measure? Should investors assess the betas of investments and use them in investment decisions? Are there alternative measures of risk that are less dependent upon stock prices? The answers to these questions have been debated widely among academics and practitioners in the past two decades. The first tests of the CAPM suggested that betas and returns were positively related, though other measures of risk (such as variance in stock prices) continued to explain differences in actual returns. This discrepancy was initially attributed to limitations in the testing techniques, but Fama and French examined the relationship between betas and returns between 1962 and 1989 and concluded that there is little or no relationship between the two.[11] While the early tests of the arbitrage pricing model and multifactor models suggested that they might provide more promise in terms of explaining differences in returns, a distinction has to be drawn between the use of these models to explain differences in past returns and their use to predict expected returns in the future. The competitors to the CAPM clearly do a much better job at explaining past returns since they do not constrain themselves to one factor, as the CAPM does. This extension to multiple factors does become more of a problem when we try to forecast expected returns for the future, since the betas and premiums of each of these factors now have to be estimated. Because the factor premiums and betas are themselves volatile, the estimation error may eliminate the benefits that could be gained by moving from the CAPM to more complex models.

---

[10]Weston and Copeland used both approaches to estimate the cost of equity for oil companies in 1989 and came up with 14.4 percent with the CAPM and 19.1 percent using the arbitrage pricing model.
[11]E. F. Fama and K. R. French, "The Cross-Section of Expected Returns," *Journal of Finance* 47 (1992): 427–466.

In summary, after 60 years of research, we are still faced with a quandary. Our models for risk are flawed, and we estimate the risk parameters within each of these models with substantial error. In the next section, we look at alternatives to conventional risk and return models.

EQUITY RISK: ALTERNATIVE MEASURES

The discomfort that practitioners and many academics feel with the theory-based risk and return models described in the preceding section has several roots. First, by starting with the premise that risk is symmetric—the upside and downside are balanced—it already seems to concede the fight to beat the market. After all, a good investment should have more upside than downside; value investors in particular build their investment strategies around the ethos of minimizing downside risk while expanding upside potential. Second, the model's dependence upon past market prices to get a measure of risk (betas come from regressions) should make anyone wary: after all, markets are often volatile for no good fundamental reason. Third, the focus on breaking down risk into diversifiable and undiversifiable risk, with only the latter being relevant for investors, does not convince some, who believe that the distinction is meaningless or should not be made.

In this section, we look at alternative approaches to assessing risk in investments. The first approach draws on information in accounting statements to evaluate the risk in a business. The second and the third approaches draw on the assumption that the market prices assets based on their risk, at least on average and over the long term. In the second, we look at the shared characteristics of companies that have generated high returns in the past, and use these characteristics as proxies for risk. In the third, we back out the returns implied in current stock prices and use these expected returns as measures of risk: riskier investments will have higher expected returns. In the fourth approach, we look at the option of adjusting cash flows for risk, either subjectively or with a model-based approach, rather than adjusting expected returns for risk. Finally, we look at building risk into a margin of safety (MOS) when making the decision on whether to buy a stock.

Accounting-Based Measures

For those who are inherently suspicious of any market-based measure, there is always accounting information that can be used to come up with a measure of risk. In particular, firms that have low debt ratios, high dividends, stable and growing earnings, and large cash holdings should be less risky to equity investors than firms without these characteristics. While the intuition is impeccable, converting it into an expected return can be problematic; however, here are three choices:

1. *Pick one accounting ratio and create scaled risk measures around that ratio.* Assume that you are assessing the risk in 3M. The median book debt-to-capital ratio for U.S. companies at the start of 2011 was 51 percent. The book debt-to-capital ratio for 3M at that time was 30.91 percent, yielding a relative risk measure of 0.61 for the company, obtained by dividing 3M's debt ratio (30.91 percent) by the market average (51 percent). The perils of this approach should be clear when applied to Apple, since the firm has no debt outstanding, yielding a relative risk of zero (which is an absurd result).

2. *Compute an accounting beta.* Rather than estimate a beta from market prices, an accounting beta is estimated from accounting numbers. One simple approach is to look at changes in accounting earnings at a firm relative to accounting earnings for the entire market. Firms that have more stable earnings than the rest of the market or whose earnings movements have nothing to do with the rest of the market will have low accounting betas. An extended version of this approach would be to estimate the accounting beta as a function of multiple accounting variables, including dividend payout ratios, debt ratios, cash balances, and earnings stability for the entire market. Plugging the values for an individual company into this regression will yield an accounting beta for the firm. While this approach looks promising, here are a couple of cautionary notes: accounting numbers are smoothed out and can hide risk, and they are estimated at most four times a year (as opposed to market numbers, which get minute-by-minute updates).

3. *Use screens.* If you are unconvinced by either of the first two approaches, the most flexible approach for incorporating accounting information into investment decisions is to screen companies that meet pre-specified screens, and choose only those among those firms that pass these screens. Thus, you may decide that you will invest only in firms that trade at less than book value, have returns on equity that exceed 20 percent, have no debt and whose earnings have grown at least 10 percent a year for the last 5 years.

In summary, with accounting risk measures, the risk measure is related to a company's fundamentals, which seems more in keeping with an intrinsic valuation view of the world. On the flip side, accounting numbers can be misleading, and the estimates can have significant errors associated with them.

Proxy Models

The conventional models for risk and return in finance (CAPM, the arbitrage pricing model, and even multifactor models) start by making assumptions about how investors behave and how markets work to derive models that measure risk and link those measures to expected returns. While these models have the advantage of having a foundation in economic theory, they seem to fall short in explaining differences in returns across investments. The reasons for the failure of these models run the gamut: the assumptions made about markets are unrealistic (no transaction costs, perfect information) and investors don't behave rationally (and behavioral finance research provides ample evidence of this).

With proxy models, we essentially give up on building risk and return models from economic theory. Instead, we start by looking at the actual returns earned by different investments and relate returns earned to observable variables. In the earlier-referenced study by Fama and French, they examined returns earned by individual stocks from 1962 to 1989, looking for company-specific variables that did a better job of explaining return differences across firms than betas, and pinpointed two variables: the *market capitalization of a firm* and its *price-to-book ratio* (the ratio of market capitalization to accounting book value for equity). Specifically, they concluded that small market cap stocks earned much higher annual returns than large market cap stocks and that low price-to-book ratio stocks earned much higher annual returns than stocks that traded at high price-to-book ratios. Rather than view this as evidence of market inefficiency, which is what prior studies that had found the same phenomena had done, they argued that if these stocks earned higher returns over long time periods, they must be riskier than stocks that earned lower returns. In effect, market capitalization and price-to-book ratios were better proxies for risk, according to their reasoning, than betas. In fact, they regressed returns on stocks against the market capitalization of a company and its price-to-book ratio to arrive at the following regression for U.S. stocks:

$$\text{Expected monthly return} = 1.77\%$$
$$- 0.11[\ln(\text{Market capitalization in millions})]$$
$$+ 0.35[\ln(\text{Book-to-price ratio})]$$

In a pure proxy model, you could plug the market capitalization and book-to-price ratio for any company into this regression to get expected returns.

In the two decades since the Fama-French paper brought proxy models to the fore, researchers have probed the data (which has become more detailed over time) to find better and additional proxies for risk. Three of the proxies are:

1. *Earnings momentum.* Equity research analysts will find vindication in research that seems to indicate that companies that have reported stronger than expected earnings growth in the past earn higher returns than the rest of the market.
2. *Price momentum.* Chartists will smile when they read this, but researchers have concluded that price momentum carries over into future periods. Thus, the expected returns will be higher for stocks that have outperformed markets in recent time periods and lower for stocks that have lagged.
3. *Liquidity.* In a nod to real-world costs, there seems to be clear evidence that stocks that are less liquid (lower trading volume, higher bid-ask spreads) earn higher returns than more liquid stocks.

Many analysts have melded the CAPM with proxy models to create composite or melded models. For instance, analysts who value small companies derive expected returns for these companies by adding a *small cap premium* to the CAPM expected return:

$$\text{Expected return} = \text{Risk-free rate} + \text{Market beta} * \text{Equity risk premium} + \text{Small cap premium}$$

The threshold for small capitalization varies across time but is generally set at the bottom decile of publicly traded companies and the small cap premium itself is estimated by looking at the historical premium earned by small-cap stocks over the market. In a 2012 paper on equity risk premiums, I estimate that companies in the bottom market cap decile earned 4.64 percent more than the overall market between 1928 and 2011.[12] Thus, the expected return (cost of equity) for a small-cap company with a beta of 1.20 (using a risk-free rate of 2% and an equity risk premium of 6%) would be:

$$\text{Expected return} = 2\% + 1.2(6\%) + 4.64\% = 13.84\%$$

---

[12]A. Damodaran, "Equity Risk Premiums: Determinants, Estimation and Implications—The 2012 Edition" (SSRN Working Paper, http://papers.ssrn.com/sol3/papers.cfm?abstract_id=2027211).

In an alternate strategy, using the Fama-French findings, the CAPM has been expanded to include market capitalization and price-to-book ratios as additional variables, with the expected return stated as:

Expected return = Risk-free rate + Market beta * Equity risk premium
+ Size beta * Small cap risk premium
+ Book-to-market beta * Book-to-market premium

The size factor and the book-to-market betas are estimated by regressing a stock's returns against the size premium and book-to-market premiums over time; this is analogous to the way we get the market beta, by regressing stock returns against overall market returns.

While the use of proxy and melded models offers a way of adjusting expected returns to reflect market reality, there are three dangers in using these models.

1. *Data mining.* As the amount of data that we have on companies increases and becomes more accessible, it is inevitable that we will find more variables that are related to returns. It is also likely that most of these variables are not proxies for risk and that the correlation is a function of the time period that we look at. In effect, proxy models are statistical models and not economic models. Thus, there is no easy way to separate the variables that matter from those that do not.
2. *Standard error.* Since proxy models come from looking at historical data, they are burdened by the noise in the data. Stock returns are extremely volatile over time, and any historical premiums that we compute (for market capitalization or any other variable) are going to have significant standard errors. For instance, the small cap premium of 4.64 percent between 1928 and 2011 has a standard error of 2.01 percent; put simply, the true premium may be less than 1 percent or higher than 7 percent. The standard errors on the size and book-to-market betas in the three-factor Fama-French model are so large that using them in practice creates more noise as it adds in precision.
3. *Pricing error or risk proxy.* For decades, value investors have argued that you should invest in stocks with low price-earnings (P/E) ratios that trade at low multiples of book value and have high dividend yields, pointing to the fact that you will earn higher returns by doing so. In fact, a scan of Benjamin Graham's screens from *Security Analysis* for cheap companies unearths most of the proxies that you see in use today. Proxy models incorporate all of these variables into the expected return and thus render these assets to be fairly priced. Using the circular logic of these models, markets are always efficient because any inefficiency that exists is just another risk proxy that needs to get built into the model.

There is a broader critique of this approach. If you believe that small-cap stocks are riskier than large-cap stocks, you have an obligation to think of fundamental or economic reasons why and build those into your risk and return model or into the parameters of the model. Adding a small cap premium is not only a sloppy (and high-error) way of adjusting expected returns but it is an abdication of the mission in intrinsic valuation, which is to build up your numbers from fundamentals.

Market-Implied Measures

As you can see from each of the alternatives laid out, there are assumptions underlying each alternative that can make users uncomfortable. So, what if you want to estimate a model-free cost of equity? There is a choice, but it comes with a catch. To see the choice, assume that you have a stock that has an expected annual dividend of $3 per share next year, with growth at 4 percent a year, and that the stock trades at $60. Using a very simple dividend discount model, you can back out the cost of equity for this company from the existing stock price:

Value of stock = Dividends next year/(Cost of equity − Growth rate)

$60 = $3.00/(Cost of equity − 4%)

Cost of equity = 9%

The mechanics of computing implied cost of equity become messier as you go from dividends to estimated cash flows and from stable-growth models to high-growth models, but the principle remains the same. You can use the current stock price and solve for the cost of equity. This cost of equity is a market-implied cost of equity. If you were required to value this company, though, using this cost of equity to value the stock would be pointless since you would arrive at a value of $60 and the not surprising conclusion that the stock is fairly priced.

So, what point is there to computing an implied cost of equity? There are three ways of incorporating these numbers into investing/valuation.

1. One is to use a conventional cost of equity in the valuation and to compare the market-implied cost of equity to the conventional one to see how much margin for error you have in your estimate. Thus, if you find your stock to be undervalued with an 8 percent cost of equity, but the implied cost of equity is 8.5 percent, you may very well decide not to buy the stock because your margin for error is too narrow; with an implied cost of equity of 14 percent, you may be more comfortable buying the stock. Think of it as a marriage of discounted cash flow valuation with a margin of safety.

2. The second is to compute a market-implied cost of equity for an entire sector and to use this cost as the cost of equity for all companies in that sector. Thus, you could compute the implied cost of equity for all banks of 9 percent, using an index of banking stocks and expected aggregate dividends on that index. You could then use that 9 percent cost of equity for any bank that I had to value. This, in effect, brings discounted cash flow valuation closer to relative valuation; after all, when we compare price-to-book ratios across banks, we are assuming that they all have the same risk (and costs of equity).

3. The third is to compute the market-implied cost of equity for the same company each period across a long period of time and to use that average as the cost of equity when valuing the company now. You are, in effect, assuming that the market prices your stock correctly over time but can be wrong in any given time period and that there are no other fundamental shifts that occurred over time that may have caused your cost of equity to change.

Risk-Adjusted Cash Flows

All of the alternatives listed in this section are structured around adjusting the discount rate for risk. Consequently, some of you may wonder why we do not risk-adjust the cash flows instead of risk-adjusting the discount rate. The answer to that question, though, depends on what you mean by risk-adjusting the cash flows. For the most part, here is what the proponents of this approach seem to mean. They will bring the possibility of bad scenarios (and the outcomes from these scenarios) into the expected cash flows, but that is not risk adjustment. To risk-adjust, you have to take the expected cash flows, replace them with *certainty equivalent* cash flows, and discount those certainty equivalent cash flows at the risk-free rate.

But what are certainty equivalent cash flows? To illustrate, consider a simple example. Assume that you have an investment, where there are two scenarios: a good scenario, where you make $80 instantly, and a bad one, where you lose $20 instantly. Assume also that the likelihood of each scenario occurring is 50 percent. The expected cash flow on this investment is $30 ($0.50 * $80 + 0.50 * -$20$). A risk-neutral investor would be willing to pay $30 for this investment, but a risk-averse investor would not. A risk-averse investor would pay less than $30, with how much less depending on how risk-averse the investor was. The amount he or she would be willing to pay would be the certainty equivalent cash flow.

Applying this concept to more complicated investments is generally difficult because there are essentially a very large number of scenarios and estimating cash flows under each one is difficult to do. Once the expected cash flow is computed, converting it into a certainty equivalent is just as complicated. There is one practical solution, which is to take the expected cash flow and discount it back at just the risk premium component of your discount rate. Thus, if your expected cash flow in one year is $100 million and your risk-adjusted discount rate is 9 percent (with the risk-free rate of 4 percent), the certainty equivalent for this cash flow would be:

Risk premium component of discount rate $= (1.09/1.04) - 1 = 4.81\%$

Certainty equivalent cash flow in year $1 = \$100/1.0481 = \$95.41$

Value today $=$ Certainty equivalent CF$/(1 + $ Risk-free rate$) = \$95.41/1.04$
$\qquad = \$91.74$

Note, though, that you would get exactly the same answer using the risk-adjusted discount rate approach:

Value today $=$ Expected CF$/(1 + $ Risk-adjusted discount rate$) = 100/1.09$
$\qquad = \$91.74$

Put differently, unless you have a creative way of adjusting expected cash flows for risk that does not use risk premiums that you have already computed for your discount rates, there is nothing gained in this exercise.

There are two practical approaches to certainty equivalent cash flows that have been used by some value investors. In the first, you consider only those cash flows from a business that you believe are safe (and you can count on) when you value the company. If you are correct in your assessment of these "safe" cash flows, you have risk adjusted the cash flows. The second variant is an interesting twist on dividends and a throwback to Ben Graham. To the extent that companies are reluctant to cut dividends once they initiate them, it can be argued that the dividends paid by a company reflect its view of how much of its earnings are certain. Thus, a firm that is very uncertain about future earnings may pay only 20 percent of its earnings as dividends whereas one that is more certain will pay 80 percent of its earnings. An investor who buys stocks based on their dividends thus has less need to worry about risk-adjusting those numbers.

The bottom line is that there are no shortcuts in risk adjustment. It is no easier (and it is often more difficult) to adjust expected cash flows for risk than it is to adjust discount rates for risk. If you do use one of the shortcuts—counting only safe cash flows or just dividends—recognize when these approaches will fail you (as they inevitably will), and protect yourself against those consequences.

Margin of Safety

Many value investors, suspicious of betas and other measures of risk that emerge from portfolio theory and market prices, argue that there is a far simpler way to incorporate risk into investment analysis, and that is to use a *margin of safety* (MOS) when assessing whether to invest.

The margin of safety has a long history in value investing. Though the term may have been in use prior to 1934, Graham and Dodd brought it into the value investing vernacular when they used it in the first edition of *Security Analysis*.[13] Put simply, they argued that investors should buy stocks that trade at significant discounts to intrinsic value, and they developed screens that would yield these stocks. In fact, many of Graham's screens in investment analysis (low PE, stocks that trade at a discount on networking capital) are attempts to put the margin of safety into practice.

In the years since, there have been value investors who have woven the margin of safety into their valuation strategies. In fact, here is how a savvy value investor uses MOS. The first step in the process requires screening for companies that meet good company criteria: solid management, good products, and sustainable competitive advantage; this is often done qualitatively but can be quantifiable. The second step in the process is the estimation of intrinsic value, but value investors use a variety of approaches in this endeavor: some use discounted cash flow, some use relative valuation, and some look at book value. The third step in the process is to compare the price to the intrinsic value, and that is where the MOS comes in: with a margin of safety of 40 percent, you would buy an asset only if its price was more than 40 percent below its intrinsic value. The term returned to center stage in 1991, when Seth Klarman, a value investing legend, wrote a book using the term as the title.[14] In the book, Klarman summarizes the margin of safety as "buying assets at a significant discount to underlying business value, and giving preference to tangible assets over intangibles."

The basic idea behind MOS is an unexceptional one. In fact, would any investor (growth, value, or technical analyst) disagree with the notion

---

[13] B. Graham and D. Dodd, *Security Analysis* (New York: McGraw-Hill, 1934).
[14] S. A. Klarman, *The Margin of Safety: Risk-Averse Value Investing Strategies for the Thoughtful Investor* (New York: HarperCollins, 1991).

that you would like to buy an asset at a significant discount to estimated value? Even the most daring growth investors would buy into the notion, though they may disagree about what to incorporate into intrinsic value. To integrate MOS into the investment process, we need to recognize its place in the process and its limitations.

- *Stage of the investment process.* Note that the MOS is used by investors at the very last stage of the investment process, once you have screened for good companies and estimated intrinsic value. Thinking about MOS while screening for companies or estimating intrinsic value is a distraction, not a help.

- MOS *is only as good as your estimate of intrinsic value.* This should go without saying, but the MOS is heavily dependent on getting good and unbiased estimates of the intrinsic value. Put differently, if you consistently overestimate intrinsic value by 100 percent or greater, having a 40 percent margin for error will not protect you against bad investment choices. That is perhaps the reason why MOS is not really an alternative to the standard risk and return measures used in intrinsic valuation (beta or betas). Beta is not an investment choice tool but an input (and not even the key one) into a discounted cash flow model. In other words, there is no reason why you cannot use beta to estimate intrinsic value and then use MOS to determine whether to buy the investment. If you don't like beta as your measure of risk, then how does using MOS provide an alternative? You still need to come up with a different way of incorporating risk into your analysis and estimating intrinsic value. Perhaps you would like to use the risk-free rate as your discount rate in discounted cash flow valuation and use MOS as a risk-adjustment measure.

  There are those who argue that you don't need to do discounted cash flow valuation to estimate intrinsic value and that there are alternatives. True, but they come with their own baggage. One alternative is to use relative valuation: assume that the multiple—price-earnings (P/E) ratio or enterprise value/earnings before interest, taxes, depreciation, and amortization (EV/EBITDA)—at which the sector is trading can be used to estimate the intrinsic value for your company. The upside of this approach is that it is simple and does not require an explicit risk adjustment. The downside is that you make implicit assumptions about risk and growth when you use a sector average multiple. The other alternative is to use book value, in stated or modified form, as the intrinsic value. This is not a bad way of doing things, if you trust accountants to get these numbers right—but do you?

- *A measure of error is needed in your intrinsic value estimate.* If you are going to use a MOS, it cannot be a constant. Intuitively, you would expect it to vary across investments and across time. Why? The reason you build in margins for error is because you are uncertain about your own estimates of intrinsic value, but that uncertainty is not the same for all stocks. Thus, you may feel perfectly comfortable using a 20 percent margin of safety when buying stock in a regulated utility where you feel secure about your estimates of cash flows, growth, and risk, whereas you would need a 40 percent margin of safety before buying stock in a small technology company, where you face more uncertainty. In a similar vein, you would have demanded a much larger margin of safety in a banking crisis, when macroeconomic uncertainty is substantial, than in a more settled market environment for the same stock. While this may seem completely subjective, it does not have to be so. If you can bring probabilistic approaches (simulations, scenario analysis) to play in intrinsic valuation, you can estimate not only intrinsic value but also the standard error in the estimates.
- *There is a cost to having a larger margin of safety.* Adding MOS to the investment process adds a constraint, and every constraint creates a cost. What, you may wonder, is the cost of investing only in stocks that have a margin of safety of 40 percent or higher? Borrowing from statistics, there are two types of errors in investing: type 1 errors, where you invest in overvalued stocks thinking that they are cheap, and type 2 errors, where you don't invest in undervalued stocks because of concerns that they might be overvalued. Adding MOS to the screening process and increasing the MOS reduces your chance of type 1 errors but increases the possibility of type 2 errors. For individual investors or small portfolio managers, the cost of type 2 errors may be small because they have relatively little money to invest and there are so many listed stocks. However, as fund size increases, the costs of type 2 errors will also go up. Many larger mutual fund managers who claim to be value investors cannot find enough stocks that meet their MOS criteria and hold larger and larger amounts in cash.

  It gets worse when a MOS is overlaid on top of conservative estimates of intrinsic value. Though the investments that make it through both tests may be wonderful, there may be very few or no investments that meet these criteria. You would love to find a company with growing earnings and no debt that is trading for less than the cash balance on the balance sheet. Who would not? But what are your chances of finding this incredible bargain? And what do you plan to do if you do not find it?

Rather than making intrinsic valuation techniques (such as DCF) the enemy and portraying portfolio theory as the black science, value investors who want to use MOS should consider incorporating useful information from both to refine MOS as an investment technique. After all, all investors have a shared objective. They want to generate better returns on their investments than the proverbial monkey with a dartboard or an S&P 500 index fund.

EQUITY RISK: ASSESSING THE FIELD

Even as we agree to disagree about the usefulness or lack of the same of betas, let us reach consensus on two fundamental facts: to ignore risk in investments is foolhardy, and not all investments are equally risky. Thus, no matter what investment strategy you adopt, you have to develop your own devices for measuring and controlling for risk. In making your choice, consider the following:

- *Explicit versus implicit.* There are plenty of analysts who steer away from discounted cash flow valuation and use relative valuation (multiples and comparable firms) because they are uncomfortable with measuring risk explicitly. However, what they fail to recognize is that they are implicitly making a risk adjustment. How? When you compare P/E ratios across banks and suggest that the bank with the lowest P/E ratio is cheapest, you are implicitly assuming that banks are all equally risky. Similarly, when you tell me to buy a technology firm because it trades at a price-earnings/growth (PEG) ratio lower than the PEG ratio for the technology sector, you are assuming that the firm has the same risk as other companies in the sector. The danger with implicit assumptions is that you can be lulled into a false sense of complacency, even as circumstances change. After all, does it make sense to assume that Citigroup and Wells Fargo, both large money center banks, are equally risky? Or that Adobe and Microsoft, both software firms, have the same risk exposure?
- *Quantitative versus qualitative.* Analysts who use conventional risk and return models are often accused of being too number oriented and not looking enough at qualitative factors. Perhaps, but the true test of a savvy investor is whether you can take the stories that you hear about companies and convert them into numbers for the future. Thus, if your argument is that a company has loyal customers, you would expect to

see the evidence in stable revenues and lots of repeat customers; as a result, the cash flows for the company will be higher and less risky. After all, at the end of the process, your dividends are not paid with qualitative dollars but with quantitative ones.

- *Simple versus complicated.* Sometimes, less is more and you get your best assessments when you keep things simple. In fact, one reason that you may stay with the CAPM is that it is a simple model at its core and you are reluctant to abandon it for more complex models until you are given convincing evidence that these models work better.

Find your own way of adjusting for risk in valuation, but refine it and question it constantly. The best feedback you get will be from your investment mistakes, since they give you indicators of the risks you missed on your original assessment. In addition, remain wedded to the fundamental principle that value is affected by risk but do not be locked into any risk and return model, since it is just a means to an end.

DEFAULT RISK

The risk that we have discussed hitherto in this chapter relates to cash flows on investments being different from expected cash flows. There are some investments, however, in which the cash flows are promised when the investment is made and the risk is that these promises will be broken. This is the case, for instance, when you lend to a business by buying a corporate bond. However, the borrower (bond issuer) may default on interest and principal payments on the borrowing. Generally speaking, borrowers with higher default risk should pay higher interest rates on their borrowing than those with lower default risk. This section examines the measurement of default risk and the relationship of default risk to interest rates on borrowing.

In contrast to the general risk and return models for equity, which evaluate the effects of market risk on expected returns, models of default risk measure the consequences of firm-specific default risk on promised returns. Diversification can be used to explain why firm-specific risk will not be priced into expected returns for equities, but the same rationale cannot be applied to securities that have limited upside potential and much greater downside potential from firm-specific events. To see what we mean by limited upside potential, consider investing in bonds issued by a company. The coupons are fixed at the time of the issue, and these coupons represent the promised cash flow on the bond. The best-case scenario for you as an investor is that you receive the promised cash flows; you are not entitled to more than these cash flows even if the company is wildly successful. All other scenarios contain only bad news, though in varying degrees, with the delivered cash flows being less than the promised cash flows. Consequently, the expected return on a corporate bond should reflect the firm-specific default risk of the firm issuing the bond.

The Determinants of Default Risk

The default risk of a firm is a function of two factors. The first factor is the firm's capacity to generate cash flows from operations, and the second factor is the magnitude of its financial obligations, including interest and principal payments.[15] Firms that generate high cash flows relative to their financial obligations should have lower default risk than firms that generate low cash flows relative to their financial obligations. Thus, firms with significant existing investments that generate relatively high cash flows will have lower default risk than firms that do not have such investments.

In addition to the size of a firm's cash flows, the default risk is also affected by the volatility in these cash flows. The more stability there is in cash flows, the lower the default risk in the firm. Firms that operate in predictable and stable businesses will have lower default risk than will other similar firms that operate in cyclical or volatile businesses. Most assessments of default risk use financial ratios to measure the cash flow coverage (i.e., the magnitude of cash flows relative to obligations) and control for industry effects to evaluate the variability in cash flows.

Bond Ratings as Measures of Default Risk

The most widely used measure of a firm's default risk is its bond rating, which is generally assigned by independent ratings agencies. The two best known are Standard & Poor's and Moody's Investors Service. Thousands of companies are rated by these two agencies, and their views carry significant weight with financial markets. The ratings assigned by these agencies are letter ratings. The process of rating a bond usually starts when the issuing company requests a rating from a bond ratings agency. The ratings agency then collects information from both publicly available sources, such

---

[15]Financial obligation refers to any payment that the firm has legally obligated itself to make, such as interest and principal payments or lease payments.

It does not include discretionary cash flows, such as dividend payments or new capital expenditures, which can be deferred or delayed without legal consequences, though there may be economic consequences.

as financial statements, and the company itself and makes a decision on the rating. If the company disagrees with the rating, it is given the opportunity to present additional information.

A rating of AAA from Standard & Poor's and Aaa from Moody's represents the highest rating granted to firms that are viewed as having the lowest default risk. As the default risk increases, the ratings decrease toward D for firms in default. A rating at or above BBB (Baa) by Standard & Poor's (Moody's) is categorized as investment grade, reflecting the view of the ratings agency that there is relatively little default risk in investing in bonds issued by these firms.

The bond ratings assigned by ratings agencies are primarily based on publicly available information, though private information conveyed by the firm to the ratings agency does play a role. The rating assigned to a company's bonds will depend in large part on financial ratios that measure the capacity of the company to meet debt payments and generate stable and predictable cash flows. A multitude of financial ratios exist, and Table 2.1 summarizes some of the key ratios used to measure default risk.

Not surprisingly, firms that generate income and cash flows significantly higher than debt payments, that are profitable, and that have low debt ratios are more likely to be highly rated than are firms that do not have these characteristics. There will be individual firms whose ratings are not consistent with their financial ratios, however, because the ratings agency does add subjective judgments into the final mix. Thus, a firm that performs poorly on financial ratios but is expected to improve its performance dramatically

TABLE 2.1 Financial Ratios Used to Measure Default Risk

Financial Ratio	Definition
EBITDA to revenues	EBITDA/Revenues
Return on invested capital (ROIC)	Earnings before interest and taxes (EBIT)/(BV of debt + BV of equity − Cash)
Interest coverage ratio	EBIT/Interest expenses
EBITDA to interest	EBITDA/Interest expenses
Funds from operations (FFO) to debt	(Net income + Depreciation)/Debt
Free operating cash flows to debt	Funds from operations/Debt
Discounted cash flows (DCF) to debt	Discounted cash flows/Debt
Debt to EBITDA	Book value (BV) of debt/EBITDA
D/(D + E)	BV of debt/(BV of debt + BV of equity)

Source: Standard & Poor's.

over the next period may receive a higher rating than is justified by its current financials. For most firms, however, the financial ratios should provide a reasonable basis for guessing at the bond rating.

What If a Firm Has No Bond Rating, and Why Do We Care?

Not all firms that borrow money have bond ratings available on them. How do you go about estimating the cost of debt for these firms? There are two choices.

- One is to look at recent borrowing history. Many firms that are not rated still borrow money from banks and other financial institutions. By looking at the most recent borrowings made by a firm, you can get a sense of the types of default spreads being charged the firm and use these spreads to come up with a cost of debt.
- The other method is to estimate a synthetic rating for the firm (i.e., use the financial ratios used by the bond ratings agencies to estimate a rating for the firm). To do this you would need to begin with the rated firms and examine the financial characteristics shared by firms within each ratings class. As an example, assume that you have an unrated firm with operating earnings of $100 million and interest expenses of $20 million. You could use the interest coverage ratio of 5.00 (100/20) to estimate a bond rating of A– for this firm.[16]

NUMBER WATCH

Ratings and default spreads: Take a look at the typical default spreads for bonds in different ratings classes.

The interest rate on a corporate bond should be a function of its default risk, which is measured by its rating. If the rating is a good measure of the default risk, higher-rated bonds should be priced to yield lower interest rates

---

[16]This rating was based on a look-up table that was developed in the mid-1990s and has been updated every two years since, by listing out all rated firms with market capitalization lower than $5 billion and their interest coverage ratios, and then sorting firms based on their bond ratings. The ranges were adjusted to eliminate outliers and to prevent overlapping ranges.

TABLE 2.2 Default Spreads and
Bond Ratings – September 2011

Rating	Spread
AAA	0.75%
AA	1.05%
A+	1.20%
A	1.35%
A–	1.55%
BBB	2.35%
BB+	4.00%
BB	5.00%
B+	5.75%
B	6.25%
B–	6.50%
CCC	10.00%
CC	11.50%
C	12.70%
D	14.00%

Source: www.bondsonline.com.

than would lower-rated bonds. The difference between the interest rate on a
bond with default risk and a default-free government bond is defined to be
the *default spread*. Table 2.2 summarizes default spreads over the treasury
for 10-year bonds in S&P's different ratings classes as of September 30,
2011.

These default spreads, when added to the riskless rate, yield the interest
rates for bonds with the specified ratings. For instance, a D-rated bond has
an interest rate about 14 percent higher than the riskless rate. This default
spread may vary by maturity of the bond and can also change from period
to period, depending on economic conditions, widening during economic
slowdowns and narrowing when the economy is strong.

CONCLUSION

Risk, as we define it in finance, is measured based on deviations of actual
returns on an investment from its expected returns. There are two types of
risk. The first, which we call equity risk, arises in investments where there
are no promised cash flows but there are expected cash flows. The second,
default risk, arises on investments with promised cash flows.

For investments with equity risk, the risk is measured by looking at the
variance of actual returns around the expected returns, with greater variance

indicating greater risk. This risk can be broken down into risk that affects one or a few investments, which we call firm-specific risk, and risk that affects many investments, which we refer to as market risk. When investors diversify, they can reduce their exposure to firm-specific risk. By assuming that the investors who trade at the margin are well diversified, we conclude that the risk we should be looking at with equity investments is the market risk. The different models of equity risk introduced in this chapter share this objective of measuring market risk, but they differ in the way they do it. In the capital asset pricing model, exposure to market risk is measured by a market beta, which estimates how much risk an individual investment will add to a portfolio that includes all traded assets. The arbitrage pricing model and the multifactor model allow for multiple sources of market risk and estimate betas for an investment relative to each source. For those who remain skeptical of risk and return models based on portfolio theory, we looked at alternatives: risk measures based on accounting ratios, using market capitalization or other proxies for risk, backing out the implied risk from market prices, risk-adjusting the cash flows, and building in a margin of safety when making investments.

On investments with default risk, risk is measured by the likelihood that the promised cash flows might not be delivered. Investments with higher default risk should have higher interest rates, and the premium that we demand over a riskless rate is the default premium. For most U.S. companies, default risk is measured by ratings agencies in the form of a company rating; these ratings determine, in large part, the interest rates at which these firms can borrow. Even in the absence of ratings, interest rates will include a default premium that reflects the lenders' assessments of default risk. These default-risk-adjusted interest rates represent the cost of borrowing or debt for a business.

EXERCISES

Pick a company that you are familiar with in terms of its business and history. Try doing the following:

1. Find an annualized standard deviation for the stock of the company over a period (a year, two years, five years). Compare it to the standard deviation in stock prices for the sector in which it operates (from my website).
2. Find a beta for your company on a service (Yahoo! Finance, Morningstar, Value Line). Better still, find the betas for your company on many services and look at the range.

   a. Compare the beta to the average beta for the sector in which the company operates.

   b. Use the beta in conjunction with a risk-free rate and equity risk premium (also available on my website) today to estimate an expected return for the stock. What does that expected return tell you? Why does it matter?

3. Check to see if your company has a bond rating. If it does, use that rating to estimate a default spread and a cost of debt for your firm.

4. If you can compute a cost of capital for your firm, do so, and compare it to the average for the sector in which it operates.

Lessons for Investors

- Your perceptions of how risky an investment is may be very different from the risk perceived by the marginal investors (the large institutional investors who set prices at the margin). The market prices assets based on the marginal investors' perceptions of risk.

- If the marginal investors in a company are well diversified, the only risk that is priced is the risk that cannot be diversified away in a portfolio. Individual risk and return models differ on how to measure this nondiversifiable risk. The capital asset pricing model tries to measure it with one beta, whereas multifactor models try to measure it with multiple betas. The measure of risk allows us to estimate an expected return on a risky investment for the future. This expected return becomes the benchmark that the investment has to beat to be a good investment.

- To the extent that you do not buy into beta or betas as measures of risk, you should consider the alternatives, which can range from using proxy measures for risk (size of the company, the industry it operates in) to accounting ratios.

- For bonds, risk is measured as default or downside risk, since there is not much potential on the upside. Bonds with higher default risk should command higher interest rates.

CHAPTER 3

Numbers Don't Lie—Or Do They?

Financial statements provide us with the fundamental information that we use to analyze firms. Although you may be able to become a successful investor without ever understanding financial statements, it does make the investment process a lot easier if you can make sense of them. It is important, therefore, that we examine the principles governing these statements and how they help us (or fail to help us) answer four questions:

1. *How valuable are the assets of a firm?* The assets of a firm can come in several forms—assets with long lives such as land and buildings, assets with shorter lives such as inventory, and intangible assets that still produce revenues for the firm, such as patents and trademarks.
2. *How did the firm raise the funds to finance these assets?* In acquiring these assets, firms can use the funds of the owners (equity) or borrowed money (debt), and the mix is likely to change as the assets age.
3. *How profitable are these assets?* To evaluate whether the investments that a firm has already made are good investments, we need to estimate what returns it is making on these investments.
4. *How much uncertainty (or risk) is embedded in these assets?* Estimating how much uncertainty there is in existing investments and the implications for a firm is clearly a first step.

We will look at the way accountants would answer these questions, and why financial statements can sometimes provide a misleading picture of a firm's health and success. Some of these distortions can be traced to the differences in objectives; accountants try to measure the current standing and immediate past performance of a firm, whereas investing is much more forward-looking.

THE BASIC ACCOUNTING STATEMENTS

There are three basic accounting statements that summarize information about a firm. The first is the *balance sheet*, shown in Figure 3.1, which

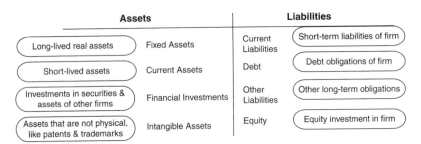

FIGURE 3.1   The Balance Sheet

summarizes the assets owned by a firm; the value of these assets; and the mix of financing—both debt and equity—used to finance these assets at a point in time.

The next is the *income statement*, shown in Figure 3.2, which provides information on the revenues and expenses of the firm, and the resulting income made by the firm, during a period. The period can be a quarter (if it is a quarterly income statement) or a year (if it is an annual report).

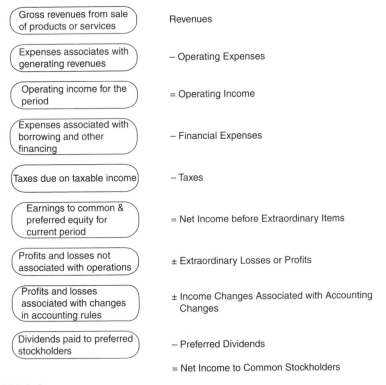

FIGURE 3.2   Income Statement

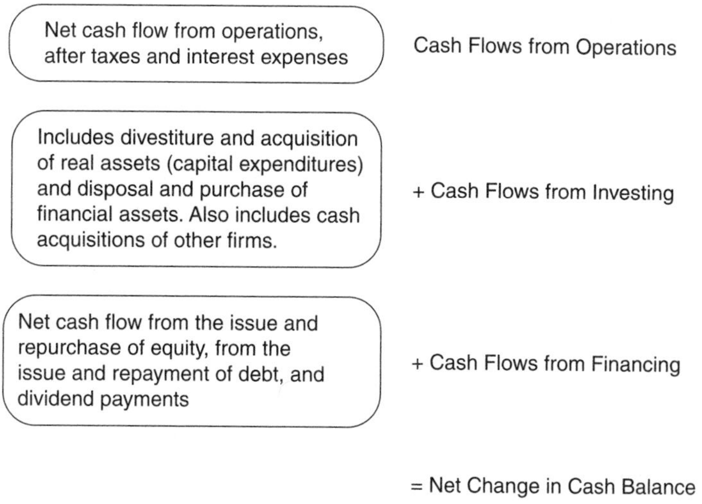

Net cash flow from operations, after taxes and interest expenses — Cash Flows from Operations

Includes divestiture and acquisition of real assets (capital expenditures) and disposal and purchase of financial assets. Also includes cash acquisitions of other firms. — + Cash Flows from Investing

Net cash flow from the issue and repurchase of equity, from the issue and repayment of debt, and dividend payments — + Cash Flows from Financing

= Net Change in Cash Balance

FIGURE 3.3 Statement of Cash Flows

Finally, there is the *statement of cash flows*, shown in Figure 3.3, which specifies the sources and uses of cash of the firm from operating, investing, and financing activities during a period.

The statement of cash flows can be viewed as an attempt to explain how much the cash flows during a period were and why the cash balance changed during the period.

ASSET MEASUREMENT AND VALUATION

When analyzing any firm, we would like to know the types of assets that it owns, the values of these assets, and the degree of uncertainty about these values. Accounting statements do a reasonably good job of categorizing the assets owned by a firm, a partial job of assessing the values of these assets, and a poor job of reporting uncertainty about asset values. In this section, we begin by looking at the accounting principles underlying asset categorization and measurement, and the limitations of financial statements in providing relevant information about assets.

Accounting Principles Underlying Asset Measurement

An asset is any resource that has the potential to either generate future cash inflows or reduce future cash outflows. While that is a general definition broad enough to cover almost any kind of asset, accountants add a caveat that for a resource to be an asset, a firm has to have acquired it in a prior transaction and be able to quantify future benefits with reasonable precision. The accounting view of asset value is to a great extent grounded in the notion of *historical cost*, which is the original cost of the asset, adjusted upward for improvements made to the asset since purchase and downward for the loss in value associated with the aging of the asset. This historical cost is called the *book value*. Though the generally accepted accounting principles for valuing an asset vary across different kinds of assets, three principles underlie the way assets are valued in accounting statements.

1. *An abiding belief in book value as the best estimate of value.* Accounting estimates of asset value begin with the book value. Unless a substantial reason is given to do otherwise, accountants view the historical cost as the best estimate of the value of an asset.
2. *A distrust of market or estimated value.* When a current market value exists for an asset that is different from the book value, accounting convention seems to view this market value with suspicion. The market price of an asset is often viewed as both much too volatile and too easily manipulated to be used as an estimate of value for an asset. This suspicion runs even deeper when values are estimated for an asset based on expected future cash flows. In recent years, though, there has been more acceptance of market value, at least in some quarters, embodied in the push toward fair value accounting.
3. *A preference for underestimating value rather than overestimating it.* When there is more than one approach to valuing an asset, accounting convention takes the view that the more conservative (lower) estimate of value should be used rather than the less conservative (higher) estimate of value.

Measuring Asset Value

The financial statement in which accountants summarize and report asset value is the balance sheet. To examine how asset value is measured, let us begin with the way assets are categorized in the balance sheet. First, there are the *fixed assets*, which include the long-term assets of the firm, such as plant, equipment, land, and buildings. Next, we have the short-term assets of the firm, including inventory (including raw materials, work in progress, and finished goods); receivables (summarizing moneys owed to the firm); and cash; these are categorized as *current assets*. We then have investments in the assets and securities of other firms, which are generally categorized as financial investments. Finally, we have what is loosely categorized as *intangible assets*. These include assets such as patents and trademarks that presumably will create future earnings and cash flows, and also uniquely accounting assets such as goodwill that arise because of acquisitions made by the firm.

Fixed Assets Generally accepted accounting principles (GAAP) in the United States require the valuation of fixed assets at historical cost, adjusted for any estimated gain or loss in value from improvements or the aging, respectively, of these assets. While in theory the adjustments for aging should reflect the loss of earning power of the asset as it ages, in practice they are much more a product of accounting rules and conventions, and these adjustments are called *depreciation*. Depreciation methods can very broadly be categorized into *straight-line* (where the loss in asset value is assumed to be the same every year over its lifetime) and *accelerated* (where the asset loses more value in the earlier years and less in the later years). While tax rules, at least in the United States, have restricted the freedom that firms have on their choice of asset life and depreciation methods, firms continue to have a significant amount of flexibility on these decisions for reporting purposes. Thus, the depreciation that is reported in the annual reports may not, and generally is not, the same depreciation that is used in the tax statements.

Since fixed assets are valued at book value and are adjusted for depreciation provisions, the value of a fixed asset is strongly influenced by both its depreciable life and the depreciation method used. Many firms in the United States use straight-line depreciation for financial reporting while using accelerated depreciation for tax purposes, since firms can report better earnings with the former,[1] at least in the years right after the asset is acquired. In contrast, Japanese and German firms often use accelerated depreciation for both tax and financial reporting purposes, leading to reported income that is understated relative to that of their U.S. counterparts.

Current Assets Current assets include inventory, cash, and accounts receivable. It is in this category that accountants are most amenable to the use of market value, especially in valuing marketable securities.

Accounts Receivable Accounts receivable represent money owed by entities to the firm on the sale of products on credit. The accounting convention is for accounts receivable to be recorded as the amount owed to the firm, based on the billing at the time of the credit sale. The only major valuation and accounting issue is when the firm has to recognize accounts receivable

---

[1]Depreciation is treated as an accounting expense. Hence, the use of straight-line depreciation (which is lower than accelerated depreciation in the first few years after an asset is acquired) will result in lower expenses and higher income.

that are not collectible. Firms can set aside a portion of their income to cover expected *bad debts* from credit sales, and accounts receivable will be reduced by this reserve. Alternatively, the bad debts can be recognized as they occur and the firm can reduce the accounts receivable accordingly. There is the danger, however, that absent a decisive declaration of a bad debt, firms may continue to show as accounts receivable amounts that they know are unlikely to ever be collected.

Cash   Cash is one of the few assets for which accountants and financial analysts should agree on value. The value of a cash balance should not be open to estimation error. Having said this, we should note that fewer and fewer companies actually hold cash in the conventional sense (as currency or as demand deposits in banks). Firms often invest the cash in interest-bearing accounts, corporate bonds or in U.S. Treasury securities, so as to earn a return on their investments. In either case, market value can deviate from book value, especially if the investments are longer term or riskier. While there is may be little default risk in these investments, interest rate movements can affect their value. We will examine the valuation of marketable securities later in this section.

Inventory   Three basic approaches to valuing inventory are allowed by GAAP: first in, first out (FIFO); last in, first out (LIFO); and weighted average.

1. *First in, first out (FIFO).* Under FIFO, the cost of goods sold is based on the cost of material bought earliest in the period, while the cost of inventory is based on the cost of material bought latest in the period. This results in inventory being valued close to the current replacement cost. During periods of inflation, the use of FIFO will result in the lowest estimate of cost of goods sold among the three valuation approaches, and the highest net income.

2. *Last in, first out (LIFO).* Under LIFO, the cost of goods sold is based on the cost of material bought latest in the period, while the cost of inventory is based on the cost of material bought earliest in the period. This results in finished goods being valued close to the current production cost. During periods of inflation, the use of LIFO will result in the highest estimate of cost of goods sold among the three valuation approaches, and the lowest net income.

3. *Weighted average.* Under the weighted average approach, both inventory and the cost of goods sold are based on the average cost of all materials bought during the period. When inventory turns over rapidly, this approach will more closely resemble FIFO than LIFO.

Firms often adopt the LIFO approach for its tax benefits during periods of high inflation. The cost of goods sold is then higher because it is based on prices paid toward to the end of the accounting period. This, in turn, will reduce the reported taxable income and net income while increasing cash flows. Studies indicate that larger firms with rising prices for raw materials and labor, more variable inventory growth, and an absence of other tax-loss carryforwards are much more likely to adopt the LIFO approach.

Given the income and cash flow effects of inventory valuation methods, it is often difficult to compare the inventory values of firms that use different methods. There is, however, one way of adjusting for these differences. Firms that choose the LIFO approach to value inventories have to specify in a footnote the difference in inventory valuation between FIFO and LIFO, and this difference is termed the *LIFO reserve*. It can be used to adjust the beginning and ending inventories, and consequently the cost of goods sold, and to restate income based on FIFO valuation.

Investments (Financial) and Marketable Securities   In the category of investments and marketable securities, accountants consider investments made by firms in the securities or assets of other firms, and other marketable securities, including Treasury bills or bonds. The way in which these assets are valued depends on the way the investment is categorized and the motive behind the investment. In general, an investment in the securities of another firm can be categorized as a *minority passive investment*, a *minority active investment*, or a *majority active investment*. The accounting rules vary depending on the categorization.

Minority Passive Investments   If the securities or assets owned in another firm represent less than 20 percent of the overall ownership of that firm, an investment is treated as a *minority passive investment*. These investments have an acquisition value, which represents what the firm originally paid for the securities and often a market value. Accounting principles require that these assets be subcategorized into one of three groups: investments that will be held to maturity, investments that are available for sale, and trading investments. The valuation principles vary for each.

1. For investments that will be held to maturity, the valuation is at historical cost or book value, and interest or dividends from this investment are shown in the income statement under net interest expenses.
2. For investments that are available for sale, the valuation is at market value, but the unrealized gains or losses are shown as part of the equity in the balance sheet and not in the income statement. Thus, unrealized

losses reduce the book value of the equity in the firm, and unrealized gains increase the book value of equity.

3. For trading investments, the valuation is at market value, and the unrealized gains and losses are shown in the income statement.

Firms are allowed an element of discretion in the way they classify investments and, subsequently, in the way they value these assets. This classification ensures that firms such as investment banks, whose assets are primarily securities held in other firms for purposes of trading, revalue the bulk of these assets at market levels each period. This is called *marking to market* and provides one of the few instances in which market value trumps book value in accounting statements.

Minority Active Investments   If the securities or assets owned in another firm represent between 20 and 50 percent of the overall ownership of that firm, an investment is treated as a *minority active investment*. While these investments have an initial acquisition value, a proportional share (based on ownership proportion) of the net income and losses made by the firm in which the investment was made is used to adjust the acquisition cost. In addition, the dividends received from the investment reduce the acquisition cost. This approach to valuing investments is called the *equity approach*.

The market value of these investments is not considered until the investment is liquidated, at which point the gain or loss from the sale, relative to the adjusted acquisition cost, is shown as part of the earnings under extraordinary items in that period.

Majority Active Investments   If the securities or assets owned in another firm represent more than 50 percent of the overall ownership of that firm, an investment is treated as a *majority active investment*.[2] In this case, the investment is no longer shown as a financial investment but is instead replaced by the assets and liabilities of the firm in which the investment was made. This approach leads to a *consolidation* of the balance sheets of the two firms, where the assets and liabilities of the two firms are merged and presented as one balance sheet. The share of the subsidiary firm that is owned not owned by the parent firm is shown as a *minority interest* on the liability side of the consolidated balance sheet. The statement of cash flows reflects the cumulated cash inflows and outflows of the combined firm. This is in contrast to the equity approach, used for minority active investments, in which only the

---

[2]Firms have evaded the requirements of consolidation by keeping their share of ownership in other firms below 50 percent.

dividends received on the investment are shown as a cash inflow in the cash flow statement.

Here again, the market value of this investment is not considered until the ownership stake is liquidated. At that point, the difference between the market price and the net value of the equity stake in the firm is treated as a gain or loss for the period.

Intangible Assets   Intangible assets include a wide array of assets ranging from patents and trademarks to goodwill. The accounting standards vary across intangible assets.

- *Patents and trademarks.* Patents and trademarks are valued differently depending on whether they are generated internally or acquired. When patents and trademarks are generated from internal sources, such as research, the costs incurred in developing the asset are expensed in that period even though the asset might have a life of several accounting periods. Thus, the intangible asset is not usually valued in the balance sheet of the firm. In contrast, when an intangible asset is acquired from an external party, it is treated as an asset.

    Intangible assets have to be amortized over their expected lives, with a maximum amortization period of 40 years. The standard practice is to use straight-line amortization. For tax purposes, however, firms are not allowed to amortize intangible assets with no specific lifetimes.
- *Goodwill.* Intangible assets are sometimes the by-products of acquisitions. When a firm acquires another firm, the purchase price is first allocated to tangible assets and then allocated to any intangible assets such as patents or trade names. Any residual becomes *goodwill*. While accounting principles suggest that goodwill captures the value of any intangibles that are not specifically identifiable, it is really a reflection of the difference between the market value of the firm owning the assets and the adjusted book value of assets. This approach is called *purchase accounting* and it creates an intangible asset (goodwill) that is usually amortized over time.

Until 2000, firms that did not want to see this charge against their earnings often used an alternative approach called *pooling accounting*, in which the purchase price never showed up in the balance sheet. Instead, the book values of the two companies involved in the merger were aggregated to create the consolidated balance sheet of the combined firm.

The rules on acquisition accounting have changed substantially in the past decade both in the United States and internationally. Not only is purchase accounting required on all acquisitions, but firms are no longer allowed to automatically amortize goodwill over long periods (as they were used to doing). Instead, an acquiring firm is required to reassess the values of the acquired entity every year; if the values have dropped since the acquisition, the value of goodwill have to be reduced (impaired) to reflect the decline in values. If the acquired firm's values have gone up, though, the goodwill cannot be increased to reflect this change.

MEASURING FINANCING MIX

The second set of questions that we would like to answer and accounting statements to shed some light on relates to the current value and subsequently the mixture of debt and equity used by the firm. The bulk of the information about these questions is provided on the liability side of the balance sheet and the footnotes.

Accounting Principles Underlying Liability and Equity Measurement

Just as with the measurement of asset value, the accounting categorization of liabilities and equity is governed by a set of fairly rigid principles. The first is a *strict categorization of financing into either a liability or equity* based on the nature of the obligation. For an obligation to be recognized as a liability, it must meet three requirements:

1. It must be expected to lead to a future cash outflow or the loss of a future cash inflow at some specified or determinable date.
2. The firm cannot avoid the obligation.
3. The transaction giving rise to the obligation has already happened.

In keeping with the earlier principle of conservatism in estimating asset value, accountants recognize as liabilities cash flow obligations that cannot be avoided.

The second principle is that the values of both liabilities and equity in a firm are *better estimated using historical costs* with accounting adjustments, rather than with expected future cash flows or market value. The process by which accountants measure the values of liabilities and equities is inextricably linked to the way they value assets. Since assets are primarily valued at historical cost or at book value, both debt and equity also get measured primarily at book value. In the section that follows, we examine the accounting measurement of both liabilities and equity.

Measuring the Value of Liabilities and Equity

Accountants categorize liabilities into current liabilities, long-term debt, and long-term liabilities that are neither debt nor equity. Next, we examine the way they measure each of these.

Current Liabilities   Current liabilities include all obligations that the firm has coming due in the next accounting period. These generally include:

- *Accounts payable*—representing credit received from suppliers and other vendors to the firm. The value of accounts payable represents the amounts due to these creditors. For this item, book value and market value should be similar.
- *Short-term borrowing*—representing short-term loans (due in less than a year) taken to finance the operations or current asset needs of the business. Here again, the value shown represents the amounts due on such loans, and the book value and market value should be similar, unless the default risk of the firm has changed dramatically since it borrowed the money.
- *Short-term portion of long-term borrowing*—representing the portion of the long-term debt or bonds that is coming due in the next year. Here again, the value shown is the actual amount due on these loans, and market value and book value should converge as the due date approaches.
- *Other short-term liabilities*— a catchall component for any other short-term liabilities that the firm might have, including wages due to its employees and taxes due to the government.

Of all the items on the liability side of the balance sheet, absent outright fraud, current liabilities should be the one for which the accounting estimates of book value and financial estimates of market value are the closest.

Long-Term Debt   Long-term debt for firms can take one of two forms. It can be a long-term loan from a bank or other financial institution, or it can be a long-term bond issued to financial markets, in which case the creditors are the investors in the bond. Accountants measure the value of long-term debt by looking at the present value of payments due on the loan or bond at the time of the borrowing. For bank loans, this will be equal to the nominal value of the loan. With bonds, however, there are three possibilities: When bonds are issued at par value, for instance, the value of the long-term debt is generally measured in terms of the nominal obligation created, in terms of principal (face value) due on the borrowing. When bonds are issued at a premium or a discount on par value, the bonds are recorded at the issue price, but the premium or discount to the face value is amortized over the life of the bond. As an extreme example, companies that issue zero coupon debt have to record the debt at the issue price, which will be significantly below the principal (face value) due at maturity. The difference between the issue price and the face value is amortized each period and is treated as a noncash interest expense.

In all of these cases, the book value of debt is unaffected by changes in interest rates during the life of the loan or bond. Note that as market interest rates rise, the present value of the loan obligations should decrease, and as interest rates fall, the loan value increases. This updated market value for debt is not shown on the balance sheet. If debt is retired prior to maturity, the difference between book value and the amount paid at retirement is treated as an extraordinary gain or loss in the income statement.

Finally, companies that have long-term debt denominated in nondomestic currencies have to adjust the book value of debt for changes in exchange rates. Since exchange rate changes reflect underlying changes in interest rates, it does imply that this debt is likely to be valued much nearer to market value than is debt in the home currency.

Other Long-Term Liabilities   Firms often have long-term obligations that are not captured in the long-term debt item. These include obligations to lessors on assets that firms have leased, to employees in the form of pension fund and health care benefits yet to be paid, and to the government in the form of taxes deferred. In the past two decades, accountants have increasingly moved toward quantifying these liabilities and showing them as long-term liabilities.

Leases   Firms often choose to lease long-term assets rather than buy them. Lease payments create the same kind of obligation that interest payments on debt create, and they must be viewed in a similar light. If a firm is allowed to lease a significant portion of its assets and keep it off its financial statements, a perusal of the statements will give a very misleading view of the company's financial strength. Consequently, accounting rules have been devised to force firms to reveal the extent of their lease obligations on their books.

There are two ways of accounting for leases. In an *operating lease*, the lessor (or owner) transfers only the right to use the property to the lessee. At the end of the lease period, the lessee returns the property to the lessor. Since the lessee does not assume the risk of ownership, the lease expense is treated as an operating expense in the income statement and the lease does not affect the balance sheet. In a *capital lease*, the lessee assumes some of the risks of ownership and enjoys some of the benefits. Consequently, the lease, when signed, is recognized both as an asset and as a liability (for the lease payments) on the balance sheet. The firm gets to claim depreciation each year on the asset and also deducts the interest expense component of the lease payment each year. In general, capital leases recognize expenses sooner than equivalent operating leases.

Since firms prefer to keep leases off the books and sometimes to defer expenses, they have a strong incentive to report all leases as operating leases. Consequently, the Financial Accounting Standards Board (FASB) has ruled that a lease should be treated as a capital lease if it meets any one of the following four conditions:

1. The lease life exceeds 75 percent of the life of the asset.
2. There is a transfer of ownership to the lessee at the end of the lease term.
3. There is an option to purchase the asset at a bargain price at the end of the lease term.
4. The present value of the lease payments, discounted at an appropriate discount rate, exceeds 90 percent of the fair market value of the asset.

The lessor uses the same criteria for determining whether the lease is a capital or operating lease and accounts for it accordingly. If it is a capital lease, the lessor records the present value of future cash flows as revenue and recognizes expenses. The lease receivable is also shown as an asset on the balance sheet, and the interest revenue is recognized over the term of the lease as it is paid.

From a tax standpoint, the lessor can claim the tax benefits of the leased asset only if it is an operating lease, though the revenue code uses slightly different criteria[3] for determining whether the lease is an operating lease.

Employee Benefits Employers provide pension and health care benefits to their employees. In many cases, the obligations created by these benefits are extensive, and a failure by the firm to adequately fund these obligations needs to be revealed in financial statements.

- *Pension plans.* In a pension plan, the firm agrees to provide certain benefits to its employees, either by specifying a defined contribution (wherein a fixed contribution is made to the plan each year by the employer, without any promises as to the benefits that will be delivered

---

[3]The requirements for an operating lease in the revenue code are as follows: (1) the property can be used by someone other than the lessee at the end of the lease term, (2) the lessee cannot buy the asset using a bargain purchase option, (3) the lessor has at least 20 percent of its capital at risk, (4) the lessor has a positive cash flow from the lease independent of tax benefits, and (5) the lessee does not have an investment in the lease.

in the plan) or a defined benefit (wherein the employer promises to pay a certain benefit to the employee). In the latter case, the employer has to put sufficient money into the plan each period to meet the defined benefits.

Under a defined contribution plan, the firm meets its obligation once it has made the prespecified contribution to the plan. Under a defined benefit plan, the firm's obligations are much more difficult to estimate, since they will be determined by a number of variables, including the benefits that employees are entitled to, the prior contributions made by the employer, the returns the plan has earned, and the rate of return that the employer expects to make on current contributions. As these variables change, the value of the pension fund assets can be greater than, less than, or equal to pension fund liabilities (which is the present value of promised benefits). A pension fund whose assets exceed its liabilities is an overfunded plan, whereas one whose assets are less than its liabilities is an underfunded plan and disclosures to that effect have to be included in financial statements, generally in the footnotes.

When a pension fund is overfunded, the firm has several options. It can withdraw the excess assets from the fund, it can discontinue contributions to the plan, or it can continue to make contributions on the assumption that the overfunding is a transitory phenomenon that could well disappear by the next period. When a fund is underfunded, the firm has a liability, though accounting standards require that firms reveal only the excess of accumulated pension fund liabilities over pension fund assets on the balance sheet.[4]

- *Health care benefits.* A firm can provide health care benefits in one of two ways: by making a fixed contribution to a health care plan without promising specific benefits (analogous to a defined contribution plan), or by promising specific health benefits and setting aside the funds to provide these benefits (analogous to a defined benefit plan). The accounting for health care benefits is very similar to the accounting for pension obligations. The key difference between the two is that firms do not have to report the excess of their health care obligations over the health care fund assets as a liability on the balance sheet, though a footnote to that effect has to be added to the financial statement.[5]

---

[4]The accumulated pension fund liability does not take into account the projected benefit obligation, where actuarial estimates of future benefits are made. Consequently, it is much smaller than the total pension liabilities.

[5]While companies might not have to report the excess of their health care obligations over assets as a liability, some firms choose to do so anyway.

Deferred Taxes Firms often use different methods of accounting for tax and financial reporting purposes, leading to a question of how tax liabilities should be reported. Since accelerated depreciation and favorable inventory valuation methods for tax accounting purposes lead to a deferral of taxes, the taxes on the income reported in the financial statements will generally be much greater than the actual tax paid. The same principles of matching expenses to income that underlie accrual accounting suggest that the deferred income tax be recognized in the financial statements. Thus a company that pays taxes of $55,000 on its taxable income based on its tax accounting, and that would have paid taxes of $75,000 on the income reported in its financial statements, will be forced to recognize the difference ($20,000) as deferred taxes in liabilities. Since the deferred taxes will be paid in later years, they will be recognized as paid.

It is worth noting that companies that actually pay more in taxes than the taxes they report in the financial statements create an asset on the balance sheet called a *deferred tax asset*. This reflects the fact that the firm's earnings in future periods will be greater as the firm is given credit for the deferred taxes.

The question of whether the deferred tax liability is really a liability is an interesting one. On one hand, firms do not owe the amount categorized as deferred taxes to any entity, and treating it as a liability makes the firm look more risky than it really is. On the other hand, the firm will eventually have to pay its deferred taxes, and treating it as a liability seems to be the conservative thing to do.

Preferred Stock

When a company issues preferred stock, it generally creates an obligation to pay a fixed dividend on the stock. Accounting rules have conventionally not viewed preferred stock as debt because the failure to meet preferred dividends does not result in bankruptcy. At the same time, the fact that the preferred dividends are cumulative makes them more onerous than common equity. Thus, preferred stock is viewed in accounting as a hybrid security, sharing some characteristics with equity and some with debt.

Preferred stock is valued on the balance sheet at its original issue price, with any cumulated unpaid dividends added on. Convertible preferred stock is treated similarly, but it is treated as equity on conversion.

Equity

The accounting measure of equity is a historical cost measure. The value of equity shown on the balance sheet reflects the original proceeds received by the firm when it issued the equity, augmented by any earnings made since (or reduced by losses, if any) and reduced by any dividends paid out during the period. While these three items go into what we can call the book value of equity, a few other items also end up in this estimate.

- When companies buy back stock for short periods, with the intent of reissuing the stock or using it to cover option exercises, they are allowed to show the repurchased stock as *treasury stock*, which reduces the book value of equity. Firms are not allowed to keep treasury stock on the books for extended periods and have to reduce their book value of equity by the value of repurchased stock if the shares remain unused. Since the stock buybacks occur at the current market price, they can result in significant reductions in the book value of equity.
- Firms that have significant losses over extended periods or carry out massive stock buybacks can end up with negative book values of equity.
- Relating back to our discussion of marketable securities, any unrealized gain or loss in marketable securities that are classified as available for sale is shown as an increase or decrease in the book value of equity in the balance sheet.

As part of their financial statements, many firms provide a summary of changes in shareholders' equity during the period, where all the changes that occurred to the accounting (book value) measure of equity value are summarized. As a final point on equity, accounting rules still seem to consider preferred stock, with its fixed dividend, as quasi equity, largely because of the fact that preferred dividends can be deferred or cumulated without the risk of default. To the extent that there can still be a loss of control in the firm (as opposed to bankruptcy), we would argue that preferred stock shares almost as many characteristics with unsecured debt as it does with equity.

OFF-BALANCE-SHEET DEBT

Toward the end of 2001, we witnessed the incredible collapse of Enron from a firm with more than $100 billion in market capitalization to a firm in bankruptcy. While there were other issues involved in the bankruptcy, one of the key ones was the failure of the firm to reveal and of analysts to find out about the billions in dollars of debt that Enron kept off its balance sheet. Enron accomplished this through the use of what are called special purpose entities—partnerships formed with the explicit objective of moving debt off the company's balance sheet. There are legitimate uses of special purpose entities, where firms carve out some of their most liquid and creditworthy assets (accounts receivable, for instance) into separate entities and let these entities borrow at a rate much lower than the rate the firm could have borrowed at.[6] Enron, however, used the partnerships to remove troublesome assets off its books, claiming the earnings from these assets and not reporting the debt backing up the assets.

When analyzing a firm, you may want to pay special attention to the footnotes and the other material contained in the filings with the Securities and Exchange Commission (SEC). While this may not give you all the information you need to estimate how much a firm owes, it may give you vital clues about the existence of debt. Firms that have multiple and complicated holding structures, with special purpose entities and partnerships, should viewed with caution. If these firms refuse to reveal fundamental information about their holdings, hiding behind accounting and legal standards, they could be hiding large obligations or toxic assets.

MEASURING EARNINGS AND PROFITABILITY

How profitable is a firm? What did it earn on the assets that it invested in? These are the fundamental questions we would like financial statements to answer. Accountants use the income statement to provide information about a firm's operating activities over a specific time period. In terms of our description of the firm, the income statement is designed to measure the earnings from assets in place. In this section, we examine the principles underlying earnings and return measurement in accounting, and the methods by which they are put into practice.

Accounting Principles Underlying Measurement of Earnings and Profitability

Two primary principles underlie the measurement of accounting earnings and profitability. The first is the principle of *accrual accounting*. In accrual

---

[6]If markets were rational, the firm's assets should now be much riskier and the rate at which it borrows should increase. If they are not rational, however, you may be able to take advantage of market frictions and end up with a much lower borrowing rate.

accounting, the revenue from selling a good or service is recognized in the period in which the good is sold or the service is performed (in whole or substantially). A corresponding effort is made on the expense side to match[7] expenses to revenues. This is in contrast to *cash accounting*, where revenues are recognized when payment is received, and expenses are recorded when they are paid.

The second principle is the categorization of expenses into operating, financing, and capital expenses. *Operating expenses* are expenses that, at least in theory, provide benefits only for the current period; the cost of labor and materials expended to create products that are sold in the current period is a good example. *Financing expenses* are expenses arising from the nonequity financing used to raise capital for the business; the most common example is interest expenses. *Capital expenses* are expenses that are expected to generate benefits over multiple periods; for instance, the cost of buying land and buildings is treated as a capital expense.

Operating expenses are subtracted from revenues in the current period to arrive at a measure of operating earnings from the firm. Financing expenses are subtracted from operating earnings to estimate earnings to equity investors or net income. Capital expenses are written off over their useful lives (in terms of generating benefits) as depreciation or amortization.

Measuring Accounting Earnings and Profitability

Since income can be generated from a number of different sources, generally accepted accounting principles (GAAP) require that income statements be classified into four sections: income from continuing operations, income from discontinued operations, extraordinary gains or losses, and adjustments for changes in accounting principles.

Generally accepted accounting principles also require the recognition of revenues when the service for which the firm is getting paid has been performed in full or substantially and for which it has received in return either cash or a receivable that is both observable and measurable. Expenses linked directly to the production of revenues (like labor and materials) are recognized in the same period in which revenues are recognized. Any expenses that are not directly linked to the production of revenues are recognized in the period in which the firm consumes the services.

While accrual accounting is straightforward in firms that produce goods and sell them, there are special cases where accrual accounting can be

---

[7]If a cost (such as an administrative cost) cannot be easily linked with a particular revenue, it is usually recognized as an expense in the period in which it is consumed.

complicated by the nature of the product or service being offered. Firms that enter into long-term contracts with their customers, for instance, are allowed to recognize revenue on the basis of the percentage of the contract that is completed. As the revenue is recognized on a percentage of completion basis, a corresponding proportion of the expense is also recognized. When there is considerable uncertainty about the capacity of the buyer of a good or service to pay for a service, the firm providing the good or service may recognize the income only when it collects portions of the selling price under the installment method.

Reverting back to our discussion of the difference between capital and operating expenses, operating expenses should reflect only those expenses that create revenues in the current period. In practice, however, a number of expenses are classified as operating expenses that do not seem to meet this test. The first is depreciation and amortization. Although the notion that capital expenditures should be written off over multiple periods is reasonable, the accounting depreciation that is computed on the original historical cost often bears little resemblance to the actual economic depreciation. The second expense is research and development (R&D) expenses, which accounting standards in the United States classify as operating expenses, but which clearly provide benefits over multiple periods. The rationale used for this classification is that the benefits cannot be counted on or easily quantified.

Much of financial analysis is built around the expected future earnings of a firm, and many of these forecasts start with the current earnings. It is therefore important that we know how much of these earnings come from the ongoing operations of the firm and how much can be attributed to unusual or extraordinary events that are unlikely to recur on a regular basis. From that standpoint, it is useful that firms categorize expenses into operating and nonrecurring expenses, since it is the earnings prior to extraordinary items that should be used in forecasting. Nonrecurring items include the following:

- *Unusual or infrequent items,* such as gains or losses from the divestiture of an asset or division and write-offs or restructuring costs. Companies sometimes include such items as part of operating expenses.
- *Extraordinary items,* which are defined as events that are unusual in nature, infrequent in occurrence, and material in impact. Examples include the accounting gain associated with refinancing high-coupon debt with lower-coupon debt, and gains or losses from marketable securities that are held by the firm.
- *Losses associated with discontinued operations,* which measure both the loss from the phaseout period and the estimated loss on the sale of

the operations. To qualify, however, the operations have to be separable from the firm.

■ *Gains or losses associated with accounting changes*, which measure earnings changes created by accounting changes made voluntarily by the firm (such as a change in inventory valuation or change in reporting period) and accounting changes mandated by new accounting standards.

Measures of Profitability

While the income statement allows us to estimate how profitable a firm is in absolute terms, it is just as important that we gauge the profitability of the firm in comparison terms or percentage returns. Two basic gauges measure profitability. One examines the profitability relative to the capital employed to get a rate of return on investment. This can be done either from the viewpoint of just the equity investors or by looking at the entire firm. Another examines profitability relative to sales by estimating a profit margin.

Return on Assets (ROA) and Return on Capital (ROC)   The *return on assets (ROA)* of a firm measures its operating efficiency in generating profits from its assets, prior to the effects of financing.

$$ROA = \frac{EBIT\,(1 - \text{Tax rate})}{\text{Total assets}}$$

NUMBER WATCH

Sector profitability: Take a look at returns on capital and operating margins, by sector, for U.S. and global firms.

Earnings before interest and taxes (EBIT) is the accounting measure of operating income from the income statement, and total assets refers to the assets as measured using accounting rules (i.e., using book value for most assets). Alternatively, return on assets can be written as:

$$ROA = \frac{\text{Net income} + \text{Interest expenses}\,(1 - \text{Tax rate})}{\text{Total assets}}$$

By separating the financing effects from the operating effects, the return on assets provides a cleaner measure of the true return on these assets.

ROA can also be computed on a pretax basis with no loss of generality, by using the earnings before interest and taxes (EBIT) and not adjusting for taxes:

$$\text{Pretax ROA} = \frac{\text{EBIT}}{\text{Total assets}}$$

This measure is useful if the firm or division is being evaluated for purchase by an acquirer with a different tax rate or structure.

Another measure of return relates the operating income to the capital invested in the firm, where capital is defined as the sum of the book value of debt and equity. This is the *return on capital (ROC)*. When a substantial portion of the liabilities is either current (such as accounts payable) or non-interest-bearing, this approach provides a better measure of the true return earned on capital employed in the business.

$$\text{After-tax ROC} = \frac{\text{EBIT}(1-t)}{\text{BV of debt} + \text{BV of equity} - \text{Cash}}$$

$$\text{Pretax ROC} = \frac{\text{EBIT}}{\text{BV of debt} + \text{BV of equity} - \text{Cash}}$$

Return on Equity While the return on capital measures the profitability of the overall firm, the *return on equity (ROE)* examines profitability from the perspective of the equity investor by relating profits to the equity investor (net profit after taxes and interest expenses) to the book value of the equity investment.

$$\text{ROE} = \frac{\text{Net income}}{\text{Book value of common equity}}$$

Since preferred stockholders have a different type of claim on the firm than do common stockholders, the net income should be estimated after preferred dividends, and the book value of common equity should not include the book value of preferred stock. This can be accomplished by using net income after preferred dividends in the numerator and the book value of common equity in the denominator.

WARNING SIGNS IN EARNINGS REPORTS

The most troubling thing about earnings reports is that we are often blindsided not by the items that get reported (such as extraordinary charges) but by the items that are hidden in other categories. We would suggest the following checklist that should be reviewed about any earnings report to gauge the possibility of such shocks.

- Is earnings growth outstripping revenue growth by a large magnitude year after year? This may well be a sign of increased efficiency, but when the differences are large and continue year after year, you should wonder about the source of these efficiencies.
- Do one-time or nonoperating charges to earnings occur frequently? The charge itself might be categorized differently each year—an inventory charge one year, a restructuring charge the next, and so on. While this may be just bad luck, it may also reflect a conscious effort by a company to move regular operating expenses into these nonoperating items.
- Do any of the operating expenses, as a percentage of revenues, swing wildly from year to year? This may suggest that the expense item—say selling, general, and administrative expenses (SG&A)—includes nonoperating expenses that should really be stripped out and reported separately.
- Does the company manage to beat analyst estimates quarter after quarter by a cent or two? Companies that beat estimates year after year are involved in earnings management and are moving earnings across time periods. As growth levels off, this practice can catch up with them.
- Does a substantial proportion of the revenues come from subsidiaries or related holdings? Although the sales may be legitimate, the prices set may allow the firm to move earnings from unit to another and give a misleading view of true earnings at the firm.
- Are accounting rules for valuing inventory or depreciation changed frequently? As true earnings growth subsides, companies seem to become much more active about using accounting discretion to pump up earnings.
- Are acquisitions followed by miraculous increases in earnings? An acquisition strategy is difficult to make successful even in the

long term. A firm that claims instant success from such as strategy requires scrutiny.

■ Is working capital ballooning as revenues and earnings surge? This can sometimes let us pinpoint those firms that generate revenues by lending at very generous terms to their own customers.

None of these factors, by themselves, suggest that we lower earnings for these firms; but combinations of the factors can be viewed as a warning signal that the earnings statement needs to be held up to greater scrutiny.

MEASURING RISK

How risky are the investments the firm has made over time? How much risk do equity investors in a firm face? These are two more questions that we would like to find the answer to in the course of an investment analysis. Accounting statements do not really claim to measure or quantify risk in a systematic way, other than to provide footnotes and disclosures where there might be risk embedded in the firm. In this section, we examine some of the ways in which accountants try to assess risk.

Accounting Principles Underlying Risk Measurement

To the extent that accounting statements and ratios do attempt to measure risk, there seem to be two common themes.

1. The first is that the risk being measured is the *risk of default*—that is, the risk that a fixed obligation, such as interest or principal due on outstanding debt, will not be met. The broader equity notion of risk, which measures the variance of actual returns around expected returns, does not seem to receive much attention. Thus, an all-equity-financed firm with positive earnings and few or no fixed obligations will generally emerge as a low-risk firm from an accounting standpoint, in spite of the fact that its earnings are unpredictable.

2. Accounting risk measures generally take a *static view of risk*, by looking at the capacity of a firm at a point in time to meet its obligations. For instance, when ratios are used to assess a firm's risk, the ratios are almost always based on one period's income statement and balance sheet.

Accounting Measures of Risk

Accounting measures of risk can be broadly categorized into two groups. The first is disclosures about potential obligations or losses in values that show up as footnotes on balance sheets, which are designed to alert potential or current investors to the possibility of significant losses. The second is the ratios that are designed to measure both liquidity and default risk.

Disclosures in Financial Statements In recent years, the number of disclosures that firms have to make about future obligations has proliferated. Consider, for instance, the case of *contingent liabilities*. These refer to potential liabilities that will be incurred under certain contingencies, as is the case when a firm is the defendant in a lawsuit. The general rule that has been followed is to ignore contingent liabilities that hedge against risk, since the obligations on the contingent claim will be offset by benefits elsewhere.[8] In recent periods, however, significant losses borne by firms from supposedly hedged derivatives positions (such as options and futures) have led to FASB requirements that these derivatives be disclosed as part of a financial statement. In fact, pension fund and health care obligations have moved from mere footnotes to actual liabilities for firms.

Financial Ratios Financial statements have long been used as the basis for estimating financial ratios that measure profitability, risk, and leverage. In the section on earnings, we looked at two of the profitability ratios—return on equity and return on capital. In this section, we look at some of the financial ratios that are often used to measure the financial risk in a firm.

Short-Term Liquidity Risk Short-term liquidity risk arises primarily from the need to finance current operations. If a firm has to make payments to its suppliers before it gets paid for the goods and services it provides, there is a cash shortfall that has to be met, usually through short-term borrowing. Though this financing of working capital needs is done routinely in most

---

[8]This assumes that the hedge is set up competently. It is entirely possible that a hedge, if sloppily set up, can end up costing the firm money.

firms, financial ratios have been devised to keep track of the extent of the firm's exposure to the risk that it will not be able to meet its short-term obligations. The two most frequently used ratios to measure short-term liquidity risk are the current ratio and the quick ratio.

The *current ratio* is the ratio of a firm's current assets (cash, inventory, accounts receivable) to its current liabilities (obligations coming due within the next period).

$$\text{Current ratio} = \frac{\text{Current assets}}{\text{Current liabilities}}$$

A current ratio below 1, for instance, would indicate that the firm has more obligations coming due in the next year than assets it can expect to turn to cash. That would be an indication of liquidity risk.

While traditional analysis suggests that firms maintain a current ratio of 2 or greater, there is a trade-off here between minimizing liquidity risk and tying up more and more cash in net working capital (Net working capital = Current assets – Current liabilities). In fact, it can be reasonably argued that a very high current ratio is indicative of an unhealthy firm that is having problems reducing its inventory. In recent years, firms have worked at reducing their current ratios and managing their net working capital better.

Reliance on current ratios has to be tempered by a few concerns. First, the ratio can be easily manipulated by firms around the time of financial reporting dates to give the illusion of safety; second, current assets and current liabilities can change by an equal amount, but the effect on the current ratio will depend on its level before the change.[9]

The *quick or acid test ratio* is a variant of the current ratio. It distinguishes current assets that can be converted quickly into cash (cash equivalents, marketable securities) from those that cannot (typically inventory, accounts receivable).

$$\text{Quick ratio} = \frac{\text{Cash} + \text{Marketable securities}}{\text{Current liabilities}}$$

The exclusion of accounts receivable and inventory is not a hard-and-fast rule. If there is evidence that either can be converted into cash quickly, it can, in fact, be included as part of the quick ratio.

---

[9]If the current assets and current liabilities increase by an equal amount, the current ratio will go down if it was greater than 1 before the increase and go up if it was less than 1.

Turnover ratios measure the efficiency of working capital management by looking at the relationship of accounts receivable and inventory to sales and to the cost of goods sold.

$$\text{Accounts receivable turnover} = \frac{\text{Sales}}{\text{Average accounts receivable}}$$

$$\text{Inventory turnover} = \frac{\text{Cost of goods sold}}{\text{Average inventory}}$$

These ratios can be interpreted as measuring the speed with which the firm turns accounts receivable into cash or inventory into sales. These ratios are often expressed in terms of the number of days outstanding.

$$\text{Days receivable outstanding} = \frac{365}{\text{Receivable turnover}}$$

$$\text{Days inventory held} = \frac{365}{\text{Inventory turnover}}$$

A similar pair of ratios can be computed for accounts payable, relative to purchases.

$$\text{Accounts payable turnover} = \frac{\text{Purchases}}{\text{Average accounts payable}}$$

$$\text{Days accounts payable outstanding} = \frac{365}{\text{Accounts payable turnover}}$$

Since accounts receivable and inventory are assets and accounts payable is a liability, these three ratios (standardized in terms of days outstanding) can be combined to get an estimate of how much financing the firm needs to fund working capital needs.

$$\begin{aligned}\text{Required financing period} = &\ (\text{Days receivable outstanding})\\ &+ (\text{Days inventory held})\\ &- (\text{Days payable outstanding})\end{aligned}$$

The greater the financing period for a firm, the greater its short-term liquidity risk.

Long-Term Solvency and Default Risk Measures of long-term solvency attempt to examine a firm's capacity to meet interest and principal payments in the long term. Clearly, the profitability ratios discussed earlier in the section are a critical component of this analysis. The ratios specifically designed to measure long-term solvency try to relate profitability to the level of debt payments, to identify the degree of comfort with which the firm can meet these payments.

The *interest coverage ratio* measures the capacity of the firm to meet interest payments from predebt, pretax earnings.

$$\text{Interest coverage ratio} = \frac{\text{EBIT}}{\text{Interest expenses}}$$

The higher the interest coverage ratio, the more secure is the firm's capacity to make interest payments from earnings. This argument, however, has to be tempered by the recognition that earnings before interest and taxes (EBIT) is volatile and can drop significantly if the economy enters a recession. Consequently, two firms can have the same interest coverage ratio but be viewed very differently in terms of risk.

The denominator in the interest coverage ratio can be easily extended to cover other fixed obligations such as lease payments. If this is done, the ratio is called a *fixed charges coverage ratio*.

$$\text{Fixed charges coverage ratio} = \frac{\text{EBIT} + \text{Other fixed charges}}{\text{Total fixed charges}}$$

Finally, this ratio, while stated in terms of earnings, can be restated in terms of cash flows by using earnings before interest, taxes, depreciation, and amortization (EBITDA) in the numerator and cash fixed charges in the denominator.

$$\text{Cash fixed charges coverage ratio} = \frac{\text{EBITDA}}{\text{Cash fixed charges}}$$

Both the interest coverage ratio and the fixed charges coverage ratio are open to the criticism that they do not consider capital expenditures, a cash flow that may be discretionary in the very short term, but not in the long term if the firm wants to maintain growth. One way of capturing the extent of this cash flow relative to operating cash flows is to compute a ratio of the two.

$$\text{Operating cash flow to capital expenditures} = \frac{\text{Cash flows from operations}}{\text{Capital expenditures}}$$

While there are a number of different definitions of cash flows from operations, the most reasonable way of defining them is to measure the cash flows from continuing operations, before interest but after taxes, and after meeting working capital needs.

$$\text{Cash flows from operations} = \text{EBIT}(1 - \text{Tax rate}) - \Delta\,\text{Working capital}$$

Debt Ratios   Interest coverage ratios measure the capacity of the firm to meet interest payments but do not examine whether it can pay back the principal on outstanding debt. *Debt ratios* attempt to do this by relating debt to total capital or to equity. The two most widely used debt ratios are:

$$\text{Debt-to-capital-ratio} = \frac{\text{Debt}}{\text{Debt} + \text{Equity}}$$

$$\text{Debt-to-equity-ratio} = \frac{\text{Debt}}{\text{Equity}}$$

The first ratio measures debt as a proportion of the total capital of the firm and cannot exceed 100 percent. The second measures debt as a proportion of equity in the firm and can be easily derived from the first.

$$\text{Debt-to-equity ratio} = \frac{\text{Debt-to-capital ratio}}{1 - \text{Debt-to-capital ratio}}$$

Although these ratios presume that capital is raised from only debt and equity, they can easily be adapted to include other sources of financing, such as preferred stock. While preferred stock is sometimes combined with common stock under the equity label, it is better to keep it separate and to compute the ratio of preferred stock to capital (which will include debt, equity, and preferred stock).

NUMBER WATCH

Leverage by sector: Take a look at book value and market value debt ratios by sector, for U.S. and global companies.

Variants on Debt Ratios There are two close variants of debt ratios. In the first, only long-term debt is used rather than total debt, with the rationale that short-term debt is transitory and will not affect the long-term solvency of the firm.

$$\text{Long-term debt-to-capital ratio} = \frac{\text{Long-term debt}}{\text{Long-term debt } + \text{Equity}}$$

$$\text{Long-term debt-to-equity ratio} = \frac{\text{Long-term debt}}{\text{Equity}}$$

Given the ease with which firms can roll over short-term debt and the willingness of many firms to use short-term financing to fund long-term projects, these variants can provide a misleading picture of the firm's financial leverage risk.

The second variant of debt ratios uses market value (MV) instead of book value, primarily to reflect the fact that some firms have a significantly greater capacity to borrow than their book values indicate.

$$\text{Market value debt-to-capital ratio} = \frac{\text{MV of debt}}{\text{MV of debt} + \text{MV of equity}}$$

$$\text{Market value debt-to-equity ratio} = \frac{\text{MV of debt}}{\text{MV of equity}}$$

Many analysts disavow the use of market value in their calculations, contending that market values, in addition to being difficult to get for debt, are volatile and hence unreliable. These contentions are open to debate. It is true that the market value of debt is difficult to get for firms that do not have publicly traded bonds, but the market value of equity is not only easy to obtain, but it is also constantly updated to reflect marketwide and firm-specific changes. Furthermore, using the book value of debt as a proxy for market value in those cases where bonds are not traded does not significantly shift most market-value-based debt ratios.[10]

---

[10]Deviations in the market value of equity from book value are likely to be much larger than deviations for debt and are likely to dominate in most debt ratio calculations.

DIFFERENCES IN ACCOUNTING STANDARDS AND PRACTICES

Differences in accounting standards across countries affect the measurement of earnings. These differences, however, are not as great as they are made out to be and they cannot explain away radical departures from fundamental principles of valuation.[11] Choi and Levich, in a survey of accounting standards across developed markets, note that most countries subscribe to basic accounting notions of consistency, realization, and historical cost principles in preparing accounting statements.[12] As countries increasingly move toward international financial reporting standards (IFRS), it is worth noting that IFRS and U.S. GAAP are more similar than dissimilar on many issues. It is true that there are areas of differences that still remain, and we note some of them in Table 3.1.

The accounting convergence notwithstanding, differences remain across accounting standards. Ratios such as price-earnings that use stated and unadjusted earnings can be misleading when accounting standards vary widely across the companies being compared. However, the information exists for us to make the adjustments needed to accounting numbers for comparisons to be valid.

CONCLUSION

Financial statements remain the primary source of information for most investors and analysts. There are differences, however, between how accounting analysis and financial analysis approach answering a number of key questions about the firm. We examined these differences in this chapter.

The first question that we examined related to the nature and the value of the assets owned by a firm. Categorizing assets into investments already made (assets in place) and investments yet to be made (growth assets), we argued that accounting statements provide a substantial amount of historical

---

[11] At the peak of the Japanese market, there were many investors who explained away the price-earnings multiples of 60 and greater in the market by noting that Japanese firms were conservative in measuring earnings. Even after taking into account the general provisions and excess depreciation used by many of these firms to depress current earnings, the price-earnings multiples were greater than 50 for many firms, suggesting either extraordinary expected growth in the future or overvaluation.

[12] F. D. S. Choi and R. M. Levich, *The Capital Market Effects of International Accounting Diversity* (New York: Dow Jones Irwin, 1990).

TABLE 3.1 Key Differences between IFRS and GAAP

	IFRS	GAAP	Net Effect
Philosophy	Principles based.	Rules based.	Firms get more discretion under IFRS to make their own choices, resulting in more differences across firms.
Revenue recognition	Revenues are recognized only when the risks and rewards of ownership have been transferred to the buyer of a product or service.	Revenues are recognized when evidence that the product or service has been delivered exists.	Revenue recognition may occur later in IFRS than in GAAP.
Long-term tangible assets	If long-term asset is made up of multiple components, each component has be capitalized and depreciated separately. Firms can choose to value entire class of assets at market value, if there is a reliable and regular source of information for market value.	Asset can be capitalized and depreciated on a consolidated basis, based on an overall life for the asset.	Computing depreciation is more work under IFRS. Net effect on depreciation is unclear. IFRS can create mix of market- and book-based valuations for assets that vary across companies.
Short-term assets	Inventory is valued at lower of cost or net realizable value. No LIFO option for valuation.	Inventory is valued at lower of cost or market value. Choice of FIFO or LIFO.	Inventory likely to be valued closer to current value under IFRS.

(continued)

TABLE 3.1 (*Continued*)

	IFRS	GAAP	Net Effect
Long-term liabilities	Convertible debt broken down into debt and equity components, based on values.	Convertible debt treated as debt, until conversion.	Debt ratios for companies with convertibles are lower under IFRS.
Consolidation	Consolidation required when you have effective control of an entity. Minority interest is reported outside of equity on balance sheet.	Consolidation required when you own 51 percent of the voting rights of an entity. Minority interest is a component of equity in balance sheet.	More consolidation under IFRS rules than GAAP rules. Shareholders' equity includes minority interest in IFRS.
Investments in other entities	Investment in securities can be classified as trading, available for sale, or held to maturity. Equity approach required for investment in businesses.	All investments, including investments in companies, can be classified as trading, available for sale, or held to maturity. Proportional consolidation is an option with joint ventures.	Holdings in other companies may sometimes be marked to market under IFRS. Only securities get marked to market under GAAP.
R&D expenses	Research costs are expensed, but development costs can be capitalized if technical and economic feasibility has been established.	Research and development costs are both expensed.	Companies that spend significant amount on R&D will see increased book value for equity.

information about the former and very little about the latter. The focus on the original price paid to acquire assets in place (book value) in accounting statements can lead to significant differences between the stated value of these assets and their market value. With growth assets, accounting rules result in low or no values for assets generated by internal research.

The second issue that we examined was the measurement of profitability. The two principles that govern how profits are measured are accrual accounting (in which revenues and expenses are shown in the period when transactions occur rather than when the cash is received or paid) and the categorization of expenses into operating, financing, and capital expenses. Operating and financing expenses are shown in income statements. Capital expenditures do not affect income in the year of the expenditure but affect income in subsequent time periods in the form of depreciation and amortization. Accounting standards miscategorize operating leases and research and development expenses as operating expenses (when the former should be categorized as financing expenses and the latter as capital expenses).

In the last part of the chapter, we examined how financial statements deal with short-term liquidity risk and long-term default risk. The emphasis in accounting statements is on examining the risk that firms may be unable to make payments that they have committed to make; there is very little focus in accounting statements on risk to equity investors.

EXERCISES

Pick a company that you are familiar with in terms of its business and history. Try the following:

1. Compute measures of profitability for your company relative to:
   a. Revenues (net profit margin, operating margin).
   b. Capital invested (return on invested capital, return on equity).
      Compare the company's measures to the averages on these measures for the sector in which it operates (from my website).
2. Compute measures of leverage for your company, by estimating the debt-to-equity and debt-to-capital ratios, on both a book value and a market value basis. Again, compare to the averages for the sector in which it operates.
3. Is the accrual income (reported in the income statement) consistent with the cash income (from the statement of cash flows)? If not, what accounts for the difference?

Lessons for Investors

- The purpose of accounting statements is to give you a measure of how a company performed in the past. Your objective in investing is to consider how a firm will perform in the future.
- Accounting rules provide significant discretion to firms in how they measure and report earnings. Firms that adopt aggressive accounting practices, even though the practices may be legal, will report higher earnings than firms that adopt more conservative practices.
- As firms age, the book value of their assets will become less and less relevant as measures of what the assets are truly worth.
- Firms with operating leases and off-balance-sheet financing owe much more than what they reveal as debt on their balance sheets.
- The footnotes to the financial statements often carry more information than the financial statements themselves.

CHAPTER 4

Show Me the Money: The Basics of Valuation

To invest wisely, you need to understand the basics of valuation. In general, you can value an asset in one of three ways. You can estimate the intrinsic value of the asset by looking at its capacity to generate cash flows in the future. You can estimate a relative value by examining how the market is pricing similar or comparable assets. Finally, you can value assets with cash flows that are contingent on the occurrence of a specific event (options).

With intrinsic valuation, the value of any asset is a function of the expected cash flows on the asset, and it is determined by the magnitude of the cash flows, the expected growth rate in these cash flows, and the uncertainty associated with receiving these cash flows. We begin by looking at assets with guaranteed cash flows over a finite period, and then we extend the discussion to cover the valuation of assets when there is uncertainty about expected cash flows. As a final step, we consider the valuation of a business with the potential, at least, for an infinite life and uncertainty in the cash flows.

With relative valuation, we begin by looking for similar or comparable assets. When valuing stocks, these are often defined as other companies in the same business. We then convert the market values of these companies to multiples of some standard variable—earnings, book value, and revenues are widely used. We then compare the valuations of the comparable companies to try to find misvalued companies.

There are some assets that cannot be valued using either discounted cash flow or relative valuation models because the cash flows are contingent on the occurrence of a specific event. These assets can be valued using option pricing models. We consider the basic principles that underlie these models.

INTRINSIC VALUE

We can estimate the value of an asset by taking the present value of the expected cash flows on that asset. Consequently, the value of any asset is a function of the cash flows generated by that asset, the life of the asset, the expected growth in the cash flows, and the riskiness associated with the cash flows. We begin this section by looking at valuing assets that have finite lives (at the end of which they cease to generate cash flows) and conclude by looking at the more difficult case of assets with infinite lives. We will also start the process by looking at firms whose cash flows are known with certainty and conclude by looking at how we can incorporate the effect of uncertainty into value.

The Mechanics of Present Value

Almost everything we do in intrinsic valuation rests on the concept of present value. The intuition of why a dollar today is worth more than a dollar a year from now is simple. Our preferences for current over future consumption, the effect of inflation on the buying power of a dollar, and uncertainty about whether we will receive the future dollar all play a role in determining how much of a discount we apply to the future dollar. In annualized terms, this discount is measured with a discount rate. However, it is worth reviewing the basic mechanics of present value before we consider more complicated valuation questions.

In general, there are five types of cash flows that you will encounter in valuing any asset. You can have a single cash flow in the future, a set of equal cash flows each period for a number of periods (annuity), a set of equal cash flows each period forever (perpetuity), a set of cash flows growing at a constant rate each period for a number of periods (growing annuity), and a cash flow that grows at a constant rate forever (growing perpetuity).

The present value (PV) of a single cash flow in the future can be obtained by discounting the cash flow back at the discount rate for the time period in question. Thus, the value of $10 million in five years with a discount rate of 15 percent can be written as:

$$\text{Present value of \$10 million in five years} = \frac{\$10}{(1.15)^5} = \$4.97 \text{ million}$$

You could read this present value to mean that you would be indifferent between receiving $4.97 million today or $10 million in five years.

What about the present value of an annuity? You have two choices. One is to discount each of the annual cash flows back to the present and add them all up. For instance, if you had an annuity of $5 million every year for the next five years and a discount rate of 10 percent, you could compute the present value of the annuity in Figure 4.1.

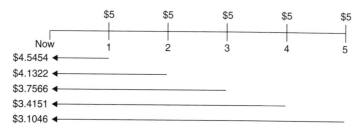

FIGURE 4.1 Cash Flows on Annuity

Adding up the present values yields $18.95 million. Alternatively, you could use a shortcut—an annuity formula—to arrive at the present value:

$$\text{PV of an annuity} = A\left[\frac{1 - \dfrac{1}{(1+r)^n}}{r}\right] = 5\left[\frac{1 - \dfrac{1}{(1.1)^5}}{0.10}\right] = \$18.95$$

Getting from the present value of an annuity to the present value of a perpetuity is simple. Setting n to ∞ in the preceding equation yields the present value of a perpetuity:

$$\text{PV of a perpetuity} = A\left[\frac{1 - \dfrac{1}{(1+r)^\infty}}{r}\right] = \frac{A}{r}$$

Thus, the present value of $5 million each year forever at a discount rate of 10 percent is $50 million ($5 million/0.10 = $50 million).

Moving from a constant cash flow to one that grows at a constant rate yields a growing annuity. For instance, if we assume that the $5 million in annual cash flows will grow 20 percent a year for the next five years, we can estimate the present value in Figure 4.2.

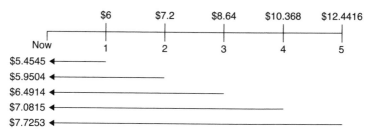

FIGURE 4.2 Cash Flows on Growing Annuity

Summing up these present values yields a total value of $32.70 million. Here again, there is a shortcut available in the form of a growing annuity formula:

$$\text{PV of a growing annuity} = A(1+g)\left[\frac{1-\dfrac{(1+g)^n}{(1+r)^n}}{r-g}\right]$$

$$= 5(1.20)\left[\frac{1-\dfrac{(1.20)^5}{(1.10)^5}}{0.10-0.20}\right] = \$32.70$$

Finally, consider a cash flow growing at a constant rate forever—a growing perpetuity. Substituting into the preceding equation, we get:

$$\text{PV of a growing perpetuity} = A(1+g)\left[\frac{1-\dfrac{(1+g)^\infty}{(1+r)^\infty}}{r-g}\right] = \frac{A(1+g)}{(r-g)}$$

Note that the fact the cash flows grow at a constant rate *forever* constrains this rate to be less than or equal to the growth rate of the economy in which you operate. Working with U.S. dollars, this growth rate should not exceed the risk-free rate in U.S. dollars, about 2 percent in 2012.

Valuing an Asset with Guaranteed Cash Flows

The simplest assets to value have cash flows that are guaranteed—that is, assets whose promised cash flows are always delivered. Such assets are riskless, and the interest rate earned on them is the *riskless rate*. The value of such an asset is the present value of the cash flows, discounted back at the riskless rate. Generally speaking, riskless investments are issued by governments that have the power to print money to meet any obligations they otherwise cannot cover. As we noted in Chapter 2, not all government obligations are without risk, since some governments have defaulted or are expected to default on promised obligations.

Default-Free Zero Coupon Bond   The simplest asset to value is a bond that pays no coupons but has a face value that is guaranteed at maturity; this

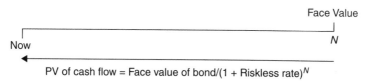

FIGURE 4.3 Cash Flows on N-Year Zero Coupon Bonds

bond is a *default-free zero coupon bond*. We can show the cash flow on this bond in Figure 4.3.

The value of this bond can be written as the present value of a single cash flow discounted back at the riskless rate where N is the maturity of the zero coupon bond. Since the cash flow on this bond is fixed, the value of the bond will increase as the riskless rate decreases, and it will decrease as the riskless rate increases.

To see an example of this valuation at work, assume that the 10-year interest rate on riskless investments is 4.55 percent, and that you are pricing a zero coupon Treasury bond, with a maturity of 10 years and a face value of $1,000. The price of the bond can be estimated as follows:

$$\text{Price of the bond} = \frac{\$1,000}{(1.0455)^{10}} = \$640.85$$

Note that the face value is the only cash flow, and that this bond will be priced well below the face value of $1,000. Such a bond is said to be *trading below par*.

Conversely, we could estimate a default-free interest rate from the price of a zero coupon Treasury bond. For instance, if the 10-year zero coupon Treasury were trading at $593.82, the default-free 10-year spot rate can be estimated as follows:

$$\text{Default-free spot rate} = \left(\frac{\text{Face value of bond}}{\text{Market value of bond}} \right)^{1/t} - 1$$

$$= \left(\frac{1,000}{593.82} \right)^{1/10} - 1 = 0.0535$$

The 10-year default-free rate is 5.35 percent.

Default-Free Coupon Bond Consider, now, a default-free coupon bond, which has fixed cash flows (coupons) that occur at regular intervals (usually

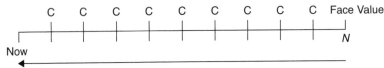

Present value of cash flows = Present value of coupons + Present value of face value

FIGURE 4.4   Cash Flows on N-Year Coupon Bonds

semiannually) and a final cash flow (face value) at maturity. The time line for this bond is shown in Figure 4.4 (with C representing the coupon each period and N being the maturity of the bond).

This bond can actually be viewed as a series of zero coupon bonds, and each can be valued using the riskless rate that corresponds to when the cash flow comes due:

$$\text{Value of bond} = \sum_{t=1}^{t=N} \frac{\text{Coupon}}{(1+r_t)^1} + \frac{\text{Face value of the bond}}{(1+r_N)^N}$$

where r_t is the interest rate that corresponds to a t-period zero coupon bond and the bond has a life of N periods.

It is, of course, possible to arrive at the same value using *some weighted average* of the period-specific riskless rates used before; the weighting will depend on how large each cash flow is and when it comes due. This weighted average rate (r) is called the *yield to maturity*, and it can be used to value the same coupon bond:

$$\text{Value of bond} = \sum_{t=1}^{t=N} \frac{\text{Coupon}}{(1+r)^1} + \frac{\text{Face value of the bond}}{(1+r)^N}$$

where r is the yield to maturity on the bond. Like the zero coupon bond, the default-free coupon bond should have a value that varies inversely with the yield to maturity. As we will see shortly, since the coupon bond has cash flows that occur earlier in time (the coupons) it should be less sensitive to a given change in interest rates than a zero coupon bond with the same maturity.

Consider now a five-year Treasury bond with a coupon rate of 5.50 percent, with coupons paid every six months. We will price this bond initially using default-free spot rates for each cash flow in Table 4.1.

TABLE 4.1   Value of Five-Year Default-Free Bond

Time	Coupon	Default-Free Rate	Present Value
0.5	$ 27.50	4.15%	$ 26.95
1	$ 27.50	4.30%	$ 26.37
1.5	$ 27.50	4.43%	$ 25.77
2	$ 27.50	4.55%	$ 25.16
2.5	$ 27.50	4.65%	$ 24.55
3	$ 27.50	4.74%	$ 23.93
3.5	$ 27.50	4.82%	$ 23.32
4	$ 27.50	4.90%	$ 22.71
4.5	$ 27.50	4.97%	$ 22.11
5	$1,027.50	5.03%	$ 803.92
Sum			$1,024.79

The default-free spot interest rates reflect the market interest rates for zero coupon bonds for each maturity. The bond price can be used to estimate a weighted-average interest rate for this bond:

$$\$1,024.78 = \sum_{t=0.5}^{t=5} \frac{\$27.50}{(1+r)^t} + \frac{\$1,000}{(1+r)^5}$$

Solving for r, we obtain a rate of 4.99 percent, which is the yield to maturity on this bond.

Bond Value and Interest Rate Sensitivity and Duration   As market interest rates change, the market value of a bond will change. Consider, for instance, the 10-year zero coupon bond and the five-year coupon bond described in the last two illustrations. Figure 4.5 shows the market value of each of these bonds as market interest rates vary from 3 percent to 10 percent.

Note that the price of the 10-year zero coupon bond is much more sensitive to interest rate changes than is the five-year coupon bond to a given change in market interest rates. The 10-year zero coupon bond loses about half its value as interest rates increase from 3 percent to 10 percent; in contrast, the five-year 5.5 percent coupon bond loses about 30 percent of its value. This should not be surprising since the present value effect of that interest rate increases the larger the cash flow and the further in the future it occurs. Thus longer-term bonds will be more sensitive to interest rate changes than shorter-term bonds with similar coupons. Furthermore,

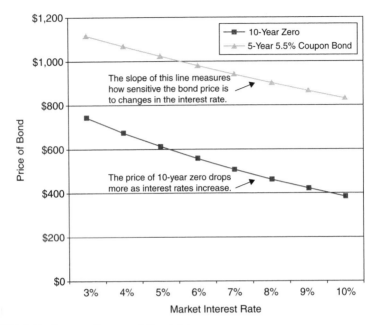

FIGURE 4.5 Interest Rates and Bond Prices

low-coupon or no-coupon bonds will be more sensitive to interest rate changes than high-coupon bonds.

The interest rate sensitivity of a bond, which is a function of both the coupon rate and the maturity of the bond, can be captured in one measure called the *duration*. The greater the duration of a bond, the more sensitive its price is to interest rate movements. The simplest measure of duration, called Macaulay duration, can be viewed as a weighted maturity of the different cash flows on the bond.

$$\text{Duration of a bond} = \frac{\displaystyle\sum_{t=1}^{t=N} t\frac{\text{CF}_t}{(1+r)^t}}{\displaystyle\sum_{t=1}^{t=N} \frac{\text{CF}_t}{(1+r)^t}}$$

where r is the yield to maturity on the bond.

For a zero coupon bond, which has only one cash flow, due at maturity, the duration is equal to the maturity.

Duration of 10-year zero coupon bond $= 10$ years

TABLE 4.2 Value of a Five-Year Coupon Bond

Time (t)	Coupon	Present Value (at 4.99%)	t * Present Value
0.5	$ 27.50	$ 26.84	$ 13.42
1	$ 27.50	$ 26.19	$ 26.19
1.5	$ 27.50	$ 25.56	$ 38.34
2	$ 27.50	$ 24.95	$ 49.90
2.5	$ 27.50	$ 24.35	$ 60.87
3	$ 27.50	$ 23.76	$ 71.29
3.5	$ 27.50	$ 23.19	$ 81.17
4	$ 27.50	$ 22.63	$ 90.53
4.5	$ 27.50	$ 22.09	$ 99.40
5	$1,027.50	$ 805.46	$4,027.28
Sum		$1,025.02	$4,558.39

Duration of 5-year 5.5% coupon bond = $4,558/$1,025 = 4.45.

The duration of the five-year coupon bond requires a few more calculations, is calculated in Table 4.2.

The longer the duration of a bond, the more sensitive it is to interest rate changes. In our previous illustrations, the 10-year coupon bond has a higher duration and will therefore be more sensitive to interest rate changes than the five-year coupon bond.

Introducing Uncertainty into Valuation

We have to grapple with two different types of uncertainty in valuation. The first arises in the context of securities like bonds, where there is a promised cash flow to the holder of the bonds in future periods. The risk that these cash flows will not be delivered is called *default risk*; the greater the default risk in a bond, given its cash flows, the less valuable the bond will become.

The second type of risk is more complicated. When we make equity investments in assets, we are generally not promised a fixed cash flow but are entitled instead to whatever cash flows are left over after other claim holders (like debt) are paid; these cash flows are called *residual cash flows*. Here, the uncertainty revolves around what these residual cash flows will be, relative to expectations. In contrast to default risk, where the risk can result only in negative consequences (the cash flows delivered will be less than promised), uncertainty in the context of equity investments can cut both ways. The actual cash flows can be much lower than expected, but they can also be much higher. For the moment, we will label this risk *equity risk* and consider, at least in general terms, how best to deal with it in the context of valuing an equity investment.

Valuing an Asset with Default Risk   We begin this section with a discussion on how we assess default risk and adjust interest rates for default risk, and then consider how best to value assets with default risk.

Measuring Default Risk and Estimating Default-Risk-Adjusted Rates When valuing investments where the cash flows are promised but there is a risk that they might not be delivered, it is no longer appropriate to use the riskless rate as the discount rate. The appropriate discount rate here will include the riskless rate and an appropriate premium for the default risk called a *default spread*. In Chapter 2, we examined how default risk is assessed by ratings agencies and the magnitude of the default spread. It is worth noting that even in the absence of bond ratings, lenders still assess default risk and charge default spreads.

Valuing an Asset with Default Risk The most common example of an asset with just default risk is a corporate bond, since even the largest, safest companies still have some risk of default. When valuing a corporate bond, we generally make two modifications to the bond valuation approach we developed earlier for a default-free bond. First, we will discount the coupons on the corporate bond, even though these no longer represent expected cash flows, but are instead promised cash flows.[1] Second, the discount rate used for a bond with default risk will be higher than that used for default-free bond. Furthermore, as the default risk increases, so will the discount rate used:

$$\text{Value of corporate coupon bond} = \sum_{t=1}^{t=N} \frac{\text{Coupon}}{(1 + k_d)^t} + \frac{\text{Face value of the bond}}{(1 + k_d)^N}$$

where k_d is the market interest rate given the default risk.

Consider, for instance, a corporate bond with a coupon rate of 8.75 percent, maturing in 35 years. Based on the default risk of the issuing company (measured by a bond rating assigned to the company by Standard & Poor's at the time of this analysis), the market interest rate on the debt is

---

[1] When you buy a corporate bond with a coupon rate of 8 percent, you are promised a payment of 8 percent of the face value of the bond each period, but the payment may be lower or nonexistent if the company defaults.

0.5 percent higher than the risk-free rate of 5.5 percent for default-free bonds of similar maturity. The price of the bond can be estimated as follows:

$$\text{Price of Corporate bond} = \sum_{t=0.5}^{t=35} \frac{43.875}{(1.06)^t} + \frac{1,000}{(1.06)^{35}} = \$1,404.25$$

The coupons are assumed to be semiannual and the present value is estimated using the annuity equation. Note that the default risk on the bond is reflected in the interest rate used to discount the expected cash flows on the bond. If Boeing's default risk increases, the price of the bond will drop to reflect the higher market interest rate.

Valuing an Asset with Equity Risk Having valued assets with guaranteed cash flows and those with only default risk, let us now consider the valuation of assets with equity risk. We begin with the introduction to the way we estimate cash flows and consider risk in investments with equity risk, and then we look at how best to value these assets.

Measuring Cash Flows for an Asset with Equity Risk Unlike the bonds that we have valued so far in this chapter, the cash flows on assets with equity risk are not promised cash flows. Instead, the valuation is based on the *expected cash flows* on these assets over their lives. We will consider two basic questions: the first relates to how we measure these cash flows, and the second to how to come up with expectations for these cash flows.

To estimate cash flows on an asset with equity risk, let us first consider the perspective of the owner of the asset (i.e., the equity investor in the asset). Assume that the owner borrowed some of the funds needed to buy the asset. The cash flows to the owner will therefore be the cash flows generated by the asset after all expenses and taxes, and also after payments due on the debt. This cash flow, which is after debt payments, operating expenses, and taxes, is called the *cash flow to equity investors*. There is also a broader definition of cash flow that we can use, where we look not just at the equity investor in the asset, but at the total cash flows generated by the asset for both the equity investor and the lender. This cash flow, which is before debt payments but after operating expenses and taxes, is called the *cash flow to the firm* (where the firm is considered to include both debt and equity investors).

Note that, since this is a risky asset, the cash flows are likely to vary across a broad range of outcomes, some good and some not so positive. In theory, to estimate the expected cash flow, we should consider all possible outcomes in each period, weight them by their relative probabilities, and arrive at an expected cash flow for that period.[2] In practice, we are much sloppier, often putting expected growth rates on current cash flows to estimate future cash flows.

Measuring Equity Risk and Estimate Risk-Adjusted Discount Rates   When we analyzed bonds with default risk, we argued that the interest rate has to be adjusted to reflect the default risk. This default-risk-adjusted interest rate can be considered the *cost of debt* to the investor or business borrowing the money. Since interest is tax deductible, the after-tax cost of debt is net of that tax saving. When analyzing investments with equity risk, we have to make an adjustment to the riskless rate to arrive at a discount rate, but the adjustment will be to reflect the equity risk rather than the default risk. Furthermore, since there is no longer a promised interest payment, we will term this rate a risk-adjusted discount rate rather than an interest rate. We label this adjusted discount rate the *cost of equity*. In Chapter 2, we looked at various approaches that can be used to estimate this value.

A firm can be viewed as a collection of assets, financed partly with debt and partly with equity. The composite cost of financing, which comes from both debt and equity, is a weighted average of the costs of debt and equity, with the weights depending upon how much of each financing is used. This cost is labeled the *cost of capital*.

For instance, consider a company that has a cost of equity of 10.54 percent and an after-tax cost of debt of 3.58 percent. Assume also that it raised 80 percent of its financing from equity and 20 percent from debt. Its cost of capital would then be:

$$\text{Cost of capital} = 10.54\%(0.80) + 3.58\%(0.20) = 9.17\%$$

Thus, for this company, the cost of equity is 10.54 percent while the cost of capital is only 9.17 percent.

If the cash flows that we are discounting are cash flows to equity investors, as defined in the previous section, the appropriate discount rate is the cost of equity. If the cash flows are prior to debt payments and therefore to the firm, the appropriate discount rate is the cost of capital.

Valuing an Asset with Equity Risk and Finite Life   Most assets have finite lives. At the end of that life, the assets are assumed to lose their operating capacity, though they might still preserve some value. To illustrate, assume that you buy an apartment building and plan to rent the apartments out to

---

[2]Note that in many cases, though we might not explicitly state probabilities and outcomes, we are implicitly doing so when we use expected cash flows.

earn income. The building will have a finite life, say 30 to 40 years, at the end of which it will have to be torn down and a new building constructed, but the land will continue to have value even if this occurs.

This building can be valued using the cash flows that it will generate (prior to any debt payments) over its life, and discounting them at the composite cost of the financing used to buy the building (i.e., the cost of capital). At the end of the expected life of the building, we estimate what the building (and the land it sits on) will be worth and discount this value back to the present, as well. In summary, the value of a finite life asset can be written as:

$$\text{Value of finite-life asset} = \sum_{t=1}^{t=N} \frac{E(\text{Cash flow on asset}_t)}{(1+k_c)^t}$$
$$+ \frac{\text{Value of asset at end of life}}{(1+k_c)^N}$$

where k_c is the cost of capital.

This entire analysis can also be done from your perspective as the sole equity investor in this building. In this case, the cash flows will be defined more narrowly as cash flows after debt payments, and the appropriate discount rate becomes the cost of equity. At the end of the building's life, we still look at how much it will be worth but consider only the cash that will be left over after any remaining debt is paid off. Thus, the value of the equity investment in an asset with a fixed life of N years, say an office building, can be written as follows:

$$\text{Value of equity in finite-life asset} = \sum_{t=1}^{t=N} \frac{E(\text{Cash flow to equity}_t)}{(1+k_e)^t}$$
$$+ \frac{\text{Value of equity in asset at end of life}}{(1+k_e)^N}$$

where k_e is the rate of return that the equity investor in this asset would demand given the riskiness of the cash flows, and the value of equity at the end of the asset's life is the value of the asset net of the debt outstanding on it. Can you extend the life of the building by reinvesting more in maintaining it? Possibly. If you choose this course of action, however, the life of the building will be longer, but the cash flows to equity and to the firm each period have to be reduced by the amount of the reinvestment needed for maintenance.[3]

---

[3]By maintaining the building better, you might also be able to charge higher rents, which may provide an offsetting increase in the cash flows.

TABLE 4.3 Value of Rental Building

Year	Expected Cash Flows	Value at End	PV at 9.51%
1	$1,050,000		$ 958,817
2	$1,102,500		$ 919,329
3	$1,157,625		$ 881,468
4	$1,215,506		$ 845,166
5	$1,276,282		$ 810,359
6	$1,340,096		$ 776,986
7	$1,407,100		$ 744,987
8	$1,477,455		$ 714,306
9	$1,551,328		$ 684,888
10	$1,628,895		$ 656,682
11	$1,710,339		$ 629,638
12	$1,795,856	$2,500,000	$ 1,444,124
Value of building =			$10,066,749

To illustrate these principles, assume that you are trying to value a rental building for purchase. The building is assumed to have a finite life of 12 years and is expected to have cash flows *before debt payments* and *after taxes* of $1 million, growing at 5 percent a year for the next 12 years. The real estate is also expected to have a value of $2.5 million at the end of the 12th year (called the salvage value). Based on your costs of borrowing and the cost you attach to the equity you will have invested in the building, you estimate a cost of capital of 9.51 percent. The value of the building can be estimated in Table 4.3.

Note that the cash flows over the next 12 years represent a growing annuity, and the present value could have been computed with a simple present value equation, as well.

$$\text{Value of building} = \frac{1,000,000(1.05)\left(1 - \frac{(1.05)^{12}}{(1.0951)^{12}}\right)}{(0.0951 - 0.05)} + \frac{2,500,000}{(1.0951)^{12}}$$

$$= \$10,066,749$$

This building has a value of $10.07 million.

Valuing an Asset with an Infinite Life

When we value businesses and firms, as opposed to individual assets, we are often looking at entities that have no finite lives. If they reinvest sufficient amounts in new assets each period, firms could keep generating cash flows forever. In this section, we value assets that have infinite lives and uncertain cash flows.

Equity and Firm Valuation   In the section on valuing assets with equity risk, we introduced the notions of cash flows to equity and cash flows to the firm. We argued that cash flows to equity are cash flows after debt payments, all expenses, and reinvestment needs have been met. In the context of a business, we will use the same definition to measure the cash flows to its equity investors. These cash flows, when discounted back at the cost of equity for the business, yield the value of the equity in the business. This is illustrated in Figure 4.6.

Note that our definition of both cash flows and discount rates is consistent—they are both defined in terms of the equity investor in the business.

There is an alternative approach in which, instead of valuing the equity stake in the asset or business, we look at the value of the entire business. To do this, we look at the collective cash flows not just to equity investors but also to lenders (or bondholders in the firm). The appropriate discount rate is the cost of capital, since it reflects both the cost of equity and the cost of debt. The process is illustrated in Figure 4.7.

Note again that we are defining both cash flows and discount rates consistently, to reflect the fact that we are valuing not just the equity portion of the investment but the investment itself.

Dividends and Equity Valuation   When valuing equity investments in publicly traded companies, you could argue that the only cash flows investors in these investments get from the firm are dividends. Therefore, the value

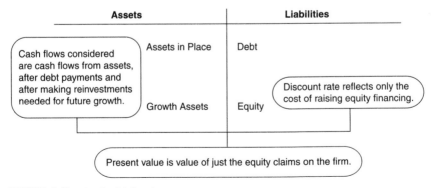

FIGURE 4.6   Equity Valuation

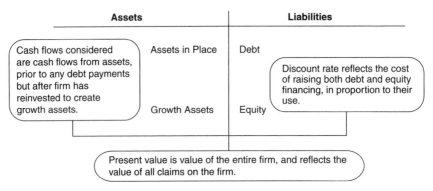

FIGURE 4.7   Firm Valuation

of the equity in these investments can be computed as the present value of
expected dividend payments on the equity.

$$\text{Value of equity (only dividends)} = \sum_{t=1}^{t=\infty} \frac{E(\text{Dividend}_t)}{(1+k_e)^t}$$

The mechanics are similar to those involved in pricing a bond, with dividend payments replacing coupon payments, and the cost of equity replacing
the interest rate on the bond. The fact that equity in a publicly traded firm
has an infinite life, however, indicates that we cannot arrive at closure on
the valuation without making additional assumptions.

One way in which we might be able to estimate the value of the equity
in a firm is by assuming that the dividends, starting today, will grow at a
constant rate forever. If we do that, we can estimate the value of the equity
using the present value formula for a perpetually growing cash flow. In fact,
the value of equity will be:

Value of equity (dividends growing at a constant rate forever)

$$= \frac{E(\text{Dividend next period})}{(k_e - g_n)}$$

This model, which is called the *Gordon growth model,* is simple but
limited, since it can value only companies that pay dividends, and only if
these dividends are expected to grow at a constant rate forever. The reason
this is a restrictive assumption is that no asset or firm's cash flows can
grow forever at a rate higher than the growth rate of the economy. If it

did, the firm would become the economy. Therefore, the constant growth rate is constrained to be less than or equal to the economy's growth rate. For valuations of firms in U.S. dollars in 2012, this puts an upper limit on the growth rate of approximately 2 to 3 percent.[4] This constraint will also ensure that the growth rate used in the model will be less than the discount rate.

NUMBER WATCH

Valuation of Consolidated Edison: See the spreadsheet that contains the valuation of Con Ed.

We will illustrate this model using Consolidated Edison, the utility that produces power for much of New York. Con Ed paid dividends per share of $2.40 in 2010. The dividends are expected to grow 2 percent a year in the long term, and the company has a cost of equity of 8 percent. The value per share can be estimated as follows:

$$\text{Value of equity per share} = \$2.40(1.02)/(0.08 - 0.02) = \$40.80$$

The stock was trading at $42 per share at the time of this valuation. We could argue that based on this valuation, the stock was mildly overvalued.

What happens if we have to value a stock whose dividends are growing at 15 percent a year? The solution is simple. We value the stock in two parts. In the first part, we estimate the expected dividends each period for as long as the growth rate of this firm's dividends remains higher than the growth rate of the economy, and sum up the present value of the dividends. In the second part, we assume that the growth rate in dividends will drop to a stable or constant rate forever sometime in the future. Once we make this assumption, we can apply the Gordon growth model to estimate the

---

[4]The nominal growth rate of the U.S. economy through the 1990s was about 5 percent. The growth rate of the global economy, in nominal U.S. dollar terms, has been about 6 percent over that period. In the last decade, growth has slowed. A good proxy for long-term nominal growth is the risk-free rate, which has dropped to about 2% in both the United States and in Europe.

present value of all dividends in stable growth. This present value is called the *terminal price* and represents the expected value of the stock in the future, when the firm becomes a stable-growth firm. The present value of this terminal price is added to the present value of the dividends to obtain the value of the stock today.

$$\text{Value of equity with high-growth dividends} = \sum_{t=1}^{t=N} \frac{E(\text{Dividends}_t)}{(1+k_e)^t}$$
$$+ \frac{\text{Terminal price}_N}{(1+k_e)^N}$$

where N is the number of years of high growth and the terminal price is based on the assumption of stable growth beyond year N.

$$\text{Terminal price} = \frac{E(\text{Dividend}_{N+1})}{(k_e - g_n)}$$

NUMBER WATCH

Valuation of Procter & Gamble: See the spreadsheet that contains the valuation of P&G.

To illustrate this model, assume that you were trying to value Procter & Gamble (P&G), one the leading consumer product companies in the world, owning some of the most valuable brands, including Gillette razors, Pampers diapers, Tide detergent, Crest toothpaste, and Vicks cough medicine. P&G reported earnings per share of $3.82 in 2010 and paid out 50 percent of these earnings as dividends that year. We will use a beta of 0.90, reflecting the beta of large consumer product companies in 2010, a risk-free rate of 3.50 percent, and a mature market equity risk premium of 5 percent to estimate the cost of equity:

$$\text{Cost of equity} = 3.50\% + 0.90(5\%) = 8.00\%$$

We estimated a 10 percent growth rate, in conjunction with earnings and dividends for the next five years, and discounting these dividends back at the cost of equity, we arrive at a cumulative value of $10.09 per share for the dividends during these five years:

	1	2	3	4	5	Sum
Earnings per share	$4.20	$4.62	$5.08	$5.59	$6.15	
Payout ratio	50.00%	50.00%	50.00%	50.00%	50.00%	
Dividends per share	$2.10	$2.31	$2.54	$2.80	$3.08	
Cost of equity	8.00%	8.00%	8.00%	8.00%	8.00%	
Present value	$1.95	$1.98	$2.02	$2.06	$2.09	$10.09

After year 5, we assume that P&G will be in stable growth, growing 3 percent a year (just below the risk-free rate). To go with the lower growth, we assume that the firm would pay out 75 percent of its earnings as dividends and face a slightly higher cost of equity of 8.5 percent.[5]

$$\text{Value per share at end of year 5} = \frac{\text{EPS}_5(1 + \text{Growth rate}_{\text{Stable}})(\text{Payout ratio}_{\text{Stable}})}{(\text{Cost of equity}_{\text{Stable}} - \text{Growth rate}_{\text{Stable}})}$$

$$= \frac{\$6.15(1.03)(0.75)}{(0.085 - 0.03)} = \$86.41$$

Discounting this price to the present at 8 percent (the cost of equity for the high-growth period) and adding to the present value of expected dividends during the high-growth period yields a value per share of $68.90.

$$\text{Value per share} = \text{PV of dividends in high growth}$$
$$+ \text{PV of value at end of high growth}$$
$$= \$10.09 + \frac{\$86.41}{1.08^5} = \$68.90$$

The stock was trading at $68 in May 2011, making it fairly valued.[6]

A Broader Measure of Cash Flows to Equity   There are two significant problems with the use of just dividends to value equity. The first is that it

---

[5]Costs of equity generally go down in stable growth, but this case is an exception. P&G is a below-average risk company during high growth. We expect it to become an average risk firm during stable growth.

[6]A. Damodaran, *Investment Valuation*, 3rd ed. (Hoboken, NJ: John Wiley & Sons, 2012).

works only if cash flows to the equity investors take the form of dividends. It will not work for valuing equity in private businesses, where the owners often withdraw cash from the business but may not call it dividends, and it may not even work for publicly traded companies if they return cash to the equity investors by buying back stock, for instance. The second problem is that the use of dividends is based on the assumption that firms pay out what they can afford to in dividends. When this is not true, the dividend discount models will misestimate the value of equity, under estimating value when they pay too little and over estimating value when they pay too much.

To counter this problem, we come up a broader definition of cash flow that we call *free cash flow to equity*, defined as the cash left over after operating expenses, interest expenses, net debt payments, and reinvestment needs. Reinvestment needs include investments in both long-term assets and short-term assets, with the former measured as the difference between capital expenditures and depreciation (net cap ex) and the latter by the change in noncash working capital. By *net debt payments*, we are referring to the difference between new debt issued and repayments of old debt. If the new debt issued exceeds debt repayments, the free cash flow to equity will be higher.

$$\text{Free cash flow to equity (FCFE)} = \text{Net income} - \text{Reinvestment needs}$$
$$- (\text{Debt repaid} - \text{New debt issued})$$

Think of this as potential dividends, or what the company could have paid out in dividends. To illustrate, in 2010, Coca-Cola reported net income of $11,809 million, capital expenditures of $2,215 million, depreciation of $1,443 million, and an increase in noncash working capital of $335 million. Incorporating the fact that Coca-Cola raised $150 million more in debt than it repaid, we can compute the free cash flow to equity as follows:

$$\begin{aligned} \text{FCFE}_{\text{Coca-Cola}} &= \text{Net income} - (\text{Cap ex} - \text{Depreciation}) \\ &\quad - \text{Change in noncash working capital} \\ &\quad - (\text{Debt repaid} - \text{New debt raised}) \\ &= 11,809 - (2,215 - 1,443) - 335 - (-150) \\ &= \$10.852 \text{ million} \end{aligned}$$

The difference between the net income and the FCFE represents the portion of net income reinvested back by equity investors in Coca-Cola in 2010.

$$\begin{aligned} \text{Equity reinvestment} &= \text{Net income} - \text{FCFE} = \$11,809 - \$10,852 \\ &= \$957 \text{ million} \end{aligned}$$

Coca-Cola paid out about $6 billion in dividends during the year, well below its free cash flow to equity. Consequently, using the dividend discount model would understate the value of equity in Coca-Cola.

NUMBER WATCH

Valuation of Coca-Cola: See the spreadsheet that contains the valuation of Coca-Cola.

Once the free cash flows to equity have been estimated, the process of estimating value parallels the dividend discount model. To value equity in a firm where the free cash flows to equity are growing at a constant rate forever, we use the present value equation to estimate the value of cash flows in perpetual growth:

$$\text{Value of equity in infinite-life asset} = \frac{E(\text{FCFE}_1)}{(k_e - g_n)}$$

All the constraints relating to the magnitude of the constant growth rate used that we discussed in the context of the dividend discount model continue to apply here.

In the more general case, where free cash flows to equity are growing at a rate higher than the growth rate of the economy, the value of the equity can be estimated again in two parts. The first part is the present value of the free cash flows to equity during the high growth phase, and the second part is the present value of the terminal value of equity, estimated based on the assumption that the firm will reach stable growth sometime in the future.

$$\text{Value of equity with high-growth FCFE} = \sum_{t=1}^{t=N} \frac{E(\text{FCFE}_t)}{(1 + k_e)^t} + \frac{\text{Terminal value of equity}_N}{(1 + k_e)^N}$$

With the FCFE approach, we have the flexibility we need to value equity in any type of business or publicly traded company. Applying this approach to Coca-Cola in 2010, we assumed that Coca-Cola's net income would grow 7.5 percent a year for the next five years and that it would reinvest 25 percent of its net income each year back into the business. In addition, we assumed

TABLE 4.4　Expected Cash Flows and Value Today

Sum	1	2	3	4	5
Expected growth rate	7.50%	7.50%	7.50%	7.50%	7.50%
Net income	$12,581	$13,525	$14,539	$15,630	$16,802
Equity reinvestment rate	25.00%	25.00%	25.00%	25.00%	25.00%
FCFE	$9,436	$10,144	$10,905	$11,722	$12,602
Cost of equity	8.45%	8.45%	8.45%	8.45%	8.45%
Cumulative cost of equity	1.0845	1.1761	1.2755	1.3833	1.5002
Present value	$8,701	$8,625	$8,549	$8,474	$8,400

that the cost of equity for Coca-Cola during this five-year period would be 8.45 percent. The resulting FCFE and the present value of these cash flows is shown in Table 4.4.

The sum of the present values of the FCFE for the next five years is $42,749 million. At the end of year 5, we assumed that Coca-Cola would be in stable growth, growing 3 percent a year, reinvesting 20 percent of its net income back into the business, with a cost of equity of 9 percent. The value of equity at the end of year 5 can then be computed:

Value of equity at end of year 10

$$= \frac{\text{Expected net income in year } 5(1 + g_{stable})(1 - \text{Equity reinvestment rate}_{stable})}{(\text{Stable cost of equity} - g_{stable})}$$

$$= \frac{\$16,802(1.03)(0.80)}{(0.09 - 0.03)} = \$230,750 \text{ million}$$

Discounting the terminal value back at the cumulated cost of equity for year 5 and adding to the present value of FCFE over the next 5 years yields an overall value for equity from operating assets.

$$\text{Value of equity today} = \text{PV of FCFE} + \text{PV of terminal value}$$
$$= \$42,749 + \$230,750/1.5002$$
$$= \$196,562 \text{ million}$$

Dividing by the number of shares outstanding (2,289.25 million) yields a value per share of $85.86, well above the prevailing stock price of $68.22 at the time of the valuation.

From Valuing Equity to Valuing the Firm　A firm is more than just its equity investors. It has other claim holders, including bondholders and banks.

When we value the firm, therefore, we consider cash flows to all of these claim holders. We define the *free cash flow to the firm* as being the cash flow left over after operating expenses, taxes, and reinvestment needs, but before any debt payments (interest or principal payments).

Free cash flow to firm (FCFF) = After-tax operating income
− Reinvestment needs

The two differences between FCFE and FCFF become clearer when we compare their definitions. The free cash flow to equity begins with net income, which is after interest expenses and taxes, whereas the free cash flow to the firm begins with after-tax operating income, which is before interest expenses. Another difference is that the FCFE is after net debt payments, whereas the FCFF is before net debt payments.

What exactly does the free cash flow to the firm measure? One interpretation is that it measures the cash flows generated by the assets before any financing costs are considered and thus is a measure of operating cash flow. Another read of it is that the free cash flow to the firm is the cash flow used to service all claim holders' needs for cash—interest and principal to debt holders and dividends and stock buybacks to equity investors.

To illustrate the estimation of free cash flow to the firm, consider Toyota in 2010. In that year, Toyota reported operating income of 933 billion yen, had a tax rate of 40 percent, and reinvested 112 billion yen in new investments (net capital expenditures and working capital). The free cash flow to the firm for Toyota in 2010 is then:

$$\text{FCFF}_{\text{Boeing}} = \text{Operating income } (1 - \text{Tax rate}) - \text{Reinvestment needs}$$
$$= 933(1 - 0.40) - 112 = 448 \text{ billion yen}$$

Note that the tax computed is a hypothetical tax, i.e., the tax that Toyota would have paid, if they had been taxed on their entire operating income.[7] Once the free cash flows to the firm have been estimated, the process of computing value follows a familiar path. If valuing a firm or business with free cash flows growing at a constant rate forever, we can use the perpetual growth equation:

$$\text{Value of firm with FCFF growing at constant rate} = \frac{E(\text{FCFF}_1)}{(k_c - g_n)}$$

---

[7]We don't count the tax benefits from interest expenses in the cash flows because it is counted in the cost of capital, through the use of an after-tax cost of debt.

In the case of Toyota, we assume a growth rate of 1.50 percent in perpetuity and a cost of capital of 6.21 percent, resulting in a value for Toyota's operating assets of 9,655 billion yen.

$$\text{Value of Toyota's operating assets} = 448(1.015)/(0.0621 - 0.015)$$
$$= 9,655 \text{ billion yen}$$

Adding Toyota's cash balance and subtracting out the debt owed will yield Toyota's estimated equity value.

There are two key distinctions between this model and the constant-growth FCFE model used earlier. The first is that we consider cash flows before debt payments in this model, whereas we used cash flows after debt payments when valuing equity. The second is that we then discount these cash flows back at a composite cost of financing (i.e., the cost of capital to arrive at the value of the firm), whereas we used the cost of equity as the discount rate when valuing equity.

To value firms where free cash flows to the firm are growing at a rate higher than that of the economy, we can modify this equation to consider the present value of the cash flows until the firm is in stable growth. To this present value, we add the present value of the terminal value, which captures all cash flows in stable growth.

$$\text{Value of high-growth business} = \sum_{t=1}^{t=N} \frac{E(\text{FCFF}_t)}{(1 + k_c)^t} + \frac{\text{Terminal value of business}_n}{(1 + k_c)^N}$$

Thus, firm valuation mirrors equity valuation, with the focus on predebt cash flows (instead of cash flows after debt payments), growth in operating income and cash flows (rather than equity income and cash flows), and a cost of capital (rather than a cost of equity).

RELATIVE VALUATION

In intrinsic valuation the objective is to find assets that are priced lower than they should be, given their cash flow, growth, and risk characteristics. In relative valuation, the focus shifts to finding assets that are cheap or expensive relative to how similar assets are being priced by the market right now. It is therefore entirely possible that an asset that is expensive on an intrinsic value basis may be cheap on a relative basis.

Standardized Values and Multiples

To compare the valuations of similar assets in the market, we need to standardize the values in some way. They can be standardized relative to the earnings that they generate, relative the book value or replacement value of the assets themselves, or relative to the revenues that they generate. Each approach is used widely and has strong adherents.

Earnings Multiples   One of the more intuitive ways to think of the value of any asset is as a multiple of the earnings generated by it. When buying a stock, it is common to look at the price paid as a multiple of the earnings per share generated by the company. This *price-earnings (P/E) ratio* can be estimated using current earnings per share (which is called a trailing P/E) or using expected earnings per share in the next year (called a forward P/E). When buying a business (as opposed to just the equity in the business), it is common to examine the value of the operating assets of the business (the enterprise value or EV) as a multiple of the *operating income (or EBIT)* or the *operating cash flow (EBITDA)*. A lower multiple is better than a higher one, but these multiples also will be affected by the growth potential and risk of the business being acquired.

Book Value or Replacement Value Multiples   While markets provide one estimate of the value of a business, accountants often provide a very different estimate of the same business in their books. This latter estimate, which is the *book value*, is driven by accounting rules and is heavily influenced by what was paid originally for the asset and any accounting adjustments (such as depreciation) made since. Investors often look at the relationship between the price they pay for a stock and the book value of equity (or net worth) as a measure of how overvalued or undervalued a stock is; the price/book value (PBV) ratio that emerges can vary widely across sectors, depending again upon the growth potential and the quality of the investments in each. When valuing businesses, this ratio is estimated using the value of the firm (the enterprise value again) and the book value of those operating assets (rather than the book value of just the equity). For those who believe that book value is not a good measure of the true value of the assets, an alternative is to use the replacement cost of the assets; the ratio of the value of the firm to replacement cost is called *Tobin's Q*.

Revenue Multiples   Both earnings and book value are accounting measures and are affected by accounting rules and principles. An alternative approach that is far less affected by these factors is to look at the relationship between the value of an asset and the revenues it generates. For equity investors, this ratio is the *price/sales ratio*, where the market value per share is divided by the revenues generated per share. For firm value, this ratio can be modified as the *value/sales ratio*, where the numerator becomes the total value of the firm. This ratio, again, varies widely across sectors, largely as a function of the profit margins in each. The advantage of using these multiples, however, is that it becomes far easier to compare firms in different markets, with different accounting systems at work.

The Fundamentals Behind Multiples

One reason commonly given for relative valuation is that it requires far fewer assumptions than does discounted cash flow valuation. In my view, this is a misconception. The difference between discounted cash flow valuation and relative valuation is that the assumptions that an analyst makes have to be made explicit in the former and they can remain implicit in the latter. Consequently, it is important that we know what the variables are that drive differences in multiples, since these are the variables we have to control for when comparing these multiples across firms.

To look under the hood, so to speak, of equity and firm value multiples, we will go back to fairly simple discounted cash flow models for equity and firm value and use them to derive our multiples. Thus, the simplest discounted cash flow model for equity, which is a stable-growth dividend discount model, would suggest that the value of equity is:

$$\text{Value of equity} = P_0 = \frac{\text{DPS}_1}{k_e - g_n}$$

where DPS_1 is the expected dividend in the next year, k_e is the cost of equity, and g_n is the expected stable growth rate. Dividing both sides by the earnings, we obtain the discounted cash flow model for the P/E ratio for a stable-growth firm:

$$\frac{P_0}{\text{EPS}_0} = \text{P/E} = \frac{\text{Payout ratio} * (1 + g_n)}{k_e - g_n}$$

Dividing both sides by the book value of equity, we can estimate the price/book value ratio for a stable-growth firm:

$$\frac{P_0}{\text{BV}_0} = \text{PBV} = \frac{\text{ROE} * \text{Payout ratio} * (1 + g_n)}{k_e - g_n}$$

where ROE is the return on equity. Dividing by the sales per share, the price/sales ratio for a stable-growth firm can be estimated as a function of its profit margin, payout ratio, profit margin, and expected growth.

$$\frac{P_0}{\text{Sales}_0} = \text{PS} = \frac{\text{Profit margin} * \text{Payout ratio} * (1 + g_n)}{k_e - g_n}$$

We can do a similar analysis from the perspective of firm valuation. The value of a firm in stable growth can be written as:

$$\text{Value of firm} = V_0 = \frac{\text{FCFF}_1}{k_c - g_n}$$

Dividing both sides by the expected free cash flow to the firm yields the value/FCFF multiple for a stable-growth firm:

$$\frac{V_0}{\text{FCFF}_1} = \frac{1}{k_c - g_n}$$

Since the free cash flow to the firm is the after-tax operating income netted against the net capital expenditures and working capital needs of the firm, the multiples of EBIT, after-tax EBIT, and EBITDA can also be similarly estimated. The value/EBITDA multiple, for instance, can be written as follows:

$$\frac{\text{Value}}{\text{EBITDA}} = \frac{(1-t)}{k_c - g} + \frac{\text{Depr }(t)/\text{EBITDA}}{k_c - g} - \frac{\text{CEx}/\text{EBITDA}}{k_c - g}$$
$$- \frac{\Delta \text{Working capital}/\text{EBITDA}}{k_c - g}$$

where Depr is depreciation and CEx is capital expenditures.

The point of this analysis is not to suggest that we go back to using discounted cash flow valuation but to get a sense of the variables that may cause these multiples to vary across firms in the same sector. An analyst who ignores these variables might conclude that a stock with a P/E of 8 is cheaper than one with a P/E of 12 when the true reason may be that the latter has higher expected growth, or that a stock with a P/BV ratio of 0.7 is cheaper than one with a P/BV ratio of 1.5 when the true reason may be that the latter has a much higher return on equity. Table 4.5 lists the multiples that are widely used and the variables driving each; the variable that is the most

TABLE 4.5 Multiples and Companion Variables (Companion Variables Are in Bold Italic Type)

Multiple	Determining Variables
Price-earnings ratio	*Growth*, payout, risk
Price/book value ratio	Growth, payout, risk, *ROE*
Price/sales ratio	Growth, payout, risk, *net margin*
EV/EBIT	Growth, *reinvestment needs*, leverage, risk
EV/EBIT$(1 - t)$	
EV/EBITDA	
EV/sales	Growth, net capital expenditure needs, leverage, risk, *operating margin*
EV/book capital	Growth, leverage, risk, *return on capital (ROC)*

significant is highlighted for each multiple. This is what we would call the *companion variable* for this multiple—the one variable we would need to know in order to use this multiple to find undervalued or overvalued assets.

The Use of Comparables

Most analysts who use multiples use them in conjunction with comparable firms to form conclusions about whether firms are fairly valued. At the risk of being simplistic, the analysis begins with two decisions: the multiple that will be used in the analysis and the group of firms that will comprise the comparable firms. The multiple is computed for each of the comparable firms, and the average (or median) is computed. To evaluate an individual firm, the analyst then compares its multiple to the average computed; if it is significantly different, the analyst makes a subjective judgment on whether the firm's individual characteristics (growth, risk, etc.) may explain the difference. Thus, a firm may have a P/E ratio of 22 in a sector where the average P/E is only 15, but the analyst may conclude that this difference can be justified by the fact that the firm has higher growth potential than the average firm in the sector. However, if, in the analyst's judgment, the difference on the multiple cannot be explained by the fundamentals, the firm will be viewed as overvalued if its multiple is higher than the average (or undervalued if its multiple is lower than the average).

Choosing Comparables   The heart of this process is the selection of the firms that comprise comparable firms. From a valuation perspective, a comparable firm is one with similar cash flows, growth potential, and risk. If life were simple, the value of a firm would be analyzed by looking at how an exactly identical firm—in terms of risk, growth, and cash flows—is priced. In most analyses, however, a comparable firm is defined to be one in the same business as the firm being analyzed. If there are enough firms in the sector to allow for it, this list will be pruned further using other criteria; for instance, only firms of similar size may be considered. Implicitly, the assumption being made here is that firms in the same sector have similar risk, growth, and cash flow profiles and therefore can be compared with considerable legitimacy. This approach becomes more difficult to apply under two conditions:

1. *There are relatively few firms in a sector.* In most markets outside the United States, the number of publicly traded firms in a particular sector, especially if it is defined narrowly, is small.
2. *The differences in risk, growth, and cash flow profiles across firms within a sector are large.* There may be hundreds of computer software companies listed in the United States, but the differences across these firms are also large.

The trade-off is therefore a simple one. Defining a sector more broadly increases the number of firms that enter the comparable firm list, but it also results in a more diverse group.

Controlling for Differences across Firms   Since it is impossible to find identical firms to the one being valued, we have to find ways of controlling for differences across firms on the relevant ways. The advantage of the discounted cash flow models introduced in the prior section is that we have a clear idea of what the fundamental determinants of each multiple are, and therefore what we should be controlling for; Table 4.5, from earlier in the chapter, provides a summary of the variables.

The process of controlling for the variables can range from very simple approaches that modify the multiples to take into account differences on one key variable to more complex approaches that allow for differences on more than one variable.

Let us start with the simple approaches. Here, the basic multiple is modified to take into account the most important variable determining that multiple. Thus, the P/E ratio is divided by the expected growth rate in earnings per share (EPS) for a company to come up with a growth-adjusted P/E ratio. Similarly, the PBV ratio is divided by the ROE to come up with a value ratio, and the price/sales ratio by the net margin. These modified ratios are then compared across companies in a sector. Implicitly, the assumption made is that these firms are comparable on all the other dimensions of value, besides the one being controlled for.

TABLE 4.6 P/E and Expected Growth: Software Companies

Company	P/E	Expected Growth Rate	Price-Earnings/ Expected Growth (PEG)
Acclaim Entertainment	13.70	23.60%	0.58
Activision	75.20	40.00%	1.88
Broderbund	32.30	26.00%	1.24
Davidson Associates	44.30	33.80%	1.31
Edmark	88.70	37.50%	2.37
Electronic Arts	33.50	22.00%	1.52
The Learning Co.	33.50	28.80%	1.16
Maxis	73.20	30.00%	2.44
Minnesota Educational	69.20	28.30%	2.45
Sierra On-Line	43.80	32.00%	1.37

We illustrate the relative valuation process in Table 4.6, which lists the P/E ratios and expected analyst consensus growth rates over five years for a selected list of software companies.

Comparisons on the P/E ratio alone do not factor in the differences in expected growth. The PEG ratio in the last column can be viewed as a growth-adjusted P/E ratio, and that would suggest that Acclaim is the cheapest company in this group and Minnesota Educational is the most expensive. This conclusion holds only if these firms are of equivalent risk, however.

NUMBER WATCH

Relative valuation of oil companies: See the spreadsheet that contains the relative valuation of oil companies used in this example.

When firms vary on more than one dimension, it becomes difficult to modify the multiples to take into account the differences across firms. It is, however, feasible to run regressions of the multiples against the variables and then use these regressions to get predicted values for each firm. This approach works reasonably well when the number of comparable firms is large and the relationship between the multiple and variable is strong. When these conditions do not hold, a few outliers can cause the coefficients to change dramatically and make the predictions much less reliable.

TABLE 4.7 PBV and ROE—Oil Companies

Company Name	PBV	ROE	Expected Growth
Total ADR B	0.90	4.10	9.50%
Giant Industries	1.10	7.20	7.81%
Royal Dutch Petroleum ADR	1.10	12.30	5.50%
Tesoro Petroleum	1.10	5.20	8.00%
Petrobras	1.15	3.37	15.00%
YPF ADR	1.60	13.40	12.50%
Ashland	1.70	10.60	7.00%
Quaker State	1.70	4.40	17.00%
Coastal	1.80	9.40	12.00%
Elf Aquitaine ADR	1.90	6.20	12.00%
Holly	2.00	20.00	4.00%
Ultramar Diamond Shamrock	2.00	9.90	8.00%
Witco	2.00	10.40	14.00%
World Fuel Services	2.00	17.20	10.00%
Elcor	2.10	10.10	15.00%
Imperial Oil	2.20	8.60	16.00%
Repsol ADR	2.20	17.40	14.00%
Shell Transport & Trading ADR	2.40	10.50	10.00%
Amoco	2.60	17.30	6.00%
Phillips Petroleum	2.60	14.70	7.50%
ENI SpA ADR	2.80	18.30	10.00%
Mapco	2.80	16.20	12.00%
Texaco	2.90	15.70	12.50%
British Petroleum ADR	3.20	19.60	8%
Tosco	3.50	13.70	14%

To provide an example, in Table 4.7 we list the price/book value ratios of oil companies and report their returns on equity and expected growth rates.

Since these firms differ on both growth and return on equity, we ran a regression of PBV ratios on both variables:

$$PBV = -0.11 + 11.22(ROE) + 7.87(\text{Expected growth}) \quad R^2 = 60.88\%$$
$$[5.79] \qquad\qquad [2.83]$$

The numbers in brackets are t-statistics and suggest that the relationships between PBV ratios and both variables in the regression are statistically significant. The R-squared indicates the percentage of the differences in PBV ratios that is explained by the independent variables. Finally, the regression itself can be used to get predicted PBV ratios for the companies in the list. Thus, the predicted PBV ratio for Repsol would be:

$$\text{Predicted PBV}_{\text{Repsol}} = -0.11 + 11.22(0.1740) + 7.87(0.14) = 2.94$$

Since the actual PBV ratio for Repsol was 2.20, this would suggest that the stock was undervalued by roughly 25 percent.

Both approaches just described assume that the relationship between a multiple and the variables driving value are linear. Since this is not necessarily true, it is possible to run nonlinear versions of these regressions.

Expanding the Comparable Firm Universe Searching for comparable firms within the sector in which a firm operates is fairly restrictive, especially when there are relatively few firms in the sector or when a firm operates in more than one sector. Since the definition of a comparable firm is not one that is in the same business but one that has the same growth, risk, and cash flow characteristics as the firm being analyzed, it is also unclear why we have to stay sector-specific. A software firm should be comparable to an automobile firm, if we can control for differences in the fundamentals.

The regression approach that we introduced in the previous section allows us to control for differences on those variables that we believe cause differences in multiples across firms. Using the minimalist version of the regression equations here, we should be able to regress P/E, PBV, and P/S ratios against the variables that should affect them:

$$\text{P/E} = a + b\,(\text{Growth}) + c\,(\text{Payout ratios}) + d\,(\text{Risk})$$
$$\text{PBV} = a + b\,(\text{Growth}) + c\,(\text{Payout ratios}) + d\,(\text{Risk}) + e\,(\text{ROE})$$
$$\text{P/S} = a + b\,(\text{Growth}) + c\,(\text{Payout ratios}) + d\,(\text{Risk}) + e\,(\text{Margin})$$

It is, however, possible that the proxies that we use for risk (beta), growth (expected growth rate), and cash flow (payout) may be imperfect and that the relationship may not be linear. To deal with these limitations, we can add more variables to the regression (e.g., the size of the firm may operate as a good proxy for risk) and use transformations of the variables to allow for nonlinear relationships.

The first advantage of this approach over the subjective comparison across firms in the same sector described in the previous section is that it does quantify, based on actual market data, the degree to which higher growth or risk should affect the multiples. It is true that these estimates can be noisy, but this noise is a reflection of the reality that many analysts choose not to face when they make subjective judgments. Second, looking at all firms in the market allows analysts operating in sectors with relatively few firms in them to make more powerful comparisons. Finally, it gets analysts past the tunnel vision induced by comparing firms within a sector, when the entire sector may be undervalued or overvalued.

VALUING AN ASSET WITH CONTINGENT CASH FLOWS (OPTIONS)

In general, the value of any asset is the present value of the expected cash flows on that asset. In this section, we consider an exception to that rule when we will look at assets with two specific characteristics:

1. They derive their value from the values of other assets.
2. The cash flows on the assets are contingent on the occurrence of specific events.

These assets are called options, and the present value of the expected cash flows on these assets will understate their true value. In this section, we describe the cash flow characteristics of options, consider the factors that determine their value, and examine how best to value them.

Cash Flows on Options

There are two types of options. A call option gives the buyer of the option the right to buy the underlying asset at a fixed price, whereas a put option gives the buyer the right to sell the underlying asset at a fixed price. In both cases, the fixed price at which the underlying asset can be bought or sold is called the *strike or exercise price*.

To look at the payoffs on an option, consider first the case of a call option. When you buy the right to purchase an asset at a fixed price, you want the price of the asset to increase above that fixed price. If it does, you make a profit, since you can buy at the fixed price and then sell at the much higher price; this profit has to be netted against the cost initially paid for the option. However, if the price of the asset decreases below the strike price, it does not make sense to exercise your right to buy the asset at a higher price. In this scenario, you lose what you originally paid for the option. Figure 4.8 summarizes the cash payoff at expiration to the buyer of a call option.

With a put option, you get the right to sell at a fixed price, and you want the price of the asset to decrease below the exercise price. If it does, you buy the asset at the current price and then sell it back at the exercise price, claiming the difference as a gross profit. When the initial cost of buying the option is netted against the gross profit, you arrive at an estimate of the net

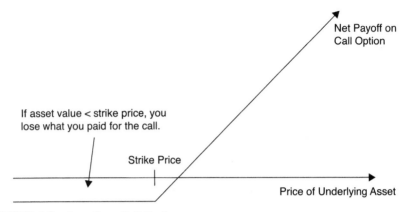

FIGURE 4.8   Payoff on Call Option

profit. If the value of the asset rises above the exercise price, you will not exercise the right to sell at a lower price. Instead, the option will be allowed to expire without being exercised, resulting in a net loss of the original price paid for the put option. Figure 4.9 summarizes the net payoff on buying a put option.

With both call and put options, the potential for profit to the buyer is significant, but the potential for loss is limited to the price paid for the option.

Determinants of Option Value

What is it that determines the value of an option? At one level, options have expected cash flows just like all other assets, and that may seem to make them good candidates for discounted cash flow valuation. The two key characteristics of options—that they derive their value from some other

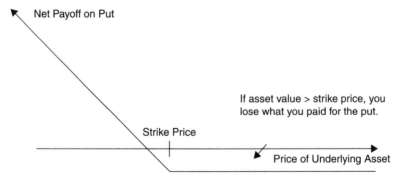

FIGURE 4.9   Payoff on Put Option

traded asset, and the fact that their cash flows are contingent on the occurrence of a specific event—do suggest an easier alternative. We can create a portfolio that has the same cash flows as the option being valued, by combining a position in the underlying asset with borrowing or lending. This portfolio is called a *replicating portfolio* and should cost the same amount as the option. The principle that two assets (the option and the replicating portfolio) with identical cash flows cannot sell at different prices is called the *arbitrage principle*.

Options are assets that derive value from an underlying asset; increases in the value of the underlying asset will increase the value of the right to buy at a fixed price and reduce the value to sell that asset at a fixed price. Conversely, increasing the strike price will reduce the value of calls and increase the value of puts.

While calls and puts move in opposite directions when stock prices and strike prices are varied, they both increase in value as the life of the option and the variance in the underlying asset's value increase. This is because the buyers of options have limited losses. Unlike traditional assets that tend to get less valuable as risk is increased, options become more valuable as the underlying asset becomes more volatile. This is so because the added variance cannot worsen the downside risk (you still cannot lose more than what you paid for the option) but increases the potential for higher profits. In addition, a longer option life just allows more time for both call and put options to appreciate in value.

The final two inputs that affect the value of the call and put options are the riskless interest rate and the expected dividends on the underlying asset. Buyers of call and put options usually pay the price of the option up front, and then wait for the expiration day to exercise. There is a present value effect associated with the fact that the promise to buy an asset for $1 million in 10 years is less onerous than paying for it now. Thus, higher interest rates will generally increase the value of call options (by reducing the present value of the price on exercise) and decrease the value of put options (by decreasing the present value of the price received on exercise). The expected dividends paid by assets make them less valuable; thus, the call option on a stock that does not pay a dividend should be worth more than a call option on a stock that does pay a dividend. The reverse should be true for put options.

CONCLUSION

In this chapter, we laid the foundations for the models that we will be using to value both assets and firms in the coming chapters. There are three classes of valuation models. The most general of these models, discounted cash flow valuation, can be used to value any asset with expected cash flows over its life. The value is the present value of the expected cash flows at a discount rate that reflects the riskiness of the cash flows, and this principle applies whether one is looking at a zero coupon government bond or equity in high-risk firms. Relative valuation models are a second set of models, where we value assets based on how similar assets are priced by the market. Third, there are some assets that generate cash flows only in the event of a specified contingency, and these assets will not be valued accurately using discounted cash flow models. Instead, they should be viewed as options and valued using option pricing models.

EXERCISES

Pick a company that you are familiar with, in terms of its business and history. Try the following:

1. Do an *intrinsic valuation* of a company. You can build your own spreadsheet or use one of mine (check under spreadsheets on my website). Here are some of your choices:
   a. A simple dividend discount model (for valuing financial service companies).
   b. A simple FCFE model (for valuing companies, using cash flows to equity).
   c. A simple FCFF model (for valuing companies, using cash flows to the firm).
2. Pick a *multiple* (P/E, price to book, value/EBITDA) and compare how your company is priced relative to the sector and to other companies within the sector. If your company trades at a much higher or lower multiple than other companies, can you think of reasons why it should?
3. Assuming that you have done both intrinsic and relative valuation, are the values similar? If not, how would you explain the difference?

Lessons for Investors

- All assets that generate or are expected to generate cash flows can be valued by discounting the expected cash flows back at a rate that reflects the riskiness of the cash flows—more risky cash flows should be discounted at higher rates.

- The value of an ongoing business is a function of four variables—how much the business generates in cash flows from existing investments, how long these cash flows can be expected to grow at a rate higher than the growth rate of the economy (high-growth period), the level of the growth rate during this period, and the riskiness of the cash flows. Companies with higher cash flows, higher growth rates, longer high-growth periods, and lower risk will have higher values.
- Alternatively, assets can be valued by looking at how similar assets are priced in the market. This approach is called relative valuation and is built on the presumption that the market is correct, on average.
- Assets whose cash flows are contingent on the occurrence of specific events are called options and can be valued using option pricing models.

CHAPTER 5

Many a Slip: Trading, Execution, and Taxes

A s investors consider different investment strategies, they have to take into account two important factors that can determine whether these strategies pay off—trading costs and taxes. It costs to trade, and some strategies create larger trading costs than others. The costs of trading clearly impose a drag on the performance of all active investors and can turn otherwise winning portfolios into losing portfolios. As we debate the extent of these costs, we need to get a measure of what the costs are, how they vary across investment strategies, and how investors can minimize these costs. In this chapter, we take an expansive view of trading costs and argue that the brokerage cost is only one and often the smallest component of trading costs. We also look at the trading costs associated with holding real assets (such as real estate) and nontraded investments (like equity in a private business). In addition, we discuss the trade-off between trading costs and trading speed.

There is a second equally important element in investment success. Investors get to take home after-tax returns and not before-tax returns. Thus, strategies that perform well before taxes may be money losers after taxes. Taxes are particularly difficult to deal with, partly because they can vary across investors and across investments for the same investor, and partly because the tax code itself changes over time, often in unpredictable ways. We will consider the evidence that many mutual funds do their investors a disservice by not considering taxes and that after-tax returns lag pretax returns considerably at these funds. We will also look at ways in which we can adjust our investment strategies to keep tax liabilities low.

THE TRADING COST DRAG

While we debate what constitutes trading costs and how to measure them, there is a fairly simple way in which we can estimate, at the minimum, how much trading costs affect the returns of the average portfolio manager. Active money managers trade because they believe that there is profit in trading, and the return to any active money manager has three ingredients to it:

Return on active money manager

$$= \text{Expected return}_{\text{Risk}} + \text{Return from active trading} - \text{Trading costs}$$

Looking across all active money managers, we can reasonably assume that the average expected return across all of them has to be equal to the return on the market index, at least in a market like the United States, where institutional investors hold 60 percent or more of all shares outstanding. Thus, subtracting the the return on the index from the average return made by active money managers should give us a measure of the payoff to active money management:

$$\text{Average return}_{\text{Active Money Managers}} - \text{Return on index}$$
$$= \text{Returns from active trading} - \text{Trading costs}$$

Here the evidence becomes quite depressing. The average active money manager has underperformed the index in the past decade by about 1 percent. If we take the view that active trading adds no excess return on average, the trading costs, at the minimum, should be 1 percent of the portfolio on an annual basis. If we take the view that active trading does add to the returns, the trading costs will be greater than 1 percent of the portfolio on an annual basis.

There are also fairly specific examples of real portfolios that have been constructed to replicate hypothetical portfolios, where the magnitude of the trading costs is illustrated starkly. For decades, Value Line has offered advice to individual investors on what stocks to buy and which ones to avoid, and has ranked stocks from 1 to 5 based on their desirability as investments. Studies by academics and practitioners found that Value Line rankings seemed to correlate with actual returns. In 1979, Value Line decided to create a mutual fund that would invest in the stocks that it was recommending to its readers. In Figure 5.1, we consider the difference in returns in the 1979 to 1991 time period between the fund that Value Line ran and the paper portfolio that Value Line has used to compute the returns that its stock picks would have had.

The paper portfolio had an annual return of 26.2 percent, whereas the Value Line fund had a return of 16.1 percent. While part of the difference can be attributed to Value Line waiting until its subscribers had a chance to

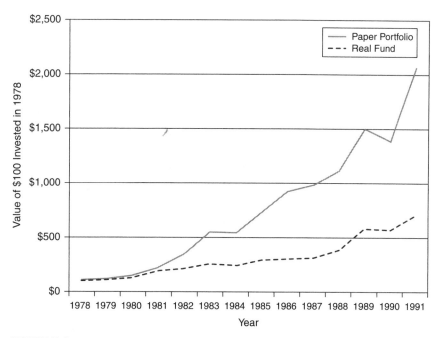

FIGURE 5.1 Value Line—Paper Portfolio versus Real Fund

trade, a significant portion of the difference can be explained by the costs of trading.

Looking at the evidence, there are a couple of conclusions that we would draw. The first is that money managers collectively either underestimate trading costs or overestimate the returns to active trading, or both. The second is that trading costs are a critical ingredient to any investment strategy, and can make the difference between a successful strategy and an unsuccessful one.

THE COMPONENTS OF TRADING COSTS: TRADED FINANCIAL ASSETS

There are some investors who undoubtedly operate under the misconception that the only cost of trading stocks is the brokerage commission that they pay when they buy or sell assets. While this might be the only cost that they pay explicitly, there are other costs that they incur in the course of trading that generally dwarf the commission cost. When trading any asset, they are three other ingredients that go into the trading costs. The first is the *spread* between the price at which you can buy an asset (the ask price) and the price at which you can sell the same asset at the same point in time (the bid price). The second is the *price impact* that an investor can create by trading on an asset, pushing the price up when buying the asset and pushing it down while selling. The third cost, which was first proposed by Jack Treynor in an article on transaction costs, is the *opportunity cost* associated with waiting to trade.[1] Although being a patient trader may reduce the first two components of trading cost, the waiting can cost profits both on trades that are made and in terms of trades that would have been profitable if made instantaneously but become unprofitable as a result of the waiting. It is the sum of these costs that makes up the total trading cost on an investment strategy.

The Bid-Ask Spread

There is a difference between what a buyer will pay and the seller will receive, at the same point in time for the same asset, in almost every traded asset market. The bid-ask spread refers to this difference. In the section that follows, we examine why this difference exists, how large it is as a cost, the determinants of its magnitude, and its effects on returns in different investment strategies.

Why Is There a Bid-Ask Spread?   In most markets, there is a dealer or market maker who sets the bid-ask spread, and there are three types of costs that the dealer faces that the spread is designed to cover. The first is the risk and the cost of holding inventory, the second is the cost of processing orders, and the final cost is the cost of trading with more informed investors. The spread has to be large enough to cover these costs and yield a reasonable profit to the market maker on his or her investment in the profession.

The Inventory Rationale   Consider market makers or specialists on the floor of the exchange who have to quote bid prices and ask prices at which they are obligated to execute buy and sell orders from investors.[2] These investors, themselves, could be trading because of information they have received (informed traders), for liquidity (liquidity traders), or based on their belief that an asset is undervalued or overvalued (value traders). In

[1] J. Treynor, "What Does It Take to Win the Trading Game?" *Financial Analysts Journal* (January–February 1981).

[2] Y. Amihud and H. Mendelson, "Asset Pricing and the Bid-Ask Spread," *Journal of Financial Economics* 17 (1986): 223–249.

such a market, if the market makers set the bid price too high, they will accumulate an inventory of the stock. If market makers set the ask price too low, they will find themselves with a large short position in the stock. In either case, there is a cost to the market makers that they will attempt to recover by increasing the spread between the bid and ask prices.

Market makers also operate with inventory constraints, some of which are externally imposed (by the exchanges or regulatory agencies) and some of which are internally imposed (due to capital limitations and risk). As the market makers' inventory positions deviate from their optimal positions, they bear a cost and will try to adjust the bid and ask prices to get back to their preferred positions.

The Processing Cost Argument Since market makers incur a processing cost when executing orders, the bid-ask spread has to cover, at the minimum, these costs. While these costs are likely to be very small for large orders of stocks traded on the exchanges, they become larger for small orders of stocks that might be traded only through a dealership market. Furthermore, since a large proportion of this cost is fixed, these costs as a percentage of the price will generally be higher for low-priced stocks than for high-priced stocks.

Technology clearly has reduced the processing cost associated with trades as computerized systems take over from traditional record keepers. These cost reductions should be greatest for stocks where the bulk of the trades are small trades—small stocks held by individual rather than institutional investors.

The Adverse Selection Problem The adverse selection problem arises from the different motives investors have for trading on an asset—liquidity, information, and views on valuation. Since investors do not announce their reasons for trading at the time of the trade, the market maker always runs the risk of trading against more informed investors. Since market makers can expect to lose on such trades, they have to charge an average spread that is large enough to compensate for such losses. This theory would suggest that spreads will be a function of three factors:

1. *The proportion of informed traders in an asset market.* As the proportion of informed traders in a market increases, the probability that the market maker will trade with an informed investor on the next trade also increases, pushing the bid-ask spread up.
2. *The differential information possessed, on average, by these traders.* The greater the differences in information possessed by different investors, the more the market maker has to worry about the magnitude of the impact.

3. *The uncertainty about future information on the asset.* The more uncertainty there is about the future, the greater the risk to the market maker from new information coming out, and thus the larger the bid-ask spread.

What Are the Factors That Determine the Bid-Ask Spread?   Given the three underlying variables that motivate the bid-ask spread, it should not be surprising that bid-ask spreads vary widely across assets and that much of the variation can be explained by systematic factors.

NUMBER WATCH
_____

Sector liquidity: See the average trading volume and other measures of liquidity, by sector, for U.S. companies.

Liquidity and Ownership Structure   The first and most critical factor determining the bid-ask spread is liquidity. Stocks that trade more heavily generally have lower bid-ask spreads than stocks that trade less frequently. Every study of bid-ask spreads finds high correlation between the magnitude of the bid-ask spread and some measure of liquidity—trading volume, turnover ratios, and so on.[3] A study of NASDAQ stocks noted the same relationship between spreads and volume, but it also uncovered an interesting new variable: stocks where institutional activity increased significantly had the biggest increase in bid-ask spreads.[4] While some of the differences can be attributed to the concurrent increase in volatility in these stocks (from institutional activity), it might also reflect the perception on the part of market makers that institutional investors tend to be informed investors with more or better information. Note, though, that institutional investors also increase liquidity, which should reduce the order-processing cost

---

[3]S. Tinic and R. West, "Competition and the Pricing of Dealer Service in the Over-the-Counter Market," *Journal of Financial and Quantitative Analysis* 7 (1972): 1707–1727; H. Stoll, "The Pricing of Security Dealer Services: An Empirical Study of Nasdaq Stocks," *Journal of Finance* 33 (1978): 1153–1172.
[4]M. Kothare and P. A. Laux, "Trading Costs and the Trading Systems for NASDAQ Stocks," *Financial Analysts Journal* 51 (1995): 42–53.

component of the bid-ask spread, and in some cases the net effect can lead to a lower spread.[5]

Riskiness   Bid-ask spreads tend to be higher on riskier assets than on safe assets, partly because the adverse selection problem is greater for more volatile stocks. Put simply, it is far more likely that there will be more informed traders, a greater information differential, and greater uncertainty about future information on these stocks. Thus, holding liquidity constant, you should expect to see larger bid-ask spreads not only on more risky stocks than on safe stocks, but also on more risky asset classes (such as equity) than on less risky ones (bonds).

Price Level   A bid-ask spread of 10 cents is trivial on a stock priced at $100 but substantial on a stock priced at $2. Not surprisingly, the bid-ask spread stated as a percentage cost tends to be higher for lower-priced stocks. Going back to the variables that underlie the bid-ask spread, the fixed processing costs will also tend to increase (in percentage terms) as the price level on a stock drops. The price level is a factor in almost every asset market, but it tends to play a bigger role in creating differences in transaction costs in markets where prices vary widely across assets. Thus, it is less of an issue in corporate bond markets, where bonds tend to have similar par values ($1,000), than in the stock market, where the price per share varies among companies. Thus, you can have shares in Berkshire Hathaway, trading in six figures, and shares in penny stocks that trade literally for pennies.

Information Transparency and Corporate Governance   Can firms have an effect on the bid-ask spreads on their stocks? There is some evidence that they can, by improving the quality of information that they disclose the financial markets, thus reducing the advantages that informed traders may have relative to the rest of the market. Heflin, Shaw, and Wild looked at 221 firms and examined the relationship between information disclosure quality (measured using disclosure quality scores assigned by the Corporate Information Committee of the Financial Analysts Federation) and the bid-ask spreads.[6] They found that bid-ask spreads decrease as information quality increases. There is also some evidence that companies with stronger

---

[5]M. K. Dey and B. Radhakrishna, "Institutional Trading, Trading Volume and Spread" (SSRN Working Paper 256104, 2001).

[6]Heflin, F., K. Shaw, and J. Wild. 2005. "Disclosure quality and market liquidity: Impact of depth quotes and order sizes." *Contemporary Accounting Research* 22 (4): 829–865.

corporate governance structures tend to have smaller bid-ask spreads than companies with weaker corporate governance, perhaps because managers in the latter group hold back critical information from the public.

Market Microstructure   Does the market in which a stock lists matter when it comes to how big the bid-ask spread should be? Studies indicate that bid-ask spreads have historically been much larger on the NASDAQ than on the New York Stock Exchange, even after controlling for differences in the variables mentioned earlier—trading volume and price level. In fact, the bid-ask spreads of stocks drop when they switch from the NASDAQ to the NYSE.[7]

A study by Christie and Schultz in 1994 provided one explanation for the phenomenon.[8] They found that there were a disproportionately large number of $1/4$ quotes and far too few $1/8$ quotes.[9] They argued that dealers on the NASDAQ were colluding to set quotes too high and that investors were therefore paying the price with larger bid-ask spreads. This triggered an investigation by the Securities and Exchange Commission (SEC), which concluded that dealers were indeed engaged in anticompetitive behavior. Eventually, the exchange settled the lawsuit for more than a billion dollars. An alternative explanation is that the higher spreads on the NASDAQ relative to the NYSE can be explained by structural differences across the markets. Consider, for example, how limit orders are handled on the two exchanges. The specialists on the floor of the New York Stock Exchange are required to reflect the limit prices in their bid-ask spread, if they are better than their own quotes, and this has the effect of reducing the bid-ask spread. On the NASDAQ, limit orders do not affect the bid-ask quotes and are executed only if prices move against the limit. You would expect larger bid-ask spreads as a consequence.[10]

---

[7]M. Barclay, "Bid-Ask Spreads and the Avoidance of Odd-Eighth Quotes on Nasdaq: An Examination of Exchange Listings," *Journal of Financial Economics* 45 (1997): 35–60.

[8]W. Christie and P. Schultz, "Why Do Nasdaq Market Makers Avoid Odd-Eighth Quotes?" *Journal of Finance* 49 (1994): 1813–1840; W. Christie and P. Schultz, "The Initiation and Withdrawal of Odd-Eighth Quotes among Nasdaq Stocks: An Empirical Analysis," *Journal of Financial Economics* 52 (1999): 409–442.

[9]If $1/8$ and $1/4$ quotes are equally likely to show up, roughly half of all quotes should be eighths ($1/8$, $3/8$, $5/8$, or $7/8$) and half should be quarters ($1/4$, $1/2$, or $3/4$).

[10]K. Chung, B. Van Ness, and R. Van Ness, "Can the Treatment of Limit Orders Reconcile the Differences in Trading Costs between NYSE and Nasdaq Issues?" *Journal of Financial and Quantitative Analysis* 36 (2001): 267–286. While they find that the treatment of limit orders does narrow the bid-ask spread on the NYSE, they conclude that collusion among dealers still leads to wider spreads on the NASDAQ.

In 2000, the New York Stock Exchange abandoned its historical practice of quoting prices in fractions ($1/8$, $1/4$, etc.) and shifted to decimal prices. Since you can get finer gradations of prices in decimals, it was hypothesized that this should lead to smaller bid-ask spreads. Studies since the shift indicate that there has been a reduction in spreads on the smaller, less liquid stocks but a much smaller impact on the more liquid listings.

How Big Is the Spread? The answer varies, depending on what asset or stock you are trading, who you are as an investor, and when and how much you trade. In this section, we first look at variations in bid-ask spreads across stocks, and then examine differences across markets and finally at differences across time.

Variation across Stocks The average bid-ask spread for a stock traded on the New York Stock Exchange in 2004 was only 5 cents, which seems trivial especially when one considers the fact that the average price of a NYSE stock is between $20 and $30. This average, however, obscures the large differences in the cost as a percentage of the price across stocks, based on capitalization, stock price level, and trading volume, and these differences get magnified if we extend the analysis to look at over-the-counter stocks.

- A study[11] by Thomas Loeb in 1983, for instance, reported the spread as a percentage of the stock price for companies as a function of their *market capitalization* for small orders. These results are summarized in Figure 5.2.

    While the dollar spread is not that different across market capitalization classes, the smallest companies also tend to have *lower-priced stocks*. Consequently, the spread is as high as 6.55 percent of the price for small-capitalization stocks and as low as 0.52 percent of the price for large-capitalization companies.
- In fact, more recent studies that classify stocks based on price level find that *lower-priced stocks* have substantially higher spreads (as a percent of stock price) than higher-priced stocks. While an argument can be made that stock price levels are correlated with other variables that affect the spread, such as illiquidity and information asymmetry, studies of bid-ask spreads around stock splits provide us with an opportunity to isolate the effects of just price levels. In these studies, where the bid-ask spread is computed as a percent of the stock price just before and after

---

[11]T. Loeb, "Trading Costs: The Critical Link between Investment Information and Results," *Financial Analysts Journal* 39 (1983): 39–44.

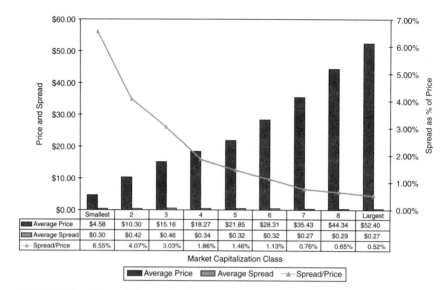

Market Capitalization Class	Smallest	2	3	4	5	6	7	8	Largest
Average Price	$4.58	$10.30	$15.16	$18.27	$21.85	$28.31	$35.43	$44.34	$52.40
Average Spread	$0.30	$0.42	$0.46	$0.34	$0.32	$0.32	$0.27	$0.29	$0.27
Spread/Price	6.55%	4.07%	3.03%	1.86%	1.46%	1.13%	0.76%	0.65%	0.52%

FIGURE 5.2   Prices and Spreads by Market Cap
Source: T. Loeb, "Trading Costs: The Critical Link between Investment Information and Results," *Financial Analysts Journal* 39 (1983): 39–44.

stock splits, the spread cost (as a percent of the stock price) increases after stock splits.

■ A study found that the stocks in the top 20 percent in terms of *trading volume* had an average spread of only 0.62 percent of the price while the stocks in the bottom 20 percent had a spread of 2.06 percent. Other studies that use different measures of liquidity, including turnover ratios, have come to the same conclusion: less liquid stocks have higher bid-ask spreads.[12]

■ Finally, the bid-ask spread seems to be a function of the *ownership structure* of a company. As insider holdings increase as a percentage of total stock outstanding, bid-ask spreads increase, reflecting lower liquidity (since insiders don't trade their holdings as frequently) and a fear that insiders may know more about the company than other investors (information asymmetry).[13]

---

[12]R. D. Huang and H. R. Stoll, "Dealer versus Auction Markets: A Paired Comparison of Execution Costs on NASDAQ and the NYSE," *Journal of Financial Economics* 41 (1996): 313–357.

[13]D. Zhou, "Ownership Structure, Liquidity and Trade Informativeness," *Journal of Finance and Accountancy* 6 (2011).

In summary, there are wide variations in bid-ask spreads across stocks, but much of the variation can be explained by differences in liquidity, price level, and information asymmetry.

Variation across Markets   If bid-ask spreads on U.S. stocks have been studied more intensively than assets listed on other markets, growth in other markets and better access to data are allowing us to explore spreads in these markets. The first extension we look at is equity markets outside the United States. Two decades ago, when liquidity in most emerging markets was very light and there was little competition to market makers in these markets, bid-ask spreads were very large in these markets. As liquidity has improved, spreads have decreased, though they remain higher than spreads in the United States. A study of 20 emerging markets spanning the globe, using data from 1996 to 2007, provides a comprehensive picture of differences in bid-ask spreads across countries in Table 5.1.[14]

There are two conclusions that we can draw from this table. The first is that the average bid-ask spread (2.16 percent), as a percentage of price, across emerging markets is much higher than the average spread across U.S. stocks. The second is that not all emerging markets are created equal, with spreads far wider in the Philippines than in China or South Korea. Much of the variation across the emerging markets can be explained by differences in liquidity, captured in two measures—the turnover ratio (trading volume/number of shares outstanding) and the percent of trading days with zero trading volume across all stocks in the market. Thus, Russia with a low turnover ratio and no trading on 40 percent of all trading days across all stocks also has large bid-ask spreads.

In some of these countries, there are variations in spreads across markets within the country. In China, for instance, there is evidence that spreads are narrower for domestic investors trading class A and B shares in Chinese companies on domestic exchanges (say, Shanghai) than for global investors trading H class shares in the same companies in Hong Kong, perhaps because information asymmetries are higher in the latter market.[15]

Moving from stock markets to other financial asset markets, we find that the key factor explaining differences in spreads is liquidity. In the bond market, for instance, the bid-ask spread is narrow in the very liquid U.S. Treasury bond market and in investment grade bonds (BBB rated or higher)

---

[14]H. Zhang, "Measuring Liquidity in Emerging Markets" (working paper, National University of Singapore, 2010).

[15]J. Cai, "Bid-Ask Spreads for Trading Chinese Stocks Listed on Domestic and International Exchanges" (working paper, 2004).

TABLE 5.1 Bid-Ask Spreads across Emerging Markets

Country	Bid-Ask Spread	Turnover	% Days with Zero Trading Volume
Argentina	2.55%	0.08	23.87%
Brazil	4.68%	1.12	29.10%
Chile	3.79%	0.17	34.19%
Mexico	2.83%	0.17	20.85%
China	0.31%	1.31	2.55%
South Korea	1.39%	3.16	4.14%
Philippines	6.61%	0.68	20.97%
Taiwan	0.63%	1.32	0.48%
India	1.90%	0.43	3.63%
Indonesia	6.17%	0.44	21.66%
Malaysia	2.43%	0.34	8.67%
Singapore	3.83%	0.37	11.61%
Thailand	2.58%	1.03	13.39%
Greece	1.81%	0.33	2.12%
Poland	1.42%	1.20	4.94%
Portugal	2.05%	0.25	7.43%
Russia	3.17%	0.15	40.06%
Turkey	1.16%	8.21	1.05%
Israel	4.17%	0.15	22.14%
South Africa	4.14%	0.16	18.44%
All	2.16%	1.73	8.88%

Source: H. Zhang, "Measuring Liquidity in Emerging Markets" (working paper, National University of Singapore, 2010).

but increases as we get to high-yield or low-rated bonds, where two factors come into play. The first factor is lower liquidity, and the other is the greater potential for information asymmetry. In the options and futures markets, the bid-ask spreads vary from a sliver in the index and commodity markets to larger values for deep-out-of-the-money options on individual stocks. Finally, spreads tend to be narrow in most currency markets, again because of high trading volume and little scope for information advantages.

Are there bid-ask spreads in the real asset market? In the commodity market, where you can buy or sell spot gold or oil, the bid-ask spreads tend to be small because of the volume of trading and the absence of information asymmetries (for the most part). With other real assets such as real estate or fine art, there is no explicit bid-ask spread, but only because the transaction cost or fee that you pay incorporates the spread. Thus, the 6 percent fee that the real estate agents split on the sale of a house plays the same role as the bid-ask spread, as does the hefty percentage of the value that has to be paid to an auction house (like Sotheby's) to sell a Picasso.

Variation across Time   If variations in liquidity and information asymmetry cause differences in bid-ask spreads across markets and, within markets, across individual assets, it stands to reason that variations over time in these factors will cause bid-ask spreads to also change over time, within any market or for any given stock.

Looking at a long time horizon, say over the last century, it is undeniable that financial markets have become more liquid over time. In the 1920s, for instance, relatively few companies were traded on stock exchanges, and trading was restricted to a few brokers (and wealthy investors). As more stocks have been listed and trading volume has increased, we have seen bid-ask spreads decrease over the past few decades. Focusing on a more recent period, the average bid-ask spread for stocks listed on the New York Stock Exchange decreased from 23 cents in 1994 to 5 cents in 2004. In fact, financial markets outside the United States have seen even larger improvements in liquidity over the past 20 to 30 years, resulting in lower bid-ask spreads in these markets.

In this generally good news story of long-term improvement in liquidity (and lower transaction costs), there have been painful interludes where liquidity has dried up and trading costs have soared. Every one of the emerging markets listed in Table 5.1 has had at least one crisis in the past few decades, where trading volume has dropped and bid-ask spreads have widened significantly. Developed markets were thought to be immune from such dramatic shifts, but the banking crisis of 2008 dispensed with that illusion. Between September and December 2008, bid-ask spreads widened across the board for all stocks and corporate bonds in the United States, often tripling and quadrupling even on large-cap, liquid stocks. One study that looked at 51 investment grade, large market cap U.S. companies and estimated the bid-ask spreads on their stocks from 2003 to 2009 found the shifts graphed in Figure 5.3.[16]

Note the spike in spreads during the banking crisis in 2008. In fact, similar spikes in spreads were reported in corporate bond and credit default swap (CDS) markets during the period.

The last point needs emphasis because it points to a clear and present danger to investment strategies. It is not just that illiquidity varies across time for individual asset classes (stocks, bonds, currencies, real assets) but

---

[16]M. Marra, "Illiquidity Commonality across Equity and Credit Markets" (doctoral thesis, Warwick Business School, 2011).

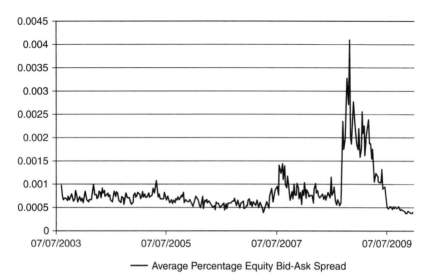

FIGURE 5.3 Bid-Ask Spreads for Stocks—51 Liquid U.S. Companies, 2003–2009
Source: M. Marra, "Illiquidity Commonality across Equity and Credit Markets" (Doctoral thesis, Warwick Business School, 2011).

that there is substantial comovement. Put differently, if bid-ask spreads soar in the stock market, it is very likely that you will also see higher spreads in the bond and real asset markets, thus increasing trading costs across the board on your investments.

Role in Investment Strategies Looking at the evidence, it is clear that bid-ask spreads will affect the returns from investment strategies, but that the effect will vary, depending on the strategy. While a strategy of buying undervalued companies in the Standard & Poor's (S&P) 500 index and holding for the long term should not be affected very much by the bid-ask spread, a strategy of buying small over-the-counter stocks or emerging market stocks after information releases and trading frequently might lose its allure when bid-ask spreads are factored into the returns.

To show the effect of the bid-ask spread on returns, consider the strategy of buying so-called loser stocks (i.e., stocks that have gone down the most over the prior year). Researchers present evidence that a strategy of buying the stocks that have the most negative returns over the previous year and holding for a five-year period earns significant positive returns.[17] A follow-up study, however, noted that many of these loser stocks were low-priced,

---

[17]W. F. M. DeBondt and R. Thaler, "Does the Stock Market Overreact?" *Journal of Finance* 40 (1985): 793–805.

and that putting in a constraint that the prices be greater than $10 on this strategy resulted in a significant drop in the excess returns. Since bid-ask spreads tend to be largest for low-priced stocks, it is an open question as to whether an investment strategy of buying loser stocks will yield excess returns in practice. In fact, similar concerns should exist about any strategy that requires investing in low-priced, illiquid, and small-cap stocks, or in asset classes that have high volatility and low liquidity.

The Price Impact

Most investors assume that trading costs become smaller as portfolios become larger. Though this is true for brokerage commissions, it is not always the case for the other components of trading costs. An investor who tries to trade a larger block may see the bid-ask spread widen, as wary market markets hold back, concerned about information asymmetries. There is one more component where larger investors bear a more substantial cost than do smaller investors, and that is in the impact that their trading has on the price level. If the basic idea behind successful investing is to buy low and sell high, pushing the price up as you buy and then down as you sell reduces the profits from investing.

Why Is There a Price Impact?   There are two reasons for the price impact when investors trade. The first is that markets are not completely liquid. A large trade can create an imbalance between buy and sell orders, and the only way in which this imbalance can be resolved is with a price change. This price change that arises from lack of liquidity will generally be temporary and will be reversed as liquidity returns to the market.

The second reason for the price impact is informational. A large trade attracts the attention of other investors in that market because it might be motivated by new information that the trader possesses. Notwithstanding claims to the contrary, investors usually assume, with good reason, that an investor buying a large block is buying in advance of good news and that an investor selling a large block has come into possession of some bad news about the company. This price effect will generally not be temporary, especially when we look across a large number of stocks where such large trades are made. Though investors are likely to be wrong a fair proportion of the time on the informational value of large block trades, there is reason to believe that they will be right often enough to make a difference.

How Large Is the Price Impact?   There is conflicting evidence on how much of an impact large trades have on stock prices. On the one hand, studies of block trades on the exchange floor seem to suggest that markets are liquid and that the price impact of trading is small and is reversed quickly.

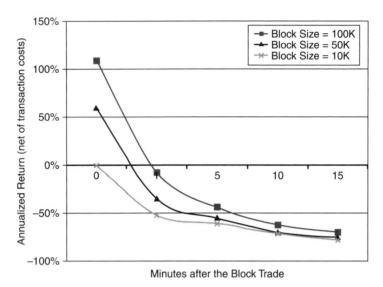

FIGURE 5.4   Annualized Returns from Buying after Block Trades
Source: L. Dann, D. Mayers, and R. Raab, "Trading Rules, Large Blocks and the
Speed of Adjustment," *Journal of Financial Economics* 4 (1977): 3–22.

These studies, however, have generally looked at heavily traded stocks at
the New York Stock Exchange. On the other hand, there are others who
argue that the price impact is likely to be large, especially for smaller and less
liquid stocks.

Studies of the price reaction to large block trades on the floor of the
exchange conclude that prices adjust within a few minutes to such trades.
An early study by Dann, Mayers, and Raab examined the speed of the price
reaction by looking at the returns an investor could make by buying stock
right around the block trade and selling later.[18] They estimated the returns
after transactions as a function of how many minutes after the block trade the
acquisition took place, and found that only trades made within a few minutes
of the block trade had a chance of making excess returns. (See Figure 5.4.)
Put another way, prices adjusted to the liquidity effects of the block trade
within five minutes of the block trade, strong evidence of the capacity of
markets to adjust quickly to imbalances between demand and supply.

This study suffers from a sampling bias—it looks at large block trades in
large-cap, liquid stocks on the exchange floor. Studies that look at smaller,

---

[18]L. Dann, D. Mayers, and R. Raab, "Trading Rules, Large Blocks and the Speed of
Adjustment," *Journal of Financial Economics* 4 (1977): 3–22.

less liquid stocks find that the price impact tends to be larger and the adjustment back to the correct price is slower than it is for the more liquid stocks.[19] There are other interesting facts about block trades that have emerged from other studies. First, while stock prices go up on block buys and go down on block sells, they are far more likely to bounce back after sell trades; when prices go up after a block buy, they are more likely to stay up.[20] Another study that looks at both liquid and illiquid stocks on the NYSE also finds a tendency on the part of markets to overshoot.[21] When a block buy is made, the price seems to go up too much, and it can take several days for it to revert back to a normal level for illiquid stocks.

These studies, while they establish a price impact, also suffer from another selection bias insofar as they look only at actual executions. The true cost of market impact arises from those trades that would have been done in the absence of a market impact but were not because of the perception that the impact would be large. In one of the few studies of how large this cost could be, Thomas Loeb collected bid and ask prices from specialists and market makers at a point in time for a variety of block sizes. Thus, the differences in the spreads as the block size increases can be viewed as an expected price impact from these trades. Table 5.2 summarizes his findings across stocks, classified by market capitalization.

The sectors refer to market capitalization and show the negative relationship between company size and price impact. Note, however, the effect of increasing block sizes on expected price impact within each sector; larger trades elicit much larger price impact than do smaller trades.

While the Loeb study suggests that price impact can create very large costs, studies of actual trades suggest that institutional investors have learned how to reduce, if not eliminate, these costs by modifying their trading behavior. First, large trades are increasingly done off the floor of the exchange, and there is some evidence that these off-floor trades have a smaller price impact than the trades on the floor. Second, to the extent that trades can be broken into smaller blocks and executed almost simultaneously, the price

---

[19]J. Hasbrouck, "Measuring the Information Content of Stock Trades," *Journal of Finance* 66 (1991): 179–207.

[20]R. W. Holthausen, R. W. Leftwich, and D. Mayers, "Large-Block Transactions, the Speed of Response, and Temporary and Permanent Stock-Price Effects," *Journal of Financial Economics* 26 (1990): 71–95; D. B. Keim and A. Madhavan, "Anatomy of the Trading Process: Empirical Evidence on the Behavior of Institutional Trades," *Journal of Financial Economics* 37 (1995): 371–398.

[21]L. Spierdijk, T. Nijman, and A. H. O. van Soest, "The Price Impact of Trades in Illiquid Stocks in Periods of High and Low Market Activity" (working paper, Tilburg University, 2002).

TABLE 5.2 Round-Trip Transaction Costs as a Function of Market Capitalization and Block Size

Sector	5	25	250	500	1,000	2,500	5,000	10,000	20,000
Smallest	17.30%	27.30%	43.80%						
2	8.90%	12.00%	23.80%	33.40%					
3	5.00%	7.60%	18.80%	25.90%	30.00%				
4	4.30%	5.80%	9.60%	16.90%	25.40%	31.50%			
5	2.80%	3.90%	5.90%	8.10%	11.50%	15.70%	25.70%		
6	1.80%	2.10%	3.20%	4.40%	5.60%	7.90%	11.00%	16.20%	
7	1.90%	2.00%	3.10%	4.00%	5.60%	7.70%	10.40%	14.30%	20.00%
8	1.90%	1.90%	2.70%	3.30%	4.60%	6.20%	8.90%	13.60%	18.10%
Largest	1.10%	1.20%	1.30%	1.71%	2.10%	2.80%	4.10%	5.90%	8.00%

Dollar Value of Block ($ thousands)

Source: T. Loeb, "Trading Costs: The Critical Link between Investment Information and Results," *Financial Analysts Journal* 39 (1983): 39–44.

impact costs can be reduced. Notwithstanding these developments, it still remains true that an investor desirous of either acquiring or divesting a large block of stock in a company will have to pay a price for immediacy.

Determinants of the Price Impact and Implications for Investment Strategies Looking at the evidence, the variables that determine that price impact of trading seem to be the same variables that drive the bid-ask spread. That should not be surprising. The price impact and the bid-ask spread are both a function of the liquidity of the market. The inventory costs and adverse selection problems are likely to be largest for stocks where small trades can move the market significantly.

Drawing on our earlier discussion of bid-ask spreads, the price impact is likely to be greater for less liquid, smaller market capitalization companies that are closely held, for the same reasons that bid-ask spreads are high for these companies. The price impact is likely to be higher in emerging markets than in developed markets and during periods of market crisis (such as the last quarter of 2008).

Since you can reduce the price impact of trades by breaking them up into smaller trades, the price impact cost is *likely to be greatest for investment strategies that require instantaneous trading*. Thus, a portfolio manager who buys small, illiquid stocks because they are undervalued is likely to face a smaller price impact cost than an investor who buys the same stocks after positive earnings announcements. The former can afford to spread the trades over time whereas the latter has to trade right after the announcement.

The price impact effect also will come into play when a small portfolio manager, hitherto successful with an investment strategy, *tries to scale up the strategy*. There are many investment strategies that deliver high risk-adjusted returns on a small scale but fail in larger portfolios because the price impact costs rise.

The Opportunity Cost of Waiting

The final component of trading costs is the opportunity cost of waiting. An investor can reduce the bid-ask spread and price impact costs of trading by trading patiently. If, in fact, there were no cost to waiting, even a large investor could break up trades into small lots and buy or sell large quantities without affecting the price or the spread significantly. There is, however, a cost to waiting. In particular, the price of an asset that an investor wants to buy because he or she believes that it is undervalued may rise while the investor waits to trade, and this, in turn, can lead to one of two consequences. One is that the investor does eventually buy, but at a much higher price, reducing expected profits from the investment. The other is that the price rises so much that the asset is no longer undervalued and the investor does not trade at all. A similar calculus applies when an investor wants to sell an asset that he or she thinks is overvalued.

The cost of waiting will depend in great part on the probability that the investor assigns that the price will rise (or fall) while he or she waits to buy (or sell). We would argue that this probability will be a function of why the investor thinks the asset is undervalued or overvalued. In particular, the following four factors should affect this probability:

1. *Is the valuation assessment based on private information or is it based on public information?* Private information tends to have a short shelf life in financial markets, and the risks of sitting on private information are much greater than the risks of waiting when the valuation assessment is based on public information. Thus, the cost of waiting is much larger when the strategy is to buy on the rumors (or information) of a possible takeover than it would be in a strategy of buying low price-earnings (P/E) ratio stocks.

2. *How active is the market for information?* Building on the first point, the risks of waiting, when one has valuable information, are much greater in markets where there are other investors actively searching for the same information. Again, in practical terms, the costs of waiting will be greater when there are dozens of analysts following the target stock than when there are few other investors paying attention to the stock.

3. *How long term or short term is the strategy?* While this generalization does not always hold, short-term strategies are more likely to be affected by the cost of waiting than longer-term strategies are. Some of this can be attributed to the fact that short-term strategies are more likely to be motivated by private information, whereas long-term strategies are more likely to be motivated by views on value.

4. *Is the investment strategy a contrarian or momentum strategy?* In a contrarian strategy, where investors are investing against the prevailing tide (buying when others are selling or selling when others are buying), the cost of waiting is likely to be smaller precisely because of this behavior. In contrast, the cost of waiting in a momentum strategy is likely to be higher since the investor is buying when other investors are buying and selling when others are selling.

In summary, the cost of waiting is likely to be greatest for short-term investment strategies, based on private information or momentum, in markets with active information gathering. It will be less of an issue for long-term investment strategies based on public information and for contrarian strategies.

TABLE 5.3 Total Round Trip Trading Costs and Market Capitalization, 1991 to 1993

Market Capitalization	Implicit Cost	Explicit Cost	Total Trading Costs (NYSE)	Total Trading Costs (NASDAQ)
Smallest	2.71%	1.09%	3.80%	5.76%
2	1.62%	0.71%	2.33%	3.25%
3	1.13%	0.54%	1.67%	2.10%
4	0.69%	0.40%	1.09%	1.36%
Largest	0.28%	0.28%	0.31%	0.40%

Source: D. B. Keim and A. Madhavan, "The Cost of Institutional Equity Trades," *Financial Analysts Journal* 54 (1998): 50–69.

Investment Strategy and Total Trading Costs

The fact that assets that have high bid-ask spreads also tend to be assets where trading can have a significant price impact makes it even more critical that we examine with skepticism investment strategies that focus disproportionately in these assets. With the price impact, the effect of the size of the portfolio becomes much more important, since large portfolios beget large trading blocks, which, in turn, have the biggest price impact. Thus, a strategy of investing in low-priced stocks that are not followed by analysts may yield excess returns, even after the bid-ask spread is considered, for a portfolio of $250 million but cease to be profitable if that same portfolio becomes $5 billion.

Keim and Madhavan examine the interrelationship between total trading costs—implicit (including price impact and opportunity costs) as well as explicit (commissions and spreads)—and investment strategies.[22] Not surprisingly, they find that strategies that require large block trades have much higher total trading costs than strategies with smaller trades. They also find that the total trading costs are much greater for investors who buy small market cap stocks as opposed to large market cap ones. Table 5.3 provides a summary of their estimates of total trading costs for small-cap and large-cap companies listed on the NYSE and NASDAQ from 1991 to 1993.

Note that the smallest companies have total round-trip trading costs that are significantly higher than the largest companies. They also find significant differences in costs between managers with different trading styles, with

---

[22] D. B. Keim, and A. Madhavan, "The Cost of Institutional Equity Trades," *Financial Analysts Journal* 54 (1998): 50–69.

technical traders having the highest costs (presumably because of their need for immediate execution) and value traders having the lowest costs.

TRADING COSTS WITH NONTRADED ASSETS

If the cost of trading stocks can be substantial, it should be even more significant if your investment strategy requires you to hold assets that are not traded regularly, such as collectibles, real estate, or equity positions in private companies. In this section, we consider these costs.

Trading Costs on Real Assets

Real assets can range from gold to real estate to fine art, and the transaction costs associated with trading these assets can also vary substantially. The smallest transaction costs are associated with commodities—gold, silver, or diamonds—since they tend to come in standardized units. With residential real estate, the commission that you have to pay a real estate broker or salesperson can be 5 to 6 percent of the value of the asset. With commercial real estate, commissions may be a smaller percentage for larger transactions, but they will still be substantial. With fine art or collectibles, the commissions become even higher. If you sell a painting through one of the auction houses, you may have to pay 15 to 20 percent of the value of the painting as a commission.

Why are the costs so high? The first reason is that there are far fewer intermediaries in real asset businesses than there are in the stock or bond markets; this reduces competition. The second is that real estate and fine art are not standardized products. In other words, one Picasso can be very different from another, and you often need the help of experts to authenticate the painting, judge value and arrange transactions. This adds to the cost in the process.

Trading Costs on Private Equity/Businesses

If your strategy requires you to take positions in private businesses—private equity, as it is called—you have to allow for the fact that lucrative though the returns from these investments may be, the investments are illiquid. It is common, in fact, for investors in private businesses to assess an illiquidity discount on value to reflect their expectation that the cost of liquidating their position will be high. In this section, we consider some of the factors that will determine this cost and empirical assessments of how big the cost may be.

Determinants of Illiquidity Cost The cost of illiquidity is likely to vary across both firms and buyers, which renders rules of thumb useless. Let us consider first four of the factors that may cause the cost to vary across firms.

1. *Liquidity of assets owned by the firm.* The fact that a private firm is difficult to sell may be rendered moot if its assets are liquid and can be sold with no significant loss in value. A private firm with significant holdings of cash and marketable securities should have a lower illiquidity cost than one with factories or other assets for which there are relatively few buyers.
2. *Financial health and cash flows of the firm.* A private firm that is financially healthy should be easier to sell than one that is not healthy. In particular, a firm with strong income and positive cash flows should be subject to a smaller illiquidity cost than one with negative income and cash flows.
3. *Possibility of going public in the future.* The greater the likelihood that a private firm can go public in the future, the lower should be the illiquidity cost. In effect, the probability of going public is built into the valuation of the private firm.
4. *Size of the firm.* If we state the illiquidity cost as a percentage of the value of the firm, it should become smaller as the size of the firm increases. In other words, the illiquidity discount should be smaller as a percentage of firm value for firms like Cargill and Koch Industries, which are worth billions of dollars, than it should be for a small firm worth a few million.

The illiquidity cost is also likely to vary across potential buyers because the desire for liquidity varies among individuals. It is likely that those buyers who have deep pockets and see little or no need to cash out their equity positions will face lower illiquidity costs than buyers that have less of a safety margin and a greater need for cash.

Empirical Evidence on Illiquidity Cost How large is the cost of being illiquid? This is a very difficult question to answer because the discount attached to an asset's value itself cannot be observed. Even if we were able to obtain the terms of all private firm transactions, note that what is reported is the price at which private firms are bought and sold. The value of these firms is not known—and the illiquidity discount is the difference between the value and the price.

In fact, much of the evidence on illiquidity discounts comes from examining *restricted stock* at publicly traded firms. Restricted securities are securities issued by a publicly traded company but not registered with the

Securities and Exchange Commission (SEC); these securities can be sold through private placements to investors but cannot be resold in the open market for a two-year holding period, and only limited amounts can be sold after that. When this stock is issued, the issue price is set much lower than the prevailing market price, which is observable, and the difference is viewed as a discount for illiquidity. There have been several studies of restricted stock, and while they vary on the degree of the discount at which restricted stocks are placed, they all report significant discounts.[23]

In summary, then, there seems to be a substantial discount attached to value, at least on average, when an investment is not liquid. Much of the practice of estimating illiquidity discounts seems to build on these averages. For instance, rules of thumb often set the illiquidity discount at 20 to 30 percent of estimated value, and there seems to be little or no variation in this discount across firms.

MANAGEMENT OF TRADING COSTS

The preceding discussion makes clear out not only how large the trading cost problem is for active money managers, but also how difficult it is to develop a strategy to minimize the collective cost. Actions taken to reduce one type of trading cost (say, the brokerage commission or bid-ask spread) may increase another (for instance, the price impact). Strategies designed to minimize the collective impact of the bid-ask spread and the price impact (such as breaking up trades and using alternative trading routes) may increase the opportunity cost of waiting. In this section, we examine ways in which trading costs can be managed within the broader construct of maximizing portfolio returns, given an investment philosophy.

Step 1: Develop a coherent investment philosophy and a consistent investment strategy.

The first step in managing trading costs is developing and staying with a coherent investment philosophy and strategy. The portfolio managers who pride themselves on style switching and moving from one investment philosophy to another are the ones who bear the biggest burden in terms of transaction costs, partly because style switching increases turnover and partly

---

[23]W. L. Silber, "Discounts on Restricted Stock: The Impact of Illiquidity on Stock Prices," *Financial Analysts Journal* 47 (1991): 60–64. The median discount on restricted stock in most of the studies that look at them is between 30 percent and 40 percent.

because it is difficult to develop a trading strategy without a consistent investment philosophy.

Step 2: Estimate the cost of waiting, given the investment strategy.

The second step in the process is determining the cost of waiting for the investment strategy that is being followed. As noted in the previous section, the cost of waiting is likely to be small for long-term, contrarian strategies and greater for short-term, information-based, and momentum strategies. If the cost of waiting is very high, then the objective has to be minimize this cost, which essentially translates into trading as quickly as one can, even if the other costs of trading increase as a consequence.

Step 3: Look at the alternatives available to minimize transaction costs, given the cost of waiting.

Once the cost of waiting has been identified, the investor can consider the third step, which is to minimize the effect of the bid-ask spread and the price impact on portfolio returns. While we have talked about trading primarily in terms of trading on the floor of the exchange, there are a number of options that an investor can use to reduce the trading costs. Rose and Cushing make some of the following suggestions to reduce trading costs on a portfolio for an institutional investor:[24]

- Take advantage of the alternatives to trading on the floor of the exchange. Among these alternatives are using the upstairs block market (where large buyers and sellers trade with each other), the dealer market (where trades are made with a dealer), and crossing networks (where trades are executed over a network). The trade-off is straightforward— the approaches that yield the most liquidity (the exchange floor and the dealer market) are also the ones that have the highest trading costs.
- Trade portfolios rather than individual stocks when multiple orders have to be placed. Portfolio trades generally result in lower trading costs and allow for better risk management and hedging capabilities.
- Use technology to reduce the paperwork associated with trading and to keep track of trades that have already been made. By allowing traders to have information on whether their trades have been executed, and on trades that have already been made, technology can help control costs.

---

[24]J. D. Rose and D. C. Cushing, "Making the Best Use of Trading Alternatives," in *Execution Techniques, True Trading Costs and the Microstructure of Markets* (AIMR, 1996).

- Be prepared prior to trading on ways to control liquidity and splits between manual and electronic trading. This pretrade analysis will allow traders to identify the least costly and most efficient way to make a trade.
- After the trade has been executed, do a posttrade analysis, where the details of the trade are provided in addition to a market impact analysis, which lists, among other information, the benchmarks that can be used to estimate the price impact, including the midpoint of the bid-ask spread before the trade and the previous day's close. These posttrade analyses can then be aggregated across types of trades, securities, and markets to give portfolio managers a measure of where their costs are greatest and how to control them.

Step 4: Stay with a portfolio size that is consistent with the investment philosophy and trading strategy that you have chosen.

While it is tempting to most portfolio managers to view portfolio growth as a positive, there is a danger that arises from allowing portfolios to become too big. How big is too big? It depends on both the portfolio strategy that has been chosen and the trading costs associated with that strategy. While a long-term value investor who focuses well-known, large-capitalization stocks might be able to allow the portfolio to increase to almost any size, an investor in small-cap, high-growth stocks or emerging market stocks may not have the same luxury, because of the trading costs we have enumerated in the earlier sections.

Step 5: Consider whether your investment strategy is yielding returns that exceed the costs.

The ultimate test of an investment strategy lies in whether it earns excess returns after transaction costs. Once an investor has gone through the first four steps, the moment of truth always arrives when the performance of the portfolio is evaluated. If a strategy consistently delivers returns that are lower than the costs associated with implementing the strategy, the investor can switch to a passive investing approach (such as an index fund) or to a different active investing strategy with higher expected returns or lower trading costs (or both).

TAXES

As has often been said, the only two things that are certain in life are death and taxes. Though investors may get a chance to pause and admire the pretax returns they make on their investment portfolios, they can spend only the returns that they have left after taxes. Strategies that yield attractive pretax returns can generate substandard after-tax returns. There are two reasons why taxes are ignored by both researchers looking at investment strategies and portfolio managers who put these strategies into practice. The first is that taxes affect different investors differently, ranging from no impact on tax-exempt investors such as pension funds to very large effects on wealthier individual investors. The second is that the complexity of the tax laws is such that the same investor may face different tax rates on different parts of his or her income (dividends versus capital gains) and different portions of his or her portfolio (pension fund versus savings).

Investment Returns and Taxes

How big of a drag are taxes on investment returns? Studies that look at returns on the U.S. stock market and government bonds show that stocks have generated much higher returns and ending values for investors than Treasury bills or bonds have. Figure 5.5 presents the ending value of $100

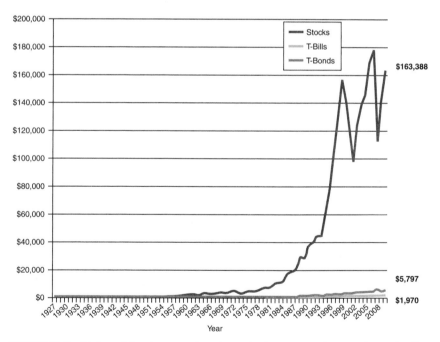

FIGURE 5.5 Value of $100 Invested at the End of 1927: Stocks, Bonds, and Bills
Source: S&P, Federal Reserve.

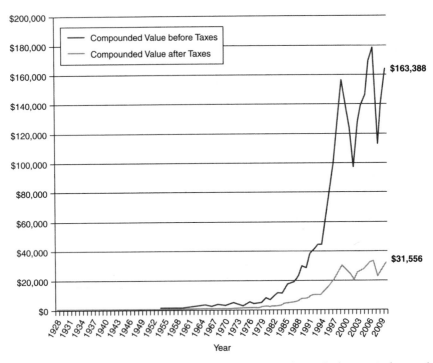

FIGURE 5.6   Value of $100 Invested in U.S. Stocks at the End of 1927: Before and
After Taxes
Source: Federal Reserve.

invested in stocks, Treasury bonds, and Treasury bills in 1928 and held
through the end of 2010.

Thus, $100 invested in stocks would have grown to $163,388, significantly higher than what your portfolio would have been worth if invested
in T-bills ($1,970) or T-bonds ($5,797). This is impressive, but it is also before taxes and transaction costs. Let us for the moment consider the effects
of taxes on these returns. Assume that the investor buying these stocks is
faced a tax rate of 35 percent on dividends and 20 percent on capital gains
over this period.[25] To compute the effect of taxes on returns, we do have
to consider how often this investor trades. If we assume that he turns over
his entire portfolio at the end of each year, he would have to pay taxes on
both dividends and the price appreciation each year. Figure 5.6 shows the

---

[25]Note that the actual tax rates on dividends and capital gains varied widely over
this period and were much higher than these values from 1950 to 1980.

effect on the portfolio value over the period and the effect of taxes on the ending portfolio.

Note that introducing taxes into returns reduces the ending value of the portfolio, assuming you invested $100 in 1927, by more than two-thirds from $163,388 to $31,556.

But what if this investor, instead of turning over the entire portfolio once every year, had turned it over once every two years (or three or five)? Trading less often does not reduce the tax bite from dividends but it does allow investors to delay paying capital gains taxes, thus increasing the ending portfolio value. This insight about the relationship between taxes and trading frequency is a key one. Since much of the return when investing in stocks comes from price appreciation, the more frequently you trade, the higher your tax bill is likely to be for any given pretax return. In fact, the effect is likely to be exacerbated by the higher tax rates on short-term capital gains (which have been generally similar to ordinary tax rates) than on long-term capital gains.

NUMBER WATCH

Historical stock returns with taxes: See the annual returns with and without taxes for U.S. stocks.

There is one final point to be made about the tax effect. Although the taxes on capital gains can be deferred by not trading on your winners, the taxes on dividends have to be paid each period that you receive dividends. Thus, a strategy of investing in stocks that have higher dividend yields than average will result in more taxes and less flexibility when it comes to tax timing, at least relative to investing in low-dividend-yield stocks for the long term. We illustrate this in Figure 5.7 for an investor by contrasting the performance of a portfolio with a dividend yield half that of the market each year to one with twice the dividend yield, keeping the total returns constant.[26]

---

[26]To provide an example, the average dividend yield across all stocks in 1996 was 3.20 percent and the total return was 23.82 percent. The half dividend yield portfolio was estimated to have a dividend yield of 1.60 percent and a price appreciation of 22.22 percent for a total return of 23.82 percent. The double dividend yield portfolio had a dividend yield of 6.40 percent and a price appreciation of 17.42 percent for a total return of 23.82 percent.

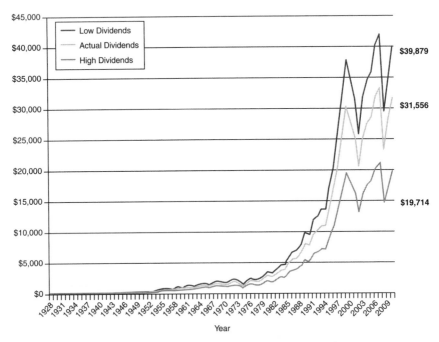

FIGURE 5.7 Dividend Yields and After-Tax Returns: U.S. Stocks
Source: Federal Reserve.

Note that the portfolio of stocks with half the dividend yield of the market has an ending value of just under $40,000 in 2010, whereas one with a dividend yield twice that of the market has an ending value of roughly half that amount.

The Tax Drag on Returns

How well do investors manage their tax liabilities? All too often, investment performance has been measured in terms of pretax returns. The rankings of mutual funds done by services such as Morningstar and *Forbes* have been based on pretax returns. Until recently, the promotional material for most funds presented the pretax returns of these funds contrasted with the S&P 500. This focus on pretax returns may be explained by the fact that different investors have very different tax profiles and it is difficult to find a typical investor, but it has also had the undesirable side effect. Money managers often adopt strategies that expose their investors to substantial tax bills because they feel that they will not be penalized for this tax exposure. Figure 5.8 presents the pretax and after-tax annual returns over the most

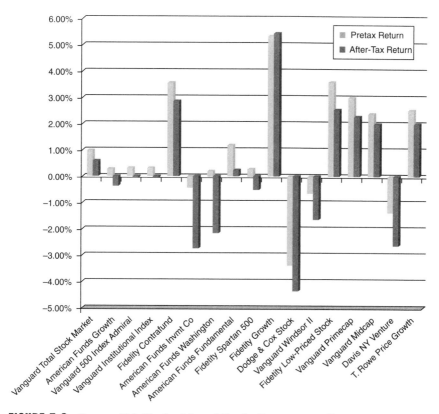

FIGURE 5.8 Largest U.S. Equity Mutual Funds: Pretax versus Posttax Returns—Five-Year Average
Source: Morningstar.

recent five-year period for some of the largest equity mutual funds in the United States in November 2011.

The after-tax returns are significantly lower than the pretax returns for all except one of the funds. Quirks in how and when mutual funds claim capital gains and losses explain the unusual phenomenon of after-tax returns exceeding pre-tax returns for Fidelity Growth.

There are encouraging signs for investors concerned about taxes. The first is that the SEC has started requiring mutual funds to report their after-tax returns in conjunction with pretax returns in their promotional material. The second is that the mutual fund families have begun offering tax-efficient funds, where the objective is to maximize after-tax rather than pretax returns. The third is that the performance evaluators, such as Morningstar, have woken up to the tax costs being imposed on investors by mutual funds.

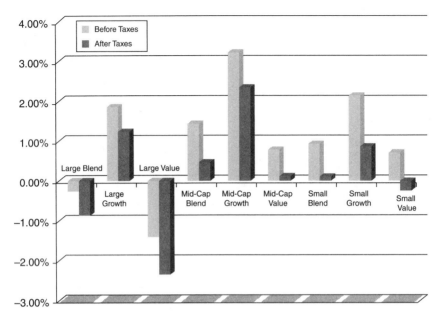

FIGURE 5.9 Mutual Funds' Annual Returns Before and After Taxes, 2006–2010
Source: Morningstar.

In fact, the latest Morningstar reports on mutual funds report not only the after-tax returns over the prior few years on these funds but also a measure of tax efficiency for each fund obtained by dividing the after-tax return by the pretax return. A fund that generates a pretax return on 9 percent and an after-tax return on 6 percent will therefore have a tax efficiency ratio of 67 percent (6 divided by 9). The final noteworthy feature is that not all mutual fund styles are equally affected by taxes. Figure 5.9 reports pretax and after-tax returns in the most recent five-year period for equity mutual funds in the United States in November 2011, categorized by style.

NUMBER WATCH

Mutual fund tax efficiency: See the average pretax and after-tax returns for mutual funds, broken down into categories.

As you can see from the graph, there are significant differences between pretax and after-tax returns at many funds, and the tax drag on returns cuts across all fund styles. While there are some funds that are tax-efficient, there are others where the after-tax return is less than 60 percent of the pretax return. What are the factors that cause the tax effect to be different? It is a function of a number of variables:

- Higher turnover ratios (and more active trading) seem to give rise to higher tax costs for investors. After all, capital gains taxes are assessed only when you sell stocks. In fact, Figure 5.10 categorizes mutual funds (both bond and equity) into six classes based on turnover ratios and reports on the difference between pretax and after-tax returns in each class.

  We measure the tax effect in each category by looking at the ratio of after-tax to pretax returns. Thus, the firms with turnover ratios that exceed 70 percent are the most tax inefficient, since the after-tax returns are only about one-third of the pretax returns. In fact, the pattern is consistent, with the tax effect generally becoming larger as the turnover ratios increase.

- The after-tax return is also affected by money flowing into the fund (inflows) and out of the fund (redemptions). Why might that be?

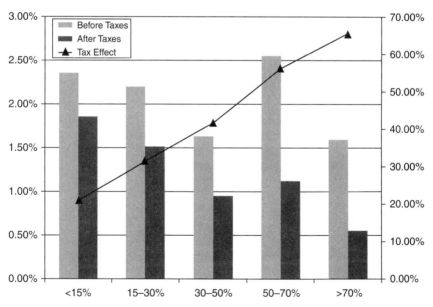

FIGURE 5.10 Turnover Ratios and Tax Effect: Annual Returns on U.S. Mutual Funds over Most Recent Five Years
Source: Morningstar.

Redemptions may require a fund to sell holdings to raise cash and, in the process, convert paper gains into taxable capital gains.

■ The tax cost will also vary depending on whether the mutual fund is actively trying to manage the cost. For instance, a fund that wants to minimize tax costs will sell a few losers when it sells winners and offset the capital losses on the former against the capital gains on the latter.

Tax Management Strategies

Tax considerations alone should not determine any investor's portfolio, but they clearly have to be a factor in how portfolios are put together and the type of investment strategies adopted. In this section, we consider ways in which investors may be able to reduce how much they lose because of taxes.

Minimal Turnover   The simplest and most effective way to reduce your taxes is to trade less often. As noted in the prior sections, portfolio turnover is a key determinant of tax costs. While you may not be able to reduce your turnover ratios to those of an index fund (which often has a turnover ratio of 5 percent or less), you can still try to minimize trading, given any strategy that you adopt. In addition, your choice of strategy should be influenced by the amount of trading that goes with it. Does this mean that you should avoid strategies that require a lot of trading? Not necessarily. If you can earn a high enough return to cover the additional taxes you have to pay, you may still choose to go with a high-trading strategy.

Tax-Based Trading   The other way to minimize taxes is to consider trades specifically for the purpose of reducing your tax bill. There are several forms of tax-based trading.

In its simplest form, you may sell stocks in your portfolio that have gone down just before a tax year ends and use the capital losses from the sale to offset capital gains on other stocks that you may have sold during the year.

If your tax status varies over time, you may choose to claim your capital gains in a year in which your tax rate is low and claim your capital losses in a year in which your tax rate is high.

In its most dangerous form, you may make investments specifically because they offer a chance to reduce your tax bill. Although such tax shelters have long been utilized by investors, you should recognize that the tax authorities usually require these entities to have an economic purpose that goes beyond tax reduction. All too often, investors are beguiled by promised tax savings in tax shelters that are never delivered.

In theory, while tax-based trading offers promise, investors have to keep it in perspective. In particular, trading purely for the purpose of reducing your tax bills strikes us as more likely to reduce than increase returns. However, augmenting a sensible trading strategy with tax considerations makes sense. Thus, if you were planning to prune and rebalance your portfolio, you should probably do it before the end of the tax year and consider the effect of these trades on your tax bill. If you are trying to decide between selling two stocks in your portfolio, the fact that one of them could reduce taxes paid by $100,000 should tip the balance.

Tax Arbitrage

The fact that all investors do not face the same tax rates and that each investor may, in fact, be taxed differently on different parts of the portfolio does raise an interesting implication. If your tax rate as an investor is much lower than the tax rates of other investors in the market, you may be able to exploit the difference to earn excess returns. To see why, consider the following scenario. Assume that you are tax exempt and that every other investor in the market faces a 40 percent tax rate on both dividends and capital gains. Let us also assume that these other investors price stocks to earn an after-tax return of 9 percent. On a pretax basis, stocks will have to earn 15 percent. As a tax-exempt investor, you will get to earn the 15 percent pretax return as well, but your after-tax returns will also be 15 percent.

Is tax arbitrage feasible if you are the only taxable investor in a tax-exempt universe? You will either have to settle for a lower after-tax return than other investors in the market or not buy stocks at all. In reality, there are both tax-exempt and taxable investors in every market, and tax rates vary widely across taxable investors. The market prices of assets will reflect the relative magnitudes of each group, and there will always be groups of assets that yield more favorable returns for each group. Thus, tax-exempt investors may find their best bargains in stocks that generate the greatest tax liabilities for other investors—high-dividend-paying stocks, for instance. High-tax-rate investors migrate toward stocks where they are penalized the least by their tax status—non-dividend-paying, high-growth stocks would be an example.

CONCLUSION

Trading costs are an integral part of any investment portfolio and can make the difference between a portfolio that beats the market and one that does not. The overall evidence suggests that trading costs impose a significant drag on portfolio returns, and may explain why active money managers underperform the market. The reason trading costs are large is that they include not just brokerage costs, but also the costs associated with the bid-ask spread, the price impact created by trading, and the cost of waiting. The reason they are difficult to control is that actions taken to reduce one component of the trading cost tend to increase the other components.

Trading costs do not impose a uniform burden on all investment strategies. They punish short-term, information-based strategies far more than they do long-term, value-based strategies; they affect strategies that focus on less liquid assets far more than they do strategies that are built around liquid assets. No matter what the strategy, though, it is the portfolio manager's job to manage trading costs, given the constraints of the strategy, and earn an excess return that covers these costs.

Taxes can also have significant implications for investment strategy. Since you get to keep only after-tax profits, the tax costs generated by different investment strategies has to be an important factor in which strategy you choose. With any given investment strategy, you can try to reduce your tax bill by trading less often, tax-based trading, or the use of tax shelters.

EXERCISES

Pick a company that you are familiar with, in terms of its business and history. Try the following:

1. Evaluate *how much trading* there was in your stock in the most recent periods by looking at:
   a. Trading volume (in shares and value) in the most recent period.
   b. Changes in trading volume over prior periods.
   c. Turnover ratios (trading volume/number of shares outstanding).
      Compare to the average turnover ratios for other companies in the sector.
2. Evaluate the *magnitude of trading costs* on your stock by:
   a. Finding the bid and ask prices currently for the stock and the resulting spread.
   b. Estimating the spread as a percentage of the current stock price.
   c. Keeping track of changes in that spread, especially during periods of market stress.
3. Break down the returns you would have made on the stock in recent years into dividends and price appreciation. Estimate *how much you would have paid in taxes* on the stock each period if you had held it in your portfolio.

Lessons for Investors

- The brokerage costs, which are often the most explicit costs of trading, represent only a small portion of the total trading cost. There are at least three other costs associated with trading: the bid-ask spread that you bear at the time of trading, the price impact that you have as a result of trading, and the cost of waiting to trade.
- While large investors may have an advantage over small investors when it comes to brokerage costs and even the bid-ask spread—they often enjoy a narrower spread—they face much larger price impact and waiting costs than small investors do.
- The drag imposed by trading costs on returns will depend on what type of stocks you invest in (it will be higher for smaller, less liquid stocks) and how much you trade (higher turnover will create higher trading costs).
- As an investor, you get to spend after-tax income, not pretax income. The portion of your returns that will be devoured by taxes will depend, like trading costs, on what you hold (dividend-paying stocks will create larger tax bills) and how much you trade (more trading will generate more taxes).

CHAPTER 6

Too Good to Be True? Testing Investment Strategies

As investors, we are constantly bombarded with sales pitches from experts claiming to have found the secret formula or the magic model that guarantees investment success. Buy stocks using this strategy, they say, and you will get a portfolio that has low risk and high returns. While you do not want to rule out the possibility that such strategies exist, it pays to be skeptical. In this chapter, we look at how to test investment strategies. In the process, we will also examine what we mean when we say that markets are efficient and cannot be beaten or that markets are inefficient and can be beaten.

Market efficiency is a concept that is controversial and attracts strong views, pro and con, partly because of differences about what it really means, and partly because it is a core belief that in large part determines how an investor approaches investing. We provide a simple definition of market efficiency and consider the implications of an efficient market for investors.

WHY DOES MARKET EFFICIENCY MATTER?

The question of whether markets are efficient, and if not, where the inefficiencies lie, is central to choosing your investment philosophy. If markets are, in fact, efficient, the market price provides the best estimate of value, and the process of valuation becomes one of justifying the market price. As an investor, you would not then try to pick undervalued or overvalued stocks or try to time the market. Instead, you would diversify across a broad band of stocks and not trade often.

If markets are not efficient, the market price may in fact be wrong, and which investment philosophy you pick will depend on why you believe markets make mistakes and how they correct them. Those investors who can find these misvalued stocks and time the market correction, then, will then be able to make higher returns than other investors, thus accomplishing the very difficult task of beating the market. But what if markets are really efficient and you mistakenly pick stocks, thinking they are inefficient? You will bear both the cost of the resources you spend (in terms of time and money) in picking stocks and the additional taxes and transaction costs of this strategy. Consequently, you will end up with a far lower return than that earned by your neighbor who invested her wealth in an index fund.

Examining where and when there are market inefficiencies can also help us in the far more prosaic task of picking investment strategies. A value investor, for example, may have to decide between low price-to-book value (PBV) ratio stocks and low price-earnings (P/E) ratio companies. The evidence may yield a clue as to which strategy is more effective in highlighting undervalued stocks, In addition, market inefficiencies can provide the basis for screening the universe of stocks to come up with a subsample that is more likely to have undervalued stocks. Given the number of stocks that you get to pick from, this not only saves time for you as an investor but increases the odds significantly of finding undervalued and overvalued stocks. For instance, studies suggest that stocks that are neglected by institutional investors are more likely to be undervalued and earn excess returns. A strategy that screens firms for low institutional investment (as a percentage of the outstanding stock) may yield a subsample of neglected firms, which can then be analyzed to arrive at a portfolio of undermisvalued firms. If the research is correct, the odds of finding undervalued firms should increase in this subsample.

EFFICIENT MARKETS: DEFINITION AND IMPLICATIONS

Market efficiency means different things to different people. To those who are true believers in efficient markets, it is an article of faith that defines how they look at or explain market phenomena. To critics, it indicates an academic notion of infallible and supremely rational investors who always know what the true value of an asset is. In this section, we first define an efficient market and then follow up with a discussion of implications for investment strategies.

What Is an Efficient Market?

In its most general sense, an efficient market is one where the market price is an unbiased estimate of the true value of the investment. Implicit in this derivation are several key concepts:

- Contrary to popular view, market efficiency does not require that the market price be equal to true value at every point in time. All it requires is that errors in the market price be unbiased—that is, that prices can be greater than or less than true value for individual stocks, as long as these deviations are random.[1]
- The fact that the deviations from true value are random implies, in a rough sense, that there is an equal chance that any given stock is undervalued or overvalued at any point in time, and that the deviation is uncorrelated with any observable variable. For instance, in an efficient market, stocks with lower price-earnings (P/E) ratios should be no more or no less likely to be undervalued than stocks with high P/E ratios.
- If the deviations of market price from true value are random, it follows that no group of investors should be able to consistently find undervalued or overvalued stocks using any investment strategy.

Market Efficiency, Investors, and Information

Definitions of market efficiency have to be specific not only about the market that is being considered but also about the investor group that is covered. It is extremely unlikely that all markets are efficient to all investors at all times, but it is entirely possible that a particular market (for instance, the New York Stock Exchange) is efficient with respect to the average investor. It is also possible that some markets are efficient while others are not, that a market is efficient with respect to some investors and not to others and in some time periods more than others. This is a direct consequence of differential tax rates and transaction costs, which confer advantages on some investors relative to others.

Definitions of market efficiency are also linked with assumptions about what information is available to investors and reflected in the price. For instance, a strict definition of market efficiency that assumes that all information, public as well as private, is reflected in market prices would imply

---

[1]Randomness implies that there is an equal chance that stocks are under- or overvalued at any point in time.

that even investors with precise inside information will be unable to beat the market. One of the earliest classifications of levels of market efficiency was provided by Eugene Fama, who argued that markets could be efficient at three levels, based on what information was reflected in prices.[2] Under weak form efficiency, the current price reflects the information contained in all past prices, suggesting that charts and technical analyses that use past prices alone would not be useful in finding undervalued stocks. Under semistrong form efficiency, the current price reflects the information contained not only in past prices but in all public information (including financial statements and news reports), and no approach predicated on using and massaging this information would be useful in finding undervalued stocks. Under strong form efficiency, the current price reflects all information, public as well as private, and no investors will be able to consistently find undervalued stocks.

Implications of Market Efficiency   An immediate and direct implication of an efficient market is that no group of investors should be able to consistently beat the market using a common investment strategy. An efficient market would also carry negative implications for many investment strategies.

- In an efficient market, equity research and valuation would be a costly task that would provide no benefits. The odds of finding an undervalued stock would always be 50–50, reflecting the randomness of pricing errors. At best, the benefits from information collection and equity research would cover the costs of doing the research.
- In an efficient market, a strategy of randomly diversifying across stocks or indexing to the market, carrying little or no information cost and minimal execution costs, would be superior to any other strategy that created larger information and execution costs. There would be no value added by portfolio managers and investment strategists.
- In an efficient market, a strategy of minimizing trading (i.e., creating a portfolio and not trading unless cash is needed) would be superior to a strategy requiring frequent trading.

It is therefore no wonder that the concept of market efficiency evokes such strong reactions on the part of portfolio managers and analysts, who view it, quite rightly, as a challenge to their very existence.

---

[2]E. F. Fama, "Efficient Capital Markets: A Review of Theory and Empirical Work," *Journal of Finance* 25 (1970): 383–417.

It is also important that there be clarity about what market efficiency does not imply. An efficient market does not imply that:

- Stock prices cannot deviate from true value; in fact, there can be large deviations from true value. The only requirement is that the deviations be random. This also implies that large market corrections (a price jump or drop is consistent with market efficiency.
- No investor will beat the market in any time period. To the contrary, approximately half of all investors,[3] prior to transaction costs, should beat the market in any period.
- No group of investors will beat the market in the long term. Given the number of investors in financial markets, the laws of probability would suggest that a fairly large number are going to beat the market consistently over long periods, not because of their investment strategies but because they are lucky. It would not, however, be consistent if a disproportionately large number of these investors used the same investment strategy.[4]

In an efficient market, the expected returns from any investment will be consistent with the risk of that investment over the long term, though there may be deviations from these expected returns in the short term.

Necessary Conditions for Market Efficiency   Markets do not become efficient automatically. It is the actions of investors, sensing bargains and putting into effect schemes to beat the market, that make markets efficient. The necessary conditions for a market inefficiency to be eliminated are as follows:

- The market inefficiency should provide the basis for a trading scheme to beat the market and earn excess returns. For this to hold true:
  - The asset or assets that are the source of the inefficiency have to be traded.
  - The transaction costs of executing the scheme have to be smaller than the expected profits from the scheme.

---

[3] Since returns are positively skewed (i.e., large positive returns can be well above 100% but the worst case scenario is that you lose 100%), less than half of all investors will probably beat the market.

[4] One of the enduring pieces of evidence against market efficiency lies in the performance records posted by many of the investors who learned their lessons from Ben Graham in the 1950s. Probability statistics would have to be stretched to explain the consistency and superiority of their records.

- There should be profit-maximizing investors who:
  - Recognize the potential for excess return.
  - Can replicate the beat-the-market scheme that earns the excess return.
  - Have the resources to trade on the asset or assets until the inefficiency disappears.

There is an internal contradiction in claiming that there is no possibility of beating the market in an efficient market and then requiring profit-maximizing investors to constantly seek out ways of beating the market and thus making it efficient. If markets were in fact efficient, investors would stop looking for inefficiencies, which would lead to markets becoming inefficient again. It thus makes sense to think about an efficient market as a self-correcting mechanism, where inefficiencies appear at regular intervals but disappear almost instantaneously as investors find them and trade on them.

Propositions about Market Efficiency   A reading of the conditions under which markets become efficient leads to general propositions about where investors are most likely to find inefficiencies in financial markets.

Proposition 1:   The probability of finding inefficiencies in an asset market decreases as the ease of trading on the asset increases. To the extent that investors have difficulty trading on an asset, either because open markets do not exist or because there are significant barriers to trading, inefficiencies can persist for long periods.

This proposition can be used to shed light on the differences between different asset markets. For instance, it is far easier to trade on stocks than it is on real estate, since stock markets are much more open, trading is in smaller units (reducing the barriers to entry for new traders), and the asset itself does not vary from transaction to transaction (one share of IBM is identical to another share, whereas one piece of real estate can be very different from another piece a stone's throw away). Based on these differences, there should be a greater likelihood of finding inefficiencies (both undervaluation and overvaluation) in the real estate market than in the stock market.

Proposition 2:   The probability of finding mispricing in an asset market increases as the transactions and information cost of exploiting the inefficiency increase. The cost of collecting information and trading varies widely across markets and even across investments in the same market. As these costs increase, it pays less and less to try to exploit these inefficiencies.

Consider, for instance, the perceived wisdom that smaller companies that are not followed by analysts or held by institutions are more likely to be undervalued. This may be true in terms of gross returns, but transaction costs are likely to be much higher for these stocks since:

- They are often unlisted or listed on a dealer market, leading to higher brokerage commissions and expenses.
- Due to their illiquidity and the fact that they are low-priced stocks, the bid-ask spread becomes a much higher fraction of the total price paid.
- Trading is often thin on these stocks, and small trades can cause prices to change, resulting in a higher buy price and a lower sell price.

Once you consider the transaction costs, you may very well find that the excess returns you perceived in these stocks are gone.

Corollary 1: Investors who can establish a cost advantage (either in information collection or in transaction costs) will be more able to exploit small inefficiencies than other investors who do not possess this advantage.

There are a number of studies that look at the effect of block trades on prices and conclude that while they affect prices, investors will not be able to exploit these inefficiencies because of the number of times they will have to trade and their transaction costs. These concerns are unlikely to hold for a specialist on the floor of the exchange, who can trade quickly, often and at no or very low costs. It should be pointed out, however, that if the market for specialists is efficient, the value of a seat on the exchange should reflect the present value of potential benefits from being a specialist.

This corollary also suggests that investors who work at establishing a cost advantage, especially in relation to information, may be able to generate excess returns on the basis of these advantages. Thus, the Templeton funds, which started investing in Japanese and other Asian markets well before other portfolio managers, were able to exploit the informational advantages they had over their peers to make excess returns in Asia in the early stages of the boom.

Proposition 3: The speed with which an inefficiency is resolved will be directly related to how easily the scheme to exploit the inefficiency can be replicated by other investors. The ease with which a scheme can be replicated itself is inversely related to the time, resources, and information needed to execute it.

Since very few investors single-handedly possess the resources to eliminate an inefficiency through trading, it is much more likely that an inefficiency will disappear quickly if the scheme used to exploit the inefficiency is transparent and can be copied by other investors. To illustrate this point, assume that stocks are consistently found to earn excess returns in the month following a stock split. Since firms announce stock splits publicly and any investor can buy stocks right after these splits, it would be surprising if this inefficiency persisted over time. This can be contrasted with the excess returns made by some funds in index arbitrage, where index futures are bought (or sold), and stocks in the index are sold short (or bought). This strategy requires that investors be able to obtain information on index and spot prices instantaneously, have the capacity (in terms of margin requirements and resources) to buy and sell index futures and to sell short on stocks, and to have the resources to take and hold very large positions until the arbitrage unwinds. Consequently, inefficiencies in index futures pricing are likely to persist at least for the most efficient arbitrageurs with the lowest execution costs and the speediest execution times.

INEFFICIENCY OR ANOMALY: A SIMPLE TEST

When you do find an investment strategy that seems to beat the market, it is always an open question as to whether you have found a market mistake that can be exploited for excess returns or just a phenomenon that occurs in financial markets that you are unable to explain because the models you use are incorrect or the data you use are incomplete or erroneous. You would categorize the first as an inefficiency and the second as an anomaly. The pragmatic difference is that you should try to make money off the first but not off the second.

One way to tell the difference is to observe what happens to the excess returns once a strategy has been uncovered and publicized. If it has uncovered an inefficiency, you should see the excess returns rapidly disappear after the strategy is made public. If it is an anomaly, you will see the excess returns continue unabated even after it is publicized.

BEHAVIORAL FINANCE: THE CHALLENGE TO EFFICIENT MARKETS

Underlying the notion of efficient markets is the belief that investors are for the most part rational and even when not so, that irrationalities cancel out in the aggregate. Starting in the mid-1970s, a challenge was mounted by a subset of economists, with backing from psychologists, that the belief in rational investors was misplaced. They pointed to the patterns that are observable in stock prices (that we will talk about in more depth in the next section), the recurrence of price bubbles in different asset markets, and the reaction to news announcements in markets as backing for their argument. In this section, we begin by considering some of the evidence accumulated by psychologists on human behavior. We will argue that almost all investment philosophies try to exploit one investor irrationality or another and that, ironically, investor failures in applying these philosophies can be traced back to other irrationalities. Put succinctly, you are your biggest enemy when it comes to investment success.

Psychological Studies

At the risk of stating the obvious, investors are human and it is not surprising that financial markets reflect human frailties. In an extraordinary book (at least for an academic economist), Robert Shiller presented some of the evidence accumulated of human behavior by psychologists that may help us understand financial market behavior.[5] He categorizes these findings into several areas, and we consider each one.

The Need for Anchors When confronted with decisions, it is human nature to begin with the familiar and use it to make judgments. Kahneman and Tversky, whose research has helped illuminate much of what is called behavioral finance, ran an experiment where they used a wheel of fortune with numbers from 1 to 100 to illustrate this point.[6] With a group of subjects, they spun the wheel to get a number and then asked the subjects numerical questions about obscure percentages—the percentage of the ancient Egyptians who ate meat, for instance. The subjects would have to guess whether the right answer was higher or lower than the number on the wheel and then provide an estimate of the actual number. They found that the answer given by subjects was consistently influenced by the outcome of the wheel spin. Thus, if the number on the wheel was 10, the answer was more likely to be 15 or 20 percent, whereas if the number on the wheel was 60 percent, it was more likely to be 45 or 50 percent. Shiller argues that market prices provide a similar anchor with publicly traded assets. Thus, an investor asked

---

[5]R. J. Shiller, *Irrational Exuberance* (Princeton, NJ: Princeton University Press, 2005).
[6]A. Tversky and D. Kahneman, "Judgment under Uncertainty: Heuristics and Biases," *Science* 185 (1974): 1124–1131.

to estimate the value of a share is likely to be influenced by the market price, with the estimated value increasing as the market price rises.

The Power of the Story For better or worse, human actions tend to be based not on quantitative factors but on storytelling. People tend to look for simple reasons for their decisions, and will often base their decision on whether these reasons exist. In a study of this phenomenon, Shafir, Simonson, and Tversky gave subjects a choice on which parent they would choose for sole custody of a child.[7] One parent was described as average in every aspect of behavior and standing whereas the other was described more completely with both positive characteristics (very close relationship with child, above-average income) and negative characteristics (health problems, travels a lot). Of the subjects studied, 64 percent picked the second. Another group of subjects was given the same choice but asked which one they would deny custody to. That group also picked the second parent. These results seem inconsistent (the first group chose the second parent as the custodian and the second group rejected the same parent, given the same facts) but suggest that investors are more comfortable with investment decisions that can be justified with a strong story than one without.

Overconfidence and Intuitive Thinking As you have undoubtedly become aware from your interactions with friends, relatives, and even strangers over time, human beings tend to be opinionated about things they are not well informed on and to make decisions based on these opinions. In an illustrative study, Fischhoff, Slovic, and Lichtenstein asked people factual questions, and found that people gave an answer and consistently overestimated the probability that they were right. In fact, they were right only about 80 percent of the time that they thought they were.[8] What are the sources of this overconfidence? One might just be evolutionary. The confidence, often in the face of poor odds, may have been what allowed us to survive and dominate as a species. The other may be more psychological. Human beings seem to have a propensity to hindsight bias; that is, they observe what happens and act as it they knew it was coming all the time. Thus, you have investors who claim to have seen the dot com crash, the housing bubble and the banking

---

[7]E. Shafir, I. Simonson, and A. Tversky, "Money Illusion," *Quarterly Journal of Economics* 112 (1997): 341–374.
[8]B. Fischhoff, P. Slovic, and S. Lichtenstein, "Knowing with Uncertainty: The Appropriateness of Extreme Confidence," *Journal of Experimental Psychology* 3 (1977): 522–564.

crisis coming during earlier years, though nothing in their behavior suggests that they did.

Herd Behavior　The tendency of human beings to be swayed by crowds has been long documented and used by tyrants over time to impose their will on us. In a fascinating experiment, Asch illustrated this by having a subject ask a group of people a question to which the answer was obvious; however, the other people in the group had been induced to provide the wrong answer deliberately.[9] Asch noted that the subject changed his own answer one-third of the time to reflect the incorrect answer given in the group. Whereas Asch attributed this to peer pressure, subsequent studies found the same phenomenon even when the subject could not see or interact with others in the group. This would suggest that the desire to be part of the crowd or share their beliefs is due to more than peer pressure.

While there is a tendency to describe herd behavior as irrational, it is worth noting that you can have the same phenomenon occur in perfectly rational markets through a process called information cascade. Shiller provides an example of two restaurants. Assume that one person picks the first restaurant at random. The second person observes the first person eating in that restaurant and is more likely to pick the same restaurant. As the number of subjects entering the market increases, you are likely to see the crowd at the first restaurant pick up, while business at the second restaurant will be minimal. Thus, a random choice by the first customer in the market creates enough momentum to make it the dominant restaurant. In investing, all too often investors at early stages in the process (initial public offering) pile into specific initial public offerings and push their prices up. Other initial public offerings are ignored and languish at low prices. It is entirely possible that the first group of stocks will be overvalued whereas the latter are undervalued. Since herd behavior is made worse by the spreading of rumors, you could argue that the coming together of the available data and media sites such as CNBC and Bloomberg has increased herd behavior.

Unwillingness to Admit Mistakes　It may be human to err, but it is also human to claim not to err. In other words, we are much more willing to claim our successes than we are willing to face up to our failures. Kahneman and Tversky, in their experiments on human behavior, noticed that subjects when presented with choices relative to the status quo often made choices

---

[9]S. E. Asch, "Effects of Group Pressure upon the Modification and Distortion of Judgment," in H. Guertzkow, ed., *Groups, Leadership, and Men* (Pittsburgh, PA: Carnegie Press, 1951).

based on unrealistic expectations. They noted that a person who has not made peace with his losses is likely to accept gambles that would otherwise be unacceptable to him. Anyone who has visited a casino will attest to this finding.

In investing, Shefrin and Statman call this the disposition effect, i.e., the tendency to hold on to losers too long and to sell winners too soon.[10] They argue that it is widespread and can cause systematic mispricing of some stocks. Terrance Odean used the trading records of over 10,000 customers at a discount brokerage house to examine whether there is evidence of this behavior among investors.[11] He noted that investors realized only 9.8 percent of their losses each year, whereas they realized 14.8 percent of their gains.[12] He also finds that investors seem to hold on to losers too long and to sell winners too soon. Overall, he argues that there is evidence of the disposition effect among investors.

The Evidence

While it is evident that human beings do not always behave rationally, it does not necessarily follow that markets will also be irrational. In fact, you could argue (as some believers in market efficiency do) that markets can be efficient even with irrational investors for several reasons. First, it is possible that there is a selection process that occurs in markets where irrational investors lose consistently to rational investors and eventually get pushed out of the market. Second, it is also possible that irrationalities cut in both directions—some leading investors to buy when they should not and others leading them to sell when they should not; if these actions offset each other, you could still have a market price that is unaffected by irrational investors. The only way to resolve this debate is to look at the evidence on the presence or absence of irrationality in market behavior.

One of the problems that we face when we test for irrationality in financial markets is the number of variables that cannot be controlled for. Investors enter and leave markets, new information arrives constantly, and the macroeconomic environment changes frequently, making it impossible to construct a controlled experiment. A few researchers have attempted to get around this problem by constructing experimental studies, similar

---

[10]H. Shefrin and M. Statman, "The Disposition to Sell Winners Too Early and Ride Losers Too Long: Theory and Evidence," *Journal of Finance* 40 (1985): 777–790.
[11]T. Odean, "Are Investors Reluctant to Realize Their Losses?" *Journal of Finance* 53 (1998): 1775–1798.
[12]The only month in which more losses are realized than gains is December.

to those used by psychologists and sociologists in the previous section, to examine how investors behave in financial markets.

The most interesting evidence from experiments is what we learn about quirks in human behavior, even in the simplest of settings. In fact, Kahneman and Tversky's challenge to conventional economic utility theory was based on their awareness of the experimental research in psychology. In this section, we cover some of the more important of these findings.

- *Framing.* Kahneman and Tversky noted that describing a decision problem differently, even when the underlying choices remain the same, can lead to different decisions and measures of risk aversion. In their classic example, they asked subjects to choose between two responses to a disease threat: the first response, they said, would save 200 people out of a population of 600, but in the second, they noted that "there is a one-third probability that everyone will be saved and a two-thirds probability that no one will be saved." While the net effect of both responses is exactly the same mathematically—400 die and 200 are saved—72 percent of the respondents picked the first option. Kahneman and Tversky termed this phenomenon "framing" and argued that both utility models and experimenters have to deal with the consequences.[13]
- *Loss aversion.* Loss aversion refers to the tendency of individuals to prefer avoiding losses to making gains. In an experiment, Kahneman and Tversky offer an example of loss aversion. The first offered subjects a choice between the following:

  Option A: A guaranteed payout of $250.

  Option B: A 25 percent chance to gain $1,000 and a 75 percent chance of getting nothing.

  Of the respondents, 84 percent chose the sure option A over option B (with the same expected payout but much greater risk), which was not surprising, given risk aversion. They then reframed the question and offered the same subjects the following choices:

  Option C: A sure loss of $750.

  Option D: A 75 percent chance of losing $1,000 and a 25 percent chance to lose nothing.

---

[13] A. Tversky and D. Kahneman, "The Framing of Decisions and the Psychology of Choice," *Science* 211 (1981): 453–458.

Now, 73 percent of respondents preferred the gamble (option D, with an expected loss of $750) over the certain loss (option C). Kahneman and Tversky noted that stating the question in terms of a gain resulted in different choices than framing it in terms of a loss.[14] Loss aversion implies that individuals will prefer an uncertain gamble to a certain loss as long as the gamble has the possibility of no loss, even though the expected value of the uncertain loss may be higher than the certain loss.

Benartzi and Thaler combined loss aversion with the frequency with which individuals checked their accounts (what they called "mental accounting") to create the composite concept of *myopic loss aversion*.[15] Haigh and List provided an experimental test that illustrates the proposition where they ran a sequence of nine lotteries with subjects, but varied how they provided information on the outcomes.[16] To one group, they provided feedback after each round, allowing them to thus react to success or failure on that round. To the other group, they withheld feedback until three rounds were completed and provided feedback on the combined outcome over the three rounds. They found that people were willing to bet far less in the frequent feedback group than in the pooled feedback group, suggesting that loss aversion becomes more acute if individuals have shorter time horizons and assess success or failure at the end of these horizons.

- *House money effect.* Generically, the house money effect refers to the phenomenon that individuals are more willing to take risks (and are thus less risk averse) with found money (obtained easily) than with earned money. Consider the experiment where 10 subjects were each given $30 at the start of the game and offered the choice of either doing nothing or flipping a coin to win or lose $9; seven chose the coin flip. Another set of 10 subjects were offered no initial funds but offered a choice of either taking $30 with certainty or flipping a coin and winning $39 if it came up heads or $21 if it came up tails. Only 43 percent chose the coin flip, even though the final consequences (ending up with $21 or $39) are the same in both experiments. Thaler and Johnson illustrate the house money effect with an experiment in which subjects were offered a

---

[14] A. Tversky and D. Kahneman, "Loss Aversion in Riskless Choice: A Reference-Dependent Model," *Quarterly Journal of Economics* 106 (1991): 1038–1061.

[15] Shlomo Benartzi and Richard Thaler, "Myopic Loss Aversion and the Equity Premium Puzzle," *Quarterly Journal of Economics* 110 (1995): 73–92.

[16] M. S. Haigh and J. A. List, "Do Professional Traders Exhibit Myopic Loss Aversion? An Experimental Analysis," *Journal of Finance* 45 (2005): 523–534.

sequence of lotteries. In the first lottery, subjects were given a chance to win $15 and were offered a subsequent lottery where they had a 50–50 chance of winning or losing $4.50. While many of these same subjects would have rejected the second lottery if it had been offered as an initial choice, 77 percent of those who won the first lottery (and made $15) took the second lottery.[17]

- *Break-even effect.* The break-even effect is the flip side of the house money effect and refers to the attempts of those who have lost money to make it back. In particular, subjects in experiments who have lost money seem willing to gamble on lotteries (that standing alone would be viewed as unattractive) that offer them a chance to break even. The study by Thaler and Johnson that uncovered the house money effect also found the break-even effect. In a study of sequenced lotteries, researchers found that subjects who lost money on the first lottery generally became more risk averse in the second lottery except when the second lottery offered them a chance to make up their first-round losses and break even.[18]

In summary, the findings from experimental studies offer grist for the behavioral finance mill. Whether or not we buy into all of the implications, it is clear that there are systematic quirks in human behavior that cannot be easily dismissed as irrational or aberrant since they are so widespread and long-standing.

As a side note, many of these experimental studies have been run using inexperienced subjects (usually undergraduate students) and professionals (traders in financial markets, experienced businesspeople) to see if age and experience play a role in making people more rational. The findings are not promising for the rational human school, since the consensus view across these studies is that experience and age do not seem to confer rationality in subjects and that some of the anomalies noted in this section are attenuated with experience. Professional traders exhibit more myopic loss aversion than undergraduate students do, for instance. The behavioral patterns indicated

---

[17]R. H. Thaler and E. J. Johnson, "Gambling with the House Money and Trying to Break Even: The Effects of Prior Outcomes on Risky Choice," *Management Science* 36 (1990): 643–660. They also document a house-loss effect, where those who lose in the initial lottery become more risk averse at the second stage, but the evidence from other experimental studies on this count is mixed.

[18]R. C. Battalio, J. H. Kagel, and K. Jiranyakul, "Testing between Alternative Models of Choice under Uncertainty: Some Initial Results," *Journal of Risk and Uncertainty* 3 (1990): 25–50.

in this section are also replicated in experiments using business settings (projects with revenues, profits, and losses) and experienced managers.[19] Finally, we should resist the temptation to label these behaviors as irrational. Much of what we observe in human behavior seems to be hardwired into our systems and cannot be easily eliminated (if at all). In fact, a study in the journal *Psychological Science* examined the decisions made by 15 people with normal IQs and reasoning skills but with damage to the portions of the brain that control emotions.[20] They confronted this group and a control group of normal individuals with 20 rounds of a lottery in which they could win $2.50 or lose a dollar, and found that the inability to feel emotions such as fear and anxiety made the brain-damaged individuals more willing to take risks with high payoffs and less likely to react emotionally to previous wins and losses. Overall, the brain-impaired participants finished with about 13 percent higher winnings than normal people who were offered the same gambles.

Testing Market Efficiency

Tests of market efficiency look at whether specific investment strategies or portfolio managers beat the market. But what does beating the market involve? Does it just imply that someone earns a return greater than what the market (say, the S&P 500) earns in a specific year? We begin by looking at what beating the market requires and define what we mean be excess returns. We will then follow up by looking at three standard ways of testing market efficiency and when and why we may choose one over the other.

Beating the Market   The fundamental question that we often attempt to answer when we test an investment strategy is whether the return we earn from the strategy is above or below a benchmark return on an alternative strategy of equivalent risk. But what should that benchmark return be? As we will see, it is almost impossible to measure the success or failure of an investment strategy without taking a point of view on how risk should be measured.

---

[19]K. Sullivan, "Corporate Managers' Risky Behavior: Risk Taking or Avoiding," *Journal of Financial and Strategic Decisions* 10 (1997): 63–74.
[20]S. Baba, G. Lowenstein, A. Bechara, H. Damasio, and A. Damasio, "Investment Behavior and the Negative Side of Emotion," *Psychological Science* 16 (2005): 435–439. The damage to the individuals was created by strokes or disease and prevented them from feeling emotions.

Performance Benchmarks   If you can estimate the returns that you could have made by adopting an investment strategy in the past or observed the returns made by a portfolio manager or investor over a period, you can evaluate those returns. To make the evaluation, you have to choose an appropriate benchmark. In this section, we consider two alternatives that are available to us in making this choice.

1. *Comparison to indexes.* When you have estimated the returns on a strategy, the simplest comparison you can make is to the returns you would have made by investing in an index. Many portfolio managers and investors still compare the returns they make on their portfolios to the returns on the S&P 500 index. While this comparison may be simple, it can also be dangerous when you have a strategy that does not have the same risk as investing in the index, and the bias can cut both ways. If you have a strategy that is riskier than investing in the index—investing in small, high-growth stocks, say—you are biasing yourself toward concluding that the strategy works (i.e., it beats the market). If you have a strategy that is much safer than investing in the index, such as buying shares of high-dividend-paying, mature companies, you are biasing yourself toward concluding that the strategy does not work.

    There are slightly more sophisticated versions of this approach that are less susceptible to this problem. For instance, some services that judge mutual funds do so by comparing them to an index of funds that have the same style as the fund being judged. Thus, a fund that invests in large market capitalization companies with low price-to-book ratios will be compared to other large-cap value funds. The peril remains, though, since categorizing investors into neat boxes is easier said than done. A fund manager may begin the year calling herself a large-cap value investor and during the course of the year shift to being an investor in high-growth, risky companies.

2. *Risk and return models.* In Chapter 2, we considered the basics of risk and put forth several risk and return models. All of these models tried to measure the risk in an investment, though they differed on how best to measure it, and related the expected return on the investment to the risk measure. You could use these models to measure the risk in an investment strategy, and then examine the returns relative to this risk measure. We will consider some of these risk-adjusted measures of performance in this section.

Mean-Variance Measures   The simplest measures of risk-adjusted performance have their roots in the mean-variance framework developed by Harry

Markowitz in the early 1950s. In the mean-variance world, the standard deviation of an investment measures its risk, and the return earned is the reward. If you compare two investments with the same standard deviation in returns, the investment with the higher average return would be considered the better one.

Sharpe Ratio Extending this concept to investment strategies, you could look at the payoff to each unit of risk taken by dividing the return earned using the strategy by the standard deviation of return, in a measure called the *Sharpe ratio*.[21]

$$\text{Sharpe ratio} = \text{Average return on strategy}/$$
$$\text{Standard deviation of returns from strategy}$$

To compute the standard deviation, you would need to track the returns on the strategy each period for several periods. For instance, the average monthly returns for a mutual fund over the past five years can be divided by the standard deviation in those monthly returns at to come up with a Sharpe ratio for that mutual fund. Once you have the Sharpe ratios for individual funds, you can compare them across funds to find the funds that earn the highest reward per unit of risk (standard deviation), or you can compare the fund's ratios to the Sharpe ratio for the entire market to make a judgment on whether active investing pays.

NUMBER WATCH

Mutual fund Sharpe ratios: See the average Sharpe ratios for mutual funds in the United States, broken down by category.

The Sharpe ratio is a versatile measure that has endured the test of time. Its focus on the standard deviation as the measure of risk does bias it against portfolios that are not diversified widely across the market. A sector-specific mutual fund (such as a biotechnology or health care fund) will tend to do

---

[21]W. F. Sharpe, "Mutual Fund Performance," *Journal of Finance* 39 (1965): 119–138.

TABLE 6.1   Sharpe Ratios for Large U.S. Mutual Funds, 2006 to 2011

Fund	Standard Deviation	Sharpe Ratio
American Funds Fundamental	19.58%	0.67
American Funds Growth	18.81%	0.63
American Funds Washington	17.76%	0.63
Davis NY	21.56%	0.49
Fidelity Contrafund	16.81%	0.82
Fidelity Growth	20.51%	0.91
Fidelity Low Priced Stocks	20.94%	0.94
Fidelity Spartan	19.57%	0.64
T. Rowe Price Growth	19.81%	0.88
Vanguard 500 Index	19.58%	0.65
Vanguard Institutional Index	19.57%	0.65
Vanguard Midcap Index	22.60%	0.86

poorly on a Sharpe ratio basis because its standard deviation will be higher due to the presence of sector-specific risk. Since investors in these funds can diversify away that risk by holding multiple funds, it does seem unfair to penalize these funds for their low Sharpe ratios.

In Table 6.1, we compute the Sharpe ratios for 12 large mutual funds in the United States in November 2011, using data from 2006 to 2011.

Using the Sharpe ratio of 0.65 for the Vanguard 500 index fund as the comparison, the Davis fund underperformed, delivering a Sharpe ratio of only 0.49. Of the Fidelity funds, the Spartan fund posted numbers very similar to the Vanguard 500 Index fund, but the three other Fidelity funds all delivered higher Sharpe ratios.

Information Ratio   A close relative of the Sharpe ratio is the *information ratio*. It is the ratio of the excess return earned by a fund over an index to the excess volatility of this fund to the volatility of the index. To measure the latter, we estimate what is commonly called *tracking error*, which measures the deviations of the fund returns from the index returns each period over several periods. In its most common form, the excess return over the S&P 500 for a fund is divided by the tracking error of the fund relative to the S&P 500.

$$\text{Information ratio} = (\text{Return on strategy} - \text{Return on index})/$$
$$\text{Tracking error versus the index}$$

Information ratios differ from Sharpe ratios because of their fidelity to an index. In other words, you can have a portfolio with low standard deviation but it can have high tracking error if it contains stocks that are not in the index. For instance, a portfolio of low-risk stocks with low market capitalization may have low standard error, but it will still have a high tracking error versus the S&P 500.

M-Squared In the 1990s, these measures were refined slightly to come up with a measure called M-squared.[22] Instead of dividing the total return of a strategy or fund by its standard deviation, you compute the expected return you would have had on the fund if you had to adjust its standard deviation down to that of the index, and compare this expected return to the return on the index. For instance, assume that you have a fund with a return of 30 percent and a standard deviation of 50 percent and that the return on the S&P 500 is 15 percent and the standard deviation of the S&P 500 is 20 percent. To make the fund's standard deviation comparable to that of the S&P 500, you would have had to invest 60 percent of your money in Treasury bills (earning 3 percent) and 40 percent in the fund:

$$\text{Adjusted standard deviation of portfolio} = 0.4(\text{Standard deviation of fund}) + 0.6(0)$$
$$= 0.4(50\%) = 20\%$$

The return on this portfolio can then be calculated:

$$\text{Expected return on portfolio} = 0.4(30\%) + 0.6(3\%) = 13.8\%$$

Since this return is lower than the S&P's return of 15 percent, you would categorize this fund as an underperformer.

This measure of performance is closely related to the Sharpe ratio and is susceptible to the same biases. Since the expected return is adjusted to make the risk of the mutual fund similar to that of the index, funds that are not diversified widely across the market will score poorly.

Capital Asset Pricing Model The capital asset pricing model (CAPM) emerged from the mean-variance framework to become the first model

---

[22]The developer of this measure was Leah Modigliani, a strategist at Morgan Stanley. Without taking anything away from her own accomplishments, it is worth noting that she is the granddaughter of Franco Modigliani, Nobel Prize winner in economics.

for risk and return in finance. In the CAPM, as described in Chapter 2, the expected return on an investment can be written as function of its beta:

Expected return = Risk-free rate

+ Beta (Expected return on market − Risk-free rate)

In Chapter 2, we used the model to estimate the expected returns for the next period, using the current risk-free rate, the beta, and the average premium earned by stocks over the risk-free rate as inputs. In this section, we consider how the capital asset pricing model can be adapted to judge past performance.

Excess Return (Alpha or Jensen's Alpha) The simplest way to use to the capital asset pricing model to evaluate performance is to compare the actual return to the return your investment or strategy should have made over the evaluation period, given its beta and given what the market did over the period. As an example, assume that you are analyzing a strategy that generated 12 percent in returns over the prior year. Assume that your calculations indicate that the strategy has a beta of 1.2, that the risk-free rate at the beginning of the past year was 4 percent, and that the return on the market over the past year was 11 percent. You can compute the excess return as follows:

Expected return over past year = 4% + 1.2(11% − 4%) = 12.4%

Excess return = Actual return − Expected return = 12% − 12.4% = −0.4%

This strategy underperformed the market, after adjusting for risk, by 0.4 percent. This excess return is also called an abnormal return.[23]

What are the differences between what we are doing here and what we did in Chapter 2 to forecast expected returns in the future? The first is that we use the risk-free rate at the beginning of the evaluation period when we do evaluation, whereas we use the current risk-free rate when making forecasts. The second is that we use the actual return on the market over the

---

[23]M. Jensen, "The Performance of Mutual Funds in the Period 1945–1964," *Journal of Finance* 23 (1967): 389–416.

period, even if it is negative, when we do evaluation rather than the expected equity premium that we use when computing forecasted returns. Finally, the beta we use in evaluation should measure the risk you were exposed to during your evaluation period, while a forward-looking beta should be used for forecasts.

The excess returns on a strategy can be computed for any return period you want—daily, weekly, monthly, or annual. You would need to adjust your risk-free rate and market return appropriately, using, for instance, the weekly risk-free rate and a weekly market return if you want to compute weekly excess returns from a strategy. An alternative approach to estimating the excess return, which should yield the same results, is to run a regression of the returns on your strategy in excess of the risk-free rate against the returns on a market index in excess of the risk-free rate.

$$\text{(Return on strategy} - \text{Risk-free rate)} = a + b \text{ (Returns on market index}$$
$$- \text{Risk-free rate)}$$

The slope of this regression gives you the historical beta, but the intercept of this regression yields the excess return by period for your strategy.[24] Using the statistical term for the intercept, the excess return is often called an *alpha*. In some quarters, it is called *Jensen's alpha*, reflecting the fact that it was first used in a study of mutual funds in the 1960s by Michael Jensen, one of the pioneers in empirical finance.

There is one final point that should be made about excess returns. When you compute excess returns by day or week over a longer period (say six months or a year), you may also want to compute how the strategy performed over the entire period. To do this, you usually look at the compounded return over the period. This compounded return is called a cumulative excess return or a cumulative abnormal return (CAR). Defining

---

[24]To see why, let's work through the algebra. The expected return in the CAPM can be written as:

$$\text{Expected return on strategy} = \text{Risk-free rate}$$
$$+ \text{Beta(Return on market} - \text{Risk-free rate)}$$

$$\text{Expected return on strategy} - \text{Risk-free rate}$$
$$= \text{Beta(Return on market} - \text{Risk-free rate)}$$

In other words, if your stock did exactly as predicted by the CAPM, the intercept should be zero. If the intercept is different from zero, that must indicate underperformance (if it is negative) or outperformance (if it is positive).

the excess return in each interval as ER_t, you can write the excess return over a period as follows:

Cumulative abnormal return over n intervals $= (1 + ER_1)(1 + ER_2)$
$(1 + ER_3) \ldots (1 + ER_n)$

A cumulative abnormal return that is greater than zero indicates that the strategy beat the market, at least over the period of your test.

Unlike the variance-based measures in the preceding section, Jensen's alpha does not penalize sector-specific funds that are not diversified, because it looks at the beta of a portfolio and not its standard deviation. The measure's fidelity to the capital asset pricing model, however, exposes it to all of the model's limitations. Since the model has historically underestimated the expected returns of small-cap stocks with low P/E ratios and low price-to-book ratios, you will tend to find that strategies that focus on stocks with these characteristics earn positive excess returns.

There are variations on Jensen's alpha that have appeared. An early variation replaced the capital asset pricing model with what is commonly called the market model, where the expected return on an investment is based on a past regression alpha.[25] In the past decade, for instance, researchers have developed a version of the measure that allows the beta to change from period to period for a strategy; these are called time-varying betas. This is clearly more realistic than assuming one beta for the entire testing period.

Treynor Index The excess return is a percentage measure. But is earning a 1 percent excess return over an expected return of 15 percent equivalent to earning a 1 percent excess return over an expected return of 7 percent? There are many who would argue that the latter strategy is a more impressive one. The *Treynor index* attempts to correct for this by converting the excess return into a ratio relative to the beta.[26] It is computed by dividing the difference between the returns on a strategy and the risk-free rate by the beta

---

[25] In the market model, the excess return is written as:

Excess return $=$ Actual return $- (a + b$ Return on Market$)$

where a is the intercept and b is the slope of a regression of returns on the stock against returns on the market index.

[26] J. L. Treynor, "How to Rate Management of Mutual Funds," *Harvard Business Review* 43 (1965): 63–70.

of the investment. This value is then compared to the difference between the returns on the market and the risk-free rate.

$$\text{Treynor index} = (\text{Return on strategy} - \text{Risk-free rate})/\text{Beta}$$

To illustrate, assume that you are considering the strategy that we described in the preceding section with a beta of 1.2 that earned a return of 12 percent in the most recent year. In that example, the return on the market over the same year was 11 percent and the risk-free rate was 4 percent. The Treynor index for this strategy would be:

$$\text{Treynor index for strategy} = (12\% - 4\%)/1.2 = 6.67\%$$

$$\text{Treynor index for market} = (11\% - 4\%)/1 = 7.00\%$$

This strategy underperformed the market.

The Treynor index is closely related to the alpha measure described in the preceding section. The measures will always agree on whether a strategy underperforms or outperforms the market, but will disagree on rankings. The Treynor index will rank lower-beta strategies higher than the alpha measure will, because it looks at excess returns earned per unit beta.

In Table 6.2, we estimate Jensen's alpha and the Treynor index for 12 large mutual funds in the United States for the five-year period ending in

TABLE 6.2 Jensen's Alpha and Treynor Index: Large Mutual Funds, 2006 to 2011

Fund	Annual Return	Beta	Jensen's Alpha	Treynor Index
American Funds Fundamental Inv	1.18%	0.99	0.86%	0.69%
American Funds Growth	0.29%	0.94	−0.04%	−0.22%
American Funds Washington	0.19%	0.90	−0.15%	−0.34%
Davis NY	−1.37%	1.08	−1.68%	−1.73%
Fidelity Contrafund	3.55%	0.83	3.20%	3.67%
Fidelity Growth	5.33%	1.00	5.01%	4.83%
Fidelity Low Priced Stocks	3.57%	1.03	3.26%	2.98%
Fidelity Spartan	0.28%	1.00	−0.04%	−0.22%
T. Rowe Price Growth	2.51%	0.96	2.18%	2.09%
Vanguard 500 Index	0.32%	1.00	0.00%	−0.18%
Vanguard Institutional Index	0.33%	1.00	0.01%	−0.17%
Vanguard Midcap Index	2.43%	1.12	2.13%	1.72%

November 2011. For simplicity, we assumed that the average annual risk-free rate during the period was 0.5 percent.

Note that this five-year period was characterized by low returns on the entire market, with the S&P delivering only 0.32 percent on an annualized basis. Since this is lower than the risk-free rate, the Treynor index value for the market is negative (it is the number we report for the Vanguard 500 Index fund). The Fidelity funds, other than the Spartan Fund, delivered positive Jensen's alphas and high Treynor index values (relative to the market number).

Arbitrage Pricing Model and Multifactor Models In Chapter 2, we noted that the assumptions that we need in order to arrive at the single market beta measure of risk in the capital asset pricing model are unrealistic and that the model itself systematically underestimates the expected returns for stocks with certain characteristics—low market capitalization and low P/E. We considered the alternative of the arbitrage pricing model (APM), which allows for multiple market risk factors that are unidentified, or a multifactor model, which relates expected returns to a number of macroeconomic factors such as interest rates, inflation, and economic growth. These models, we argued, allow us more flexibility when it comes to estimating expected returns.

You could use either the arbitrage pricing model or a multifactor model to estimate the return you would have expected to earn over a period on a portfolio and compare this return to the actual return earned. In other words, you could compute an excess return or alpha for a strategy or portfolio using these models instead of the capital asset pricing model.

To the extent that the arbitrage pricing model and multifactor models are less likely to yield biased returns for small-cap and low-P/E stocks, you could argue that the excess returns from these models should give you better measures of performance. The biggest problem that you run into in using these models to evaluate the excess returns earned by a portfolio manager or a strategy is that the portfolios themselves may be constantly shifting. What you measure as an alpha from these models may really reflect your failure to correct for the variation in exposure to different market risk factors over time. Although this is also a problem with the capital asset pricing model, it is far easier to adjust a single beta over time than it is to work with multiple betas.

Proxy and Composite Models The alternative to conventional risk and return models is the use of a proxy model, where the returns on stocks are correlated with observable financial characteristics of the firm. Perhaps the best-known proxy model was the one developed by Fama and French that we presented in Chapter 2.[27] They found that between 1962 and 1989 stocks with lower market capitalizations and price-to-book ratios consistently earned higher returns than larger market capitalization companies with higher price-to-book ratios. In fact, market capitalization and price-to-book ratio differences across firms explained far more of the variation in actual returns than betas did.

Building on this theme, traditional risk and return models may fall short when it comes to estimating expected returns for portfolios that have disproportionately large exposures to small-cap or low price-to-book value stocks. These portfolios will look like they earn excess returns. Using a proxy model in which the returns on the portfolio are conditioned on the market cap of the stocks held in the portfolio and their price-to-book ratios may eliminate this bias:

$$\text{Expected return on portfolio} = a + b\,(\text{Average market capitalization})_{\text{Portfolio}}$$
$$+ c\,(\text{Average price-to-book ratio})_{\text{Portfolio}}$$

This model can even be expanded to include a conventional market beta, yielding what is often called a three-factor model:

$$\text{Expected return on portfolio} = a + b\,(\text{Market beta})$$
$$+ c\,(\text{Average market capitalization})_{\text{Portfolio}}$$
$$+ d\,(\text{Average price-to-book ratio})_{\text{Portfolio}}$$

The peril of incorporating variables such as market capitalization and price-to-book ratios into expected returns is that you run a risk of creating a self-fulfilling prophecy. If markets routinely misprice certain types of companies—small companies, for instance—and we insist on including these variables in the expected return regressions, we will be biased, with a complete-enough model, toward finding that markets are efficient. In fact, in recent years researchers have added a fourth factor, price momentum, to these factor models because of recent findings that companies that have done well in the recent past are likely to continue doing well in the future.

Closing Thoughts   There are two closing points that we emphasize about the use of risk and return models and tests of market efficiency. The first is that a test of market efficiency is a joint test of market efficiency and the efficacy of the model used for expected returns. When there is evidence of

---

[27]E. F. Fama and K. R. French, "The Cross-Section of Expected Returns," *Journal of Finance* 47 (1992): 427–466.

excess returns in a test of market efficiency, this can indicate that markets are inefficient or that the model used to compute expected returns is wrong, or both. Although this may seem to present an insoluble dilemma, if the conclusions of the study are insensitive to different model specifications, it is much more likely that the results are being driven by true market inefficiencies and not just by model misspecifications.

In terms of which approach you should use to come up with expected returns, it is worth noting that each approach has its own built-in biases that you need to be aware of. Table 6.3 summarizes the alternative approaches to evaluating returns and the types of strategies and portfolios that they are likely to be biased toward and against.

TABLE 6.3   Performance Evaluation Measures and Biases

Performance Evaluation Measure	Computation	Biases
Sharpe ratio	Average return on strategy/ Standard deviation of returns from strategy	Against portfolios that are not broadly diversified. Sector-specific funds and strategies will be penalized.
Information ratio	(Return on strategy – Return on index)/Tracking error versus index	Against portfolios that deviate from the index by holding stocks not in the index.
M-squared	Return on strategy (with riskless investment to have same standard deviation as market) – Return on market	Same as Sharpe ratio.
Jensen's alpha	Actual return – [Risk-free rate + Beta * (Return on market – Risk-free rate)]	Toward small-cap, low-P/E, low PBV ratio strategies.
Treynor index	(Return on strategy – Risk-free rate)/Beta	All of the biases of Jensen's alpha but slight tilt toward lower-beta strategies.
Excess return (APM and multifactor)	Actual return – Expected return (from APM or multifactor model)	Mismeasurement of alpha for strategies where portfolio changes substantially over periods.
Proxy models	Actual return – [$a + b$ (Average market capitalization)$_\text{Portfolio}$ + c (Average PVB ratio)$_\text{Portfolio}$]	Against portfolios that try to take advantage of systematic market mispricing of some variables such as market capitalization.

Strategies for Testing Market Efficiency

There are a number of different ways of testing for market efficiency, and the approach used will depend in great part on the investment scheme being tested. A scheme based on trading on information events (stock splits, earnings announcements, or acquisition announcements) is likely to be tested using an *event study* where returns around the event are scrutinized for evidence of excess returns. A scheme based on trading on an observable characteristic of a firm (price-earnings ratios, price-to-book value ratios, or dividend yields) is likely to be tested using a *portfolio study* approach, where portfolios of stocks with these characteristics are created and tracked over time to see if, in fact, they make excess returns. An alternative way of testing to see if there is a relationship between an observable characteristic and returns is to run a regression of the latter on the former. This approach allows for more flexibility if you are testing for interactions among variables. The following pages summarize the key steps involved in each of these approaches, and some potential pitfalls to watch out for when conducting or using these tests.

Event Study An event study is designed to examine market reactions to and excess returns around specific information events. The information events can be marketwide, such as macroeconomic announcements, or firm-specific, such as earnings or dividend announcements. The steps in an event study are:

1. *The event to be studied is clearly identified, and the date on which the event was announced is pinpointed.* The presumption in event studies is that the timing of the event is known with a fair degree of certainty. Since financial markets react to the information about an event rather than the event itself, most event studies are centered around the announcement date for the event.[28]

Announcement Date

2. *Once the event dates are known, returns are collected around these dates for each of the firms in the sample.* In doing so, two decisions have to be made. First, you have to decide whether to collect weekly, daily, or shorter-interval returns around the event. This will, in part, be decided

---

[28]In most financial transactions, the announcement date tends to precede the event date by several days, and sometimes weeks.

by how precisely the event date is known (the more precisely it is known, the more likely it is that shorter return intervals can be used) and by how quickly information is reflected in prices (the faster the adjustment, the shorter the return interval to use). Second, you have to determine how many periods of returns before and after the announcement date will be considered as part of the event window. That decision also will be determined by the precision of the event date, since more imprecise dates will require longer windows.

$$R_{-jn} \dots\dots\dots\dots\dots\dots\dots\dots\dots\dots R_{j0}\dots\dots\dots\dots\dots\dots\dots\dots\dots\dots R_{+jn}$$

Return window: $-n$ to $+n$

where

$Rjt =$ Returns on firm j for period t $(t = -n, \dots, 0, \dots +n)$

3. The returns, by period, around the announcement date are adjusted for market performance and risk to arrive at excess returns for each firm in the sample. You could use any of the risk and return models described in the preceding section to estimate excess returns. For instance, if the capital asset pricing model is used to control for risk:

Excess return on period $t =$ Return on day $t -$ (Risk-free rate

$+$ Beta $*$ Return on market on day t)

$$ER_{-jn} \dots\dots\dots\dots\dots\dots\dots\dots ER_{j0}\dots\dots\dots\dots\dots\dots\dots\dots ER_{+jn}$$

Return window: $-n$ to $+n$

where

$ERjt =$ Excess returns on firm j for period t $(t = -n, \dots, 0, \dots +n)$

You can also look at how a portfolio held over multiple periods would have done by measuring a cumulated abnormal return (CAR) by compounding the excess returns over the periods. Thus, if your excess return on day 1 is $+2$ percent, day 2 is -1 percent, and day 3 is $+1.5$ percent, your cumulative excess return over all three days would be:

Cumulated excess return $= (1 + ER_1)(1 + ER_2)(1 + ER_3) - 1$

$= (1.02)(0.99)(1.015) - 1 = 1.02495$ or 2.495%

4. *Once the excess returns are estimated for each firm in the sample, the average excess returns can be computed across the firms*, and it will

almost never be equal to zero. To test to see whether this number is
significantly different from zero, however, you need a statistical test.
The simplest is to compute a standard deviation in the excess returns
across the sampled firms, and to use this to estimate a t-statistic. Thus,
if you have N firms in your sample and you have computed the excess
returns each day for these firms:

$$\text{Average excess return on day } t = \sum_{J=1}^{J=N} \frac{\text{ER}_{Jt}}{N}$$

$$\text{T-statistic for excess return on day } t = \text{Average excess return} / \text{Standard error}$$

You can then check to see if the t-statistics are statistically significant.
For instance, if the t-statistic is 2.33 or higher, there is a 99 percent chance
that the average excess return is different from zero. If the average is positive,
the event increases stock prices, whereas if the average is negative, the event
decreases stock prices.

Consider the following illustrative example. Academics and practitioners have long argued about the consequences of option listing for stock price
volatility. On the one hand, there are those who argue that options attract
speculators and hence increase stock price volatility. This higher risk, they
argue, should lead to lower stock prices. On the other hand, there are others who argue that options increase the available choices for investors and
increase the flow of information to financial markets, and thus lead to lower
stock price volatility and higher stock prices.

One way to test these alternative hypotheses is to do an event study,
examining the effects of listing options on the underlying stocks' prices. In
1989, Conrad did such a study, following these steps:[29]

Step 1: The dates on which the announcements were made that options would be listed on the Chicago Board Options Exchange on
individual stocks was collected.

Step 2: The prices of the underlying stocks (j) were collected for each of
the 10 days prior to the option listing announcement date, the day
of the announcement, and each of the 10 days after.

Step 3: The returns on the stock (Rjt) were computed for each of these
trading days.

---

[29] J. Conrad, "The Price Effect of Option Introduction," *Journal of Finance* 44 (1989):
487–498.

Step 4: The beta for the stock (β_j) was estimated using the returns from a time period outside the event window (using 100 trading days from before the event and 100 trading days after the event).

Step 5: The returns on the market index (Rmt) were computed for each of the 21 trading days.

Step 6: The excess returns were computed for each of the 21 trading days:

$$\text{ER}_{jt} = R_{jt} - \beta_j R_{mt} \ldots t = -10, -9, -8, \ldots, +8, +9, +10$$

The excess returns were cumulated for each trading day.

Step 7: The average and standard error of excess returns across all stocks with option listings were computed for each of the 21 trading days. The t-statistics were computed using the averages and standard errors for each trading day. Table 6.4 summarizes the average excess returns and t-statistics around option listing announcement dates.

TABLE 6.4 Excess Returns around Option Listing Announcement Dates

Trading Day	Average Excess Return	Cumulative Excess Return	T-Statistic
−10	0.17%	0.17%	1.30
−9	0.48%	0.65%	1.66
−8	−0.24%	0.41%	1.43
−7	0.28%	0.69%	1.62
−6	0.04%	0.73%	1.62
−5	−0.46%	0.27%	1.24
−4	−0.26%	0.01%	1.02
−3	−0.11%	−0.10%	0.93
−2	0.26%	0.16%	1.09
−1	0.29%	0.45%	1.28
0	0.01%	0.46%	1.27
1	0.17%	0.63%	1.37
2	0.14%	0.77%	1.44
3	0.04%	0.81%	1.44
4	0.18%	0.99%	1.54
5	0.56%	1.55%	1.88
6	0.22%	1.77%	1.99
7	0.05%	1.82%	2.00
8	−0.13%	1.69%	1.89
9	0.09%	1.78%	1.92
10	0.02%	1.80%	1.91

Based on these excess returns, there is no evidence of an announcement effect on the announcement day alone, but there is mild[30] evidence of a positive effect over the entire announcement period.

HOW DIFFERENT IS DIFFERENT? STATISTICAL VERSUS ECONOMIC SIGNIFICANCE

If you compare two samples on any dimension, you will get different results. Thus, you could compare the average returns on portfolios of companies with tall CEOs to the average returns of portfolios of companies with short CEOs, and you would find them to be different. But what should we read into the difference? If the average return on companies headed by tall CEOs is higher, should we rush out to buy stock in those companies? Not quite yet, because the differences often arise purely from chance.

The first test that you can run is a statistical test, where you apply the laws of probability to estimate the likelihood that the difference you are observing is purely random. This is what we do, for instance, when we compute a t-statistic on abnormal returns. If the t-statistic is 2.33, for example, we are saying that there is only a 1 percent chance that the difference we are observing is random and a 99 percent chance that returns are higher on companies with tall CEOs. If the t-statistic has been only 0.50, there would have been a 31 percent chance that the difference was purely random. In fact, it is common to test for statistical significance at the 1 percent or 5 percent levels; that is, only differences where the probability of randomness is less than 1 percent or 5 percent would be viewed as statistically significant.

The second test is for economic significance. When the difference between two samples is economically significant, you can make money off the difference. In the example that we have used, you could buy stocks with tall CEOs and sell stocks with short CEOs and make excess returns on your investment. Statistical significance does not always equal economic significance. First, you may have transaction costs that are much higher than the difference in returns between the two groups. Note that the larger the sample you use, the more likely it is that even small differences can be statistically significant. Thus, a

---

[30]The t-statistics are marginally significant at the 5 percent level.

difference of 0.20 percent may be statistically significant, but it clearly is not sufficient to cover execution costs. Second, you have the thorny issue of causation not being equal to correlation. In other words, all you have established is a correlation between returns and CEO height, but you have not established causation. Do firms with tall CEOs earn higher returns or do firms with higher returns hire tall CEOs? If it is the latter, you may very well find statistical significance but not economic profits.

Portfolio Study In some investment strategies, firms with specific characteristics are viewed as more likely to be undervalued, and therefore to have excess returns, than firms without these characteristics. In these cases, the strategies can be tested by creating portfolios of firms possessing these characteristics at the beginning of a time period and examining returns over the time period. To ensure that these results are not colored by the idiosyncrasies of one time period, this analysis is repeated for a number of periods. The seven steps in doing a portfolio study are:

1. The variable on which firms will be classified is defined, using the investment strategy as a guide. This variable has to be observable, though it does not have to be numerical. Examples would include market value of equity, bond ratings, stock prices, price-earnings ratios, and price-to-book value ratios.
2. The data on the variable is collected for every firm in the defined sample[31] at the *start* of the testing period, and firms are classified into portfolios based on the magnitude of the variable. Thus, if the price-earnings ratio is the screening variable, firms are classified on the basis of P/E ratios into portfolios from lowest P/E to highest P/E classes. The number of classes will depend on the size of the sample, since there have to be sufficient firms in each portfolio to get some measure of diversification.
3. The returns are collected for each firm in each portfolio for the testing period, and the returns for each portfolio are computed, making an

---

[31]Though there are practical limits on how big the sample can be, care should be taken to make sure that no biases enter at this stage of the process. An obvious one would be to pick only stocks that have done well over the time period for the universe.

assumption about how stocks will be weighted—some studies use equal weightings whereas others are value weighted.

4. The beta (if using a single-factor model like the CAPM) or betas (if using a multifactor model like the arbitrage pricing model) of each portfolio are estimated, either by taking the average of the betas of the individual stocks in the portfolio or by regressing the portfolio's returns against market returns over a prior time period (for instance, the year before the testing period).

5. The excess returns earned by each portfolio are computed, in conjunction with the standard error of the excess returns.

6. There are a number of statistical tests available to check whether the average excess returns are, in fact, different across the portfolios. Some of these tests are parametric[32] (they make certain distributional assumptions about excess returns) and some are nonparametric.[33]

7. As a final test, the extreme portfolios can be matched against each other to see whether there are statistically significant differences across these portfolios.

To illustrate this process, consider the following. Practitioners have claimed that low price-earnings ratio stocks are generally bargains and do much better than the market or stocks with high price-earnings ratios. This hypothesis can be tested using a portfolio approach:

Step 1: Using data on price-earnings ratios from the end of 1987, firms on the New York Stock Exchange were classified into five groups, the first group consisting of stocks with the lowest P/E ratios and the fifth group consisting of stocks with the highest P/E ratios. Firms with negative price-earnings ratios were ignored.

Step 2: The returns on each portfolio were computed using data from 1988 to 1992. Stocks that went bankrupt or were delisted were assigned a return of –100 percent.

Step 3: The betas for each stock in each portfolio were computed using monthly returns from 1983 to 1987, and the average beta for each

---

[32] One parametric test is an F test, which tests for equality of means across groups. This test can be conducted assuming either that the groups have the same variance or that they have different variances.

[33] An example of a nonparametric test is a rank sum test, which ranks returns across the entire sample and then sums the ranks within each group to check whether the rankings are random or systematic.

TABLE 6.5 Excess Returns from 1988 to 1992 for P/E Ratio Portfolios

P/E Class	1988	1989	1990	1991	1992	1988–1992
Lowest	3.84%	−0.83%	2.10%	6.68%	0.64%	2.61%
2	1.75%	2.26%	0.19%	1.09%	1.13%	1.56%
3	0.20%	−3.15%	−0.20%	0.17%	0.12%	−0.59%
4	−1.25%	−0.94%	−0.65%	−1.99%	−0.48%	−1.15%
Highest	−1.74%	−0.63%	−1.44%	−4.06%	−1.25%	−1.95%

portfolio was estimated. The portfolios were assumed to be equally weighted.[34]

Step 4: The returns on the market index were computed each year from 1988 to 1992.

Step 5: The excess returns on each portfolio were computed each year, using the actual returns estimated from step 2, the betas estimated from step 3, and the market returns from step 4:

Excess return in year t = Actual return on portfolio in year t

$-$ [Risk-free rate at the start of year t

$-$ Beta $*$ (Return on market in year t

$-$ Risk-free rate at the start of year t)]

Table 6.5 summarizes the excess returns each year from 1988 to 1992 for each portfolio.

Step 6: While the ranking of the returns across the portfolio classes seems to confirm our hypothesis that low-P/E stocks earn a higher return, we have to consider whether the differences across portfolios are statistically significant. There are several tests available, but these are a few:

■ An F test can be used to accept or reject the hypothesis that the average returns are the same across all portfolios. A high F score would lead us to conclude that the differences are too large to be random.

F statistic for difference across P/E portfolios between 1988 and 1992 = 14.75

---

[34]This will be a function of your strategy. If your strategy requires market-cap-weighted holdings, you would have to modify the test accordingly.

This suggests that there is less than a 1 percent chance that the difference between the portfolios is random.

■ A chi-squared test is a nonparametric test that can be used to test the hypothesis that the means are the same across the five portfolio classes.

Chi-squared statistic for difference across P/E portfolios, 1988–1992 = 36.16

This confirms our conclusion from the F test that the differences are statistically significant.

■ We could isolate just the lowest P/E and highest P/E stocks and estimate a t-statistic that the averages are different across these two portfolios. In this case, the t-statistics that we obtain when we compare the returns on the lowest and highest P/E ratio classes is 5.61. This difference is also statistically significant.

Regressions   One of the limitations of portfolio studies is that they become increasing unwieldy as the number of variables that you use in your strategy increases. For instance, assume that you pick stocks that have low P/E ratios and low institutional investment, and whose stock prices have done well in the past six months. You could categorize all firms in your sample into five portfolios, based on each variable, but you would end up with 125 portfolios overall because of the potential interactions among the variables. The other problem with portfolio studies is that you group firms into classes and ignore differences across firms within each class. Thus, the stocks in the lowest P/E ratio class may have P/E ratios that range from 4 to 12. If you believe that these differences may affect the expected returns on your strategy, you could get a better measure of the relationship by running a multiple regression. Your dependent variable would be the returns on stocks, and the independent variables would include the variables that form your strategy. There are four steps to running a regression:

Step 1: Identify your dependent variable. This is the variable that you are trying to explain. In most investment schemes, it will be a measure of the return you would make on the investment, but you have to make at least two judgments. The first is whether you plan to use total returns or excess returns; with the latter, you would adjust the returns for risk and market performance, using one the measures discussed earlier in the chapter. The second decision you have to make is on the return interval you will be using—monthly, quarterly, annual, or five-year, for instance. This choice will be determined both by your investment strategy—long-term strategies require long-term returns—and by the ease with which you can get data on your independent variables for the intervals. For instance, if you use accounting variables such as earnings or book value as independent variables, you will be able to get updates only once every quarter for these variables.

Step 2: Decide on how you will measure the variables that will underlie you strategy. For instance, in the example cited earlier, you will have to define P/E ratios, institutional investment, and stock price momentum with more specificity. With P/E ratios, you will have to choose between different measures of earnings—primary or diluted, before or after extraordinary items, current or trailing. With institutional investment, you could measure the institutional holdings as a percentage of outstanding stock or as a percentage of float (stock that is traded), and you will also have to decide whether you will consider all institutional investors or only certain kinds (mutual funds, pension funds, etc.). With stock price momentum, you may have to choose between percent changes over the previous six months, which will bias you toward lower-priced stocks, or absolute changes, which will bias you toward higher-priced stocks. Once you have determined your independent variables, you will have to collect information on them at the beginning of each of your testing periods. For instance, if you decide that annual returns in the year 2000 will be your dependent variable, you will have to collect information on P/E ratios and institutional holdings from January 1, 2000, and stock price momentum from June 30, 1999, to January 1, 2000.[35]

Step 3: You should check for the nature of the relationship between the dependent variable and each independent variable. A scatter plot provides a simple graphical tool for doing this. You are checking to see not only if there is a relationship but also for whether the relationship is linear. Figure 6.1 presents two scatter plots.

Panel A represents a scatter plot with a linear relationship, but Panel B is more consistent with a nonlinear relationship. If you

---

[35]For institutional holdings, you will have to use whatever values you would have been able to obtain from public sources as of January 1, 2000. Since there is a delay before institutions file with the SEC, you may not know the holdings as of January 1 until much later in the year.

Panel A: Linear Relationship

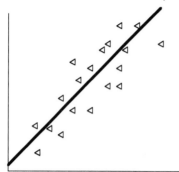

Panel B: Nonlinear Relationship

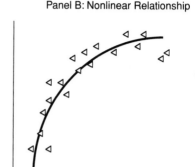

FIGURE 6.1 Scatter Plots—Linear and Nonlinear Relationships

observe the latter, you may have to transform the variable to make the relationship more linear.[36]

Step 4: You can now run the regression of the dependent variable against the independent variables, with or without transformations. In the example noted before, for instance, you would regress returns against P/E ratios, institutional holdings as a percentage of the stock outstanding, and the price change over the past six months:

Return on stock $= a + b$ (P/E)
$+ c$ (Institutional holdings as % of stock)
$+ d$ (Stock price change over past six months)

If your hypothesis is right, you should expect to see the following:

$b < 0$: Stocks with higher P/E ratios should have lower returns.

$c < 0$: Stocks with higher institutional holdings should have lower returns.

$d > 0$: Stocks that have done well over the past six months should have higher returns.

---

[36]Transformation requires you to convert a number by taking a mathematical function of it. Some commonly used transformations include the natural log, square root, and square. The natural log transformation is probably the most useful one in financial research.

Once you run the regression, you have to pass it through the tests for statistical significance. In other words, even if all of the coefficients have the right signs, you have to check to ensure that they are significantly different from zero. In most regressions, statistical significance is estimated with a t-statistic for each coefficient. This t-statistic is computed by dividing the coefficient by the standard error of the coefficient. You can also compute an F statistic to measure whether the regression collectively yields statistically significant results.

The regression described here, where you look for differences across observations (firms, funds, or countries) at a point in time, is called a cross-sectional regression. You can also use regressions to analyze how a variable changes over time as other variables change. For instance, it also long been posited that P/E ratios for all stocks go up as interest rates go down and economic growth increases. You could look at the P/E ratios for the entire market each year for the past 40 years, for instance, and examine whether P/E ratios have changed as interest rates and economic growth have changed. This regression is called a time series regression. Some inventive analysts even combine cross-sectional and time series data to create pooled regressions.

THE LIMITS OF REGRESSIONS

Regressions are powerful tools to examine relationships, but they have their limits when it comes to testing market efficiency. The first problem that they share with all other tools is that they are only as good as the data that go into them. If your data are filled with errors, you should expect the regression output to reflect that. The second problem is that you make assumptions about the nature of the relationship between the dependent and independent variables that may not be true. For instance, if you run a regression of returns against institutional holdings as a percentage of outstanding stock, you are assuming a linear relationship between the two—that is, that returns will change by the same magnitude if holdings go from 10 to 20 percent as they would if holdings went from 20 to 30 percent. The third problem arises when you run multiple regressions. For the regression coefficients to be unbiased, the independent variables should be uncorrelated with each other. In reality, it is difficult to find independent variables that have this characteristic.

The Cardinal Sins in Testing Market Efficiency

In the process of testing investment strategies, there are a number of pitfalls that have to be avoided. Some of them are:

- *Using anecdotal evidence to support or reject an investment strategy.* Anecdotal evidence is a double-edged sword. It can be used to support or reject the same hypothesis. Since stock prices are noisy and all investment schemes (no matter how absurd) will succeed sometimes and fail at other times, there will always be cases where the scheme works.
- *Testing an investment strategy on the same data and time period from which it was extracted.* This is the tool of choice for the unscrupulous investment adviser. An investment scheme is extracted from hundreds through an examination of the data for a particular time period. This investment scheme is then tested on the same time period, with predictable results. (The scheme does miraculously well and makes immense returns.) An investment scheme should always be tested on a time period different from the one it is extracted from or on a universe different from the one used to derive the scheme.
- *Sampling biases.* Since there are thousands of stocks that could be considered part of the testable universe of investments, researchers often choose to use a smaller sample. When this choice is random, this does limited damage to the results of the study. If the choice is biased, it can provide results that are not true in the larger universe. Biases can enter in subtle ways. For instance, assume that you decide to examine whether stocks with low prices are good investments, and you test this by estimating the returns over the past year for stocks that have low prices today. You will almost certainly find that this portfolio does badly, but not because your underlying hypothesis is false. Stocks that have gone down over the past year are more likely to have low stock prices today than stocks that have gone up. By looking at low stock prices today, you created a sample that is biased toward poorly performing stocks. You could very easily have avoided this bias by looking at stock prices at the start of your return period (rather than the end of the period).
- *Failure to control for market performance.* A failure to control for overall market performance can lead you to conclude that your investment scheme works just because it makes good returns or does not work just because it makes poor returns. Most investment strategies will generate good returns in a period in which the market does well and few will do so when the market does badly. It is crucial, therefore, that investment schemes control for market performance during the period of the test.

- *Failure to control for risk.* A failure to control for risk leads to a bias toward accepting high-risk investment schemes and rejecting low-risk investment schemes, since the former should make higher returns than the market and the latter should make lower returns, without implying any excess returns. For instance, a strategy of investing in the stock of bankrupt companies may generate annual returns that are much higher than returns on the S&P 500, but it is also a much riskier strategy and has to be held to a higher standard.

- *Mistaking correlation for causation.* Statistical tests often present evidence of correlation, rather than causation. Consider the study on P/E stocks cited in the earlier section. We concluded that low-P/E stocks tend to have higher excess returns than high-P/E stocks. It would be a mistake to conclude that a low price-earnings ratio, by itself, causes excess returns, since the high returns and the low P/E ratio themselves might have been caused by the high risk associated with investing in the stocks. In other words, high risk might be the causative factor that leads to both of the observed phenomena—low P/E ratios on the one hand and high returns on the other. This insight would make us more cautious about adopting a strategy of buying low-P/E stocks in the first place.

Some Lesser Sins That Can Be a Problem

While the errors in the last section can be fatal, there are lesser errors that researchers make that can color their conclusions. Here is a partial list.

- *Data mining.* The easy access that we have to huge amounts of data on stocks today can be a double-edged sword. While it makes it far easier to test investment strategies, it also exposes us to the risk of what is called data mining. When you relate stock returns to hundreds of variables, you are bound to find some that seem to predict returns, simply by chance. This will occur even if you are careful to sample without bias and test outside your sample period.

- *Survivor or survival bias.* Most researchers start with an existing universe of publicly traded companies and work back through time to test investment strategies. This can create a subtle bias since it automatically eliminates firms that failed during the period, with obvious negative consequences for returns. If the investment scheme is particularly susceptible to picking firms that have high bankruptcy risk, this may lead to an overstatement of returns on the scheme. For example, assume that the investment scheme recommends investing in stocks that have very negative earnings, using the argument that these stocks are most likely to benefit from a turnaround. Some of the firms in this portfolio will go bankrupt, and a failure to consider these firms will overstate the returns from this strategy.

■ *Not allowing for transaction costs.* Some investment schemes are more expensive than others because of transaction costs—execution fees, bid-ask spreads, and price impact. A complete test will take these into account before it passes judgment on the strategy. This is easier said than done, because different investors have different transaction costs, and it is unclear which investor's trading cost schedule should be used in the test. Most researchers who ignore transaction costs argue that individual investors can decide for themselves, given their transaction costs, whether the excess returns justify the investment strategy.

■ *Not allowing for difficulties in execution.* Some strategies look good on paper but are difficult to execute in practice, either because of impediments to trading or because trading creates a price impact. Thus a strategy of investing in very small companies may seem to create excess returns on paper, but these excess returns may not exist in practice because the price impact is significant.

A SKEPTIC'S GUIDE TO INVESTMENT STRATEGIES

At the start of this chapter, we noted that investors are bombarded with sales pitches for "can't miss" investment strategies. Increasingly, these strategy sales pitches come with what look like impressive back-tests that show that the strategy in question handily beats the market. If the proof is in the actual performance, it is also clear that most of these strategies really do not work and that we as investors need to develop ways of separating the wheat from the chaff. Here is a checklist that may help the next time you review a strategy.

Can the investment strategy be tested and implemented?

There are some investment strategies that sound good but are difficult to test and even more difficult to implement. There are two reasons for this. The first is that the strategy is based on qualitative factors that are nebulous and subject to interpretation. For instance, a strategy that requires you to invest in well-managed companies but does not specify what qualifies as good management is essentially useless. The second is that the strategy requires you to have access to information that you could not possess unless you were a time traveler. Thus, a market timing strategy that requires you to invest in stocks at the start of each year if the real economic growth in the last quarter of the prior year exceeds 4 percent has a fatal flaw, since the government does not report on the last quarter until February or March of the next year.

If the strategy can be tested, is the test that has been devised a fair one of the strategy?

When testing a strategy, you have to make judgment calls on a number of dimensions. You have to decide first on the time period over which you will assess the strategy, and that choice should reflect the selling point of the strategy. Thus, if an investment strategy is presented as one that protects you during market downturns, it has to be tested over a period in which there was enough market turbulence to test that claim. In general, testing an investment strategy over a period in which the market has generally moved in one direction (bullish or bearish) is dangerous, since the future will almost certainly deliver a mix of both good and bad times. You also have to make measurement choices on the variables you will use to capture the essence of the strategy. Those choices will be easy for those strategies that are built around clearly defined variables (price-to-book value ratio, for instance) but is more complicated for those strategies built around variables that can be captured with different measures (high growth, for example, can be defined as growth in revenues or earnings, and can be computed from the past or be an estimate for the future).

Does it pass the statistical tests?

In the preceding sections, we laid out the cardinal and lesser sins that bedevil the statistical tests of investment strategies. When looking at any back-test of a strategy, you should start by looking at the size of the sample (larger samples are better than smaller samples) and sampling bias (checking in particular for whether the way in which the sample was created is likely to skew the final conclusions). You should follow up by looking at how statistical significance is being established and whether there are features to the data that may contaminate the statistical tests being used to make the case.

Does it pass the economic significance tests?

As we noted earlier, what passes for statistical significance, especially with large samples, may not pass the economic significance test. In particular, there are three checks that should be performed. The first is on the magnitude of the additional returns; thus a strategy may claim to beat the market, but does it beat it by 0.2 percent, 2 percent, or 20 percent a year? The second is in the risk adjustments. We listed a number of different risk-adjustment measures that can be used; in addition, there is a commonsense test that should always be applied. Take a look at the stocks (or other assets) that come through as the ones to buy based on the strategy, and see if they reflect the study's claims on the risk exposure. Thus, a strategy that claims to have average or low risk will be undermined if most of the stocks that show up on the list are young, high-growth companies. Finally, you should consider the potential trading costs that you will be exposed to on the strategy, given the types of stocks or assets it requires you to invest in and how often and when you have to trade.

Has it been tried before?

There is truth to the saying that almost everything that is marketed as new and different in investing has been tried before, sometimes successfully and sometimes not. While investors often view market history as obscure and irrelevant, especially given how much markets have changed over time, you can learn by looking at how investors in the past fared with strategies similar to the one that is being tested. If it worked, how long and how well did it work? If it did not work, why did it fail? If there is a new twist or variant that is being incorporated into the strategy, will it help to avoid repeating that failure? If you do have an investment strategy that has never been tried before, it is worth asking why. It is possible that the new assets or markets have made it feasible for the first time, but it is also possible that there is a fatal flaw to the strategy that you don't see yet.

CONCLUSION

The question of whether markets are efficient will always be a provocative one, given the implications that efficient markets have for investment management and research. If an efficient market is defined as one where the market price is an unbiased estimate of the true value, it is quite clear that some markets will always be more efficient than others and that markets will always be more efficient to some investors than to other investors. The capacity of a market to correct inefficiencies quickly will depend, in part, on the ease of trading, the transaction costs, and the vigilance of profit-seeking investors in that market.

Market efficiency can be tested in a number of different ways. The three most widely used tests to test efficiency are event studies, which examine market reactions to information events; portfolio studies, which evaluate the returns of portfolios created on the basis of observable characteristics; and regressions that relate returns to firm characteristics either at a point in time or across time. It does make sense to be vigilant, because bias can enter these studies, intentionally or otherwise, in a number of different ways and can lead to unwarranted conclusions and, worse still, to wasteful investment strategies.

EXERCISES

Pick an investment strategy that intrigues you. It can be a strategy that you have used before or that you have read about.

1. Is the strategy testable? If it is not, would you still use it? Why or why not?
2. Assuming that it is testable, what type of test you would need to run to evaluate the strategy—an event study, a portfolio study, or something else?
3. Once you have decided on the type of test, consider the details of how you would go about running the test. (You may not actually have the resources to run the test, but you can still think about how you would do it if you did have the resources.)
   a. Over what time period would you test the strategy?
   b. How big does your sample have to be for you to feel comfortable with the results?
   c. Once you have chosen a time period and sample size, what are the steps involved in running the test?
   d. How do you plan to incorporate risk and transaction costs into your analysis?
   e. Assuming that the strategy generates excess returns, what residual concerns would you still have in implementing the strategy?

Lessons for Investors

- An efficient market makes mistakes, but the mistakes tend to be random. In other words, you know that some stocks are undervalued and some are overvalued, but you have no way of identifying which group each stock falls into.
- You are more likely to find inefficiencies in markets that are less liquid and where information is less easily available or accessible.
- In an inefficient market, you can use publicly available information to find undervalued and overvalued stocks and trade on them to earn returns that are consistently greater than what you would have earned on a randomly selected portfolio of equivalent risk.
- To create portfolios of equivalent risk, you have to use models for risk and return. To the extent that your model for risk is misspecified, you may uncover what look like inefficiencies but really represent the failures of your model.

CHAPTER 7

Smoke and Mirrors?
Price Patterns, Volume Charts,
and Technical Analysis

S ome investors believed that price charts provide signals of the future, and pore over them looking for patterns that will predict future price movements. Notwithstanding the disdain with which they are viewed by other investors and many academics, easy access to data combined with an increase in computing capabilities—charting and graphing programs abound—has meant that more investors look at charts now than ever before. In addition, data on trading volume and from derivatives markets have provided chartists with new indicators to pore over.

In this chapter, we look at the basis of charting by examining the underlying premise in charting and technical analysis, which is a belief that there are systematic and often irrational patterns in investor behavior and that technical indicators and charts provide advance warning of shifts in investor behavior. While we will not attempt to describe every charting pattern and technical indicator (there are hundreds), we will categorize them based on the view of human behavior that underlies them. In the process, we will see if there are lessons in charts that even nonbelievers can take away and cautionary notes for true believers about potential inconsistencies.

RANDOM WALKS AND PRICE PATTERNS

In many ways, the antithesis of charting is the notion that prices follow a random walk. In a random walk, the stock price reflects the information in past prices, and knowing what happened yesterday is of no consequence to what will happen today. Since the random walk comes in for a fair degree

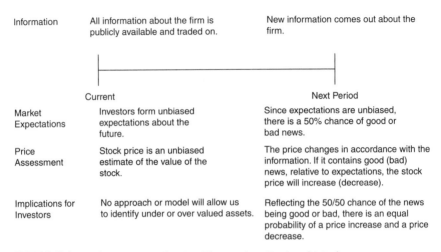

Information	All information about the firm is publicly available and traded on.	New information comes out about the firm.
	Current	Next Period
Market Expectations	Investors form unbiased expectations about the future.	Since expectations are unbiased, there is a 50% chance of good or bad news.
Price Assessment	Stock price is an unbiased estimate of the value of the stock.	The price changes in accordance with the information. If it contains good (bad) news, relative to expectations, the stock price will increase (decrease).
Implications for Investors	No approach or model will allow us to identify under or over valued assets.	Reflecting the 50/50 chance of the news being good or bad, there is an equal probability of a price increase and a price decrease.

FIGURE 7.1 Information and Price Changes in a Rational Market

of abuse from technical analysts, some justified and some not, we will begin by looking at what the random walk is and its implications.

The Basis for Random Walks

To understand the argument for prices following a random walk, we have to begin with the presumption that investors at any point in time estimate the value of an asset based on expectations of the future, and that these expectations are both unbiased and rational, given the information that investors have at that point in time. Under these conditions, the price of the asset changes only as new information comes out about it. If the market price at any point in time is an unbiased estimate of value, the next piece of information that comes out about the asset should be just as likely to contain good news as bad.[1] It therefore follows that the next price change is just as likely to be positive as it likely to be negative. The implication of course is that each price change will be independent of the previous one, so knowing an asset's price history will not help form better predictions of future price changes. Figure 7.1 summarizes the assumptions.

The random walk is not magic, but there are two prerequisites for it to hold. The first is that investors are rational and form unbiased expectations of the future, based on all of the information that is available to them at the

---

[1] If the probability of good news is greater than the probability of bad news, the price should increase before the news comes out. Technically, it is the expected value of the next information release that is zero.

time. If expectations are set too low or set too high consistently—in other words, investors are too optimistic or too pessimistic—information will no longer have an equal chance of being good or bad news, and prices will not follow a random walk. The second is that price changes are caused by new information. If investors can cause prices to change by just trading, even in the absence of information, you can have price changes in the same direction rather than a random walk.

The Basis for Price Patterns

Chartists are not alone in believing that there is information in past prices that can be useful in forecasting future price changes. There are some fundamental investors who use technical and charting indicators, albeit as secondary factors, in picking stocks. They disagree with the basic assumptions made by random walkers and argue that:

- Investors are not always rational in the way they set expectations. These irrationalities may lead to expectations being set too low for some assets at some times and too high for other assets at other times. Thus, the next piece of information is more likely to contain good news for the first asset and bad news for the second.
- Price changes themselves may provide information to markets. Thus, the fact that a stock has gone up strongly the past four days may be viewed as good news by investors, making it more likely that the price will go up today rather than down.

The debate about whether price changes are random has continued for the past 50 years, ever since researchers were able to access price data on stocks. The initial tests were almost all conducted by those who believed that prices follow a random walk, and, not surprisingly, they found no price patterns. In the past two decades, there has been an explosion in both the amount of data available and in the points of view of researchers. One of the biggest surprises (at least to those who believed the prevailing dogma of efficient and rational markets) has been the uncovering of numerous price patterns, though it is not clear whether these are evidence of irrational markets and whether they offer the potential for profits.

EMPIRICAL EVIDENCE

As the studies of the time series properties of prices have proliferated, the evidence can be classified based on the periods over which researchers examine asset prices, with some studies focusing on very short-term changes (minute to minute, or hour to hour) at one extreme, and other studies looking at longer-term returns (over many months or even years). Since the findings are sometimes contradictory, we will present them separately. We will also present evidence on seasonal patterns in stock prices that seem to persist not only over many periods but also across most markets.

The Really Short Term: Mild Price Patterns

The notion that today's price change conveys information about tomorrow's price change and that there are detectable patterns in stock prices is deeply rooted in most investors' psyches. All too often, these patterns are backed up by anecdotal evidence, with the successful experiences on one or a few stocks in one period extrapolated to form rules about all stocks over other time periods. Even in a market that follows a perfect random walk, you will see price patterns on some stocks that seem to defy probability. The entire market may go up 10 days in a row, or down, for no other reason than pure chance. Given that this is often true, how do we test to see if there are significant price patterns? We consider two ways in which researchers have examined this question.

Serial Correlation   If today is a big up day for a stock, what does this tell us about tomorrow? There are three different points of view. The first is that the momentum from today will carry into tomorrow, and that tomorrow is more likely to be an up day than a down day. The second is that there will be profit taking as investors cash in their profits, and that the resulting correction will make it more likely that tomorrow will be a down day. The third is that each day we begin anew, with new information and new worries, and that what happened today has no implications for what will happen tomorrow.

Statistically, the serial correlation measures the relationship between price changes in consecutive time periods, whether hourly, daily, or weekly, and is a measure of how much the price change in any period depends on the price change over the previous time period. A serial correlation of zero would therefore imply that price changes in consecutive time periods are uncorrelated with each other, and can thus be viewed as a rejection of the hypothesis that investors can learn about future price changes from past ones. A serial correlation that is positive, and statistically significant, could be viewed as evidence of price momentum in markets, and would suggest that returns in a period are more likely to be positive if the prior period's returns were positive or negative if the previous returns were negative. A serial correlation that is negative, and statistically significant, could be evidence of price reversals, and would be consistent with a market in which positive returns are more likely to follow negative returns and vice versa.

From the viewpoint of investment strategy, serial correlations can sometimes be exploited to earn excess returns. A positive serial correlation would be exploited by a strategy of buying after periods with positive returns and selling after periods with negative returns. A negative serial correlation would suggest a strategy of buying after periods with negative returns and selling after periods with positive returns. Since these strategies generate transaction costs, the correlations have to be large enough to allow investors to generate profits to cover these costs. It is therefore entirely possible that there be serial correlation in returns without any opportunity to earn excess returns for most investors.

The earliest studies[2] of serial correlation all looked at large U.S. stocks and concluded that the serial correlation in stock prices was small. One of the first, for instance, found that 8 of the 30 stocks listed in the Dow had negative serial correlations and that most of the serial correlations were less than 0.05.[3] Other studies confirmed these findings of very low correlation, positive or negative, not only for smaller stocks in the United States, but also for other markets. For instance, Jennergren and Korsvold reported low serial correlations for the Swedish equity market,[4] and Cootner concluded that serial correlations were low in commodity markets as well.[5] While there may be statistical significance associated with some of these correlations, it is unlikely that there is enough correlation in short-period returns to generate excess returns after you adjust for transaction costs.

The serial correlation in short-period returns is also affected by market liquidity and the presence of a bid-ask spread. Not all stocks in an index are liquid, and, in some cases, stocks may not trade during a period. When the stock trades in a subsequent period, the resulting price changes can create positive serial correlation in market indices. To see why, assume that the market is up strongly on day 1, but that three stocks in the index do not

---

[2] S. S. Alexander, "Price Movements in Speculative Markets: Trends or Random Walks," in *The Random Character of Stock Market Prices* (Cambridge, MA: MIT Press, 1964); P. H. Cootner, "Stock Prices: Random versus Systematic Changes," *Industrial Management Review* 3 (1962): 24–45.

[3] E. F. Fama, "The Behavior of Stock Market Prices," *Journal of Business* 38 (1965): 34–105.

[4] L. P. Jennergren and P. E. Korsvold, "Price Formation in the Norwegian and Swedish Stock Markets—Some Random Walk Tests," *Swedish Journal of Economics* 76 (1974): 171–185.

[5] P. H. Cootner, "Common Elements in Futures Markets for Commodities and Bonds," *American Economic Review* 51, no. 2 (1961): 173–183.

trade on that day. On day 2, if these stocks are traded, they are likely to go up to reflect the increase in the market the previous day. The net result is that you should expect to see positive serial correlation in short-term returns in illiquid market indexes. The bid-ask spread creates a bias in the opposite direction if transaction prices are used to compute returns, since prices have a equal chance of ending up at the bid or the ask price. The bounce that this induces in prices will result in negative serial correlations in returns.[6] For very short return intervals, this bias induced in serial correlations might dominate and create the mistaken view that price changes in consecutive time periods are negatively correlated.

There are some recent studies that find evidence of serial correlation in returns over short time periods, but the correlation is different for high-volume and low-volume stocks. With high-volume stocks, stock prices are more likely to reverse themselves over short periods (i.e., have negative serial correlation). With low-volume stocks, stock prices are more likely to continue to move in the same direction (i.e., have positive serial correlation).[7] None of these studies suggest that you can make money of these correlations.

Runs Tests Once in a while a stock has an extended run where prices go up several days in a row or down several days in a row. While this, by itself, is completely compatible with a random walk, you can examine a stock's history to see if these runs happen more frequently or less frequently than they should. A runs test is based on a count of the number of runs (i.e., sequences of price increases or decreases) in price changes over time. Thus, the following time series of price changes, where U is an increase and D is a decrease would result in these runs:

UUU DD U DDD UU DD U D UU DD U DD UUU DD UU D UU D

There were 18 runs in this price series of 33 periods. This actual number of runs in the price series is compared against the number that can be

---

[6]Roll provides a simple measure of this relationship:

$$\text{Bid-ask spread} = -\sqrt{2} \ (\text{Serial covariance in returns})$$

where the serial covariance in returns measures the covariance between return changes in consecutive time periods. See R. Roll, "A Simple Measure of the Effective Bid-Ask Spread in an Efficient Market," *Journal of Finance* 39 (1984): 1127–1139.
[7]J. S. Conrad, A. Hameed, and C. Niden, "Volume and Autocovariances in Short-Horizon Individual Security Returns," *Journal of Finance* 49 (1994): 1305–1330.

expected in a series of this length, assuming that price changes are random.[8] If the actual number of runs is greater than the expected number, there is evidence of negative correlation in price changes. If it is lower, there is evidence of positive correlation. A study of price changes in the Dow 30 stocks, assuming daily, four-day, nine-day, and 16-day return intervals, provided the following results.

	Differencing Interval			
	Daily	Four-day	Nine-day	16-day
Actual runs	735.1	175.7	74.6	41.6
Expected runs	759.8	175.8	75.3	41.7

The actual number of runs in four-day returns (175.7) is almost exactly what you would expect in a random process. There is slight evidence of positive correlation in daily returns but no evidence of deviations from randomness for longer return intervals.

Again, while the evidence is dated, it serves to illustrate the point that long strings of positive and negative changes are, by themselves, insufficient evidence that markets are not random, since such behavior is consistent with price changes following a random walk. It is the recurrence of these strings that can be viewed as evidence against randomness in price behavior.

HIGH-FREQUENCY TRADING

High-frequency trading generally references automated trading, usually in high volume, often by institutional investors. While that may not sound unique or even new, high-frequency trading is entirely driven by computer algorithms, rather than by human insight or decisions. Thus, if there are patterns in stock prices and information in trading volume, even over very short time periods, computer algorithms can be written to instantaneously take advantage of these patterns to make money. While the profits generated per share may be tiny, they can amount to sizable values over very large trades.

(continued)

---

[8]There are statistical tables that summarize the expected number of runs, assuming randomness, in a series of any length.

High-frequency trading has created its own share of headlines, most of which have been negative. It has been blamed for so-called flash crashes, where a mistake in the computer algorithm or faulty data can result in price instability. A drop in U.S. stocks of almost 5 percent during a 30-minute period on May 6, 2010, for instance, was at least partially attributed to high-frequency trading in index futures. It has also become as a symbol of how uneven the playing field is for individual investors, who do not have the resources for high-frequency trading and have to compete with institutional investors who do.

We believe that the criticism is overblown. First, high-frequency trading has exacerbated some of the volatility in markets, but the rise in stock market volatility in the post-2008 time period has more to do with increases in macroeconomic uncertainty than with trading mechanisms. Second, individual investors should never be trying to exploit minute-to-minute movements in stock prices in the first place, with or without high-frequency trading. As for the institutional investors who use high-frequency trading, it is possible that the first entrants in this game claimed some surplus from short-term price movements, but as it has become more common, the payoff has become more modest.

The Short Term: Price Reversal   As you move from hours and days to weeks or months, there seems to be some evidence that prices reverse. In other words, stocks that have done well over the last month are more likely to do badly in the next one, and stocks that have done badly over the last month are more likely to bounce back.[9] The reasons given are usually rooted in market overreaction; the stocks that have gone up (or down) the most over the most recent month are ones where markets have overreacted to good (or bad) news that came out about the stock over the month. The price reversal then reflects markets correcting themselves.

A study looked at the differential returns that would have been generated by a strategy of selling short the top decile of stocks based on how well they did in the past month, and buying the stocks in the bottom decile, with a

---

[9]N. Jegadeesh, "Evidence of Predictable Behavior of Security Returns," *Journal of Finance* 45 (1990): 881–898; B. N. Lehmann, "Fads, Martingales, and Market Efficiency," *Quarterly Journal of Economics* 105 (1990): 1–28.

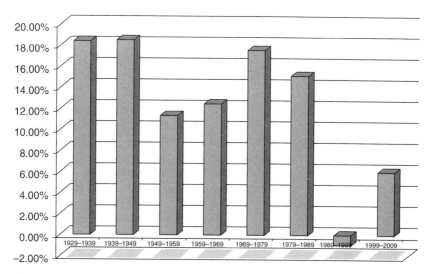

FIGURE 7.2 Annual Returns to Short-Term Reversal Strategy, 1929 to 2009
Source: D. Blitz, J. Huij, S. Lansdorp and M. Verbeek, "Short-Term Residual Return" (SSRN Working Paper 1911449, 2010).

holding period of a month.[10] The annualized returns from this strategy are presented in Figure 7.2. The strategy would have generated substantial profits, before adjusting for transaction costs and risk, in all but one decade (1989–1999) out of the last eight decades.

Studies that have looked at short-term price reversal do present three caveats that should play a role in whether you should invest based on the phenomenon. The first is that this strategy can skew toward buying small market cap companies with low price-to-book ratios, at least in some periods. To the extent that these companies are riskier, the excess returns on this strategy have to be scaled down. The second is that this is a high trading/turnover strategy and the transaction costs can eat into the excess returns significantly, especially if the stocks being traded are small market cap companies. The third is that to the extent that this is a strategy built around market overreaction to news, it may be more effective to build it around actual news announcements. For instance, we will look at a strategy of trading after earnings announcements in Chapter 10 that represents a much more direct way of exploiting market overreaction.

---

[10]D. Blitz, J. Huij, S. Lansdorp, and M. Verbeek, "Short-Term Residual Return" (SSRN Working Paper 1911449, 2010).

The Mid Term: Price Momentum

When time is defined as many months or a year rather than a single month, there seems to be a tendency toward positive serial correlation. Jegadeesh and Titman present evidence of what they call "price momentum" in stock prices over time periods of several months—stocks that have gone up in the past six months tend to continue to go up, whereas stocks that have gone down in the past six months tend to continue to go down.[11] Between 1945 and 2008, if you classified stocks into deciles based on price performance over the previous year, the annual return you would have generated by buying the stocks in the top decile and holding for the next year was *16.5 percent higher* than the return you would have earned on the stocks in the bottom decile. To add to the allure of the strategy, the high-momentum stocks also had less risk (measured as price volatility) than the low-momentum stocks.[12]

Figure 7.3 shows the allure to a momentum strategy by looking at the annual returns, from 1927 to 2010, to investing in stocks classified into momentum classes based on the most recent year's performance.

The momentum effect is just as strong in the European markets, though it seems to be weaker in emerging markets.[13] In the United Kingdom, Dimson, Marsh, and Staunton looked at the 100 largest stocks on the British market and compared the value of a portfolio composed of the 20 best performers over the previous 12 months with the 20 worst performers over the same period; £1 invested in the best performers in 1900 would have grown to £2.3 million at the end of 2009, whereas £1 invested in the worst performers would have grown to only £49.

What may cause this momentum? One potential explanation is that mutual funds are more likely to buy past winners and dump past losers, and they tend to do this at the same time, thus generating price continuity.[14] In

---

[11]N. Jegadeesh and S. Titman, "Returns to Buying Winners and Selling Losers: Implications for Stock Market Efficiency," *Journal of Finance* 48, no. 1 (1993): 65–91; N. Jegadeesh and S. Titman, "Profitability of Momentum Strategies: An Evaluation of Alternative Explanations," *Journal of Finance* 56, no. 2 (2001): 699–720.

[12]K. Daniel, "Momentum Crashes" (SSRN Working Paper 1914673, 2011).

[13]G. K. Rouwenhorst, "International Momentum Strategies," *Journal of Finance* 53 (1998): 267–284; G. Bekaert, C. B. Erb, C. R. Harvey, and T. E. Viskanta, "What Matters for Emerging Market Equity Investments," *Emerging Markets Quarterly* (Summer 1997): 17–46.

[14]M. Grinblatt, S. Titman, and R. Wermers, "Momentum Investment Strategies, Portfolio Performance, and Herding: A Study of Mutual Fund Behavior," *American Economic Review* 85 (1995): 1088–1105.

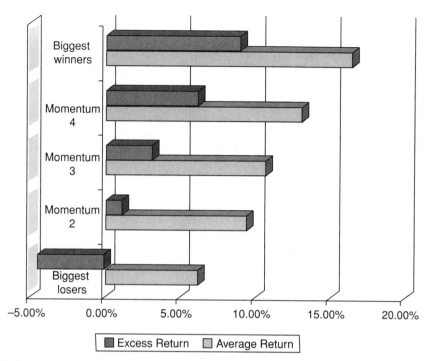

FIGURE 7.3   Annual Returns to Momentum from 1927 to 2010—U.S. Stocks Momentum Classes Based on Prior Year's Performance
Source: Raw data from Ken French's Data Library (Dartmouth College).

recent years, as more research has been done on the momentum effect, four interesting patterns are emerging:

1. Price momentum that is accompanied by higher trading volume is both stronger and more sustained than price momentum with low trading volume.[15]
2. There are differences in opinion on the relationship between momentum and firm size. While some of the earlier studies suggest that momentum is stronger at small market cap companies, a more recent study that looks at U.S. stocks from 1926 to 2009 finds the relationship to be a weak

---

[15]K. Chan, A. Hameed, and W. Tong, "Profitability of Momentum Strategies in the International Equity Markets," *Journal of Financial and Quantitative Analysis* 35 (2000): 153–172.

one, though it does confirm that there are subperiods (e.g., 1980–1996) where momentum and firm size are correlated.[16]

3. There also seem to be differences in opinion on whether momentum is stronger on the upside (as prices are rising) or on the downside (as prices are falling). The conclusions seem to vary, depending on the time period examined, with upside momentum dominating over very long time periods (1926–2009) and downside momentum winning out over some subperiods (such as 1980–1996).

4. Price momentum is more sustained and stronger for higher-growth companies with higher price-to-book ratios than for more mature companies with lower price-to-book ratios.

Researchers looking at other asset markets have found evidence that momentum is not restricted to stock markets. There is evidence of price momentum in commodity markets, currency markets, and real estate, and many investment strategies are built around that phenomenon.

The Long Term: Price Reversal Again!

When the long term is defined in terms of many years, there is substantial negative correlation in returns, suggesting that markets reverse themselves over long periods. Fama and French examined five-year returns on stocks from 1941 to 1985 and presented evidence of this phenomenon.[17] They found that serial correlation is more negative in five-year returns than in one-year returns, and is much more negative for smaller stocks rather than larger stocks. Figure 7.4 summarizes one-year and five-years serial correlation by size class for stocks on the New York Stock Exchange.

This phenomenon has also been examined in other markets, and the findings have been similar.

Given the findings of little or no correlation in the short term and substantial correlation in the long term, it is interesting that so many technical analysts focus on predicting intraday or daily prices. The bigger payoff seems to be in looking at price patterns over much longer periods, though there are caveats we will present in the next chapter on these long-term strategies.

---

[16]R. Israel and T. J. Moskowitz, "The Role of Shorting, Firm Size, and the Time on Market Anomalies" (working paper, University of Chicago, 2011).

[17]E. F. Fama and K. R. French, "Permanent and Temporary Components of Stock Prices," *Journal of Political Economy* 96: 246–273.

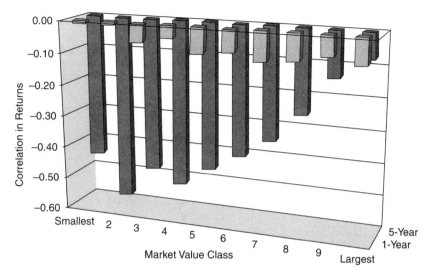

FIGURE 7.4   One-Year and Five-Year Correlations: Market Value Class: 1941 to 1985
Source: Fama and French (1988).

The Tipping Point   If there is price momentum in asset markets that lasts for months but there is price reversal over years, there has to be a tipping point, where momentum breaks and reversal starts to dominate. That tipping point is not just of academic interest, since it is the key to the success of a momentum-based strategy. After all, the biggest danger you face in any momentum strategy is missing the inflection point where the momentum changes direction.

NUMBER WATCH

Price momentum by sector: See the returns in prior periods for U.S. stocks, broken down by sector.

There have been a few attempts to gauge when this inflection point occurs by looking at past data and examining the relationship between holding periods and returns on a momentum strategy. These studies seem to indicate that momentum profits continue (and thus increase returns) for between six and nine months, suggesting that this is the optimal holding period for a momentum-based strategy. The nature of momentum strategies

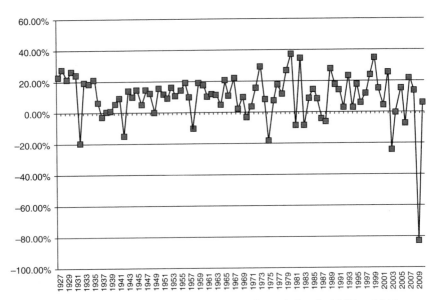

FIGURE 7.5 Returns to a Momentum Strategy for U.S. Stock: 1927 to 2010
Source: Raw data from Ken French's Data Library (Dartmouth College).

is that investors tend to make money consistently for long periods while momentum lasts, but then lose large amounts when momentum shifts. Using data from Fama and French on the difference in returns between the top and bottom deciles of stocks, based on momentum, we can see this danger in Figure 7.5.

Note that a strategy of buying winners (high-momentum stocks) initiated in 1990 would have beat losers (low-momentum stocks) in 17 of the next 20 years, but the losses in the three years (especially in 2009) would have wiped out a great deal of the profits from the profitable years.

Price Correlation Run Amok: Market Bubbles

Looking at the evidence on price patterns, there is evidence of both price momentum (in the medium term) and price reversal (in the short term and really long term). Read together, you have the basis for price bubbles: the momentum creates the bubble and the crash represents the reversal. Through time markets have boomed and busted, and in the aftermath of every bust, irrational investors have been blamed for the crash. As we will see in this section, it is not that simple. You can have bubbles in markets with only rational investors, and assessing whether you are in a bubble is

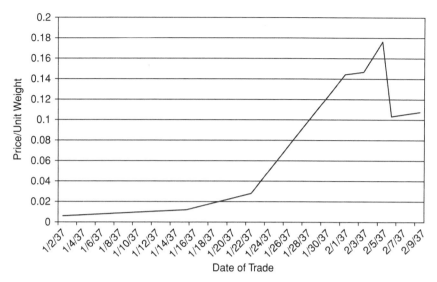

FIGURE 7.6   Price of a Tulip Bulb (Switzer)—January and February 1637
Source: Raw data from P. M. Garber, "Who Put the Tulip in Tulipmania?" in *Crashes and Panics: The Lessons of History*, ed. Eugene N. White (New York: Dow Jones Irwin/McGraw-Hill, 1990).

significantly more difficult, while you are in the midst of one, than after it bursts.

A Short History of Bubbles   As long as there have been markets, there have been bubbles. Two of the earliest bubbles to be chronicled occurred in the 1600s in Europe. One was the boom in prices of tulip bulbs in Holland that began in 1634. A single tulip bulb (Semper Augustus was one variety) sold for more than 5,000 guilders (the equivalent of more than $60,000 today) at the peak of the market. Stories abound, though many of them may have been concocted after the fact, of investors selling their houses and investing the money in tulip bulbs. As new investors entered the market in 1636, the frenzy pushed bulb prices up even more until the price peaked in early February. Figure 7.6 presents the price of one type of bulb (Switzers) in January and February of 1637.[18]

---

[18]P. M. Garber, "Who Put the Tulip in Tulipmania?" in *Crashes and Panics: The Lessons of History*, ed. Eugene N. White (New York: Dow Jones Irwin/McGraw-Hill, 1990).

Note that the price peaked on February 5, 1637, but investors who bought tulip bulbs at the beginning of the year saw their investments increase almost 30-fold over the next few weeks.

A little later in England, a far more conventional bubble was created in securities of a firm called the South Sea Corporation, a firm with no assets that claimed to have the license to mint untold riches in the South Seas. The stock price was bid up over the years before the price plummeted. The crash, which is described in vivid detail in Charles Mackay's classic book *Extraordinary Popular Delusions and the Madness of Crowds*, left many investors in England poorer.[19]

Through the 1800s, there were several episodes of boom and bust in the financial markets in the United States, and many of these were accompanied by banking panics.[20] As markets became broader and more liquid in the 1900s, there was a renewed hope that liquidity and more savvy investors would make bubbles a phenomenon of the past, but it was not to be. In 1907, J. P. Morgan had to intervene in financial markets to prevent panic selling, a feat that made his reputation as the financier of the world. The 1920s saw a sustained boom in U.S. equities, and this boom was fed by a number of intermediaries ranging from stockbrokers to commercial banks and sustained by lax regulation. The crash of 1929 precipitated the Great Depression, and created perhaps the largest raft of regulatory changes in the United States, ranging from restrictions on banks (the Glass-Steagall Act) to the creation of the Securities and Exchange Commission.

The period after World War II ushered in a long period of stability for the United States, and while there was an extended period of stock market malaise in the 1970s, the bubbles in asset prices tended to be tame relative to past crashes. In emerging markets, though, bubbles continued to form and burst. In the late 1970s, speculation and attempts by some in the United States to corner the precious metals markets did create a brief boom and bust in gold and silver prices. By the mid-1980s, there were some investors who were willing to consign market bubbles to history. On October 19, 1987, the U.S. equities market lost more than 20 percent of its value in one day, the worst single day in market history, suggesting that investors,

---

[19]C. Mackay, *Extraordinary Popular Delusions and the Madness of Crowds*, 1852; reprinted by John Wiley & Sons, New York. To get a flavor of financial markets in England at the time of the South Sea bubble, you should look at *A Conspiracy of Paper*, a novel set in the era by David Liss (New York: Ballantine Books, 2001). Also see E. Chancellor, *Devil Takes the Hindmost* (New York: Plume, 2000).

[20]The crash of 1873 was precipitated by the failure of firm called Jay Cooke, a financial services firm in Philadelphia. The New York Stock Exchange was closed for 10 days and several banks closed their doors in the aftermath.

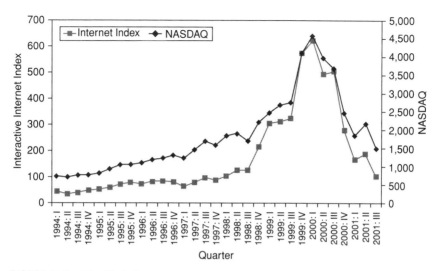

FIGURE 7.7   The Tech Boom
Source: Raw data from Bloomberg.

notwithstanding technological improvements and more liquidity, still shared a great deal with their counterparts in the 1600s. In the 1990s, we witnessed another in this cycle of market bubbles in the dramatic rise and fall of the dot-com sector. New technology companies with limited revenues and large operating losses went public at staggering prices (given their fundamentals) and their stock prices kept increasing. After peaking with a market value of $1.4 trillion in early 2000, this market, too, ran out of steam and lost almost all of this value in the subsequent year or two. Figure 7.7 summarizes the Internet index and the NASDAQ from 1994 to 2001.

The chart again has the makings of a bubble, as the value of the Internet index increased almost tenfold over the period, pulling the tech-heavy NASDAQ up with it.

Rational Bubbles?   A rational bubble sounds like an oxymoron, but it is well within the realms of possibility. Perhaps the simplest way to think of a rational bubble is to consider a series of coin tosses, with a head indicating a plus day and a tail a minus day. You would conceivably get a series of plus days pushing the stock price above the fair value, and the eventual correction is nothing more than a reversion back to a reasonable value. Note too that it is difficult to tell a bubble from a blunder. Investors in making their assessments for the future can make mistakes in pricing individual assets, either because they have poor information or because the actual outcomes (in terms of growth and returns) do not match expected values. If this is the

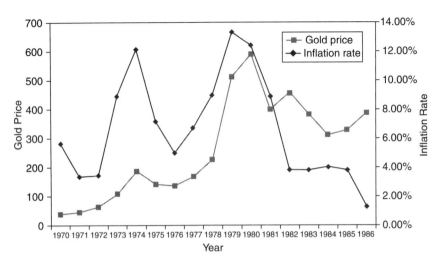

FIGURE 7.8   Gold Prices from 1970 to 1986
Source: Raw data from Bloomberg.

case, you would expect to see a surge in prices followed by an adjustment to a fair value. In fact, consider what happened to gold prices in the late 1970s. As inflation increased, many investors assumed (incorrectly in hindsight) that high inflation was here to stay, and they pushed gold prices up accordingly. Figure 7.8, which graphs gold prices from 1970 to 1986, looks very much like a classic bubble, but may just indicate our tendencies to look at things in the rearview mirror after they happen.

The surge in gold prices closely followed the increase in inflation in the late 1970s, reflecting gold's value as a hedge against inflation. As inflation declined in the 1980s, gold prices followed. It is an open question, therefore, whether this should be even considered a bubble.

Bubble or Blunder: Tests   There are some researchers who argue that you can separate bubbles from blunders by looking at how prices build up over time. Santoni and Dwyer, for instance, argue that you need two elements for a bubble: positive serial correlation in returns and a delinking of prices and fundamentals as the bubble forms.[21] They tested the periods prior to the 1929 and 1987 crashes to examine whether there is evidence of bubbles forming in those periods. Based on their analysis, there is no evidence of

---

[21]G. J. Santoni and G. P. Dwyer, "Bubbles or Fundamentals: New Evidence from the Great Bull Markets," in *Crashes and Panics: The Lessons of History*, ed. Eugene N. White (New York: Dow Jones Irwin/McGraw-Hill, 1990).

positive serial correlation in returns or of a reduction in the correlation between prices and fundamentals (which they define as dividends) in either period. Therefore, they argue that neither period can be used as an example of a bubble.

While there is truth to the underlying premise, these tests may be too weak to capture bubbles that form over long periods. For instance, Santoni and Dwyer's conclusion of no serial correlation seems to be sensitive to both the time periods examined and the return interval used. In addition, detecting a delinking of prices and fundamentals statistically may be difficult to do if it happens gradually over time. In short, these may be useful indicators but they are not conclusive.

Bubbles: From Inception to Crash   One or the more fascinating questions in economics examines how and why bubbles form and what precipitates their bursting. Though each bubble has its own characteristics, there seem to be four phases to every bubble.

Phase 1: The Birth of the Bubble   Most bubbles have their genesis in a kernel of truth. In other words, at the heart of most bubbles is a perfectly sensible story. Consider, for instance, the dot-com bubble. At its center was a reasonable argument that as more and more individuals and businesses gained online access, they would also be buying more goods and services online. The bubble builds as the market provides positive reinforcement to some investors and businesses for irrational or ill-thought-out actions. Using the dot-com phenomenon again, you could point to the numerous start-up companies with half-baked ideas for e-commerce that were able to go public with untenable market capitalizations and the investors who made profits along the way.

A critical component of bubbles building is the propagation of the news of the success to other investors in the market, who on hearing the news also try to partake in the bubble. In the process, they push prices up and provide even more success stories that can be used to attract more investors, thus providing the basis for a self-fulfilling prophecy. In the days of the tulip bulb craze, this would have had to be word of mouth, as successful investors spread the word, with the success being exaggerated in each retelling of the story. Even in this century, until very recently, the news of the success would have reached investors through newspapers, financial newsmagazines, and the occasional business show on television. In the dot-com bubble, we saw two additional phenomena that allowed news and rumors to spread even more quickly. The first was the Internet itself, where chat rooms and websites allowed investors to tell their success stories (or make them up as they went along). The second was the creation of cable stations such as CNBC, where analysts and money managers could present their views to millions of investors.

Phase 2: The Sustenance of the Bubble   Once a bubble forms, it needs sustenance. Part of the sustenance is provided by the institutional parasites that make money of the bubble and develop vested interests in preserving and expanding the bubbles. Among these parasites, you could include:

- *Investment banks*. Bubbles in financial markets bring with them a number of benefits to investment banks, starting with a surge in initial public offerings of firms but expanding to include further security issues and restructurings on the part of established firms that do not want to be shut out of the party.
- *Brokers and analysts*. A bubble generates opportunities for brokers and analysts selling assets related to the bubble. In fact, the ease with which investors make money as asset prices go up, often with no substantial reason, relegates analysis to the back burner.
- *Portfolio managers*. As a bubble forms, portfolio managers initially watch in disdain as investors they view as naive push asset prices up. At some point, though, even the most prudent portfolio managers seem to get caught up in the craze and partake of the bubble, partly out of greed and partly out of fear.
- *Media*. Bubbles make for exciting business news and avid investors. While this is especially noticeable in the dot-com bubble, with new books, television shows, and magazines directly aimed at investors in these stocks, even the earliest bubbles had their own versions of CNBC.

In addition to the institutional support that is provided for bubbles to grow, intellectual support is usually also forthcoming. There are both academics and practitioners who argue, when confronted with evidence of overpricing, that the old rules no longer apply. New paradigms are presented justifying the high prices, and those who disagree are disparaged as old-fashioned and out of step with reality.

Phase 3: The Bursting of the Bubble   All bubbles eventually burst, though there seems to be no single precipitating event that causes the reassessment. Instead, there is a confluence of factors that seem to lead to the price implosion. The first is that bubbles need ever more new investors (or at least new investment money) flowing in for sustenance. At some point, you run out of suckers as the investors who are the best targets for the sales pitch become fully invested. The second is that each new entrant into the bubble is more outrageous than the previous one. Consider, for instance, the dot-com bubble. While the initial entrants like America Online and Amazon.com might have had a possibility of reaching their stated goals, the new dot-com companies that were listed in the late 1990s were often idea companies with no vision of how to generate commercial success. As these new firms flood the market, even those who are apologists for high prices find themselves exhausted trying to explain the unexplainable.

The first hint of doubt among the true believers turns quickly to panic as reality sets in. Well-devised exit strategies break down as everyone heads for the exit doors at the same time. The same forces that created the bubble cause its demise, and the speed and magnitude of the crash mirror the formation of the bubble in the first place.

Phase 4: The Aftermath   In the aftermath of the bursting of the bubble, you initially find investors in complete denial. In fact, one of the amazing features of postbubble markets is the difficulty of finding investors who lost money in the bubble. Investors claim either that they were one of the prudent ones who never invested in the bubble in the first place or that they were one of the smart ones who saw the correction coming and got out in time.

As time passes and the investment losses from the bursting of the bubble become too large to ignore, the search for scapegoats begins. Investors point fingers at brokers, investment banks, and the experts who nurtured the bubble, arguing that they were misled.

Finally, investors draw lessons that they swear they will adhere to from this point on. "I will never invest in a tulip bulb again" or "I will never invest in a dot-com company again" becomes the refrain you hear. Given these resolutions, you may wonder why price bubbles show up over and over. The reason is simple: no two bubbles look alike. Thus investors, wary about repeating past mistakes, make new ones, which in turn create new bubbles in new asset classes.

Upside versus Downside Bubbles   Note that most investors think of bubbles in terms of asset prices rising well above fair value and then crashing. In fact, all of the bubbles we have referenced from the tulip bulb craze to the dot-com phenomenon were upside bubbles. But can asset prices fall well below fair market value and keep falling? In other words, can you have bubbles on the downside? In theory, there is no reason why you could not, and this makes the relative scarcity of downside bubbles, at least in the popular literature, surprising. One reason may be that investors are more likely to blame external forces—the bubble, for instance—for the money they lose when they buy assets at the peak of an upside bubble and are more likely to claim the returns they make when they buy stocks when they are at the bottom of a downside bubble as evidence of their investment prowess.

Another may be that it is far easier to create investment strategies to take advantage of an underpriced asset than it is to take advantage of an overpriced one. With the former, you can always buy the asset and hold until the market rebounds. With the latter, your choices are both more limited and more likely to be time limited. You can borrow the asset and sell it (short the asset), but not for as long as you want—most short selling is for a few months. If there are options traded on the asset, you may be able to buy puts on the asset, though until recently, only of a few months' duration. In fact, there is a regulatory bias in most markets against such investors, who are often likely to be categorized as speculators. As a consequence of these restrictions on betting against overpriced assets, bubbles on the upside are more likely to persist and become bigger over time, whereas bargain hunters operate as a floor for downside bubbles.

A Closing Assessment   Based on our reading of history, it seems reasonable to conclude that there are bubbles in asset prices, though only some of them can be attributed to market irrationality. Whether investors can take advantage of bubbles to make money seems to be a more difficult question to answer. One reason for the failure to exploit bubbles seems to stem from the desire to partake in the short term profits; even investors who believe that assets are overpriced want to make money off the bubble. Another reason is that it is difficult and dangerous to go against the crowd. Overvalued assets may get even more overvalued and these overvaluations can stretch over years, thus imperiling the financial well-being of any investor who has bet against the bubble. Finally, there is also an institutional interest on the part of investment banks, the media, and portfolio managers, all of whom feed of the bubble, to perpetuate the bubble.

Seasonal and Temporal Patterns in Prices

One of the most puzzling phenomena in asset prices is the existence of seasonal and temporal patterns in stock prices that seem to cut across all types of asset markets. As we will see in this section, stock prices seem to go down more on Mondays than on any other day of the week and do better in January than in any other month of the year. What is so surprising about this phenomenon, you might ask? It is very difficult to justify the existence of patterns such as these in a rational market; after all, if investors know that stocks do better in January than in any other month, they should start buying the stock in December and shift the positive returns over the course of the year. Similarly, if investors know that stocks are likely to be marked down on Monday, they should begin marking them down on Friday and hence shift the negative returns over the course of the week.

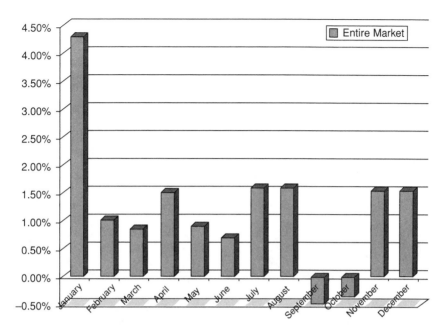

FIGURE 7.9 Returns by Month of the Year: U.S. Stocks from 1927 to 2011
Source: Raw data from Ken French's Data Library (Dartmouth College).

The January Effect Studies of returns in the United States and other major financial markets consistently reveal strong differences in return behavior across the months of the year. Figure 7.9 reports average returns by month of the year from 1927 to 2011.

Returns in January are significantly higher than returns in any other month of the year. This phenomenon is called the year-end or January effect, and it can be traced specifically to the first two weeks in January.

The January effect is much more pronounced for small firms than for larger firms, and Figure 7.10 graphs returns in January for the smallest firms (bottom 10 percent), the largest firms (top 10 percent) and the small cap premium (the difference between the smallest company returns and the entire market) from 1927 to 2011. We will return to examine this phenomenon in Chapter 9, where we take a closer look at investing in small-cap stocks as a strategy.

Note that the bulk of the small cap premium is earned in January and that small-cap stocks underperform the market for last quarter of each calendar year.

The universality of the January effect is illustrated in Figure 7.11, which reports on returns in January versus the other months of the year in several

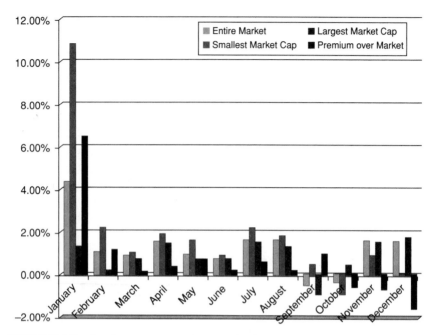

FIGURE 7.10   Small Cap Premium by Month of Year: U.S. Stocks from 1927 to 2011

Source: Raw data from Ken French's Data Library (Dartmouth College).

major financial markets, and finds strong evidence of a January effect in every market.[22]

In fact, researchers have unearthed evidence of a January effect in bond and commodity markets as well as stocks.

A number of explanations have been advanced for the January effect, but few hold up to serious scrutiny. One is that there is tax-loss selling by investors at the end of the year on stocks that have gone down to capture the capital gain, driving prices further down, presumably below true value, in December, and a buying back of the same stocks in January, resulting in the high returns.[23] The fact that the January effect is accentuated for

---

[22]R. Haugen and J. Lakonishok, *The Incredible January Effect* (Homewood, IL: Dow-Jones Irwin, 1988).

[23]It is to prevent this type of trading that the Internal Revenue Service has a "wash sale rule" that prevents you from selling and buying back the same stock within 45 days. To get around this rule, there has to be some substitution among the stocks. Thus investor 1 sells stock A and investor 2 sells stock B, but when it comes time to buy back the stock, investor 1 buys stock B and investor 2 buys stock A.

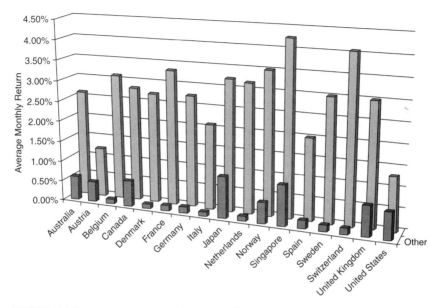

FIGURE 7.11   The International January Effect
Source: R. Haugen and J. Lakonishok, *The Incredible January Effect* (Homewood, IL: Dow-Jones Irwin, 1988).

stocks that have done worse over the prior year is offered as evidence for this explanation. There are several pieces of evidence that contradict it, though. First, there are countries (like Australia) that have a different tax year but continue to have a January effect. Second, the January effect is no greater, on average, in years following bad years for the stock market than in other years.

A second rationale is that the January effect is related to institutional trading behavior around the turn of the year. It has been noted, for instance, that the ratio of buys to sells for institutions drops significantly below average in the days before the turn of the year and picks up to above average in the months that follow.[24] It is argued that the absence of institutional buying pushes prices down in the days before the turn of the year and pushes prices up in the days after. Again, while this may be true, it is not clear why other investors do not step in and take advantage of these quirks in institutional behavior.

---

[24]Institutional buying drops off in the last 10 days of the calendar year, and picks up again in the first 10 days of the next calendar year.

The Summer Swoon   If you take a closer look at Figure 7.9, where we look at return by month of the year, note that there is a pronounced swoon in returns in the later months of the year, especially in September and October. The returns from May 1 to October 30 (summer months) are lower than the returns from November 1 to April 30 (winter months). An investor who invested $1,000 in the S&P 500 but left it in the index only in the winter months would have seen the portfolio grow to almost $39,000 by the end of 2006. In contrast, an investor who invested $1,000 in the S&P 500 but left it in the index only for the summer months would have only $916 by the end of 2006; that investor would have lost money over the period.

The late summer swoon is not restricted to U.S. stocks. A study of 37 foreign equity markets found that the returns in the winter months were higher than the returns in summer months in 36 of the markets, with returns in the summer months averaging less than half the return in winter months. In many of these markets, just as with the January effect, the summer swoon has interactions with other pricing effects and is more pronounced for small market cap companies than for large market cap ones.

The Weekend Effect   Are stock returns consistently higher on some days of the week than others? A surprising feature of stock returns is the existence of what is called the weekend effect, another return phenomenon that has persisted over extraordinarily long periods and over a number of international markets. It refers to the differences in returns between Mondays and other days of the week. The significance of the return difference is brought out in Figure 7.12, which graphs returns by days of the week from 1927 to 2001.

The returns on Mondays are, on average, negative, whereas the returns on every day of the week are not. In addition, returns on Mondays are negative more often than returns on any other trading day. There are a number of other findings on the Monday effect that researchers have fleshed out.

- The Monday effect is really a weekend effect since the bulk of the negative returns are manifested in the Friday close to Monday open returns. In other words, the negative returns on Monday are generated by the fact that stocks tend to open lower on Mondays rather than by what happens during the day. The returns from intraday returns on Monday (the price changes from open to close on Monday) are not the culprits in creating the negative returns.
- The Monday effect is worse for small stocks than for larger stocks. This mirrors our findings on the January effect.

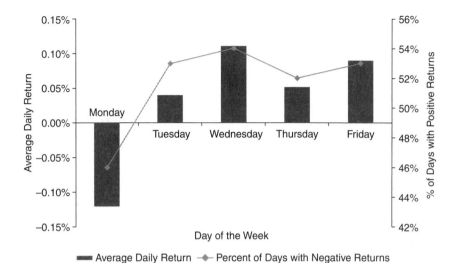

FIGURE 7.12 Returns by Day of the Week, 1927 to 2001
Source: Raw data from the Center for Research in Security Prices (CRSP).

- The Monday effect is no worse following three-day weekends than two-day weekends.
- Monday returns are more likely to be negative if the returns on the previous Friday were negative. In fact, Monday returns are, on average, positive following positive Friday returns, and are negative 80 percent of the time following negative Friday returns.[25]

The weekend effect is strong in the rest of the world as well as the United States, with the returns on Monday lower than returns on other days of the week for every international market examined.

Since many of these studies are at least a decade old, it is worth asking whether the weekday effect persists. Looking at just the daily returns on the S&P 500 from 1981 and 2010 and breaking down the weekday returns by day of the week, we estimated the weekday effect for five-year subperiods in Figure 7.13. Note that to make the comparisons across the periods, we netted out the average daily return over each subperiod from the daily average returns by weekday; thus, the returns on Mondays were, on average, 0.13 percent lower than the average daily returns in the 1981 to 1985 subperiod.

---

[25]A. Abraham and D. L. Ikenberry, "The Individual Investor and the Weekend Effect," *Journal of Financial and Quantitative Analysis* 29 (1994): 263–277.

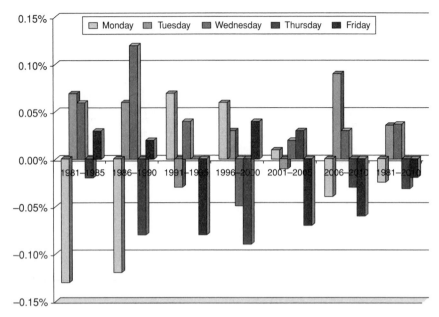

FIGURE 7.13 Returns by Weekday: S&P 500 from 1981 to 2010
Source: Standard & Poor's.

Interestingly, the weekend effect has been muted for much of the past two decades. In fact, Thursdays and Fridays deliver roughly comparable returns to Mondays over the entire period. One hypothesis that we would offer for the dissipation of the weekday effect is that global listings and virtual trading platforms have allowed trading to become almost round-the-clock. The notion that trading on a stock or an index comes to a complete stop from Friday close to Monday open is almost quaint in today's marketplace.

Volume Patterns

Though the random walk hypothesis is silent about the relationship between trading volume and prices, it does assume that all available information is incorporated in the current price. Since trading volume is part of publicly available information, there should therefore be no information value to knowing how many shares were traded yesterday or the day before.

As with prices, there is evidence that trading volume carries information about future stock price changes. Datar, Naik, and Radcliffe show that low-volume stocks earn higher returns than high-volume stocks, though they

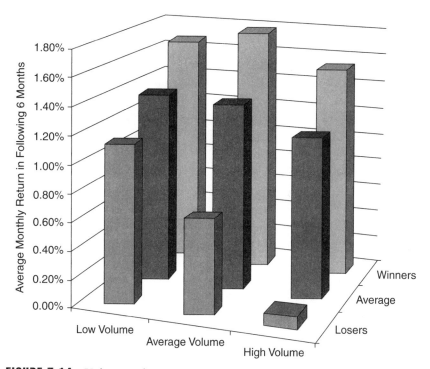

FIGURE 7.14   Volume and Price Interaction: NYSE and AMEX Stocks, 1965 to 1995
Source: C. M. C. Lee and B. Swaminathan, "Price Momentum and Trading Volume," *Journal of Finance* 5 (2000): 2016–2069.

attribute the differential return to a liquidity premium on the former.[26] A more surprising result comes from Lee and Swaminathan, who look at the interrelationship between price and trading volume.[27] In particular, they examine the price momentum effect that was documented by Jegadeesh and Titman—that stocks that go up are more likely to keep going up and stocks that go down are more likely to keep dropping in the months after—and show that it is much more pronounced for high-volume stocks. Figure 7.14 classifies stocks based on how well or badly they have done in the past six months (winners, average stocks, and losers) and their trading volume (low,

---

[26]V. Datar, N. Naik, and R. Radcliffe, "Liquidity and Asset Returns: An Alternative Test," *Journal of Financial Markets* 1 (1998): 205–219.
[27]C. M. C. Lee and B. Swaminathan, "Price Momentum and Trading Volume," *Journal of Finance* 5 (2000): 2016–2069.

average, and high) and looks at returns on these stocks in the following six months.

Note that the price momentum effect is strongest for stocks with high trading volume. In other words, a price increase or decrease that is accompanied by strong volume is more likely to continue into the next period. Stickel and Verecchia confirm this result with shorter-period returns; they conclude that increases in stock prices that are accompanied by high trading volume are more likely to carry over into the next trading day.[28]

In summary, the level of trading volume in a stock, changes in volume, and volume accompanied by price changes all seem to provide information that investors can use to pick stocks. It is not surprising that trading volume is an integral part of technical analysis.

DATA MINING OR ANOMALIES

When looking at the evidence on seasonal and temporal anomalies in stock price data, we are faced with an interesting dilemma. As stock price data has become both richer (we have gone from annual to intraday data and from just equity markets to bond and derivatives markets) and easier to access and use, it is not surprising that the number of inefficiencies and anomalies discovered has also increased. You could argue that some of these findings can be attributed to the sheer volume of data that is available to us. As hundreds of researchers pore over this data, using finer and finer microscopes, they will find patterns depending on the portion of the data that they are looking at.

In a spirited defense of efficient markets, Fama presents the argument that almost all of the anomalies and inefficiencies that researchers have detected over the past 40 years can be attributed purely to chance, rather than irrational or inefficient investors. In fact, he makes the interesting point that those researchers who claim to find inefficiencies cannot seem to agree on whether the inefficiencies indicate a market that overreacts or one that underreacts to new information.[29]

---

[28]S. Stickel and R. Verecchia, "Evidence That Trading Volume Sustains Stock Price Changes," *Financial Analysts Journal* (November–December 1994): 57–67.
[29]E. F. Fama, "Market Efficiency, Long-Term Returns, and Behavioral Finance," *Journal of Financial Economics* 49 (September 1998): 283–306.

THE FOUNDATIONS OF TECHNICAL ANALYSIS

It is best to let technical analysts provide the basis for their approach in their own words. Edwards and Magee, in their classic book on technical analysis, made the following argument:

> *It is futile to assign an intrinsic value to a stock certificate. One share of U.S. Steel, for example, was worth $261 in the early fall of 1929, but you could buy it for only $22 in June 1932. By March 1937 it was selling for $126 and just one year later for $38.... This sort of thing, this wide divergence between presumed value and intrinsic value, is not the exception; it is the rule; it is going on all the time. The fact is that the real value of U.S. Steel is determined at any given time solely, definitely and inexorably by supply and demand, which are accurately reflected in the transactions consummated on the floor of the exchange.[30]*

If we were to summarize the assumptions that underlie technical analysis, we would list the following:

- *Market value is determined solely by the interaction of supply and demand.* We do not think that nonchartists would have any quarrels with this assumption, which describes how prices are set in any market.
- *Supply and demand are governed by numerous factors, both rational and irrational.* The market continually and automatically weighs all these factors. Note that a random walker would have no qualms about this assumption, either, but would point out that any irrational factors are just as likely to be on one side of the market as on the other.
- *Disregarding minor fluctuations in the market, stock prices tend to move in trends that persist for an appreciable length of time.* This is where non-chartists would part ways with chartists. In a rational or even a reasonably sensible market, any trend that can be discerned by investors using charts should provide profit opportunities that when taken advantage of should eliminate the trend.
- *Changes in trend are caused by shifts in demand and supply.* These shifts, no matter why they occur, can be detected sooner or later in the action of the market itself. This is at the core of technical analysis.

---

[30]R. Edwards and J. Magee, *Technical Analysis of Stock Trends* (Boca Raton, FL: St. Lucie Press, 2001).

Charts, the believers argue, send advance warning of shifts in demand and supply in the form of price and volume patterns.

The views of technical analysts are best described by another quote from Edwards and Magee:

> *The market price reflects not only the differing fears and guesses and moods, rational and irrational, of hundreds of potential buyers and sellers, but it also reflects their needs and resources—in total, factors which defy analysis and for which no statistics are obtainable. These are nevertheless all synthesized, weighted and finally expressed in the one precise figure at which a buyer and seller get together and make a deal. The resulting price is the only figure that counts.*

Both the anecdotal and the empirical evidence seem to suggest that investors often are irrational, at least based on the economic definition of rationality. Whether this irrationality results in systematic price patterns is a little more difficult to assess, though the serial correlation in prices over both short and long periods and the periodic appearance of price bubbles in asset markets seem to indicate that irrational behavior has price effects. Finally, even if there are systematic price patterns caused by irrationality, there is the question of whether you can take advantage of these price patterns. It is entirely possible that the price patterns are so unpredictable that no investor can take advantage of them to earn excess returns. Technical analysts and chartists would disagree.

TECHNICAL INDICATORS AND CHARTING PATTERNS

Over the years, technical analysts have developed hundreds of technical indicators and detected dozens of chart patterns that they contend help them forecast future price changes. While we cannot describe or even list all of them, we can categorize them based on the nature of irrationality that we attribute to markets. Consolidating all of the irrationalities that have been attributed to financial markets, we have created five groupings:

1. **Market participants overreact to new information.** If this is true (i.e., prices rise too much on good news and fall too much on bad news), you would draw on contrarian indicators that would help you to gauge the direction in which the crowd is going and to go against it.
2. **Market participants are slow learners.** In many ways, this is the polar opposite of the first grouping. If investors are slow learners, prices will

underreact to new information and you would expect price direction to persist; you would therefore use momentum strategies, which would gauge market direction and move with it.

3. Investors change their minds frequently and often irrationally, causing significant shifts in demand and supply that cause prices to move. If you believe that this is the way markets work, you would use technical indicators and charting patterns to detect these shifts.

4. There are certain investors who lead markets, and finding out when and what they are buying and selling can provide a useful leading indicator of future price movements. If this is what you believe about markets, you would track the trading of these leading investors and try to follow them.

5. There are external forces that govern up and down movements in markets that override fundamentals and investor preferences. Technical indicators and charting patterns that allow us to see the larger cycles in stock prices can allow us to get ahead of other investors.

Within each group, we can consider different technical indicators that we can broadly categorize into three groups: price indicators, which are based on past price movements; volume indicators, which look at trading volume; and sentiment indicators, which use qualitative measures of how bullish or bearish investors are about stocks.

Markets' Overreaction—Contrarian Indicators

There are many practitioners and some economists, especially in the behavioral school, who believe that investors overreact to new information. This, in turn, can create patterns in stock prices that can be exploited by investors to earn excess returns. In this section, we consider some of the indicators, which we label contrarian, that have been developed by analysts who subscribe to this view.

The Basis for Overreaction and Implications

Why would markets overreact to new information? Some researchers in experimental psychology suggest that people tend to overweight recent information and underweight prior data in revising their beliefs when confronted with new information. Others argue that a few investors tend to panic when confronted with new information, and they take the rest of the market with them. As evidence, you could point to the strong evidence of price reversals over long periods that we presented earlier in this chapter.

If markets overreact, it follows that large price movements in one direction will be followed by large price movements in the opposite direction.

In addition, the more extreme the initial price movement, the greater will be the subsequent adjustment. If markets overreact, the road to investment success seems clear. You buy assets when others are most bearish about them, and sell assets when other investors are most optimistic and buying. If your assumption about market overreaction is correct, you will earn excess returns as markets correct themselves over time.

Technical Trading Rules Based on Contrarian Opinion   There are a number of indicators, some based on price patterns, some based on trading volume, and some based on market views, that are designed to provide you with a sense of market direction. The objective is to not follow the market direction but to go against it, and these are contrarian indicators. We consider three widely used indicators in this section, each of which is focused on a different subset of investors.

Trades that are in lots of less than 100 are called odd lots and are usually made by small investors. There are data services that track the number of *odd-lot trades*—both buys and sells—in individual stocks and in the market. As small investors become more enthusiastic about a stock, odd-lot buys increase relative to sells. When they become pessimistic, the reverse occurs. To the extent that you view small investors as more likely to overreact to information, you would sell as odd lot buying increases and buy as odd lot selling decrease.

But what if you believe that it is institutional investors who panic and not small investors? After all, large price movements are usually caused by *institutional buying and selling*, rather than by individual traders. There are indicators that track the stocks that institutions are selling and buying, with the objective of doing the opposite. There are also indicators that track the percentage of mutual fund portfolios that are invested in cash and near-cash investments, a good indicator of how bullish or bearish mutual fund investors are. When mutual funds are optimistic about the market, cash holdings tend to fall, whereas cash holdings increase as they become more pessimistic. If you believe that mutual fund managers overreact, you would buy when they are bearish and sell when they are bullish.

Finally, you could look at investment advisers who claim to have divined the future. *Investment advisory services* often have their lists of most desirable and least desirable stocks. Value Line and Standard & Poor's categorize stocks into classes based on their perceived attractiveness as investments. In keeping with the notion that the market is usually wrong, you would sell those stocks that investment advisers are most bullish on and buy those stocks they are most bearish on.

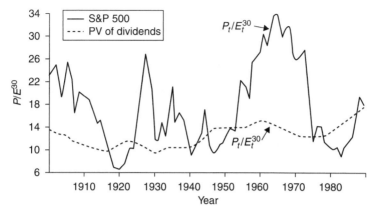

FIGURE 7.15 Are Markets Too Volatile?
Source: R. Shiller, *Market Volatility* (Cambridge, MA: MIT Press, 1990).

Shifting Demand

Technical analysts often argue that the greatest profits are to be made at what can be called inflection points—a fancy term for shifts in price trends from positive to negative or vice versa. Since price is ultimately determined by demand and supply, analysts often look for leading indicators of shifts in demand, especially when those shifts are caused my emotion rather than fundamentals. If they succeed, they will make money.

The Basis for Shifting Demand and Implications   The basis for the shifting demand argument is that demand shifts cause price changes and that these demand shifts often have no basis in economic fundamentals. The anecdotal evidence seems to bear out this view. Markets often move for no discernible reason, and the volatility in stock prices seems to vastly exceed the volatility in underlying value. The empirical evidence also backs up the view that prices are more volatile than fundamental value. Shiller compared stock price movements over time to movements in the present value of dividends (which he viewed as a measure of fundamental value) and concluded that stock prices were significantly more volatile (see Figure 7.15).[31]

Note that the smoothed-out line is the present value (PV) of dividends, whereas the volatile line represents the S&P 500.

It should be noted, though, that neither the anecdotal evidence nor Shiller's study conclusively proves that stock price is too volatile. In fact,

---

[31] R. Shiller, *Market Volatility* (Cambridge, MA: MIT Press, 1990).

some researchers have argued that if the value of a stock is based on expectations, small news announcements can cause big shifts in expectations and stock prices.

Technical Trading Rules Aimed at Detecting Shifting Demand There are numerous pricing patterns and indicators that chartists claim provide advance warning of shifting demand. We will consider four broad measures here. The first relates to the entire market, and measures the breadth of the market by looking at the *number of stocks that advance relative to those that decline*. The argument here is that a market that goes up with limited breadth (a few stocks are creating much of the upward momentum, while the rest are flat or declining) is a market where demand (and prices) is likely to decline soon. In fact, an extension of this measure is the *advance/decline line*, which is reported in many financial newspapers, where you graph the ratio of the number of stocks that have gone up to the number of stocks that have dropped. Here again, analysts argue that a divergence between index levels and the advance/decline line—a drop in the index accompanied by an improvement in the advance/decline line—may indicate an upcoming shift toward buying.

The second is the presence (at least perceived presence) of *support and resistance lines* in prices. A resistance line is an upper bound on the price whereas a support line represents a lower bound on the price. Both are extracted by looking at past prices. Thus, a stock that has tended to move between $20 and $40 over the last few periods has a support line at $20 and a resistance line at $40. It may be pure coincidence (though we think not), but support and resistance lines often are nice round numbers—you very seldom see a resistance line at $39.88 and a support line at $21.13. Figure 7.16 provides a chart with support and resistance lines.

The fact that the stock stays below the resistance line and above the support line is not news, but a stock that breaks through either gets attention. When a stock breaks through the resistance line, technical analysts view it as a sign of a shift in demand upward and the beginning of a sustained upward movement in prices. Conversely, when a stock falls below the support line, analysts view it as a breakdown in demand and the precursor of a further decline in prices. While the notion of arbitrary support and resistance lines strikes us as fanciful, if enough investors buy into their existence, there can be a self-fulfilling prophecy. To see why, assume that a stock with a resistance line of $40 sees its stock price go up to $40.50. Investors who believe that this is a beginning of a surge in prices will all try to buy the stock on the event, causing the stock price to continue going up. Whether such a price increase can be sustained for more than a few days is an open question. In the graph in Figure 7.16, you can also see another widely followed chart

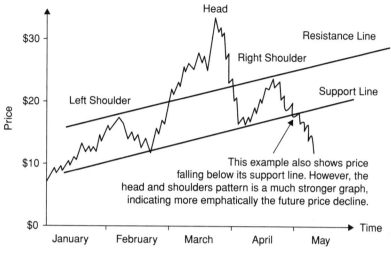

FIGURE 7.16   Support and Resistance Lines

pattern, called head and shoulders. In fact, there are hundreds of patterns that chartists have uncovered over time that they have offered as leading indicators of price changes.[32]

Central to much of technical analysis is a reverence for *moving averages* (i.e., averages of stock prices over the past few months or weeks). Often, you will see price charts with a moving average line superimposed on actual prices. Again, analysts view any deviation of stock prices from a moving average line as an indication of an underlying shift in demand that can be exploited for profits. As with many technical indicators, there are numerous variants that have developed around the concept of the simple moving average, where the average is computed over a moving time window—for example, time-weighted moving averages, where you weight recent prices more than older observations.

In recent years, information on *trading volume* for individual stocks has become increasingly accessible. Technical analysts now routinely look at trading volume for clues of future price movements, either in conjunction with price changes or by itself. For instance, an increase in the stock price that is accompanied by heavy trading volume is considered a more positive prognosticator of future price increases than one generated on light volume.

---

[32]R. Colby and T. Myers, *The Encyclopedia of Technical Market Indicators* (New York: Dow Jones Irwin/McGraw-Hill, 1988).

Empirical Evidence on Technical Indicators There is not much empirical evidence for or against many of the individual charting patterns. Part of the reason for this is that many of these patterns are so subjectively defined (different analysts use different and often shifting definitions of what comprises a support or a resistance line, for instance) that they cannot be tested empirically, which serves both sides of the argument very well. Supporters of charting can then use their own tests, which are often biased, to offer proof that their patterns work. Opponents of technical analysis can rest secure in their absolute conviction that charting is for the naive and the misguided and not worry about evidence to the contrary.

It is quite ironic that some of the best defenses of technical analysis have been offered by academics, who would not categorize themselves as chartists or technical analysts. Lo, Wang, and Mamaysky present a fairly convincing defense of technical analysis from the perspective of financial economists.[33] They use daily returns of stocks on the New York Stock Exchange and NASDAQ from 1962 and 1996 and employ the most sophisticated computational techniques (rather than human visualization) to look for pricing patterns. They find that the most common patterns in stocks are double tops and bottoms, followed by the widely used head and shoulders pattern. In other words, they find evidence that some of the most common patterns used by technical analysts exist in prices. Lest this be cause for too much celebration among chartists, they also point out that these patterns offer only marginal incremental returns (an academic code word for really small) and offer the caveat that these returns may not survive transaction costs.

ARE CURRENCY MARKETS DIFFERENT?

While there is little empirical evidence to back the use of charts in the stock market, a number of studies claim to find that technical indicators may work in currency markets. To name a few:

- Filter rules, where you buy a currency if it goes up by X percent and sell if it goes down by the same amount earned substantial

---

[33] A.W. Lo, H. Mamaysky, and J. Wang, "Foundations of Technical Analysis: Computational Algorithms, Statistical Inference, and Empirical Implementation," *Journal of Finance* 55 (2000): 1705–1765.

profits in the deutsche mark, yen, and sterling markets between 1973 and 1981.[34]

■ Moving average rules would have generated excess returns in foreign currency markets.[35]

■ Head and shoulders patterns would have generated excess returns in the pound sterling, Canadian dollar, French franc, and Swiss franc markets between 1973 and 1994.[36]

Though there are dissenting voices, there clearly seem to be more opportunities for technical analysis in currency markets. Some attribute it to central bank intervention. When central banks target exchange rates, especially in conflict with the fundamentals, they can generate speculative profits for investors.

Slow Learning Markets: Momentum Indicators

If investors are slow to assess the effects of new information on stock prices, you can see sustained up or down movements in stock prices after news comes out about the stock—up movements after good news and down movements after bad news. There are analysts who contend that this is indeed the case and create trading rules that take advantage of this slow learning process. Since these rules are based on the assumption that trends in prices tend to continue for long periods, they can be categorized as momentum rules.

The Basis for Slow Learning and Implications   What is the evidence that markets learn slowly? The best support for slow learning markets comes from studies that look at information events such as earnings announcements or acquisitions. As we will see later in this book, there is evidence that markets continue to adjust to the information well after it has come out.

---

[34]M. P. Dooley and R. Shafer, "Analysis of Short-Run Exchange Rate Behavior: March 1973 to November 1981," in *Exchange Rate and Trade Instability, Causes, Consequences and Remedies* (Ballinger, 1983).

[35]B. C. Kho, "Time-Varying Risk Premia, Volatility, and Technical Trading Rule Profits," *Journal of Financial Economics* 41 (1996): 246–290.

[36]C. L. Osler and P. H. K. Chang, "Head and Shoulders: Not a Flaky Pattern" (Staff Paper, Federal Reserve Bank of New York, 1995).

For instance, a firm that reports much better than expected earnings will generally see its stock price jump on the announcement and continue to drift upward for the next few days. The same seems to occur to a target firm in an acquisition. While there are alternative explanations for price drifts, one potential explanation is that markets learn slowly and it takes them a while to assimilate the information.

If markets learn slowly, you should expect to see prices move in the same direction after a precipitating action. If the initial news was good—a good earnings report or an earnings upgrade from an analyst—you should expect to see upward price momentum. If the news was bad, you should expect to see the opposite. In fact, recent empirical studies (referenced in the earlier part of this chapter) have found evidence of price momentum in equity markets in the United States at least in the short term.

Technical Indicators to Take Advantage of Slow Learning Markets Momentum investors firmly believe that the trend is your friend and that it is critical that you look past the day-to-day movements in stock prices at the underlying long-term trends. The simplest measure of trend is a *trend line*. Figure 7.17 contains two trend lines—the graph on the left is for Apple Computers from 2008 to 2012 and the graph on the right is for Nokia over the same time period.

NUMBER WATCH

Sectors with highest relative strength: Take a look at the relative strength numbers for U.S. companies, categorized by sector.

In this Apple Computer chart to the left, you see an uptrend line, as the stock moved strongly upwards during the period. On the right, you see Nokia's price follow a downtrend line as the stock prices dropped over the perio. As momentum investors, you would buy stocks that are going up and staying above the uptrend line. If the price falls below the uptrend line, it is viewed as a negative sign. Conversely, if the price rises above a downtrend line, it is considered a bullish sign.

A closely followed momentum measure is called *relative strength*, which is the ratio of the current price to an average over a longer period (say six months or a year). Stocks that score high on relative strength are therefore stocks that have gone up the most over the period, whereas those that score low are stocks that have gone down. The relative strength can be used in

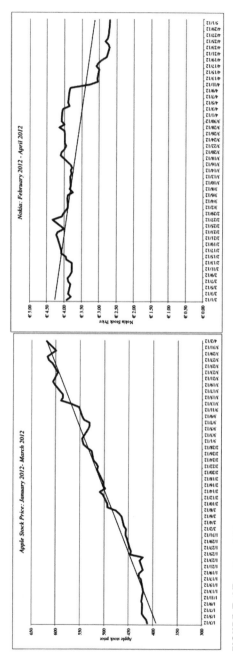

FIGURE 7.17 Trend Lines

absolute terms, where only stocks that have gone up over the period would be considered good investments. Alternatively, the relative strength can be compared across stocks, and you would invest in stocks that show the highest relative strength (i.e., have gone up the most relative to other stocks).

Following the Informed Investors: Leading Indicators   This approach is the flip side of the contrarian approach. Instead of assuming that investors, on average, are likely to be wrong, you assume that they are right. To make this assumption more palatable, you do not look at all investors but only at the investors who presumably know more than the rest of the market.

The Basis for Following Smart Investors and Implications   Are some investors smarter and better informed than others? Undoubtedly. Do they make higher returns as a consequence? Not necessarily. As John Maynard Keynes was fond of pointing out, a stock market is a beauty contest in which the prize goes to the person who best gauges who the other judges in the contest will pick as the winner. In investment terminology, the high returns often go to the investor who can best pick the stocks that other investors will buy.

There are two keys to making a strategy of following other investors work. The first is identifying the smart investors, who may not always be the largest or best known. It stands to reason that investors who have access to the best information are most likely to beat the market and would be the ones you should follow. The second is to find out when and what these smart investors are trading in a timely fashion, so you can imitate them. This is often difficult to do. Even though insiders and institutions have to file with the Securities and Exchange Commission (SEC), providing details about their trades, the filings are made several weeks after the trades occur.

Technical Indicators for Followers   There are several technical indicators that attempt to pinpoint what better-informed investors are buying and selling. Here, we consider two. The first looks at *short sales made by market specialists*. Since these specialists are close to the action and have access to information that the rest of us cannot see (such as the order book and trading on the floor), it can be argued that they should have an inside track on overpriced and underpriced stocks. Thus, a surge in specialist short sales in a stock would be a precursor for bad news on the stock and a big price drop. Some analysts look at all short sales made on a stock, arguing that only larger, more sophisticated investors can short stock in the first place. A study by Senchack and Starks provides some support for this indicator by noting that stock returns tend to me more negative for stocks in which the short interest (short sales as a percent of the outstanding stock) is higher.[37]

In the past few years, the SEC has speeded up the process of recording transactions by insiders and has made this data more easily accessible to the public. You can therefore look up stocks where *insider buying* or *selling* has increased the most. In fact, the ratio of insider buying to selling is often tracked for stocks with the idea that insiders who are buying must have positive information about a stock whereas insiders who are selling are likely to have negative information.

Long-Term Cycles: Mystical Indicators

The final set of technical indicators includes those that are based on long-term cycles in prices that exercise an inexorable hold on how prices move. Since these long-term cycles operate independently of fundamentals, it is very difficult to explain them without resorting to mysticism.

Basis for Long-Term Cycles and Implications   There are two ways in which you can defend the use of long-term cycles. One is to abandon any basis in rationality and argue that there are a number of phenomena in nature that cannot be explained with models.[38] You can think of such investors as subscribers to the karmic theory of investing. In other words, everything that happens has already been predestined and there is nothing that we can do to stop it. This requires an almost religious belief that cycles will replicate themselves. The other defense is based on market behavior. You can argue that investors, even though they might be separated over time, behaved in very much the same way in the South Sea bubble as they did in the dot-com bubble. Consequently, long-term cycles reflect the pricing mistakes that investors make and remake over time. As a cautionary note, you should realize that if you look for patterns too intently in charts, you will find them, especially if you use visual techniques (rather than statistical ones).

Technical Indicators Based on Cycles   There are numerous cycles that analysts see in stock prices, but we will consider only two in this section. In the first, the *Dow Theory*, the market is considered to have three movements, all going at the same time. The first is the narrow movement (daily fluctuations)

---

[37]A. J. Senchack Jr. and L. T. Starks, "Short-Sale Restrictions and Market Reaction to Short-Interest Announcements," *Journal of Financial and Quantitative Analysis* 28, no. 2 (June 1993): 177–194.

[38]Scientists would undoubtedly disagree.

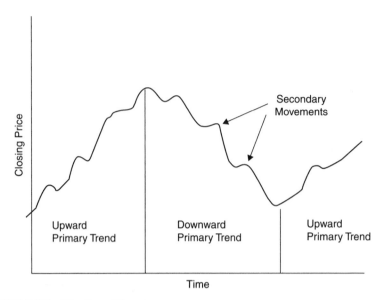

FIGURE 7.18 The Dow Theory

from day to day. The second is the short swing (secondary movements) running from two weeks to a few months; and the third is the main movement (primary trends) covering several years in duration. Proponents of the theory claim that you can tell where you are in the primary cycle by charting the industrial and transportation components of the Dow index and looking for confirmation (i.e., both indexes moving in the same direction). In Figure 7.18, the latter two movements of the Dow Theory are presented.

In 1922, William Hamilton wrote a book titled *The Stock Market Barometer* about the Dow Theory, in which he presented evidence on the measure's efficacy at predicting market movements. A study that appraised Hamilton's predictions in the *Wall Street Journal* between 1901 and 1929 concluded that he had far too many correct calls than could be attributed to chance and that you would have earned excess returns followings his advice.[39]

While the Dow Theory has been around for almost a century, the *Elliott Wave* acquired a wide following in the 1980s. R. N. Elliott's theory was that the market moves in waves of various sizes, from those encompassing only individual trades to those lasting centuries, perhaps longer. In the classic

---

[39]S. J. Brown, W. N. Goetzmann, and A. Kumar, "The Dow Theory: William Peter Hamilton's Track Record Reconsidered" (SSRN Working Paper 58690, 1998).

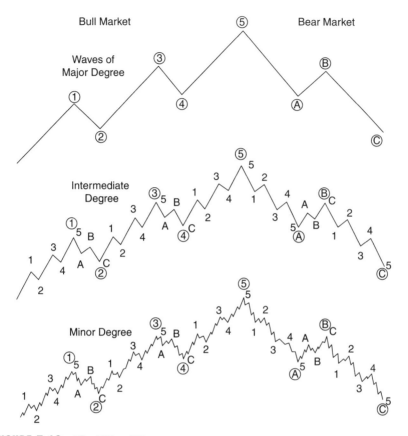

FIGURE 7.19   The Elliott Wave

Elliott wave, a cycle lasts 200 years and has eight wave segments—five up and three down—with smaller cycles within each of these waves. By classifying these waves and counting the various classifications (see Figure 7.19), he argued that it was possible to determine the relative positions of the market at all times.

In the aftermath of the 1987 crash, there were several newsletters based on the Elliott Wave.[40] Most of them faded in the years after, as the predictive power of the model was found to be wanting.

---

[40] A. J. Frost and R. R. Prechter Jr., *The Elliott Wave Principle: Key to Market Behavior* (Gainesville, GA: New Classics Library, 1998). For a critical look, see F. Gehm, "Who Is R. N. Elliott and Why Is He Making Waves?" *Financial Analysts Journal* (January–February 1983): 51–58.

Other cycles include the *Kitchen cycle* (inventories, three to five years); the *Juglar cycle* (fixed investment patterns, 7 to 11 years); and the *Kuznets cycle* (building patterns, 15 to 25 years). A more controversial theory is the *Kondratyev cycle* (also called the long economic cycle, about 54 years) in three stages of upswing, crisis, and depression. The *Babson chart* of business barometers uses statistics and charts to model a 20-year cycle in four stages: overexpansion, decline, depression, and improvement.

Determinants of Success at Charting and Technical Analysis

Can you succeed with technical indicators and charts? The answer that has been long given by academics and fundamentals is no, but that answer may need to be reassessed in light of the research on price patterns (especially price momentum) and trading volume in recent years. There seems to be enough evidence now for us to conclude that it is foolhardy to ignore recent price movements and changes in trading volume when investing in a stock. So what are the essential ingredients for success with technical analysis? These seem to be a few:

- If you decide to use a charting pattern or technical indicator, you need to be aware of the investor behavior that gives rise to its success. This is not just to satisfy your curiosity but also to ensure that you can modify or abandon the indicator if the underlying behavior changes.
- It is important that you back-test your indicator to ensure that it delivers the returns that are promised. In running these tests, you should pay particular attention to the volatility in performance over time and how sensitive the returns are to holding periods. There are some strategies that work only in bull markets, for example, and only for specific holding periods—say one month or less.
- The excess returns on many of the strategies that we described in this chapter seem to depend on timely trading. In other words, to succeed at some of these strategies, you may need to monitor prices continuously, looking for the patterns that would trigger trading.
- Building on the theme of time horizons, success at charting can be very sensitive to how long you hold an investment. Recall, for instance, that momentum indicators seem to work for only a few months and that reversals seem to occur beyond that time period. Finding the optimal holding period and staying disciplined seem to be key to earning the returns that we sometimes see on paper.
- The strategies that come from technical indicators are generally short-term strategies that require frequent and timely trading. With some

strategies, you may need to trade several times during the course of a day or a week. Not surprisingly, these strategies also generate large trading costs that can very quickly eat into any excess returns you may have.

In summary, investors who can track markets continuously and trade cheaply may be able to take advantage of price patterns and volume indicators to earn excess returns, if they can pinpoint the right indicators and stay disciplined. As price and volume data become increasingly available to all investors, though, it is likely that these strategies will be more useful as secondary strategies, used to augment returns on a primary strategy. For instance, growth investors who buy stocks with rising earnings may also consider adding price momentum to the mix of variables that they look at before making their investment choices. Investors who cannot or do not want to track markets continuously are unlikely to earn enough returns on these strategies to cover transaction costs.

CONCLUSION

Investors have always claimed to find patterns in charts that help them make better investment decisions. Skeptics have viewed these claims as fiction and have argued that there is no basis to technical analysis. In recent years, evidence has steadily accumulated that there is information in past price movements and trading volume and that there may be a foundation for some of the claims made by chartists. In particular, stocks that have done well in the recent past seem to be more likely to do well in the near future (price momentum), and trading volume changes seem to lead price changes in some markets.

All technical indicators have their basis in quirks in human behavior. We categorize technical trading indicators based on the type of behavior that may lead to their success. Contrarian indicators such as mutual fund holdings or odd-lot ratios, where you track what investors are buying and selling with the intention of doing the opposite, are grounded in the belief that markets overreact. A number of technical indicators are built on the presumption that investors often change their views collectively, causing shifts in demand and prices, and that patterns in charts—support and resistance lines, price relative to a moving average—can predict these changes. With momentum indicators, such as relative strength and trend lines, you are assuming that markets often learn slowly and that it takes time for prices to adjust to true values. If you believe that there are some traders who trade ahead of the market because they have better analysis tools or information, your indicators will follow these traders (specialist short sales and insider buying/selling, for instance) with the objective of piggybacking on their trades. Finally, if you believe that there are long-term cycles in stock prices, your investment strategy may be driven by the cycle you subscribe to and where you believe you are in the cycle.

If you are a short-term investor with the discipline to stick with a tested indicator, low trading costs, and continuous access to information, you may be able to use technical indicators as the basis for your investment strategy. Even those who do not want to build their entire strategy around price patterns and trading volume may still find them useful to augment returns on their primary strategies.

EXERCISES

Pick a few stocks that you are interested in following or investing in and follow through:

1. For these stocks, look at price charts of
   a. daily prices, to see if there is price momentum in the stock and if so, in which direction.
   b. monthly prices, to see if there is price momentum in the stock and if so, in which direction.
   c. annual prices, to see if there is price momentum in the stock and if so, in which direction.
   With each chart, draw a trend line and compute the relative strength value (Price today/Price in the past).
2. Look at trends in trading volume on your stocks, in the short term (daily, weekly) and the long term.
3. Find out the short interest in your stock and what experts (or at least analysts) think about it as an investment.
4. Find the percent of stock held by institutions and whether they were net buyers or sellers in the most recent periods.

Lessons for Investors

To be a successful technical analyst, you need to:

- *Understand human nature:* Investors are human and display all of the foibles of human nature. Some of them tend to be overconfident and to overreact and move in herds. At the same time, others display too little confidence, learn too slowly, or are born contrarians. What happens in markets represents the tug and the pull between these groups. When you use an indicator, you need to understand the assumption about human behavior that underlies it.

- *Not mistake random price movements for price patterns:* Even when prices move randomly, you can generate charts that look like they have patterns. Even bubbles and crashes, which are used by many analysts as evidence of irrationality, can exist in rational markets.
- *Have a time horizon that matches your indicator:* Some indicators require time horizons of a few hours, others require a few weeks, and some may even stretch to a few months.
- *Be disciplined:* If you decide to use a technical indicator to pick stocks, assuming you have back-tested the indicator, you will need to stay within your specified strategy.

CHAPTER 8

Graham's Disciples: Value Investing

Value investors are bargain hunters, and many investors describe themselves as such. But who is a value investor? In this chapter, we begin by addressing this question, and argue that value investors come in many forms. Some value investors use specific criteria to screen for what they categorize as undervalued stocks and invest in these stocks for the long term. Other value investors believe that bargains are best found in the aftermath of a sell-off, and that the best time to buy a stock is when it is down in price. Still others adopt a more activist approach, where they buy large stakes in companies that look undervalued and mismanaged and push for changes that they believe will unleash this value.

Value investing is backed by academic research and also by anecdotal evidence—the successes of value investors like Benjamin Graham and Warren Buffett are legendary—but it is not for all investors. We will consider what investors need to bring to the table to succeed at value investing.

WHO IS A VALUE INVESTOR?

In 2011, Morningstar, a widely used source of mutual fund information, categorized 2,152 equity mutual funds, out of 8,277 domestic equity funds, as value funds. But how did it make this categorization? It did so based on a simple measure: any fund that invested in stocks with low price-to-book value ratios or low price-earnings (P/E) ratios and high dividend yields, relative to the market, was categorized as a value fund. This is a fairly conventional approach, but we believe that it is too narrow a definition of value investing and misses the essence of value investing.

Another widely used definition of value investors suggests that they are investors interested in buying stocks for less than what they are worth. But that is too broad a definition since you could potentially categorize most active investors as value investors on this basis. After all, growth investors also want to buy stocks for less than what they are worth.

So what is the essence of value investing? To understand value investing, we have to begin with the proposition that the value of a firm is derived from two sources: investments that the firm has already made (assets in place) and expected future investments (growth opportunities). What sets value investors apart is their desire to buy firms for less than what their assets in place are worth. Consequently, value investors tend to be leery of large premiums paid by markets for growth opportunities and try to find their best bargains in more mature companies that are out of favor.

Even with this definition of value investing, there are three distinct strands that we see in value investing. The first and perhaps simplest form of value investing is passive screening, where companies are put through a number of investment screens—low P/E ratios, assets that are easily marketable, low risk, and so forth—and those that pass the screens are categorized as good investments. In its second form, you have contrarian value investing, where you buy assets that are viewed as untouchable by other investors because of poor past performance or bad news about them. In its third form, you become an activist value investor, who buys equity in undervalued or poorly managed companies but then uses the power of your position (which has to be a significant one) to push for change that will unlock this value.

THE PASSIVE SCREENER

There are many investors who believe that stocks with specific characteristics, some quantitative (say low-P/E ratios) and some qualitative (such as good management), outperform other stocks, and that the key to investment success is to identify what these characteristics are. Benjamin Graham, in his classic book on security analysis (with David Dodd), converted these factors into screens that could be used to find promising investments.[1] In recent years, as data has become more easily accessible and computing power has

---

[1] B. Graham and D. Dodd, *Security Analysis* (New York: McGraw-Hill, 1934).

expanded, these screens have been refined and extended, and variations are used by many portfolio managers and investors to pick stocks.

Ben Graham: The Father of Screening

Many value investors claim to trace their antecedents to Ben Graham and to use the book *Security Analysis* that he coauthored with David Dodd in 1934 as their investment bible. But who was Ben Graham, and what were his views on investing? Did he invent screening, and do his screens still work?

Graham's Screens Ben Graham started his business life as a financial analyst and later was part of an investment partnership on Wall Street. He was successful on both counts, but his reputation was made in the classroom. He taught at Columbia University and the New York Institute of Finance for more than three decades, and during that period developed a loyal following among his students. In fact, much of his fame comes from the success enjoyed by his students in the market.

It was in the first edition of *Security Analysis* that Ben Graham put his mind to converting his views on markets to specific screens that could be used to find undervalued stocks. While the numbers in the screens did change slightly from edition to edition, they preserved their original form and are summarized here:

1. Earnings-to-price ratio that is double the AAA bond yield.
2. P/E of the stock has to be less than 40 percent of the average P/E for all stocks over the past five years.
3. Dividend yield > two-thirds of the AAA corporate bond yield.
4. Price < two-thirds of tangible book value.[2]
5. Price < two-thirds of net current asset value (NCAV), where net current asset value is defined as liquid current assets including cash minus current liabilities.
6. Debt-equity ratio (book value) has to be less than 1.
7. Current assets > twice current liabilities.
8. Debt < twice net current assets.
9. Historical growth in earnings per share (EPS) over the past 10 years > 7 percent.

---

[2]Tangible book value is computed by subtracting the value of intangible assets such as goodwill from the total book value.

10. No more than two years of declining earnings over the previous 10 years.

Any stock that passes all 10 screens, Graham argued, would make a worthwhile investment. It is worth noting that while there have been a number of screens that have been developed by practitioners since these first appeared, many of them are derived from or are subsets of these original screens.

The Performance How well do Ben Graham's screens work when it comes picking stocks? Henry Oppenheimer: studied the portfolios obtained from these screens from 1974 to 1981 and concluded that you could have made an annual return well in excess of the market.[3] As we will see later in this section, academics have tested individual screens—low P/E ratios and high dividend yields, to name two—in recent years and have found that they indeed yield portfolios that deliver higher returns. Mark Hulbert, who evaluates the performance of investment newsletters, found that newsletters that sought to follow Graham did much better than other newsletters.

The only jarring note is that an attempt to convert the screens into a mutual fund that would deliver high returns did fail. In the 1970s, an investor name James Rea was convinced enough of the value of these screens that he founded a fund called the Rea-Graham fund, which would invest in stocks based on the Graham screens. Though it had some initial successes, the fund floundered during the 1980s and early 1990s and was ranked in the bottom quartile for performance.

The best support for Graham's views on value investing doesn't come from academic studies or the Rea-Graham fund but from the success of many of his students at Columbia. Though they chose diverse paths, many of them ended up managing money and posting records of extraordinary

---

[3]H. R. Oppenheimer, "A Test of Ben Graham's Stock Selection Criteria," *Financial Analysts Journal* 40 (1984): 68–74.

success. In the section that follows, we look at the most famous of his students—Warren Buffett.

GRAHAM'S MAXIMS ON INVESTING

Janet Lowe, in her biography of Ben Graham, notes that while his lectures were based on practical examples, he had a series of maxims that he emphasized on investing.[4] Since these maxims can be viewed as the equivalent of the first commandments of value investing, they are worth revisiting.

1. Be an investor, not a speculator. Graham believed that investors bought companies for the long term, but speculators looked for short-term profits.
2. Know the asking price. Even the best company can be a poor investment at the wrong (too high) price.
3. Rake the market for bargains. Markets make mistakes.
4. Stay disciplined and buy the formula:

$$E(2g + 8.5) * T\text{-bond rate}/Y$$

where E is earnings per share, g is expected growth rate in earnings, Y is the yield on AAA-rated corporate bonds, and 8.5 is the appropriate multiple for a firm with no growth. For example, consider a stock with $2 in earnings in 2012 and 10 percent growth rate, when the Treasury bond rate was 2 percent and the AAA bond rate was 3 percent. The formula would have yielded the following price:

$$\text{Price} = \$2.00[2(10) + 8.5] * (2/3) = \$38.00$$

If the stock traded at less than this price, you would buy the stock.
5. Regard corporate figures with suspicion, advice that carries resonance in the aftermath of recent accounting scandals.
6. Diversify. Don't bet it all on one or a few stocks.
7. When in doubt, stick to quality.

(continued)

---

[4]J. C. Lowe, *Benjamin Graham on Value Investing: Lessons from the Dean of Wall Street* (Chicago: Dearborn Financial, 1994).

8. Defend your shareholder's rights. This was another issue on which Graham was ahead of his time. He was one of the first advocates of corporate governance.
9. Be patient. This follows directly from the first maxim.

It was Ben Graham who created the figure of Mr. Market that was later much referenced by Warren Buffett. As described by Graham, Mr. Market was a manic-depressive who does not mind being ignored, and is there to serve and not to lead you. Investors, he argued, could take advantage of Mr. Market's volatile disposition to make money.

Warren Buffett: Sage from Omaha

No investor is more lionized or more relentlessly followed than Warren Buffett. The reason for the fascination is not difficult to fathom. He has risen to become one of the wealthiest men in the world with his investment acumen, and the pithy comments on the markets that he makes at stock-holder meetings and in annual reports for his companies are widely read. In this section, we consider briefly Buffett's rise to the top of the investment world, and examine how he got there.

Buffett's History How does one become an investment legend? Warren Buffett started a partnership with seven limited partners in 1956, when he was 25, with $105,000 in funds. He generated a 29 percent return over the next 13 years, developing his own brand of value investing during the period. One of his most successful investments during the period was an investment in American Express after the company's stock price tumbled in the early 1960s. Buffett justified the investment by pointing out that the stock was trading at far less than what American Express had generated in cash flows for a couple of years. By 1965, the partnership was at $26 million and was widely viewed as successful.

The event that made Buffett's reputation was his disbanding of the partnership in 1969 because he could not find any stocks to buy with his value investing approach. At the time of the disbanding, he said:[5]

On one point, I am clear. I will not abandon a previous approach whose logic I understand, although I might find it difficult to apply, even though it may mean forgoing large and apparently easy profits

---

[5]Buffett Partnership letter, May 29, 1969.

> *to embrace an approach which I don't fully understand, have not practiced successfully and which possibly could lead to substantial permanent loss of capital.*

The fact that a money manager would actually put his investment philosophy above short-term profits, and the drop in stock prices in the years following this action, played a large role in creating the Buffett legend.

Buffett then put his share of partnership (about $25 million) into Berkshire Hathaway, a textile company whose best days seemed to be in the past. He used Berkshire Hathaway as a vehicle to acquire companies (GEICO in the insurance business and noninsurance companies such as See's Candies, Blue Chip Stamps, and the *Buffalo News*) and to make investments in other companies (American Express, the *Washington Post*, Coca-Cola, Disney). His golden touch seemed to carry over, and Figure 8.1 captures Berkshire Hathaway's success over the past few decades.

An investment of $100 in Berkshire Hathaway in December 1988 would have grown to $2,500 by the end of 2010, five times more than what you would have made investing in the S&P 500.

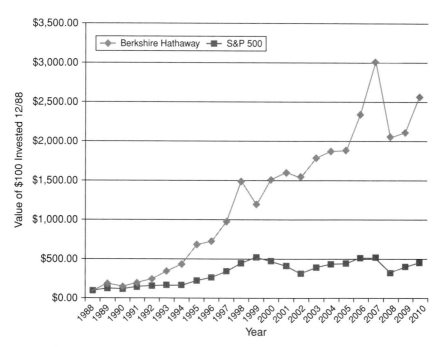

FIGURE 8.1   Value of $100 Invested in 1988: Berkshire Hathaway versus S&P 500
Source: Raw data from Bloomberg.

As CEO of the company, Buffett broke with the established practices of other firms in many ways. He refused to fund the purchase of expensive corporate jets and chose to keep the company in spartan offices in Omaha, Nebraska. He also refused to split the stock as the price went ever higher to the point that relatively few individual investors could afford to buy a round lot in the company. On December 31, 2010, a share of Berkshire Hathaway stock was trading at over $120,000, making it by far the highest-priced listed stock in the United States. He insisted on releasing annual reports that were transparent and included his views on investing and the market, stated in terms that could be understood by all investors.

BUFFETT'S TENETS

Roger Lowenstein, in his excellent book on Buffett, suggests that his success can be traced to his adherence to the basic notion that when you buy a stock, you are buying an underlying business, and to the following tenets:[6]

Business Tenets

- The business the company is in should be simple and understandable. In fact, one of the few critiques of Buffett was his refusal to buy technology companies, whose business he said was difficult to understand.
- The firm should have a consistent operating history, manifested in operating earnings that are stable and predictable.
- The firm should be in a business with favorable long-term prospects.

Management Tenets

- The managers of the company should be candid. As evidenced by the way he treated his own stockholders, Buffett put a premium on managers he trusted. Part of the reason he made an investment in the *Washington Post* was the high regard that he had for Katherine Graham, who inherited the paper from her husband, Phil Graham.

---

[6]R. Lowenstein, *Buffett: The Making of an American Capitalist* (New York: Doubleday, 1996).

- The managers of the company should be leaders and not followers. In practical terms, Buffett was looking for companies that mapped out their own long-term strategies rather than imitating other firms.

Financial Tenets

- The company should have a high return on equity, but rather than base the return on equity on accounting net income, Buffett used a modified version of what he called owners' earnings:

Owners' earnings = Net income + Depreciation and amortization
$$- \text{ Maintenance capital expenditures}$$

Harking back to Chapter 4, where we looked at valuation, note that this is very close to a free cash flow to equity.

- The company should have high and stable profit margins and a history of creating value for its stockholders.

Market Tenets

- In determining value, much has been made of Buffett's use of a risk-free rate to discount cash flows. Since he is known to use conservative estimates of earnings and since the firms he invests in tend to be stable firms, it looks to us like he makes his risk adjustment in the cash flows rather than the discount rate.[7]
- In keeping with Buffett's views of Mr. Market as capricious and moody, even valuable companies can be bought at attractive prices when investors turn away from them.

Assessing Buffett It may be presumptuous to assess an investor who has acquired mythic status, but is Warren Buffett the greatest investor ever? If so, what accounts for his success, and can it be replicated? His reputation

---

[7]In traditional capital budgeting, this approach is called the certainty equivalent approach, where each expected cash flow is replaced with a lower cash flow, representing its certainty equivalent.

as a great investor is well deserved, and his extended run of success cannot be attributed to luck. He has had his bad years, but he has always bounced back in subsequent years. The secret to his success seems to rest on the long view he brings to companies and his discipline—the unwillingness to change investment philosophies even in the midst of short-term failure.

Much has been made about the fact that Buffett was a student of Ben Graham at Columbia University, and their adherence to value investing. Warren Buffett's investment strategy is more complex than Graham's original passive screening approach. Unlike Graham, whose investment strategy was inherently conservative, Buffett's strategy seems to extend across a far more diverse range of companies, from high-growth firms like Coca-Cola to staid firms such as Blue Chip Stamps. While they both may use screens to find stocks, the key difference, as we see it, between the two men is that Graham strictly adhered to quantitative screens whereas Buffett has been more willing to consider qualitative screens. For instance, he has always put a significant weight on both the credibility and the competence of top managers when investing in a company.

In more recent years, he has had to struggle with two by-products of his success and a third one that has its roots in recent market crises.

1. His record of picking winners has attracted publicity and a crowd of imitators who follow his every move, buying everything be buys and making it difficult for him to accumulate large positions at attractive prices.

2. At the same time the larger funds at his disposal imply that he is investing far more than he did two or three decades ago in each of the companies that he takes a position in, creating a larger price impact (and lower profits).

3. The crises that have beset markets over the past few years have been both a threat and an opportunity for Buffett. As markets have staggered through the crises, the biggest factors driving stock prices and investment success have become macroeconomic unknowns (sovereign risk, interest rate volatility, and commodity prices) and not the company-specific factors that Buffett has historically viewed as his competitive edge (assessing a company's profitability and cash flows). At the same time, Buffett has lent both his credibility and liquidity to companies that have been perceived to be in trouble (American Express, Goldman Sachs) and earned substantial profits on his investments.

In the past two years, facing the one enemy that he cannot beat, his mortality, Buffett has sought out successors who would manage Berkshire

Hathaway when he is not there. Needless to say, they will have big shoes to fill.

Be like Buffett?   Warren Buffett's approach to investing has been examined in detail and it is not a complicated one. Given his track record, you would expect a large number of imitators. Why, then, do we not see other investors using his approach replicate his success? There are four reasons:

1. Markets have changed since Buffett started his first partnership. His greatest successes did occur in the 1960s and the 1970s, when relatively few investors had access to information about the market and institutional money management was not dominant. We think that Buffett would have difficulty replicating his success if he were starting anew in today's market, where information on companies and trading is widely available and dozens of money managers claim to be looking for bargains in value stocks.
2. In recent years, Buffett has adopted a more activist investment style (albeit with a soft touch) and has succeeded with it. To succeed with this style as an investor, though, you would need substantial resources and have the credibility that comes with investment success. There are few investors, even among successful money managers, who can claim this combination.
3. As noted in the preceding section, Buffett's style was honed during a period where macroeconomic risks were mild (at least for mature markets like the United States) and investors could focus just on the quality of a company when deciding whether to make an investment. If the shift toward macroeconomic risk is a permanent one, adopting a Buffett strategy of buying good companies at low prices and holding for the long term may not deliver the results it used to.
4. The final ingredient of Buffett's success has been patience. As he has pointed out, he does not buy stocks for the short term but businesses for the long term. He has often been willing to hold stocks that he believes to be undervalued through disappointing years. In those same years, he has faced no pressure from impatient investors, since stockholders in Berkshire Hathaway have such high regard for him. Many money managers who claim to have the same long time horizon that Buffett has come under pressure from investors wanting quick results.

In short, it is easy to see what Warren Buffett did right over the past half century but it will be very difficult for an investor to replicate that success. In the sections that follow, we will examine both the original value investing approach that brought him success in the early part of his investing life and the more activist value investing that has brought him success in recent years.

Value Screens

The Graham approach to value investing is a screening approach, where investors adhere to strict screens (like the ones described earlier in the chapter) and pick stocks that pass those screens. Since the data needed to screen stocks are widely available today, the key to success with this strategy seems to be picking the right screens. In this section, we consider a number of screens used to pick value stocks and the efficacy of these screens.

Book Value Multiples The book value of equity measures what accountants consider to be the value of equity in a company. The market value of equity is what investors attach as a value to the same equity. Investors have used the relationship between price and book value in a number of investment strategies, ranging from the simple to the sophisticated. In this section, we begin by looking at a number of these strategies and the empirical evidence on their success.

Buy Low Price-to-Book Value Companies Some investors argue that stocks that trade at low price-to-book value ratios are undervalued, and there are several studies that seem to back this strategy. Rosenberg, Reid, and Lanstein looked at stock returns in the United States between 1973 and 1984 found that the strategy of picking stocks with high book-to-price ratios (low price-book values) would have yielded an excess return of about 4.5 percent a year.[8] In another study of stock returns between 1963 and 1990, firms were classified on the basis of book-to-price ratios into 12 portfolios, and firms in the lowest book-to-price (highest PBV) class earned an average annual return of 3.7 percent a year, while firms in the highest book-to-price (lowest PBV) class earned an average annual return of 24.31 percent for the 1963 to 1990 period.[9] We updated these studies to consider how well a strategy of buying low price-to-book value stocks would have done in the past two decades and compared these returns to returns in earlier time periods. The results are summarized in Figure 8.2.

---

[8] B. Rosenberg, K. Reid, and R. Lanstein, "Persuasive Evidence of Market Inefficiency," *Journal of Portfolio Management* 11 (1985): 9–17.

[9] E. F. Fama and K. R. French, "The Cross-Section of Expected Returns," *Journal of Finance* 47 (1992): 427–466. They found that the price-to-book ratio explained more of the variation across stock returns than any other fundamental variable, including market capitalization.

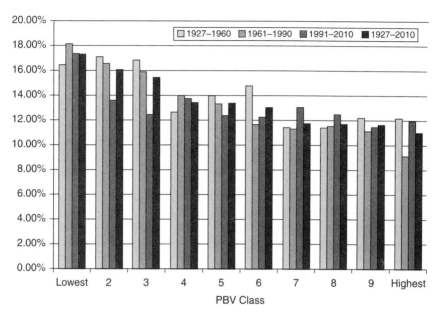

FIGURE 8.2 PBV Classes and Returns, 1927 to 2010
Source: Raw data from Ken French's Data Library (Dartmouth College).

The lowest price-to-book value stocks earned 6.24 percent more, on an annualized basis, than the high price-to-book stocks across the entire time period (1927–2010); they continued to earn higher annual returns (5.44 percent) than the high price-to-book value stocks between 1991 and 2010.

These findings are not unique to the United States. A study found that the book-to-market ratio had a strong role in explaining the cross-section of average returns on Japanese stocks.[10] Another study extended the analysis of price-book value ratios across other international markets, and found that stocks with low price-book value ratios earned excess returns in every market that was analyzed, between 1981 and 1992.[11] In their annual update of historical returns on equity markets, Dimson, Marsh, and Staunton report on the returns earned by low price-to-book value stocks in 20 different markets, relative to the market, and find that low price-to-book stocks have

---

[10]L. K. Chan, Y. Hamao, and J. Lakonishok, "Fundamentals and Stock Returns in Japan," *Journal of Finance* 46 (1991): 1739–1789. They concluded that low price-to-book value stocks in Japan earned a considerable premium over high price-to-book value stocks.

[11]C. Capaul, I. Rowley, and W. F. Sharpe, "International Value and Growth Stock Returns," *Financial Analysts Journal* 49 (1993): 27–36.

earned a premium in 16 of 20 markets between 1975 and 2010, with the magnitude of the premium exceeding 4 percent in seven of these markets.[12]

Thus, a strategy of buying low price-to-book value stocks seems to hold out much promise. Why don't more investors use it, then? you might ask. We will consider some of the possible problems with this strategy in the next section and screens that can be added on to reduce these problems.

What Can Go Wrong?   Stocks with low price-to-book value ratios earn excess returns relative to high price-to-book stocks if we use conventional measures of risk and return, such as betas. But, as noted in earlier chapters, these conventional measures of risk are imperfect and incomplete. Low price-book value ratios may operate as a measure of risk, since firms that trade well below book value are more likely to be in financial trouble and go out of business. Investors therefore have to evaluate whether the additional returns made by such firms justify the additional risk taken on by investing in them.

NUMBER WATCH

Price-to-book ratios by sector: Take a look at the average price-to-book ratios, by sector, for U.S. companies.

The other limitation of a strategy of buying low price-to-book value stocks is that the low book value multiples may be well deserved if companies earn and are expected to continue earning low returns on equity. In fact, we considered the relationship between price-to-book value ratios and returns on equity in Chapter 5. For a stable-growth firm, for instance, the price-to-book value ratio can be written as follows:

$$\text{Price/book} = \frac{(\text{Return on equity} - \text{Expected growth rate})}{(\text{Return on equity} - \text{Cost of equity})}$$

Stocks with low returns on equity should trade at low price-to-book value ratios. In fact, a firm that is expected to earn a return on equity that is less than its cost of equity in the long term should trade at a discount on book value. In summary, then, as an investor you would want stocks with

---

[12]E. Dimson, P. Marsh, and M. Staunton, *Credit Suisse Global Investment Return Sourcebook 2011* (London: London Business School, 2011).

low price-to-book ratios that also have reasonable (if not high) returns on equity and limited exposure to risk.

If low price-to-book value ratios may yield riskier stocks than average or stocks that have lower returns on equity, a more discerning strategy would require us to find mismatches—stocks with low price-to-book ratios, low default risk, and high returns on equity. If we used debt ratios as a proxy for default risk and the accounting return on equity in the past year as the proxy for the returns that will be earned on equity in the future, we would expect companies with low price-to-book value ratios, low debt ratios, and high return on equity to be undervalued.

Market Value to Replacement Cost—Tobin's Q Tobin's Q provides an alternative to the price-to-book value ratio, by relating the market value of the firm to the replacement value of the assets in place. When inflation has pushed up the price of the assets, or where technology has reduced the price of the assets, this measure may provide a better measure of undervaluation.

$$\text{Tobin's Q} = \text{Market value of assets/Replacement value of assets in place}$$

The value obtained from Tobin's Q is determined by two variables—the market value of the firm and the replacement cost of assets in place. In inflationary times, when the cost of replacing assets increases significantly, Tobin's Q will generally be lower than the unadjusted price-book value ratio. Conversely, if the cost of replacing assets declines much faster than the book value (technology might be a good example), Tobin's Q will generally be higher than the unadjusted price-book value ratio.

Many studies in recent years have suggested that a low Tobin's Q is indicative of an undervalued or a poorly managed firm that is more likely to be taken over. One study concludes that firms with a low Tobin's Q are more likely to be taken over for purposes of restructuring and increasing value.[13]

While this measure has some advantages in theory, it does have practical problems. The first is that the replacement value of some assets may be difficult to estimate, largely because they are so specific to each firm. The second is that, even where replacement values are available, substantially more information is needed to construct this measure than the traditional price-book value ratio. In practice, analysts often use shortcuts to arrive at

---

[13]L. H. Lang, R. M. Stulz, and R. A. Walkling, "Managerial Performance, Tobin's Q, and the Gains from Successful Tender Offers," *Journal of Finance* 24 (1989): 137–154.

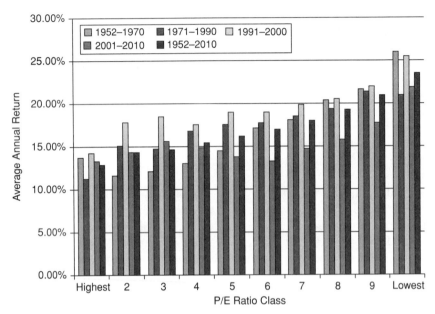

FIGURE 8.3 Returns on P/E Ratio Classes, 1952 to 2010
Source: Raw data from Ken French's Data Library (Dartmouth College).

Tobin's Q, using book value of assets as a proxy for replacement value. In these cases, the only distinction between this measure and the price-to-book value ratio is that this ratio is stated in terms of the entire firm (rather than just the equity).

Earnings Multiples   Investors have long argued that stocks with low price-earnings ratios are more likely to be undervalued and earn excess returns. In fact, it was the first of Ben Graham's 10 screens for undervalued stocks. In this section, we examine whether the screen stands up to the promises made by its proponents.

Empirical Evidence on Low-P/E Stocks   Studies that have looked at the relationship between P/E ratios and excess returns have consistently found that stocks with low P/E ratios earn significantly higher returns than stocks with high P/E ratios over long time horizons. Figure 8.3 summarizes annual returns by P/E ratio classes for stocks from 1952 to 2010. Firms were classified into 10 deciles based on P/E ratios at the beginning of each year, and returns were measured during the course of the year.

NUMBER WATCH

Sector average P/E ratios: Take a look at the average PE ratio, by sector, for U.S. companies.

Firms in the lowest P/E ratio class earned 12.21 percent more each year than the stocks in the highest P/E class between 1952 and 1970, about 9.74 percent more each year, on average, between 1971 and 1990, and about 9.9 percent more each year, on average, between 1991 and 2010.

The high returns earned by low P/E ratio stocks also persist in other international markets. Table 8.1 summarizes the results of studies looking at this phenomenon in markets outside the United States.

Thus, the results seem to hold up as we go across time and markets, notwithstanding the fact the findings have been widely disseminated for more than 20 years.

What Can Go Wrong? Given the types of returns that low P/E ratio stocks earn, should we rush out and buy such stocks? While such a portfolio may

TABLE 8.1 Excess Returns on Low P/E Ratio Stocks by Country, 1989 to 1994

Country	Annual Premium Earned by Lowest P/E Stocks (bottom quintile) over the market
Australia	3.03%
France	6.40%
Germany	1.06%
Hong Kong	6.60%
Italy	14.16%
Japan	7.30%
Switzerland	9.02%
United Kingdom	2.40%

Annual premium: Premium earned over an index of equally weighted stocks in that market between January 1, 1989, and December 31, 1994. These numbers were obtained from a Merrill Lynch Survey of Proprietary Indexes.

include a number of undervalued companies, it may also contain other less desirable companies.

- *Companies with high-risk earnings.* The excess returns earned by low price-earnings ratio stocks can be explained using a variation of the argument used for small stocks—that the risk of low P/E ratio stocks is understated in the capital asset pricing model (CAPM). It is entirely possible that a portfolio of low-P/E stocks will include stocks where there is a great deal of uncertainty about future operating earnings. A related explanation, especially in the aftermath of the accounting scandals of recent years, is that accounting earnings are susceptible to manipulation. If earnings are high not because of a firm's operating efficiency but because of one-time items such as gains from divestitures or questionable items such as income from pension funds, you may not be getting bargains by buying these stocks.
- *Tax costs.* A second possible explanation that can be given for this phenomenon, which is consistent with an efficient market, is that low PE ratio stocks generally have large dividend yields, which would have created a larger tax burden for investors since dividends were taxed at higher rates during much of this period.
- *Low growth.* A third possibility is that the price-earnings ratio is low because the market expects future growth in earnings to be low or even negative. Many low P/E ratio companies are in mature businesses where the potential for growth is minimal or even negative. As an investor, therefore, you have to consider whether the trade-off of a lower P/E ratio for lower growth works in your favor.

Finally, many of the issues we raised about how accountants measure earnings will also be issues when you use P/E ratios. For instance, the fact that research and development (R&D) is expensed at technology firms rather than capitalized may bias their earnings down (and their P/E ratios upward).

ENTERPRISE VALUE TO EBITDA MULTIPLES

The earnings per share of a firm reflect not just the earnings from operations of a firm but all other income as well. Thus, a firm with substantial holdings of cash and marketable securities may generate enough income on these investments to push earnings up. In addition, earnings per share and equity multiples are affected by how much debt a firm has and what its interest expenses are. These concerns, in con-junction with the volatility induced in earnings by noncash expenses (such as depreciation) and varying tax rates, has led some investors to seek a more stable, cash-based measure of predebt earnings. One measure that has acquired a following is called the enterprise value (EV) to EBITDA multiple, and is defined as follows:

Enterprise value to EBITDA

$$= \frac{\text{Market value of equity} + \text{Market value of debt} - \text{Cash and marketable securities}}{\text{Earnings before interest, taxes, depreciation, and amortization}}$$

Why, you might wonder, do we add back debt and subtract out cash? Since EBITDA is before interest expenses, you would be remiss if you did not add back debt. Analysts who look at Price/EBITDA will conclude, for instance, that highly levered firms are cheap. Since we do not count the income from the cash and marketable securities in EBITDA, we net it out of the numerator as well.

The sectors where this multiple makes the most sense tend to be heavy infrastructure businesses; steel, telecommunications, and cable are good examples. In these sectors, you can screen for stocks with low enterprise value to EBITDA ratios. As a note of caution, though, in many cases firms that look cheap on an enterprise value to EBITDA basis often have huge reinvestment needs (capital expenditures eat up much of the EBITDA) and poor returns on capital. Thus, we would recommend adding two more screens when you use this multiple—low reinvestment needs and high return on invested capital (ROIC).

Revenue Multiples As investors have become more wary about trusting accounting earnings, an increasing number have started moving up the in-come statement looking for numbers that are less susceptible to accounting decisions. Not surprisingly, many have ended up screening for stocks that trade at low multiples of revenues. But how well have revenue multiples worked at picking undervalued stocks? In this section, we begin by looking at that evidence and then consider some of the limitations of this strategy.

Empirical Evidence on Price-to-Sales Ratios There is far less empirical ev-idence, either for or against, on revenue multiples than there is on price-earnings or price-to-book value ratios. In one of the few direct tests of the price-sales ratio, Senchack and Martin compared the performance of low price-sales ratio portfolios with low price-earnings ratio portfolios, and concluded that the low price-sales ratio portfolio outperformed the market but not the low price-earnings ratio portfolio.[14] They also found that the low price-earnings ratio strategy earned more consistent returns than a low price-sales ratio strategy, and that a low price-sales ratio strategy was more biased toward picking smaller firms. In 1988, Jacobs and Levy tested the value of low price-sales ratios (standardized by the price-sales ratio of the industries in which the firms operated) as part of a general effort to disentangle the forces influencing equity returns. They concluded that stocks with low price-sales ratios, by themselves, yielded an excess return of about 2 percent a year between 1978 and 1986. Even when other factors were thrown into the analysis, the price-sales ratios remained a significant factor in explaining excess returns (together with price-earnings ratio and size).[15]

What Can Go Wrong? While firms with low price-to-sales ratios may deliver excess returns over long periods, it should be noted, as with low price-to-book and price-earnings ratios, that there are firms that trade at low price-to-sales ratios that deserve to trade at those values. In addition to risk being the culprit again (higher-risk companies should have lower price-to-sales ratios) there are two other possible explanations.

1. *High leverage.* One of the problems with using price-to-sales ratios is that you are dividing the market value of equity by the revenues of the firm. When a firm has borrowed substantial amounts, it is entirely possible that its market value will trade at a low multiple of revenues. If you pick stocks with low price-to-sales ratios, you may very well end up with a portfolio of the most highly levered firms in each sector.
2. *Low margins.* Firms that operate in businesses with little pricing power and poor profit margins will trade at low multiples of revenues. The reason is intuitive. Your value ultimately comes not from your capacity to generate revenues but from the earnings that you have on those revenues.

---

[14]A. J. Senchack Jr. and J. D. Martin, "The Relative Performance of the PSR and PER Investment Strategies," *Financial Analysts Journal* 43 (1987): 46–56.
[15]B. I. Jacobs and K. N. Levy, "Disentangling Equity Return Irregularities: New Insights and Investment Opportunities," *Financial Analysts Journal* 44 (1988): 18–44; B. I. Jacobs and K. N. Levy, "On the Value of 'Value,'" *Financial Analysts Journal* 44 (1988): 47–62.

The simplest way to deal with the first problem is to redefine the revenue multiple. If you use enterprise value (which adds debt to the numerator and subtracts out cash) instead of market value of equity in the numerator, you will remove the bias toward highly levered firms.

The significance of profit margins in explaining price-to-sales ratios suggests that screening on the basis of both price-sales ratios and profit margins should be more successful at identifying undervalued securities. You want to buy stocks that trade at low revenue multiples while earnings sizeable profit margins.

Dividend Yields While P/E ratios, price-to-book ratios, and price-to-sales ratios might be the most widely used value screens, there are some investors who view the dividend yield as the only secure measure of returns. Earnings, they argue, are not only illusory but are also out of reach for most investors in stocks since a significant portion may get reinvested. Following up on this logic, stocks with high dividend yields should be better investments than stocks with low dividend yields.

Does this approach yield results? Between 1952 and 2010, for instance, stocks with high dividend yields earned higher annual returns than stocks with low dividend yields, but the relationship is neither as strong nor as consistent as the results obtained from the P/E ratio or the PBV ratio screens. Figure 8.4 summarizes returns earned by dividend yield class from 1952 to 2010, broken down by subperiods.

The results are mixed, with high dividend yield stocks generating higher returns than low dividend yield stocks only between 2001 and 2010. In each of the other subperiods, the high dividend yield portfolio either under-performs or matches the returns on non–dividend payers and low dividend yield stocks.

NUMBER WATCH

Dividend yields by sector: Take a look at the average dividend yields, by sector, for companies in the United States.

Notwithstanding this evidence, there are some conservative investors who continue to believe that buying high-dividend stocks is a low-risk, high-return strategy. An extreme version of this portfolio is the strategy of investing in the "Dogs of the Dow," the 10 stocks with the highest dividend yields in the Dow Jones Industrial Average. Proponents of this strategy claim

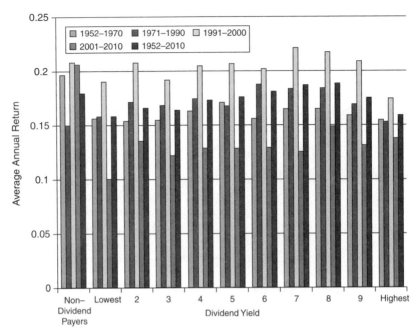

FIGURE 8.4 Returns on Dividend Yield Classes, 1952 to 2010
Source: Raw data from Ken French's Data Library (Dartmouth College).

that they generate excess returns from it, but they compare the returns to what you would have made on the Dow 30 and the S&P 500 and do not adequately adjust for risk. A portfolio with only 10 stocks in it is likely to have a substantial amount of firm-specific risk. McQueen, Shields, and Thorley examined this strategy and concluded that while the raw returns from buying the top dividend-paying stocks are higher than the rest of the index, adjusting for risk and taxes eliminates all of the excess return.[16] A later study by Hirschey also indicates that there are no excess returns from this strategy after you adjust for risk.[17]

There are three final considerations in a high-dividend strategy. The first is that you will have a much greater tax cost on this strategy, if dividends are taxed at a higher rate than capital gains. That was the case prior to 2003 and may very well be true again starting in 2013. The second is that some

[16]G. McQueen, K. Shields, and S. R. Thorley, "Does the Dow-10 Investment Strategy Beat the Dow Statistically and Economically?" *Financial Analysts Journal* (July/August 1997): 66–72.
[17]M. Hirschey, "The 'Dogs of the Dow' Myth," *Financial Review* 35 (2000): 1–15.

stocks with high dividend yields may be paying much more in dividends than they can afford and the market is building in the expectation of a dividend cut, into the stock price. The third is that any stock that pays a substantial portion of its earnings as dividends is reinvesting less and can therefore expect to grow at a much lower rate.

Determinants of Success

If all we have to do to earn excess returns is invest in stocks that trade at low multiples of earnings, book value, or revenues, shouldn't more investors employ these screens to pick their portfolios? And assuming that they do, should they not beat the market by a healthy amount?

To answer the first question, a large number of portfolio managers and individual investors employ either the screens we have referred to in this section or variants of these screens to pick stocks. Unfortunately, their performance does not seem to match up to the returns that we see earned on the hypothetical portfolios. Why might that be? We can think of several reasons.

- *Time horizon.* All of the studies quoted earlier look at returns over time horizons of five years or greater. In fact, low price-to-book value stocks have underperformed high price-to-book value stocks over shorter time periods. The same can be said about P/E ratios and price-to-sales ratios.
- *Dueling screens.* If one screen earns you excess returns, three should do even better seems to be the attitude of some investors who proceed to multiply the screens they use. They are assisted in this process by the easy access to both data and screening technology. There are websites (many of which are free) that allow you to screen stocks (at least in the United States) using multiple criteria.[18] The problem, though, is that the use of one screen may undercut the effectiveness of others, leading to worse rather than better portfolios.
- *Absence of diversification.* In their enthusiasm for screens, investors sometimes forget the first principles of diversification. For instance, it is not uncommon to see stocks from one sector disproportionately represented in portfolios created using screens. A screen from low-P/E stocks may deliver a portfolio of banks and utilities, whereas a screen of low price-to-book ratios and high returns on equity may deliver stocks

---

[18]Stockscreener.com, run by Hoover, is one example. You can screen all listed stocks in the United States using multiple criteria, including all of the criteria discussed in this chapter.

from a sector with high infrastructure investments that has had bad sector-specific news come out about it.

- *Taxes and transaction costs.* As in any investment strategy, taxes and transaction costs can take a bite out of returns, although the effect should become smaller as your time horizon lengthens. Some screens, though, can increase the effect of taxes and transaction costs. For instance, screening for stocks with high dividends and low P/E ratios will yield a portfolio that may have much higher tax liabilities (because of the dividends).
- *Success and imitation.* In some ways, the worst thing that can occur to a screen (at least from the viewpoint of investors using the screen) is that its success is publicized and that a large number of investors begin using that same screen at the same time. In the process of creating portfolios of the stocks they perceive to be undervalued, they may very well eliminate the excess returns that drew them to the screen in the first place.

To be a successful screener, you would need to be able to avoid or manage these problems. In particular, you need to have a long time horizon, pick your combination of screens well, and ensure that you are reasonably diversified. If a screen succeeds, you will probably need to revisit it at regular intervals to ensure that market learning has not reduced the efficacy of the screen.

Tools for Success

Passive value investors know that there are no sure winners in investing. Buying low P/E or low price-to-book value ratios may have generated high returns in the past but there are pitfalls in every strategy. Since value investors are bound by a common philosophy, which is that you should minimize your downside risk without giving up too much of your upside potential, they have devised tools to put this philosophy into practice in the past few decades.

Accounting Checks   The two most widely used multiples used to find cheap stocks, P/E and price-to-book ratios, both have accounting numbers in the denominator—accounting earnings in the case of P/E, and accounting book value in the case of price-to-book. To the extent that these accounting numbers are unsustainable, manipulated, or misleading, the investment choices that follow will reflect these biases. Thus, a company that reports inflated earnings, either because it had an unusually good year (a commodity company after a spike in the price of the commodity) or because of accounting choices (which can range from discretion within the accounting rules to fraud), will look cheap on a price-earnings ratio basis. Similarly, a firm that takes a large restructuring charge and writes down its book value of assets (and equity) will look expensive on a price-to-book basis.

To combat the problem, value investors have developed ways of correcting both earnings and book value. With accounting earnings, there are three widely used alternatives to the actual earnings. The first is normalized earnings, where value investors look at the average earnings earned over a five- or 10-year period rather than earnings in the most recent year. With commodity and cyclical companies, this will allow for smoothing out of cycles and result in earnings that are much lower than actual earnings (if earnings are at a peak) or higher than actual earnings (if earnings have bottomed out). The second is adjusted earnings, where investors who are willing to delve through the details of company filings and annual reports often devise their own measures of earnings that correct for what they see as shortcomings in conventional accounting earnings. The adjustments usually include eliminating one-time items (income and expenses) and estimating expenses for upcoming liabilities (underfunded pension or health care costs). Finally, we noted Buffett's use of a modified version of owner's earnings, where depreciation, amortization, and other noncash charges are added back and capital expenditures needed to maintain existing assets are subtracted out to get to "owners' earnings." In effect, this replaces earnings with a cash flow after maintenance investments have been made.

With book value, value investors have to deal with two problems. The first is that the book value of a company's assets and equity will generally be inflated after it acquires another company, because you are required to show the price you paid and the resulting goodwill as an asset. Netting goodwill out of assets will reduce book value and make acquisitive companies look less attractive on a price-to-book basis. Consequently, value investors often use tangible book value, rather than total book value, where

Tangible book value = Book value − Goodwill − Other intangible assets

The second is that book value does not equate to liquidation value; in other words, some assets are easier to liquidate (and convert to cash at or close to their book value) than other assets. To compensate for the difficulty of converting book value to cash for some assets, value investors also look at narrower measures of book value with greater weight given to liquid assets. In one of its most conservative versions, some value investors look at only current assets (on the assumption that accounts receivable and inventory can be more easily sold at close to book value) and compute a *net net value* (Book value of current assets − Book value of current liabilities − Book value of long-term debt). Buying a company for less than its net net value is thus considered an uncommon bargain, since you can liquidate its current assets, pay off its outstanding liabilities, and pocket the difference.

The Moat When you buy a stock at a low price-earnings ratio or because it has a high dividend yield, you are implicitly assuming that it can continue generating these earnings (and paying dividends) in the long term. For this to occur, the firm has to be able to hold on to (and hopefully even strengthen) its market share and margins in the face of competition. The "moat" is a measure of a company's competitive advantages; the stronger and more sustainable a company's competitive advantages, the more difficult it becomes for others to breach the moat and the safer the earnings stream becomes.

But how do you measure this moat? Some value investors look at the company's history, arguing with some legitimacy that a history of stable earnings and steady growth is evidence of a deep moat. Others use qualitative factors, such as the presence of an experienced and competent management team, the possession of a powerful brand name, or the ownership of a license or patent. With either approach, the objective is to look at the underpinnings of reported earnings to see if they can be sustained in the future.

Margin of Safety In Chapter 2, we included an extensive section on margin of safety. Summarizing, the margin of safety (MOS) is the buffer that value investors build into their investment decision to protect themselves against risk. Thus, a MOS of 20 percent would imply that an investor would buy a stock only if its price is more than 20 percent below the estimated value (estimated using a multiple or a discounted cash flow model).

Value investors use the margin of safety as their protection from being wrong on two levels. The first is in their assessment of the *intrinsic value* of a company, where the errors can come from erroneous assumptions about the future of the company or unforeseen macroeconomic risks. The second is in the market price adjustment; after all, there is no guarantee that the stock price will move toward the intrinsic value, even if the intrinsic value is right. Extending the logic, the margin of safety should be larger for riskier companies where there is more uncertainty about the future. It should also widen during periods of market crisis, when macroeconomic risks become larger, and in inefficient or illiquid markets, where the price adjustment may take more time.

THE CONTRARIAN VALUE INVESTOR

The second strand of value investing is contrarian value investing. In this manifestation of value investing, you begin with the belief that stocks that are beaten down because of the perception that they are poor investments (because of their own poor investments, default risk, or bad management) tend to get punished too much by markets, just as stocks that are viewed as good investments get pushed up too much. Within contrarian investing, we would include several strategies ranging from relatively unsophisticated ones like buying the biggest losers in the market in the prior period to vulture and distressed security investing, where you use sophisticated quantitative techniques to highlight securities (both stocks and bonds) issued by troubled firms that may be undervalued.

Basis for Contrarian Investing

Do markets overreact to new information and systematically overprice stocks when the news is good and underprice stocks when the news is bad? There is some evidence for this proposition, especially in the long term, and, as we noted in Chapter 7, studies do find that stocks that have done exceptionally well or badly in a period tend to reverse course in the following period, but only if the period is defined in terms of years rather than weeks or months.

Strategies and Evidence

Contrarian investing takes many forms, but we will consider just three strategies in this section. We will begin with the simple strategy of buying stocks that have gone down the most over the previous period; move on to a slightly more sophisticated process of playing the expectations game, buying stocks where expectations have been set too low and selling stocks where expectations are too high; and end the section by looking at a strategy of investing in securities issued by firms in significant operating and financial trouble.

Buying the Losers   In Chapter 7, we presented evidence that stocks reverse themselves over long periods in the form of negative serial correlation; that is, stocks that have gone up the most over the past five years are more likely to go down over the next five years. Conversely, stocks that have gone down the most over the past five years are more likely to go up. In this section, we consider a strategy of buying the latter and selling or avoiding the former.

The Evidence   How would a strategy of buying the stocks that have gone down the most over the past few years perform? To isolate the effect of price reversals on the extreme portfolios, DeBondt and Thaler constructed a winners portfolio of 35 stocks that had gone up the most over the prior year, and a losers portfolio of 35 stocks that had gone down the most over

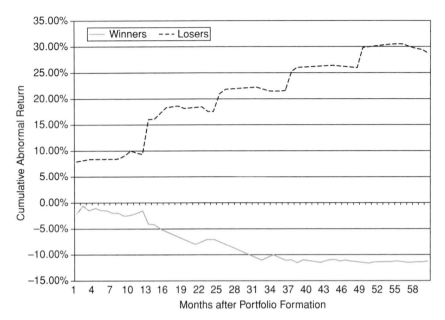

FIGURE 8.5   Cumulative Abnormal Returns—Winners versus Losers
Source: W. F. M. DeBondt and R. Thaler, "Further Evidence on Investor Over-reaction and Stock Market Seasonality," *Journal of Finance* 42 (1987): 557–581.

the prior year, each year from 1933 to 1978.[19] They examined returns on these portfolios for the 60 months following the creation of the portfolio. Figure 8.5 graphs the returns on both the loser and winner portfolios.

This analysis suggests that an investor who bought the 35 biggest losers over the previous year and held for five years would have generated a cumulative abnormal return of approximately 30 percent over the market and about 40 percent over an investor who bought the winners portfolio.

This evidence is consistent with market overreaction and suggests that a simple strategy of buying stocks that have gone down the most over the past year or years may yield excess returns over the long term. Since the strategy relies entirely on past prices, you could argue that this strategy shares more with charting (consider it a long-term contrarian indicator) than it does with value investing.

---

[19]W. F. M. DeBondt and R. Thaler, "Further Evidence on Investor Overreaction and Stock Market Seasonality," *Journal of Finance* 42 (1987): 557–581.

Caveats   There are many academics as well as practitioners who suggest that these findings are interesting but that they overstate potential returns on loser portfolios for several reasons:

- There is evidence that loser portfolios are more likely to contain low-priced stocks (selling for less than $5), which generate higher transaction costs and are also more likely to offer heavily skewed returns; that is, the excess returns come from a few stocks making phenomenal returns rather than from consistent performance.
- Studies also seem to find that loser portfolios created every December earn significantly higher returns than portfolios created every June. This suggests an interaction between this strategy and tax-loss selling by investors. Since stocks that have gone down the most are likely to be sold toward the end of each tax year (which ends in December for most individuals), their prices may be pushed down by the tax-loss selling.
- There seems to be a size effect when it comes to the differential returns. When you do not control for firm size, the loser stocks outperform the winner stocks; but when you match losers and winners of comparable market value, the only month in which the loser stocks outperform the winner stocks is January.[20]
- The final point to be made relates to time horizon. As we noted in the preceding chapter, while there may be evidence of price reversals in long periods (three to five years), there is evidence of price momentum (losing stocks are more likely to keep losing and winning stocks to keep winning) if you consider shorter periods (six months to a year). An earlier study that we referenced, by Jegadeesh and Titman, tracked the difference between winner and loser portfolios by the number of months that you held the portfolios.[21] Their findings are summarized in Figure 8.6.

There are two interesting findings in this graph. The first is that the winner portfolio actually outperforms the loser portfolio in the first 12 months. The second is that while loser stocks start gaining ground on winning stocks after 12 months, it took them 26 months in the 1941–1964 time

---

[20]P. Zarowin, "Size, Seasonality and Stock Market Overreaction," *Journal of Financial and Quantitative Analysis* 25 (1990): 113–125.

[21]N. Jegadeesh and S. Titman, "Returns to Buying Winners and Selling Losers: Implications for Stock Market Efficiency," *Journal of Finance* 48, no. 1 (1993): 65–91.

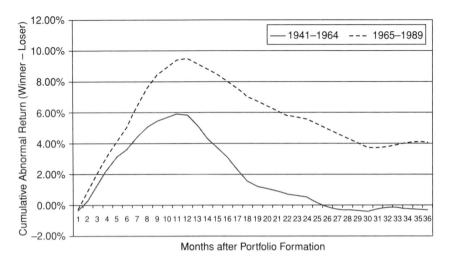

FIGURE 8.6 Differential Returns—Winner versus Loser Portfolios
Source: N. Jegadeesh and S. Titman, "Returns to Buying Winners and Selling Losers: Implications for Stock Market Efficiency," *Journal of Finance* 48, no. 1 (1993): 65–91.

period to get ahead of them, and the loser portfolio does not start outperforming the winner portfolio even with a 36-month time horizon in the 1965–1989 time period. The payoff to buying losing companies may depend heavily on whether you have the capacity to hold these stocks for long time periods.

Playing the Expectations Game A more sophisticated version of contrarian investing is to play the expectations game. If you are right about markets overreacting to recent events, expectations will be set too high for stocks that have been performing well and too low for stocks that have been doing badly. If you can isolate these companies, you can buy the latter and sell the former. In this section, we consider a couple of ways in which you can invest on expectations.

Bad Companies Can Be Good Investments Any investment strategy that is based on buying well-run, good companies and expecting the growth in earnings in these companies to carry prices higher is dangerous, since it ignores the possibility that the current price of the company already reflects the quality of the management and the firm. If the current price is right (and the market is paying a premium for quality), the biggest danger is that the

TABLE 8.2 Excellent versus Unexcellent Companies—Financial Comparison

	Excellent Companies	Unexcellent Companies
Growth in assets	10.74%	4.77%
Growth in equity	9.37%	3.91%
Return on capital	10.65%	1.68%
Return on equity	12.92%	−15.96%
Net margin	6.40%	1.35%

firm loses its luster over time and the premium paid will dissipate. If the market is exaggerating the value of the firm, this strategy can lead to poor returns even if the firm delivers its expected growth. It is only when markets underestimate the value of firm quality that this strategy stands a chance of making excess returns.

There is some evidence that well-managed companies do not always make good investments. Tom Peters, in his widely read book on excellent companies a few years ago, outlined some of the qualities that he felt separated excellent companies from the rest of the market.[22] Without contesting his standards, a study went through the perverse exercise of finding companies that failed on each of the criteria for excellence—a group of unexcellent companies—and contrasting them with a group of excellent companies. Table 8.2 provides summary statistics for both groups.[23]

The excellent companies clearly are in much better financial shape and are more profitable than the unexcellent companies, but are they better investments? Figure 8.7 contrasts the returns that would have been made on these companies versus the excellent ones.

The excellent companies may be in better shape financially, but the unexcellent companies would have been much better investments, at least over the time period considered (1981–1985). An investment of $100 in unexcellent companies in 1981 would have grown to $298 by 1986, whereas $100 invested in excellent companies would have grown to only $182. While this study did not control for risk, it does present some evidence that good companies are not necessarily good investments, whereas bad companies can sometimes be excellent investments.

The second study used a more conventional measure of company quality. Standard & Poor's, the ratings agency, assigns quality ratings to stocks

---

[22]T. Peters, *In Search of Excellence: Lessons form America's Best Run Companies* (New York: Warner Books, 1988).
[23]M. Clayman, "Excellence Revisited," *Financial Analysts Journal* (May/June 1994): 61–66.

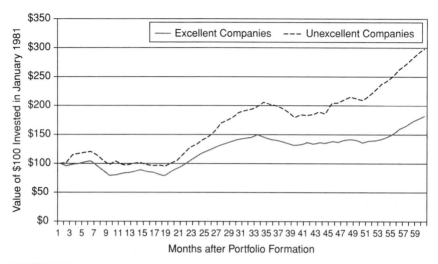

FIGURE 8.7   Excellent versus Unexcellent Companies
Source: M. Clayman, "Excellence Revisited," *Financial Analysts Journal* (May/June 1994): 61–66.

that resemble its bond ratings. Thus, an A-rated stock, according to S&P, is a higher-quality investment than a stock rated B+, and the ratings are based on financial measures (such as profitability ratios and financial leverage). Figure 8.8 summarizes the returns earned by stocks in different ratings classes, and as with the previous study, the lower-rated stocks had higher returns than the higher-rated stocks.

Again, the study is not definitive because the differences in returns may well reflect the differences in risk across these companies, but it indicates that investors who bought the higher-rated stocks expecting to earn higher returns would have been sorely disappointed.

One version, perhaps an extreme one, of contrarian investing is vulture investing. In vulture investing, you buy the equity and bonds of companies that are in bankruptcy and bet on either a restructuring or a recovery. This is a high-risk strategy where you hope that a few big winners offset the many losers in your portfolio.

Caveats   As with the previous strategy of buying losers, a strategy of buying companies that rank low on financial criteria is likely to require a long time horizon and expose you to more risk, both from financial default and from volatility. In addition, though, the following factors should be kept in mind while putting together a portfolio of "bad" companies.

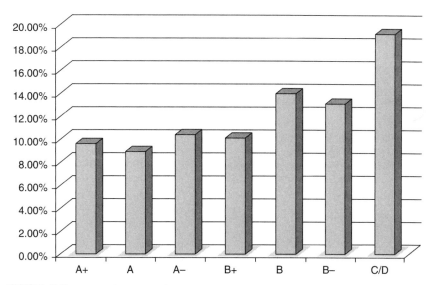

FIGURE 8.8 Annual Returns for S&P Stock Ratings Classes

The first is that not all companies that are poor performers are badly managed. Many are in sectors that are in long-term decline and have no turnaround in sight. It is entirely likely that these companies will continue to be poor performers in the future. Your odds of success are usually higher if you buy a poorly performing company in a sector where other companies are performing well. In other words, you are more likely to get the upside if there is potential for improvement.

Even if companies have potential for improvement, part of the reason for the poor performance of the companies may be poor management. If the management of the company is entrenched, either because the managers hold a significant portion of the equity—at least the voting shares—or because of antitakeover amendments in place, there may be little chance of improved performance in the future. You may have a better chance of succeeding in your investments, if you direct your investments to poorly managed firms where there is a high (or at least a reasonable) chance of removing incumbent management. You would, for instance, avoid poorly managed companies with unequal voting rights (voting and nonvoting shares), substantial holdings by incumbent managers, or antitakeover amendments in place.

Finally, risk-averse investors who wait for the absolute bottom before they invest often fail because timing the bottom is just about impossible. You will have to accept the fact that bad companies will sometimes (or often) become worse before they become better, and that this will create some short-term damage to your portfolio.

Determinants of Success

The caveats presented in the preceding section suggest that success from buying shares in losers or bad companies is not guaranteed and may prove elusive. In particular, you need the following:

- *Long time horizon.* To succeed by buying shares in these companies, you need to have the capacity to hold the stocks for several years. This is necessary not only because these stocks require long time periods to recover, but also to allow you to spread the high transaction costs associated with these strategies over more time. Note that having a long time horizon as a portfolio manager may not suffice if your clients can put pressure on you to liquidate holdings at earlier points. Consequently, you need either clients who think like you do and agree with you or clients who have made enough money with you in the past that their greed overwhelms any trepidation they might have in your portfolio choices.
- *Diversification.* Since poor stock price performance is often precipitated or accompanied by operating and financial problems, it is very likely that quite a few of the companies in the loser portfolio will cease to exist. If you are not diversified, your overall returns will be extremely volatile as a result of a few stocks that lose all of their value. Consequently, you will need to spread your bets across a large number of stocks in a large number of sectors. One variation that may accomplish this is to buy the worst-performing stock in each sector, rather than the worst-performing stocks in the entire market.
- *Personal qualities.* This strategy is not for investors who are easily swayed or stressed by bad news about their investments or by the views of others (analysts, market watchers, and friends). Almost by definition, you will read little that is good about the firms in your portfolio. Instead, there will be bad news about potential default, management turmoil, and failed strategies at the companies you own. In fact, there might be long periods after you buy the stock when the price continues to go down further as other investors give up on the company. Many investors who embark on this strategy find themselves bailing out of their investments early, unable to hold on to these stocks in the face of the drumbeat of negative information. In other words, to succeed with this strategy you need both the self-confidence to stand your ground as others bail out and a stomach for short-term volatility (especially the downside variety).

ACTIVIST VALUE INVESTING

One of the more frustrating aspects of passive contrarian investing is that you, as an investor, do not control your destiny. Thus, you could invest in a poorly managed company expecting management to change, but it may never happen, leaving you with an investment that wilts over time. In activist value investing, you acquire a large stake in an undervalued or poorly managed company, and then use your position as a large stockholder to push for changes that will release this value. In other words, you act as the catalyst for change, and enrich yourself in the process.

Strategies and Evidence

The strategies used by you as an activist value investor are diverse, and will reflect why the firm is undervalued in the first place. If a business has investments in poorly performing assets or businesses, shutting down, divesting, or spinning off these assets will create value for its investors. When a firm is being far too conservative in its use of debt, you may push for a recapitalization (where the firm borrows money and buys back stock). Investing in a firm that could be worth more to someone else because of synergy, you may push for it to become the target of an acquisition. When a company's value is weighed down because it is perceived as having too much cash, you may demand higher dividends or stock buybacks. In each of these scenarios, you may have to confront incumbent managers who are reluctant to make these changes. In fact, if your concerns are broadly about management competence, you may even push for a change in the top management of the firm.

Asset Redeployment/Restructuring   While few firms make investments expecting to generate substandard returns, shifts in the business or the economy can make this a reality. If a firm finds itself with a significant portion of capital invested in assets that earn less than the cost of funding them, redeploying or restructuring these assets may create value for stockholders. In this section, we assess various asset restructuring strategies—ranging from splitting the firm into individual parts to divestitures of selected assets—and the consequences for value.

Asset Deployment and Value   The relationship between investment decisions and value creation is a simple one. To fund an investment, a firm has to raise capital (from either equity investors or lenders), and there is a cost associated with this capital (a cost of capital) that reflects the risk of the investments that the firm plans to make. That capital is invested in assets that generate a return on the invested capital; if that return is greater than the cost of capital, the assets are creating value, and if it is less, the assets are destroying value. Thus, you could make an inventory of all assets that a firm has on its books and classify them into value-creating, value-neutral, and value-destroying investments.

The puzzle to some may be the last category. Why, you may wonder, would any firm take on investments that are value destroying? There are many possible reasons, some occurring even before the investment is made and many happening in the aftermath:

- *Ego, overconfidence, and bias.* While we tend to think of investment decisions as based primarily on the numbers, it is inevitable that human nature enters into the decision process. In too many cases, the decision maker enters the process with preconceptions and biases that color the analysis (altering the numbers), thus making the final decision a foregone conclusion. If you add to this the fact that many decision makers are overconfident about their own abilities and their egos make it difficult to back down, you have the recipe for bad investments. In fact, all of these tendencies get exaggerated as the decisions get larger, and for decision makers who are higher in the ranks. As a consequence, the most egregious distortions occur when firms make large investments (acquisitions, large joint ventures, entering new businesses).

- *Failure to adjust for changing risk.* Earlier, we noted that the cost of capital for a firm is set by investors who make their assessments about the risk in the firm based on its business model and past history. Thus, a firm that operates in a safe business and has generated stable earnings over time will have a low cost of capital. Using that cost of capital as the benchmark on new investments makes sense only if these investments continue in the same vein: stable investments in safe businesses. If the firm enters new businesses that are riskier and continues to use its old cost of capital as its hurdle rate, it may very well be taking on bad investments; the return on capital on these investments may exceed the old cost of capital but doesn't match up to the correct risk-adjusted cost of capital that should have been used in the assessment.

- *Business spread.* Companies often spread themselves across multiple businesses, sometimes attracted by higher returns and oftentimes by the stability that they see from operating in diversification. At the limit, you have conglomerates like General Electric and Siemens that operate in dozens of businesses. While there may be some benefits, there is also a potential cost. By spreading themselves thinly across multiple businesses, it is possible that some of these businesses may be run less efficiently than if they were stand-alone businesses, partly because accountability is weak and partly because of cross subsidies. Researchers have looked at the question of whether conglomerates trade at a premium or discount to their parts. To make this judgment, they value the pieces of a conglomerate using the typical multiple that independent firms in each business trade at. Thus, you could break GE down into individual businesses and value each one based on the enterprise value-to-EBITDA or P/E ratio that other firms in that business trade at. You can then add up the values of the parts and compare the total to the value of the conglomerate. In this comparison, the evidence seems to indicate that conglomerates trade at significant discounts (ranging from 5 to 10 percent, depending on the study) to their piecewise values.[24]

■ *Changes in sector or business.* Even firms that make unbiased and well-reasoned judgments about their investments, at the time that they make them, can find that unanticipated changes in the business or sector can turn good investments into bad ones. Thus, a pharmaceutical firm that made the decision to develop a new drug in 2006, based on its expectation of high drug prices and returns, may find that a change in the health care law or a new drug introduced by a rival company in 2010 lowers returns on the investment to below the cost of capital.

■ *Macroeconomic changes.* In a similar vein, value-creating investments made in assets when the economy is doing well can reverse course quickly if the economy slows down or goes into a recession. In fact, the banking crisis in 2008 ushered in a period of macroeconomic shocks (sovereign defaults, regulatory changes, political risk) that rendered useless even the best investment analyses from prior periods.

For any of the reasons listed, a firm can find itself with a large proportion of its investments delivering returns well below what it costs to fund them.

Asset Deployment: Value-Enhancement Actions   Assuming that some or a large portion of the assets of a firm are in the value-destroying column, earning less than their cost of capital, what should companies (or investors

---

[24]See Philip G. Berger and Eli Ofek, "Diversification's Effect on Firm Value," *Journal of Financial Economics* 37 (1995): 39–65; Larry H. P. Lang and René M. Stulz, "Tobin's Q, Corporate Diversification, and Firm Performance," *Journal of Political Economy* 102 (1994): 1248–1280.

in these companies) try to do? The choices range across the spectrum and reflect why the investment went bad in the first place.

- *Shutdown/liquidation.* When an asset is earning less than its cost of capital, the most obvious solution would seem to be to be to shut it down; but does that make sense? It does, but only in two cases. The first is if the asset is losing money and is expected to generate negative cash flows with no end in sight. Shutting down a factory or a product line where the operating costs exceed the revenues is a clear gain for investors in the firm, even though there may be large social costs (laid-off employees, devastated company towns, costs for taxpayers). The second is if the firm can reclaim the capital originally invested in the asset by shutting it down. This is more difficult than it looks. A firm that invests $100 million in an asset, expecting to generate 12 percent a year, is unlikely to be able to get the investment back if the asset is generating only 6 percent in returns each year.

- *Divestitures.* In a divestiture, a firm sells assets or a division to the highest bidder. To see how a divestiture affects value, you would need to compare the price received on the divestiture to the present value of the expected cash flows that would have been generated from the firm continuing to operate the divested asset. There are three possible scenarios:

  1. If the divestiture value is equal to the present value of the expected cash flows, the divestiture will have no effect on the divesting firm's value.
  2. If the divestiture value is greater than the present value of the expected cash flows, the value of the divesting firm will increase on the divestiture.
  3. If the divestiture value is less than the present value of the expected cash flows, the value of the firm will decrease on the divestiture.

  The divesting firm receives cash in return for the assets and can choose to retain the cash and invest it in marketable securities, invest the cash in other assets or new investments, or return the cash to stockholders in the form of dividends or stock buybacks. This action, in turn, can have a secondary effect on value.

  There are at least three reasons for a firm to divest its assets or a division. The first is that the divested assets may have a higher value to the buyer of these assets. For assets to have a higher value, they have to either generate higher cash flows for the buyers or result in lower risk (leading to a lower discount rate). The higher cash flows can occur because the buyer is more efficient at utilizing the assets, or because the buyer finds synergies with its existing businesses. The lower discount rate may reflect the fact that the owners of the buying firm are more diversified that the owners of the firm selling the assets. In either case, both sides can gain from the divestiture and share in the increased value. The second reason for divestitures is less value-driven and more a result of the immediate cash flow needs of the divesting firm. Firms that find themselves unable to meet their current operating or financial expenses may have to sell assets to raise cash. For instance, many leveraged acquisitions in the 1980s were followed by divestitures of assets. The cash generated from these divestitures was used to retire and service debt. The third reason for divestitures relates to the assets *not* sold by the firm rather than the divested assets. In some cases, a firm may find the cash flows and values of its core businesses affected by the fact that it has diversified into unrelated businesses. This lack of focus can be remedied by selling assets or businesses that are peripheral to the main business of a firm.

A number of empirical questions are worth asking about divestitures. What types of firms are most likely to divest assets? What happens to the stock price when assets are divested? What effect do divestitures have on the operating performance of the divesting firm? Let us look at the evidence on each of these questions. Linn and Rozeff examined the price reaction to announcements of divestitures by firms and reported an average excess return of 1.45 percent for 77 divestitures between 1977 and 1982.[25] They also noted an interesting contrast between firms that announce the sale price and motive for the divestiture at the time of the divestiture, and those that do not: in general, markets react much more positively to the first group than to the second, as shown in Table 8.3.

It appears that financial markets view with skepticism firms that are evasive about the reasons for and use of the proceeds from divestitures. This finding was confirmed by Klein, when she noted that that the excess returns are positive only for those divestitures where the price is announced at the same time as the divestiture.[26] She extended the study and concluded that the magnitude of the excess return is a function of the size of the divestiture. For example, when the divestiture is less than 10 percent of the equity of the firm, there is no significant price effect,

---

[25]Scott C. Linn and Michael S. Rozeff, "The Effect of Voluntary Spin-Offs on Stock Prices: The Anergy Hypothesis," *Advances in Financial Planning and Forecasting* 1, no. 1 (1985): 265–292.

[26]A. Klein, "The Timing and Substance of Divestiture Announcements: Individual, Simultaneous and Cumulative Effects," *Journal of Finance* 41 (1986): 685–696.

TABLE 8.3 Market Reaction to Divestiture Announcements

	Motive Announced	
Price Announced	Yes	No
Yes	3.92%	2.30%
No	0.70%	0.37%

whereas if it exceeds 50 percent, the stock price increases by more than 8 percent.

Studies that have looked at the performance of firms after they divest assets report improvements in a number of operating measures: operating margins and returns on capital increase, and stock prices tend to outperform the rest of the sector. In summary, firms that have lost focus often are most likely to divest noncore assets, markets respond positively to these divestitures if information is provided at the time of the divestiture, and operating performance tends to improve after divestitures.

■ *Spin-offs, split-offs, and split-ups.* In a spin-off, a firm separates out assets or a division and creates new shares with claims on this portion of the business. Existing stockholders in the firm receive these shares in proportion to their original holdings. They can choose to retain these shares or sell them in the market. In a split-up, which can be considered an expanded version of a spin-off, the firm splits into different business lines, distributes shares in these business lines to the original stockholders in proportion to their original ownership in the firm, and then ceases to exist. A split-off is similar to a spin-off, insofar as it creates new shares in the undervalued business line. In this case, however, the existing stockholders are given the option to exchange their parent company stock for these new shares, which changes the proportional ownership in the new structure.

There are two primary differences between a divestiture and a spin-off. The first is that there is often no cash generated for the parent firm in a spin-off. The second is that the division being spun off usually becomes an independent entity, often with existing management in place. As a consequence, the first two reasons given for divestitures—a buyer who generates higher value from the assets than the divesting firm and the need to meet cash flow requirements—do not apply to spin-offs. Improving the focus of the firm and returning to core businesses, which we offered as reasons for divestitures, can be arguments for spin-offs as well. There are four other reasons:

1. A spin-off can be an effective way of creating value when subsidiaries or divisions are less efficient than they could be and the fault lies with the parent company, rather than the subsidiaries. For instance, Miles and Woolridge consider the case of Cyprus Minerals, a firm that was a mining subsidiary of Amoco in the early 1980s.[27] Cyprus was never profitable as an Amoco subsidiary. In 1985, it was spun off after losing $95 million in the prior year. Cyprus cut overhead expenses by 30 percent and became profitable within six months of the spin-off. Since the management of Cyprus remained the same after the spin-off, the losses prior to it can be attributed to the failures of Amoco's management. When a firm has multiple divisions and the sum of the divisional values is less than what the parent company is valued at, you have a strong argument for a split-off, with each division becoming an independent unit.

2. The second advantage of a spin-off or split-off, relative to a divestiture, is that it might allow the stockholders in the parent firm to save on taxes. If spin-offs and split-offs are structured correctly, they can save stockholders significant amounts in capital gains taxes. In 1992, for instance, Marriott spun off its hotel management business into a separate entity called Marriott International; the parent company retained the real estate assets and changed its name to Host Marriott. The entire transaction was structured to pass the tax test, and stockholders in Marriott were not taxed on any of the profits from the transaction.

3. The third reason for a spin-off or split-off occurs when problems faced by one portion of the business affect the earnings and valuation of other parts of the business. As an example, consider the pressure brought to bear on the tobacco firms, such as Philip Morris (Altria) and RJR Nabisco, to spin off their food businesses because of investor perception that the lawsuits faced by the tobacco businesses weighed down the values of their food businesses as well.

4. Finally, spin-offs and split-offs can also create value when a parent company is unable to invest or manage its subsidiary businesses optimally because of regulatory constraints. For instance, AT&T, when it was a partially regulated telecommunications firm, found itself constrained in

---

[27] J. Miles and J. R. Woolridge, *Spin-Offs & Equity Carve-Outs* (Morristown, NJ, Financial Executives Research Foundation, 1999).

decision making in its research and computer divisions. In 1995, AT&T spun off both divisions: the research division (Bell Labs) was renamed Lucent Technologies, and the computer division reverted back to its original name of NCR.

Why would a firm use a split-up instead of spin-off or split-off? By giving existing stockholders an option to exchange their parent company stock for stock in the split-up unit, the firm may get a higher value for the assets of the unit. This is so because those stockholders who value the unit the most will be most likely to exchange their stock. The approach makes sense when there is wide disagreement among stockholders on how much the unit is worth.

Two issues have been examined by researchers who have looked at spin-offs. The first relates to the stock price reaction to the announcement of spin-offs. In general, these studies find that the parent company's stock price increases on the announcement of a spin-off. A study by Schipper and Smith examined 93 firms that announced spin offs between 1963 and 1981 and reported an average excess return of 2.84 percent in the two days surrounding the announcement.[28] Further, there is evidence that the excess returns increase with the magnitude of the spun off entity. Schipper and Smith also find evidence that the excess returns are greater for firms in which the spin-off is motivated by tax and regulatory concerns.

The second set of studies look at the performance of both the spun-off units and the parent companies after the spin-offs. These studies, which are extensively documented in Miles and Woolridge, can be summarized as follows:

- Cusatis, Miles, and Woolridge report that both the spun-off units and the parent companies report positive excess returns in the three years after the announcement of the spin-offs. Figure 8.9 reports the total returns and the returns adjusted for overall industry returns in the three years after the spin-off.[29]
- Both groups are much more likely to be acquired, and the acquisition premiums explain the overall positive excess returns.

---

[28]K. Schipper and A. Smith, "Effects of Recontracting on Shareholder Wealth: The Case of Voluntary Spin-Offs," *Journal of Financial Economics* 12 (1983): 437–468; see also G. L. Hite and J. E. Owers, "Security Price Reactions around Corporate Spin-Off Announcements," *Journal of Financial Economics* 12 (1983): 409–436.
[29]P. J. Cusatis, J. A. Miles, and J. R. Woolridge, "Restructuring Through Spin Offs: The Stock Market Evidence," *Journal of Financial Economics* 33 (1993): 293–311.

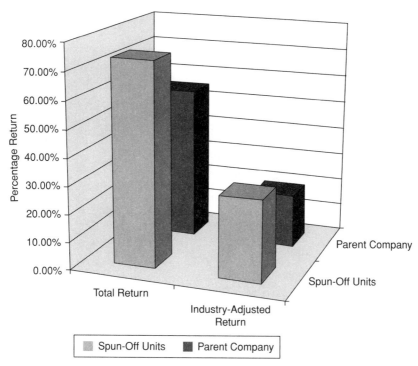

FIGURE 8.9 Returns at Spin-Offs and Parent Company
Source: P. J. Cusatis, J. A. Miles, and J. R. Woolridge, "Restructuring Through Spin Offs: The Stock Market Evidence," *Journal of Financial Economics* 33 (1993): 293–311.

There is a significant improvement in operating performance at the spun-off units in the three years after the spin-off. Figure 8.10 reports on the change in revenues, operating income, total assets, and capital expenditures at the spun-off units in the three years after the spin-off, before and after adjusting for the performance of the sector.

Note that the spun-off units grow faster than their peers in terms of revenues and operating income; they also reinvest more in capital expenditures than other firms in the industry.

Capital Structure/Financing Choices In corporate finance, there has long been a debate about whether firms can become more valuable as a result of changing the mix of debt and equity that they use to fund their businesses. There is one school of thought, attributed to Miller and Modigliani, that argues that value is unaffected by financial leverage, but only in a world

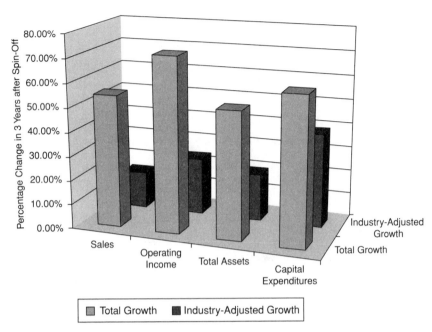

FIGURE 8.10 Operating Performance of Spun-Off Units
Source: J. Miles and J. R. Woolridge, *Spin-Offs & Equity Carve-Outs* (Financial Executives Research Foundation, 1999).

without taxes and default risk.[30] Another school of thought argues that in the presence of taxes and default risk, there is an optimal amount of debt that a firm can carry, and value is maximized at that point. Finally, there is a school of thought that argues that firms should not use debt since it is risky, and less debt is always better than more debt.

Capital Structure and Value The trade-off on using debt and the consequences for value is a straightforward one. Interest expenses are tax deductible and cash flows to equity are not, making debt more attractive, relative to equity, as the marginal tax rate rises. Debt can also operate as a disciplinary mechanism on managers in mature firms; managers are less likely to take bad investments if they have to make interest expenses each period. On the other side of the ledger, debt has two disadvantages. The first is an *expected bankruptcy cost*, since as debt increases, so does the probability of bankruptcy. But what is the cost of bankruptcy? One is the direct

---

[30]F. Modigliani and M. Miller, "The Cost of Capital, Corporation Finance and the Theory of Investment," *American Economic Review* 48 (1958): 261–297.

cost of going bankrupt, such as legal fees and court costs, which can eat up a significant portion of the value of a bankrupt firm. The more devastating cost is the effect of being perceived as being in financial trouble: customers may stop buying your products, suppliers may demand cash for goods, and services and employees may leave, creating a downward spiral for the firm that can destroy it. The second disadvantage is an *agency cost*, arising from different and competing interests of equity investors and lenders in a firm. Equity investors see more upside from risky investments than lenders do. As lenders become aware of this potential, they protect themselves by either writing covenants into loan agreements or charging higher interest rates. Putting this trade-off into practice requires us to try to quantify both the costs and benefits of debt.

NUMBER WATCH

Financial leverage by sector: Take a look at the average debt ratios and costs of capital, in market value terms, by sector.

In the cost of capital approach, the optimal financing mix is the one that minimizes a company's cost of capital. Replacing equity with debt has the positive effect of replacing a more expensive mode of funding (equity) with a less expensive one (debt), but in the process the increased risk in both debt and equity will push up the costs of both components. The cost of capital approach relies on sustainable cash flow to determine the optimal debt ratio. The more stable and predictable a company's cash flow and the greater the magnitude of these cash flows—as a percentage of enterprise value—the higher the company's optimal debt ratio can be. Furthermore, the most significant benefit of debt is the tax benefit. Higher tax rates should lead to higher debt ratios.

Bradley, Jarrell, and Kim analyzed whether differences in debt ratios can be explained by some of the trade-off variables (taxes, bankruptcy costs) listed above.[31] They noted that the debt ratio was lower for firms with more volatile operating income. Since these firms are also likely to face much higher likelihood of bankruptcy, this finding is consistent with the proposition that firms with high bankruptcy costs borrow less. They also looked at firms with high advertising and R&D expenses; lenders to these

---

[31] M. Bradley, G. A. Jarrell, and E. H. Kim, "On the Existence of an Optimal Capital Structure: Theory and Evidence," *Journal of Finance* 39 (1984): 857–878.

firms are likely to be much more concerned about recouping their debt if the firm gets into trouble, because the assets of these firms are intangible (brand names or patents) and difficult to liquidate. These firms, consistent with the theory, have much lower debt ratios. They also find that there is a significant number of firms whose debt ratios are much lower and much higher than predicted by the cross-sectional relationship.

A simple test of whether financing mix affects value is to look at the market reactions to firms that change their financing mixes, either increasing their debt ratios or lowering them. The studies that have looked at this question are in agreement that stock prices do change in response to financing mix changes, and that they tend to increase around leverage-increasing actions and decrease on the announcement of leverage-decreasing actions. Taken in sum, this would suggest that markets view more firms as underleveraged than overleveraged and that increasing debt is viewed as adding to value.

Capital Structure: Value-Enhancement Strategies   Assume that you are a firm that has chosen the wrong mix of debt and equity in funding your assets. What are the ways in which you can (or an activist can try to make you) fix this problem? There is a continuum from small actions that nudge the debt ratio over a period of time toward the right mix to decisive ones where the change is large and occurs abruptly.

- *Marginal recapitalization.* Even if a firm is reluctant to revisit its funding of existing investments, it can change the way it finances new investments. Thus, a firm that is underleveraged (with an actual debt ratio of 10 percent and an optimal ratio of 40 percent) can fund its new investments with a debt ratio of 40 percent or even higher. Similarly, an overleveraged firm can fund its new projects predominantly or entirely with equity from retained earnings or new equity issues, and see its debt ratio decline. Over time, the debt ratio for the firm will drift toward the optimal ratio though the rate of drift will depend on how much the firm is investing in new projects. Unfortunately, for larger, mature firms, the rate of change will be glacial, since new investments will tend to be small relative to existing investments.
- *Total recapitalization.* In a recapitalization, a firm changes its financial mix of debt and equity without substantially altering its investments or asset holdings. If you are underleveraged, you can recapitalize in many ways. For instance, you can increase your debt ratio by borrowing money and paying a dividend or by buying back stock. Alternatively, you can swap debt for equity, where equity investors in your firm are offered equivalent amounts (in market value terms) in debt. If you want

to reduce your debt ratio, you would reverse these actions, raising equity and reducing debt. The boom in debt for equity recapitalization occurred in the late 1980s. A study that looked at these recapitalizations came to two conclusions. The first was that almost every one of them was triggered by the threat of a hostile takeover. In other words, it is external pressure that forces managers to increase financial leverage. The second was that the average stock price reaction to recapitalizations is very positive. On average, in the sample of 45 recapitalizations studied, the stock price increased by 21.9 percent. This finding is not restricted to just stock buybacks. A study of 52 offers to exchange debt for equity found that stock prices increased by 14 percent.

If you are overleveraged, your choices will parallel the underleveraged firm's actions. You can try to raise new equity (by issuing new stock or equity options) and pay down your debt. You can cut back or eliminate dividends, assuming that you are still paying them. You can also try to convince your lenders to swap their debt holding for equity investments in the company. The problem is that recapitalization is likely to be more difficult for a firm with too much debt than one with too little. In an overleveraged firm, investors are less willing to buy your equity offerings, it is unlikely that you are paying substantial dividends, and lenders remain wary of holding equity in your firm.

- *Leveraged acquisitions.* If a firm is underleveraged and the existing management is too conservative and stubborn to change, there is an alternative. An acquirer can borrow money, implicitly using the target firm's debt capacity, and buy out the firm. This is, of course, the phenomenon of the leveraged buyout, where a group of investors raises debt against the assets of a publicly traded firm, preferably one with stable earnings and marketable assets, and uses the debt to acquire the outstanding shares in the firm. If they succeed in their endeavor, the firm becomes a private company, and the debt is partly or substantially paid down with the firm's cash flows or from asset sales over time. Once the firm has been nursed back to health and efficiency, it is taken public again, reaping (at least if all goes according to plan) substantial payoffs for the equity investors in the deal. Studies of leveraged acquisitions suggest that they do, on average, deliver significant returns to their investors. However, some of the leveraged buyouts done toward the end of the 1980s and just before the banking crisis of 2008 failed spectacularly, highlighting again that leverage is a two-edged sword, elevating returns in good times and reducing them in bad times.

Is there a similar nuclear option available against overleveraged firms where managers are unable or unwilling to reduce debt? While there is no explicit analogue to the leveraged buyout, there is a far more conventional route that can be followed, in which the operating assets of an overleveraged firm (which can still have significant value) can be acquired by an investor or a healthy company and the troubled firm is put into liquidation.

Dividend Policy/Cash Balances In November 2011, Apple reported a cash balance in excess of $80 billion, the most eye-catching example of a more general cash buildup at U.S. companies during the prior years. With the cash buildup has come the question of whether this cash accumulation helps or hurts investors in the firms in question, and if it hurts them, whether the cash should be returned to stockholders in the form of higher dividends or stock buybacks. In this section, we provide a nuanced answer, where the cash buildup can help investors in some companies, leave investors in other companies unaffected, and hurt investors in some companies. It is the last group that should be targeted for higher dividends and/or buybacks by investors.

NUMBER WATCH

Cash holdings by sector: See the cash balances as a percentage of revenues and value, by sector, for U.S. companies.

Cash and Value To some investors/analysts, the question of whether cash hurts or helps them seems like an easy one to answer. After all, cash is usually invested in liquid and riskless or near-riskless investments, earning a low rate of return. Since that return is generally much lower than the returns that the company makes on its operating investments or its cost of capital, cash looks like a bad investment. That misses a key point about investment assessment, which is that investment returns should be compared against a hurdle rate that reflects the risk of the investment. Since cash is a riskless, liquid investment, the cost of capital for cash is the risk-free rate, and cash invested in Treasury bills or commercial paper is thus value neutral. So cash, by itself, is neither value creating nor value destroying.

So, how does cash affect value? Put differently, how much cash is too much cash? To answer these questions, you have to start off with a clear sense of how or why cash balances affect equity investors in a company. Rather than worry about the low returns that cash generates, investors should redirect their attention to what the company may do with the cash. While cash invested in Treasury bills, earning a low rate of return, does not hurt value, that same cash invested in projects earning 6 percent, if the cost of capital for those projects is 9 percent, will destroy value. To make a judgment on whether to attach a discount to cash, investors should look at a company's track record, discounting cash balances in the hands of companies that have a history of poor investments and bad acquisitions. They should not discount cash balances in the hands of companies where managers are selective in their investments and have earned high returns (on both projects and for their investors).

While it may seem outlandish to argue that the market values cash balances differently in the hands of different companies, there is empirical evidence that backs this proposition. Pinkowitz and Williamson tried to estimate the value that markets were attaching to cash by regressing the market values of firms against fundamental variables that should determine value (including growth, leverage, and risk) and adding cash as an independent variable.[32] They concluded that the market values a dollar in cash at about $1.03, across all companies, with a standard error of $0.093. Consistent with the motivations for holding cash, they found that cash is valued more highly (>$1.20 for $1 in cash) in the hands of high-growth companies with more uncertainty about future investment needs than in the hands of larger, more mature companies that earn less than their cost of capital (where a dollar in cash is valued at about 70 cents).

Cash: Value-Enhancement Strategies   If you are a company with a poor track record of taking bad investments, trust in management will be a scarce commodity and your cash holdings will be discounted by the market. The path to value enhancement, whether you choose to take it or activist investors push you along the path, is to return the cash to the stockholders, either by paying higher dividends or by buying back stock.

- *Dividends.* The conventional path to returning cash to stockholders is to pay it out as dividends. For firms that have never paid dividends before, this will mean initiating dividends for the first time; for firms that have been paying dividends, this will translate into increasing dividends. If the cash balance to be returned is very large, it may take the form of a special dividend.

---

[32]L. Pinkowitz and R. Williamson, "What Is a Dollar Worth? The Market Value of Cross Holdings" (working paper, Georgetown University, 2002).

The arguments for and against dividends are well rehearsed and have been heard over time. On the plus side, dividends fit into the value investor's vision of safe cash flows, predictable and stable, and are a positive signal since only firms that feel confident about their future will initiate or increase regular dividends. On the minus side, for much of the past century, investors in the United States have been penalized by the tax code for dividends, with dividends being taxed at much higher rates than capital gains. In addition, taxes on dividends are unavoidable in the sense that investors holding the stock have to receive the dividend and pay taxes on them, even if they have no need for the cash.

- *Stock buybacks.* The alternative to using cash to pay dividends is to use it to buy back stock. In the United States, at least, the shift away from dividends to stock buybacks has been dramatic over the past two decades, as evidenced in Figure 8.11.

Note that aggregate dividends amounted to $100 billion in 1988 and aggregate stock buybacks were $50 billion in that year. During the 1990s, buybacks increased dramatically, and in 1999, cash returned in buybacks exceeded cash paid out in dividends in the aggregate. The trend continued uninterrupted through 2008, with 2007 representing a high-water mark for

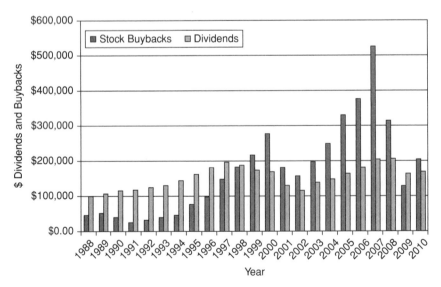

FIGURE 8.11 Stock Buybacks and Dividends: Aggregate for U.S. Firms, 1988 to 2010
Source: Standard & Poor's.

buybacks. The market collapse and economic fears that followed induced companies to hold back on buybacks in 2009, but it was clearly just a pause, not a stop to the trend, as the return to buybacks in 2010 indicates.

So, what has caused this movement away from dividends in the past two decades? Dividends have been taxed at much higher rates than capital gains going back to the early decades of the past century. In fact, in 1979, the highest marginal tax rate on dividends was 70 percent, while it was only 28 percent on capital gains. The changes in the tax laws in the past three decades have reduced the tax disadvantage of dividends—in fact, capital gains and dividends have both been taxed at 15 percent from 2003 to 2012—and cannot therefore be a rationale for the surge in buybacks. It also cannot be attributed to companies thinking that their stock prices were too low, since these buyback surges occurred during the bull markets of the 1990s and 2004 to 2007, not during down markets. There are four possible explanations.

1. *Management compensation.* The shift toward using options in management compensation at many firms has altered managerial incentives on whether to pay dividends or buy back stock. When you buy back stock, your stock price generally increases, partly because there are fewer shares outstanding after the buyback. When you pay a dividend, your stock will drop on the ex-dividend day. As an investor, you may not care because you get a dividend to compensate for the price drop. As a manager with options, you do care, since your option value will decrease with the stock price.

2. *Uncertainty about earnings.* The second explanation is that dividends are sticky: once you initiate or increase a dividend, you are expected to keep paying that dividend. Buybacks are flexible: companies can buy back stock in one year without creating expectations about future years. Companies that are uncertain about future earnings will therefore be more likely to buy back stock than pay dividends. Deregulation (of telecommunications, airlines, and a host of other businesses) in conjunction with globalization (and the concurrent loss of secure local markets) has resulted in less predictability in earnings across the board.

3. *Changing investor profiles.* The expansion of hedge funds and private equity investors has changed investor profiles in the stock market. These investors may be focused on price appreciation (rather than dividends) and may prefer buybacks to dividends.

4. *The dilution delusion.* A stock buyback reduces the number of shares outstanding and generally increases earnings per share. Applying the current P/E ratio to the higher earnings per share should result in a stock price. If this logic held, stock buybacks would be magic bullets

that companies could use to push their stock prices up. The flaw with this logic, of course, is that it assumes that the price-earnings ratio will not change for the company as it pays cash out to stockholders and makes itself a riskier enterprise.

Corporate Governance Both conglomerate discounts and underleverage are manifestations of a larger problem, which is that managers at some publicly traded companies do not put stockholder interests first. While you can fashion specific solutions to these issues, they may not be sufficient in a firm where the source of the problem is poor management. For such firms, the only long-term solution to value generation is a new management team.

Corporate Governance and Value   In most publicly traded firms, there is a separation between the ownership of the firm (stockholders) and the managers of the firm. *Corporate governance* is a term that we use to capture how accountable managers are to stockholders and the mechanisms in place to make this accountability real. The relationship between corporate governance, in this abstract form, and value is therefore not clearly defined; there is no input in an intrinsic valuation for whether you have a strong and independent board of directors in a valuation model. However, if we view corporate governance as the power that stockholders possess to change bad management, there is a way to bring corporate governance into value by approaching valuation in two steps. In the first step, you value the company run by the existing managers, warts and all, and call this the status quo value. In the second step, you value the company run by optimal management and term this the optimal value. To the extent that there are at least some dimensions where the incumbent managers are falling short, the latter should be higher than the former. The price at which the stock will trade in a reasonably efficient market will be a weighted average of these two values:

Traded value

= (Probability of no change in management) (Status quo value)

+ (Probability of change in management) (Optimal value)

With strong corporate governance, the probability of change in management should be high and the stock should trade close to its optimal value; with weak corporate governance, the traded value will approach the status quo value. Any action that improves corporate governance (eliminating differences in voting rights across shares; a new, more independent board; the entry of an activist investor) will therefore increase the traded value.

Gompers, Ishi, and Metrick studied the effect of corporate governance on stock prices by developing a corporate governance index, based on 24 factors, for 1,500 firms; higher scores on the index translated into weaker corporate governance.[33] They found that the stocks with the weakest stockholder power earned 8.4 percent less in annual returns than stockholders with the strongest stockholder power. They also found that an increase of 1 percent in the poor governance index translated into a decline of 2.4 percent in the firm's Tobin's Q, which is the ratio of market value to replacement cost. In other words, we would expect a firm where stockholders have strong powers to replace and change managers to trade at a higher market value than an otherwise similar firm (in terms of risk, growth, and cash flow characteristics) where stockholders have limited or no power over managers. Corporate governance systems are stronger in some countries than others, and there have been a few studies that have looked at the relationship between firm performance/value and corporate governance across countries. Klapper and Love looked at 14 emerging markets with wide differences in corporate governance and legal systems. They find that countries with weaker legal systems tend to have weaker corporate governance systems. They also conclude that firms with stronger corporate governance systems have higher market values and report better operating performance.[34] Finally, they find that the strength of corporate governance matters more in countries with weak legal systems.

While there seems to be support for the argument that companies with better corporate governance trade at higher values, this does not make them better investments per se, since it's the change in the value that determines returns. In fact, the relationship between corporate governance and returns is weak, with little evidence backing the proposition that investors earn higher returns from investing in companies with stronger corporate governance.

Combining the two sets of findings, though, does offer an opening for investors. If you can invest in companies ahead of an event that strengthens corporate governance (removal of disproportionate voting rights on shares, the election of a more activist board, removal of antitakeover clauses in corporate charters), you will gain from the increase in value that should accompany the change in governance. In an interesting twist on this concept, Bris and Cabolis looked at target firms in 9,277 cross-border mergers, where

---

[33]P. A. Gompers, J. L. Ishi, and A. Metrick, "Corporate Governance and Equity Prices," *Quarterly Journal of Economics* 118 (2003): 107–155.

[34]Leora F. Klapper and Inessa Love, "Corporate Governance, Investor Protection and Performance in Emerging Markets," *Journal of Corporate Finance* 10 (2004): 703–728.

the corporate governance system of the target was in effect replaced by the corporate governance system of the acquirer. Since corporate governance systems vary across countries, this gives the researchers an opportunity to examine the effect on stock prices of changing the corporate governance system. They find that stock prices increase for firms in an industry when a firm or firms in that industry are acquired by foreign firms from countries with better corporate governance.[35]

Corporate Governance: Value-Enhancement Actions   If the key to succeeding with activist investing is to change the way a company is run, strengthening corporate governance is an important first step. The actions that activist investors take to accomplish this range from challenging incumbent managers at annual meetings to trying to acquire the firm with the intent of replacing the top managers.

- *Proxy contests.* At large publicly traded firms with widely dispersed stock ownership, annual meetings are lightly attended. For the most part, stockholders in these companies tend to stay away from meetings and incumbent managers usually get their votes by default, thus ensuring management-approved boards. In some companies, activist investors compete with incumbent managers for the proxies of individual investors, with the intent of getting their nominees for the board elected. While they may not always succeed at winning majority votes, they do put managers on notice that they are accountable to stockholders. There is evidence that proxy contests occur more often in companies that are poorly run, and that they sometimes create significant changes in management policy and improvements in operating performance.[36]
- *Changing top management.* If you are an activist investor in a firm with incompetent management, how would you go about instituting change? Needless to say, you will not have the cooperation of the existing management, whom you have labeled as not up to the job. If you are able to harness enough stockholders to your cause, though, you may be able to

---

[35]A. Bris and C. Cabolis, "Corporate Governance Convergence by Contract: Evidence from Cross Border Mergers" (Yale Working Paper No. 02-32, 2002). Firms of English or Scandinavian origin tend to score higher on corporate governance measures.

[36]J. H. Mulherin and A. B. Poulsen, "Proxy Contests and Corporate Change: Implications for Shareholder Wealth," *Journal of Financial Economics* 47 (1998): 279–313. They find that the bulk of the wealth from proxy contests stems from firms that are subsequently acquired or where management is changed.

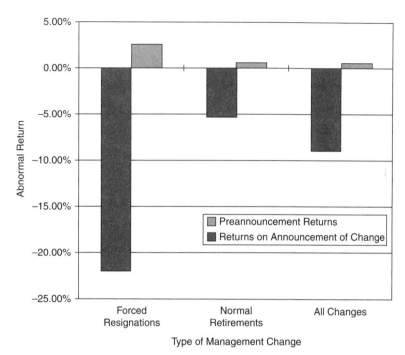

FIGURE 8.12 Returns around Management Changes
Source: E. P. H. Furtado and V. Karan, "Causes, Consequences, and Shareholder Wealth Effects of Management Turnover: A Review of the Empirical Evidence." *Financial Management* 19 (1990): 60–75.

increase the pressure on the top management to step down. While some may view the loss of top managers in a company as bad news, it really depends on the market's perception of the management. The overall empirical evidence suggests that changes in management are generally viewed as good news.[37] In Figure 8.12, we examine how stocks react when a firm's CEO is replaced.

The stock price goes up, on average, when top management is changed. However, the impact of management changes is greatest when the change is forced. Management is more likely to be forced out in the aftermath of poor performance (operating and stock price), and stock prices increase after the change is announced.

---

[37]E. P. H. Furtado and V. Karan, "Causes, Consequences, and Shareholder Wealth Effects of Management Turnover: A Review of the Empirical Evidence," *Financial Management* 19 (1990): 60–75.

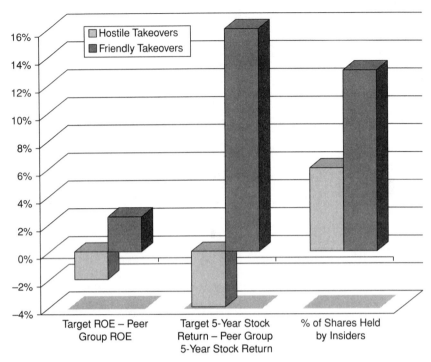

FIGURE 8.13 Friendly versus Hostile Takeover Target Characteristics
Source: A. Bhide, "The Causes and Consequences of Hostile Takeovers," *Journal of Applied Corporate Finance* 2 (1989): 36–59.

- *Hostile acquisitions.* If you cannot get top management to leave the firm, you can actively seek out hostile acquirers for the firm. If others share your jaundiced view of the management of the firm, you may very well succeed. There is evidence that indicates that badly managed firms are much more likely to be targets of acquisitions than well-managed firms. Figure 8.13 summarizes key differences between target firms in friendly and hostile takeovers.[38] Note that target firms in hostile takeovers, relative to their peer group, generally have lower returns on equity on projects, have done worse for their stockholders, and have less insider holdings than target firms in friendly takeovers. Needless to say, the

---

[38]A. Bhide, "The Causes and Consequences of Hostile Takeovers," *Journal of Applied Corporate Finance* 2 (1989): 36–59.

payoff to being the stockholder of a firm that is the target of a hostile takeover is large.

Classes of Activist Investors

If the essence of activist investing is that you invest in a poorly managed company and then try to get it to change (by either running it yourself or putting pressure on management), it follows that activist investors can take different forms. Some are lone wolves, entrepreneurs on the lookout for turnaround candidates; others are institutional investors (mutual funds and pension funds) that don't want to follow the "sell and move on" strategy; and still others are hedge funds or private equity funds.

Lone Wolves   In the movie *Wall Street*, Michael Douglas plays the role of a hostile raider, proclaiming that greed is good and eager to profit at any cost. His character was modeled on Ivan Boesky, one of many individuals during the 1980s who raised the profile of activist investors by targeting public companies, sometimes taking them over and at other times just scaring managers enough to get them to change their ways and profiting along the way. While Hollywood has since found other bogeymen in the finance business, Bill Ackman, Carl Icahn, and Nelson Peltz are just a few high-profile investors who continue the practice.

These successful raiders share some common features. The first is that they target the right companies, picking firms that have underperformed their peer groups both in profitability and in stock price performance. The second is that they are not shy about rocking the boat, challenging incumbent managers on their fundamental business decisions: where they invest, how they raise funds, and how much they return to stockholders. The third is that they are willing to do the legwork and expend the resources required to contest management, from gathering proxies to trying to build alliances with unhappy investors and portfolio managers. The fourth is that they are persistent, willing to fight for long periods to accomplish what they set out to do, while recognizing when to give up (or give in) on fights that they cannot win.

Institutional Activists   Activist investing does not come naturally to mutual funds and pension funds for many reasons. Its confrontational style riles managers in targeted firms (who may be clients or potential clients for mutual fund firms in other businesses), and it requires time and resources that fund managers who have a hundred or more companies in their portfolios are unwilling to expend. Consequently, the typical professional money manager remains a passive investor who votes with his or her feet, selling stock in companies that he or she does not like and moving on.

There are and have been some exceptions to this general rule. The California Public Employees' Retirement System (CalPERS) was one of the first funds to take an activist investing stance in the mid-1980s. Not only did it generate an annual list of worst-managed firms in the United States, but it then took positions in these firms and sought to change the way they were run. In the past two decades, other mutual funds have taken on the activist role, but they remain a small subset of the overall universe of funds.

Activist Hedge Funds/Private Equity Funds   The explosion in private equity and hedge funds in the past few decades has opened a new front in activist investing. A subset of private equity funds have made their reputations (and wealth) at least in part by investing in (and sometimes buying outright) publicly traded companies that they feel are managed less than optimally, changing the way they are managed, and cashing out in the marketplace.

A key difference between these funds and the other two classes of activist investors is that they have an ambivalent relationship with incumbent managers. Rather than challenge them as incompetent, they often team up with managers in taking public companies into the private domain, at least temporarily. In effect, they are arguing that the key reasons for poor management are the separation of ownership from management (prevalent at most publicly traded companies) and the pressures brought to bear by investors and analysts on public companies to deliver results quickly.

Empirical Evidence on Activist Investing

So, what types of firms do activist investors target? Once they take large positions in these firms or take them over, do they live up to the stereotype of short-term, greedy investors who destroy businesses, or do they have a more positive impact on how companies are run? Finally, do activist investors make large profits, after adjusting for the risks that they are exposed to?

Whom Do They Target and Why?   If activist investors hope to generate their returns from changing the way companies are run, they should target poorly managed companies for their campaigns. Institutional and individual activists do seem to focus on poorly managed companies, targeting companies that are less profitable and that have delivered lower returns than their peer group. Hedge fund activists seem to focus their attention on a different group. A study of 888 campaigns mounted by activist hedge funds between 2001 and 2005 finds that the typical target companies are small-cap to mid-cap companies, have above-average market liquidity, trade at low price-to-book value ratios, are profitable with solid cash flows, and pay their

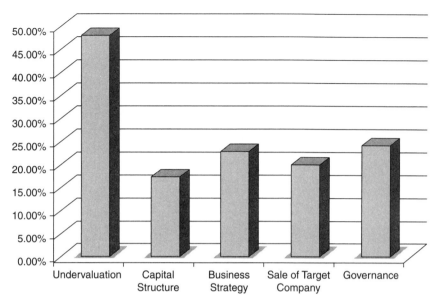

FIGURE 8.14 Motives for Hedge Fund Activism
Source: A. Brav, W. Jiang, and H. Kim, "Hedge Fund Activism: A Review," *Foundations and Trends in Finance*, NOW (2010).

CEOs more than other companies in their peer group. Thus, they are more likely to be undervalued companies than poorly managed ones. A paper that examines hedge fund motives behind the targeting provides more backing for this general proposition in Figure 8.14.[39]

In summary, the typical activist hedge fund behaves more like a passive value investor looking for undervalued companies than like an activist investor looking for poorly managed companies.

What Do They Do? The essence of activist investing is that incumbent management is challenged, but on what dimensions? And how successfully? A study of 1,164 activist investing campaigns between 2000 and 2007 documents some interesting facts about activism:[40]

- Two-thirds of activist investors quit before making formal demands on the target. The failure rate in activist investing is very high.

---

[39] A. Brav, W. Jiang, and H. Kim, "Hedge Fund Activism: A Review," *Foundations and Trends in Finance*, NOW (2010).
[40] N. Gantchev, "The Costs of Shareholder Activism: Evidence from a Sequential Decision Model" (SSRN Working Paper 1646471, 2011).

- Among those activist investors who persist, less than 20 percent request a board seat, about 10 percent threaten a proxy fight, and only 7 percent carry through on that threat.
- Activists who push through and make demands on managers are most successful when they demand the taking private of a target (41 percent success rate), the sale of a target (32 percent), restructuring of inefficient operations (35 percent), or additional disclosure (36 percent). They are least successful when they ask for higher dividends/buybacks (17 percent success rate), removal of the CEO (19 percent), or executive compensation changes (15 percent). Overall, activists succeed about 29 percent of the time in their demands on management.

The review paper on hedge fund activism, that we used as the basis for Figure 8.14, finds that the median holding for an activist hedge fund is 6.3 percent, and even at the 75th percentile the holding is about 15 percent. Put differently, most activist hedge funds try to change management practices with well below a majority holding in the company. The same paper also documents an average holding period of about two years for an activist investment, though the median is much lower (about 250 days).

In general, the market reaction to activist investors, whether they are hedge funds or individuals, is positive. A study that looked at stock returns in targeted companies in the days around the announcement of activism, came up with the summary results that are reported in Figure 8.15.

Note that the bulk of the excess return (about 5 percent of the total of 7 percent) is earned in the 20 days before the announcement and that the post-announcement drift is small. There is also a jump in trading volume prior to the announcement, which does pose interesting (and troubling) questions about insider information and trading. The study also documents that the average returns around activism announcements have been drifting down over time, from 14 percent in 2001 to less than 4 percent in 2007.

Following through and looking at companies that have been targeted and sometimes controlled by activist investors, we can classify the changes at these companies into the four groups that we listed earlier (as potential value enhancement):

1. *Asset deployment and operating performance.* There is mixed evidence on this count, depending on the type of activist investor group looked at and the time period. Divestitures of assets do pick up after activism, albeit not dramatically, for targeted firms. There is evidence that firms targeted by individual activists do see an improvement in return on capital and other profitability measures relative to their peer groups, whereas firms targeted by hedge fund activists don't see a similar jump in profitability measures.

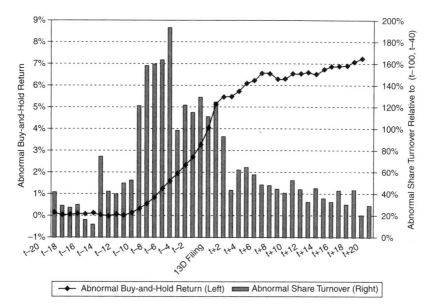

FIGURE 8.15 Excess Returns and Trading Volume around Activism Announcements

Note: The solid line (left axis) plots the average buy-and-hold return around the Schedule 13D filing, in access of the buy-and-hold return of the value-weight market, from 20 days prior the 13D file date to 20 days afterward. The bars (right axis) plot the increase (in percentage points) in the share trading turnover during the same time window compared to the average turnover rate during the preceding $(-100, -40)$ event window.

Source: A. P. Brav, W. Jiang, F. Portnoy, and R. S. Thomas, "The Returns to Hedge Fund Activism" (SSRN Working Paper 1111778, 2008).

2. *Capital structure.* On financial leverage, there is a moderate increase of about 10 percent in debt ratios at firms that are targeted by activist hedge funds, but the increase is not dramatic or statistically significant. There are dramatic increases in financial leverage at a small subset of firms that are targets of activism, but the conventional wisdom that activist investors are proponents of outlandishly high debt ratios is not borne out in the overall sample. One study does note a troubling phenomenon, at least for bondholders in targeted firms, with bond prices dropping about 3 to 5 percent in the years after firms are targeted by activists and a higher likelihood of bond rating downgrades.[41]

---

[41]H. Aslan and H. Maraachlian, "The New Kids on the Block: Wealth Effects of Hedge Fund Activism on Bondholders" (working paper, University of Houston, 2009).

3. *Dividend policy.* The firms that are targeted by activists generally increase their dividends and return more cash to stockholders, with the cash returned as a percentage of earnings increasing by about 10 percent to 20 percent.
4. *Corporate governance.* The biggest effect is on corporate governance. The likelihood of CEO turnover jumps at firms that have been targeted by activists, increasing 5.5 percent after the targeting. In addition, CEO compensation decreases in the targeted firms in the years after the activism, with pay tied more closely to performance.

In summary, activist investors seem to improve profitability mildly, increase financial leverage (and distress costs) somewhat, raise cash payout to stockholders, and make managers more responsive to stockholders. One study that tracks activist investments through 2009 (most of the studies stop in 2005 or 2006) finds that the end results are disappointing, both in terms of the changes that are made at the target firms and the returns earned by activist hedge funds.[42] Activist hedge funds seem to derive more of their returns from value investing and less from activism, whereas activist individual investors get a bigger share of value from activism (and changing corporate policy).

What Returns Do They Generate for Themselves?　The overall evidence on whether activist investors make money is mixed and varies depending on which group of activist investors is studied and how returns are measured.

- Activist mutual funds seem to have had the lowest payoff to their activism, with little change accruing to the corporate governance, performance, or stock prices of targeted firms.[43] Markets seem to recognize this, with studies that have examined proxy fights finding that there is little or no stock price reaction to proxy proposals by activist institutional investors. Activist hedge funds, however, seem to earn substantial excess returns, ranging from 7 or 8 percent on an annualized

---

[42]W. W. Bratton, "Hedge Funds and Governance Targets: Long-Term Results" (working paper, University of Pennsylvania Institute for Law & Economic Research, 2010).
[43]Stuart Gillan and Laura Starks, "The Evolution of Shareholder Activism in the United States," *Journal of Applied Corporate Finance* 19 (2007): 55–73; D. Yermack, "Shareholder Voting and Corporate Governance," *Annual Review of Financial Economics* 2 (2010): 103–125.

basis at the low end to 20 percent or more at the high end.[44] Individual activists seem to fall somewhere in the middle, earning higher returns than institutions but lower returns than hedge funds.[45]

- While the average excess returns earned by hedge funds and individual activists is positive, there is substantial volatility in these returns and the magnitude of the excess return is sensitive to the benchmark used and the risk-adjustment process. Put in less abstract terms, activist investors frequently suffer setbacks in their campaigns, and the payoff is neither guaranteed nor predictable.
- Targeting the right firms, acquiring stock in these companies, demanding board representation, and conducting proxy contests are all expensive, and the returns made across the targeted firms have to exceed the costs of activism for these funds to generate value. While none of the studies that we have reference hitherto factored these costs, the Gantchev paper referenced earlier concluded that the cost of an activist campaign at an average firm was $10.71 million and that the net returns to activist investing, if these costs are considered, shrink toward zero.
- The average returns across activist investors obscures a key component, which is that the distribution is skewed with the most positive returns being delivered by the activist investors in the top quartile; the median activist investor may very well just break even, especially after accounting for the cost of activism.

Can You Make Money Following Activist Investors?   Given that most individual investors do not have the resources to be activist investors, this strategy may seem to be unreachable, but there is one possible way in which you may be able to partake in their success. If you could invest in companies that have been targeted for hedge fund investors and ride their coattails to higher stock prices, you could indirectly be a beneficiary of activist investing.

Figure 8.15, which we used to illustrate the immediate market reaction to activism, answers the question, at least for the very short term. Since the bulk of the excess returns are earned in the days before the announcement of activism, there is little to be gained in the short term by investing in a stock after it has been targeted by activist investors. As for whether you can

[44]A. Brav, W. Jiang, F. Partnoy, and R. Thomas, "Hedge Fund Activism, Corporate Governance, and Firm Performance," *Journal of Finance* 63, no. 4 (2008): 1729–1773.

[45]A. Klein and Z. Emanuel, "Entrepreneurial Shareholder Activism: Hedge Funds and Other Private Investors," *Journal of Finance* 63, no. 1 (2009): 187–229.

make money by investing in stocks targeted by activists and holding for the longer term, the evidence on whether hedge fund investors themselves make money in the long term provides some answers and direction:

- *The right activists.* If the median activist hedge fund investor essentially breaks even, as the evidence suggests, a blunderbuss approach of investing in a company targeted by any activist investor is unlikely to generate value. However, if you are selective about the activist investors you follow, targeting only the most effective activists and investing only in companies that they target, your odds improve.
- *Performance cues.* To the extent that the excess returns from this strategy come from changes made at the firm to operations, capital structure, dividend policy, and/or corporate governance, you should keep an eye on whether and how much change you see on each of these dimensions at the targeted firms. If the managers at these firms are able to stonewall activist investors successfully, the returns are likely to be unimpressive as well.
- *A hostile acquisition windfall?* A study by Greenwood and Schor notes that while a strategy of buying stocks that have been targeted by activist investors generates excess returns, almost all of those returns can be attributed to the subset of these firms that get taken over in hostile acquisitions.[46]

Overall, though, a strategy of following activist investors is likely to yield modest returns at best, because you will be getting the scraps from the table.

There is an alternate strategy worth considering that may offer higher returns and that also draws on activist investing. You can try to identify companies that are poorly managed and run, and thus most likely to be targeted by activist investors. In effect, you are screening firms for low returns on capital, low debt ratios, and large cash balances (representing screens for potential value enhancement), and for aging CEOs, corporate scandals, and/or shifts in voting rights (operating as screens for management change). If you succeed, you should be able to generate higher returns when some of these firms change because of pressure either from within (from an insider or an assertive board of directors) or from without (activist investors or a hostile acquisition).

---

[46]R. Greenwood and M. Schor, "Hedge Fund Investor Activism and Takeovers," *Journal of Financial Economics* 92, no. 3 (2009): 362–375.

Determinants of Success

Activist value investors have an advantage over passive value investors since they can provide the catalysts for value creation. So, what is it that stops all of us from being activist value investors? When we consider some of the prerequisites for being a successful value investor, we can also see why there are so few successful ones.

- This power of activist value investing usually comes from having the capital to buy significant stakes in poorly managed firms and using these large stockholder positions to induce management to change its behavior. Managers are unlikely to listen to small stockholders, no matter how persuasive their case may be.
- In addition to capital, though, activist value investors need to be willing to spend substantial time fighting to make themselves heard and pushing for change. This investment in time and resources implies that an activist value investor has to pick relatively few fights and be willing to invest substantially in each fight.
- Activist value investing, by its very nature, requires a thorough under-standing of target firms, since you have to know where each of these firms is failing and how you would fix these problems. Not surprisingly, activist value investors tend to choose a sector that they know really well and take positions in firms within that sector. It is clearly not a strategy that will lead to a well-diversified portfolio.
- Finally, activist value investing is not for the fainthearted. Incumbent managers are unlikely to roll over and give in to your demands, no matter how reasonable you may think them to be. They will fight, and sometimes fight dirty, to win. You have to be prepared to counter and be the target for abuse. At the same time, you have to be adept at forming coalitions with other investors in the firm since you will need their help to get managers to do your bidding.

If you consider all these requirements for success, it should come as no surprise that most conventional mutual funds steer away from activist value investing. Even though they might have the capital to be activist investors, they do not have the stomach or the will to go up against incumbent man-agers. The most successful activist value investors have either been wealthy and motivated individuals, small, focused mutual funds; or activist hedge funds that are willing to work with managers on changing the way their firms are run. As a small individual investor, you can try to ride their coattails and hope that they succeed, but it is unlikely that you will match their success. Offering more promise is a strategy of screening for companies that are ripe for activist intervention: poorly managed companies with the catalysts in place for management change.

HOW DIVERSIFIED SHOULD YOU BE?

A question that investors of all stripes face is whether you should spread your bets across many investments, and if so, how many? The debate is an old one and there is a range of views that fall between two extremes. At one extreme is the maxim that you should be maximally diversified, propagated by those who believe in efficient markets. At the other is the "go all in" investor, who believes that if you find a significantly undervalued company, you should put all or most of your money in that company, rather than dilute your upside potential by spreading your bets.

So, should you diversify? And if so, how much should you diversify? The answers to these questions depend on two factors: (1) how certain you feel about your assessment of value for individual assets and (2) how certain you are about the market price adjusting to that value within your specified time horizon.

- At one limit, if you are absolutely certain about your assessment of value for an asset and that the market price will adjust to that value within your time horizon, you should put all of your money in that investment. That is the case, for instance, if you find an option trading for less than its exercise value: you should invest all of your money in buying as many options as you can and exercise those options to make the profit. In general, this is what we term *pure arbitrage* (which we cover in Chapter 11), and it is feasible only with finite-lived assets (such as options, futures, and fixed income securities), where the maturity date provides an end point at which the price adjustment has to occur. On a more cynical note, this could also be the case if you are the recipient of private information about an upcoming news release (earnings, acquisition), where there is no doubt about the price impact of the release (at least in terms of direction) and the timing of the news release. The fact that you may very well be on the wrong side of the legal divide may also operate as a crimp on this strategy.

■ At the other limit, if you have no idea what assets are cheap and which ones are expensive (which is the efficient market proposition), you should be as diversified as you can get, given transaction costs. After all, you gain nothing by holding back on diversification and your portfolio will deliver less return per unit of risk taken.

Most active investors tend to fall between these two extremes. If you invest in equities, at least, it is almost inevitable that you have to diversify, for two reasons. The first is that you can never value an equity investment with certainty; the expected cash flows are estimates, and risk adjustment is not always precise. The second is that even if your valuation is precise, there is no explicit date by which market prices have to adjust; there is no equivalent to a maturity date or an option expiration date for equities. A stock that is underpriced can stay underpriced for a long time, and even get more underpriced.

Building on that theme, the degree of diversification across equities will depend on how your investment strategy is structured, with an emphasis on the following dimensions:

■ *Uncertainty about investment value.* If your investment strategy requires you to buy mature companies that trade at low price-earnings ratios, you may need to hold fewer stocks than if it requires you to buy young growth companies (where you are more uncertain about value). In fact, you can tie the margin of safety (referenced earlier in this chapter) to how much you need to diversify; if you use a higher margin of safety when investing, you should feel more comfortable holding a less diversified portfolio.

■ *Market catalysts.* To make money, the market price has to adjust toward your estimated value. If you can provide a catalyst for the market adjustment (nudging or forcing the price toward value), you can hold fewer investments and be less diversified than a completely passive investor who has no choice but to wait for the market adjustment to happen. Thus, you will need to hold fewer stocks as an activist investor than as an investor who picks stocks based on a P/E screen.

(continued)

■ *Time horizon.* To the extent that the price adjustment has to happen over your time horizon, having a longer time horizon should allow you to have a less diversified portfolio.

In summary, then, there is nothing irrational about holding just a few stocks in your portfolio, if it is composed of mature companies and you have built in a healthy margin of safety, and especially if you have the power to move markets. By the same token, it makes complete sense for investors to spread their bets widely if they are investing in companies where there is substantial uncertainty about the future and are unclear about how and when the market price will adjust to the anticipated value.

CONCLUSION

Value investing comes in many stripes. First, there are the screeners, whom we view as the direct descendants of the Ben Graham school of investing. They look for stocks that trade at low multiples of earnings, book value, or revenues, and argue that these stocks can earn excess returns over long periods. It is not clear whether these excess returns are truly abnormal returns, rewards for having a long time horizon, or just the appropriate rewards for risk that we have not adequately measured. Second, there are contrarian value investors, who take positions in companies that have done badly in terms of stock prices and/or have acquired reputations as poorly managed or badly run companies. They are playing the expectations game, arguing that it is far easier for firms such as these to beat market expectations than firms that are viewed as successful firms. Finally, there are activist investors who take positions in undervalued and/or badly managed companies and by virtue of their holdings are able to force changes in corporate policy or management that unlock this value.

What, if anything, ties all of these different strands of value investing together? In all of its forms, the common theme of value investing is that firms that are out of favor with the market, either because of their own performance or because the sector that they are in is in trouble, can be good investments.

EXERCISES

1. Would you classify yourself as a value investor? If yes, what type of value investor are you (passive, contrarian, activist)?

2. Assuming that you are a passive value investor, come up with two screens that you would use to find cheap stocks.
   a. Use those screens to find cheap stocks.
   b. Take a look at your list of cheap stocks. Do you see any potential problems with a portfolio composed of these stocks?
   c. Add a screen or screens that would help you avoid the problem stocks.
3. Assuming that you are a contrarian value investor, come up with two screens that you would use to find cheap stocks.
   a. Use those screens to find cheap stocks.
   b. Take a look at your list of cheap stocks. Do you see any potential problems with a portfolio composed of these stocks?
   c. Add a screen or screens that would help you avoid the problem stocks.
4. Assuming that you are trying to find stocks that will be targeted by activist investors, come up with two screens that you would use to find cheap stocks.
   a. Use those screens to find cheap stocks.
   b. Take a look at your list of cheap stocks. Do you see any potential problems with a portfolio composed of these stocks?
   c. Add a screen or screens that would help you avoid the problem stocks.

Lessons for Investors

To be a value investor, you should have:

- *A long time horizon:* While the empirical evidence is strongly supportive of the long-term success of value investing, the key phrase is *long term*. If you have a time horizon that is less than two or three years, you may never see the promised rewards to value investing.
- *Be willing to bear risk:* Contrary to popular opinion, value investing strategies can entail a great deal of risk, at least in the short term from price movements. Firms that look cheap on a price-to-earnings or price-to-book basis can be exposed to both earnings volatility and default risk.

In addition to these, to be a contrarian value investor, you need:

- *A tolerance for bad news:* As a contrarian investor who buys stocks that are down and out, you should be ready for more bad news to come out about these stocks. In other words, things will often get worse before they get better.

In addition to all of these requirements, to be an activist value investor, you have to:

- *Be willing to fight:* Incumbent managers in companies that you are trying to change will seldom give in without a fight.
- *Have significant resources:* To get the attention of incumbent managers, you have to acquire a large stake in the company.

CHAPTER 9

The Allure of Growth: Small Cap and Growth Investing

There is a widespread belief that while value investing is for the risk averse, growth investing is the investment philosophy of those who like to take risk. Though there is nothing wrong with seeking out risk, taking on risk for the sake of doing so is foolhardy. Growth clearly has value, but the real issue is whether you can buy it at a reasonable price. In this chapter, we examine the basis of growth investing and dispense with the notion that all growth investors are risk seekers. As with value investing, we will look at the various strands of growth investing and examine what you would need to be a successful growth investor.

WHO IS A GROWTH INVESTOR?

Many services define a growth investor as one who buys stocks that trade at high multiples of earnings. Though this may be a convenient way to categorize investors, it is not an accurate one. In fact, it leaves us with the misleading picture of growth investors as being uninterested in the value of what they are buying. While this may be true for some growth investors, does anyone really believe that Peter Lynch, who built Fidelity Magellan by focusing on growth companies, cares less about value than Warren Buffett does?

We will define growth investors as those who invest in companies based on how the market is valuing their growth potential, rather than as existing investments. With our categorization, note that growth investors care just as much about value as value investors do. What then, you might wonder, is the distinction between growth and value investors? The key difference lies in where the focus for finding value lies. As we argued in the preceding chapter, value investors believe that you are more likely to find

329

undervaluation of assets in place and tend to invest in mature firms with substantial existing assets, albeit underperforming ones. Growth investors believe that their competitive edge is in assessing the value of growth and that they are more likely to find bargains in growth investments.

In the sections that follow, we consider the different strands of growth investing. We begin by looking at passive growth investing strategies, where we focus on investing in stocks that pass a specific screen—small companies, initial public offerings, and stocks that trade at low price-earnings (P/E) ratios relative to growth. We will then consider activist growth investing strategies, where investors not only take large positions in growth companies, but also actively involve themselves in the management of these companies. It is in this category that we consider venture capital and some elements of private equity investing.

PASSIVE GROWTH INVESTING

In passive growth investing, as in passive value investing, we use screens to find stocks that are undervalued by the market. The simplest version of passive growth investing is investing in small companies, with *small* defined in terms of market capitalization. Next, we look at investing in initial public offerings (IPOs), with the intent of capturing any excess returns associated with the stock going up after the offering. Finally, we consider more conventional growth investing strategies, by first looking at a strategy of buying companies with high growth; we then evaluate a strategy of buying high-P/E stocks, and finally a more nuanced strategy of buying growth stocks, but only at a reasonable price (GARP).

Small Cap Investing

One of the most widely used passive growth strategies is the strategy of investing in small companies, with *small* defined in terms of market capitalization. You could construct a value-oriented small cap portfolio, but most small cap portfolios tend to be tilted toward growth companies, so we believe that this category fits better in this chapter. We begin by reviewing the empirical evidence on small cap investing, and then look at the requirements for success at this strategy.

The Small Cap Effect Studies have consistently found that smaller firms (in terms of market value of equity) earn higher returns than larger firms of equivalent risk, where risk is defined in terms of the market beta. Figure 9.1 summarizes annual returns for stocks in 10 market value classes,

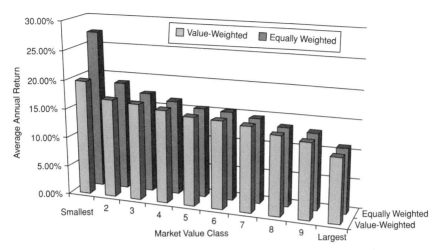

FIGURE 9.1   Annual Returns by Market Value Class, 1927 to 2010
Source: Raw data from Ken French's Data Library (Dartmouth College).

for the period from 1927 to 2010.[1] The portfolios were reconstructed at the end of each year based on the market values of stock at that point in time, and held for the subsequent year.

If we look at value-weighted portfolios, the smallest stocks earned an annual return of about 20 percent between 1927 and 2010, as contrasted with the largest stocks, which earned an annual return of 11 percent. If we use an equally weighted portfolio, the small firm premium is much larger, an indication that the premium is being earned by the smallest stocks. In other words, to capture the small cap premium, you would have to invest in the smallest companies in the market. Nevertheless, these results are impressive and provide a rationale for the number of portfolio managers who focus on buying small-cap stocks. Before we conclude that small cap investing is the way to go, though, we do have to consider some of the details of the small stock premium.

Small Cap Cycles   On average, have small-cap stocks outperformed large-cap stocks over this period? Absolutely, but, success from this strategy is by no means guaranteed in every time period. While small-cap stocks have done better than large-cap stocks in more periods than not, there have been extended periods where small-cap stocks have underperformed large-cap

---

[1]These annual returns were obtained from the annual returns data set maintained by Kenneth French and Eugene Fama on market value classes.

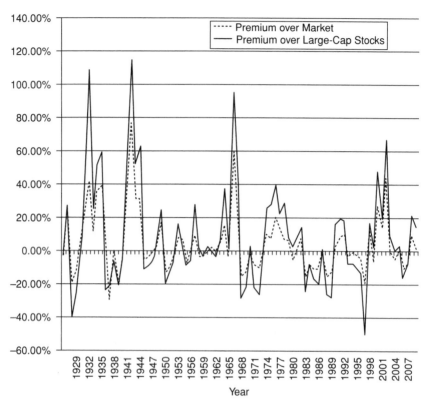

FIGURE 9.2 Small Cap Premium over Time, 1927 to 2010
Source: Raw data from Ken French's Data Library (Dartmouth College).

stocks. Figure 9.2 graphs the premium earned by small-cap stocks (those in the lowest decile in terms of market capitalization) over both the market and large-cap stocks (in the highest decile in terms of market capitalization) from 1927 to 2010.

Note that the premium is negative in a significant number of years—small stocks earned lower returns than large stocks in those years. In fact, during the 1980s and the middle of the last decade, large market cap stocks outperformed small-cap stocks by a significant amount, creating a debate about whether this was a long-term shift in the small stock premium or just a temporary dip. On the one side, Jeremy Siegel argues that the small stock premium can be almost entirely attributed to the performance of small stocks in the late 1970s.

Pradhuman takes a close look at the small cap premium in his book on the topic and divides the 1926–1999 time period into 11 subperiods, with

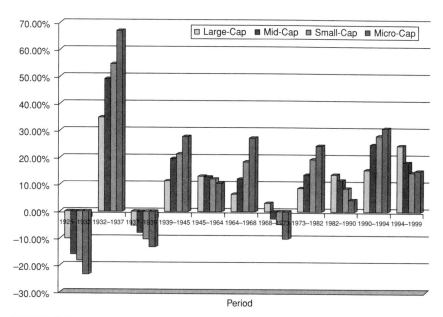

FIGURE 9.3 Small Cap Cycles over Time
Source: S. Pradhuman, *Small Cap Dynamics* (Princeton, NJ: Bloomberg Press, 2000).

small-cap stocks outperforming in five periods and underperforming in six periods.[2] Figure 9.3 summarizes his findings by period.

Pradhuman notes that small-cap stocks tend to do much better than large-cap stocks when the yield curve is downward sloping and inflation is high, which may explain why the premium was high in the 1970s. He also finds that the small cap premium tends to be larger when default spreads on corporate bonds narrow. In summary, there is a return premium for small-cap stocks but it is a volatile one. While the premium clearly exists over long time periods, it also disappears over extended periods.

Deconstructing the Small Cap Effect   A number of studies have tried to take a closer look at the small cap effect to see where the premium comes from. The following are some of the conclusions:

- The small cap effect is greatest in the micro-cap companies (i.e., the really small companies). In fact, many of these companies have market capitalizations of $250 million or lower. All too often these are also

---

[2]S. Pradhuman, *Small Cap Dynamics* (Princeton, NJ: Bloomberg Press, 2000).

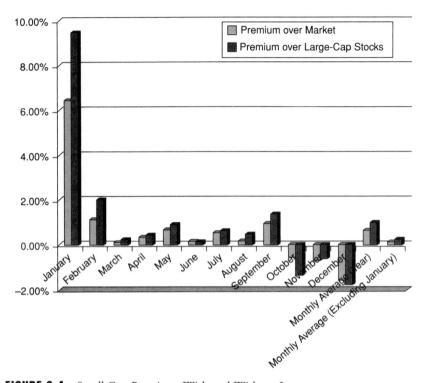

FIGURE 9.4 Small Cap Premium: With and Without January
Source: Raw data from Ken French's Data Library (Dartmouth College).

companies that have low-priced and illiquid stocks and are not followed by equity research analysts.

- A significant proportion of the small cap premium is earned in January. Figure 9.4 presents the contrast between small-cap stocks and the market and the contrast between small-cap and large-cap companies in January and for the rest of the year between 1927 and 2010.

- In fact, you cannot reject the hypothesis that there is no small cap premium from February to December. Many of the other temporal anomalies that we noted in Chapter 7, such as the weekend effect, also seem to be greater for small-cap companies. There is evidence of a small firm premium in markets outside the United States. Studies find small cap premiums of about 7 percent from 1955 to 1984 in the United Kingdom,[3]

---

[3]E. Dimson and P. R. Marsh, "Event Studies and the Size Effect: The Case of UK Press Recommendations," *Journal of Financial Economics* 17 (1986): 113–142.

8.8 percent in France, and a much smaller size effect in Germany,[4] and a premium of 5.1 percent for Japanese stocks between 1971 and 1988.[5] Dimson, Marsh, and Staunton examine the small cap premium across 20 equity markets around the world and find that small-cap stocks earn premiums in 19 of 20 markets over long time periods; the average annualized small cap premium between 2001 and 2010 across the 20 markets was 8.5 percent.[6]

Explanations for the Small Stock Premium The persistence of the small stock premium in empirical studies has led many to argue that what looks like a premium comes from the failure to allow for transaction costs and measure risk correctly in firms. There is truth in these arguments, though it is unclear whether the small stock premium would disappear even if they were considered.

Transaction Costs The transaction costs of investing in small stocks are significantly higher than the transaction costs of investing in larger stocks, and the premiums are estimated prior to these costs. In Chapter 5, for instance, we looked at the bid-ask spread as a percentage of the stock price and noted that it tended to be higher for smaller companies. In addition, the price impact from trading is also higher for small-cap stocks because they are less liquid. Can the difference in transaction costs overwhelm the small cap premium? The answer has to depend on your time horizon. With short time horizons, the transaction costs can wipe out any perceived excess returns associated with small-cap companies. With longer time horizons, though, you can spread the costs over your holding period and the excess returns may persist.

In a telling illustration of the difficulties associated with replicating the small firm premiums that are observed in the studies in real time, in Figure 9.5 we compare the returns on a hypothetical small firm portfolio (CRSP Small Stocks) with the actual returns on one of the best-known small cap mutual funds (DFA Small Stock Fund), which passively invests in the same small stocks.

---

[4]E. F. Fama and K. R. French, "Value versus Growth: The International Evidence," *Journal of Finance* 53 (1998): 1975–1999.

[5]L. K. Chan, Y. Hamao, and J. Lakonishok, "Fundamentals and Stock Returns in Japan," *Journal of Finance* 46 (1991): 1739–1789.

[6]E. Dimson, P. Marsh, and M. Staunton, *Credit Suisse Global Investment Return Sourcebook 2011* (London: London Business School, 2011).

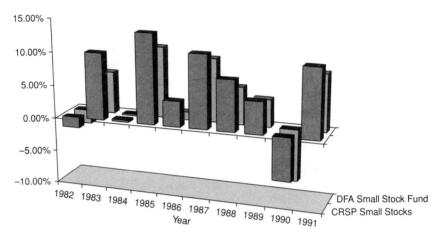

FIGURE 9.5   Returns on CRSP Small Stocks versus DFA Small Stock Fund
Source: Morningstar.

Note that the returns on the DFA fund lag the returns on the hypothetical portfolio by about 1 percent, reflecting the transaction and execution costs faced by the fund. Updating these results for the 20 years ending in 2010, the DFA micro-cap fund earned 13.42 percent a year, while the small-cap firms in the CRSP hypothetical portfolio generated 14.52 percent a year. Thus, the transactions costs amounted to 1.10 percent for even a passive, small cap fund and will be much larger for more active, small cap investors.

Failure to Consider Liquidity and Estimation Risk   Many of the studies that uncover a small cap premium measure the risk of stocks using a market beta and the capital asset pricing model (CAPM). It is entirely possible that the capital asset pricing model is not the right model for risk, and betas underestimate the true risk of small stocks. Thus, the small firm premium may really reflect the failure of the market beta to capture risk. The additional risk associated with small stocks may come from several sources. First, the estimation risk associated with estimates of beta for small firms is much greater than the estimation risk associated with beta estimates for larger firms, partly because of the fact that small companies tend to change more over time and partly because of their short histories. The small firm premium may be a reward for this additional estimation risk.[7] Second, there may be

---

[7]The problem with this argument is that it does not allow for the fact that estimation risk cuts both ways—some betas will be underestimated and some will be overestimated—and should be diversifiable.

much greater liquidity risk associated with investing in small companies. This risk, which is also partially responsible for the higher transaction costs noted in the previous section, is not captured in betas.

While the argument that liquidity and estimation risk can be significant problems for small-cap stocks seems unexceptional, there is one problem with at least the estimation risk component. Note that portfolios of small-cap stocks do not carry the same risk as individual stocks and that estimation risk, in particular, should be diversifiable. Estimation risk will lead you to underestimate the risk (or betas) of some small companies and overestimate the risk (or betas) of other small companies. The beta of a portfolio of such companies should still be predictable, because the estimation errors should average out. With illiquidity, the diversification argument is tougher to make, since it manifests itself as a higher cost (bid-ask spread or price impact) for all small stocks, especially if it is systematic. Thus, the illiquidity risk will show up as higher transaction costs in a small-cap portfolio and will increase as trading in the portfolio increases and during market crises.

Information Risk   When investing in publicly traded companies, we tend to rely not only on the financial reports filed by the company but also on the opinions of analysts following the company. We expect these analysts, rightly or wrongly, to collect information about the firm and reveal this information in their reports. With a large and widely held firm, it is not un-common to see 25 or 30 analysts following the firm and substantial external information on the firm. Many small-cap firms are followed by only one or two analysts and many are not followed by any, as you can see in Figure 9.6.

With some small-cap firms, you may find that the only source of infor-mation is the firm itself. Though the firm may follow all of the regulatory requirements, the information revealed is unlikely to be unbiased, and it is entirely possible that bad news about the firm's operations may be withheld. Since you cannot diversify away this risk, you may demand a premium when investing in these companies.

Determinants of Success in Small Cap Investing   Let us concede, notwith-standing the period in the 1980s when the premium waned, that small-cap stocks earn a premium over large-cap stocks when we adjust for risk using conventional measures like beta. Given the discussion in the preceding sec-tion about potential explanations for this premium, what do you need to do to succeed in small cap investing?

- The first and most critical factor seems to be a *long time horizon*, given the ups and downs of small cap premium. In Figure 9.7, we examine the percentage of time a small cap investor would have outstripped a

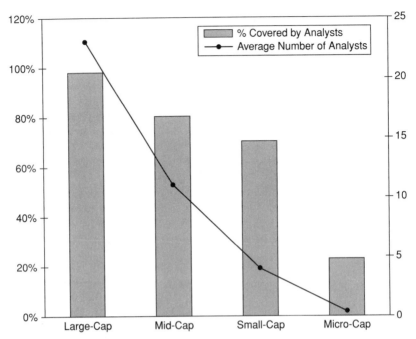

FIGURE 9.6   Analyst Coverage
Source: Capital IQ.

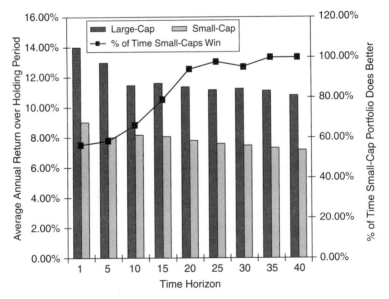

FIGURE 9.7   Time Horizon and the Small Firm Premium

large cap investor with different time horizons. Note that the number is close to 50 percent for time horizons up to five years, no different from a random strategy. Beyond five years, though, small cap investing wins decisively.

A long time horizon will also go a long way toward reducing the bite taken out of returns by transaction costs.

■ The importance of discipline and diversification become even greater if you are a small cap investor. Since small-cap stocks tend to be concentrated in a few sectors, you will need a much larger portfolio to be diversified with small-cap stocks.[8] In addition, diversification should also reduce the impact of estimation risk and some information risk.

■ When investing in small-cap stocks, the responsibility for due diligence will often fall on your shoulders as an investor, since there are often no analysts following the company. You may have to go beyond the financial statements and scour other sources (local newspapers, the firm's customers, and its competitors) to find relevant information about the company.

If you combine the need for more stocks in your portfolio with additional research on each, you can see that small cap investing is likely to be more time and resource intensive than most other investment strategies. If you are willing to expend these resources and have a long time horizon, you should be able to claim a portion of the small cap premium going forward.

SMALL CAP VALUE INVESTING

While we have considered small cap investing as a strand of growth investing, you can be a small-cap value investor if you focus on small companies that trade with low P/E or low PBV ratios, the conventional measures of value companies. Investors who do this hope to combine the excess returns that have been uncovered for buying stocks that trade at low multiples of earnings and book value with the excess returns associated with small cap investing.

(continued)

---

[8]The conventional rule of thumb for being diversified (where you diversify away 95 percent of the firm-specific risk) with large-cap stocks is about 25 stocks. With small-cap stocks, you would need to hold more stocks. How many more? It will depend on your strategy, but you should consider holding at least 40 to 50 stocks.

Pradhuman, in his book on small cap investing, contrasts a strategy of buying small-cap value stocks with small-cap growth stocks and presents several results. First, the excess return on a small-cap value strategy is less than the sum of the excess return on a value strategy and the excess return on a small-cap strategy. In other words, there is some leakage in returns from both strategies when you combine them. Second, the difference in returns between value and growth small-cap stocks mirrors the difference in returns between value and growth large-cap stocks, but the cycles are exaggerated. In other words, when value stocks outperform (or underperform) growth stocks across the market, small-cap value stocks outperform (or underperform) small-cap growth stocks by an even larger magnitude. Third, the excess returns in the past two decades on a small-cap value strategy seem to be more driven by the value component than by the small cap component.[9]

Initial Public Offerings

In initial public offerings (IPOs), private firms make the transition to being publicly traded firms by offering their shares to the public. In contrast with equity issues by companies that are already publicly traded, where there is already a market price for the stock that acts as an anchor, an initial public offering has to be priced by an investment banker based on perceptions of demand and supply. There are some investors who believe that they can exploit both the uncertainty in the process and the biases brought to the pricing by investment bankers to make excess returns.

The Process of an Initial Public Offering   When a private firm becomes publicly traded, the primary benefit it gains is increased access to financial markets and to capital for projects. This access to new capital is a significant gain for high-growth businesses with large and lucrative investment opportunities. A secondary benefit is that the owners of the private firm are able to cash in on their success by attaching a market value to their holdings. These benefits have to be weighed against the potential costs of being publicly

---

[9]He came to this conclusion by regressing excess returns on stocks against market capitalization and price-to-book ratio. The latter explained far more of the differences in excess returns than the former.

traded. The most significant of these costs is the loss of control that may ensue from being a publicly traded firm. Other costs associated with being a publicly traded firm are the information disclosure requirements and the legal requirements.[10] Assuming that the benefits outweigh the costs, there are several steps involved in an initial public offering.

Once the decision to go public has been made, a firm generally cannot approach financial markets on its own. This is so because it may be largely unknown to investors and does not have the expertise to go public without help. Therefore, a firm has to pick intermediaries to facilitate the transaction. These intermediaries are usually investment banks which provide several services.

First, they help the firm meet the information disclosure and filing requirements of the public markets. In order to make a public offering the United States, a firm has to file a registration statement and prospectus with the SEC, providing information about the firm's financial history, its forecasts for the future, and how it plans to use the funds it raises from the initial public offering. The prospectus provides information about the riskiness and prospects of the firm for prospective investors in its stock. Second, they provide the credibility a small and unknown private firm may need to induce investors to buy its stock. Third, they provide their advice on the valuation of the company and the pricing of the new issue. Fourth, they absorb some of the risk in the issue by guaranteeing an offer price on the issue; this guarantee is called an underwriting guarantee. Finally, they help sell the issue by assembling an underwriting syndicate, who try to place the stock with their clients. The underwriting syndicate is organized by one investment bank, called the lead investment bank, and private firms tend to pick investment bankers based on reputation and expertise, rather than price. A good reputation provides the credibility and the comfort level needed for investors to buy the stock of the firm; expertise applies not only to the pricing of the issue and the process of going public but also to other financing decisions that might be made in the aftermath of a public issue. The investment banking agreement is then negotiated, rather than opened up for competition.

Once the firm chooses an investment banker to take it public, the next step is to estimate a value for the firm. This valuation is generally done by the lead investment bank, with substantial information provided by the issuing firm. The value is sometimes estimated using discounted cash flow

---

[10]The costs are twofold. One is the cost of producing and publicizing the information itself. The other is the loss of control over how much and when to reveal information about the firm to others.

models, similar to those described in Chapter 5. More often, though, the value is estimated by using a pricing multiple, estimated by looking at comparable firms that are already publicly traded. Whichever approach is used, the absence of substantial historical information, in conjunction with the fact that these are small companies with high growth prospects, makes the estimation of value an uncertain one at best. The other decision the firm has to make relates to the size of the initial issue and the use of the proceeds. In most cases, only a portion of the firm's stock is offered at the initial public offering; this reduces the risk on the underpricing and enables the owners to test the market before they try to sell more stock. In most cases, the firm uses the proceeds from the initial stock issue to finance new investments.

The next step in this process is to set the value per share for the issuer. To do so, the equity in the firm is divided by the number of shares, which is determined by the price range the issuer would like to have on the issue. If the equity in the firm is valued at $50 million, for example, the number of shares would be set at 5 million to get a target price range of $10 per share, or at 1 million shares to get a target price range of $50 per share. The final step in this process is to set the offering price per share. Most investment banks set the offering price below the estimated value per share for two reasons. First, it reduces the bank's risk exposure, since it ensures that the shares will be bought by investors at the offering price. (If the offering price is set too high and the investment bank is unable to sell all of the shares being offered, it has to use its own funds to buy the shares at the offering price.) Second, investors and investment banks view it as a good sign if the stock increases in price in the immediate aftermath of the initial issue. For the clients of the investment banker who get the shares at the offering price, there is an immediate payoff; for the issuing company, the ground has been prepared for future issues. In setting the offering price, investment bankers have the advantage of first checking investor demand. This process, which is called building the book, involves polling institutional investors prior to pricing an offering to gauge the extent of the demand for an issue. It is also at this stage in the process that the investment banker and issuing firm will present information to prospective investors in a series of presentations called road shows. In this process, if the demand seems very strong, the offering price will be increased; in contrast, if the demand seems weak, the offering price will be lowered. In some cases, a firm will withdraw an initial public offering at this stage[11] if investors are not enthusiastic about it.

---

[11] One study of initial public offerings between 1979 and 1982 found that 29 percent of firms terminated their initial public offerings at this stage in the process.

Once the offering price has been set, the die is cast. If the offering price has indeed been set below the true value, the demand will exceed the offering, and the investment banker will have to choose a rationing mechanism to allocate the shares. On the offering date—the first date the shares can be traded—there will generally be a spurt in the market price. However, if the offering price has been set too high, as is sometimes the case, the investment bankers will have to discount the offering to sell it and make up the difference to the issuer because of the underwriting agreement.

IPO Pricing: The Evidence How well do investment bankers price initial public offerings? One way to measure this is to compare the price when the stock first starts trading to the offering price. Precise estimates vary from year to year, but the average initial public offering seems to be underpriced by about 10 percent to 15 percent. The underpricing also seems to be greater for smaller public offerings. One study estimates the underpricing as a function of the issue proceeds for 1,767 IPOs between 1990 and 1994, and the results are presented in Figure 9.8.[12]

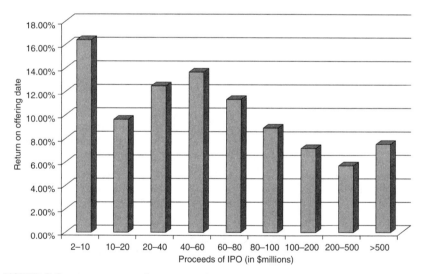

FIGURE 9.8 Average Initial Return and Issue Size
Source: I. Lee, S. Lockhead, J. R. Ritter, and Q. Zhao, "The Costs of Raising Capital," *Journal of Financial Research* 19 (1996): 59–74.

---

[12]I. Lee, S. Lockhead, J. R. Ritter, and Q. Zhao, "The Costs of Raising Capital," *Journal of Financial Research* 19 (1996): 59–74.

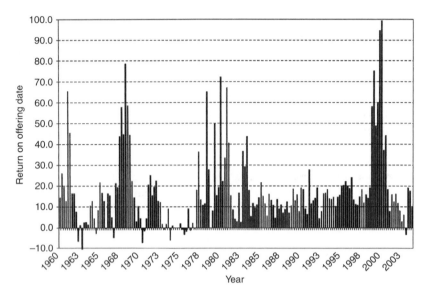

FIGURE 9.9 IPO Underpricing over Time
Source: A. Ljundquist, *IPO Underpricing*, Handbooks in Corporate Finance: Empirical Corporate Finance, edited by Espen Eckbo (Elsevier/North Holland Press (2004)).

The smaller the issue, the greater the underpricing; the smallest offerings often are underpriced by more than 17 percent, but the underpricing is much less for the larger issues.

In a comprehensive survey article on IPO underpricing in 2004, Ljundquist presents two additional findings about the phenomenon.[13] First, he notes that the degree of underpricing has varied widely over time in the United States and presents the average offering date returns (a rough measure of underpricing) across time in Figure 9.9.

Note the dramatic underpricing in 1999 and 2000, when the average IPO jumped by 71 percent and 57 percent on the opening date respectively, and that IPO markets move in cycles, with underpricing increasing in the hot periods and shrinking during other periods. Second, Ljundquist expands the analysis to look at public offerings in 19 European markets in Figure 9.10, and notes that IPOs are underpriced, on average, in every single one. As attention shifts toward emerging markets, initial public offerings have boomed in Asia and Latin America in the past few years. Boulton, Smart, and

---

[13] A. Ljundquist, *IPO Underpricing*, Handbooks in Corporate Finance: Empirical Corporate Finance, edited by Espen Eckbo (2004).

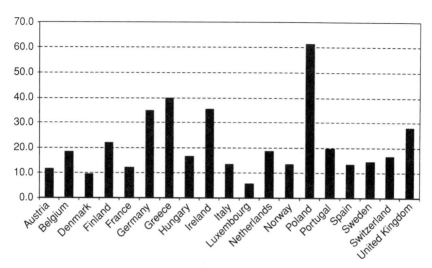

FIGURE 9.10 IPO Underpricing in European Markets
Source: A. Ljundquist, *IPO Underpricing*, Handbooks in Corporate Finance: Empirical Corporate Finance, edited by Espen Eckbo (Elsevier/North Holland Press (2004)).

Zutter estimate the degree of underpricing across 37 countries, including many emerging markets, and evaluate reasons for differences.[14] In particular, they find that IPO underpricing decreases with earnings quality; the underpricing is greatest in countries with poor information disclosure standards and opaque financial statements. The price jumps about 121 percent on the offering date for a typical Chinese IPO but only about 7 percent for the average Brazilian IPO.

While the evidence that initial public offerings go up in price on the offering date is strong, it is not clear that these stocks are good investments in the years after. Loughran and Ritter tracked returns on 5,821 IPOs in the five years after the offerings and contrasted them with returns on nonissuers in Figure 9.11. Note that the IPO firms consistently underperform the nonissuing firms and that the underperformance is greatest in the first few years after the offering. This phenomenon is less pronounced for larger initial public offerings, but it still persists. Put succinctly, the primary payoff to investing in IPOs comes from getting the shares at the offering price and not from buying the shares in the after market.

---

[14]T. J. Boulton, S. B. Smart, and C. J. Zutter, "Earnings Quality and International IPO Underpricing," *Accounting Review* 86 (2010): 483–505.

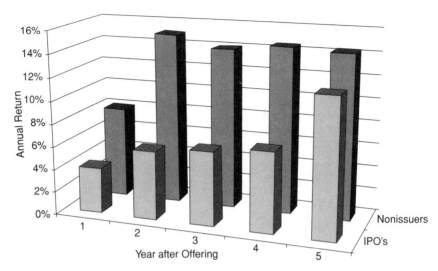

FIGURE 9.11 Postissue Returns—IPOs versus Non-IPOs
Source: T. Loughran and J. R. Ritter, "The New Issues Puzzle," *Journal of Finance* 50, 23–51.

Investment Strategies Given the evidence on underpricing of IPOs and the substandard returns in the years after, are there investment strategies that can be constructed to make money on IPOs? In this section, we consider two. In the first, we adopt the bludgeon approach, trying to partake in every initial public offering and hoping to benefit from the offering day jump (chronicled in the preceding studies). In the second, we adopt a variant of momentum investing, riding IPOs in hot markets and avoiding them in cold markets. In the last, we look at refinements that allow us to invest selectively in those IPOs where the odds best favor investors.

The Bludgeon Strategy: Invest in Every IPO If initial public offerings, on average, are underpriced, an obvious investment strategy is to subscribe to a large number of initial public offerings and to construct a portfolio based on allotments of these offerings. There is, however, a catch in the allotment process that may prevent this portfolio from earning excess returns from the average underpricing. When investors subscribe to initial public offerings, the number of shares that they are allotted will depend on whether and by how much the offering is underpriced. If it is significantly underpriced, you will get only a fraction of the shares that you requested. However, if the offering is correctly priced or overpriced, you will get all of the shares that you requested. Thus, your portfolio will be underweighted in underpriced initial public offerings and overweighted in overpriced offerings.

Is there a way in which you can win this allotment game or in the post-offering market? There are two strategies that you can adopt, though neither guarantees success. The first is to be the beneficiary of a biased allotment system, where the investment bank gives you more than your share of your requested shares in underpriced offerings. The second is to bet against the herd and sell short on IPOs just after they go public, hoping to make money from the price decline in the following months. The peril with this strategy is that the newly listed stocks are not always liquid, and selling short can be both difficult and dangerous.

Ride the Wave: Invest Only in Hot Markets Initial public offerings ebb and flow with the overall market, with both the number of offerings and the degree of underpricing moving in waves. There are periods when the market is flooded with initial public offerings, with significant underpricing, and periods when there are very few offerings, with a concurrent drop-off in underpricing as well. Contrast, for instance, the salad days of the late 1990s, when firms went public at an extraordinary pace, and 2001, when the number slowed to a trickle. Figure 9.12 provides a summary of the

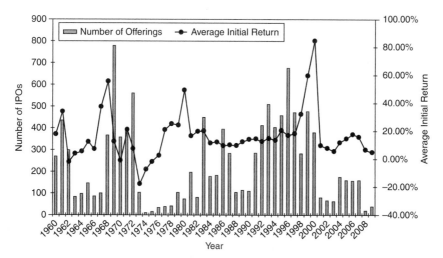

FIGURE 9.12 Number of IPOs and Average Initial Return
Source: A. Ljundquist, *IPO Underpricing*, Handbooks in Corporate Finance: Empirical Corporate Finance, edited by Espen Eckbo (Elsevier/North Holland Press, 2004)). For the most recent years, we used data from IPOcentral.com, a website that tracks IPOs.

number of offerings made each year from 1960 to 2010 and the average initial returns on those offerings.

Note that the number of offerings drops to almost zero in the early 1970s and the returns to IPOs drop as well. The same phenomenon occurs after the dot-com crash of 2001–2002 and the banking crisis of 2008–2010. A strategy of riding the IPO wave would therefore imply investing when the IPO market is hot, with lots of offerings and significant underpricing, and steering away from IPOs in the lean years.

This strategy is effectively a momentum strategy, and the risks are similar. First, while it is true that the strategy generates returns, on average, across the entire hot period, whether you make money or not depends largely upon how quickly you recognize the beginning of a hot IPO market (with delayed entry translating into lower returns) and its end (since the IPO listings toward the very end of the hot market are the ones most likely to fail). Second, the initial public offerings during any period tend to share a common sector focus. For instance, the bulk of the initial public offerings during 1999 were of young technology and telecom firms. Investing only in these public offerings will result in a portfolio that is not diversified in periods of plenty, with an overweighting in whichever sector is in favor at that point in time.

The Discriminating IPO Investor If the biggest danger of an IPO investment strategy is that you may be saddled with overpriced stocks (either because you received your entire allotment of an overpriced IPO or because you are approaching the end of a hot IPO cycle), incorporating a value focus may allow you to avoid some of the risk. Thus, rather than invest in every IPO listing across time or in hot markets, you will invest only in those IPOs where the odds of underpricing are greatest. This will require an investment of time and resources prior to the offering, where you use the information in the prospectus and other public filings to value the company, employing either intrinsic or relative valuation models. You will then use the value estimates from your analysis to decide on which IPOs to invest in and which ones to avoid.

There are two potential pitfalls with this strategy. The first is that your valuation skills have to be well honed, because valuing a company going public is generally much more difficult than valuing one that is already listed. While companies going public have to provide information on their financial standing and what they plan to use the offering proceeds for, they also tend to be younger, high-growth firms. As a consequence, not only is there less of a financial history for the firm, but that history is not as useful in forecasting the future. The second is that, as we noted in the earlier section, IPO markets go through cycles, with the number of underpriced offerings dropping to a handful in cold markets. Thus, your task may end up being finding the least overpriced IPOs rather than underpriced ones, and then working out an exit strategy for selling these stocks before the correction hits.

Determinants of Success   A strategy of investing in initial public offerings makes more sense as an ancillary strategy rather than a primary strategy, partly because of the sector concentration of initial public offerings during hot periods and partly because of the absence of offerings during cold periods. Assuming that it is used as an ancillary strategy, you would need to do the following to succeed:

- Have the valuation skills to value companies with limited information and considerable uncertainty about the future, so as to be able to identify public offerings that are underpriced or overpriced.
- Since this is a short-term strategy, often involving getting the shares at the offering price and flipping the shares shortly after the offering date, you will have to gauge the market mood and demand for each offering, in addition to assessing its value. In other words, a shift in market mood can leave you with a large allotment of overpriced shares in an initial public offering.
- Play the allotment game well, asking for more shares than you want in companies that you view as severely underpriced and fewer or no shares in firms that are overpriced or that are priced closer to fair value.
- Be ready to be a global investor, as initial public offerings increasingly shift to emerging markets in Asia and Latin America.

In recent years, investment banks have used the allotment process to reward selected clients. In periods when demand for initial public offerings is high, they have also been able to punish favored investors who flip shares for a quick profit by withholding or rationing future allotments. If you are required to hold these stocks for the long term to qualify for the initial offering, you may very well find that the superior performance of these stocks in the initial offering period can very quickly be decimated by poor returns in subsequent periods.

Growth Screens

If you are a portfolio manager whose choices come from a very large universe of stocks, your most effective way of building a portfolio may be to screen stocks and pick those that pass specific screens. In other words, you do with growth stocks what Ben Graham did with value stocks. In this section, we consider three screening strategies: a strategy of buying stocks with high expected growth rates in earnings; the highflier strategy, where you pick stocks with high P/E ratios; and the growth at a reasonable price (GARP) strategy, where you pick growth stocks that trade at low prices, given their expected growth.

High Earnings Growth Strategy   The strategy that follows most logically for most growth investors is to buy stocks with high growth rates in earnings. You can look at past growth in earnings as a predictor of future growth and buy companies with high historical earnings growth rates, or you can look for companies where analysts are predicting high expected earnings growth.

Historical Growth   Is the growth rate in the past a good indicator of growth in the future? Not necessarily. Past growth rates may be used by many investors as forecasts of future growth, but there are two problems.

1. The first problem is that past growth rates are volatile and are noisy predictors of future growth. In a 1962 study of the relationship between past growth rates and future growth rates, Little coined the term "higgledy piggledy growth" because he found little evidence that firms that grew fast in one period continued to grow fast in the next period.[15] In the process of running a series of correlations between growth rates in earnings in consecutive periods of different length, he frequently found negative correlations between growth rates in the two periods, and the average correlation across the two periods was close to zero (0.02). If past growth in earnings is not a reliable indicator of future growth at the average firm, it becomes even less so at smaller firms. The growth rates at smaller firms tend to be even more volatile than growth rates at other firms in the market. The correlation between growth rates in earnings in consecutive time periods (five years, three years, and one year) for firms in the United States, categorized by market value, is reported in Figure 9.13.

   While the correlations tend to be higher across the board for one-year growth rates than for three-year or five-year growth rates in earnings, they are also consistently lower for smaller firms than they are

---

[15]I. M. D. Little, *Higgledy Piggledy Growth* (Oxford, UK: Institute of Statistics, 1962).

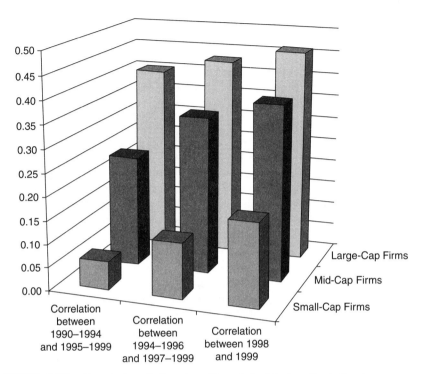

FIGURE 9.13 Correlations in Earnings Growth by Market Capitalization
Source: Capital IQ.

for the rest of the market. This would suggest that you should be more cautious about using past growth, especially in earnings, for forecasting future growth at these firms.

NUMBER WATCH

Historical earnings growth: Take a look at average growth rate over the past five years in earnings, by sector, for U.S. companies.

- The second problem is that there is mean reversion in earnings growth rates. In other words, companies that are growing fast will see their growth rates decline toward the market or industry average, whereas below average growth companies will see their growth rates increase.

This tendency is chronicled by Dreman and Lufkin when they track companies in the highest and lowest earnings growth classes for five years after the portfolios are formed.[16] Although the highest earnings growth companies have an average growth rate that is 20 percent higher than the average growth rate for the lowest earnings growth companies in the year the portfolio is formed, the difference is close to zero five years later.

In general, revenue growth tends to be more persistent and predictable than earnings growth. This is because accounting choices have far smaller effects on revenues than they do on earnings. Consequently, revenue growth is more correlated over time than earnings growth. The implication is that historical growth in revenues is a far more useful number when it comes to forecasting than historical growth in earnings.

There are some investors who believe that it is not earnings growth per se that you should be looking at but momentum in growth. In other words, you want to invest in stocks whose earnings growth is accelerating. This is, in fact, a big component of what Value Line's acclaimed stock picking measures are based on. While Value Line may have been successful with this strategy in its earlier years, much of what we have said about earnings growth also applies to earnings momentum.

In summary, past earnings growth is not a reliable indicator of future growth, and investing in companies with high past growth does not yield significant returns. In fact, if there is mean reversion and you pay a large premium for companies with high growth, you will find yourself with a losing portfolio.

Expected Earnings Growth Value is ultimately driven by future growth and not past growth. It seems reasonable, therefore, that you would be better served investing in stocks whose expected growth is high rather than historical growth. Here, you do run into a practical problem. In a market as large as that of the United States, you cannot estimate expected growth for each firm in the market. Instead, you have to rely on analyst estimates of expected growth for companies. That information, though, is freely accessible now to most investors, and you could buy stocks with high expected growth rates in earnings. But will such a strategy generate excess returns?

---

[16]D. Dreman and E. Lufkin, "Do Contrarian Strategies Work within Industries?" *Journal of Investing* (Fall 1997): 7–29; D. Dreman and E. Lufkin, "Investor Overreaction: Evidence That Its Basis Is Psychological," *Journal of Psychology and Financial Markets* 1 (2000): 61–75.

Consider what you would need for this strategy to be successful. First, analysts have to be proficient at forecasting long-term earnings growth. Second, the market price should not already reflect or price this growth. If it does, your portfolio of high-growth companies will not generate excess returns. On both conditions, the evidence works against the strategy. When it comes to forecasting growth, analysts have a tendency to base long-term growth forecasts on past growth, and the forecast errors are high for long-term forecasts. In fact, some studies find that time series models match or even outperform analysts when it comes to forecasting long-term growth. As for pricing growth, markets historically have been more likely to overprice growth than underprice it, especially during periods of high earnings growth for the market.

High-P/E Strategy   The easiest growth strategy, albeit the riskiest, is to buy the stocks with the highest P/E ratios on the market, on the assumption that these are growth companies whose growth will deliver the excess returns in the future.

The Overall Evidence   We should begin by noting that the overall evidence on beating the market with high P/E ratio stocks is grim. As we argued in Chapter 8, buying low P/E ratio stocks seems to outperform high P/E ratio stocks by significant margins. Figure 9.14 presents the difference in annual returns from buying low P/E ratio and high P/E ratio portfolios from 1952 to 2010.

On both an equally weighted and a value-weighted basis, high P/E ratio stocks have underperformed low P/E ratio stocks. In fact, it is this consistent underperformance of high P/E ratio stocks that has led to the value-investing bias that we often see in both academic and practitioner research.

The Growth Investors' Case   Given this sorry performance, you might wonder what attracts investors to this strategy. The answer lies in market cycles. There have been extended time periods in which high-P/E stocks have outperformed low-P/E stocks. For instance, growth investing seems to do much

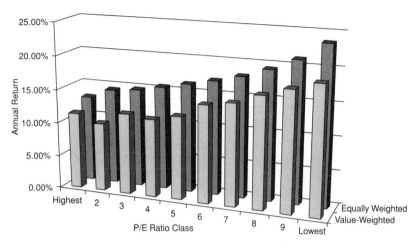

FIGURE 9.14 P/E Ratios and Stock Returns, 1952 to 2010
Source: Raw data from Ken French's Data Library (Dartmouth College).

better when the earnings growth in the market is low, whereas value investing tends to do much better when earnings growth is high. In Figure 9.15,
we have graphed the difference between a low-P/E and a high-P/E portfolio
and the growth in earnings in each period.

We measure the performance of growth versus value by looking at the
difference between the returns earned on a portfolio of stocks in the top

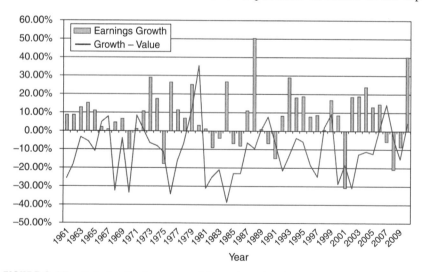

FIGURE 9.15 Relative Performance of Growth and Value versus Earnings Growth
Source: Raw data from Ken French's Data Library (Dartmouth College).

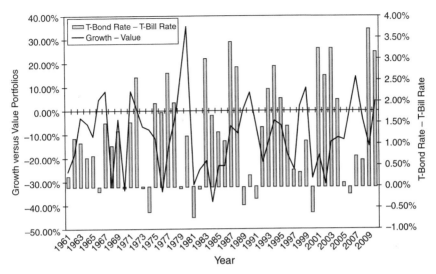

FIGURE 9.16 Relative Performance of Growth Stocks versus Yield Curve
Source: Raw data from Ken French's Data Library (Dartmouth College), Federal Reserve.

decile in terms of P/E (growth) and a portfolio of stocks in the lowest decile (value). Thus, a positive value indicates that high-P/E stocks outperformed low-P/E stocks in that year. Growth investing does best in years when earnings growth is low. This may be due to the fact that growth stocks are more desirable in periods when earnings growth is low, because growth is scarce. By the same token, when companies are reporting high earnings growth, investors seem to be unwilling to pay a premium for growth.

Growth investing also seems to do much better when the yield curve is flat or downward sloping, and value investing does much better when the yield curve is upward sloping. Figure 9.16 presents the relationship between the slope of the yield curve and the performance of growth investing.

The most interesting evidence on growth investing, however, lies in the percentage of active money managers who beat their respective indexes. When measured against their respective indexes, active growth investors seem to beat growth indexes more often than active value investors beat value indexes. In his paper on mutual funds in 1995, Malkiel provides additional evidence on this phenomenon.[17] He notes that between 1981 and 1995, the average actively managed value fund outperformed the average

---

[17]B. G. Malkiel, "Returns from Investing in Equity Mutual Funds 1971 to 1991," *Journal of Finance* 50 (1995): 549–572.

actively managed growth fund by only 16 basis points a year, whereas the value index outperformed a growth index by 47 basis points a year. He attributes the 31 basis point difference to the contribution of active growth managers relative to value managers. We will look at this evidence in more detail in Chapter 13.

PETER LYNCH: FINDING VALUE IN GROWTH STOCKS

If Warren Buffett is the icon for value investors, Peter Lynch occupies a similar position for growth investors. His reputation was made during his stewardship of Fidelity Magellan, a small high-growth fund that he took over in 1977 and made into the largest equity mutual fund in the world over the next decade. The reason for its growth was its performance. An investment of $10,000 in the Magellan fund would have grown 20-fold over the next 10 years. During that period, Lynch also helped dispel the notion that growth investors were incurable optimists who bought stocks on promises. He introduced the rigors of value investing to growth investing, and he described much of what he did in his books on investing and his articles for *Worth*, a financial magazine.

Looking at his writings, you can summarize his views on growth investing in the following maxims. The first is that numbers matter more than stories and that the allure of a growth company has to be measured by the results it delivers and not just by its promise. The second is that it takes far more work and effort to monitor a growth company than it does a value company. Thus, spreading your bets across too many companies can hurt you. The third is that you have to take a stand early in a growth company's life to make profits, since waiting to invest until a growth company has clearly established its presence is usually too late. The fourth is that you need to be patient; even with the right growth companies, it may take a while for the returns to manifest themselves. Finally, good growth companies are rare, and finding one good growth company may require you to research a dozen or more companies.

GARP Strategies There are many growth investors who would blanch at the strategy of buying high-P/E stocks. Their mission, they would argue, is to buy high-growth stocks whose growth is undervalued. To find these stocks, they have developed a number of strategies in which you consider both expected growth and the current pricing of the stock. We consider two of these strategies in this section: buying stocks with a P/E less than the expected growth rate and buying stocks with a low ratio of P/E to growth (called a PEG ratio).

PE Less Than Growth Rate   The simplest growth at a reasonable price (GARP) strategy is to buy stocks that trade at a P/E ratio less than the expected growth rate. Thus, a stock that has a P/E ratio of 12 and an expected growth rate of 8 percent would be viewed as overvalued, whereas a stock with a P/E of 40 and an expected growth rate of 50 percent would be viewed as undervalued. While this strategy clearly has the benefit of simplicity, it can be dangerous for several reasons.

- *Interest rate effect.* Since growth generates earnings in the future, the value created by any given growth rate will be greater when interest rates are low (which makes the present values higher) than when interest rates are high. Thus, the stock with a P/E of 40 and an expected growth rate of 50 percent when interest rates are 7 percent may find itself with a P/E of 60 if interest rates drop to 5 percent. It is not surprising, therefore, that portfolio managers who use this strategy not only find far more underpriced stocks when interest rates are high but also find stocks in many emerging markets (where interest rates tend to be high) to be cheap. The effect of interest rates on the relationship between P/E and growth can be best illustrated by looking at the percentage of firms that trade at less than their expected growth rate as a function of the Treasury bond rate. In 1981, when Treasury bond rates hit 12 percent, more than 65 percent of firms traded at P/E ratios less than the expected growth rate. In 1991, when rates had dropped to about 8 percent, the percentage of stocks trading at less than the expected growth rate also dropped to about 45 percent. By the end of the 1990s, with the Treasury bond rate dropping to 5 percent, the percentage of stocks that traded at less than the expected growth rate had dropped to about 25 percent.
- *Growth rate estimates.* When this strategy is used for a large number of stocks, you have no choice but to use the growth rate estimates of others. In some cases, the consensus growth rates estimated by all analysts following a firm are obtained from a data service. When you do this, you have to wonder both about the differences in the quality of the growth estimates across different analysts and about their comparability. Given that these estimated growth rates are at most for five years, you may penalize companies that have expected growth for much longer periods by focusing just on the five-year rate.

It is also possible that in low interest rate scenarios, very few stocks pass this screen and you will end up with little to invest in.

PEG Ratios An alternative approach that seems to offer more flexibility than just comparing the P/E ratio to expected growth rates is to look at the ratio of the P/E to expected growth. This ratio, called the PEG ratio, is widely used by analysts and portfolio managers following growth companies.

Defining the PEG Ratio The PEG ratio is defined to be the price-earnings ratio divided by the expected growth rate in earnings per share:

$$PEG\ ratio = \frac{P/E\ ratio}{Expected\ growth\ rate}$$

For instance, a firm with a P/E ratio of 40 and a growth rate of 50 percent is estimated to have a PEG ratio of 0.80. There are some who argue that only stocks with PEG ratios less than 1.00 are desirable, but this strategy is equivalent to the strategy of comparing the P/E to the expected growth rate.

NUMBER WATCH

Sector average PEG ratios: Take a look at the average PEG ratio, by sector, for U.S. companies.

Consistency requires the growth rate used in this estimate be the growth rate in earnings per share. Given the many definitions of the P/E ratio, which one should you use to estimate the PEG ratio? The answer depends on the base on which the expected growth rate is computed. If the expected growth rate in earnings per share is based on earnings in the most recent year (current earnings), the P/E ratio that should be used is the current P/E ratio. If it based on trailing earnings, the P/E ratio used should be the trailing P/E ratio. The forward P/E ratio should generally not be used in this computation, since it may result in a double counting of growth.[18] Building upon the theme of uniformity, the PEG ratio should be estimated using the same growth

---

[18]If the forward earnings are high because of high growth in the next year, and this high growth results in a high growth rate for the next five years, you have effectively counted the growth rate next year twice.

estimates for all firms in the sample. You should not, for instance, use five-year growth rates for some firms and one-year growth rates for others. One way of ensuring uniformity is to use the same source for earnings growth estimates for all the firms in the group. For instance, both I/B/E/S and Zacks provide consensus estimates from analysts of earnings per share growth over the next five years for most U.S. firms. Many analysts who use PEG ratios, though, prefer to use short-term growth rates in earnings in their computations.

Using the PEG Ratio   How do analysts use PEG ratios? A stock with a low PEG ratio is considered cheap, because you are paying less for the growth. It is viewed as a growth-neutral measure that can be used to compare stocks with different expected growth rates. In a study concluded in 1998, Morgan Stanley found that a strategy of buying stocks with low PEG ratios yielded returns that were significantly higher than what you would have made on the S&P 500. The researchers came to this conclusion by looking at the 1,000 largest stocks on the U.S. and Canadian exchanges each year from January 1986 through March 1998, and categorizing them into deciles based on the PEG ratio. They found that the 100 stocks with the lowest PEG ratios earned an annual return of 18.7 percent during the period, higher than the market return of about 16.8 percent over the period. While no mention was made of risk adjustment, it was argued that the difference was larger than could be justified by the risk adjustment.

We updated this study to examine how this strategy would have done from 1991 to 2010, creating five portfolios at the end of each year based on the PEG ratio and examining the returns in the following year. Figure 9.17 summarizes the average annual returns on PEG ratio classes in the 1991 to 1996, 1997 to 2001, and 2002 to 2010 time periods.

A strategy of investing in low PEG ratio stocks would have generated an average return about 2 to 3 percent higher than the average returns on a high PEG ratio portfolio, before adjusting for risk, during all of the time periods.

Potential Problems   There are two potential problems with PEG ratios that may lead us to misidentify riskier stocks with higher growth rates as undervalued. The first and most obvious problem is that the PEG ratio is obtained by dividing the P/E ratio by the expected growth rate, and the uncertainty about that expected growth rate is not factored into the number. Intuitively, you would expect riskier stocks for any given growth rate to have lower P/E ratios. Thus, a stock that looks cheap on a PEG ratio basis may be, in fact, correctly valued or even overvalued. The relationship between risk and growth can be illustrated in two ways. The first is by computing the

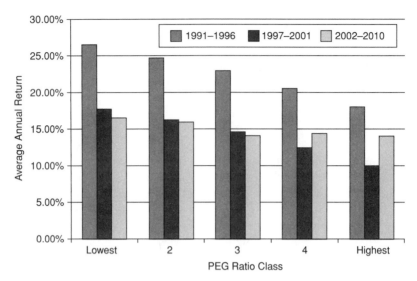

FIGURE 9.17 PEG Ratios and Annual Returns
Source: Value Line.

P/E ratio for a hypothetical firm, holding growth and cash flows constant, but varying the risk.[19] In Figure 9.18, for instance, we vary the beta of a stock with an expected growth rate of 25 percent for five years and 8 percent forever thereafter, and compute the PEG ratio.

Note that the PEG ratio for the safe firm, with a beta of 0.75, is almost four times higher than the PEG ratio for the risky firm (with the same growth rate) with a beta of 2.00. You can also see the relationship between risk and PEG ratios by computing the average PEG ratios for all stocks listed in the United States and categorizing them based on their riskiness. Figure 9.19 classifies all firms in the United States into 10 risk classes[20] and computes the average PEG ratios for firms in each class in January 2011.

---

[19]To do this, you first have to compute the P/E ratio based on fundamentals and then divide by the expected growth rate. A more detailed exposition is provided in my book *Investment Valuation*, but the PEG ratio in a two-stage dividend discount model can be written as

$$\text{PEG} = \frac{(\text{Payout ratio}) (1 + g) \left(1 - \dfrac{(1 + g)^n}{\left(1 + k_{e,hg}\right)^n} \right)}{g \left(k_{e,hg} - g\right)} + \frac{(\text{Payout ratio}_n) (1 + g)^n (1 + g_n)}{g (k_{e,st} - g_n) (1 + k_{e,hg})^n}$$

[20]This categorization was based on stock price standard deviation, but we did try alternate measures such as beta and obtained similar results.

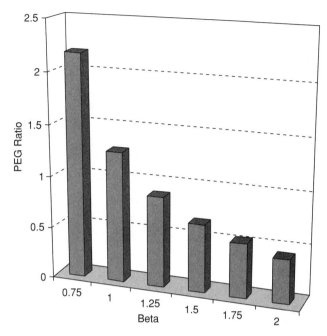

FIGURE 9.18 PEG Ratios and Beta: Firm with 25 Percent Growth for Next Five Years, 8 Percent Thereafter

The highest-risk firms have the lowest PEG ratios in the market, reflecting the downward pressure exerted by risk on PEG ratios. Thus, a portfolio of the stocks with the lowest PEG ratios will tend to include a large number of high-risk stocks. The second potential problem with PEG ratios is less obvious but just as dangerous. When we use PEG ratios, we make the implicit assumption that as growth doubles, the P/E ratio doubles, and if it is halved, the P/E ratio will be halved as well. In other words, we assume a linear relationship between P/E and expected growth, and this clearly is not correct. To see why, consider what should happen to the P/E as expected growth drops to zero. If you have a firm that has a dollar in earnings that it pays out in dividends and you expect to get this dollar in dividends in perpetuity, you would still be willing to pay a price for its stock. In other words, your P/E does not go to zero. On the other side, you will find that P/E ratios increase as you increase the expected growth rate, but at a decreasing rate. In other words, your P/E ratio will change much more dramatically when your expected growth rate goes from 3 to 4 percent than when it goes from 23 to 24 percent. Again, the effect on PEG ratio of varying the growth rate can be shown in one of two ways. Using the same process that we used to

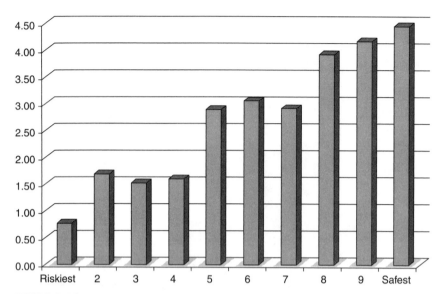

FIGURE 9.19 PEG Ratios by Risk Class in January 2011: U.S. Stocks
Source: Capital IQ.

examine the relationship between PEG ratios and risk, we can estimate the PEG ratio for a hypothetical firm in Figure 9.20 as you change the expected growth rate during its high-growth phase.

The PEG ratio is highest when the expected growth rate is low, but is lower at higher expected growth rates. Clearly, the problem is greatest when you are comparing high-growth firms to low-growth firms, since PEG ratios will be understated for the former and overstated for the latter. It is less of an issue if you are comparing PEG ratios across firms with high growth rates, since the effect is muted.

In short, picking stocks based on low PEG ratios can leave you with a portfolio of stocks with high risk and high growth that are not undervalued. Can you correct for these errors? You can adjust for risk by either considering it as a separate factor (you pick stocks with low PEG ratios and low risk) or modifying the PEG ratio. Morgan Stanley, for example, aware of the potential bias toward risk in the PEG ratio, modified it to include the dividend yield in the denominator to create a new ratio called the PEGY ratio:

$$PEGY = \frac{P/E}{(\text{Expected growth rate} + \text{Dividend yield})}$$

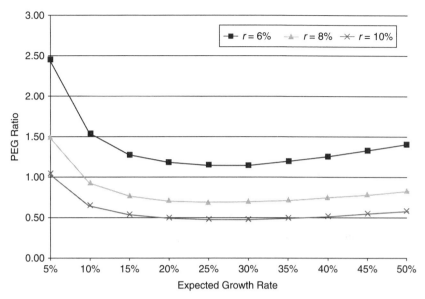

FIGURE 9.20 PEG Ratios and Expected Growth Rate over Next Five Years

Thus, a firm with a P/E ratio of 12, an expected growth rate of 5 percent, and a dividend yield of 4 percent would have a PEGY ratio of 1.33 [12/(5 + 4)]. Intuitively, adding the dividend yield to the denominator counteracts the tilt toward high-growth companies that PEG ratios expose you to, but it is not an easy multiple to work with, especially in today's market, in which companies replace dividends with buybacks.

Determinants of Success at Passive Growth Investing The overall empirical evidence on the efficacy of screens is much less favorable for growth screens than it is for value screens. While there are cycles during which growth screens like low PEG ratios and high P/E ratios yield excess returns, they are trumped over longer periods by value screens such as low P/E or low price-to-book value ratios. From our perspective, there are four key determinants of success at this strategy:

1. Since growth is the key dimension of value in these companies, obtaining better estimates of expected growth should improve your odds of success. If you are a growth investor following a fairly small set of companies, you may try to estimate growth yourself. If you can estimate growth more precisely than the overall market, you should get a payoff. If this is not a feasible option because you do not have the resources to estimate expected growth rates for the hundreds of firms that you

follow, you should compare the different sources that you have for this input to see which one has the best track record.

2. If your underlying strategy is sound, a long time horizon increases your chances of earning excess returns. In other words, if you conclude after careful analysis that buying stocks that have P/E ratios less than the expected growth rate would have yielded high returns over the past two decades, you will be more likely to replicate these results if you have a five-year horizon than a one-year horizon.

3. There seem to be interactions between growth potential and the stock price momentum that we referenced in Chapter 7, with momentum being stronger at high-growth companies. Thus, combining a passive growth screen with a momentum screen (such as relative strength) may augment the returns to the strategy.

4. Finally, there are extended cycles where the growth screens work exceptionally well and other cycles where they are counterproductive. If you can time these cycles, you could augment your returns substantially. Since many of these cycles are related to how the overall market is doing, this boils down to your market timing ability.

ESTIMATING GROWTH FROM FUNDAMENTALS

If obtaining better estimates of growth is key to successful growth investing, you may want to consider breaking your dependence on estimates of growth made by equity research analysts. As we will see in the next chapter, analysts often do not estimate long-term growth, and even when they do, they provide biased estimates. One alternative that may yield better and more robust estimates is to link the expected growth to fundamental aspects of how a firm is run. In fact, the expected growth rate in earnings for a firm comes from two sources: its willingness to reinvest its earnings back into new projects and assets and its capacity to earn high returns on these investments. The growth rate in earnings for a firm in the long term should be a product of the proportion of its earnings that are reinvested back in the business and the return on this investment. For equity earnings, it can be computed as follows:

$$\text{Growth rate in earnings per share} =$$
$$(1 - \text{Dividends/Earnings})(\text{Return on equity})$$

Consider, for instance, a company that pays no dividends and earns about 25 percent on its equity. Its expected growth rate, if it can sustain these numbers, will be 25 percent. In contrast, a company that pays about 50 percent of its earnings as dividends and earns 16 percent as its return on equity will have an expected growth rate of 8 percent.

When computing growth in operating earnings, you will have to modify the equation to make it consistent:

Growth rate in operating earnings = [(Capital expenditures − Depreciation + Change in working capital)/EBIT(1 − t)] ∗ Return on capital

Thus, a company that reinvests 80 percent of its after-tax operating income and earns a return on capital of 40 percent will be able to post a growth rate of 32 percent a year.

ACTIVIST GROWTH INVESTING

In activist growth investing, you not only take a position in a growth business but you also play an active role in making it successful. Since most growth businesses start off as small and privately owned, the most common forms of activist growth investing involve taking positions in these businesses before they go public and in nurturing them toward eventual public offerings and large profits. In this section, we consider venture capital and private equity investing as examples of activist growth investing.

Description

In venture capital investing, you provide equity financing to small and often risky businesses in return for a share of the ownership of the firm. The size of your ownership share will depend on two factors. First, at the minimum, you will demand an ownership share based on how much capital you contribute to the firm, relative to total firm value. For instance, if you provide $2 million and the estimated value of the firm is $10 million, you will expect to own at least 20 percent of the firm. Second, if the business can raise the funds from other sources, its bargaining position will be stronger, and it may be able to reduce your share down to a small premium over the minimum just specified. If a business has no other options available to raise the equity financing, however, its bargaining position is considerably weaker, and the owner of the business will have to give up a disproportionate share of the ownership to get the required funding. In general, the capacity to raise funds from alternative sources or to go public will increase with the size of the firm and decrease with the uncertainty about its future prospects. Thus, smaller and riskier businesses are more likely to seek venture capital and are also more likely to be asked to give up a greater share of the value of the firm when receiving the venture capital.

The Market for Private Equity and Venture Capital

Until a few decades ago, venture capital was provided by individuals or groups that tended to specialize in a sector, invest in relatively few firms, and take an active role in the operations of these firms. In recent decades, though, as the market for venture capital has expanded, you have seen three categories emerge.

The first are *venture capital funds* that trace their lineage back to the 1950s. One of the first was American Research and Development, which provided seed money for the founding of Digital Equipment Corporation. During the 1960s and 1970s, these funds multiplied and helped start and expand companies such as Intel and Apple that were then taken public. The second are *large publicly traded companies*, like Intel and Microsoft, that have substantial resources (cash and/or the capacity to raise capital) and relatively few internal investment opportunities. They have invested in small companies with promising technologies, hoping to either use these technologies internally or to profit from taking these companies public. More recently, we have seen the growth of *private equity funds* that pool the wealth of individual investors and invest in private firms that show promise. This has allowed investors to invest in private businesses without taking an active role in managing these firms. Pension funds and institutional investors, attracted by the high returns earned by investments in private firms, have also set aside portions of their overall portfolios to invest in private equity.

Most private equity funds are structured as private limited partnerships, where the managers of the fund are the general partners and the investors in the fund—both individual and institutional—are limited partners. The general partners hold on to the power on when and where to invest and are generously compensated, with annual compensation a percentage of the total capital invested with an additional bonus, specified as a percent of the excess profits generated on that capital. These partnerships typically last from 10 to 12 years, and limited partners have to agree to make capital commitments for periods of five to seven years.

The Process of Venture Capital Investing

Venture capital can prove useful at different stages of a private firm's existence. *Seed-money venture capital*, for instance, is provided to start-up firms that want to test a concept or develop a new product, while *start-up venture capital* allows firms that have established products and concepts to develop and market them. Additional rounds of venture capital allow private firms that have more established products and markets to expand. There are five steps associated with how venture capital gets to be provided to firms, and how venture capitalists ultimately profit from these investments.

Provoke Equity Investor's Interest   There are hundreds of small firms interested in raising finance from private equity investors, and relatively few venture capitalists and private equity investors. Given this imbalance, the first step that a private firm wanting to raise private equity has to take is to get private equity investors interested in investing in it. There are a number of factors that help the private firm at this stage. One is the *type of business* that the private firm is in, and how attractive this business is to private equity investors. In the late 1980s and early 1990s, for instance, firms in biotechnology were the favored targets for private equity investors. By the late 1990s, the focus had shifted to Internet and technology stocks.

Another factor is the track record of the top manager or managers of the firm. Top managers who have a track record of converting private businesses into publicly traded firms have an easier time raising private equity capital. Thus, it is not uncommon to see serial entrepreneurs, who start, nurture and take public multiple companies sequentially, with easy access to venture capital.

Valuation and Return Assessment   Once private equity investors become interested in investing in a firm, the value of the private firm has to be assessed by looking at both its current and expected prospects. While venture capitalists sometimes use discounted cash flow models to value firms, they are much more likely to value private businesses using what is called the *venture capital method*. Here, the earnings of the private firm are forecast for a future year when the company can be expected to go public. These earnings, in conjunction with a price-earnings multiple estimated by looking at publicly traded firms in the same business, is used to assess the value of the firm at the time of the initial public offering; this is called the exit or terminal value.

For instance, assume that a small private software firm is expected to have an initial public offering in three years, and that the net income in three years for the firm is expected to be $4 million. If the price-earnings ratio of publicly traded software firms is 25, this would yield an estimated exit value of $100 million. This value is discounted back to the present at what venture capitalists call a *target rate of return*, which measures what venture capitalists believe is a justifiable return, given the risk that they are exposed to. This target rate of return is usually set at a much higher level[21] than the traditional cost of equity for the firm.

$$\text{Discounted terminal value} = \text{Estimated exit value}/(1 + \text{Target return})^n$$

In this example, if the venture capitalists require a target return on 30 percent on the investment, the discounted terminal value for the firm would be:

$$\text{Discounted terminal value} = \$100 \text{ million}/1.30^3 = \$45.52 \text{ million}$$

Structuring the Deal   In structuring the deal to bring private equity into the firm, the private equity investor and the firm have to negotiate two items. First, the private equity investor has to determine what proportion of the value of the firm he or she will demand in return for the private equity investment. The owners of the firm, in turn, have to determine how much of the firm they are willing to give up in return for the same capital. In these assessments, the amount of new capital being brought into the firm has to be measured against the estimated firm value. In the software firm example, assuming that the venture capitalists are considering investing $12 million, they would want to own at least 26.36 percent of the firm.[22]

$$\text{Ownership proportion} = \text{Capital provided}/\text{Estimated value}$$
$$= \$12/\$45.52 = 26.36\%$$

Second, the private equity investors will often impose constraints on the managers of the firm in which the investment is being made. This is to ensure that the private equity investors are protected and that they have a say in how the firm is run.

Postdeal Management   Once the private equity investment has been made, the private equity investor will often take an active role in the management of the firm. Private equity investors and venture capitalists bring not only a wealth of management experience to the process, but also contacts that can be used to raise more capital and get fresh business for the firm.

---

[21]By 1999, for instance, the target rate of return for private equity investors was in excess of 30 percent.
[22]Private equity investors draw a distinction between what a firm will be worth without their capital infusion (premoney) and what it will be worth with the infusion (postmoney). Optimally, they would like their share of the firm to be based on the premoney valuation, which will be lower.

Exit   Private equity investors and venture capitalists invest in private businesses because they are interested in earning a high return on these investments. There are three ways in which a private equity investor can profit from an investment in a business. The first and usually the most lucrative alternative is an initial public offering made by the private firm. While venture capitalists do not usually liquidate their investments at the time of the initial public offering, they can sell at least a portion of their holdings once shares are traded.[23] The second alternative is to sell the private business to another firm; the acquiring firm might have strategic or financial reasons for the acquisition. The third alternative is to withdraw cash flows from the firm and liquidate the firm over time. This strategy would not be appropriate for a high-growth firm, but it may make sense if investments made by the firm no longer earn excess returns.

The Payoff to Venture Capital and Private Equity Investing

Note that the act of seeking and receiving venture capital is voluntary, and both sides enter into the relationship with the hope of gaining from it. The business gains access to funds that would not have been available otherwise; these funds in turn might enable the firm to bridge the gap until it can become a publicly traded firm. The venture capitalist might contribute management and organizational skills to the venture and provide the credibility needed for the business to raise more financing. The venture capitalist also might provide the know-how needed for the firm to eventually make a public offering of its equity. If the venture capitalist picks the right businesses to fund and provides good management skills and advice, there can be large returns on the initial investment. While the venture capitalist may reap returns from the private business itself, the largest payoff occurs if and when the business goes public and the venture capitalist is able to convert his or her stake into cash at the market price.

How well do venture capital and private equity investors do, relative to the market? There is clearly anecdotal evidence that some venture capital investors do very well on individual deals and over time. There are also periods of time when venture capital and private equity investing collectively

---

[23]B. S. Black and R. J. Gilson, "Venture Capital and the Structure of Capital Markets: Banks versus Stock Markets," _Journal of Financial Markets_ 47 (1998): 243–277. They argue that one of the reasons why venture capital is much more active in the United States than in Japan or Germany is because the option to go public is much more easily exercised in the United States.

TABLE 9.1 Private Equity Performance Index (PEPI) (Returns as of June 30, 2011)

Fund Type	1 Year	3 Years	5 Years	10 Years	15 Years	20 Years
Early/seed venture capital	27.60%	3.76%	6.87%	−0.44%	41.23%	31.44%
Balanced venture capital	32.73%	11.21%	13.15%	4.99%	13.53%	21.71%
Later-stage venture capital	22.06%	2.54%	5.88%	3.25%	28.56%	24.60%
All venture capital	26.34%	4.31%	7.37%	1.25%	30.89%	27.35%
Russell 2000	37.41%	7.77%	4.08%	6.27%	7.37%	9.82%
NASDAQ Composite	31.49%	6.55%	5.01%	2.53%	5.83%	9.21%
S&P 500	30.69%	3.34%	2.94%	2.72%	6.50%	8.73%

Source: Cambridge Associates.

earns extraordinary returns. During the 1990s, for instance, venture capital funds earned an average return of 29.5 percent, compared to the S&P 500's annual return of 15.1 percent, but there are three potential problems with this comparison. The first is that the appropriate comparison would really be to the NASDAQ, which boomed during the 1990s and contained companies much like those in a venture capital portfolio—young technology firms. The second and related point is that these returns (both on the venture capital funds and on the NASDAQ) are before we adjust for the substantial risk associated with the types of companies in their portfolios. The third is that the returns on the venture capital funds are suspect because they are often based on assessments of value (often made by the venture capitalists) of nontraded investments. In fact, many of these venture capital funds were forced to confront both the risk and self-assessment issues in 2000 and 2001 as many of their investments, especially in new technology businesses, were written down to true value. From September 2000 to September 2001, for instance, venture capital funds lost 32 percent of their value, private equity funds lost 21 percent, and buyout funds lost 16 percent of their value.

When we look at the longer period returns on private equity and venture capital investing over the past two decades, what emerges is the sobering evidence that the strategy has a mixed record. Cambridge Associates, a data service that tracks the returns on venture capital investments, reported short-term and long-term returns on private equity investments as of June 2011, presented in Table 9.1.

Over the past 20 years, venture capital funds have outperformed public equity indexes, but all of the outperformance can be traced to the 1991–2000 period. In the past decade, every category of venture capital has underperformed the equity indexes, sometimes by large amounts. Ljundquist and Richardson examined private equity funds and conclude that they did make modest excess returns between 1981 and 2001, but attribute the higher returns to compensation for illiquidity.[24] In a more recent study, Phalippou and Gottschalg document that average reported returns for private equity funds tend to be biased upward, because of the failure to incorporate the effects of funds that closed down and for accounting overstatement. Making these adjustments, they show that the typical fund underperforms the S&P 500 by about 3 percent.[25]

There is one final point worth making about private equity and venture capital investments. The average returns just reported are pushed up by the presence of a few investments that make very high returns. In general, the highest-return venture capital investments tend to be in (relatively few) companies that eventually go public. Most private equity and venture capital investments generate low or negative returns, and the median (rather than the average) return indicates this propensity. Consider, for instance, the glory years of 1997 through 1999. The conventional wisdom is that private equity investments did well in those years. In 1999, the weighted-average internal rate of return on private equity investments was 119 percent, but the median return in that year was 2.9 percent. The median venture capital investor trailed the average investor badly in most other years as well, indicating the chasm between the best venture capital/private equity investors and the rest of the segment.

Determinants of Success in Activist Growth Investing

While venture capital and private equity investing, in general, is not a recipe for guaranteed high returns, there are some venture capital and private equity investors who succeed and earn extraordinary returns. What set them apart, and how can you partake in their success? The keys seem to be the following:

- *Pick your companies (and managers) well.* Many small private businesses do not survive, either because the products or services they offer do not find a ready audience or because of poor management. Good

---

[24] A. Ljundquist and M. Richardson, "The Cash Flow, Return and Risk Characteristics of Private Equity" (SSRN Working Paper, 2003).
[25] L. Phalippou and O. Gottschalg, "The Performance of Private Equity Funds," *Review of Financial Studies* 22 (2009): 1747–1776.

venture capitalists seem to have the capacity to find the combination of ideas and management that makes success more likely.

- *Diversify.* The rate of failure is high among private equity investments, making it critical that you spread your bets. The earlier the stage of financing—seed money, for example—the more important it is that you diversify.
- *Support and supplement management.* Venture capitalists are also management consultants and strategic advisers to the firms that they invest in. If they do this job well, they can help the managers of these firms convert ideas into commercial success.
- *Protect your investment as the firm grows.* As the firm grows and attracts new investment, you as the venture capitalist will have to protect your share of the business from the demands of those who bring in fresh capital.
- *Know when to get out.* Having a good exit strategy seems to be as critical as having a good entrance strategy. Know how and when to get out of an investment is critical to protecting your returns.

As a successful venture capitalist, you will still find yourself holding not only a risky portfolio but a relatively undiversified one, with large stakes in a number of small and volatile businesses. In short, activist growth investing is best suited for investors who possess substantial capital, have long time horizons, and are willing to take risks.

CONCLUSION

If value investors bet on the market getting it wrong when pricing assets in place, growth investors place their bets on misassessments of the value of growth. While some categorize growth investors based on their willingness to buy high P/E ratio stocks, that characterization does not capture the diversity of growth investors. In this chapter, we began by looking at investing in small-cap stocks and initial public offerings as growth investing strategies. We then considered a variety of growth screens used by investors to find undervalued growth, ranging from high P/E ratios to low PEG ratios. While the empirical evidence is not as supportive of growth screens as it is for value screens, investors who are disciplined, have long time horizons, and are good at gauging market cycles can earn significant excess returns.

In the last part of the chapter, we examined venture capital and private equity investing and categorized them as activist growth investing strategies, since they require taking large positions in young growth businesses and then taking an active role in their operations. While there are some venture capital and private equity investors who earn huge returns, the overall returns to private equity investing reflect only a modest premium over investing in publicly traded stocks. A large appetite for risk and a long time horizon are prerequisites for success.

EXERCISES

1. Do you think that a growth stock can be cheap? If yes, how or why would that happen? If not, why not?
2. Assume that you are intrigued by the small-cap stock strategy.
   a. What do you see as the biggest benefit of the strategy? What do you see as the biggest dangers from investing in small-cap companies?
   b. Given the evidence and caveats presented in this chapter on small cap investing, how would you adapt your stock picking to maximize your returns?
3. Assume that you are interested in making money off initial public offerings.
   a. What do you see as the biggest benefit of the strategy? What do you see as the biggest dangers from investing in IPOs?
   b. Given the evidence and caveats presented in this chapter on IPO investing, how would you adapt your stock picking to maximize your returns?
4. Assuming that you are interested in buying growth at a reasonable price (GARP), come up with two screens that you would use to find cheap GARP stocks.
   a. Use those screens to find cheap stocks.
   b. Take a look at your list of cheap stocks. Do you see any potential problems with a portfolio composed of these stocks?
   c. Add a screen or screens that would help you avoid the problem stocks.

Lessons for Investors

To be a growth investor, you need to:

- *Make better estimates of growth, and price it well:* The success of growth investing ultimately rests on your capacity to forecast growth and to price it right. If you are better at these roles than the market, you improve your odds of success.
- *Catch growth cycles when they occur:* Growth investing has historically done best when earnings growth in the market is low and investors are pessimistic about the future.

To be an activist growth investor, you need to:

- *Accept skewed returns:* Private equity and venture capital investing may offer a few investors spectacular returns, but the average returns to all investors in these categories are low (relative to investing in publicly traded stocks).
- *Invest in the right businesses:* To succeed at private equity investing, you have to pick the right businesses to make the investments in, diversify your bets, and have a well-devised exit strategy.

CHAPTER 10

Information Pays: Trading on News

Information affects stock prices. This undeniable fact is brought home every day as we watch financial markets react to news announcements about firms. When firms report better than anticipated earnings, stock prices go up, whereas firms that announce plans to cut or eliminate dividends see their stock prices go down. Given this reality, any investor who is able to gain access to information prior to it reaching the market can buy or sell ahead of the information, depending on whether it is good or bad news, and make money. There is a catch, though. Information that has not yet been made available to markets may be viewed as inside information, and trading on it can then be illegal.

For any portfolio manager who wants to trade on information legally, there are three alternatives. One is to use the rumor mills that always exist in financial markets, screening the rumors for credibility (based on both the news in the rumors and the source of the rumors) and then trading on credible rumors. Another is to wait until the information reaches the market and then to trade on the market reaction. Implicit in this approach is the assumption that markets react inappropriately to news items and that it is possible to take advantage of these mistakes. The third alternative is to use information that is publicly available to anticipate future news announcement. Thus, if you can read the tea leaves correctly and predict which firms are likely to surprise markets by reporting higher or lower than expected earnings, you have the foundations of a very successful investment strategy.

In this chapter, we begin by considering the individuals who are most likely to have access to private information—insiders and equity research analysts—and consider whether they use it to earn high returns. We then move on to consider information announcements made by firms—earnings and dividend announcements, acquisitions and investment announcements, for instance—and how markets react to that information, and whether there is a possibility of profiting on information by trading after the announcement. In the final part of the chapter, we consider the essential ingredients of a successful information-based trading strategy.

INFORMATION AND PRICES

The market price of an asset is an estimate of its value. Investors in the market make assessments of value based on their expectations for the future; they form these expectations using the information that is available to them, and this information can arrive in different forms. It can be public information available in financial statements or filings with the Securities and Exchange Commission (SEC), or information available to one or a few investors. In this section, we will begin by drawing a distinction between private and public information, and then considering how an efficient market should react to information.

Private and Public Information

While the steps in the pricing process—receive information, process the information to form expectations, and trade on the asset—may be the same for all investors, there can be wide variations across investors in when they receive information, how much information they are provided and how they process the information. Some investors have access to more information than others. For instance, an equity research analyst whose job it is to evaluate a stock as an investment may have access to more information about the firm than a small investor making the same decision, or at least get the information in a more timely fashion. These differences in information are compounded by the different ways in which investors use the information to form expectations. Some investors build complex quantitative models, converting the information into expected earnings and cash flows, and then value the investments. Other investors use the same information to make comparisons across traded investments. The net effect is that, at any point in time, investors will disagree on how much an asset is worth. Those who think that it is worth more will be the buyers of the asset, and those who think it is worth less will sell the asset. The market price represents the price at which the market clears—that is, where demand (buying) is equal to supply (selling).

Let us now consider the relationship between price and value. In Chapter 4, we argued that the value of an asset is the present value of the expected cash flows over its lifetime. The price of that asset represents the product of a process in which investors use the information available on the asset to form expectations about the future. The price can and usually will deviate from the value for three reasons. First, the information available may be insufficient or incorrect; then expectations based on this information will also be wrong. Second, investors may not do a good job of processing the information to arrive at expectations. Third, even if the information is correct and investors, on average, form expectations properly, there might still be investors who are willing to trade at prices that do not reflect these expectations. Thus, an investor who assesses the value of a stock to be $50 might still be willing to buy the stock for $60 because he or she believes that it can be sold to someone else later for $75.

Information Efficiency: How Stock Prices React to News

In Chapter 6, we took a close look at the characteristics of an efficient market. There are three ways of measuring or defining market efficiency, at least as it relates to information. One is to look at how much and for how long prices deviate from true value. The second is to measure how quickly and completely prices adjust to reflect new information. The third is to measure whether some investors in markets consistently earn higher returns than others who are exposed to the same amount of risk. It is the last definition that we used in Chapter 6.

If we define market efficiency in terms of how much the price of an asset deviates from a firm's true value, the smaller and less persistent the deviations are, the more efficient a market is. Market efficiency does not require that the market price be equal to true value at every point in time. All it requires is that errors in the market price be unbiased; that is, prices can be greater than or less than true value, as long as these deviations are random. Another way of assessing market efficiency is to look at how quickly and how well markets react to new information. The value of an asset should increase when new information that affects any of the inputs into value—the cash flows, the growth, or the risk—reaches the market. In an efficient market, the price of the asset will adjust instantaneously and, on average, correctly to the new information, as shown in Figure 10.1.[1]

The adjustment will be slower if investors are slow in assessing the impact of the information on value. In Figure 10.2, we show the price of an asset adjusting slowly to new information. The drift in prices that we observe after the information arrives is indicative of a slow learning market.

---

[1]K. C. Brown, W. V. Harlow, and S. M. Tinic, "Risk Aversion, Uncertain Information, and Market Efficiency," *Journal of Financial Economics* 22 (1988): 355–385.

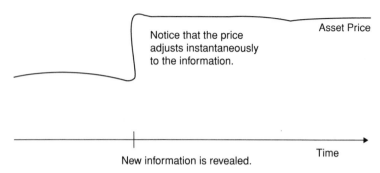

Notice that the price adjusts instantaneously to the information.

Asset Price

New information is revealed.

Time

FIGURE 10.1 Price Adjustment in an Efficient Market

In contrast, the market could adjust instantaneously to the new information but overestimate the effect of the information on value. Then, the price of the asset will increase by more than it should given the effect of the new positive information on value, or drop by more than it should with negative information. Figure 10.3 shows the drift in prices in the opposite direction after the initial overreaction.

TRADING ON PRIVATE INFORMATION

Are investors who have information that no one else has access to (i.e., private information) able to use this information to profit? While the answer seems obvious, it is difficult to test whether they do. The reason for this is that the insider trading laws, at least in the United States, specifically forbid trading in advance of significant information releases. Thus, insiders who follow the law and register their trades with the SEC are not likely to be trading on specific information in the first place. Notwithstanding this selection bias, we will begin by looking at whether insider buying and

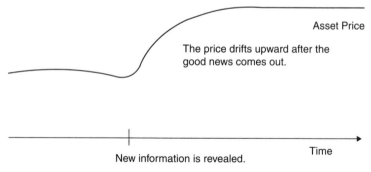

Asset Price

The price drifts upward after the good news comes out.

New information is revealed.

Time

FIGURE 10.2 A Slow Learning Market

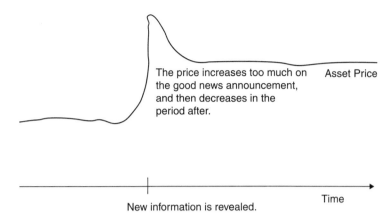

FIGURE 10.3 An Overreacting Market

selling operate as signals of future price movements, since insiders may still know more about the firm than outsiders do; insider trading laws do not bar you from trading on assessments of value that are based upon your knowledge (and not information). We will then look at the more difficult question of whether those who trade illegally on private information make excess returns. While this may seem like an impossible test to run, we can at least draw inferences about this trading by looking at trading volume and price movements prior to major news announcements.

Insiders

The SEC defines an insider as an employee, an officer, a director of the firm or a major stockholder (holding more than 5 percent of the outstanding stock in the firm). Insiders are barred from trading in advance of specific information on the company and are required to file with the SEC when they buy or sell stock in the company. In this section, we will begin by looking at the relationship between these insider trading reports and subsequent stock price changes, and then consider whether noninsiders can use information on insider trading to earn excess returns themselves.

NUMBER WATCH

Insider holdings by sector: Take a look at the insider holdings as a percentage of shares outstanding, by sector, for U.S. companies.

FIGURE 10.4 Cumulative Returns Following Insider Trading: Buy versus Sell Group
Source: J. Jaffe, "Special Information and Insider Trading," *Journal of Business* 47 (1974): 410–428.

Insider Trading and Stock Prices If it is assumed, as seems reasonable, that insiders have better information about the company, and consequently better estimates of value, than other investors, the decisions by insiders to buy and sell stock should signal future movements in stock prices. Figure 10.4, derived from an early study of insider trading by Jaffe, examines excess returns on two groups of stock, classified on the basis of insider trades.[2] The buy group includes stocks where insider buys exceeded sells by the biggest margin, and the sell group includes stocks where insider sells exceeded buys by the biggest margin.

Note that the returns are much more positive in the twenty months after insiders buy than in the period after insider sells. This would suggest that insiders are more likely to buy stocks in their companies, if they view them as under valued. Subsequent studies support this finding,[3] but it is worth noting that insider buying is a noisy signal; about 4 in 10 stocks where insiders are buying turn out to be poor investments, and even on average,

---

[2] J. Jaffe, "Special Information and Insider Trading," *Journal of Business* 47 (1974): 410–428.

[3] See J. E. Finnerty, "Insiders and Market Efficiency," *Journal of Finance* 31 (1976): 1141–1148; N. Seyhun, "Insiders' Profits, Costs of Trading, and Market Efficiency," *Journal of Financial Economics* 16 (1986): 189–212; M. Rozeff and M. Zaman, "Market Efficiency and Insider Trading: New Evidence," *Journal of Business* 61 (1988): 25–44.

the excess returns earned are not very large. Lakonishok and Lee took a closer look at the price movements around insider trading. They found that firms with substantial insider selling had stock returns of 14.4 percent over the subsequent 12 months, which was significantly lower than the 22.2 percent earned by firms with insider buying. However, they found that the link between insider trading and subsequent returns was greatest for small companies and that there was almost no relationship at larger firms. They also noted that it was far weaker for long-term returns than for short-term returns.

Over the past two decades, there have been two developments that have affected the profitability of insider trading in the United States. The first is that the SEC has become more expansive in its definition of what constitutes insider information (to include any material nonpublic information, rather than just information releases from the firm) and more aggressive in its enforcement of insider trading laws. The second is that companies, perhaps in response to the SEC's hard line on insider trading, have adopted more stringent policies restricting insiders from trading on information. Perhaps as a consequence, the price effect of insider trading has decreased over time, and one study finds that the price effect of (legal) insider trading has almost disappeared since 2002, with the adoption of Regulation Fair Disclosure (Regulation FD), which restricts selective information disclosure by companies to a few investors or analysts, and Sarbanes-Oxley, which increased scrutiny of insider trading.[4]

Is insider trading more informative (and profitable) in some firms than in others? A study that looked at differences across firms finds that insider trading is more profitable in less transparent firms and where analyst disagreement about future earnings growth is greatest.[5] In a related finding, Aboody and Lev note that insider trades are more profitable at firms with significant research and development (R&D) expenditures than at firms without these expenditures; arguably, the payoff and likely success of R&D investments are more difficult for outsiders to assess.[6]

In the past few years, there have been attempts to examine the returns earned by insiders in other markets, and the results are consistent with findings in the United States over time. In markets like the United

---

[4]I. Lee, M. Lemmon, Y. Li, and J. M. Sequeira, "The Effects of Regulation on the Volume, Timing, and Profitability of Insider Trading" (SSRN Working Paper 1824185, 2011).

[5]Y. Wu and Q. Zhu, "When Is Insider Trading Informative?" (SSRN Working Paper 1917132, 2011).

[6]D. Aboody and B. Lev, "Information Asymmetry, R&D, and Insider Gains," *Journal of Finance* 56 (2000): 2747–2766.

Kingdom, where insider trading is expansively defined and strongly enforced, the profits to insider trading are minimal.[7] In many emerging markets, where insider trading is defined narrowly and/or it is not prosecuted with vigor, insider buying is associated with subsequent price increases, and selling with price decreases.

Can You Follow Insiders?   If insider trading offers advance warning, albeit a noisy one, of future price movements, can we as outside investors use this information to make better investment decisions? In other words, when looking for stocks to buy, should we consider the magnitude of insider buying and selling on the stock? To answer this question, we first have to recognize that since the SEC does not require an immediate filing of insider trades, investors will find out about insider trading on a stock with a lag of a few weeks or even a few months. In fact, until recently, it was difficult for an investor to access the public filings on insider trading. As these filings have been put online in recent years, this information on insider trading has become available to more and more investors.

A study of insider trading examined excess returns around both the date the insiders report to the SEC and the date that information becomes available to investors in the official summary.[8] Figure 10.5 presents the contrast between the two event studies.

Given the opportunity to buy on the date the insider reports to the SEC, investors could have marginal excess returns (of about 1 percent), but these returns diminish and become statistically insignificant if investors are forced to wait until the official summary date. If you control for transaction costs, there are no excess returns associated with the use of insider trading information. Does this mean that insider trading information is useless? It may be so if we focus on total insider buying and selling, but there may be value added if we can break down insider trading into more detail. Consider the following propositions:

- Not all insiders have equal access to information. Top managers and members of the board should be privy to much more important information, and thus their trades should be more revealing. A study by Bettis, Vickrey, and Vickrey finds that investors who focus only on large

---

[7]D. Andriosopoulos and H. Hoque, "Information Content of Aggregate and Individual Insider Trading" (SSRN Working Paper 1959549, 2010).
[8]H. N. Seyhun, "Insiders' Profts, Costs of Trading and Market Efficiency," *Journal of Financial Economics* 16 (1986): 189–212.

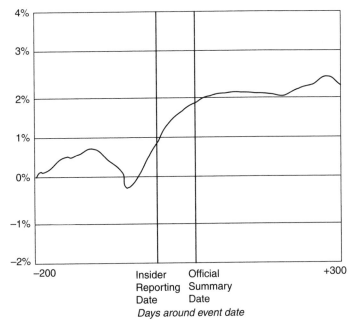

FIGURE 10.5 Abnormal Returns around Reporting Day: Official Summary
Availability Day
Source: H. N. Seyhun, "Insiders' Profts, Costs of Trading and Market Efficiency,"
Journal of Financial Economics 16 (1986): 189–212.

trades made by top executives rather than total insider trading may, in
fact, be able to earn excess returns.[9]

- As investment alternatives to trading on common stock have multiplied,
insiders have also become more sophisticated about using these alternatives. As an outside investor, you may be able to add more value by
tracking these alternative investments. For instance, Bettis, Bizjak, and
Lemmon find that insider trading in derivative securities (options specifically) to hedge their common stock positions increases immediately
following price run-ups and prior to poor earnings announcements. In
addition, they find that stock prices tend to go down after insiders take
these hedging positions.[10]

[9]J. Bettis, D. Vickrey, and Donn Vickrey, "Mimickers of Corporate Insiders Who
Make Large Volume Trades," *Financial Analysts Journal* 53 (1997): 57–66.
[10]J. C. Bettis, J. M. Bizjak, and M. L. Lemmon, "Insider Trading in Derivative
Securities: An Empirical Investigation of Zero Cost Collars and Equity Swaps by
Corporate Insiders" (SSRN Working Paper 167189, 1999).

- Knowledge about insider trading is more useful in some companies than in others. Insider buying or selling is likely to contain less information (and thus be less useful to investors) in companies where information is plentiful (both because of disclosure by the company and analysts following the company) and easy to assess. It will be most useful in companies where there is little external information (because the company is small and lightly followed) or difficult to assess (either because its investments are uncertain or difficult to evaluate, like R&D).

Illegal Insider Trading   None of the studies quoted so far in this chapter answers the question of whether insiders themselves make excess returns. The reporting process, as set up now by the SEC, is biased toward legal and less profitable trades and away from illegal and more profitable trades. Though direct evidence cannot be easily offered for this proposition, it seems likely that insiders trading illegally on private information make excess returns. To support this proposition, we can present three pieces of evidence.

1. The first (and weakest) is anecdotal. When insiders are caught trading illegally, they almost invariably have made a killing on their investments. Clearly, some insiders made significant returns off their privileged positions. The reason that it has to be viewed as weak evidence, though, is because the SEC looks for large profits as one of the indicators of whether it will prosecute someone for insider trading. In other words, insiders who trade illegally on information may be breaking the law but are less likely to be prosecuted for the act if they lose money.
2. Almost all major news announcements made by firms are preceded by a price run-up (if it is good news) or a price drop (if it is bad news). Thus, you see that the stock price of a target firm starts to drift up before the actual takeover announcement, and that the stock price of a firm reporting disappointing earnings drops in the days prior to the earnings report. While this may indicate a prescient market, it is much more likely that someone with access to the privileged information (either at the firm or the intermediaries helping the firm) is using the information to trade ahead of the news. In fact, the other indicator of insider trading is the surge in trading volume in both the stock itself and derivatives prior to big news announcements.[11]
3. In addition to having access to information, insiders are often in a position to time the release of relevant information to financial markets.

---

[11] It is for this reason that the SEC tracks trading volume. Sudden increases in volume often trigger investigations of insiders at firms.

Knowing that they are not allowed to trade ahead of this information, insiders often adjust information disclosure to make it less likely that they will be targeted by the SEC. One study finds that insiders sell stock between three and nine quarters before their firms report a break in consecutive earnings increases.[12] It also finds that insider selling increases at growth firms prior to periods of declining earnings.

Using Insider Trading in Investment Decisions   As the information on insider trades has become more accessible, it has also become less useful. In addition, the spurt in the use of options in management compensation schemes has introduced a substantial amount of noise in the reporting system, since a large proportion of insider trades now are associated with managers exercising options and then selling a portion of their stock holdings for liquidity and diversification reasons. For information on insider trading to pay off, you need to look beyond the total insider trading numbers at the insiders themselves, focusing on large trades by top managers at smaller, less followed firms. Even then, you should not expect miracles, since you are using publicly available information.

While illegal insider trading is impossible to track, there are indirect measures that investors can use to at least guess when it is most prevalent, at least with smaller, lightly traded companies. A surge in trading volume, accompanied by a price change, can often be an indicator at these companies of insider activity; a doubling of trading volume with an increase in price may be indicative of insider buying, whereas a price decrease may be indicative of insider selling. This relationship between trading volume and private information may provide an intuitive rationale for the use of some of the volume/price momentum measures described in Chapter 7 as technical indicators.

Analysts

Analysts clearly hold a privileged position in the market for information, operating at the nexus of private and public information. Using both types of information, analysts make earnings forecasts for the firms that they follow, and issue buy and sell recommendations to their clients, who trade on the basis of those recommendations. In this section, we consider if there is useful information in these forecasts and recommendations and whether incorporating them into investment decisions leads to higher returns.

---

[12]B. Ke, S. Huddart, and K. Petroni, "What Insiders Know about Future Earnings and How They Use It: Evidence from Insider Trades," *Journal of Accounting & Economics* 35, no. 3 (August 2003): 315–346.

NUMBER WATCH

Analyst following by sector: Take a look at the number of analysts who follow the typical company, by sector, for the United States.

Who Do Analysts Follow? The number of analysts tracking firms varies widely across firms. At one extreme are firms like Apple, GE, Google, and Microsoft that are followed by dozens of analysts. At the other extreme, there are hundreds of firms that are not followed by any analysts. Why are some firms more heavily followed than others? These seem to be some of the determinants:

- *Market capitalization.* The larger the market capitalization of a firm, the more likely it is to be followed by analysts.
- *Institutional holding.* The greater the percentage of a firm's stock that is held by institutions, the more likely it is to be followed by analysts. The open question, though, is whether analysts follow companies because institutions own them or whether institutions invest in companies that are more heavily tracked by analysts. Given that institutional investors are the biggest clients of equity research analysts, the causality probably runs both ways.
- *Trading volume.* Analysts are more likely to follow liquid stocks. Here again, though, it is worth noting that the presence of analysts may play a role in increasing trading volume.

We capture all of these factors in Figure 10.6, where we classify firms into market value classes and look at the number of analysts and the institutional holding (as a percent of outstanding stock) in each class. The largest companies tend to be held more by institutions and followed by more equity research analysts.

SELL-SIDE AND BUY-SIDE ANALYSTS: A PRIMER

There are thousands of financial analysts who try to value stocks, and most of them toil anonymously. The analysts who receive the most attention are the sell-side analysts who work for investment banks. Their research is primarily for external consumption and their roles are complex. They interact with the firms they research and sell their research to portfolio managers and individual investors. Buy-side analysts, in contrast, work for money management companies like Fidelity. Their research is intended primarily for internal consumption and is designed to help portfolio managers pick better stocks.

Why does it matter? Sell-side equity research may have a higher profile than buy-side research, but it is also buffeted by far more conflicts of interest and bias. The fact that the investment banks that churn out the research do not have to invest in the stocks that they recommend should give pause to individual investors who intend to follow these recommendations. In addition, sell-side analysts have to spend substantially more time selling than buy-side analysts do.

Earnings Forecasts Analysts spend a considerable amount of time and resources forecasting earnings per share for the companies that they follow,

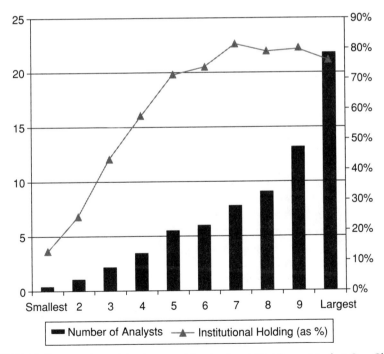

FIGURE 10.6 Number of Analysts and Institutional Holdings: Market Cap Class
Source: Capital IQ.

for the next quarter and for the next financial year. Presumably, this is where their access to company management and sector knowledge should generate an advantage. Thus, when analysts revise their forecasts upward or downward, they convey information to financial markets, and prices should react. In this section, we examine how markets react to analyst forecast revisions and whether there is a potential for investors to take advantage of this reaction.

The Information in Analyst Forecasts   There is a simple reason to believe that analyst forecasts of growth in earnings should be better than using historical growth rates in earnings. Analysts, in addition to using historical data, can avail themselves of other information that may be useful in predicting future growth.

- *Firm-specific information that has been made public since the last earnings report.* Analysts can use information that has come out about the firm since the last earnings report to make predictions about future growth. This information can sometimes lead to significant reevaluation of the firm's expected earnings and cash flows.
- *Macroeconomic information that may impact future growth.* The expected growth rates of all firms are affected by economic news on gross domestic product (GDP) growth, interest rates, and inflation. Analysts can update their projections of future growth as new information comes out about the overall economy and about changes in fiscal and monetary policy. Information, for instance, that shows the economy growing at a faster rate than forecast will result in analysts increasing their estimates of expected growth for cyclical firms.
- *Information revealed by competitors on future prospects.* Analysts can also condition their growth estimates for a firm on information revealed by competitors on pricing policy and future growth. For instance, a negative earnings report by one automotive firm can lead to a reassessment of earnings for other automotive firms.
- *Private information about the firm.* Analysts sometimes have access to private information about the firms they follow that may be relevant in forecasting future growth. In an attempt to restrict this type of information leakage, the SEC issued Regulation Fair Disclosure (Regulation FD) to prevent firms from selectively revealing information to a few analysts or investors. Outside the United States, however, firms routinely convey private information to analysts following them.
- *Public information other than earnings.* Models for forecasting earnings that depend entirely upon past earnings data may ignore other publicly available information that is useful in forecasting future earnings. It has

been shown, for instance, that other financial variables such as earnings retention, profit margins, and asset turnover are useful in predicting future growth. Analysts can incorporate information from these variables into their forecasts.

In summary, it is logical to expect that the resources that are expended in the care and feeding of equity research analysts provide a payoff on one of their primary tasks, forecasting earnings, if not in the long term, at least in the near term.

The Quality of Earnings Forecasts   If analysts are indeed better informed than the rest of the market, the forecasts of growth from analysts should be better than estimates based on either historical growth or other publicly available information. But is this presumption justified? Are analyst forecasts of growth superior to other estimates?

The general consensus from studies that have looked at short-term forecasts (one quarter ahead to four quarters ahead) of earnings is that analysts provide better forecasts of earnings than models that depend purely upon historical data. The mean relative absolute error, which measures the absolute difference between the actual earnings and the forecast for the next quarter, in percentage terms, is smaller for analyst forecasts than it is for forecasts based on historical data.

Two studies shed further light on the value of analysts' forecasts. An early study examined the relative accuracy of forecasts in the *Earnings Forecaster*, a publication from Standard & Poor's that summarizes forecasts of earnings from more than 50 investment firms.[13] This study measured the squared forecast errors by month of the year and computed the ratio of analyst forecast error to the forecast error from time-series models of earnings. It found that the time-series models actually outperform analyst forecasts from April until August, but underperform them from September through January. The authors of the study hypothesize that this is because there is more firm-specific information available to analysts during the latter part of the year. A later study compares consensus analyst forecasts from the Institutions Brokers Estimate System (I/B/E/S) with time-series forecasts from one quarter ahead to four quarters ahead.[14] The analyst forecasts outperform

---

[13]T. Crichfield, T. Dyckman, and J. Lakonishok, "An Evaluation of Security Analysts Forecasts," *Accounting Review* 53 (1978): 651–668.
[14]P. O'Brien, "Analyst's Forecasts as Earnings Expectations," *Journal of Accounting and Economics* 10 (1988): 53–83.

the time-series model for one-quarter-ahead and two-quarters-ahead forecasts, do as well as the time-series model for three-quarters-ahead forecasts, and do worse than the time-series model for four-quarters-ahead forecasts. Thus, the advantage gained by analysts from firm-specific information seems to deteriorate as the time horizon for forecasting is extended.

Dreman and Berry examined analyst forecasts from 1974 to 1991 and found that in more than 55 percent of the forecasts examined, analyst estimates of earnings were off by more than 10 percent from actual earnings.[15] One potential explanation given for this poor forecasting is that analysts are routinely over optimistic about future growth. Chopra finds that a great deal of this forecast error comes from the failure of analysts to consider large macroeconomic shifts. In other words, analysts tend to overestimate growth at the peak of a recovery and underestimate growth in the midst of a recession.[16] A study that compares analyst forecast errors across seven countries finds, not surprisingly, that analysts are more accurate and less biased in countries that mandate more financial disclosure.[17]

Most of these studies look at short-term forecasts (usually the next quarter), and there is little evidence to suggest that analysts provide superior forecasts of earnings when the forecasts are over the long term (three or five years). A study by Cragg and Malkiel compared long-term forecasts by five investment management firms in 1962 and 1963 with actual growth over the following three years to conclude that analysts were poor long-term forecasters.[18] This view was contested in a later study by Vander Weide and Carleton, who found that the consensus predictions of five-year growth from analysts were superior to historically oriented growth measures in predicting future growth.[19] In general, though, only a small proportion of analysts who follow firms make long-term forecasts.

There is an intuitive basis for arguing that analyst predictions of growth rates must be better than time-series or other historical-data-based models simply because they use more information. The evidence indicates, however,

---

[15]D. N. Dreman and M. Berry, "Analyst Forecasting Errors and Their Implications for Security Analysis," *Financial Analysts Journal* (May/June 1995): 30–41.

[16]V. K. Chopra, "Why So Much Error in Analyst Forecasts?" *Financial Analysts Journal* (November–December 1998): 35–42.

[17]H. N. Higgins, "Analyst Forecasting Performance in Seven Countries," *Financial Analysts Journal* 54 (May/June 1998): 58–62.

[18]J. G. Cragg and B. G. Malkiel, "The Consensus and Accuracy of Predictions of the Growth of Corporate Earnings," *Journal of Finance* 23 (1968): 67–84.

[19]J. H. Vander Weide and W. T. Carleton, "Investor Growth Expectations: Analysts vs. History," *Journal of Portfolio Management* 14 (1988): 78–83.

that this superiority in forecasting is surprisingly small for long-term forecasts and that past growth rates play a significant role in determining analyst forecasts.

Market Reaction to Earnings Forecast Revisions   In Chapter 7, we considered the price momentum strategies in which investors buy stocks that have gone up the most in recent periods, expecting the momentum to carry forward into future periods. You could construct similar strategies based on earnings momentum. While some of these strategies are based purely on earnings growth rates, most of them are based on how earnings measure up to analyst expectations. In fact, one strategy is to buy stocks where analysts are revising earnings forecasts upward, and hope that stock prices follow these earnings revisions.

A number of studies in the United States conclude that it is possible to use forecast revisions made by analysts to earn excess returns. In one of the earliest studies of this phenomenon, Givoly and Lakonishok created portfolios of 49 stocks in three sectors based on earnings revisions, and reported earning an excess return on 4.7 percent over the following four months on the stocks with the most positive revisions.[20] Hawkins, Chamberlin, and Daniels reported that a portfolio of stocks with the 20 largest upward revisions in earnings on the I/B/E/S database would have earned an annualized return of 14 percent, as opposed to the index return of only 7 percent.[21] In another study, Cooper, Day, and Lewis reported that much of the excess returns is concentrated in the weeks around the revision (1.27 percent in the week before the forecast revision, and 1.12 percent in the week after), and that analysts that they categorize as leaders (based on timeliness, impact, and accuracy) have a much greater impact on both trading volume and prices.[22] In 2001, Capstaff, Paudyal, and Rees expanded the research to look at earnings forecasts in other countries and concluded that you could have earned excess returns of 4.7 percent in the United Kingdom, 2 percent in France, and 3.3 percent in Germany from buying stocks with the most positive revisions.[23]

---

[20]D. Givoly and J. Lakonishok, "The Quality of Analysts' Forecasts of Earnings," *Financial Analysts Journal* 40 (1984): 40–47.

[21]E. H. Hawkins, S. C. Chamberlin, and W. E. Daniel, "Earnings Expectations and Security Prices," *Financial Analysts Journal* (September/October 1984): 20–38.

[22]R. A. Cooper, T. E. Day, and C. M. Lewis, "Following the Leader: A Study of Individual Analysts Earnings Forecasts," *Journal of Financial Economics* 61 (2001): 383–416.

[23]J. Capstaff, K. Paudyal, and W. Rees, "Revisions of Earnings Forecasts and Security Returns: Evidence from Three Countries" (SSRN Working Paper 253166, 2000).

As researchers have probed the earnings revision data, there are some interesting facts that are coming to the fore. First, forecast revisions that diverge more from the consensus (i.e., bold forecasts) have a much biggest impact on price and are more likely to be accurate than forecast revisions that stay close to the pack. However, bold forecasts are uncommon, since most analysts tend to go with the herd, revising earnings in the same direction and about the same magnitude as others following the stock.[24] Second, timeliness matters, with analysts who revise their earnings estimates earlier having a much bigger price impact than those revisions that occur later in the cycle. Third, earnings revisions made by analysts who work at bigger banks or brokerage houses have a much bigger price impact, perhaps because they have wider reach and exposure, than analysts who work with smaller entities.

Potential Pitfalls The limitation of an earnings revision strategy is its dependence on two of the weakest links in financial markets: earnings reports that come from firms, and analyst forecasts of those earnings. In recent years, we have become increasingly aware of the capacity of firms not only to manage their earnings but also to manipulate them using questionable accounting ploys. At the same time, we have discovered that analysts' forecasts are biased, partly because of their closeness to the firms that they follow.

Even if the excess returns persist, you also need to consider why they might exist in the first place. To the extent that analysts influence trades made by their clients, there will be a price effects when analysts revise earnings. The more influential analysts are, the greater the effect they will have on prices, but the question is whether the effect is lasting. One way you may be able to earn higher returns from this strategy is to identify key analysts and build an investment strategy around forecast revisions made by them, rather than looking at consensus estimates made by all analysts. In particular, focusing on more influential analysts and trading on bolder, timelier revisions offers greater odds for success.

Finally, you should recognize that it is a short-term strategy that yields fairly small excess returns over investment horizons ranging from a few weeks to a few months. The increasing skepticism of markets toward both earnings reports from firms and forecasts by analysts bodes ill for these strategies. Therefore, while forecast revisions and earnings surprises by themselves are unlikely to generate lucrative portfolios, they can augment other more long-term screening strategies.

---

[24]C. Gleason and C. Lee, "Analyst Forecast Revisions and Market Price Discovery," *Accounting Review* 78 (2003): 193–225.

Analyst Recommendations The centerpieces of analyst reports are the recommendations that they make on stock, and these range from very positive (strong buy) to very negative (strong sell), with intermediate positions (weak buys, weak sells). You would expect stock prices to react to changes in analyst recommendations, if for no other reason than for the fact that some investors will follow these recommendations, pushing up stock prices on buy recommendations and pushing them down on sell recommendations. In this section, we consider some key empirical facts about analyst recommendations first and then consider how markets react to these recommendations. We close with an analysis of whether investors can use analyst recommendations to make money in the short term and the long term.

The Recommendation Game There are four empirical facts that need to be laid on the table about recommendations before we start examining how markets react to them.

1. If we categorize analyst recommendations into buy, sell, and hold, the overwhelming number are buy recommendations. In 2011, for instance, buy recommendations outnumbered sell recommendations for U.S. stocks by a 7 to 1 margin, but that was a marked improvement over the 25 to 1 margin that we saw in the boom market of the 1990s. While there are many reasons for this bias, the most significant one is that analysts who issue sell recommendations find themselves shunned not only by the companies in question but sometimes by the brokerage houses that they work for.

2. Part of the reason for this imbalance between buy and sell recommendations is that analysts often have many more layers beyond buy, sell, and hold. Some investment banks, for instance, have numerical rating systems in which stocks are classified from 1 to 5 (as is the case with Value Line), whereas others break buy and sell recommendations into subclasses (strong buy, weak buy). What this allows analysts to do is not only rate stocks on a finer scale, but also send sell signals without ever saying the word (sell). Thus, an analyst downgrading a stock from a strong buy to a weak buy is suggesting that investors sell the stock. In November 2011, for instance, we looked at the recommendations made by analysts on U.S. companies, categorized into five groups: from highest (strong buy or equivalent) to lowest (strong sell or equivalent); the numbers are presented in Figure 10.7.

   Note that the positive recommendations vastly outnumber negative recommendations, and that the skew toward the positive is greater for small firms than for large ones.

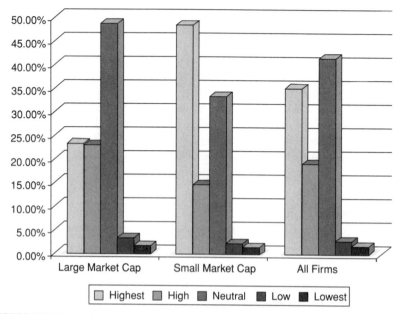

FIGURE 10.7 Analyst Recommendations for U.S. Companies, November 2011
Source: Capital IQ.

3. As with earnings forecasts, there is herd behavior when it comes to recommendations. Thus, when one analyst upgrades a stock from a weak buy to a strong buy, there tends to be a rush of other analyst upgrades in the following days.
4. Analysts also seem to be players of the momentum game, with buy recommendations becoming more numerous and stronger after a sustained run-up in the stock price of a company, and sell recommendations (infrequent as they are) showing up only after a stock price has had a disastrous decline.

The Market Reaction to Recommendations How do markets react to recommendations made by analysts? A study by Womack examined the stock price response to buy and sell recommendations on the day of the recommendation and in the weeks following.[25] While both buy and sell recommendations affect stock prices, sell recommendations affect prices much more than buy recommendations. This should not be surprising when you

---

[25]K. Womack, "Do Brokerage Analysts' Recommendations Have Investment Value?" *Journal of Finance* 51 (1996): 137–167.

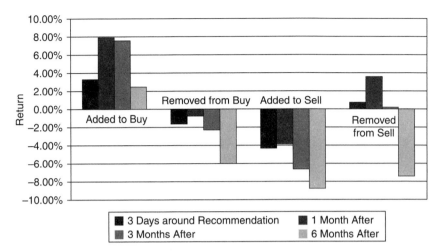

FIGURE 10.8 Market Reaction to Recommendations, 1989 to 1990
Source: K. Womack, "Do Brokerage Analysts' Recommendations Have Investment Value?" *Journal of Finance* 51 (1996): 137–167.

remember that buy recommendations vastly outnumber sell recommendations. Interestingly, this study also documents that the price effect of buy recommendations tends to be immediate and there is no evidence of price drifts after the announcement, whereas prices continue to trend down after sell recommendations. Figure 10.8 graphs the study's findings. Stock prices increase by about 3 percent on buy recommendations, whereas they drop by about 4 percent on sell recommendations at the time of the recommendations (three days around reports). In the six months following, prices decline an additional 5 percent for sell recommendations, while leveling off for buy recommendations.

Other studies of analyst recommendations find that investors react not only to the recommendations but to revisions made to target prices and to the qualitative arguments made in the report; a buy recommendation accompanied by an increase in the target price and a stronger qualitative argument, i.e., a story, has a much more positive impact on stock prices.[26]

One of the key issues that faces both equity research analysts and investors who use their assessments is the extent to which recommendations are perceived to be driven not by views on the stock itself but as cheerleading for the companies followed by the analysts. In some cases, this bias is made

---

[26]A. Brav and R. Lehavy, "An Empirical Analysis of Analysts' Target Prices: Short-Term Informativeness and Long-Term Dynamics," *Journal of Finance* 58 (2003): 1933–1968.

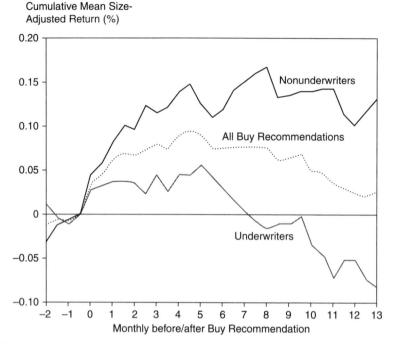

FIGURE 10.9 Performance Comparison for Companies Receiving New Buy Recommendations within One Year of IPO, 1990 to 1991
Source: R. Michaely and K. L. Womack, "Conflicts of Interests and the Credibility of Underwriter Analysts Recommendation," *Review of Financial Studies* 12 (1999): 635–686.

worse by other businesses that the equity research analysts' employers have with the firm in question. Michaely and Womack tested this proposition by looking at the stock price performance of buy recommendations after initial public offerings and comparing buy recommendations made by analysts who worked for the underwriters on these offerings and recommendations from analysts who did not. Their findings are summarized in Figure 10.9.[27]

Note that stock prices go up much more following buy recommendations made by nonunderwriter analysts than after buy recommendations by underwriter analysts. While this may seem obvious, many investors

---

[27]R. Michaely and K. L. Womack, "Conflicts of Interests and the Credibility of Underwriter Analysts Recommendation," *Review of Financial Studies* 12 (1999): 635–686.

overlook the connections between analysts and the firms that they analyze and pay a significant price for the omission.[28]

Potential and Perils of Analyst Recommendations   Can you make money off analyst recommendations? The answer seems to be yes, at least in the short term. Even if there were no new information contained in recommendations, there is the self-fulfilling prophecy created by clients who trade on these recommendations, pushing up stock prices after buy recommendations and pushing them down after sell recommendations.[29] If this is the only reason for the stock price reaction, though, the returns are not only likely to be small but could very quickly dissipate, leaving you with large transaction costs and little to show as excess returns. In fact, that is the conclusion that Barber, Lehavy, McNichols, and Trueman arrive at in their study of whether investors can profit from following analysts.[30]

To incorporate analyst recommendations into an investment strategy, you need to adopt a more nuanced approach.

- You should begin by identifying the analysts who not only are the most influential but also have the most content (private information) in their recommendations. Recommendations that are backed up by numbers and a solid story have more heft to them than recommendations that do not.
- Optimally, you would want to screen out analysts where the potential conflicts of interest are too large for the recommendations to be unbiased. Since that will leave you with a relatively short list, you should also pay particular attention to recommendations that go against the grain (i.e., a sell recommendation from a normally bullish analyst or a buy recommendation from an analyst known for a bearish view).

---

[28]In June 2002, Merrill Lynch agreed to pay $100 million to settle with New York State, after the state uncovered e-mails sent by Henry Blodget, Merrill's well-known Internet analyst, that seemed to disparage stocks internally as he was recommending them to outside clients. The fact that many of these stocks were being taken to the market by Merrill added fuel to the fire. Merrill agreed to make public any potential conflicts of interest it may have on the firms followed by its equity research analysts.
[29]This can be a significant factor. When the *Wall Street Journal* publishes its Dartboard column, it reports on the stocks being recommended by the analysts its picks. These stocks increase in price by about 4 percent in the two days after they are picked but reverse themselves in the weeks that follow.
[30]B. Barber, R. Lehavy, M. NcNichols, and B. Trueman, "Can Investors Profit from the Prophets? Security Analyst Recommendations and Stock Returns," *Journal of Finance* 56 (2001): 531–563.

- You should invest based on the recommendations, preferably at the time the recommendations are made.[31]
- Assuming that you still attach credence to the views of the recommending analysts, you should watch analysts for signals that they have changed or are changing their minds. Since these signals are often subtle, you can easily miss them.

FINDING THE BEST ANALYSTS

How does one go about finding the best analysts following a stock? You could go with the analysts chosen in popularity contests, where other analysts and/or portfolio managers vote for the "best" analysts. One example is the All-America analyst team from Institutional Investor, where the star analysts are picked in each sector. But do not fall for the hype. The highest-profile analysts on this list are not always the best, and some are notorious for self-promotion. The best sources of information on analysts tend to be outside services without an ax to grind. The *Wall Street Journal* has a special section on sell-side equity research analysts, where it evaluates analysts on the quality of their recommendations and ranks them on that basis. There are a few online services that track equity research forecasts and recommendations and report on how close actual earnings numbers were to their forecasts.

There are qualitative factors to consider as well. Analysts who have clear, well-thought-out analyses that show a deep understanding of the businesses that they analyze should be given more weight that analysts who make spectacular recommendations based on surface-level assessments. Most importantly, good analysts should be just as willing to stand up to the management of companies and disagree with them (and issue sell recommendations).

TRADING ON PUBLIC INFORMATION

Most of us do not have access to private information about firms, but we all share access to public information about a firm. Some of this public

---

[31]This might not be your choice to make, since analysts reveal their recommendations first to their clients. If you are not a client, you will often learn about the recommendation only after the clients have been given a chance to take positions on the stock.

information takes the form of periodic earnings reports and dividend announcements, made four times every year by most firms in the United States and less frequently elsewhere, and some of it is news made by the firm when it announces that it is taking over another firm (or being taken over) or making a major investment or divestiture. In some cases, the information comes from a regulatory authority governing the firm's fortunes, as is the case when the Food and Drug Administration (FDA) announces that it has approved (or not approved) a drug for treatment. In each of these cases, we would expect the stock price to react to the news contained in the announcement. If the market reaction is appropriate, there is little that we can do to make money off the news, but if the market reaction is not appropriate, we may be able to exploit it with specific trading strategies.

Earnings Announcements

When firms make earnings announcements, they convey information to financial markets about their current and future prospects. The magnitude of the information in the report, and the size of the market reaction to it, should depend on how much the earnings report exceeds or falls short of investor expectations. In an efficient market, there should be an instantaneous reaction to the earnings report if it contains surprising information, and prices should increase following positive surprises and move down following negative surprises.

Earnings Surprises and Price Reaction   Since actual earnings are compared to investor expectations, one of the key parts of an earnings event study is the measurement of these expectations. Some of the earlier studies of the phenomenon used earnings from the same quarter in the prior year as a measure of expected earnings; that is, firms that report increases in quarter-to-quarter earnings provide positive surprises and those that report decreases in quarter-to-quarter earnings provide negative surprises. In more recent studies, analyst estimates of earnings have been used as a proxy for expected earnings and have been compared to the actual earnings. Figure 10.10 is a graph of price reactions to earnings surprises, classified on the basis of magnitude into different classes, from most negative earnings reports to most positive earnings reports.[32]

---

[32]The original study of this phenomenon was in R. Ball and P. Brown, "An Empirical Evaluation of Accounting Income Numbers, *Journal of Accounting Research* 6 (1968): 159–178. That study was updated by Bernard and Thomas (1989), with daily data around quarterly earnings announcements. (V. Bernard and J. Thomas,

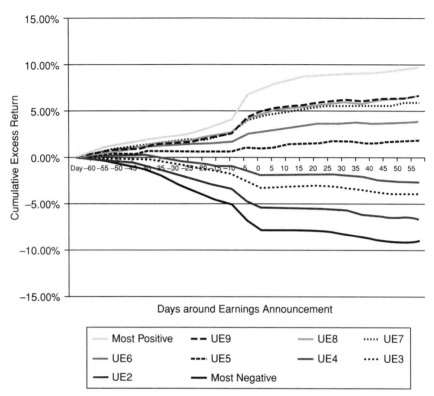

FIGURE 10.10 Market Reaction to Unexpected Quarterly Earnings Surprises: U.S. Companies from 1988 to 2002
Source: D. C. Nichols and J. M. Wahlen, "How Do Accounting Numbers Relate to Stock Returns: A Review of Classic Accounting Research with Updated Numbers," *Accounting Horizons* 18 (2004): 263–286.

The evidence contained in this graph is consistent with the evidence in most earnings announcement studies.

- The earnings announcement clearly conveys valuable information to financial markets; there are positive excess returns (cumulative abnormal

"Post-Earnings Announcement Drift: Delayed Price Response or Risk Premium?" *Journal of Accounting Research* 27 (1989): 1–48.) This graph is developed from an update of that study by Nichols and Wahlen (2004). (D. C. Nichols and J. M. Wahlen, "How Do Accounting Numbers Relate to Stock Returns: A Review of Classic Accounting Research with Updated Numbers," *Accounting Horizons* 18 (2004): 263–286.)

returns) around positive surprises (actual earnings > expected earnings) and negative excess returns around negative surprises (actual earnings < expected earnings).

■ There is some evidence of a price drift in the days immediately prior to the earnings announcement, which is consistent with the nature of the announcement; that is, prices tend to go up on the days before positive announcements and down on the days before negative announcements. This can be viewed as evidence of either insider trading, information leaking out to the market, or getting the announcement date wrong.[33]

■ There is some evidence of a price drift in the days following an earnings announcement. This can be seen by isolating only the postannouncement effect of earnings reports in Figure 10.11.

Thus, a positive (or negative) report evokes a positive (or negative) market reaction on the announcement date, and there are positive excess returns in the days and weeks following the earnings announcement.

■ The price changes around earnings reports are also accompanied by a jump in trading volume in the days immediately before and after earnings reports.

The studies just quoted looked at all earnings announcements, but there is research that indicates that the returns associated with earnings surprises are more pronounced with some types of stocks than with others. For instance:

■ A study of value and growth stocks found that the returns in the three days around earnings announcements were much more positive for value stocks (defined as low-P/E and low-PBV stocks) than for growth stocks across all earnings announcements—positive as well as negative. This suggests that you are much more likely to get a positive surprise with a value stock than with a growth stock, indicating perhaps that markets tend to be overly optimistic in their expectations of earnings for growth companies.

■ Earnings announcements made by smaller firms seem to have a larger impact on stock prices on the announcement date, and prices are more likely to drift after the announcement.

---

[33]The *Wall Street Journal* or Compustat are often used as information sources to extract announcement dates for earnings. For some firms, news of the announcement may actually cross the newswire the day before the *Wall Street Journal* announcement, leading to a misidentification of the report date and the drift in returns the day before the announcement.

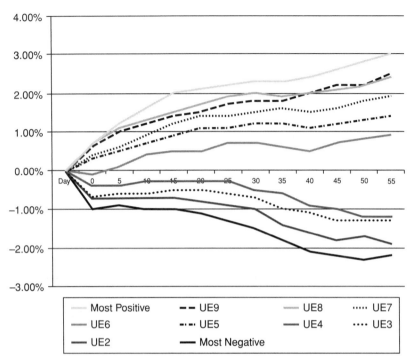

FIGURE 10.11 Postannouncement Drift after Unexpected Quarterly Earnings Surprises: U.S. Companies from 1988 to 2002
Source: D. C. Nichols and J. M. Wahlen, "How Do Accounting Numbers Relate to Stock Returns: A Review of Classic Accounting Research with Updated Numbers," *Accounting Horizons* 18 (2004): 263–286.

- As with analyst reports, there seems to be evidence that the market reaction to earnings reports is a function of not only the earnings number reported but also the accompanying management commentary.[34]
- There is some evidence that the market reaction to earnings reports is greater at firms with high institutional ownership, with one rationale being offered that institutional investors tend to be more short term in their focus and thus more likely to respond to quarterly earnings reports.

In summary, the fact that stock prices go up when earnings are better than expected and go down when they are worse than expected is not

---

[34]E. A. Demers and C. Vega, "Soft Information in Earnings Announcements: News or Noise?" (SSRN Working Paper, 2008).

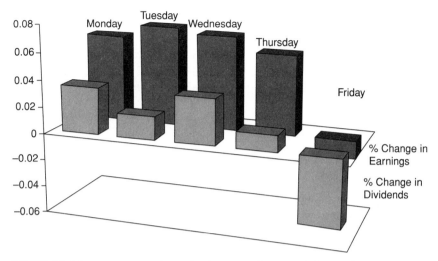

FIGURE 10.12 Earnings and Dividend Reports by Day of the Week
Source: A. Damodaran, "The Weekend Effect in Information Releases: A Study of Earnings and Dividend Announcements," *Review of Financial Studies* 2 (1989): 607–623.

unexpected. It is the drift in the days after the announcements that is surprising, since it suggests that investors can trade after announcements and generate profits.

Earnings Delays, Industry Effects, and Price Reaction The management of a firm has some discretion on the timing of earnings reports, and there is some evidence that the timing affects expected returns. A study of earnings reports, classified by the day of the week that the earnings are reported, reveals that earnings and dividend reports on Fridays are much more likely to contain negative information than announcements on any other day of the week.[35] This is shown in Figure 10.12.

Announcements made on Friday are more likely to contain bad news—earnings drops and dividend cuts—than announcements on any other day of the week, and a significant number of these announcements come out after close of trading on Friday. This may provide an interesting link to the weekend effect described in Chapter 7.

---

[35]A. Damodaran, "The Weekend Effect in Information Releases: A Study of Earnings and Dividend Announcements," *Review of Financial Studies* 2 (1989): 607–623.

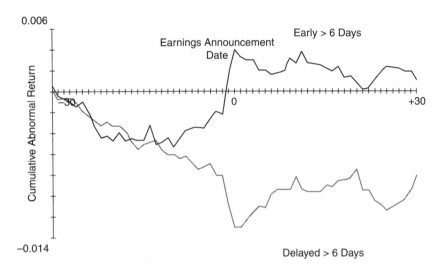

FIGURE 10.13 Cumulated Abnormal Returns around Earnings Reports: Day 0 Is Earnings Announcement Date
Source: A. E. Chambers and S. H. Penman, "Timeliness of Reporting and the Stock Price Reaction to Earnings Announcement," *Journal of Accounting Research* 22: 21–47.

There is also some evidence, as seen in Figure 10.13, that earnings announcements that are delayed, relative to the expected announcement date,[36] are much more likely to contain bad news than earnings announcements that are early or on time.

Earnings announcements that are more than six days late relative to the expected announcement date are much more likely to contain bad news and evoke negative market reactions than earnings announcements that are on time or early. It may be worth the while of investors who build their investment strategies around earnings announcements to keep track of expected earnings announcement dates.

Finally, investors do learn about earnings prospects for a company from earnings announcements made by other companies in the sector. Thus, the announcement by an automobile company of higher earnings will lead investors to reassess (and increase) expectations of earnings at other automobile companies that are yet to report earnings. As a consequence, the price

---

[36]Firms in the United States tend to be consistent about the date each year that they reveal their quarterly earnings. The delay is computed relative to this expected date. See A. E. Chambers and S. H. Penman, "Timeliness of Reporting and the Stock Price Reaction to Earnings Announcement," *Journal of Accounting Research* 22: 21–47.

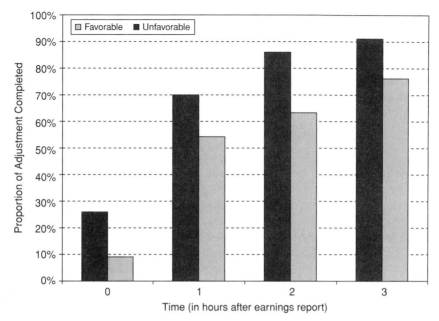

FIGURE 10.14 Price Adjustment by Hour after Earnings Report
Source: Catherine S. Woodruff and A. J. Senchack Jr., "Intradaily Price-Volume Adjustments of NYSE Stocks to Unexpected Earnings," *Journal of Finance* 43, no. 2 (1988): 467–491.

impact of earnings surprises will be higher for companies that announce earlier in the cycle than for later announcers.

Intraday Price Reaction Studies have examined the speed with which prices react to earnings announcements within the day of the announcement. There, the evidence is mixed. Woodruff and Senchack examined price adjustment by transaction after favorable earnings reports (surprise > 20 percent) and unfavorable earnings reports (surprise < –20 percent), and reported the proportion of the eventual adjustment that had occurred by the hour after the earnings report for each category (in Figure 10.14).[37]

As Figure 10.14 illustrates, approximately 91 percent of the eventual adjustment occurs within three hours of the report for the most positive

---

[37]Catherine S. Woodruff and A. J. Senchack Jr., "Intradaily Price-Volume Adjustments of NYSE Stocks to Unexpected Earnings," *Journal of Finance* 43, no. 2 (1988): 467–491.

earnings surprises, while only 76 percent of the eventual adjustment occurs during the same period for the most negative earnings announcements. This would seem to indicate that markets are much more efficient about assessing good news than bad news. If nothing else, this also illustrates the importance of trading promptly after an earnings announcement. Investors who wait to read about the announcement the next day or even later in the day will find that the bulk of the adjustment has occurred by the time that they trade.

Earnings Quality and Market Reaction   The strategy of investing on earnings surprises has come under some pressure because firms have learned to play the earnings game. In the past two decades, concerns have been raised by some about the phenomenon of earnings management at companies, and whether it has led to deterioration in the informativeness of earnings reports. While there is evidence that companies manage earnings more, manifested in the higher frequency with which firms are able to beat earnings estimates from analysts, earnings reports still seem to evoke strong price responses. In fact, at least according to some studies, the market responses to earnings reports have increased over time.[38] One reason is that markets have learned that companies manage earnings, so they adjust expectations accordingly. Thus, to evoke a positive response, markets have to report earnings that exceed so-called whispered earnings and that are higher than the consensus analyst estimate by a margin, with the margin depending on the company's history. Another reason is that increased disclosure requirements have increased the information contained in earnings reports and thus the price response.

As firms play the earnings game, the quality of earnings has also diverged across companies. A firm that beats earnings estimates because it has more efficient operations should be viewed more favorably than one that beats estimates because it changed the way it values inventory. Does the market distinguish appropriately between the two? The evidence indicates that it does not, at least on the date of the announcement, but that it eventually corrects for poor quality earnings. In a study of this phenomenon, Chan, Chan, Jegadeesh, and Lakonishok examined firms that reported high accruals (i.e., a measure of cash earnings and argued that firms that report high earnings without a matching increase in cash flows have poorer quality

---

[38]W. D. Collins, O. Li, and H. Xie, "What Drives the Increased Informativeness of Earnings Announcements over Time?" *Review of Accounting Studies* 14 (2009): 1–30.

earnings.[39] When they tracked a portfolio composed of these firms, they discovered that the high-accrual year was usually the turning point in the fortunes of this firm, with subsequent years bringing declining earnings and negative stock returns.

Can You Make Money off Earnings Announcements? Financial markets get much of their firm-specific information from earnings announcements, and there are collectively thousands of earnings announcements each year. There are some portfolio managers whose investment strategies are based primarily or largely on trading on or after these announcements. There are three strategies that can be built around earnings announcements:

1. The first strategy is to buy immediately on the announcement and hope to make money intraday on the slow price adjustment (shown in Figure 10.14). This is a very short-term, high-turnover strategy and will generally make sense only if you can track information in real time, trade instantly, and control your transaction costs.
2. The second strategy is to buy stocks that report large positive earnings surprises, hoping to benefit from the drift. The returns can be augmented by selling short on stocks that report negative earnings surprises, hoping again as these stocks continue to drift down. This is a slightly more long-term strategy with holding periods measured in weeks rather than hours, but there is potential for excess returns, even after transaction costs. How would you refine this strategy to harvest higher returns? You could draw on the empirical evidence and concentrate only on earnings announcements made by smaller, less liquid companies where the drift is more pronounced. In addition, you can try to direct your money toward companies with higher-quality earnings surprises by avoiding firms with large accruals (i.e., firms that report increasing earnings and decreasing cash flows).
3. Your potential for large returns is greatest if you can forecast which firms are most likely to report large positive earnings surprises, and invest in those firms prior to their earnings announcements. Impossible, without insider information, you say! Not quite, if you remember that price and volume drift up before the actual announcement and that firms that report their earnings later than expected are more likely to report bad news. Even if you are right only 55 percent of the time, you should be able to post high excess returns.

---

[39]K. Chan, L. K. C. Chan, N. Jegadeesh, and J. Lakonishok, "Earnings Quality and Stock Returns," *Journal of Business* 79 (2006): 1041–1082.

BUY ON THE RUMOR, SELL ON THE NEWS

Wall Street adages should always be taken with a grain of salt, but they usually do have a kernel of truth to them. This particular one on rumor and news has particular relevance when we look at how prices run up before the news announcement and how little is left on the table after the announcement. An investor who has access to high-quality gossip (if that is not an oxymoron) may be able to buy stocks before good news comes out and sell before bad news. But high-quality gossip is difficult to come by, especially on Wall Street, where a dozen false news stories circulate for every true one.

Acquisitions

The investment announcements that usually have the most effect on value and stock prices are acquisition announcements, simply because acquisitions are large relative to other investments. In this section, we begin with an analysis of how the announcement of an acquisition affects the market price of the target and acquiring firm on the day of the acquisition, follow up by looking at the postacquisition performance (operating and stock price) of the acquiring firm, and conclude with the question of whether there is anything in this process that can be exploited by an investor for gain.

The Acquisition Date　The big price movements associated with acquisitions occur around the date the acquisition is announced and not when it is actually consummated. While much of the attention in acquisitions is focused on the target firms, we will argue that what happens to the acquiring firm is just as interesting, if not more so.

The Announcement Effect: Targets and Bidders　The evidence indicates that the stockholders of target firms are the clear winners in takeovers—they earn significant excess returns[40] not only around the announcement of the acquisitions, but also in the weeks leading up to it. Jensen and Ruback reviewed 13 studies that look at returns around takeover announcements and reported an average excess return of 30 percent to target stockholders in

---

[40]The excess returns around takeover announcements to target firms are so large that using different risk and return models seems to have no effect on the overall conclusions.

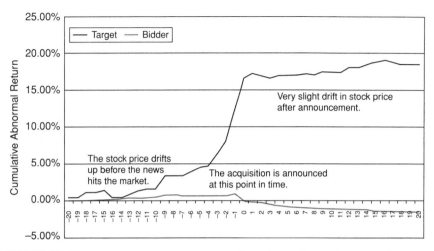

FIGURE 10.15 Acquisition Announcement: Cumulative Excess Returns—Target and Acquirer

successful tender offers and 20 percent to target stockholders in successful mergers.[41] Jarrell, Brickley, and Netter examined the results of 663 tender offers made between 1962 and 1985 and noted that premiums averaged 19 percent in the 1960s, 35 percent in the 1970s, and 30 percent between 1980 and 1985.[42] The price behavior of a typical target firm in an acquisition is illustrated in Figure 10.15, from one of the studies, which summarizes the target firm stock price in the 10 days before, the day of, and the 10 days after an acquisition announcement.[43]

Note that about half the premium associated with the acquisition is already incorporated in the target's stock price by the time the acquisition is announced. This suggests that information about acquisitions is leaked to some investors, who trade on that information. On the acquisition date, there is a decided jump in the stock price, but the drift afterward is mild.

If we categorize acquisitions based on how the acquiring firm pays for them, we find that the stock prices of target firms tend to do much better on the announcement of cash-based acquisitions (where the acquirer uses only

[41]M. C. Jensen and R. S. Ruback, "The Market for Corporate Control," *Journal of Financial Economics* 11 (1983): 5–50.

[42]G. A. Jarrell, J. A. Brickley, and J. M. Netter, "The Market for Corporate Control: The Empirical Evidence since 1980," *Journal of Economic Perspectives* 2 (1988): 49–68.

[43]Dennis, D. D. and J. J. McConnell, "Corporate Mergers and Security Returns," *Journal of Financial Economics* 16 (1986): 143–188.

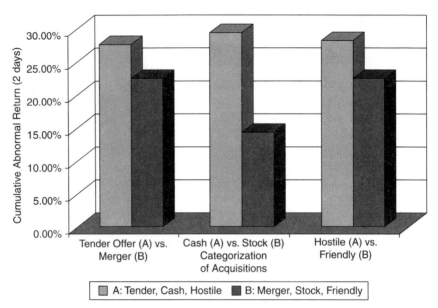

FIGURE 10.16 Target Firm Premiums in Acquisition
Source: R. D. Huang and R. Walkling, "Acquisition Announcements and Abnormal Returns," *Journal of Financial Economics* 19 (1987): 329–350.

cash to pay for the acquired company's stock) than stock-based acquisitions (where the acquirer pays some or all of the price with shares). We also find that the premiums in hostile acquisitions are larger than the premiums on friendly mergers and that the premiums on tender offers are slightly higher than the premiums on mergers. Figure 10.16, extracted from one study, provides an illustration of the magnitude of the differences.[44]

Some attempts at takeovers fail, either because the bidding firm withdraws the offer or because the target firm fights it off. Bradley, Desai, and Kim analyzed the effects of takeover failures on target firm stockholders and found that, while the initial reaction to the announcement of the failure is negative, albeit statistically insignificant, a substantial number of target firms are taken over within 60 days after the failure of the first takeover, with shareholders in these firms earning significant excess returns (50 percent to 66 percent).[45]

---

[44]R. D. Huang and R. Walkling, "Acquisition Announcements and Abnormal Returns," *Journal of Financial Economics* 19 (1987): 329–350.
[45]M. Bradley, A. Desai, and E. H. Kim, "The Rationale behind Interfirm Tender Offers," *Journal of Financial Economics* 11 (1983): 183–206.

Bidding Firms The effect of takeover announcements on bidder firm stock prices is not as clear-cut as it is for target firms. In Figure 10.15, the cumulative excess returns to bidding firms in takeovers is close to zero. Jensen and Ruback report excess returns of 4 percent for bidding firm stockholders around tender offers and no excess returns around mergers. Jarrell, Brickley, and Netter, in their examination of tender offers from 1962 to 1985, note a decline in excess returns to bidding firm stockholders from 4.4 percent in the 1960s to 2 percent in the 1970s to −1 percent in the 1980s.[46] Other studies indicate that approximately half of all bidding firms earn negative excess returns around the announcement of takeovers, suggesting that shareholders are skeptical about the perceived value of the takeover in a significant number of cases.

When an attempt at a takeover fails, Bradley, Desai, and Kim report negative excess returns of 5 percent to bidding firm stockholders around the announcement of the failure. When the existence of a rival bidder in figured in, the studies indicate significant negative excess returns (of approximately 8 percent) for bidder firm stockholders who lose out to a rival bidder within 180 trading days of the announcement, and no excess returns when no rival bidder exists.

Considering the evidence, it is quite clear that bidding firm stockholders often do not share the enthusiasm of managers in these firms for mergers and acquisitions. While managers would argue that this is because they are not privy to the information that is available only to insiders, we will see in the next section that many mergers fail and that stockholders are perhaps more prescient than managers are.

After the Acquisition Many studies examine the extent to which mergers and acquisitions succeed or fail after the firms combine. These studies generally conclude that mergers often fail to deliver on their promises of efficiency and synergy, and even those that do deliver seldom create value for the acquirers' stockholders.

McKinsey & Company examined 58 acquisition programs between 1972 and 1983 for evidence on two questions: (1) Did the return on the amount invested in the acquisition exceed the cost of capital? (2) Did the acquisition help the parent company outperform the competition? They concluded that 28 of the 58 programs failed both tests, and six more failed at least one test. In a follow-up study of 115 mergers in the United Kingdom

---

[46]G. A. Jarrell, J. A. Brickley, and J. M. Netter, "The Market for Corporate Control: The Empirical Evidence since 1980," *Journal of Economic Perspectives* 2 (1988): 49–68.

and the United States in the 1990s, McKinsey concluded that 60 percent of the transactions earned returns on capital less than the cost of capital, and that only 23 percent earned excess returns.[47] In 1999, KPMG examined 700 of the most expensive deals between 1996 and 1998 and concluded that only 17 percent created value for the combined firm, 30 percent were value neutral, and 53 percent destroyed value.[48]

A study looked at the eight largest bank mergers in 1995 and concluded that only two (Chase/Chemical, First Chicago/NBD) subsequently outperformed the bank-stock index.[49] The largest, Wells Fargo's acquisition of First Interstate, was a significant failure. In an incisive book on the topic titled *The Synergy Trap*, Sirower took a detailed look at the promises and failures of synergy and drew the gloomy conclusion that synergy is often promised but seldom delivered.[50]

The most damaging piece of evidence on the outcome of acquisitions is the large number of acquisitions that are reversed within fairly short time periods. Mitchell and Lehn note that 20.2 percent of the acquisitions made between 1982 and 1986 were divested by 1988.[51] In a later study, Kaplan and Weisbach found that 44 percent of the mergers they studied were reversed, largely because the acquirer paid too much or because the operations of the two firms did not mesh.[52] Studies that have tracked acquisitions for longer time periods (10 years or more) have found the divestiture rate of acquisitions rises to almost 50 percent, suggesting that many firms do not enjoy the promised benefits from acquisitions.

Takeover-Based Investment Strategies

There are three broad classes of investment strategies that can be constructed around takeovers. The first and most lucrative, if you can pull it off, is to

[47]This study was referenced in an article titled "Merger Mayhem" that appeared in *Barron's* on April 20, 1998.
[48]KPMG, *Unlocking Shareholder Value: The Keys to Success*, KPMG Global Research Report, 1999. KPMG measured the success at creating value by comparing the postdeal stock price performance of the combined firm to the performance of the relevant industry segment for a year after the deal was completed.
[49]This study was done by Keefe, Bruyette and Woods, an investment bank. It was referenced in an article titled "Merger Mayhem" in *Barron's*, April 20, 1998.
[50]M. L. Sirower, *The Synergy Trap* (New York: Simon & Schuster, 1996).
[51]M. L. Mitchell and K. Lehn, "Do Bad Bidders Make Good Targets?" *Journal of Applied Corporate Finance* 3 (1990): 60–69.
[52]S. Kaplan and M. S. Weisbach, "The Success of Acquisitions: The Evidence from Divestitures," *Journal of Finance* 47 (1992): 107–138.

find a way to invest in a target firm before the acquisition is announced. The second is to wait until after the takeover is announced and then try to take advantage of the price drift between the announcement date and the day the deal is consummated. This is often called risk arbitrage and we will take a closer look at it in the next chapter. The third is also a postannouncement strategy, but it is a long-term strategy in which you invest in firms that you believe have the pieces in place to deliver the promised synergy or value creation.

Preannouncement Investing   Looking at the stock price reaction of target firms both immediately prior to and immediately after the acquisition announcement, it is quite clear that the real money to be made in acquisitions comes from investing in firms before they become targets rather than after. Absent inside information, is this doable? There may be a way, and the answer lies in looking at firms that typically become target firms.

Research indicates that the typical target firm in a hostile takeover has the following three characteristics:[53]

1. It has underperformed other stocks in its industry and the overall market, in terms of returns to its stockholders in the years preceding the takeover.
2. It has been less profitable than firms in its industry in the years preceding the takeover.
3. It has a much lower stock holding by insiders than do firms in its peer groups.

Other studies provide tantalizing clues about typical target firms. Lang, Stulz, and Walkling find, for instance, that stocks that trade at low market values relative to their replacement costs (a low Tobin's Q) are much more likely to be taken over than firms that trade at high market values.[54] The odds of being taken over also increase if the firm has a smaller market capitalization, does not have shares with different voting classes, and has no antitakeover amendments on its books.

There are two ways in which we can use the findings of these studies to identify potential target firms. The first is to develop a set of screens that incorporate the variables mentioned earlier. You could, for instance, invest in

---

[53]This research, drawn from a paper by Bhide, was also referenced in Chapter 8.
[54]L. H. Lang, R. M. Stulz, and R. A. Walkling, "Managerial Performance, Tobin's Q, and the Gains from Successful Tender Offers," *Journal of Finance* 24 (1989): 137–154.

small market cap firms with low insider holdings, depressed valuations (low price-to-book ratios), and low returns on equity. The second and slightly more sophisticated variant is to estimate the probability of being taken over for every firm in the market using statistical techniques.[55]

Postannouncement Investing   In this strategy, you buy companies after acquisitions or mergers are completed because you believe that they will be able to deliver what they promise at the time of the merger—higher earnings growth and synergy. As we noted in the earlier section on synergy, it shows up in relatively few mergers. Can we identify those mergers that are most likely to succeed and invest only in those? Again, the clues may lie in history.

Some studies find improvements in operating efficiency after mergers, especially hostile ones. Healy, Palepu, and Ruback found that the median postacquisition cash flow returns improve for firms involved in mergers, though 25 percent of merged firms lag industry averages after transactions.[56] Parrino and Harris examined 197 transactions between 1982 and 1987 and categorized the firms based on whether the management is replaced (123 firms) at the time of the transaction, and the motive for the transaction.[57] They found that:

- On average, in the five years after the transaction, merged firms earned 2.1 percent more than the industry average.
- Almost all this excess return occurred in cases where the CEO of the target firm is replaced within one year of the merger. These firms earned 3.1 percent more than the industry average, whereas when the CEO of the target firm continued in place the merged firm did not do better than the industry.

In addition, a few studies examine whether acquiring related businesses (i.e., synergy-driven acquisitions) provides better returns than acquiring

---

[55] A probit, for instance, resembles a regression but estimates probabilities based on specified independent variables. In this case, you could run a probit across firms in the market using the variables identified by earlier studies—low return on equity (ROE), poor stock returns, and low market cap—as independent variables. You will get as output the probability of being taken over for each firm in the market. You could follow up by constructing a portfolio of stocks where this probability is highest.

[56] P. M. Healy, K. G. Palepu, and R. S. Ruback, "Does Corporate Performance Improve after Mergers?" *Journal of Financial Economics* 31 (1992): 135–176.

[57] J. D. Parrino and R. S. Harris, "Takeovers, Management Replacement and Post-Acquisition Operating Performance: Some Evidence from the 1980s," *Journal of Applied Corporate Finance* 11: 88–97.

unrelated businesses (i.e., conglomerate mergers), and come to conflicting conclusions. While some corporate strategy studies suggest that conglomerates create value for stockholders, Nail, Megginson, and Maquieira examined 260 stock swap transactions and categorized the mergers as either a conglomerate or a "same-industry" transaction.[58] They found no evidence of wealth benefits for either stockholders or bondholders in conglomerate transactions. However, they did find significant net gains for both stockholders and bondholders in the case of mergers of related firms.

Finally, on the issue of synergy, the KPMG study of the 700 largest deals from 1996 to 1998 concludes the following:

- Firms that evaluate synergy carefully before an acquisition are 28 percent more likely to succeed than firms that do not.
- Cost-saving synergies associated with reducing the number of employees are more likely to be accomplished than new product development or R&D synergies. For instance, only a quarter to a third of firms succeeded on the latter, whereas 66 percent of firms were able to reduce head count after mergers.

Considering all the contradictory evidence contained in different studies, we would draw the following conclusions about the odds of success in mergers.[59]

- Mergers of equals (firms of equal size) seem to have a lower probability of succeeding than acquisitions of a smaller firm by a much larger firm.[60]
- Cost-saving mergers where the cost savings are concrete and immediate seem to have a better chance of delivering on synergy than mergers based on growth synergy.
- Acquisition programs that focus on buying small private businesses for consolidations have had more success than acquisition programs that concentrate on acquiring publicly traded firms.
- Hostile acquisitions seem to do better at delivering improved postacquisition performance than friendly mergers.

---

[58]L. A. Nail, W. L. Megginson, and C. Maquieira, "Wealth Creation versus Wealth Redistributions in Pure Stock-for-Stock Mergers," *Journal of Financial Economics* 48 (1998): 3–35.
[59]Some of this evidence is anecdotal and is based on the study of just a few mergers.
[60]This might well reflect the fact that failures of mergers of equals are much more visible than failures of the small firm/large firm combinations.

As investors, then, we should steer away from firms that follow low-odds acquisition strategies (buying large market cap, publicly traded firms with growth synergy objectives) and toward firms that adopt disciplined, high-odds strategies (buying small private businesses with cost-cutting programs in place).

Other Announcements

While earnings and acquisition announcements may offer the best opportunities for trading profits for investors trading on information, the market reacts to other announcements made by firms as well.

Stock Splits A stock split increases the number of shares outstanding without changing the current earnings or cash flows of the firm. As a purely cosmetic event, a stock split should not affect the value of the firm or value of outstanding equity. Rather, the price per share will go down to reflect the stock split, since there are more shares outstanding. Figure 10.17 summarizes the results of the first event studies, which examined the stock price reaction

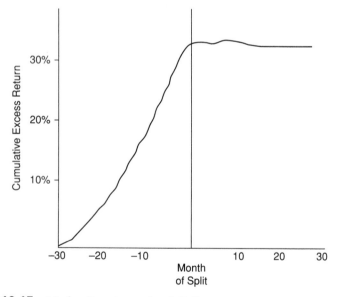

FIGURE 10.17 Market Reaction to Stock Splits
Source: E. F. Fama, L. Fisher, M. C. Jensen, and R. Roll, "The Adjustment of Stock Prices to New Information," *International Economic Review* 10, no. 1 (1969): 1–21.

to 940 stock splits between 1927 and 1959 by cumulating excess returns in the 60 months around the actual split date.[61]

On average, this study found that stock splits tended to follow periods of excess returns; this is not surprising, since splits typically follow price run-ups. They also found no evidence of excess returns around the splits themselves, suggesting that the splits were value neutral events. One of the limitations of the study was its use of monthly returns rather than daily returns. More recent studies that look at the daily price reaction to stock splits find a mild positive effect: stock prices go up when splits are announced. One study that looked at all two-for-one stock splits between 1975 and 1990 estimated that stock prices increase, on average, 3.38 percent on the announcement of a stock split and that the announcement effect is much greater for small market cap stocks (10.04 percent) than for large market cap stocks (1.01 percent).[62] Researchers attribute this to a signaling effect (i.e., only companies that expect their stock prices to go up in the future will announce stock splits).

In recent years, a few studies have pointed out that stock splits may have an unintended negative effect on stockholders by raising transaction costs. For instance, the bid-ask spread, which is one component of the transaction cost, is a much larger percentage of the price for a $20 stock than it is for a $40 stock.[63] Copeland chronicles the increase in transaction costs and the decline in trading volume following splits.[64] This additional cost has to be weighed off against the potential signaling implications of a stock split.[65]

Dividend Changes   Financial markets examine every action a firm takes for implications for future cash flows and firm value. When firms announce changes in dividend policy, they are conveying information to markets,

---

[61]E. F. Fama, L. Fisher, M. C. Jensen, and R. Roll, "The Adjustment of Stock Prices to New Information," *International Economic Review* 10, no. 1 (1969): 1–21.

[62]D. L. Ikenberry, G. Rankine, and E. K. Stice, "What Do Stock Splits Really Signal?" *Journal of Financial and Quantitative Analysis* 31 (1996): 357–375. They report that stocks that split continue to earn excess returns in the two years after the split— 7.93 percent in the first year and 12.15 percent in the second year.

[63]The bid-ask spread refers to the difference between the price at which a security can be bought (the ask price) or sold (the bid price) at any point in time.

[64]T. E. Copeland, "Liquidity Changes Following Stock Splits," *Journal of Finance* 34, no. 1 (1979): 115–141.

[65]See G. Charest, "Split Information, Stock Returns and Market Efficiency—I," *Journal of Financial Economics* 6 (1978): 265–296; M. S. Grinblatt, R. W. Masulis, and S. Titman, "The Valuation Effects of Stock Splits and Stock Dividends," *Journal of Financial Economics* 13 (1984): 461–490.

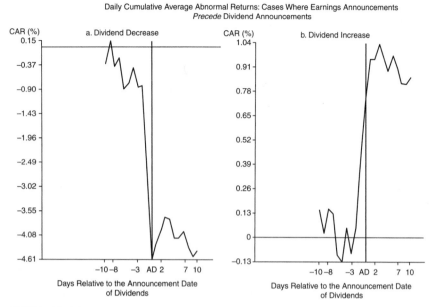

Daily Cumulative Average Abnormal Returns: Cases Where Earnings Announcements
Precede Dividend Announcements

FIGURE 10.18 Excess Returns around Announcements of Dividend Changes
Source: J. Aharony and I. Swary, "Quarterly Dividends and Earnings Announcements and Stockholders' Returns: An Empirical Analysis," *Journal of Finance* 36 (1981): 1–12.

whether they intend to or not. An increase in dividends is generally viewed as a positive signal, since firms that increase dividends must believe that they have the capacity to generate these cash flows in the future. Decreasing dividends is a negative signal, largely because firms are generally very reluctant to cut dividends. Thus, when a firm cut or suspend dividends, markets see it as an indication that this firm is in substantial and long-term financial trouble. The empirical evidence concerning price reactions to dividend increases and decreases is consistent, at least on average, with this signaling theory. Figure 10.18 summarizes the average excess returns around dividend changes for firms found in a 1981 study. On average, stock prices go up when dividends are increased and go down when dividends are decreased, though the price reaction to the latter seems much more intense—a drop of more than 4.5 percent on dividend decreases and an increase of only about 1 percent on dividend increases.[66]

---

[66] J. Aharony and I. Swary, "Quarterly Dividends and Earnings Announcements and Stockholders' Returns: An Empirical Analysis," *Journal of Finance* 36 (1981): 1–12.

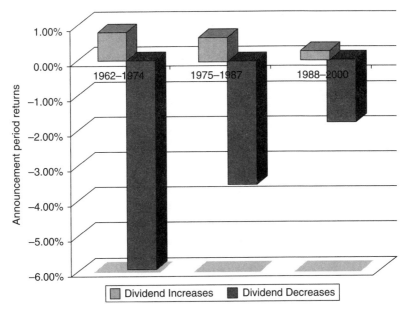

FIGURE 10.19 Market Reaction to Dividend Changes over Time: U.S. Companies
Source: Y. Amihud and K. Li, "The Declining Information Content of Dividend Announcements and the Effect of Institutional Investors" (SSRN Working Paper 482563, 2002).

Since the study, though, U.S. companies have dramatically changed the way they return cash to stockholders. Rather than pay higher regular dividends, many companies have instead turned to stock buybacks. In response or perhaps independently, investors have also become less focused on dividends when assessing stocks. A study that looked at the market reaction to dividend changes by period reports a significant drop-off in the market reaction to dividend changes over time, as evidenced in Figure 10.19.[67]

Note that while the patterns remain unchanged—dividend increases (or decreases) evoke price increases (or decreases), and dividend decreases have a bigger impact than dividend increases—the effect has declined over time.

A subclass of dividend changes that has drawn special attention is firms that either start paying dividends for the first time (dividend initiations) and stop paying dividends altogether (dividend cessations). The evidence here is consistent with studies reporting, on average, that dividend initiation is

---

[67]Y. Amihud and K. Li, "The Declining Information Content of Dividend Announcements and the Effect of Institutional Investors" (SSRN Working Paper 482563, 2002).

accompanied by a price increase (and cessation by a decrease). However, there is some evidence that dividend initiations are viewed as bad news in some companies; the stock price drops at about 40 percent of companies that initiate dividends. That should come as no surprise, since growth firms that start paying dividends are sending a signal that their best growth is behind them and that they no longer have the investment opportunities they used to have.[68]

Finally, what about cash returned by companies to stockholders on an irregular basis? This may have taken the form of special dividends until a few decades ago, but it has generally been replaced with stock buybacks at U.S. companies. The initial price reaction to a buyback announcement is positive, with the magnitude of the reaction increasing with the magnitude of the stock buyback.[69] While early studies suggested that this positive price effect carries over into subsequent periods,[70] more recent studies contest that finding,[71] noting that companies that buy back stock do not outperform the market or their peer group in the periods following the buyback.

Can investors use the information in dividend changes and buybacks to make higher returns? While the price change on the dividend announcement itself might not offer opportunities for investors (unless they have access to inside information), a study that looked at the price drift after dividend changes are announced noted that stock prices continue to drift up after dividend increases and drift down after dividend decreases for long periods and especially so after dividend omissions. Investors may be able to take advantage of this drift and augment returns on their portfolios. With buybacks, as with acquisitions, the bigger payoff to investors comes from identifying companies that are likely to buy back stock before the companies announce these buybacks: companies that generate low returns on equity or capital (relative to their cost of equity and capital), have high cash balances, trade at low valuation multiples, and have low financial leverage. Since these

---

[68]R. Michaely, R. H. Thaler, and K. L. Womack, "Price Reactions to Dividend Initiations and Omissions: Overreaction or Drift?" *Journal of Finance* 50 (1995): 573–608.

[69]An interesting exception was the first quarter of 2009. Companies that bought back stock in this quarter, shortly after the banking crisis of 2008, were punished rather than rewarded, with stock prices dropping about 1.6 percent on average.

[70]D. Ikenberry, J. Lakonishok, and T. Vermaelen, "Market Underreaction to Open Market Share Repurchases," *Journal of Financial Economics* 39 (1995): 181–208. They find a strong positive excess return over a five-year period from holding shares in companies that buy back their own stock.

[71]A. C. Eberhart and A. R. Siddique, "Why Are Stock Buyback Announcements Good News?" (SSRN Working Paper 647843, 2004).

were characteristics that we suggested should be used by value investors in picking companies, buybacks may be one way in which a value investing strategy can deliver higher returns.

IMPLEMENTING AN INFORMATION-BASED INVESTMENT STRATEGY

If you decide to center your investment strategy around information releases—earnings reports, acquisition announcements, or other news—you have to recognize that it is much more difficult to deliver the returns on an actual portfolio than it is in a hypothetical portfolio. To succeed at this strategy, you have to:

- *Identify the information around which your strategy will be built.* Since you have to trade on the announcement, it is critical that you determine in advance the information that will trigger a trade. To provide an example, you may conclude that your best potential for returns comes from buying shares in small companies that report earnings that are much higher than expected. However, you have to go further and specify what constitutes a small company (market cap less than $1 billion? $5 billion?) and by how much the actual earnings need to beat expectations (10 percent higher than expectations? 20 percent higher than expectations?). This is necessary because you will not have to the time for analysis after the report comes out.
- *Invest in an information system that will deliver the information to you instantaneously.* Many individual investors receive information with a time lag—15 to 20 minutes after it reaches the trading floor and institutional investors. While this may not seem like a lot of time, the biggest price changes after information announcements occur during these periods.
- *Execute quickly.* Getting an earnings report or an acquisition announcement in real time is of little use if it takes you 20 minutes to trade. Immediate execution of trades is essential to succeeding with this strategy.
- *Keep a tight lid on transaction costs.* Speedy execution of trades usually goes with higher transaction costs, but these transaction costs can very easily wipe out any potential you may see for excess returns, especially because you will be trading a lot (as with any short-term strategy).
- *Know when to sell.* Almost as critical as knowing when to buy is knowing when to sell, since the price effects of news releases may begin to fade or even reverse after a while. Thus, if you buy stock of firms after positive earnings announcements, you have to determine at the time you

buy the stock when you will sell it. While this may seem to take away your flexibility, the alternative of holding on to stocks too long, hoping that they will go up, can be even more damaging.

If you consider the requirements for success—immediate access to information, and instantaneous and cheap execution—it is not surprising that information-based investing was for a long time profitable only for institutional investors. In recent years, however, online access to information and trading has made it feasible for individual investors to join the party. This is a mixed blessing, though, since the more investors trade on information, the less returns there are from these strategies.

CONCLUSION

As investors, we all dream of receiving that important news release ahead of the market and making lucrative profits on it. Information is the key to investment success, and this chapter explores the possibility of acquiring and using information to augment portfolio returns. We began by looking at how market prices move in response to information, and noted that in an efficient market, the price reaction to new information is instantaneous. In such a market, investing in an asset after the information has been released is a neutral strategy. In an inefficient market, you can make money after the information is released, buying after good news if it is a slow learning market, or selling after good news if it is an overreacting market.

To examine whether it is possible to use information profitably, we first looked at the two groups of individuals most likely to have access to privileged or private information. Insiders in firms, especially top managers, clearly know more about their firms than do investors in markets. Insider trading does seem to provide a signal of future price movements—insider buying seems to precede stock price increases and selling seems to occur ahead of price drops—but the signal is noisy and the returns are small. This may, however, reflect the fact that the really profitable insider trades—the illegal ones—are never filed with the SEC. Equity research analysts also have access to information that most other investors do not have, and reflect this information in earnings forecasts and recommendations. Here again, while upward revisions in earnings and buy recommendations generally lead to stock price increases, and downward revisions and sell recommendations are followed by poor stock price performance, the returns are surprisingly small. The difficulty that both insiders and analysts have in converting information to returns should be a cautionary note to any investor considering an information-based investment strategy.

In the second part of the chapter, we looked at earnings reports, acquisition announcements, and other firm-specific announcements. These announcements affect prices significantly: positive (or negative) earnings reports are associated with price increases (or decreases), target company stock prices jump on acquisition announcements, and stock prices generally increase when there are stock splits or dividend increases. Unless you can anticipate these news releases, though, this price increase cannot be translated into a large profit. There does seem to be some evidence of a price drift after earnings announcements, and there are investors who try to take advantage of this drift by buying after positive earnings reports and selling after negative reports. To succeed with information-based trading, you have to be selective and disciplined in your investment choices and efficient in your execution.

EXERCISES

1. Do you think markets respond appropriately to new information? If yes, what makes them responsive? If no, what types of mistakes do you think they make and why?
2. Do you believe that insiders in companies know more than you do about the value of the company? If yes, what is the source of their advantage?
   a. Assuming that insiders do know more than you do and trade on that information, do you think that you can make money by following their trading?
   b. Given the information on insider trading in this chapter, how would you refine this strategy to generate higher returns for yourself?
3. Do you believe that analysts following companies know more than you do about the value of the company? If yes, what is the source of their advantage?
   a. Assuming that analysts do know more than you do and trade on that information, do you think that you can make money by following their earnings forecasts and recommendations?
   b. Given the information on analyst reports in this chapter, how would you refine this strategy to generate higher returns for yourself?
4. Stock prices clearly move on earnings announcements, with the movement beginning before the announcement, accelerating on the announcement, and continuing afterward.
   a. If you believe that you can make money off this price movement, what portion of the price movement (before, contemporaneous, after) do you think you can best exploit?

b. How would you go about doing it?

c. What would your concerns be with this strategy, and how would you go about meeting them?

Lessons for Investors

To be a successful trader on information, you need to:

- *Find a reliable source of information:* It goes without saying that good information is the key to success with any information-based trading strategy. (To stay on the right side of the law, make sure that your reliable source is not an insider.)
- *Have a clearly defined strategy for trading on information:* Since you will have to trade quickly, you will not have the time after information comes out to assess and analyze it. You will need to make a prejudgment on when you will be trading.
- *Be disciplined:* Don't deviate from your trading strategy, and do stick to the time horizon that you have chosen for yourself. Holding on to a stock for a few days more hoping to recoup your losses can make a bad situation worse.
- *Control your trading costs:* Since you will be trading frequently and immediate execution is key, your trading costs can be large. As the funds at your disposal increase, the price impact you have as you trade can be substantial.

CHAPTER 11

A Sure Profit: The Essence
of Arbitrage

A rbitrage represents the holy grail of investing because it allows investors to invest no money, take no risk, and walk away with sure profits. In other words, it is the ultimate money machine that investors hope to access. In this chapter, we consider three types of arbitrage. The first is pure arbitrage, where, in fact, you risk nothing and earn more than the riskless rate. For pure arbitrage to be feasible, you need two assets with identical cash flows, different market values at the same point in time, and a given point in time in the future at which the values have to converge. This type of arbitrage is most likely to occur in derivatives markets—options and futures—and in some parts of the bond market. The second is near arbitrage, where you have assets that have identical or almost identical cash flows, trading at different prices, but there is no guarantee that the prices will converge and there exist significant constraints on forcing convergence. The third is speculative arbitrage, which is really not arbitrage in the first place. Here, investors take advantage of what they see as mispriced and similar (though not identical) assets, buying the cheaper one and selling the more expensive one. If they are right, the difference should narrow over time, yielding profits. It is in this category that we consider hedge funds in their numerous forms.

PURE ARBITRAGE

If you have two assets that have exactly the same cash flows over the same time period, they should trade at the same price. If they do not, you would buy the cheaper asset, sell short on the more expensive asset, hold on to the differences in prices, and not have any risk exposure in the future. That is pure arbitrage, and, needless to say, it is rare for many reasons. First, identical assets are not common in the real world, especially if you are an equity investor. Second, assuming two identical assets exist, you have to wonder why pricing differences would persist in markets where investors can see those differences. If, in addition, we add the constraint that there is a point in time when the market prices have to converge, it is not surprising that pure arbitrage is most likely to occur with derivative assets—options and futures—and in fixed income markets, especially with default-free government bonds.

Futures Arbitrage

A futures contract is a contract to buy (and sell) a specified asset at a fixed price in a future time period. There are two parties to every futures contract: the seller of the contract, who agrees to deliver the asset at the specified time in the future, and the buyer of the contract, who agrees to pay a fixed price and take delivery of the asset. If the asset that underlies the futures contract is traded and is not perishable, you can construct a pure arbitrage if the futures contract is mispriced. In this section, we consider the potential for arbitrage first with storable commodities and then with financial assets, and then look at whether such arbitrage is possible and profitable.

The Arbitrage Relationships   The basic arbitrage relationship can be derived fairly easily for futures contracts on any asset by estimating the cash flows on two strategies that deliver the same end result—the ownership of the asset at a fixed price in the future. In the first strategy, you buy the futures contract, wait until the end of the contract period, and buy the underlying asset at the futures price. In the second strategy, you borrow the money and buy the underlying asset today, and then store it for the period of the futures contract. In both strategies, you end up with the asset at the end of the period and are exposed to no price risk during the period—in the first because you have locked in the futures price and in the second because you bought the asset at the start of the period. Consequently, you should expect the cost of setting up the two strategies to be exactly the same. Across different types of futures contracts, there are individual details that cause the final pricing relationship to vary: commodities have to be stored and create storage costs, whereas stocks may pay a dividend while you are holding them.

Storable Commodities   The distinction between storable and perishable goods is that storable goods can be acquired today at the spot price and stored until the expiration of the futures contract, which is the practical equivalent of buying a futures contract and taking delivery at expiration. Since the two approaches provide the same result in terms of having possession of the commodity at expiration, the futures contract, if priced right, should cost the same as a strategy of buying and storing the commodity. The two additional costs of the latter strategy are as follows:

1. Since the commodity has to be acquired now, rather than at expiration, there is an added financing cost associated with borrowing the funds needed for the acquisition now.

$$\text{Added interest cost} = (\text{Spot price}) \left[(1 + \text{Interest rate})^{\text{Life of futures contract}} - 1 \right]$$

2. If there is a storage cost associated with storing the commodity until the expiration of the futures contract, this cost has to be reflected in the strategy as well. In addition, there may be a benefit to having physical ownership of the commodity. This benefit is called the convenience yield and will reduce the futures price. The net storage cost is defined as the difference between the total storage cost and the convenience yield.

If F is the futures contract price, S is the spot price, r is the annualized interest rate, t is the life of the futures contract, and k is the net annual storage costs (as a percentage of the spot price) for the commodity, the two equivalent strategies and their costs can be written as follows.

Strategy 1: Buy the futures contract. Take delivery at expiration. Pay \$F.

Strategy 2: Borrow the spot price (S) of the commodity and buy the commodity. Pay the additional costs.

- Interest cost $= S[(1+r)^t - 1]$
- Cost of storage, net of convenience yield $= Skt$

If the two strategies have the same costs,

$$F^* = \begin{aligned} & S\left[(1+r)^t - 1\right] + Skt \\ & = S\left[(1+r)^t + kt\right] \end{aligned}$$

This is the basic arbitrage relationship between futures and spot prices. Note that the futures price does not depend on your expectations of what will happen to the spot price over time but on the spot price today. Any deviation from this arbitrage relationship should provide an opportunity for arbitrage (i.e., a strategy with no risk and no initial investment) and for positive profits. These arbitrage opportunities are described in Figure 11.1.

This arbitrage is based on several assumptions. First, investors are assumed to borrow and lend at the same rate, which is the riskless rate. Second,

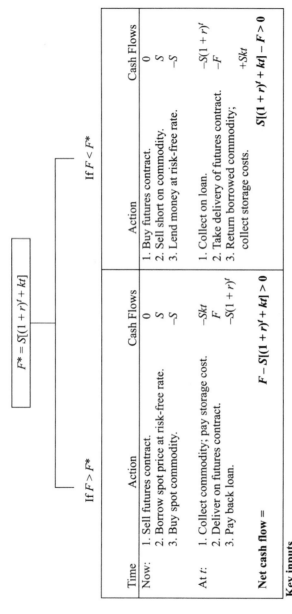

$$F^* = S[(1 + r)^t + kt]$$

If F > F*

Time	Action	Cash Flows
Now:	1. Sell futures contract.	0
	2. Borrow spot price at risk-free rate.	S
	3. Buy spot commodity.	$-S$
At t:	1. Collect commodity; pay storage cost.	$-Skt$
	2. Deliver on futures contract.	F
	3. Pay back loan.	$-S(1 + r)^t$
Net cash flow =		$F - S[(1 + r)^t + kt] > 0$

If F < F*

Action	Cash Flows
1. Buy futures contract.	0
2. Sell short on commodity.	S
3. Lend money at risk-free rate.	$-S$
1. Collect on loan.	$-S(1 + r)^t$
2. Take delivery of futures contract.	$-F$
3. Return borrowed commodity; collect storage costs.	$+Skt$
	$S[(1 + r)^t + kt] - F > 0$

Key inputs

F^* = Theoretical futures price
F = Actual futures price
S = Spot price of commodity
r = Riskless rate of interest (annualized)
t = Time to expiration of futures contract
k = Annualized carrying cost, net of convenience yield (as % of spot price)

Key assumptions

1. The investor can lend and borrow at the riskless rate.
2. There are no transaction costs associated with buying or selling short the commodity.
3. The short seller can collect all storage costs saved because of the short selling.

FIGURE 11.1 Storable Commodity Futures: Pricing and Arbitrage

when the futures contract is overpriced, it is assumed that the seller of the futures contract (the arbitrageur) can *sell short* on the commodity and can recover from the owner of the commodity the storage costs that are saved as a consequence. To the extent that these assumptions are unrealistic, the bounds on prices within which arbitrage is not feasible expand. Assume, for instance, that the rate of borrowing is r_b and the rate of lending is r_a, and that the short seller cannot recover any of the saved storage costs and has to pay a transaction cost of t_s. The futures price will then fall within a bound.

$$(S - t_s)(1 + r_a)^t < F^* < S\left[(1 + r_b)^t + kt\right]$$

If the futures price falls outside this bound, there is a possibility of arbitrage, and this is illustrated in Figure 11.2.

Stock Index Futures Futures on stock indexes have become an important and growing part of most financial markets. Today, you can buy or sell futures on most equity indices in the United States, as well as many indices in other countries. An index futures contract entitles the buyer to any appreciation in the index over and above the index futures price and the seller to any depreciation in the index from the same benchmark. To evaluate the arbitrage pricing of an index futures contract, consider the following strategies.

> *Strategy 1:* Sell short on the stocks in the index for the duration of the index futures contract. Invest the proceeds at the riskless rate. This strategy requires that the owners of the stocks that are sold short be compensated for the dividends they would have received on the stocks.
>
> *Strategy 2:* Sell the index futures contract.

Both strategies require the same initial investment, have the same risk, and should provide the same proceeds. Again, if S is the spot price of the index, F is the futures price, y is the annualized dividend yield on the stock, and r is the riskless rate, the arbitrage relationship for a futures contract that pays off in time period t can be written as follows:

$$F^* = S(1 + r - y)^t$$

If the futures price deviates from this arbitrage price, there should be an opportunity for arbitrage. This is illustrated in Figure 11.3.

This arbitrage is also conditioned on several assumptions. First, we assume that investors can lend and borrow at the riskless rate. Second, we

Modified Assumptions

1. Investor can borrow at r_b ($r_b > r$) and lend at r_a ($r_a < r$).
2. The transaction cost associated with selling short is t_s (where t_s is the dollar transaction cost).
3. The short seller does not collect any of the storage costs saved by the short selling.

$$F_h^* = S[(1 + r_b)^t + kt]$$
$$F_1^* = (S - t_s)(1 + r_a)^t$$

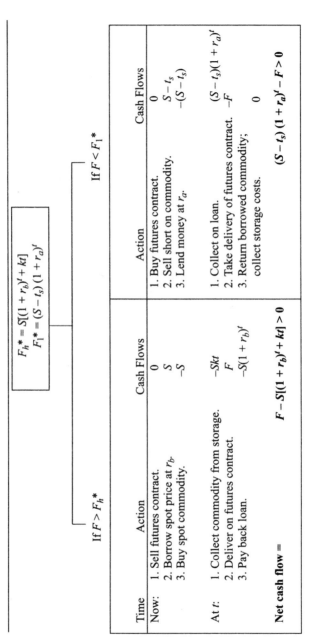

If $F > F_h^*$

Time	Action	Cash Flows
Now:	1. Sell futures contract.	0
	2. Borrow spot price at r_b.	S
	3. Buy spot commodity.	$-S$
At t:	1. Collect commodity from storage.	$-Skt$
	2. Deliver on futures contract.	F
	3. Pay back loan.	$-S(1 + r_b)^t$
Net cash flow =		$F - S[(1 + r_b)^t + kt] > 0$

If $F < F_1^*$

Time	Action	Cash Flows
Now:	1. Buy futures contract.	0
	2. Sell short on commodity.	$S - t_s$
	3. Lend money at r_a.	$-(S - t_s)$
At t:	1. Collect on loan.	$(S - t_s)(1 + r_a)^t$
	2. Take delivery of futures contract.	$-F$
	3. Return borrowed commodity; collect storage costs.	0
Net cash flow =		$(S - t_s)(1 + r_a)^t - F > 0$

F_h = Upper limit for arbitrage bound on futures prices F_1 = Lower limit for arbitrage bound on futures prices

FIGURE 11.2   Storable Commodity Futures: Pricing and Arbitrage with Modified Assumptions

$$F^* = S(1 + r - y)^t$$

If $F > F^*$

Time	Action	Cash Flows
Now:	1. Sell futures contract.	0
	2. Borrow spot price of index at risk-free rate.	S
	3. Buy stocks in index.	$-S$
At t:	1. Collect dividends on stocks.	$S[(1 + y)^t - 1]$
	2. Delivery on futures contract.	F
	3. Pay back loan.	$-S(1 + r)^t$
Net cash flow =		$F - S(1 + r - y)^t > 0$

If $F < F^*$

Time	Action	Cash Flows
Now:	1. Buy futures contract.	0
	2. Sell short stocks in the index.	S
	3. Lend money at risk-free rate.	$-S$
At t:	1. Collect on loan.	$S(1 + r)^t$
	2. Take delivery of futures contract.	$-F$
	3. Return borrowed stocks; pay forgone dividends.	$-S[(1 + y)^t - 1]$
		$S(1 + r - y)^t - F > 0$

Key inputs

$F^* =$ Theoretical futures price
$F =$ Actual futures price
$S =$ Spot level of index

$r =$ Riskless rate of interest (annualized)
$t =$ Time to expiration of futures contract
$y =$ Dividend yield over lifetime of futures contract (as % of current index level)

Key assumptions

1. The investor can lend and borrow at the riskless rate.
2. There are no transaction costs associated with buying or selling short stocks.
3. Dividends are known with certainty.

FIGURE 11.3 Stock Index Futures: Pricing and Arbitrage

ignore transaction costs on both buying stock and selling short on stocks. Third, we assume that the dividends paid on the stocks in the index are known with certainty at the start of the period. If these assumptions are unrealistic, the index futures arbitrage will be feasible only if prices fall outside a band, the size of which will depend on the seriousness of the violations in the assumptions.

Thus, if we assume that investors can borrow money at r_b and lend money at r_a and that the transaction cost of buying stock is t_c and selling short is t_s, the band within which the futures price must stay can be written as:

$$(S - t_s)(1 + r_a - y)^t < F^* < (S + t_c)(1 + r_b - y)^t$$

The arbitrage that is possible if the futures price strays outside this band is illustrated in Figure 11.4.

In practice, one of the issues that you have to factor in is the seasonality of dividends since the dividends paid by stocks tend to be higher in some months than others. Figure 11.5 graphs out cumulative dividends paid by stocks in the S&P 500 index on U.S. stocks in 2009 and 2010 by month of the year.

Thus, dividend yields seem to peak in February, May, August, and November in both years. An index futures contract coming due in these months is much more likely to be affected by dividends, especially as maturity draws closer.

Treasury Bond Futures   The Treasury bond futures traded on the Chicago Board of Trade (CBOT) require the delivery of any government bond with a maturity greater than 15 years, with a no-call feature for at least the first 15 years. Since bonds of different maturities and coupons will have different prices, the CBOT has a procedure for adjusting the price of the bond for its characteristics. The conversion factor itself is fairly simple to compute and is based on the value of the bond on the first day of the delivery month, with the assumption that the interest rate for all maturities equals a preset rate per annum (with semiannual compounding). For instance, if the preset rate is 8 percent, you can compute the conversion factor for a 9 percent coupon bond with 18 years to maturity. Working in terms of a $100 face value of the bond, the value of the bond can be written as follows, using the interest rate of 8 percent.

$$\text{PV of bond} = \sum_{t=0.5}^{t=20} \frac{4.50}{(1.08)^t} + \frac{100}{(1.08)^{20}} = \$111.55$$

Modified Assumptions

1. Investor can borrow at r_b ($r_b > r$) and lend at r_a ($r_a < r$).
2. The transaction cost associated with selling short is t_s (where t_s is the dollar transaction cost), and the transaction cost associated with buying the stocks in the index is t_c.

$$F_h^* = (S + t_c)(1 + r_b - y)^t$$
$$F_1^* = (S - t_s)(1 + r_a - y)^t$$

If $F > F_h^*$ If $F < F_1^*$

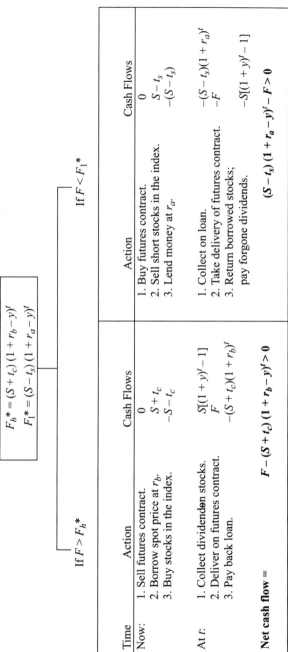

Time	Action	Cash Flows
Now:	1. Sell futures contract.	0
	2. Borrow spot price at r_b.	$S + t_c$
	3. Buy stocks in the index.	$-S - t_c$
At t:	1. Collect dividends on stocks.	$S[(1 + y)^t - 1]$
	2. Deliver on futures contract.	F
	3. Pay back loan.	$-(S + t_c)(1 + r_b)^t$
Net cash flow =	$F - (S + t_c)(1 + r_b - y)^t > 0$	

Time	Action	Cash Flows
Now:	1. Buy futures contract.	0
	2. Sell short stocks in the index.	$S - t_s$
	3. Lend money at r_a.	$-(S - t_s)$
At t:	1. Collect on loan.	$-(S - t_s)(1 + r_a)^t$
	2. Take delivery of futures contract.	$-F$
	3. Return borrowed stocks; pay forgone dividends.	$-S[(1 + y)^t - 1]$
Net cash flow =	$(S - t_s)(1 + r_a - y)^t - F > 0$	

F_h = Upper limit for arbitrage bound on futures prices

F_1 = Lower limit for arbitrage bound on futures prices

FIGURE 11.4 Stock Index Futures: Pricing and Arbitrage with Modified Assumptions

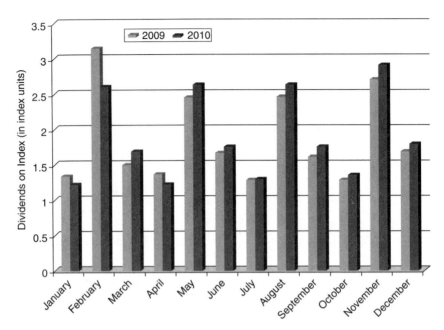

FIGURE 11.5   Dividends by Month on the S&P 500, 2009 and 2010
Source: Bloomberg.

The conversion factor for this bond is 111.55. Generally, the conversion factor will increase as the coupon rate increases and with the maturity of the delivered bond.

This feature of Treasury bond futures (i.e., that any one of a menu of Treasury bonds can be delivered to fulfill the obligation on the bond) provides an advantage to the seller of the futures contract. Naturally, the cheapest bond on the menu, after adjusting for the conversion factor, will be delivered. This *delivery option* has to be priced into the futures contract. There is an additional option embedded in Treasury bond futures contracts that arises from the fact that the seller does not have to notify the clearinghouse until 8 p.m. about his intention to deliver. If bond prices decline after the close of the futures market, the seller can notify the clearinghouse of his intention to deliver the cheapest bond that day. If not, the seller can wait for the next day. This option is called the *wild card option*.

The valuation of a Treasury bond futures contract follows the same lines as the valuation of a stock index future, with the coupons of the Treasury bond replacing the dividend yield of the stock index. The theoretical value of a futures contract should be:

$$F^* = (S - \text{PVC})(1 + r)^t$$

where $F^* =$ Theoretical futures price for Treasury bond futures
contract
$S =$ Spot price of Treasury bond
PVC $=$ Present value of coupons during life of futures contract
$r =$ Risk-free interest rate corresponding to futures life
$t =$ Life of futures contract

If the futures price deviates from this theoretical price, there should be the opportunity for arbitrage. These arbitrage opportunities are illustrated in Figure 11.6.

This valuation ignores the two options described earlier—the option to deliver the cheapest-to-deliver bond and the option to have a wild card play. These give an advantage to the seller of the futures contract and should be priced into the futures contract. One way to build this into the valuation is to use the cheapest deliverable bond to calculate both the current spot price and the present value of the coupons. Once the futures price is estimated, it can be divided by the conversion factor to arrive at the standardized futures price.

Currency Futures   In a currency futures contract, you enter into a contract to buy a foreign currency at a price fixed today. To see how spot and futures currency prices are related, note that holding the foreign currency enables the investor to earn the risk-free interest rate (R_f) prevailing in that country while the domestic currency earns the domestic risk-free rate (R_d). Since investors can buy currency at spot rates, and assuming that there are no restrictions on investing at the risk-free rate, we can derive the relationship between the spot and futures prices. *Interest rate parity* relates the differential between futures and spot prices to interest rates in the domestic and foreign market.

$$\frac{\text{Futures price}_{d,f}}{\text{Spot price}_{d,f}} = \frac{(1 + R_d)}{(1 + R_f)}$$

where futures price$_{d,f}$ is the number of units of the domestic currency that will be received for a unit of the foreign currency in a forward contract, and spot price$_{d,f}$ is the number of units of the domestic currency that will be received for a unit of the same foreign currency in a spot contract. For instance, assume that the one-year interest rate in the United States is 2 percent and the one-year interest rate in Switzerland is 1 percent. Furthermore, assume that the spot exchange rate is $1.10 per Swiss Franc. The one-year futures price, based on interest rate parity, should be as follows:

$$\frac{\text{Futures price}_{\$,\text{Sfr}}}{\$1.10} = \frac{(1.02)}{(1.01)}$$

This results in a futures price of $1.1109 per Swiss franc.

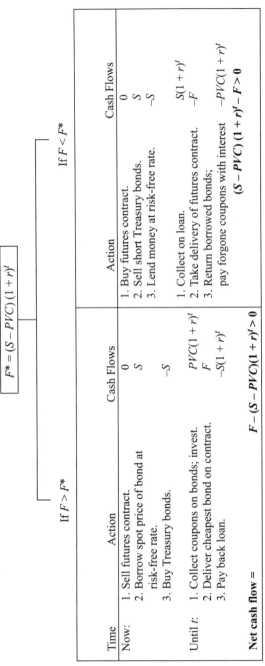

$$F^* = (S - PVC)(1 + r)^t$$

If F > F*

Time	Action	Cash Flows
Now:	1. Sell futures contract.	0
	2. Borrow spot price of bond at risk-free rate.	S
	3. Buy Treasury bonds.	$-S$
Until t:	1. Collect coupons on bonds; invest.	$PVC(1 + r)^t$
	2. Deliver cheapest bond on contract.	F
	3. Pay back loan.	$-S(1 + r)^t$

Net cash flow = $F - (S - PVC)(1 + r)^t > 0$

If F < F*

Action	Cash Flows
1. Buy futures contract.	0
2. Sell short Treasury bonds.	S
3. Lend money at risk-free rate.	$-S$
1. Collect on loan.	$S(1 + r)^t$
2. Take delivery of futures contract.	$-F$
3. Return borrowed bonds; pay forgone coupons with interest	$-PVC(1 + r)^t$

$(S - PVC)(1 + r)^t - F > 0$

Key inputs

F^* = Theoretical futures price
F = Actual futures price
S = Spot level of Treasury bond

r = Riskless rate of interest (annualized)
t = Time to expiration of futures contract
PVC = Present value of coupons on bond during life of futures contract

Key assumptions
1. The investor can lend and borrow at the riskless rate.
2. There are no transaction costs associated with buying or selling short bonds.

FIGURE 11.6 Treasury Bond Futures: Pricing and Arbitrage

TABLE 11.1 Arbitrage When Currency Futures Contracts Are Mispriced

Forward Rate Mispricing	Actions to Take Today	Actions at Expiration of Futures Contract
If futures price > $1.1109 (e.g., $1.12)	1. Borrow the spot price ($1.10) in the U.S. domestic markets @ 2%. 2. Convert the $1.10 into a Swiss franc at spot price. 3. Invest the Swiss francs @ 1%. 4. Sell futures contract on Sfr for proceeds for Sfr investment @ $1.12	1. Collect 1.01 Sfr on Swiss franc investment. 2. Convert 1.01 Sfr into dollars at futures price of 1.12. $1.01 * 1.12 = 1.1312$ 3. Repay dollar borrowing with interest. $1.10 * 1.02 = \$1.1220$ **Profit = \$1,1312– \$1.220 = \$0.0090**
If futures price < $1.1109 (e.g., $1.105)	1. Borrow a Swiss franc @ 1%. 2. Convert the Swiss franc into dollars at spot rate of $1.10. 3. Invest $1.10 in the U.S. market @ 2%. 4. Buy a futures contract on Sfr for proceeds on U.S. $ investment @ 1.105.	1. Collect on dollar investment. $\$1.10 * 1.02 = \$1.122$ 2. Convert $1.122 into Swiss francs at futures price of $1.105. $\$1.122/1.105 \ \$/Sfr = 1.0154 \ Sfr$ 3. Repay Sfr borrowing with interest. $1 * 1.01 = 1.01 \ Sfr$ **Profit = 1.0154 Sfr – 1.01 Sfr = 0.0054 Sfr**

Why does this have to be the futures price? If the futures price were greater than $1.1109, say $1.12, an investor could take advantage of the mispricing by selling the futures contract, completely hedging against risk, and ending up with a return greater than the risk-free rate. The actions the investor would need to take are summarized in Table 11.1, with the cash flows associated with each action next to the action.

The first arbitrage of Table 11.1 results in a riskless profit of $0.0092, with no initial investment. The process of arbitrage will push the futures price down toward the equilibrium price.

If the futures price were lower than $1.1109, the actions would be reversed, with the same final conclusion. Investors would be able to take no risk, invest no money, and still end up with a positive cash flow at expiration. In the second arbitrage of Table 11.1, we lay out the actions that would lead to a riskless profit of 0.0054 Sfr.

Special Features of Futures Markets   There are two special features of futures markets that can make arbitrage tricky. The first is the existence of margins. While we assumed when constructing the arbitrage that buying and selling futures contracts would create no cash flows at the time of the transaction, you have to put up a portion of the futures contract price (about 5 percent to 10 percent) as a margin in the real world. To compound the problem, this margin is recomputed every day based on futures prices that day (this process is called *marking to market*) and you may be required to come up with more margin if the price moves against you (down if you are a buyer, and up if you are a seller). If this margin call is not met, your position can be liquidated and you may never get to see your arbitrage profits.

NUMBER WATCH

Price limits and contract specifications: Take a look at the price limits and contract specifications on widely traded futures contracts.

The second feature is that the futures exchanges generally impose price movement limits on most futures contracts. If the price of the contract drops or increases by the amount of the price limit, trading is generally suspended for the day, though the exchange reserves the discretion to reopen trading in the contract later in the day. The rationale for introducing price limits is to prevent panic buying and selling on an asset based on faulty information or rumors, and to prevent overreaction to real information. By allowing investors more time to react to extreme information, it is argued, the price reaction will be more rational and reasoned. In the process, though, you can create a disconnect between the spot markets, where no price limits exist, and the futures markets, where they do.

Feasibility of Arbitrage and Potential for Success   If futures arbitrage is so simple, you may ask, how in a reasonably efficient market would arbitrage opportunities even exist? In the commodity futures market, for instance, Garbade and Silber find little evidence of arbitrage opportunities, and their findings are echoed in other studies.[1] In the financial futures markets, there is evidence that indicates that arbitrage is indeed feasible but only to a subset of investors. Differences in transaction costs seem to explain most of the differences. Large institutional investors, with close to zero transaction costs and instantaneous access to both the underlying asset and futures markets, may be able to find arbitrage opportunities where most individual investors would not. In addition, these investors are also more likely to meet the requirements for arbitrage—being able to borrow at rates close to the riskless rate and sell short on the underlying asset.

Note, though, that the returns are small even to these large investors and that arbitrage will not be a reliable source of profits, unless you can establish a competitive advantage on one of three dimensions.[2] First, you can try to establish a transaction cost advantage over other investors, which will be difficult to do since you are competing with other large institutional investors. Second, you may be able to develop an information advantage over other investors by having access to information earlier than others. However, much of the information is pricing information and is public. Third, you may find a quirk in the data or pricing of a particular futures contract before others learn about it. As a consequence, the arbitrage possibilities seem to be greater when futures contracts are first introduced on an asset, since investors take time to understand the details of futures pricing. For instance, it took investors a while to learn to incorporate the effect of uneven dividends into stock index futures and the wild card option into Treasury bond futures. Presumably, investors who learned faster than the market would have been able to take advantage of the mispricing of futures contracts in these early periods and earn excess returns.

Options Arbitrage

As derivative securities, options differ from futures in a very important respect. They represent rights rather than obligations; calls give you the right to buy, and puts give you the right to sell. Consequently, a key feature of options is that the losses on an option position are limited to what you paid for the option, if you are a buyer. Since there is usually an underlying asset that is traded, you can, as with futures contracts, construct positions that essentially are risk-free by combining options with the underlying asset.

---

[1] K. D. Garbade and W. L. Silber, "Price Movements and Price Discovery in Futures and Cash Markets," *Review of Economics and Statistics* 115 (1983): 289–297.
[2] A study of 835 index arbitrage trades on the S&P 500 futures contracts estimated that the average gross profit from such trades was only 0.30 percent.

Exercise Arbitrage   The easiest arbitrage opportunities in the option market exist when options violate simple pricing bounds. No option, for instance, should sell for less than its exercise value. Thus, the minimal arbitrage conditions are as follows:

With a call option: Value of call > Value of underlying asset − Strike price
With a put option: Value of put > Strike price − Value of underlying asset

For instance, a call option with a strike price of $30 on a stock that is currently trading at $40 should never sell for less than $10. If it did, you could make an immediate profit by buying the call for less than $10 and exercising right away to make $10.

In fact, you can tighten these bounds for call options if you are willing to create a portfolio of the underlying asset and the option and hold it through the option's expiration. The bounds then become:

With a call option: Value of call > Value of underlying asset − Present value of strike price

With a put option: Value of put > Present value of strike price − Value of underlying asset

To see why, consider the call option in the previous example. Assume that you have one year to expiration and that the riskless interest rate is 10 percent.

$$\text{Present value of strike price} = \$30/1.10 = \$27.27$$
$$\text{Lower bound on call value} = \$40 - \$27.27 = \$12.73$$

The call has to trade for more than $12.73. What would happen if it traded for less, say $12? You would sell short a share of stock for $40, buy the call for $12, and invest the remaining proceeds from the short sale of $28 ($40 − $12) at the riskless rate of 10 percent. Consider what happens a year from now:

If the stock price > strike price ($30): You first collect the proceeds from the riskless investment [$28(1.10) = $30.80], exercise the option (buy the share at $30), and cover your short sale. You will then get to keep the difference of $0.80.

If the stock price < strike price ($30): You collect the proceeds from the riskless investment ($30.80), buy a share in the open market for the prevailing price then (which is less than $30), and keep the difference.

In other words, you invest nothing today and are guaranteed a positive payoff in the future. You could construct a similar example with puts.

The arbitrage bounds work best for non-dividend-paying stocks and for options that can be exercised only at expiration (European options). Most options in the real world can be exercised prior to expiration (American options) and are on stocks that pay dividends. Even with these options, though, you should not see short-term options trading violating these bounds by large margins, partly because exercise is so rare even with listed American options and dividends tend to be small. As options become long-term and dividends become larger and more uncertain, you may very well find options that violate these pricing bounds, but you may not be able to profit off them.

Replicating Portfolio   One of the key insights that Fischer Black and Myron Scholes had about options in the 1970s that revolutionized option pricing was that a portfolio composed of the underlying asset and the riskless asset could be constructed to have exactly the same cash flows as a call or put option.[3] This portfolio is called the replicating portfolio. In fact, Black and Scholes used the arbitrage argument to derive their option pricing model by noting that since the replicating portfolio and the traded option have the same cash flows, they would have to sell at the same price.

To understand how replication works, let us consider a very simple model for stock prices where prices can jump to one of two points in each time period. This model, which is called a binomial model, allows us to model the replicating portfolio fairly easily. In the diagram, we have the binomial distribution of a stock, currently trading at $50, for the next two time periods. Note that in two time periods, this stock can be trading for as much as $100 or as little as $25. Assume that the objective is to value a call with a strike price of $50, which is expected to expire in two time periods.

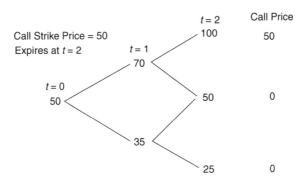

[3] F. Black and M. Scholes, "The Valuation of Option Contracts and a Test of Market Efficiency," *Journal of Finance* 27 (1972): 399–417.

Now assume that the interest rate is 11 percent. In addition, define:

$$\Delta = \text{Number of shares in the replicating portfolio}$$

$$B = \text{Dollars of borrowing in replicating portfolio}$$

The objective is to combine Δ shares of stock and B dollars of borrowing to replicate the cash flows from the call with a strike price of $50. Since we know the cash flows on the option with certainty at expiration, it is best to start with the last period and work backward through the binomial tree.

Step 1: Start with the end nodes and work backward. Note that the call option expires at $t = 2$, and the gross payoff on the option will be the difference between the stock price and the exercise price if the stock price $>$ exercise price, and zero if the stock price $<$ exercise price.

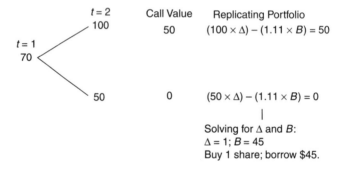

The objective is to construct a portfolio of Δ shares of stock and B in borrowing at $t = 1$, when the stock price is $70, that will have the same cash flows at $t = 2$ as the call option with a strike price of $50. Consider what the portfolio will generate in cash flows under each of the two stock price scenarios after you pay back the borrowing with interest (11 percent per period) and set the cash flows equal to the cash flows you would have received on the call.

If stock price $= \$100$: Portfolio value $= 100\Delta - 1.11B = 50$

If stock price $= \$50$: Portfolio value $= 50\Delta - 1.11B = 0$

We can solve for both the number of shares of stock you will need to buy (1) and the amount you will need to borrow ($45) at $t = 1$. Thus, if the stock price is $70 at $t = 1$, borrowing $45 and buying one share of the stock will give the same cash flows as buying the call. To prevent arbitrage, the value of the call at $t = 1$, if the stock price is $70, has to be equal to the cost (to you as an investor) of setting up the replicating position:

Value of call = Cost of replicating position = $70\Delta - B = (70)(1) - 45 = \$25$

Considering the other leg of the binomial tree at $t = 1$,

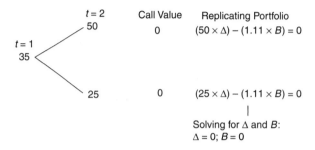

If the stock price is 35 at $t = 1$, then the call is worth nothing.

Step 2: Now that we know how much the call will be worth at $t = 1$ ($25 if the stock price goes to $70 and $0 if it goes down to $35), we can move backward to the earlier time period and create a replicating portfolio that will provide the values that the option will provide.

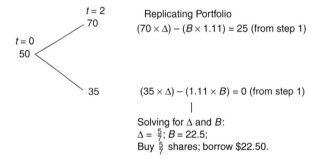

In other words, borrowing $22.50 and buying $\frac{5}{7}$ of a share today will provide the same cash flows as a call with a strike price of $50. The value of the call therefore has to be the same as the cost of creating this position.

$$\text{Value of call} = \text{Cost of replicating position}$$
$$= \left(\frac{5}{7}\right) (\text{Current stock price}) - 22.5$$
$$= \left(\frac{5}{7}\right) (50) - 22.5 = \$13.21$$

Consider for the moment the possibilities for arbitrage if the call traded at less than $13.21, say $13.00. You would buy the call for $13.00, sell the replicating portfolio for $13.21, and claim the difference of $0.21. Since the cash flows on the two positions are identical, you would be exposed to no risk and you make a certain profit. If the call traded for more than $13.21, say $13.50, you would buy the replicating portfolio, sell the call, and claim the $0.29 difference. Again, you would not have been exposed to any risk. You could construct a similar example using puts. The replicating portfolio in that case would be created by selling short on the underlying stock and lending the money at the riskless rate. Again, if puts are priced at a value different from the replicating portfolio, you could capture the difference and be exposed to no risk.

What are the assumptions that underlie this arbitrage? The first is that both the underlying asset and the option are traded, that you can be long or short on either, and that you can trade simultaneously in both markets, thus locking in your profits. However, the very assumption that you can constantly or dynamically replicate the cash flows on the option by using the underlying asset and riskless asset has been vigorously contested by many, thus breaching a fundamental requirement for arbitrage.[4] The second assumption is that there are no (or at least very low) transaction costs. If transaction costs are large, prices will have to move outside the band created by these costs for arbitrage to be feasible. The third assumption is that you can borrow at the riskless rate and sell short, if necessary. If you cannot, arbitrage may no longer be feasible.

Arbitrage Across Options   When you have multiple options listed on the same asset, you may be able to take advantage of relative mispricing—how one option is priced relative to another—and lock in riskless profits. We will look first at the pricing of calls relative to puts and then consider how options with different exercise prices and maturities should be priced relative to each other. We will close the section by looking at returns from buying versus selling options.

Put-Call Parity   When you have a put and a call option with the same exercise price and the same maturity, you can create a riskless position by selling the call, buying the put, and buying the underlying asset at the same time. To see why, consider selling a call and buying a put with exercise price K and expiration date t, and simultaneously buying the underlying asset

---

[4]E. Derman and N. N. Taleb, "The Illusions of Dynamic Replication" (SSRN Working Paper 720581, 2005).

at the current price S. The payoff from this position is riskless and always yields a cash flow of K at expiration t. To see this, assume that the stock price at expiration is S^*. The payoff on each of the positions in the portfolio can be written as follows:

Position	Payoffs at t If $S^* > K$	Payoffs at t If $S^* < K$
Sell call	$-(S^* - K)$	0
Buy put	0	$K - S^*$
Buy stock	S^*	S^*
Total	K	K

Since this position yields K with certainty, the cost of creating this position must be equal to the present value of K at the riskless rate $(K\,e^{-rt})$.

$$S + P - C = Ke^{-rt}$$
$$C - P = S - Ke^{-rt}$$

This relationship between put and call prices is called put-call parity. If it is violated, you have arbitrage.

If $C - P > S - K^{-rt}$, you would sell the call, buy the put, and buy the stock. You would earn more than the riskless rate on a riskless investment.

If $C - P < S - K^{-rt}$, you would buy the call, sell the put, and sell short the stock. You would then invest the proceeds at the riskless rate and end up with a riskless profit at maturity.

Note that violations of put-call parity create arbitrage opportunities only for options that can be exercised only at maturity (European options) and may not hold if options can be exercised early (American options).

Does put-call parity hold up in practice, or are there arbitrage opportunities? An early study examined option pricing data from the Chicago Board Options Exchange from 1977 to 1978 and found potential arbitrage opportunities in a few cases.[5] However, the arbitrage opportunities were small and persisted only for short periods. Furthermore, the options examined were American options, where arbitrage may not be feasible even if put-call parity is violated. A study by Kamara and Miller of options on the S&P 500 (which are European options) between 1986 and 1989 found that

---

[5]R. C. Klemkosky and B. G. Resnick, "Put-Call Parity and Market Efficiency," *Journal of Finance* 34 (1979): 1141–1155.

there were few violations of put-call parity, and that the deviations tend to be small.[6]

Mispricing across Strike Prices and Maturities   A spread is a combination of two or more options of the same type (call or put) on the same underlying asset. You can combine two options with the same maturity but different exercise prices (bull and bear spreads), two options with the same strike price but different maturities (calendar spreads), two options with different exercise prices and maturities (diagonal spreads), and more than two options (butterfly spreads). You may be able to use spreads to take advantage of relative mispricing of options on the same underlying stock.

- *Strike prices.* A call with a lower strike price should never sell for less than a call with a higher strike price, assuming that they both have the same maturity. If it did, you could buy the lower strike price call and sell the higher strike price call, and lock in a riskless profit. Similarly, a put with a lower strike price should never sell for more than a put with a higher strike price and the same maturity. If it did, you could buy the higher strike price put, sell the lower strike price put, and make an arbitrage profit.
- *Maturity.* A call (put) with a shorter time to expiration should never sell for more than a call (put) with the same strike price with a long time to expiration. If it did, you would buy the call (put) with the shorter maturity and sell the call (put) with the longer maturity (i.e., create a calendar spread) and lock in a profit today. When the first call expires, you will either exercise the second call (and have no cash flows) or sell it (and make a further profit).

Even a casual perusal of the option prices listed in the newspaper or on the Internet each day should make it clear that it is very unlikely that pricing violations that are this egregious will exist in a liquid options market.

There are riskier strategies that do not require the blatant mispricing that pure arbitrage does but do require relative mispricing, either across options or over time. For instance, there is evidence that investors are not rational in their behavior just before ex-dividend days and often choose not to exercise call options when they should. In particular, rational exercise would require the exercise of options when the time value on the option is less than the expected dividend, and Hao, Kalay, and Mayhew find that

---

[6]A. Kamara and T. W. Miller, "Daily and Intradaily Tests of European Put-Call Parity," *Journal of Financial and Quantitative Analysis* 30, no. 4 (1995): 519–541.

about 30 percent of call options that should have been exercised are not, leading to windfall profits for those who sold these options.[7]

Long versus Short Positions   Studies that have looked at the profit opportunities from trading on options have uncovered an irregularity. In general, strategies that require selling options seem to offer much better returns, given their risk, than equivalent strategies that require buying options. There are, however, three potential roadblocks to using this strategy to generate arbitrage profits in the long term. The first is the transaction costs of these strategies tend to be high, wiping out a large portion of the profits over time. The second is that the margin requirements (and the resultant margin calls) if the stock price moves in the wrong direction can limit how much an investor can invest in a strategy and also sometimes force the investor to close down positions prematurely. Finally, these strategies also suffer from exposure to extreme events: risks that occur infrequently but when they do cause major and even catastrophic losses.

VOLATILITY VIEWS AND OPTIONS

Option prices are determined by expected volatility, and there are strategies that are designed to profit from views on the future direction of volatility or from mispricing of volatility across options on the same underlying asset. These strategies are not riskless and thus don't fit into the arbitrage spectrum. They can, however, still be profitable.

Taking the volatility timing strategies, there are patterns to volatility over time that investors may be able to exploit. In particular, just as prices and P/E ratios often revert back to historic norms, there is evidence that volatility does as well. A strategy of buying options (straddles or other positions that minimize exposure to stock price direction) when the implied volatility in option prices is lower than the historic realized volatility generates significant excess returns for investors, with option positions in the highest decile (in terms of difference between historic realized volatility and implied volatility) earning 0.21 percent a month more than expected. However, allowing

(continued)

---

[7]J. Hao, A. Kalay, and S. Mayhew, "Ex-Dividend Arbitrage in Options Markets," *Review of Financial Studies* 23 (2010): 271–303.

for transaction costs lowers that excess return to just under 0.08 percent a month. A strategy of selling options when the implied volatility is much higher than the realized volatility generates excess returns of about 0.16 percent a month, but incorporating transaction costs wipes out most of those returns.[8]

There is clear evidence that the implied volatilities in option prices are different for different options on the same underlying asset at the same time; this is clearly not consistent with conventional option pricing models. In particular, there seems to be evidence of a volatility smile, where options at-the-money for a given underlying asset and option maturity have lower implied volatilities than options that are deep-in-the-money or deep-out-of-the-money. To the extent that this consistently shows up in different option markets and across time, most analysts incorporate the smile into their option pricing models, using higher volatilities when valuing deep-in-the-money or deep-out-of-the-money options. However, to the extent that a smile is exaggerated (the difference in implied volatilities between at-the-money and deep-in-the-money or deep-out-of-the money options is too high), selling straddles can be profitable, assuming the smile will revert back to normal levels.

Fixed Income Arbitrage

Fixed income securities lend themselves to arbitrage more easily than equities because they have finite lives and contractually specified cash flows. This is especially so when you have default-free bonds, where the contractual cash flows are also guaranteed. Consider one very simple example. You could replicate a 10-year Treasury bond's cash flows by buying zero coupon Treasuries with expirations matching those of the coupon payment dates on the Treasury bond. For instance, if you invest $100 million in a 10-year Treasury bond with an 8 percent coupon rate, you can expect to get cash flows of $4 million every six months for the next 10 years and $100 million at the end of the tenth year. You could have obtained exactly the same cash flows by buying zero coupon Treasuries with face values of $4 million, expiring every six months for the next 10 years, and an additional 10-year

---

[8]A. Goyal and A. Saretto, "Option Returns and Volatility Mispricing," *Journal of Financial Economics* 94 (2009): 310–326.

zero coupon bond with a face value of $100 million. Since the cash flows are identical, you would expect the two positions to trade for the same price. If they do not trade at the same price, you would buy the cheaper position and sell the more expensive one, locking in the profit today and having no cash flow or risk exposure in the future.

With corporate bonds, you have the extra component of default risk. Since no two firms are exactly identical when it comes to default risk, you may be exposed to some risk if you are using corporate bonds issued by different entities. In fact, two bonds issued even by the same entity may not be equivalent because of differences in how they are secured and structured. There are some arbitrageurs who argue that bond ratings are a good proxy for default risk, and that buying one AA-rated bond and selling another should be effectively riskless, but bond ratings are not perfect proxies for default risk. In fact, you see arbitrage attempted on a wide variety of securities with promised cash flows, such as mortgage-backed bonds. While you can hedge away much of the cash flow risk, the nature of the cash flow claims will still leave you exposed to some risk. With mortgage-backed bonds, for instance, the unpredictability of prepayments by homeowners has exposed many so-called riskless positions to risk.

Is there any evidence that investors are able to find Treasuries mispriced enough to generate arbitrage profits? Grinblatt and Longstaff, in an assessment of the Treasury Strips program (a program allowing investors to break up a Treasury bond and sell its individual cash flows) note that there are potential arbitrage opportunities in these markets but find little evidence of trading driven by these opportunities.[9] A study by Balbás and López of the Spanish bond market also sheds some light on this question. Examining default-free and option-free bonds in the Spanish market between 1994 and 1998, they conclude that there were arbitrage opportunities, especially surrounding innovations in financial markets.[10] We would extend their findings to argue that opportunities for arbitrage with fixed income securities are probably greatest when new types of bonds are introduced—mortgage-backed securities in the early 1980s, inflation-indexed Treasuries in the late 1990s, and the Treasury Strips program in the late 1980s. As investors become more informed about these bonds and how they should be priced, arbitrage opportunities seem to subside.

---

[9]M. Grinblatt and F. A. Longstaff, "Financial Innovation and the Role of Derivative Securities: An Empirical Analysis of the U.S. Treasury's Strips Program," *Journal of Finance* 55 (2000): 1415–1436.

[10]A. Balbás and S. López, "Financial Innovation and Arbitrage in the Spanish Bond Market" (SSRN Working Paper 264575, 2001).

Determinants of Success

The nature of pure arbitrage—two identical assets that are priced differently—makes it likely that it will be short lived. In other words, in a market where investors are on the lookout for riskless profits, it is very likely that small pricing differences will be exploited quickly and in the process disappear. Consequently, the first two requirements for success at pure arbitrage are access to real-time prices and instantaneous execution. It is also very likely that the pricing differences in pure arbitrage will be very small—often a few hundredths of a percent. To make pure arbitrage feasible, therefore, you can add two more conditions. The first is access to substantial debt at favorable interest rates, since it can magnify the small pricing differences. Note that many of the arbitrage positions require you to be able to borrow at the riskless rate. The second is economies of scale, with transactions amounting to millions or hundreds of millions of dollars rather than thousands. Institutions that are successful at pure arbitrage often are able to borrow several times their equity at the riskless rate to fund arbitrage transactions, using the guaranteed profits on the transaction as collateral.

With these requirements, it is not surprising that individual investors have generally not been able to succeed at pure arbitrage. Even among institutions, pure arbitrage is feasible only to a few, and even to those, it is a transient source of profits in two senses. First, you cannot count on the existence of pure arbitrage opportunities in the future, since it requires that markets repeat their errors over time. Second, the very fact that some institutions make profits from arbitrage attracts other institutions into the market, reducing the likelihood of future arbitrage profits. To succeed in the long term with arbitrage, you will need to be constantly on the lookout for new arbitrage opportunities.

Thus, an investment strategy that is predicated on pure arbitrage will run dry more often than not. At the same time, a strategy that assumes that arbitrage opportunities never come along may miss incredible investment opportunities. So, it is best to be opportunistic on arbitrage opportunities. Have an investment strategy built around something that has higher odds of success—a momentum, value, or growth investing strategy—and keep an eye open for arbitrage opportunities. If one does show up on the horizon, jump on it and use it to augment your investment returns.

NEAR ARBITRAGE

In near arbitrage, you have either two assets that are very similar but not identical and that are priced differently, or identical assets that are mispriced but with no guaranteed price convergence. No matter how sophisticated your trading strategies may be in these scenarios, your positions will no longer be riskless.

Same Security, Multiple Markets

In today's global markets, there are a number of stocks that are listed on more than one market. If you can buy the same stock at one price in one market and simultaneously sell it at a higher price in another market, you can lock in a riskless profit. As we will see in this section, things are seldom this simple.

Dual and Multiple Listings   Many large companies such as Royal Dutch, General Electric, and Microsoft trade on multiple markets on different continents. Since there are time periods during the day when there is trading occurring on more than one market on the same stock, it is conceivable (though not likely) that you could buy the stock for one price in one market and sell the same stock at the same time for a different (and higher) price in another market. The stock will trade in different currencies, and for this to be a riskless transaction, the trades have to occur at precisely the same time and you have to eliminate any exchange rate risk by converting the foreign currency proceeds into the domestic currency instantaneously. Your trade profits will also have to cover the different bid-ask spreads in the two markets and transaction costs in each.

There are some exceptional cases where the same stock trades in different markets in one country. Swaicki and Hric examine 84 Czech stocks that trade on the two Czech exchanges—the Prague Stock Exchange (PSE) and the Registration Places System (RMS)—and find that prices adjust slowly across the two markets and arbitrage opportunities exist (at least on paper); the prices in the two markets differ by about 2 percent.[11] These arbitrage opportunities seem to increase for less liquid stocks. The authors consider transaction costs, but they do not consider the price impact that trading itself would have on these stocks and whether the arbitrage profits would survive the trading.

The risks do increase if there are differences in voting rights and dividends across shares, since any price differences can then reflect these fundamental variations rather than arbitrage opportunities. A study of intraday pricing of 100 pairs of dual-class shares, with the same cash flows, albeit

---

[11] J. Swaicki and J. Hric, "Arbitrage Opportunities in Parallel Markets: The Case of the Czech Republic" (SSRN Working Paper 269017, 2001).

with different voting rights, in the United States from 1993 to 2006 uncovered at least 3,687 cases where the bid price of one class of shares exceeded the ask price of the other class by at least 1 percent. Buying the cheaper class and selling the more expensive one generated excess returns in excess of 30 percent a year, after adjusting for cost of the bid-ask spread.[12]

NUMBER WATCH

Most widely traded American depositary receipts (ADRs): Take a look at the 50 most widely traded ADRs on the U.S. market.

Depositary Receipts   Many Latin American, Asian, and European companies have *American depositary receipts (ADRs)* listed on the U.S. market. These depositary receipts create a claim equivalent to the one you would have had if you had bought shares in the local market and should therefore trade at a price consistent with the local shares. What makes them different and potentially riskier than the stocks with dual listings is that ADRs are not always directly comparable to the common shares traded locally—one ADR on Telmex, the Mexican telecommunications company, is convertible into 20 Telmex shares. In addition, converting an ADR into local shares can be both costly and time consuming. In some cases, there can be differences in voting rights as well. In spite of these constraints, you would expect the price of an ADR to closely track the price of the shares in the local market, albeit with a currency overlay since ADRs are denominated in dollars.

In a study that looks at the link between ADRs and local shares, Kin, Szakmary, and Mathur conclude that about 60 to 70 percent of the variation in ADR prices can be attributed to movements in the underlying share prices and that ADRs overreact to events in the U.S. market and underreact to changes in exchange rates and information about the underlying stock.[13] However, they also conclude that investors cannot take advantage of the pricing errors in ADRs because convergence does not occur quickly or in predictable ways. With a longer time horizon and/or the capacity to convert

---

[12]P. Schultz and S. Shive, "Mispricing of Dual-Class Shares: Profit Opportunities, Arbitrage and Trading" (SSRN Working Paper 1338885, 2009).

[13]M. Kin, A. C. Szakmary, and I. Mathur, "Price Transmission Dynamics between ADRs and Their Underlying Foreign Securities," *Journal of Banking and Finance* 24 (2000): 1359–1382.

ADRs into local shares, though, you should be able to take advantage of significant pricing differences.

Studies that have looked at ADRs on stocks in a series of emerging markets, including Brazil, Chile, Argentina, and Mexico, seem to arrive at common conclusions. There are often persistent deviations from price parity, and there seems to be a potential for excess returns, sometimes of significant magnitude, for investors who exploit unusually large price divergences.[14] Every one of these studies also sounds notes of caution: convergence can sometimes be slow in coming, there are high transaction costs, and illiquidity in the local market can be a serious concern. Studies that have looked at developed markets such as Germany, Canada, and the United Kingdom also document occasional price differences between the local listing and the ADR, though the differences tend to be smaller and price convergence occurs more quickly.[15]

Closed-End Funds

In a conventional mutual fund, the number of shares increases and decreases as money comes into and leaves the fund, and each share is priced at net asset value (NAV)—the market value of the securities of the fund divided by the number of shares. Closed-end mutual funds differ from other mutual funds in one very important respect. They have a fixed number of shares that trade in the market like other publicly traded companies, and the market price can be different from the net asset value.

In both the United States and the United Kingdom, closed-end mutual funds have shared a common characteristic. When they are created, the price is usually set at a premium on the net asset value per share. As closed-end funds trade, though, the market price tends to drop below the net asset value and stay there. Figure 11.7 provides the distribution of premiums and discounts (computed by comparing the net asset value to the market price) for all closed-end funds in the United States in November 2011.

---

[14]For Argentina and Chile, see R. Rabinovitch, A. C. Silva, and R. Susmel, "Returns on ADRs and Arbitrage in Emerging Markets," *Emerging Markets Review* 4 (2003): 225–328; for Mexico, see S. Koumkwa and R. Susmel, "Arbitrage and Convergence: Evidence from Mexican ADRs" (SSRN Working Paper, 2005); for Brazil, see O. R. de Mederos and M. E. de Lima, "Brazilian Dual-Listed Stocks, Arbitrage and Barriers" (SSRN Working Paper, 2007); for India, see S. Majumdar, "A Study of International Listing by Firms of Indian Origin" (SSRN Working Paper, 2007).

[15]See C. Eun and S. Sabberwal, "Cross-Border Listing and Price Discovery: Evidence from U.S. Listed Canadian Stocks," *Journal of Finance* 58 (2002): 549–577; K. A. Froot and E. Dabora, "How Are Stock Prices Affected by the Location of Trade?" *Journal of Financial Economics* 53 (1999): 189–216.

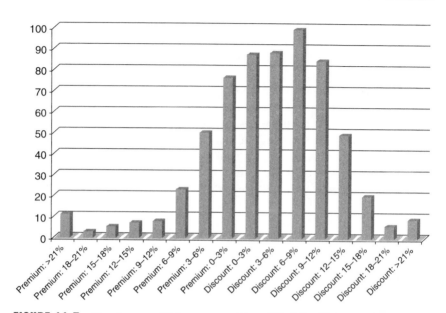

FIGURE 11.7 Premiums and Discounts on Closed-End Funds, November 2011
Source: www.closed-endfunds.com.

Note that 442 of the 626 closed-end funds trade at a discount to net asset value, and that the median discount is about 4.33 percent.

So what? you might ask. Lots of firms trade at less than the estimated market value of their assets. That might be true, but closed-end funds are unique for two reasons. First, the assets are all traded stocks and the market value is therefore known at any point in time and is not an estimate. Second, liquidating a closed-end fund's assets should not be difficult to do, since you are selling marketable securities. Thus, liquidation should be neither costly nor time consuming. Given these two conditions, you may wonder why you should not buy closed-end funds that trade at a discount and either liquidate them yourself or hope that someone else will liquidate them. Alternatively, you may be able to push a closed-end fund to open end and see prices converge on net asset value. Figure 11.8 reports on the performance of closed-end funds when they open end, based on a study of 94 UK closed-end funds that open ended.[16]

Note that as you get closer to the open-ending date (day 0), the discount becomes smaller relative to the average closed-end fund. For instance, the

---

[16]Carolina Minio-Paluello, "The UK Closed-End Fund Discount" (PhD thesis, London Business School, 1998).

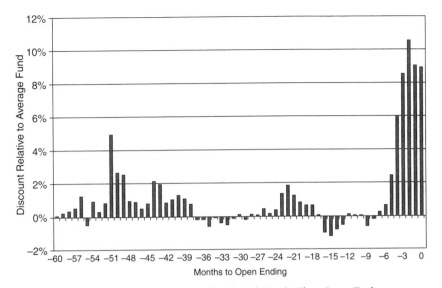

FIGURE 11.8   Relative Discount on Closed-End Funds That Open End
Source: Carolina Minio-Paluello, "The UK Closed-End Fund Discount" (PhD thesis, London Business School, 1998).

discount goes from being on par with the discount on other funds to being about 10 percent lower than the typical closed-end fund.[17]

So what is the catch? In practice, taking over a closed-end fund while paying less than net asset value for its shares seems to be very difficult to do for several reasons, some related to corporate governance and some related to market liquidity. The potential profit is also narrowed by the mispricing of illiquid assets in closed-end fund portfolios (leading to an overstatement of the NAV) and tax liabilities from liquidating securities. There have been a few cases of closed-end funds being liquidated, but they remain the exceptions.

NUMBER WATCH

Most discounted closed-end funds: Take a look at the 50 closed-end funds with the largest discounts.

---

[17]E. Dimson and C. Minio-Kozerzki, "Closed-End Funds: A Survey" (working paper, London Business School, 1998).

What about the strategy of buying discounted funds and hoping that the discount disappears? This strategy is clearly not riskless, but it does offer some promise. In one of the first studies of this strategy, Thompson studied closed-end funds from 1940 to 1975 and reports that you could earn an annualized excess return of 4 percent from buying discounted funds.[18] A later study reports excess returns from a strategy of buying closed-end funds whose discounts had widened and selling funds whose discounts had narrowed—a contrarian strategy applied to closed-end funds.[19] Extending the analysis, Pontiff reports that closed-end funds with a discount of 20 percent or higher earn about 6 percent more than other closed-end funds.[20] These, as well as studies in the United Kingdom, seem to indicate a strong mean-reversion component to discounts at closed-end funds. Figure 11.9, which is from a study of the discounts on closed-end funds in the United Kingdom, tracks relative discounts on the most discounted and least discounted funds over time.

Note that the discounts on the most discounted funds decrease whereas the discounts on the least discounted funds increase, and the difference narrows over time.

Reviewing all of the evidence, it is clear that if there are profits to be made from investing in closed-end funds, they are neither riskless nor particularly large. Many closed-end funds trade at permanent discounts on their net asset values, and arbitrage opportunities are uncommon.

Convertible and Capital Structure Arbitrage

In both convertible and capital structure arbitrage, investors attempt to take advantage of relative mispricing of a firm's different security offerings. In convertible arbitrage, the focus is on securities that have options embedded in them. Thus, when companies have convertible bonds or convertible preferred stock outstanding in conjunction with common stock, warrants, preferred stock, and conventional bonds, it is entirely possible that you could find one of these securities mispriced relative to the others, and be able to construct a low-risk strategy by combining two or more of the securities in a portfolio.

---

[18] Rex Thompson, "The Information Content of Discounts and Premiums on Closed-End Fund Shares," *Journal of Financial Economics* 6 (1978): 151–186.
[19] Seth C. Anderson, "Closed-End Funds versus Market Efficiency," *Journal of Portfolio Management* 13 (1986): 63–65.
[20] Jeffrey Pontiff, "Costly Arbitrage: Evidence from Closed-End Funds," *Quarterly Journal of Economics* 111 (1996): 1135–1151.

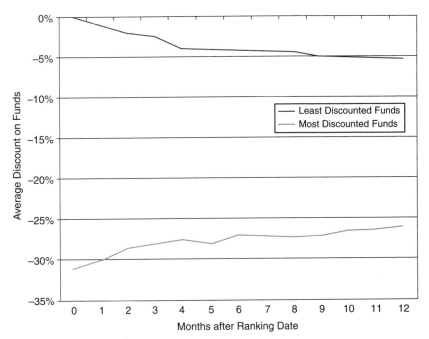

FIGURE 11.9 Discounts on Most Discounted and Least Discounted Funds over Time
Source: E. Dimson and C. Minio-Kozerski, "Closed-End Funds: A Survey" (working paper, London Business School, 1998).

In a simple example, note that since the conversion option is a call option on the stock, you could construct a synthetic convertible bond by combining holdings in the common stock of the company, a riskless investment, and a straight bond issued by the firm. Once you can do this, you can take advantage of differences between the pricing of the convertible bond and synthetic convertible bond and potentially make profits. In the more complex forms, when you have warrants, convertible preferred, and other options trading simultaneously on a firm, you could look for options that are mispriced relative to each other, and then buy the cheaper option and sell the more expensive one.

In practice, there are several possible impediments. First, many firms that issue convertible bonds do not have straight bonds outstanding, and you have to substitute a straight bond issued by a company with similar default risk. Second, companies can force conversion of convertible bonds, which can wreak havoc on arbitrage positions. Third, convertible bonds have long maturities. Thus, there may be no convergence for long periods, and you have to be able to maintain the arbitrage position over these periods. Fourth, transaction costs and execution problems (associated with trading the different securities) may prevent arbitrage.

In capital structure arbitrage, you cast a wider net and look to see if a company's debt is mispriced relative to its equity. Thus, for a distressed firm, if debt is being underpriced by bond investors while stock is being overpriced by equity investors, you would buy bonds and sell stock in the same company, hoping to gain from a convergence. The growth of the credit default swap (CDS) market has added another dimension to capital structure arbitrage. In its typical form, investors estimate what the theoretical CDS spread for a company should be, based on the stock price and how much debt the firm has, and compare this spread to the actual price for a CDS on that company in the market; if the CDS is priced too low, they buy the CDS; if it is priced too high, they sell it.[21]

The evidence on whether this strategy delivers risk-adjusted returns over time is mixed. A study of 135,759 CDS spreads across 261 different issuers from 2001 to 2005 found that while the strategy delivered profits at the portfolio level, individual trades were exposed to significant risk, especially from large movements in the CDS spreads.[22] Another study that tried alternate structural models to estimate the correct CDS spread came to the conclusion that the structural models did well at forecasting changes in the CDS spread and that investors could earn significant excess returns, with those returns increasing for lower-credit-quality companies.

Determinants of Success

Studies that have looked at closed-end funds, dual-listed stocks, and the relative pricing of a firm's securities all seem to conclude that there are pockets of inefficiency that can exploited to make money. However, there is residual risk in all of these strategies, arising sometimes from the fact that the assets are not perfectly identical (convertibles versus synthetic convertibles) or because there are no mechanisms for forcing the prices to converge (closed-end funds).

---

[21] There are several structural models that can be used to make this estimate. Many of them use variants of a pricing model developed by Merton, where equity is treated as a call option on the company and an option pricing model is used to extract the correct values for equity and the appropriate credit spread for debt. See R. C. Merton, "On the Pricing of Corporate Debt: The Risk Structure of Interest Rates," *Journal of Finance* 29 (1974): 449–470.

[22] F. Yu, "How Profitable Is Capital Structure Arbitrage?" (SSRN Working Paper 687436, 2005).

So, what would you need to succeed with near arbitrage strategies? The first thing to note is that these strategies will not work for small investors or for very large investors. Small investors will be stymied both by transaction costs and by execution problems. Very large investors will quickly drive discounts to parity and eliminate excess returns. If you decide to adopt these strategies, you need to refine and focus your strategies on those opportunities where convergence is most likely to occur quickly. For instance, if you decide to try to exploit the discounts of closed-end funds, you should focus on the closed-end funds that are most discounted and concentrate especially on funds where there is the potential to bring pressure on management to open end the funds. You should also avoid funds with substantial illiquid or nontraded stocks in their portfolios, since the net asset values of these funds may be significantly overstated.

THE LIMITS OF ARBITRAGE

In a perfect world (at least for financial economists), any relative mispricing of assets attracts thousands of investors who borrow risklessly and take advantage of the arbitrage. In the process, they drive it out of existence. In the real world, it is much more likely that any assets that are mispriced are not perfectly identical (thus introducing some risk into the mix) and that only a few large investors have the capacity to access low-cost debt and take advantage of arbitrage opportunities. There are two other factors that may allow arbitrage opportunities to persist:

1. *Behavioral factors.* It is entirely possible, then, that near arbitrage opportunities will be left unexploited because these large investors are unwilling to risk their capital in these investments. Vishny and Shleifer provide a fascinating twist on this argument. They note that the more mispriced assets become on a relative basis, the greater the risk to arbitrageurs that the mispricing will move against them.[23] Hence, they argue that arbitrageurs will pull back from investing in the most mispriced assets, especially if there are thousands of other traders in the market who are pushing prices in the opposite direction.

(continued)

---

[23] Andrei Shleifer and Robert W. Vishny, "The Limits of Arbitrage," *Journal of Finance* 52 (1997): 35–55.

> **2.** *Market crisis.* A study of market movements during the banking crisis of 2008 showed that arbitrage opportunities not only were available but could have generated large profits for investors who were willing to take them. However, the liquidity and funding constraints that investors found themselves under during the crisis prevented them from exploiting these opportunities.

SPECULATIVE ARBITRAGE

The word *arbitrage* is used much too loosely in investments, and there are a large number of strategies that are characterized as arbitrage but actually expose investors to significant risk. In fact, the strategies covered in this section would probably be better characterized as pseudo arbitrage strategies.

Paired Arbitrage

In classic arbitrage, you buy an asset at one price and sell an exactly identical asset at a different (and higher) price. In paired arbitrage, you buy one stock (say General Motors) and sell another stock that you view as very similar (say Ford), and argue that you are not that exposed to risk. Clearly, this strategy is not riskless since no two equities are exactly identical, and even if they were very similar, there may be no convergence in prices.

Let us consider first how you pair up stocks. The conventional practice among those who have used this strategy on Wall Street has been to look for two stocks whose prices have historically moved together (i.e., have high correlation over time). This often leads to two stocks in the same sector, such as GM and Ford. Once you have paired the stocks, you compute the spread between them and compare this spread to historic norms. If the spread is too wide, you buy the cheaper stock and short the more expensive stock. In many cases, the strategy is self-financing. For example, if Ford is trading at $20 and GM is trading at $40 and you believe that GM is overpriced relative to Ford, you would buy two shares of Ford and sell short one share of GM. If you are right and the spread narrows between the shares, you will profit on your paired position.

Can such a simplistic strategy, based entirely on past prices, make excess returns? Gatev, Goetzmann, and Rouwenhorst tested a variety of trading rules based on pairs trading from 1962 to 2002, using the following process:[24]

- Screening first for only stocks that traded every day, the authors found a matching partner for each stock by looking for the stock with the minimum squared deviation in normalized price series.[25] Intuitively, note that if two stocks move together all the time, the squared distance in returns should be zero. Once they had paired all the stocks, they studied the pairs with the smallest squared deviation separating them.
- With each pair, they tracked the normalized prices of each stock and took a position on the pair if the difference exceeded the historical range by two standard deviations, buying the cheaper stock and selling the more expensive one.

Over the period, the pairs trading strategy did significantly better than a buy-and-hold strategy. Strategies of investing in the top 20 pairs earned an annualized excess return of about 11 percent, and although the returns drop off for the pairs below the top 20, you continue to earn excess returns. When the pairs are constructed by industry group (rather than just based on historical prices), the excess returns persist but they are smaller. Controlling for the bid-ask spread in the strategy reduces the excess returns by about a fifth, but the returns are still significant.

Looking more closely at when pairs trading pays off provides some interesting insights. A study found that the profits to pairs trading were highest when the initial price divergence is caused by an absence of liquidity on one of the stocks or by a common news item affecting both companies that is absorbed more quickly in the market for one stock than the other. The profits tended to be lower when the divergence was caused by information affecting just one of the stocks. In addition, the convergence happens more quickly for smaller, less liquid and more volatile stocks.[26]

While the overall trading strategy looks promising, there are three points worth emphasizing that should also act as cautionary notes about this

---

[24]E. G. Gatev, W. N.Goetzmann, and K. G. Rouwenhorst, "Pairs Trading, Performance of a Relative Value Arbitrage Rule" (SSRN Working Paper, 1999); E. Gatev, W. Goetzmann, and K. Rouwenhorst, "Pairs Trading: Performance of a Relative Value Arbitrage Rule," *Review of Financial Studies* 19 (2006): 797–827.

[25]If you use absolute prices, a stock with a higher price will always look more volatile. You can normalize the prices around 1 and use these series.

[26]J. Engelberg, P. Gao, and R. Jagannathan, "An Anatomy of Pairs Trading: The Role of Idisyncratic News, Common information and Liquidity" (SSRN Working Paper 1330689, 2009).

strategy. The first is that the study quoted earlier found that the pairs trading strategy created negative returns in about one out of every six periods, and that the difference between pairs often widened before it narrowed. In other words, it is a risky investment strategy that also requires the capacity to trade instantaneously and at low cost. The second is that the success of the strategy requires nimbleness and quick adjustments. For instance, the profits from the strategy increase if you close out pair positions where no convergence happens within 10 days. Third, the earlier referenced study by Gatev et al. found that the profits to the strategy vary across time, suggesting that there is a fundamental economic factor underlying the excess returns. Given how much of the returns come from liquidity, we would argue that this strategy is likely to be most profitable in periods of overall market illiquidity and less profitable when liquidity is plentiful. In fact, studies that look at pairs trading in less liquid markets find much higher excess returns to the strategy than the studies that look at U.S. stocks, with a study of pairs trading in Finnish stock finding annualized excess returns in excess of 200 percent.[27] Finally, the strategy may have been too successful for its own good, as evidenced in an observation from a well-known quantitative analyst, David Shaw, who bemoaned the fact that by the late 1990s the pickings for quantitative strategies (like pairs trading) had become slim because so many investment banks were adopting the strategies. As the novelty wears off, the profitability of pairs trading may also decline.

Merger Arbitrage

As we noted in the preceding chapter, the stock price of a target company jumps on the announcement of a takeover. However, it trades at a discount usually to the price offered by the acquiring company. The difference between the postannouncement price and the offer price is called the arbitrage spread, and there are investors who try to profit off this spread in a strategy called merger or risk arbitrage. If the merger succeeds, the arbitrageur captures the arbitrage spread, but if it fails, he or she could suffer a substantial loss. In a more sophisticated variant in stock mergers (where shares of the acquiring company are exchanged for shares in the target company), the arbitrageur will sell the acquiring firm's stock in addition to buying the target firm's stock.

To begin with, we should note that the term *risk arbitrage* is misleading. It is clearly not arbitrage in the classic sense since there are no guaranteed

---

[27]K. Rinne and M. Suominen, "How Some Bankers Made a Million by Trading Just Two Securities" (SSRN Working Paper 1796064, 2011).

profits and it is not quite clear why the prefix *risk* is attached to it. Notwithstanding this quarrel with terminology, we can examine whether risk arbitrage delivers the kinds of returns we often hear about anecdotally, and if it does, is it compensation for risk (that the merger may not go through) or is it an excess return? Mitchell and Pulvino use a sample of 4,750 mergers and acquisitions to examine this question.[28] They conclude that there are excess returns associated with buying target companies after acquisition announcements of about 9.25 percent annually, but that you lose about two-thirds of these excess returns if you factor in transaction costs and the price impact that you have when you trade (especially on the less liquid companies).

While the overall strategy returns look attractive, Mitchell and Pulvino also point to one unappealing aspect of this strategy. The strategy earns moderate positive returns much of the time, but earns large negative returns when it fails. Does this make it a bad strategy? Not at all, but it points to the dangers of risk arbitrage when it is restricted to a few big-name takeover stocks (as it often is); an investor who adopts this strategy is generally one big failure away from seeing his or her profits wiped out. If you use leverage to do risk arbitrage, the dangers are multiplied.

Determinants of Success

The fact that we categorize the strategies in this section as speculative arbitrage is not meant to be a negative comment on the strategies. We believe that these are promising investment strategies that have a history of delivering excess returns, but they are not risk-free. More ominously, it is easy for those who have done pure arbitrage to drift into near arbitrage and then into speculative arbitrage as they have more funds to invest. In doing so, however, there are two caveats that have to be kept in mind:

1. The use of financial leverage has to be scaled to reflect the riskiness of the strategy. With pure arbitrage, you can borrow 100 percent of what you need to put the strategy into play. In futures arbitrage, for instance, you borrow 100 percent of the spot price and borrow the commodity. Since there is no risk, the leverage does not create any damage. As you move to near and speculative arbitrage, this leverage has to be reduced. The extent to which it has to be reduced will depend on both the degree of risk in the strategy and the speed with which you think prices will

---

[28] M. Mitchell and T. Pulvino, "Characteristics of Risk in Risk Arbitrage," *Journal of Finance* 56 (2001): 2135–2175.

converge. The more risky a strategy and the less certain you are about convergence, the less debt you should take on.

2. These strategies work best if you can operate without a market impact. As you get more funds to invest and your strategy becomes more visible to others, you run the risk of driving out the very mispricing that attracted you to the market in the first place.

In many ways, the rise and fall of Long Term Capital Management (see box) should stand as testimony to how even the brightest minds in investing can sometimes either miss or willfully ignore these realities. Long Term Capital Management's eventual undoing can be traced to many causes, but the immediate cause was the number of speculative arbitrage positions they put in place—pairs trading, interest rate bets—with tremendous leverage.

THE FALL OF LONG TERM CAPITAL MANAGEMENT

Investors considering arbitrage as their preferred investment philosophy should pay heed to the experiences of Long Term Capital Management (LTCM). The firm, which was founded in the early 1990s by ex-Salomon trader John Meriwether, promised to bring together the best minds in finance to find and take advantage of arbitrage opportunities around the world. Delivering on the first part of the promise, Meriwether lured the best bond traders from Salomon and brought on board two Nobel Prize winners—Myron Scholes and Bob Merton. In the first few years of its existence, the firm also lived up to the second part of the promise, earning extraordinary returns for the elite of Wall Street. In those years, LTCM was the envy of the rest of the Street as it used low-cost debt to lever up its capital and invest in pure and near arbitrage opportunities.

As the funds at their disposal got larger, the firm had to widen its search to include pseudo arbitrage investments. By itself, this would not have been fatal, but the firm continued to use the same leverage on these riskier investments as it did on its safe investments. It bet on paired trades in Europe and decreasing spreads in country bond markets, arguing that the sheer number of investments it had in its portfolio would create diversification: if it lost on one investment, it would gain on another. In 1997, the strategy unraveled as collapses in one market (Russia) spread into other markets as well. As the portfolio dropped in value, LTCM found itself facing the downside of its size and high leverage. Unable to unwind its large positions without affecting market prices, and facing the pressures of lenders, LTCM faced certain bankruptcy. Fearing that it would bring down other investors in the market, the Federal Reserve engineered a bailout of the firm by its creditors while its positions were liquidated.

What are the lessons that we can learn from the fiasco? Besides the cynical one that it is good to have friends in high places, you could argue that the fall of LTCM teaches us that:

- Size can be a double-edged sword. While it gives you economies of scale in transaction costs and lowers the cost of funding, it also makes it more difficult for you to unwind positions that you have taken.
- Leverage can make low-risk positions into high-risk investments, since small moves in the price can translate into large changes in equity.
- The most brilliant minds in the world and the best analytical tools cannot insulate you from the vagaries of the market.[29]

LONG/SHORT STRATEGIES—HEDGE FUNDS

In the past few years, hedge funds have become one of the fastest-growing parts of the money management business. Largely unregulated, headed at the outset by outsized personalities like George Soros and Julian Robertson, and seemingly delivering huge returns to their investors, hedge funds became serious players in the money management game. At the outset of this section, we have to note that it is probably not quite accurate to categorize hedge funds as having any specific strategy, since you can have hedge funds specializing in almost every strategy we have listed in this book. You can have value and growth investing hedge funds, hedge funds that specialize in market timing, hedge funds that invest on information, and hedge funds that do convertible arbitrage. The reason that we consider it in this chapter is because it lends itself particularly well to arbitrage strategies, which require that you buy some assets and sell short on others at the same time. In this section, we will take a closer look at hedge fund strategies and how well they really have performed.

---

[29]R. Lowenstein, *When Genius Failed: The Rise and Fall of Long Term Capital Management* (New York: Random House, 2000).

Background, History, and Structure

What makes a fund into a hedge fund? The common characteristic shared by all hedge funds is that they not only buy assets that they feel are undervalued, but they simultaneously sell short on assets that they believe to be overvalued. Defined this way, hedge funds have probably been around as long as stock markets have been in existence, though they have traditionally been accessible only to the very wealthy. In the past decade, however, hedge funds have taken a larger and larger market share of total investment funds. While the magnitude of the funds under hedge fund management is disputed, it is estimated that more than two trillion dollars in assets were managed by hedge funds in 2011.

Performance

Are the storied returns to investing in hedge funds true? Are small investors who are often shut out from investing in hedge funds losing out because of this? To answer these questions, we need to look not at anecdotal evidence or the performance of the best hedge funds, but at all hedge funds. In an early study of all offshore hedge funds from 1989 to 1995, Brown, Goetzmann, and Ibbotson chronicled the returns in Table 11.2.[30]

There are several interesting numbers in this table. First, the average hedge fund earned a lower return (13.26 percent) over the period than the S&P 500 (16.47 percent), but it also had a lower standard deviation in returns (9.07 percent) than the S&P 500 (16.32 percent). Thus, it seems to offer a better payoff to risk, if you divide the average return by the standard deviation (this is the commonly used Sharpe ratio for evaluating money managers). Second, these funds are much more expensive than traditional mutual funds, with much higher costs and incentive fees that take away one out of every five dollars of excess returns. In a study that examined 2,016 hedge funds from 1990 to 1999, the overall conclusions were similar—that is, that hedge funds earned a lower return than the S&P 500 (14.2 percent versus 18.8 percent), they were less risky, and they had higher Sharpe ratios (0.41 for the hedge funds versus 0.27 for the S&P 500).[31]

The hedge fund business has expanded both in terms of money under management and in types of funds. A study that looked at hedge funds from 1994 to 2009 and chronicled the returns on different types of hedge funds

---

[30]Stephen J. Brown, William N. Goetzmann, and Roger G. Ibbotson, "Offshore Hedge Funds: Survival and Performance, 1989–1995," *Journal of Business* 72, no. 1 (1999): 91–119.

[31]B. Liang, "Hedge Fund Performance: 1990–1999," *Financial Analysts Journal* 57 (2001): 11–18.

TABLE 11.2 Offshore Hedge Fund Returns, 1989 to 1995

Year	Number of Funds in Sample	Arithmetic Average Return	Median Return	Return on S&P 500	Average Annual Fee (as % of assets under management)	Average Incentive Fee (as % of excess returns)
1988–1989	78	18.08%	20.30%		1.74%	19.76%
1989–1990	108	4.36%	3.80%		1.65%	19.52%
1990–1991	142	17.13%	15.90%		1.79%	19.55%
1991–1992	176	11.98%	10.70%		1.81%	19.34%
1992–1993	265	24.59%	22.15%		1.62%	19.10%
1993–1994	313	−1.60%	−2.00%		1.64%	18.75%
1994–1995	399	18.32%	14.70%		1.55%	18.50%
Entire period		13.26%		16.47%		

Note: Returns are net of fees.

over that period arrived at the measures of gross and net returns reported in Figure 11.10.[32]

First, note that the returns net of fees are significantly lower than the gross returns at every hedge fund category, a testimonial again to the cost created for investors in these funds. Second, on a net return basis, the average hedge fund underperformed the S&P 500, but as with the earlier study, the lower risk associated with these funds results in positive risk-adjusted returns and attractive risk/return trade-offs (Sharpe ratios). Third, the study looked at all funds that had returns for at least 24 months, but then broke the funds down into live funds and funds that ceased to exist. Out of the 3,000 funds in the sample, only 1,300 were live in 2010, and the failed or liquidated funds had lower gross and net returns than the surviving funds.

The market crises of the past decade have put hedge funds to multiple tests, and revealed some key components of what separates successful funds from those that do not make it. First, a significant proportion of the differences in returns across hedge funds seems to be associated with liquidity risk, with the less liquid funds delivering the higher risk-adjusted returns.[33] However, during crises (such as the last quarter of 2008), these same less liquid funds came under the most pressure and suffered the greatest carnage.

---

[32]S. Feng, "A Comparison of Hedge Fund Gross and Net Performance" (SSRN Working Paper 1929213, 2011).

[33]R. Sadka, "Hedge Fund Performance and Liquidity Risk," *Journal of Investment Management* (forthcoming).

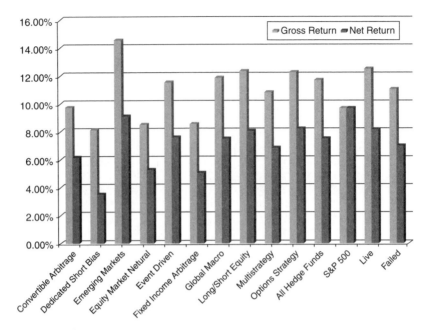

FIGURE 11.10 Annualized Returns on Hedge Funds by Category, 1994 to 2009
Source: S. Feng, "A Comparison of Hedge Fund Gross and Net Performance" (SSRN Working Paper 1929213, 2011).

Second, investors in hedge funds are much more reactive to bad performance, withdrawing money out at a rate three times higher than mutual fund investors. As a consequence, hedge funds are more likely to liquidate positions quickly than mutual funds are; it is estimated that hedge funds sold about 29 percent of their overall holdings in the last quarter of 2008, largely in response to margin calls and redemption requests.[34]

In summary, what are we to make of these findings? First, the biggest advantage of hedge funds does not seem to lie in the delivery of high returns but in lower risk. Every study that we have quoted finds that hedge funds underperform the market, especially over bull markets, but that they are more efficient in their risk taking.[35] Second, the high costs and failure

---

[34]I. Ben-David, F. Franzoni, and R. Moussawi, "Hedge Fund Stock Trading in the Financial Crisis of 2007–2009" (working paper, Ohio State University, 2011).

[35]A contrary viewpoint is offered by three hedge fund managers at AQR Capital Management in Chicago. They argue that the returns on many hedge funds are based on self-assessments of value for illiquid securities. The resulting smoothing out of returns creates the illusion of low or no correlation with the market and low standard deviations.

rate of hedge funds have to be factored into any investment strategy. The fee structure is tilted toward management, and the expenses are larger for hedge funds. Since many hedge fund strategies are successful only on the small scale, they are put to the test as they scale up. Third, a significant hidden risk (at least hidden in good times) of investing in hedge funds is illiquidity. During crises, investors in hedge funds are more likely to demand redemption, which in turn can cause hedge funds to try to liquidate positions, exacerbating losses and creating a downward spiral.

CONCLUSION

For many practitioners, the promise of being able to invest no money, take no risk, and still make a profit remains alluring. That is essentially what arbitrage allows you to do. In pure arbitrage, you buy a security at one price and sell an exactly identical security at a higher price, thus ensuring yourself a riskless profit. The markets where pure arbitrage is feasible tend to be the derivatives markets, since you can construct equivalent securities using the underlying asset and lending or borrowing. In futures markets, for instance, you can attain equivalent results by borrowing money; buying the underlying asset (storable commodity, stock, or bond); and storing it until the maturity of a futures contract; or buying the futures contract directly. In the options markets, you can replicate a call option by borrowing money and buying the underlying asset and a put option, by selling short on the underlying asset and lending at the riskless rate. Pure arbitrage may also be feasible with default-free bonds. If opportunities exist for pure arbitrage, they are likely to be few and far between and available only to a subset of large institutional investors with very low transaction costs and the capacity to take on very high leverage at close to riskless rates.

Near arbitrage refers to scenarios where either the two assets being bought and sold are not exactly identical or there is no point in time when prices have to converge. We considered three examples: equities on the same company that trade in different markets at different prices, closed-end funds that trade at a discount on the net asset value of the securities in the fund, and convertible bonds that trade at prices that are inconsistent with the prices of other securities issued by the company. In each, the mispricing may be obvious but the profits are not guaranteed because you cannot force convergence (liquidating the closed-end fund or converting the ADR into local shares) or because you cannot create exactly identical securities (convertible arbitrage). You may still be able to construct low-risk strategies that earn high returns, but riskless profits are not feasible.

In the final section, we examined what we term speculative or pseudo arbitrage. In pairs trading, two stocks that tend to move together are paired up and traded when the price difference moves out of a historical range; you sell the more expensive stock and you buy the cheaper one. In merger arbitrage, you buy stocks of target firms after acquisitions are announced and hope to make the difference between the postannouncement price and the offer price. While both these strategies offer promising returns, neither is close to being riskless.

In closing, we looked at the part of the money management business that is closest in philosophy to arbitrage, the hedge fund business. Though they share the common characteristics of a long/short strategy, hedge funds come in all varieties. On average, they have returns that are lower than a strategy of buying and holding stocks, but have risk that is significantly lower. As hedge funds use this finding to bring in more money, they run the risk of being the victims of their own success, since it is not clear whether many hedge fund strategies will scale up.

As a final note, the one constant that shows up across different arbitrage strategies is liquidity. Investors who need liquidity less (and thus value it less) have a clear advantage over those who do need liquidity, and the advantage grows during market crises. In fact, the profits on many arbitrage strategies, whether real, near, or pseudo, seem to represent illiquidity premiums rather than come from market mistakes. Put differently, only investors who can afford to stay illiquid and thus have lower transaction costs can take advantage of these arbitrage strategies.

EXERCISES

1. Do you believe that pure arbitrage opportunities exist in markets?
   a. If they do exist, who are the beneficiaries? (Are they big institutional investors, insiders, or tax-exempt investors?)
   b. What is the source of their advantage? (Is it luck, low transaction costs, the capacity to trade quickly, or something else?)
   c. What markets/time periods are pure arbitrage opportunities most likely to show up in?
2. Do you believe that near arbitrage opportunities exist in markets?
   a. If they do exist, where (in what markets) would you look for them? (Dual-listed stocks? Bonds? Real estate? Currencies?)
   b. Assuming you find these near arbitrage opportunities, what may be the biggest impediments to your making money on these opportunities?
3. Paired trades are a simple example of pseudo arbitrage.
   a. Can you find a pair of stocks that move together?
   b. How would you confirm that they do?

   c. Are they mispriced relative to each other now?

   d. If you decide to take advantage of the mispricing, what would be the biggest threats to your succeeding with this strategy?

Lessons for Investors

To be a successful arbitrageur, you need to:

- *Understand that near arbitrage is more likely than pure arbitrage:* Pure arbitrage opportunities, if they exist, are most likely to be found in derivatives and government bond markets and will be very quickly exploited. Near arbitrage, where you have two almost identical assets that are priced differently or where you have no forced convergence, should be more common.
- *Have excellent execution capabilities and low execution costs:* Arbitrage requires you to trade large quantities instantaneously in two or more markets.
- *Have access to low-cost debt:* The pricing differences between two similar assets, even if they exist, are likely to be very small and can be made into substantial returns only by using leverage.
- *Be a liquidity provider:* To succeed with many of the arbitrage strategies listed in this chapter, you have to be willing to invest in cheaper, illiquid assets when liquidity is at a premium, and make your profits as the prices recover.

If you decide to move to pseudo arbitrage, you need to:

- *Keep leverage under control:* As you move from pure to near arbitrage and from near to pseudo arbitrage, the risk in your strategy will increase and you should reduce the financial leverage in your strategy accordingly.
- *Recognize that size is a double-edged sword:* As you get more funds to invest, you may be able to reduce your execution costs, but you will also have a much more difficult time getting into and out of your positions quickly and without a price impact.

CHAPTER 12

The Impossible Dream?
Timing the Market

It is every investor's dream to time the market, for obvious reasons. A successful market timer does not have to have any skill at picking stocks since market timing alone will deliver extraordinary returns. In fact, we begin this chapter by looking at the immense payoff that can come from timing the market well, and this payoff to timing the market makes all of us easy victims for the next market-timing sales pitch.

The problem with market timing, notwithstanding its potential for delivering huge returns, is that it is so difficult to do, on a consistent basis. We look at a range of market timing strategies, from technical indicators to fundamental indicators to macroeconomic variables, and we note the pitfalls with each one. We also look at the assumptions underlying each indicator and why they sometimes help us predict market movements and more importantly, why they fail so frequently.

MARKET TIMING: PAYOFFS AND COSTS

The question of whether market timing has a big payoff and what its costs are arouses strong views from both practitioners and academics. While academics are fairly unified in their belief that market timing is not worth the time and resources that are expended on it, practitioners feel deeply on both sides of the issue. We begin by looking at the payoffs to market timing and then consider the costs.

The Payoff to Market Timing

In a 1986 article, a group of researchers[1] raised the hackles of many an active portfolio manager by estimating that as much as 93.6 percent of the variation in quarterly performance at professionally managed portfolios could be explained by the mix of stocks, bonds, and cash at these portfolios.[2] In a different study in 1992, Shilling examined the effect on your annual returns of being able to stay out of the market during bad months.[3] He concluded that an investor who would have missed the 50 weakest months of the market between 1946 and 1991 would have seen his annual returns almost double from 11.2 percent to 19 percent. Ibbotson examined the relative importance of asset allocation and security selection of 94 balanced mutual funds and 58 pension funds, all of which had to make both asset allocation and security selection decisions. Using 10 years of data through 1998, Ibbotson finds that about 40 percent of the differences in returns across funds can be explained by their asset allocation decisions and 60 percent by security selection. Collectively, these studies suggest that the asset allocation decision has important consequences for your returns, and its importance increases with your time horizon.

While how much of actual portfolio returns are due to asset allocation is open to debate, there can be no denying its importance to overall portfolio returns. While most researchers looked at the allocation across financial assets alone, we would define the asset allocation decision much more broadly to include real assets, including real estate, and in the most general case, human capital. The asset allocation decision follows logically from the assessment of the risk preferences, cash needs, and tax status of the investor. The portfolio manager has to decide on the mix of assets that maximizes the after-tax returns subject to the risk and cash flow constraints of the investor. This is what we would term the *passive approach* to asset allocation, where the investor's characteristics determine the right mix for the portfolio. In coming up with the mix, we draw on the lessons of diversification; asset

---

[1]G. Brinson, L. R. Hood, and G. Beebower, "Determinants of Portfolio Performance," *Financial Analysts Journal* 42 (1986): 39–44; G. Brinson, B. Singer, and G. Beebower, "Determinants of Portfolio Performance II: An Update," *Financial Analysts Journal* 47 (1991): 40–47.

[2]J. A. Nuttall and J. Nuttall, "Asset Allocation Claims—Truth or Fiction?" (working paper, 1998). A survey found that of 50 writers who quoted this study, 37 misread it to indicate that 93% of the total return came from asset allocation.

[3]A. Shilling, "Market Timing: Better than a Buy-and-Hold Strategy," *Financial Analysts Journal* 48 (1992): 46–50.

classes tend to be influenced differently by macro economic events, and do not move in tandem. This, in turn, implies that diversifying across asset classes will yield better trade-offs between risk and return than investing in any one asset class. The same can be said about expanding portfolios to include both domestic and foreign assets.

There is, however, an active component to asset allocation, which leads portfolio managers to deviate from the passive mix just defined, and one factor is market timing. To the extent that portfolio managers believe that they can time markets (i.e., determine which markets are likely to go up more than expected and which less than expected), they will alter the asset mixes accordingly. Thus, a portfolio manager who believes that the stock market is overvalued and is ripe for a correction while real estate is undervalued may reduce the proportion of the portfolio that is allocated to equities and increase the proportion allocated to real estate. It should be noted that there are some who differentiate between these actions, which they call tactical asset allocation, and more drastic switches from stock to cash, which they call market timing. We see only a difference in degree and will draw no such distinction.

The Cost of Market Timing

If market timing were costless, you could argue that everyone should try to time markets, given the huge returns to getting it right. There are, however, significant costs associated with trying to time markets (and getting it wrong):

- In the process of switching from stocks to cash and back, you may miss the best years of the market. In an article titled "The Folly of Stock Market Timing," Jeffrey examined the effects of annually switching from stock to cash and back from 1926 to 1982 and concluded that the potential downside vastly exceeds the potential upside.[4] In his article on market timing in 1975, Bill Sharpe suggested that unless you can tell a good year from a bad year 7 times out of 10, you should not try market timing.[5] This result is confirmed by Chua, Woodward, and To, who use Monte Carlo simulations on the Canadian market and confirm you

---

[4]R. Jeffrey, "The Folly of Stock Market Timing," *Financial Analysts Journal* (July–August 1984): 102–110.
[5]W. F. Sharpe, "Are Gains Likely from Market Timing," *Financial Analysts Journal* 31 (1975): 60–69.

have to be right 70 to 80 percent of the time to break even from market timing.[6]

■ These studies do not consider the additional transaction costs that inevitably flow from market timing strategies, since you will trade far more extensively with these strategies. At the limit, a stock/cash switching strategy will mean that you will have to liquidate your entire equity portfolio if you decide to switch into cash and start from scratch again the next time you want to be in stocks.

■ A market timing strategy will also increase your potential tax liabilities. To see why, assume that you have a strategy of selling your stocks after two good years in the market, based on your belief that a bad year is more likely to follow. You will have to pay capital gains taxes when you sell your stocks, and over your lifetime as an investor, you will pay far more in taxes. The costs will get even higher if the market timing strategy is short term, since short-term capital gains have been taxed at higher tax rates, at least in the United States.

In Summary

The perceived payoff from market timing is large and apparent, whereas the costs are often less visible. This must explain why so many portfolio managers and investors, their protestations to the contrary, engage in some market timing. In addition, the high profiles of market strategists at all of the major investment firms suggest that the asset allocation decision is perceived to be an important one.

Its appeal to investors notwithstanding, market timing remains an elusive dream for most. Looking back at market history, there have been far fewer successful market timers than successful stock selectors, and it is not clear whether even the few successes that are attributed to market timing should be attributable to luck. Why is it so difficult to succeed at market timing? One very important reason is that there are fewer potential differential advantages that investors can build on when it comes to timing markets. For instance, it is unlikely that one can acquire an informational advantage over other investors at timing markets, but it may still be possible, with sufficient research and private information, to get an informational advantage at picking stocks. Market timers contend that they can take existing information and use it more creatively or in better models to arrive at predictions for

---

[6]J. H. Chua, R. S. Woodward, and E. C. To, "Potential Gains from Stock Market Timing in Canada," *Financial Analysts Journal* 43, no. 5 (September/October 1987): 50–56.

markets, but such approaches can be easily imitated, and imitation is the kiss of death for successful investment strategies.

MARKET TIMING APPROACHES

There are probably as many market timing approaches as there are investors. Some of these approaches are based on nonfinancial indicators, some on charts and technical measures, some on the assumption that stock and bond prices revert to a normal range, some on macroeconomic variables such as interest rates and business cycles; and some draw on the valuation tools that we used to analyze individual stocks: discounted cash flow and relative valuation models.

Market Timing Based on Nonfinancial Indicators

Through the decades, there are some investors who have claimed to foretell the market's future by looking at nonfinancial indicators. Some of these indicators, such as whether the NFC or AFC team wins the Super Bowl, are clearly of dubious origin and would fall into a category that we title spurious indicators. Other indicators such as the hemline index, which relates stock prices to the level of hemlines on skirts, fall into the grouping of feel-good indicators that measure the overall mood of people in the economy, who after all are both the consumers who act as the engine for the economy and the investors determining prices. Finally, there are the hype indicators that measure whether market prices are becoming disconnected from reality by looking at investor chatter and behavior.

Spurious Indicators Analysts, researchers, and investors all pore over stock market movements, hoping to find patterns and it is not surprising that they find variables that seem to predict what the market will do in the next period. Consider one very widely talked-about indicator—who wins the Super Bowl.[7] In the 44 years that the Super Bowl has been played from 1966 to 2010, the winner has come from the old National Football League 29 times, whereas an American Football League team has won 13 times; in two of the years, the Super Bowl has been won by teams not in existence in the 1960s. In the 30 years that a team from the old National Football

---

[7]For those unfamiliar with the Super Bowl, it is played between the winner of the American Football Conference (AFC) and the winner of the National Football Conference (NFC), on the last Sunday in January.

League has won, the S&P 500 has increased, on average, 12.3 percent in the subsequent year, and has gone up in 26 of the years. In the 13 years that the AFL team has won, the market has been down an average of 2.35 percent in the subsequent year, and has declined in six of the years. In fact, there are academic researchers who claim that if you define success as getting the market direction right, the success rate of 70 percent (31 out of 44 years) is far too high to due to chance.[8]

So why not invest in the market after observing who wins the Super Bowl? There are several potential problems. First, we disagree that chance cannot explain this phenomenon. When you have hundreds of potential indicators that you can use to time markets, there will be some that show an unusually high correlation purely by chance. Second, a forecast of market direction (up or down) does not really qualify as market timing, since how much the market goes up clearly does make a difference. Third, you should always be cautious when you can find no economic link between a market timing indicator and the market. There is no conceivable reason that who wins the Super Bowl should affect or be correlated with overall economic performance. Indicators such as these may make for amusing anecdotes at parties but can be lethal to your portfolio as market timing devices.

Feel-Good Indicators When people feel optimistic about the future, it is not just stock prices that are affected by this optimism. Often, there are social consequences as well, with styles and social mores influenced by the fact that investors and consumers feel good about the economy. In the 1920s, for instance, as the economy grew and times were good, people partied and the markets zoomed up. In the 1980s, in another big bull market, you had the storied excesses of Wall Street, documented in books like *Liar's Poker* and movies like *Wall Street*.

It is not surprising, therefore, that people have discovered linkages between social indicators and Wall Street. Consider, for instance, an index that has been around for decades called the hemline index that finds a correlation between the hemlines on women's skirts and the stock market. This politically incorrect index is based on the notion that shorter dresses and skirts are associated with rising stock prices whereas longer dresses are predictors of stock market decline. Assuming the index works, we would argue that

---

[8]T. Krueger and W. Kennedy, "An Examination of the Superbowl Stock Market Predictor," *Journal of Finance* 45 (1991): 691–697. For a more up-to-date study, see George W. Kester, "What Happened to the Super Bowl Stock Market Predictor?" *Journal of Investing* 19, no. 1 (Spring 2010): 82–87.

you are seeing a manifestation of the same phenomenon. As people get more upbeat, fashions do seem to get more daring (with higher hemlines following) and markets also seem to go up. You could undoubtedly construct other indexes that have similar correlations. For instance, you should expect to see a high correlation between crowds at expensive nightclubs at New York City (or wherever young investment bankers and traders congregate) and the market.

The problem with feel-good indicators, in general, is that they tend to be contemporaneous or lagging rather than leading indicators. In other words, the hemlines don't drop before the markets drop but in conjunction with or after a market drop. As an investor, these indicators are of little use, since your objective is to get out before the market drops and to get in before the market goes up.

Hype Indicators It is said that Joseph Kennedy, a well-known speculator on stocks in his own time, knew it was time to get out of the market when he heard his shoeshine boy talking about stocks. In our own time, there are some who believe that the market peaked when the ratings of business TV channels (such as CNBC) exceeded those of long-running soap operas. In fact, one indicator called the "cocktail party chatter" indicator tracks three measures: the time elapsed at a party before talk turns to stocks, the average age of the people discussing stocks, and the fad component of the chatter. According to the indicator, the less time it takes for the talk to turn to stocks, the lower the average age of the market discussants, and the greater the fad component, the more negative you should be about future stock price movements.

Harking back to our discussion of bubbles, remember that propagation is critical to bubbles getting bigger. In our media world, this will involve print, television, and online, and an overflow into day-to-day conversations. Thus, the discussion at the watercooler in a typical business is more likely to be about stocks than about football or other such daily (and more normal) obsessions when markets are buoyant. As investors increasingly turn to social media (Facebook, Twitter, etc.), researchers are probing the data that is coming from these forums to see if they can be used to get a sense of market mood (and future direction). A study of almost 10 million tweets in 2008 found that a relationship between the collective mood on the tweets predicted stock price movements, and a hedge fund, Derwent Capital, moved quickly to try to take advantage.[9]

---

[9] J. Bollen, H. Mao, and X. Zeng, "Twitter Mood Predicts the Stock Market," *Journal of Computer Science* 2 (2011): 2–8.

While hype indicators, of all nonfinancial indicators, offer the most promise as predictors of the market, they do suffer from several limitations. For instance, defining what constitutes abnormal can be tricky in a world where standards and tastes are shifting—a high rating for CNBC may indicate too much hype or may be just reflecting the fact that viewers find financial markets to be both more entertaining and less predictable than a typical soap opera. Even if we decide that there is an abnormally high interest in the market today and you conclude (based on the hype indicators) that stocks are overvalued, there is no guarantee that stocks will not get more overvalued before the correction occurs. In other words, hype indicators may tell you that a market is overvalued, but they don't tell you when the correction will occur.

Market Timing Based on Technical Indicators

In Chapter 7, we examined a number of chart patterns and technical indicators used by analysts to differentiate between undervalued and overvalued stocks. Many of these indicators are also used by analysts to determine whether and by how much the entire market is under- or overvalued. In this section, we consider some of these indicators.

Past Prices We looked at evidence of price patterns in individual company stock prices in Chapter 7: reversals in very short time periods, momentum in the medium term, and reversals in the long term. Studies do not seem to find similar evidence when it comes to the overall market. If markets have gone up significantly in the most recent years, there is no evidence that market returns in future years will be negative. If we consolidate stock returns from 1871 to 2011 into five-year periods, we find a mild positive correlation of 0.1323 between five-year period returns; in other words, positive returns on stocks over the past five years are slightly more likely to be followed by positive returns than negative returns in the next five years.

NUMBER WATCH

Returns for U.S. market: Take a look at annual returns for the U.S. stock market from 1871 to today.

In Table 12.1, we report on the probabilities of an up year and a down year following a series of scenarios, ranging from two down years in a

TABLE 12.1   Market Performance

Priors	Number of Occurrences	Average Return in Year After	% of Up Years (Following)
After two down years	21	2.63%	61.90%
After one down year	32	10.95%	53.13%
After one up year	31	8.35%	80.65%
After two up years	55	2.24%	56.36%
All	139	5.66%	61.87%

row to two up years in a row, based on actual stock price data from 1871 to 2001.

There is no discernible pattern, as far as we can see. There is mild evidence for both price momentum: an up year is more likely to be followed by an up year and price reversal, with the highest returns coming after a down year. The return in the year following two up years doesn't look good, but neither does the return following two down years. In summary, there is little information that we can see in past market returns that allow us to make reasoned judgments about the future.

Another price-based indicator that receives attention, at least from the media at the beginning of each calendar year, is the *January indicator*. The indicator posits that as January goes, so goes the year—if stocks are up, the market will be up for the year, but a bad beginning usually precedes a poor year.[10] According to the venerable *Stock Trader's Almanac* that is compiled every year by Yale Hirsch, this indicator has worked 88 percent of the time. Note, though, that if you exclude January from the year's returns and compute the returns over the remaining 11 months of the year, the signal becomes much weaker and returns are negative only 50 percent of the time after a bad start in January. Thus, buying stocks after stocks have gone up (or selling after they have gone down) in January may hurt you just as often as it helps you.

Trading Volume   There are some analysts who believe that trading volume can be a much better indicator of future market returns than past prices. Volume indicators are widely used to forecast future market movements. In fact, price increases that occur without much trading volume are viewed as less likely to carry over into the next trading period than those that are

---

[10]Note that there are narrower versions of the January indicator, using just the first 5 or 10 days of January.

accompanied by heavy volume. At the same time, very heavy volume can also indicate turning points in markets. For instance, a drop in the index with very heavy trading volume is called a *selling climax* and may be viewed as a sign that the market has hit bottom. This supposedly removes most of the bearish investors from the mix, opening the market up presumably to more optimistic investors. On the other hand, an increase in the index accompanied by heavy trading volume may be viewed as a sign that market has topped out.

Another widely used indicator looks at the trading volume on puts as a ratio of the trading volume on calls. This ratio, which is called the *put-call ratio,* is often used as a contrarian indicator. When investors become more bearish, they buy more puts, and this (as the contrarian argument goes) is a good sign for the future of the market.

Technical analysts also use *money flow*, which is the difference between uptick volume and downtick volume, as a predictor of market movements. An increase in the money flow is viewed as a positive signal for future market movements whereas a decrease is viewed as a bearish signal. Using daily money flows from July 1997 to June 1998, Bennett and Sias find that money flow is highly correlated with returns in the same period, which is not surprising.[11] While they find no predictive ability with short-period returns—five-day returns are not correlated with money flow in the previous five days—they do find some predictive ability for longer periods. With 40-day returns and money flow over the prior 40 days, for instance, there is a link between high money flow in the first 40 days and positive stock returns in the next 40 days.

Chan, Hameed, and Tong extend this analysis to global equity markets. They find that equity markets show momentum: markets that have done well in the recent past are more likely to continue doing well, whereas markets that have done badly remain poor performers. They also find that the momentum effect is stronger for equity markets that have high trading volume and weaker in markets with low trading volume.[12]

Volatility In recent years, a number of studies have uncovered a relationship between changes in market volatility and future returns. One study by Haugen, Talmor, and Torous found that increases in market volatility cause

---

[11]J. A. Bennett and R. W. Sias, "Can Money Flows Predict Stock Returns?" *Financial Analysts Journal* 57 (2001).

[12]K. Chan, A. Hameed, and W. Tong, "Profitability of Momentum Strategies in the International Equity Markets," *Journal of Financial and Quantitative Analysis* 35 (2000): 153–172.

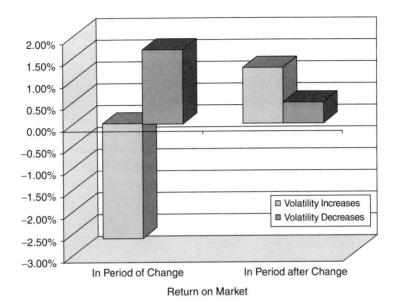

FIGURE 12.1 Returns around Volatility Changes
Source: R. A. Haugen, E. Talmor, and W. N. Torous, "The Effect of Volatility Changes on the Level of Stock Prices and Subsequent Expected Returns," *Journal of Finance* 46 (1991): 985–1007.

an immediate drop in stock prices but that stock returns increase in subsequent periods.[13] They examined daily price volatility from 1897 through 1988 and looked for time periods where the volatility has increased or decreased significantly, relative to prior periods.[14] They then looked at returns both at the time of the volatility change and in the weeks following for both volatility increases and decreases, and their results are summarized in Figure 12.1.

Note that volatility increases cause stock prices to drop but that stock prices increase in the following four weeks. With volatility decreases, stock prices increase at the time of the volatility change, and they continue to increase in the weeks after, albeit at a slower pace.

---

[13]R. A. Haugen, E. Talmor, and W. N. Torous, "The Effect of Volatility Changes on the Level of Stock Prices and Subsequent Expected Returns," *Journal of Finance* 46 (1991): 985–1007.

[14]Daily price volatility is estimated over four week windows. If the volatility in any four week window exceeds (falls below) the volatility in the previous four-week window (at a statistical significance level of 99%), it is categorized as an increase (decrease) in volatility.

In the past decade, the growth in trading in volatility indexes such as the Chicago Board Options Exchange (CBOE) Market Volatility Index (VIX) has offered investors a forward-looking measure of volatility, and researchers have started looking at the relationship between the levels of expected volatility and future price movements. Copeland and Copeland looked at one-day percentage changes of the VIX from its 75-day historical average and chronicle two findings. The first is that an increase in the VIX, relative to the historical average, is accompanied by negative returns in the period in which it happens but is a predictor of positive market returns in the future, consistent with the findings of realized volatility. The second is that value stocks and large-cap stocks do much better than growth stocks and small-cap stocks when the VIX is high, and worse when the VIX is low. In other words, higher volatility is a precursor to positive returns for the entire market, but particularly so for large-cap stocks.[15]

Does this mean that you should buy stocks after an increase in volatility (actual or expected)? Not necessarily. The increase in returns in the weeks following a volatility increase may just reflect the reality that stocks are riskier. However, if you believe that a surge in volatility is temporary and that stock volatility will revert back to normal levels, a strategy of buying stocks after an increase in equity market volatility may bear fruit. Since it is a short-term strategy, there will be transaction costs, but they can be controlled by using index futures or options.

NUMBER WATCH

VIX, by quarter: Take a look at the VIX on a quarterly basis, from its inception to today.

Other Technical Indicators There are a number of nonprice indicators that are used by analysts to forecast future market movements. As with stock-specific technical indicators, marketwide indicators are often used in contradictory ways by momentum and contrarian analysts, with an increase in a specific indicator being viewed as bullish by one group and bearish by the other. Since we did cover technical indicators in depth in Chapter 7, we

---

[15]M. M. Copeland and T. E. Copeland, "Market Timing: Style and Size Rotation using the VIX," *Financial Analysts Journal* 55 (1999): 73–81.

will make only a short mention of some of these indicators in this section, categorized into price and sentiment indicators:

- Price indicators include many of the pricing patterns that we discussed in Chapter 7. Just as support and resistance lines and trend lines are used to determine when to move in and out of individual stocks, they are also used to decide when to move in and out of the stock market.
- Sentiment indicators try to measure the mood of the market. One widely used measure is the *confidence index,* which is defined as the ratio of the yield on BBB-rated bonds to the yield on AAA-rated bonds. If this ratio increases, investors are becoming more risk averse or at least demanding a higher price for taking on risk, which is negative for stocks. An indicator that is viewed as bullish for stocks is *aggregate insider buying* of stocks. When this measure increases, according to its proponents, stocks are more likely to go up.[16] Other sentiment indicators include *mutual fund cash positions* and the degree of bullishness among investment advisers and newsletters. These are often used as contrarian indicators—an increase in cash in the hands of mutual funds and more bearish market views among mutual funds are viewed as bullish signs for stock prices.[17]

While many of these indicators are used widely, they are mostly backed with anecdotal rather than empirical evidence.

Market Timing Based on Normal Ranges (Mean Reversion) There are many investors who believe that prices tend to revert back to what can be called normal levels after extended periods in which they might deviate from these norms. With the equity market, the normal range is usually defined in terms of price-earnings (P/E) ratios, whereas with the bond market a normal range of interest rates is used to justify betting on market direction.

---

[16]M. Chowdhury, J. S. Howe, and J. C. Lin, "The Relation between Aggregate Insider Transactions and Stock Market Returns," *Journal of Financial and Quantitative Analysis* 28 (1993): 431–437. They find a positive correlation between aggregate insider buying and market returns but report that a strategy based upon the indicator would not earn enough to cover transaction costs.

[17]K. L. Fisher and M. Statman, "Investor Sentiment and Stock Returns," *Financial Analysts Journal* 56 (2000): 16–23. They examined three sentiment indicators—the views of Wall Street strategists, investment newsletters and individual investors—and concluded that there is indeed evidence supporting a contrarian investment strategy.

Is There a Normal Range for P/E Ratios?   Buy if the P/E drops below 12 and sell if it rises above 18. You will see variations of this advice in many market timing newsletters. A more academic version of this argument was made by Campbell and Shiller, who looked at P/E ratios from 1871 to recent years and concluded that stocks revert back to a P/E ratio of about 16 times normalized earnings. They defined normalized earnings as the average earnings over the previous 10 years.[18] The implicit belief here is that there is a normal range for P/E ratios and that if the P/E rises above the top end of the range, stocks are likely to be overvalued, whereas if they fall below the bottom of the range, they are likely to be undervalued. While the approach is straightforward, where does the normal range of P/E ratios come from? In most cases, it seems to come from looking at history and attaching a subjective judgment on the upper and lower limits. A slightly more sophisticated approach to estimating a range would require us to estimate the variation (standard deviation) in P/E ratios over time and use it to compute a range; two standard deviations on either side of the average would give you a range outside which you should fall only 5 percent of the time by chance.

Consider, for instance, Figure 12.2, which presents P/E ratios for the S&P 500 going back to 1960. Note that P/E ratios have varied widely over the years, hitting single digits in the late 1970s and rising to more than 25 in the late 1990s. Using the distribution over time as our guide, we could hazard a guess that the normal range of P/E ratios for the United States is between 13 (the 25th percentile) and 18 (the 75th percentile). Shiller uses a much longer data series (going back to 1870) and inflation-adjusted and normalized earnings (computed as an average of the previous 10 years of inflation-adjusted earnings) to estimate P/E ratios across time in Figure 12.3.

As we noted earlier, Shiller arrived at an average normalized P/E across time for U.S. stocks of about 16, and a range of between 12 and 20; numbers above this range would represent an overvalued market and numbers below this range an undervalued market.

NUMBER WATCH

P/E ratios for U.S. stocks: Take a look at the P/E ratio for the S&P 500 each year going back to 1960.

---

[18] J. Campbell and R. Shiller, "Valuation and the Long-Run Stock Market Outlook," *Journal of Portfolio Management* 24 (1998): 11–26.

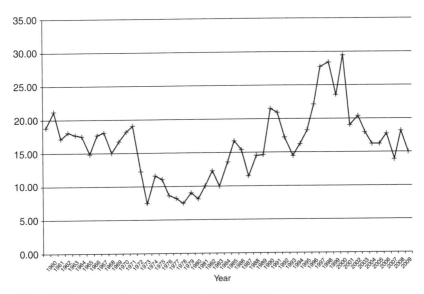

FIGURE 12.2 P/E Ratios for S&P 500, 1960–2010
Source: Bloomberg.

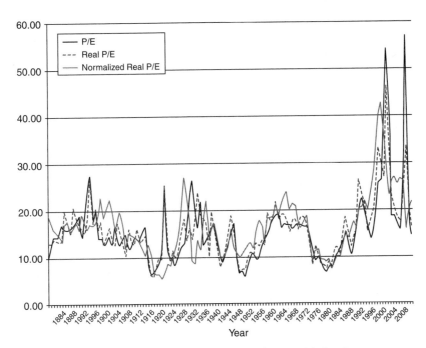

FIGURE 12.3 P/E, Real P/E, and Normalized Real P/E—U.S. Stocks
Source: Raw data from Robert Shiller's website at Princeton.

The limitations of this approach should be obvious. In addition to trusting history to repeat itself, you are making two other assumptions. The first is that you can identify a normal trading range by looking at historical data. As you can see from the graph, you will not get any consensus—someone else looking at this graph might end up with a different band for P/E, using a different time period and a different confidence interval. The second assumption is that the fundamentals have not shifted significantly over time. If interest rates are much lower today than they have been historically, you would expect stocks to trade at much higher P/E ratios than they have historically. How much higher? We will look at this question in more detail in the later parts of this chapter.

Normal Range of Interest Rates   Some analysts hypothesize that market interest rates move within a normal range. Under this hypothesis, when interest rates approach the high end of the range, they are more likely to decrease, and when they approach the low end of the range, they are more likely to increase. This hypothesis is corroborated by two pieces of evidence:

1. *Slope of the yield curve.* The yield curve, which reflects future expectations about interest rates, is more likely to be downward sloping when interest rates are high than when they are low. Thus, investors are more likely to expect interest rates to come down if they are high now and go up if they are low now. Table 12.2 summarizes the frequency of downward-sloping yield curves as a function of the level of interest rates.

   This evidence is consistent with the hypothesis that maintains that interest rates move within a normal range; when they approach the upper end of the normal range, the yield curve is more likely to be downward sloping, and when rates approach the lower end of the normal range, the curve is more likely to be upward sloping.

2. *Interest rate level and expected change.* More significantly, investors' expectations about future interest rate movements seem to be borne out by actual changes in interest rates. When changes in interest rates are

TABLE 12.2   Yield Curves and the Level of Interest Rates

Period	1-Year T-Bill Rate	Upward	Flat	Downward
1900–1970	>4.40%	0	0	20
	3.25–4.4%	10	10	5
	<3.25%	26	0	0
1971–2010	>8%	4	1	3
	<8%	20	10	2

regressed against the current level of interest rates, there is a negative and significant relationship between the level of the rates and the change in rates in subsequent periods; that is, there is a much greater likelihood of a drop in interest rates next period if interest rates are high in this one, and a much greater chance of rates increasing in future periods if interest rates are low in this one. For instance, using Treasury bond rates from 1927 to 2010 and regressing the change in interest rates (Δ Interest rate$_t$) in each year against the level of rates at the end of the prior year (Interest rate$_{t-1}$), we arrive at the following results:

$$\Delta \text{ Interest rate}_t = 0.0032 - 0.0622 \quad \text{Interest rate}_{t-1} \quad R^2 = 0.0309$$
$$[1.40] \qquad [1.60]$$

This regression suggests two things. One is that the change in interest rates in this period is negatively correlated with the level of rates at the end of the prior year; if rates were high, they were more likely to decrease (if low, they would increase). Second, for every one percent increase in the level of current rates, the expected drop in interest rates in the next period increases by 0.0622 percent.

This evidence has to be considered with some caveats. The first is that the proportion of interest rate changes in future periods explained by the current level of rates is relatively small (about 3.09 percent); there are clearly a large number of other factors, most of which are unpredictable, that affect interest rate changes. The second is that the normal range of interest rates, which is based on past experience, might shift if the underlying expectations of inflation change dramatically as they did in the 1970s in the United States. Consequently, many firms that delayed borrowing in the early part of that decade, because they thought that interest rates were at the high end of the range, found themselves facing higher and higher rates in each of the following years. Similarly, firms that borrowed large amounts in 2007, thinking that interest rates were at historic lows, found that they went down further in the next few years.

HINDSIGHT IS 20/20

Market timing always seems simple when you look back in time. After the fact, you can always find obvious signals of market reversals—bull markets turning to bear markets or vice versa. Thus, in 2001 there

(continued)

were investors who looked back at 1999 and bemoaned the fact that they missed getting out of stocks when the market topped at the end of that year. At that time, though, the signs were not so obvious. There were analysts who argued that the market was overvalued and indicators that supported that point of view, but there were just as many analysts, if not more, who saw the market continuing to rise and had supporting models.

In practice, there is almost never a consensus among investors on whether markets have hit bottom or peaked at the time that it occurs. It is an interesting fact that optimism about the future is greatest just as markets top out and the market mood is darkest just as markets turn around. To succeed at market timing, you cannot wait until a bottom has been established before buying or for a market top before selling. If you do, you will miss much of the subsequent payoff.

Market Timing Based on Fundamentals

Just as the prices of individual stocks must reflect their cash flows, growth potential, and risk, entire markets (equity, bond, and real asset) have to reflect the fundamentals of these assets. If they do not, you can argue that they are misvalued. In this section, we consider two ways in which we can bring fundamentals into market timing models. In the first, we try to develop market timing strategies based on the level of fundamental variables—interest rates and economic growth, for instance. In the second, we try to extend the valuation techniques developed for individual stocks to markets.

Fundamental Indicators   You can try to time markets by developing simple signals based on macroeconomic variables. In this section, we consider some of these signals—a few old and some new—that have been used by portfolio managers as market timing tools.

Short-Term Interest Rates   Buy stocks when short-term rates (Treasury bills) are low and sell them when short-term rates are high, or so goes the conventional wisdom. But is there a basis to this advice? In Table 12.3, we examine stock returns under four Treasury bill scenarios: after a decline in rates of more than 1 percent over the prior year, a drop of between 0 and 1 percent, an increase in rates of less than 1 percent, and an increase of more than 1 percent between 1928 and 2001.

TABLE 12.3 Stock Returns and Treasury Bill Rates

| | | Stock Returns in Following Year | |
Change in T-Bill Rate	Number of Years	% of Up Years	Average Annual Returns
Drop by more than 1%	12	66.67%	9.65%
Drop between 0 and 1%	28	75.00%	12.90%
Increase between 0 and 1%	28	71.43%	12.37%
Increase more than 1%	15	66.67%	11.78%

In this case, there is little evidence backing up the proposition that a drop in the Treasury bill rate seems to predict high stock market returns. Generally speaking, markets are just as likely to go up in years after the Treasury bill rate has increased and earn higher returns for investors as in years after Treasury bill rates have decreased.[19]

This link has been examined by a number of academic studies. Ang and Bekaert documented that Treasury bill rates dominate other variables as a predictor of short-term stock market movements.[20] A study by Breen, Glosten, and Jagannathan evaluated a strategy of switching from stock to cash and vice versa, depending on the changes in the Treasury bill rate, and conclude that such a strategy would have added about 2 percent in excess returns to an actively managed portfolio.[21] In a 2002 study that does raise cautionary notes about this strategy, Abhyankar and Davies examine the correlation between Treasury bill rates and stock market returns in subperiods from 1929 to 2000. They find that almost all of the predictability of stock market returns comes from the 1950 to 1975 time period, and that short-term rates have had almost no predictive power for the stock market since 1975. They also conclude that short-term interest rates have more predictive power with the durable goods sector and with smaller companies than they do with the entire market.[22]

---

[19]You could do a similar study using the level of rather than the change in Treasury bill rates, but Treasury bill rates were much lower prior to the Second World War.

[20]A. Ang and G. Bekaert, "Stock Return Predictability: Is It There?" *Review of Financial Studies* 20 (2007): 651–707.

[21]W. Breen, L. R. Glosten, and R. Jagannathan, "Economic Significance of Predictable Variations in Stock Index Returns," *Journal of Finance* 44 (1989): 1177–1189.

[22]A. Abhyankar and P. R. Davies, "Return Predictability, Market Timing and Volatility: Evidence from the Short Rate Revisited" (SSRN Working Paper 305224, 2002).

In conclusion, then, you should be aware of how high or low short-term rates are when you invest in the market, but the value of short-term rates as a predictor of stock market movements has decreased over the past few decades. Its remaining predictive power seems to be restricted to the very short term and to subsectors of the market.

Treasury Bond Rate   Intuitively, it is the Treasury bond rate—the long-term riskless rate—that should have a much stronger impact on stock prices, since it offers a direct alternative to investing in stocks for the long term. If you can make 8 percent investing risklessly in Treasuries for the next 30 years, why would you settle for less when investing in stocks? Thus, we should expect to see stock prices go up if the Treasury bond rate comes down and go down if the rate goes up. Figure 12.4 presents a scatter plot of returns on stock returns each year and the T-bond rate at the end of the prior year.

In 1981, for instance, the Treasury bond rate at the start of the year was 14 percent and the return on the stock index during the year was 20 percent. In 1930, the Treasury bond rate at the start of the year was 3 percent and the

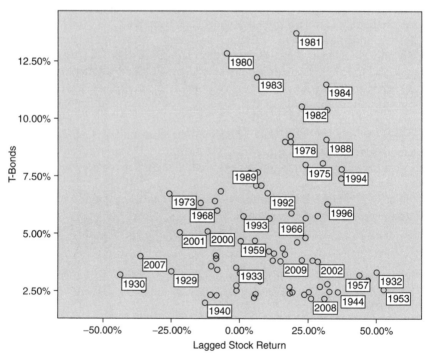

FIGURE 12.4   T-Bond Rates versus Stock Returns in the Following Year, 1928–2010
Source: Federal Reserve.

return on stocks during the year was –40 percent. If there is a relationship between Treasury bond rates at the start of a period and stock returns during the period, it is not strong enough to be obvious, and there seems to be little support for the proposition that stock returns are high following periods when interest rates are low and low when interest rates are high. In fact, stocks did very well in 1982, even though interest rates were very high at the beginning of the year, and did very badly in 1961, notwithstanding the fact that the Treasury bond rate was only 2 percent at the end of the prior year.

This link between Treasury bond rates and stock returns can also be examined if we consider how much we can earn as a return on stocks. You could define this return narrowly as the dividend yield (dividends/current stock prices) or use a much broader measure, such as earnings yield, which looks at the overall earnings on the market as a percentage of the current level of the index. The earnings yield is the inverse of the price-earnings ratio and is used widely by market strategists. Rather than focus on the level of the Treasury bond rate, market strategists often look at the difference between earnings yields and the Treasury bond rate. In simpler terms, they believe that it is best to invest in stocks when earnings yields are high relative to the Treasury bond rate. In fact, there are some strategists who believe that stocks are overvalued when the earnings yield is lower than the Treasury bond rate. To examine this proposition, we looked at the difference between the earnings yield and the T-bond rate at the end of every year from 1960 to 2010 and the returns on the S&P 500 in the following year (see Table 12.4).

The relationship is tenuous at best. When the earnings yield exceeds the Treasury bond rate by more than 2 percent, which has occurred in 10 out of the 51 years, the return on the S&P 500 in the following year has averaged 11.91 percent. However, the returns are almost as good when the earnings yield has lagged the Treasury bond rate by zero to 1 percent. It is true that the annual returns are only 3.04 percent in the five years following periods

TABLE 12.4 Earnings Yield, T-Bond Rates, and Stock Returns, 1960 to 2010

Earnings Yield – T-Bond Rate	Number of Years	Stock Returns			
		Average	Standard Deviation	Maximum	Minimum
>2%	10	11.91%	15.56%	31.55%	−11.81%
1% to 2%	11	1.72%	20.44%	26.38%	−38.49%
0% to 1%	3	16.14%	6.21%	20.26%	8.99%
−1% to 0%	6	11.21%	12.93%	27.25%	−11.36%
−2% to 1%	16	7.74%	18.69%	34.11%	−23.37%
<−2%	5	3.04%	8.40%	12.40%	−10.14%

when the earnings yield was lower than the Treasury bond rate by more than 2 percent, but the annual returns were also very low in the 11 years when the earnings yield exceeded the Treasury bond rate by 1 to 2 percent. Thus, there seems to be little historical support for using earnings yield and Treasury bond rates to predict future stock market movements.

Business Cycles   As with Treasury bonds, there is an intuitive link between the level of stock prices and economic growth. You would expect stocks to do much better in economic booms than during recessions. What makes this relationship tricky, however, is that market movements are based on predictions of changes in economic activity in the future, rather than levels of activity. In other words, you may see stock prices rising in the depths of a recession if investors expect the economy to begin recovering in the next few months. Alternatively, you may see stock prices drop even in the midst of robust economic growth, if the growth does not measure up to expectations. In Figure 12.5, we have graphed the S&P 500 index and gross domestic product (GDP) growth going back to 1929.

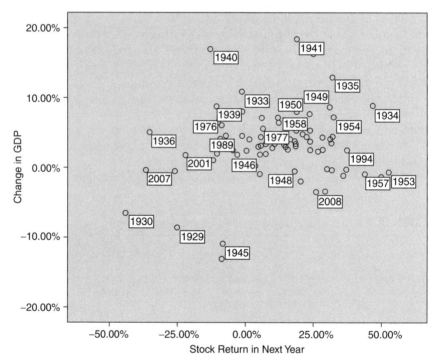

FIGURE 12.5   Real GDP Growth and Market Returns
Source: Federal Reserve.

TABLE 12.5   Real Economic Growth as a Predictor of Stock Returns, 1929 to 2010

GDP Annual Growth	Number of Years	Stock Returns in Next Year			
		Average Return	Standard Deviation in Returns	Best Year	Worst Year
>5%	23	10.04%	19.42%	46.74%	−35.34%
3.5% to 5%	25	13.38%	12.26%	31.86%	−9.03%
2% to 3.5%	9	14.08%	16.41%	37.20%	−10.46%
0% to 2%	7	−3.40%	11.50%	7.44%	−21.97%
<0%	17	15.11%	29.84%	52.56%	−43.84%
All years	82	11.16%	20.02%	52.56%	−43.84%

There is a positive relationship between real GDP growth during a year and stock returns during the year, but there is also a lot of noise in the relationship. Even if the relationship were strong enough to pass muster, you cannot use it for market timing unless you can forecast real economic growth. The real question then becomes whether you can make forecasts of future stock market movements after observing economic growth in the past year. To examine whether there is any potential payoff to investing after observing economic growth in the prior year, we looked at the relationship between economic growth in a year and stock returns in the following year, using data from 1929 to 2010 in Table 12.5.

There seems to be no clearly discernible relationship between returns next year and GDP growth this year. It is true that the years with negative GDP growth are followed by the most extreme years (in terms of positive and negative returns) and higher volatility, but the average stock returns in this scenario are higher than the average returns you would have earned if you had bought after the best economic growth years (growth exceeds 5 percent).

NUMBER WATCH

Historical macroeconomic numbers: Take a look at inflation and GDP growth over the past few decades in the United States.

If you can forecast future growth in the economy, it is useful at two levels. One is in overall market timing, since you will steer more of your funds into stocks prior to better-than-expected economic growth and away from stocks when you foresee the economy slowing. You can also use the information to overinvest in those sectors that are most sensitive to the economic cycle—automobile and housing stocks, for instance—if you believe that robust economic growth is around the corner.

Intrinsic Value Models   One way in which we can take the individual fundamentals that we considered in the preceding section and consolidate them into one market view is to do an intrinsic valuation of the entire market. What, you might ask, is an intrinsic valuation? Back in Chapter 4, we considered how an individual stock can be valued using a discounted cash flow (DCF) model as the present value of expected cash flows in the future. A market is composed of individual assets, and if individual assets can be valued using discounted cash flow models, we see no reason why the entire market cannot be valued as the present value of expected cash flows. In this section, we consider how best to extend discounted cash flow models to valuing the market, and the value that may be added from doing so.

Extending DCF Models to the Market   Consider, for instance, the dividend discount model that we introduced in Chapter 4. We argued that the value of a stock can be written as the present value of the expected dividends from owning the stock, discounted back at the cost of equity. Extending this argument to an index, the value of an index can also be written as the present value of the expected dividends on the index. Thus, if the dividends on the entire stock index are expected to be $40 next year, the expected growth rate in perpetuity is expected to be 4 percent and the cost of equity for the average-risk stock is expected to be 9 percent, you could value the index as follows:

$$\text{Value of index} = \text{Expected dividends next year}/$$
$$(\text{Cost of equity} - \text{Expected growth rate})$$
$$= 40/(0.09 - 0.04) = 800$$

As with an individual stock, this model can be extended to allow for high growth. Thus, if you expected dividends to grow 10 percent a year for the next five years and then expect the growth rate to drop to 4 percent in perpetuity, the value of the index can be computed in Table 12.6.

Note that the dividends grow at 10 percent until year 5 and that the terminal value of the index is based on a 4 percent growth rate forever.

$$\text{Terminal value} - 58.56(1.04)/(0.09 - 0.04) = \$1,218.13$$

We noted that one limitation of dividend discount models is that companies may not pay out what they can afford to in dividends or may choose

TABLE 12.6   Valuing an Index with High Growth

	Dividends	Terminal Value	Present Value
1	$40.00		$ 36.70
2	$44.00		$ 37.03
3	$48.40		$ 37.37
4	$53.24		$ 37.72
5	$58.56	$1,218.13	$829.76
Value of index =			$978.59

alternative ways of returning cash to stockholders (stock buybacks, for instance). You can modify this model by replacing dividends with potential dividends (free cash flows to equity for the index) or by augmenting dividends with stock buybacks on the index.

Some Caveats   While the building blocks for discounted cash flow valuation may remain the same for individual stocks and the markets, there are some cautionary notes that need to be added when valuing entire markets.

- We allowed for the possibility of high growth in the preceding section, but you should be much more cautious about assuming high growth—in terms of both the growth rate and how long high growth will continue— for a market than you would be for an individual stock, especially when the market is broadly based. Consider, for instance, the S&P 500. Since it includes the 500 companies with the largest market capitalizations, arguing that earnings for these companies will grow at a rate much higher than the growth rate of the economy implies that the profit margins of these companies will increase over time. While this is feasible in the short term, especially if the economy is coming out of a recession or if firms are restructuring, we do not see how this can be sustained in the long term.
- The cost of equity that we are considering here is the cost of equity for the entire index. If we are considering a broadly based equity index, this cost of equity should reflect the riskless rate and the risk premium that investors demand for investing in equities as a class.

NUMBER WATCH

Intrinsic value of S&P 500 index: Take a look at the most recent valuation of the S&P 500.

On the plus side, you should have less trouble forecasting earnings and dividends for an index than you should with individual stocks. After all, you have the luxury of diversification. In other words, you may overestimate earnings on some stocks and underestimate earnings on other stocks, but your overall measure of earnings can still be fairly precise.

An Illustration: Valuing the S&P 500 in January 2011   To illustrate this process, on January 1, 2011, the S&P 500 was trading at 1,257.64 and the dividends on the index amounted to $23.12 over the previous year. On the same date, analysts were estimating an expected growth rate of 6.95 percent in earnings for the index for the following five years. Assuming that dividends grow at the same rate as earnings, we obtain the following:

Year	2011	2012	2013	2014	2015
Expected dividends =	$24.73	$26.44	$28.28	$30.25	$32.35

To estimate the cost of equity, we assume a beta of 1 for the index and use the risk-free rate on January 1, 2011, of 3.29 percent and an equity risk premium of 5 percent:

$$\text{Cost of equity} = 3.5\% + 5\% = 8.5\%$$

After year 5, earnings and dividends are expected to grow at 3.29 percent, the same nominal rate as the economy (assumed to be equal to the risk-free rate). The value that we obtained for the index is:

$$\text{Value of index} = \frac{24.73}{1.085} + \frac{26.44}{1.085^2} + \frac{28.28}{1.085^3} + \frac{30.25}{1.085^4} + \frac{32.35}{1.085^5}$$
$$+ \frac{32.35(1.0329)}{(0.085 - 0.0329)1.085^5} = 560.15$$

This would suggest that the index was massively overvalued on January 1, 2011.

Since many of the companies in the index have chosen to return cash in the form of stock buybacks, rather than dividends, a more realistic estimate of value would incorporate these expected buybacks. To do so, we added the buybacks in 2010 to the dividends to arrive at a value of 53.96 for augmented dividends on the index. Applying the same parameters that we used for conventional dividends (growth rate of 6.95 percent for the next five years and 3.29 percent beyond year 5), we estimate a new value for the index:

$$\text{Value of index} = \frac{57.72}{1.085} + \frac{61.73}{1.085^2} + \frac{66.02}{1.085^3} + \frac{70.60}{1.085^4} + \frac{75.51}{1.085^5}$$

$$+ \frac{75.51(1.0329)}{(0.085 - 0.0329)1.085^5} = 1{,}307.48$$

With buybacks incorporated, the index looked slightly undervalued.

How Well Do Intrinsic Valuation Models Work? How well would a strategy of buying the index when it is intrinsically undervalued and selling when it is intrinsically overvalued do? It is difficult to answer this question because it depends on the inputs you estimate for the intrinsic valuation model and your time horizon. Generally speaking, the odds of success increase as the quality of your inputs improves and your time horizon lengthens. Eventually, markets seem to revert back to intrinsic value, but "eventually" can be a long time coming.

There is, however, a cost associated with using intrinsic valuation models when they find equity markets to be overvalued. If you take the logical next step of not investing in stocks when they are overvalued, you will have to invest your funds in either other securities that you believe are fairly valued (such as short-term government securities) or in other asset classes. In the process, you may end up out of the stock market for extended periods while the market is, in fact, going up. For instance, most intrinsic value models would have suggested that the equity market in the United States was overvalued starting in 1994. If you had followed through and not invested in equities until 2002 (when the models suggested that valuations were fair again), you would have lost far more (by not investing in the bull market between 1994 and 2000) than you would have gained (by not investing in the down markets of 2001 and 2002).

The problem with intrinsic value models is their failure to capture permanent shifts in attitudes toward risk or investor characteristics. This is because so many of the inputs for these models come from looking at the past. Thus, the risk premium used to come up with the cost of equity may have been estimated looking at historical data on stock and bond returns, and dividends may reflect what companies did last year. If one or both have changed as a consequence of shifts in the market, you will get a misleading signal from intrinsic valuation models. In fact, many investors who used intrinsic value models bought stocks during the early 1970s as stock prices dropped and failed to take into account the seismic shifts created by the high inflation of that period.

Relative Value Models   In relative value models, you examine how markets are priced relative to other markets and to fundamentals. How is this different from intrinsic value models? While the two approaches share some characteristics, this approach is less rigid insofar as it does not require that you work within the structure of a discounted cash flow model. Instead, you make comparisons either of markets over time (the S&P in 2012 versus the S&P in 1990) or of different markets at the same point in time (U.S. stocks in 2012 versus European stocks in 2012).

Comparisons across Time   In its simplest form, you can compare the way stocks are priced today to the way they used to be priced in the past and draw conclusions on that basis. Thus, as we noted in the section on historic norms, many analysts argue that stocks today, priced at 13 times earnings in early 2012, are cheap because stocks historically have been priced at 15 to 16 times earnings.

While reversion to historic norms remains a very strong force in financial markets, we should be cautious about drawing too strong a conclusion from such comparisons. As the fundamentals (interest rates, risk premiums, expected growth, and payout) change over time, the P/E ratio will also change. Other things remaining equal, for instance, we would expect the following.

- An increase in interest rates should result in a higher cost of equity for the market and a lower P/E ratio.
- A greater willingness to take risk on the part of investors will result in a lower risk premium for equity and a higher P/E ratio across all stocks.
- An increase in expected growth in earnings across firms will result in a higher P/E ratio for the market.

In other words, it is difficult to draw conclusions about P/E ratios without looking at these fundamentals. A more appropriate comparison is therefore not between P/E ratios across time, but between the actual P/E ratio and the predicted P/E ratio based on fundamentals existing at that time.

Figure 12.6 summarizes the earnings/price ratios (or earnings yield) for S&P 500, Treasury bond rates, and the difference between bond and bill rates at the end of each year from 1960 to 2010.

You do not need to be a statistician to note that earnings-to-price ratios are high (and P/E ratios are low) when the Treasury bond rates are high, and the earnings-to-price ratios decline when Treasury bond rates drop. This strong positive relationship between E/P ratios and T-bond rates is evidenced by the correlation of 0.69 between the two variables. In addition, there is evidence that the term structure also affects the E/P ratio. In the following

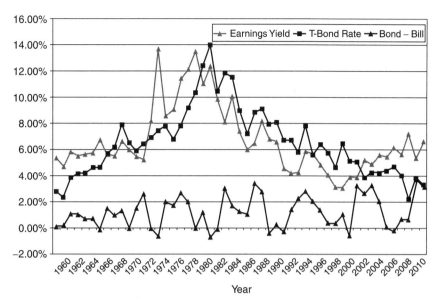

FIGURE 12.6   E/P Ratios and Interest Rates
Source: Bloomberg.

regression, we regress E/P ratios against the level of T-bond rates and the yield spread (T-bond – 3 month T-bill rate), using data from 1960 to 2000.

$$E/P = 0.0266 + 0.6746 \text{ T-bond rate} - 0.3131 \text{ (T-bond rate} - \text{T-bill rate)}$$
$$[3.37] \quad [6.41] \quad\quad\quad\quad [-1.36] \quad R^2 = 0.476$$

Other things remaining equal, this regression suggests that:

- Every 1 percent increase in the T-bond rate increases the E/P ratio by 0.6746 percent. This is not surprising, but it quantifies the impact that higher interest rates have on the P/E ratio.
- Every 1 percent increase in the difference between T-bond and T-bill rates reduces the E/P ratio by 0.3131 percent. Flatter or negatively sloping term yield curves seem to correspond to lower P/E ratios, and upward-sloping yield curves correspond to higher P/E ratios. While at first sight this may seem surprising, the slope of the yield curve, at least in the United States, has been a leading indicator of economic growth, with more upward-sloped curves going with higher growth.

Based on this regression, we can predict the E/P ratio for the S&P 500 in November 2011, with the T-bill rate at 0.2 percent and the T-bond rate at 2.2 percent.

$$E/P_{2011} = 0.0266 + 0.6746(0.022) - 0.3131(0.022 - 0.02)$$
$$= 0.0408 \text{ or } 4.08\%$$

$$P/E_{2000} = \frac{1}{E/P_{2011}} = \frac{1}{0.0408} = 24.50$$

NUMBER WATCH

Relative value of S&P 500 index: Take a look at the most recent relative valuation of the S&P 500.

Since the S&P 500 was trading at a multiple of 15 times earnings in November 2011, this would have indicated a significantly undervalued market. This regression can be enriched by adding other variables (which should be correlated to the price-earnings ratio), such as expected growth in GDP and payout ratios, as independent variables. The biggest uncertainty is whether the multiple market crises from 2008 to 2011 have rendered historical relationships between P/E ratios and interest rates meaningless, at least for the United States.

Comparisons across Markets Comparisons are often made between price-earnings ratios in different countries with the intention of finding undervalued and overvalued markets. Markets with lower P/E ratios are viewed as undervalued, and those with higher P/E ratios are considered overvalued. Given the wide differences that exist between countries on fundamentals, it is clearly misleading to draw these conclusions. For instance, you would expect to see the following, other things remaining equal:

- Countries with higher real interest rates should have lower P/E ratios than countries with lower real interest rates.
- Countries with higher expected real growth should have higher P/E ratios than countries with lower real growth.
- Countries that are viewed as riskier (and thus command higher risk premiums) should have lower P/E ratios than safer countries.

■ Countries where companies are more efficient in their investments (and earn a higher return on these investments) should trade at higher P/E ratios.

We will illustrate this process to compare P/E ratios across markets. Table 12.7 summarizes P/E ratios across different developed markets in July 2000, together with dividend yields and interest rates (short term and long term) at the time.

A naive comparison of P/E ratios suggests that Japanese stocks, with a P/E ratio of 52.25, are overvalued, while Belgian stocks, with a P/E ratio of 14.74, are undervalued. There is, however, a strong negative correlation between P/E ratios and 10-year interest rates (−0.73) and a positive correlation between the P/E ratio and the yield spread (0.70). A cross-sectional regression of the P/E ratio on interest rates and expected growth yields the following.

$$\text{P/E ratio} = 42.62 - 360.9\,(\text{10-year rate}) + 846.6\,(\text{10-year rate} - \text{2-year rate})$$
$$[2.78] \quad [-1.42] \qquad\qquad [1.08] \quad R^2 = 59\%$$

The coefficients are of marginal significance, partly because of the small size of the sample. Based on this regression, the predicted P/E ratios for the countries are shown in Table 12.8.

From this comparison, Belgian and Swiss stocks would be the most undervalued, while U.S. stocks would be the most overvalued.

TABLE 12.7 P/E Ratios for Developed Markets, July 2000

Country	P/E	Dividend Yield	2-Year Rate	10-Year Rate	10-Year – 2-Year
United Kingdom	22.02	2.59%	5.93%	5.85%	−0.08%
Germany	26.33	1.88%	5.06%	5.32%	0.26%
France	29.04	1.34%	5.11%	5.48%	0.37%
Switzerland	19.60	1.42%	3.62%	3.83%	0.21%
Belgium	14.74	2.66%	5.15%	5.70%	0.55%
Italy	28.23	1.76%	5.27%	5.70%	0.43%
Sweden	32.39	1.11%	4.67%	5.26%	0.59%
Netherlands	21.10	2.07%	5.10%	5.47%	0.37%
Australia	21.69	3.12%	6.29%	6.25%	−0.04%
Japan	52.25	0.71%	0.58%	1.85%	1.27%
United States	25.14	1.10%	6.05%	5.85%	−0.20%
Canada	26.14	0.99%	5.70%	5.77%	0.07%

TABLE 12.8 Predicted P/E Ratios for Developed Markets, July 2000

Country	Actual P/E	Predicted P/E	Under- or Overvalued
United Kingdom	22.02	20.83	5.71%
Germany	26.33	25.62	2.76%
France	29.04	25.98	11.80%
Switzerland	19.60	30.58	−35.90%
Belgium	14.74	26.71	−44.81%
Italy	28.23	25.69	9.89%
Sweden	32.39	28.63	13.12%
Netherlands	21.10	26.01	−18.88%
Australia	21.69	19.73	9.96%
Japan	52.25	46.70	11.89%
United States	25.14	19.81	26.88%
Canada	26.14	22.39	16.75%

This example is extended to examine P/E ratio differences across emerging markets at the end of 2000. In Table 12.9, the country risk factor is estimated for the emerging markets.[23] It is scaled from 0 (safest) to 100 (riskiest).

The regression of P/E ratios on these variables provides the following:

$$P/E = 16.16 - 7.94 \text{ Interest rates} + 154.40 \text{ Real growth} - 0.112 \text{ Country risk}$$
$$[3.61] \; [-0.52] \qquad\qquad [2.38] \qquad\qquad [-1.78] \quad R^2 = 74\%$$

Countries with higher real growth and lower country risk have higher P/E ratios, but the level of interest rates seems to have only a marginal impact. The regression can be used to estimate the price-earnings ratio for Turkey.

$$\text{Predicted P/E for Turkey} = 16.16 - 7.94(0.25) + 154.40(0.02) - 0.112(35)$$
$$= 13.35$$

At a P/E ratio of 12, the market can be viewed as slightly undervalued.

---

[23]These estimates come from the *Economist*.

TABLE 12.9   P/E Ratios and Key Statistics: Emerging Markets

Country	P/E Ratio	Interest Rates	GDP Real Growth	Country Risk
Argentina	14	18.00%	2.50%	45
Brazil	21	14.00%	4.80%	35
Chile	25	9.50%	5.50%	15
Hong Kong	20	8.00%	6.00%	15
India	17	11.48%	4.20%	25
Indonesia	15	21.00%	4.00%	50
Malaysia	14	5.67%	3.00%	40
Mexico	19	11.50%	5.50%	30
Pakistan	14	19.00%	3.00%	45
Peru	15	18.00%	4.90%	50
Philippines	15	17.00%	3.80%	45
Singapore	24	6.50%	5.20%	5
South Korea	21	10.00%	4.80%	25
Thailand	21	12.75%	5.50%	25
Turkey	12	25.00%	2.00%	35
Venezuela	20	15.00%	3.50%	45

Interest rates: Short-term interest rates in these countries.

Determinants of Success

Can you time markets by comparing stock prices now to prices in the past or to how stocks are priced in other markets? Though you can make judgments about market under- or overvaluation with these comparisons, there are two problems with this analysis.

1. Since you are basing your analysis by looking at the past, you are assuming that there has not been a significant shift in the underlying relationship. Structural or permanent shifts wreak havoc on these models.
2. Even if you assume that the past is prologue and that there will be reversion back to historic norms, you do not control this part of the process. In other words, you may find stocks to be overvalued on a relative basis, but they become more overvalued over time. Thus convergence is neither timed nor even guaranteed.

How can you improve your odds of success? First, you can try to incorporate into your analysis those variables that reflect the shifts that you believe have occurred in markets. For instance, if you believe that the influx of hedge fund money into the equity markets over the past two decades has changed the fundamental pricing relationship, you can include the percentage of stock held by hedge funds in your regression. Second, you can have a longer time horizon, since you improve your odds on convergence.

THE INFORMATION LAG WITH FUNDAMENTALS

If you are considering timing the market using macroeconomic variables such as inflation or economic growth, you should also take into account the time lag before you will get this information. Consider, for instance, a study that shows that there is high positive correlation between GDP growth in a quarter and the stock market's performance in the next. An obvious strategy would be to buy stocks after a quarter of high GDP growth and sell after a quarter of negative or low GDP growth. The problem with the strategy is that the information on GDP growth will not be available to you until you are two months into the next quarter.

If you use a market variable such as the level of interest rates or the slope of the yield curve to make your market forecasts, you are in better shape since this information should be available to you contemporaneously with the stock market. In building these models, you should be careful and ensure that you are not building a model where you will have to forecast interest rates in order to forecast the stock market. To test for a link between the level of interest rates and stock market movements, you would look at the correlation between interest rates at the beginning of each year and stock returns over the year. Since you can observe the former before you make your investment decision, you would have the basis for a viable strategy if you find a correlation between the two. If you had run the test between the level of interest rates at the end of each year and stock returns during the year, implementing an investment strategy even if you find a correlation would be problematic since you would have to forecast the level of interest rates first.

THE EVIDENCE ON MARKET TIMING

While we have looked at a variety of ways in which investors try to time markets from technical indicators to fundamentals, we have not asked a more fundamental question: Do those who claim to time markets actually succeed? In this section, we consider a broad range of investors who try to time markets and examine whether they succeed.

Mutual Fund Managers

Most equity mutual funds do not lay claims to market timing, but, in our view, they do try to time markets at the margin. We will begin by looking at whether they succeed on average. There are some mutual funds that claim market timing as their primary skill, and these funds are called tactical asset allocation funds. We will look at the track records of these funds and pass judgment on whether their claims hold up.

Cash Holdings How do we know that mutual funds try to time markets? While all equity mutual funds need to hold some cash—investments in Treasuries and commercial paper—to meet redemption needs and for day-to-day operations, they collectively hold much more cash than is necessary. In fact, the only explanation for the cash balances that we observe at equity mutual funds is that mutual funds use them to signal their views of future market movements: they hold more cash when they are bearish and less cash when they are bullish. In Figure 12.7, we present the average cash balance at mutual funds at the start of each year from 1980 to 2010 and the returns on the S&P 500 each year.

Note that the cash balances seem to increase after bad years for the market and decrease after good years, but there is little predictive power in the level of cash holdings. For instance, cash holdings by mutual funds decreased as the market went up in the 1990s and were lowest at the start of the year that the market boom ended. Similarly, the cash balance at mutual

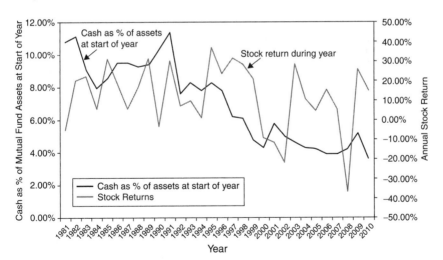

FIGURE 12.7 Mutual Fund Cash Holdings and Stock Returns
Source: Investment Company Institute.

funds decreased dramatically in 2008, largely in reaction to the market drop in that year.

The question of whether mutual funds are successful at market timing has been examined widely in the literature going back four decades. A study in 1966 by Treynor and Mazuy suggested that we look at whether the betas of funds increase when the market return is large in absolute terms by running a regression of the returns on a fund against both market and squared market returns:[24]

$$R_{\text{Fund, Period } t} = a + b \text{ Return}_{\text{Market, } t} + c \text{ Return}_{\text{Market, } t}^{2}$$

If a fund manager has significant market timing abilities, they argued, the coefficient c on squared returns should be positive. This approach, when tested out on actual mutual fund returns, yields negative values for the coefficient on squared returns, indicating negative market timing abilities rather than positive ones. In 1981, Merton and Henrikkson modified this equation to consider whether funds earned higher returns in periods when the market was positive, and found little evidence of market timing as well.[25]

Tactical Asset Allocation and Other Market Timing Funds   In the aftermath of the crash of 1987, a number of mutual funds sprang up claiming that they could have saved investors the losses from the crash by steering them out of equity markets prior to the crash. These funds were called tactical asset allocation funds and made no attempt to pick stocks. Instead, they argued that they could move funds between stocks, Treasury bonds, and Treasury bills in advance of major market movements and allow investors to earn high returns. Since 1987, though, the returns delivered by these funds have fallen well short of their promises. Figure 12.8 compares the returns on a dozen large tactical asset allocation funds over 5-year and 10-year periods (1989–1998) to the overall market as well as to fixed mixes—50 percent in both stocks and bonds, and 75 percent stocks/25 percent bonds. We call the last two couch potato mixes, reflecting the fact that we are making no attempt to time the market. The tactical asset allocation funds under perform the overall market and the couch potato funds.

---

[24]Jack L. Treynor and Kay Mazuy, "Can Mutual Funds Outguess the Market?" *Harvard Business Review* 44 (1966): 131–136.

[25]Roy D. Henriksson and Robert C. Merton, "On Market Timing and Investment Performance, II: Statistical Procedures for Evaluating Forecasting Skills," *Journal of Business* 54 (1981): 513–533.

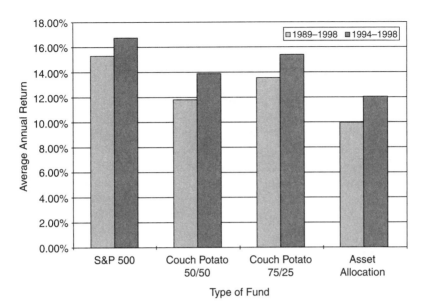

FIGURE 12.8 Performance of Unsophisticated Strategies versus Asset Allocation Funds
Source: Money magazine.

One critique of this study may be its focus on a few tactical asset allocation funds. Becker, Ferson, Myers, and Schill examined a much larger sample more than 100 asset allocation funds between 1990 and 1995 and also find little evidence of success at market timing at these funds.[26] Updating these studies, it does not look like tactical asset allocation funds have become better at market timing over time. Looking at the 1999 to 2010 time period, for instance, tactical asset allocation funds generated an annual return of 5.2 percent, lower than the return you would have generated by investing 60 percent of your portfolio in stocks and 40 percent in bonds at the start of 1999 and leaving that portfolio untouched until December 31, 2010.

Hedge Funds In the preceding chapter, we looked at the aggregate evidence on whether hedge funds beat the market. In this section, we focus on a whether hedge funds show market timing skills. A paper looking at the ability of hedge funds to time markets in their focus groups (which

---

[26]C. Becker, W. Ferson, D. Myers, and M. Schill, "Conditional Market Timing with Benchmark Investors," *Journal of Financial Economics* 52 (1999): 119–148.

may be commodities, currencies, fixed income, or arbitrage) found some evidence (albeit not overwhelming) of market timing payoff in bond and currency markets but none in equity markets.[27] In contrast, a more recent and comprehensive evaluation of just 221 market timing hedge funds found evidence that a few of these funds are able to time both market direction and volatility, and generate abnormal returns as a consequence.[28]

Building on the theme of liquidity, there is also evidence that what separates successful hedge funds from those that fail is their capacity to adjust market exposure ahead of market liquidity changes, reducing exposure prior to periods of high illiquidity. The funds that do this best outperform funds that don't make the adjustment by 3.6 to 4.9 percent a year after adjusting for risk.[29]

Investment Newsletters

There are hundreds of investment newsletters that investors subscribe to for sage advice on investing. Some of these investment newsletters are centered on suggesting individual stocks for investors, but some are directed toward timing the market. For a few hundred dollars, we are told, we too can be privy to private signals of market movements.

Graham and Harvey examined the market timing abilities of investment newsletters by examining the stock/cash mixes recommended in 237 newsletters from 1980 to 1992.[30] If investment newsletters are good market timers, you should expect to see the proportion allocated to stocks increase prior to the stock market going up. When the returns earned on the mixes recommended in these newsletters are compared to a buy-and-hold strategy, 183 or the 237 newsletters (77 percent) delivered lower returns than the buy-and-hold strategy. One measure of the ineffectuality of the market timing recommendations of these investment newsletters lies in the fact that while equity weights increased 58 percent of the time before market upturns, they also increased by 53 percent before market downturns. There is some evidence of continuity in performance, but the evidence is much stronger

---

[27] Y. Chen, "Timing Ability in the Focus Market of Hedge Funds" (working paper, Boston College, 2005).

[28] Y. Chen and B. Liang, "Do Market Timing Hedge Funds Time the Market?" *Journal of Financial and Quantitative Analysis* 42 (2007): 827–856.

[29] C. Cao, Y. Chen, B. Liang, and A. Lo, "Can Hedge Funds Time Market Liquidity?" (SSRN Working Paper 1537925, 2011).

[30] John R. Graham and Campbell Harvey, "Market Timing Ability and Volatility Implied in Investment Newsletters' Asset Allocation Recommendations," *Journal of Financial Economics* 42 (1996): 397–421.

for negative performance than for positive performance. In other words, investment newsletters that give bad advice on market timing are more likely to continue to give bad advice than are newsletters that give good advice to continue giving good advice.[31]

The only hopeful evidence on market timing comes from a study of professional market timers who are investment advisers. These timers provide explicit timing recommendations only to their clients, who then adjust their portfolios accordingly—shifting money into stocks if they are bullish and out of stocks if they are bearish. A study by Chance and Hemler looked at 30 professional market timers who were monitored by MoniResearch Corporation, a service that monitors the performance of such advisers, and found evidence of market timing ability.[32] It should be noted that the timing calls were both short term and frequent. One market timer had a total of 303 timing signals between 1989 and 1994, and there were, on average, about 15 signals per year across all 30 market timers. Notwithstanding the high transaction costs associated with following these timing signals, following their recommendations would have generated excess returns for investors.[33]

Market Strategists

The market strategists at major investment banks represent perhaps the most visible symbols of market timing. Their prognostications about the market are widely disseminated not only by their investment banks but also by the media. While much of what market strategists say about markets cannot be easily categorized as bullish or bearish—good market strategists are difficult to pin down when it comes to explicit forecasts—they also make specific recommendations on preferred asset allocation mixes that are made public.

Given that this is the primary mission of market strategists, how do these allocation mixes yield market predictions? One way is to look at the percentage allocated to stocks. More bullish market strategists will recommend a larger proportion of the portfolio be invested in stocks, whereas bearish strategists will overweight cash and bonds. The other is to look at changes in

---

[31]A good market timing newsletter is likely to repeat its success about 50% of the time. A poor market timing newsletter has a 70% chance of repeating its poor performance.

[32]D. M. Chance and M. L. Hemler, "The Performance of Professional Market Timers: Daily Evidence from Executed Strategies," *Journal of Financial Economics* 62 (2001): 377–411.

[33]The study looked at excess returns after transactions costs but before taxes. By its very nature, this strategy is likely to generate large tax bills, since almost all of your gains will be taxed at the ordinary tax rate.

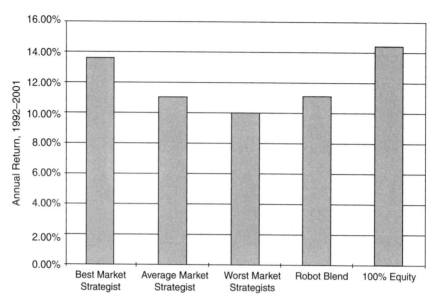

FIGURE 12.9   Annual Return from Market Strategies Mixes, 1992–2001
Source: Wall Street Journal.

holdings recommended by the same strategist from period to period—an increase in the proportion allocated to stocks would indicate more bullishness. On both dimensions, the market timing skills of strategists are questionable. The *Wall Street Journal*, in addition to reporting the asset allocation mixes of strategists, also compares the returns that would have been generated by following each bank's allocation advice to the returns you would have made by being fully invested in stocks over 1-year, 5-year, and 10-year periods. To counter the argument that it is unfair to compare a 100 percent equity portfolio to a asset allocation mix, the *Journal* also reports on the returns on a robot mix—a fixed allocation across stocks, bonds, and bills. Figure 12.9 summarizes the returns on all three from 1992 to 2001, as well as the returns you would have earned by following the strategist who had the best mixes over the period and the one with the worst mixes.

Note that the returns on the robot mix are slightly higher than the average returns generated by following the average market strategists. Of the 16 banks that the *Wall Street Journal* tracks, only five would have generated returns higher than the robot mix over the period, and even those would have been well within a statistical margin for error. Finally, even the best strategist's asset mix would have underperformed a strategy of being fully invested in stocks. Overall, the evidence indicates that the market timing skills of leading market strategies are vastly overstated.

MARKET TIMERS: FROM LIVERMORE TO ACAMPORA

Market timers are the meteors of the investment universe. They attract a great deal of attention when they streak, but they fade quickly. Looking at the high-profile market timers (market gurus) over time, we find a diverse group.[34] Some were chartists, some used fundamentals, and some were mysterious about their methods, but there are three common characteristics that they seem to share:

1. *A capacity to see the world in black and white.* Market gurus do not prevaricate. Instead, they make bold statements that seem outrageous when they make them about where the market will be six months or a year from now. Ralph Acampora, for instance, made his reputation with his call that the Dow would hit 7,000 (it was at 3,500 at the time).
2. *A correct call on a big market move.* All market timers make their reputations by calling at least one big market move. For Jesse Livermore, it was the market crash of 1929, and for Acampora, it was the bull market of the 1990s.
3. *Outsize personalities.* Market gurus are born showmen who use the media of their time as megaphones to publicize not only their market forecasts but the news of their successes. In fact, part of their success can be attributed to their capacity to make other investors act on their predictions, making these predictions, at least in the near term, self-fulfilling prophecies.

So why do great market gurus stumble? The very same factors that contribute to their success seem to underlie their failures. Their absolute conviction in their market timing abilities and their past successes seems to feed into more outrageous calls that ultimately destroy their reputations. Joe Granville, one of the market gurus of the late 1970s, for instance, spent all of the 1980s recommending that people sell stocks and buy gold, and his newsletter was ranked among the worst in terms of performance for the decade.

---

[34]One of the best books on Livermore is the classic *Reminiscences of a Stock Market Operator* by Edwin LeFèvre, reprinted by John Wiley & Sons in 2006 (Hoboken, NJ).

MARKET TIMING STRATEGIES

If you can time markets, how can you take advantage of this skill? Market timing strategies range across the spectrum, from being narrowly focused on one market (usually stocks) or just protecting your portfolio from adverse market movements to broader strategies that stretch across markets and try to profit from market movements.

The Big Picture

In the past few decades, market timing has become much broader in its scope, partly because of new investors entering the market (hedge funds and global mutual funds) and partly because of new instruments for trading on markets (derivatives, exchange-traded funds, credit default swaps). Market timing strategies can be generally categorized on the following dimensions:

- *Time horizon.* Market strategies can range from very short term, measured in minutes or even seconds, to very long term, where investors are betting on markets turning around over a period of years.
- *Single market versus multiple markets.* A few decades ago, market timing was defined almost exclusively in terms of equity markets, with an even tighter focus on domestic equities. Today, there are investors who not only look across global equity markets but across asset classes, buying and selling currencies, commodities, fixed income, and equities, depending on their views on each market.
- *Defensive versus aggressive market timing.* In defensive market timing, your key objective is protecting your portfolio from markets moving in the wrong direction. Thus, if you are invested in stocks and believe that equity markets are poised to decline, you may sell stocks or buy put options on stocks to protect yourself from losses. With aggressive market timing, your objectives are broader and you hope to use your market views to add to your returns.

Until a few years ago individual investors were restricted to narrower market timing strategies by cost and access restrictions, but now it is possible for anyone to be a macro market timer.

The Details

There are at least four ways you can time markets, with varying degrees of risk associated with each. The first way is to adjust your mix of assets, allocating more than you normally would (given your time horizon and risk preferences) to markets that you believe are undervalued and less than you normally would to markets that are overvalued. The second approach is to switch investment styles and strategies within a market (usually stocks) to reflect expected market performance. The third is to shift your funds within the equity market from sector to sector, depending on your expectations of future economic and market growth. The fourth and most risky way to time markets is to speculate on market direction, using either borrowed money (leverage) or derivatives to magnify profits.

Asset Allocation The simplest way of incorporating market timing into investment strategies is to alter the mix of assets—stocks, cash, bonds, and other assets—in your portfolio. In fact, we judged the capacity of mutual fund managers and investment newsletters to time the market by looking at whether changes that they recommended in the asset allocation mix were useful predictors or future market movements. The limitation of this strategy is that it can be costly to alter holdings in individual asset classes, since you may have to liquidate assets in one class and invest in assets in another. It can also take time to put into practice. As a consequence, asset allocation works better with long-term than with short-term market timing.

Style Switching There are some investment strategies that do well in bull markets and others that do better in bear markets. If you can identify when markets are overvalued or undervalued, you could shift from one strategy to another or even from one investment philosophy to another just in time for a market shift.

For instance, in our discussion of growth versus value strategies in Chapter 9, we noted the research done by Richard Bernstein, which showed that growth investing does better that value investing when earnings growth is low for the entire market and that value investing beats growth investing when earnings growth is high. Bernstein also notes that growth investing tends to do much better when the yield curve is flat or downward sloping. In a related result, Pradhuman presents evidence that small cap investing yields higher returns than value investing when inflation is high and bond default spreads are low. You could take advantage of your market timing skills to shift from growth to value investing if you believe that markets are overvalued and headed for a correction, or from value to growth investing if you consider them undervalued and likely to go up. In a paper that examines the payoff to style timing, Kao and Shumaker estimate the returns an investor would have made if she had switched with perfect foresight from 1979 to 1997 from value to growth stocks and back for both small-cap and large-cap stocks.[35] The annual returns from a perfect foresight strategy each year would have been 20.86 percent for large-cap stocks and 27.30 percent for small-cap stocks. In contrast, the average annual return across all stocks was only 10.33 percent over the period.

While this strategy looks promising, there may be less to it than meets the eye. In addition to the higher transaction costs and taxes that come with switching from one investment style to another, you also have the problem that most switches occur after the fact, reflecting not market timing skills but reaction to market performance. Thus, value investors seem to switch to growth investing after a market slowdown has occurred and not in advance of a slowdown, and growth investors switch to value investing well into a bull market. If, in fact, if you do have skills as a market timer that make you confident enough to switch investment styles, you could argue that you would get a much bigger payoff by speculating, using index futures or options.

Sector Rotation   There are some investors who believe that staying out of the market because of their views on the market—that it is either too costly (because of the possibility that they could be wrong) or not feasible (because they are required to invest in the market). They may be able to parlay their market timing skills into superior returns by switching across sectors of the market as their view of the market changes. Thus, if they believe that the market will increase in the coming periods, due to stronger than expected real economic growth, they may switch into cyclical sectors. Alternatively, if their view is that interest rates will go up in the coming year and this will cause the market to drop, they may switch out of financial stocks into companies that are less sensitive to interest rates (e.g., consumer products).

While there are undoubtedly differences across sector rotation models, Stovall provides an excellent summary of the conventional wisdom on which sectors do best at each stage of the market in his book on sector rotation.[36] Figure 12.10 is extracted from his book.

Note that the market lead is captured by the fact that the market both bottoms out and peaks before the economy. Your sector bets reflect this leading effect. You invest in cyclicals as the economy enters a recession (and the market hits bottom) and you shift into industrial and energy companies as the economy improves. If you can pick the right sectors to invest in each period, you would undoubtedly earn very high returns. For instance, a

---

[35]D. Kao and R. D. Shumaker, "Equity Style Timing (Corrected)," *Financial Analysts Journal* 55 (1999): 37–48.
[36]S. Stovall, *Sector Investing* (New York: McGraw-Hill, 1996).

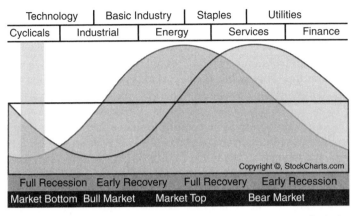

FIGURE 12.10 Sector Rotation—Sector Emphasis as a Function of Market Cycle
Source: S. Stovall, *Sector Investing* (New York: McGraw-Hill, 1996).

strategy where you would have invested in only the best-performing sectors each year from 1970 to 1977 instead of the S&P 500 would have generated excess returns of 289 percent.[37] While this may not be feasible, investing in sectors that have done well in recent periods seems to provide at least short-term excess returns to investors.[38]

Building on the last point, sector rotation is not always based on market timing views. There are some investors who use the stock selection approaches described in earlier chapters to pick sectors to invest in. For instance, investors who believe in price momentum may invest in sectors that have done well in the recent past, whereas those who are contrarians may invest in the sectors that delivered the worst performance in prior periods.

Speculation The most direct way to take advantage of your market timing abilities is to buy assets in a market that you believe is undervalued and sell assets in one that you believe is overvalued. In the past decade, this is the strategy that has been adopted by market timing hedge funds to trade across equity, bond, and currency markets to take advantage of what they see as potential mispricing, with varying degrees of success. Success can generate large returns because you have relatively little equity invested and because

[37] J. Farreell, "Homogeneous Stock Groupings: Implications for Portfolio Management," *Financial Analysts Journal* 31 (1975): 50–62.

[38] E. H. Sorensen and T. Burke, "Portfolio Returns from Active Industry Group Rotation," *Financial Analysts Journal* 46 (1986): 43–50. They report superior returns for at least two quarters from investing in industry groups that have done well in recent periods.

you benefit from both sides of the transactions—the undervalued markets increasing and the overvalued markets decreasing.

What can go wrong? The high leverage implicit in strategies where you buy some investments and sell short others exaggerates the effects of both success and failure. Thus, while the payoff to predicting markets is very large, the cost of failure is also very large. Whether you should adopt a speculative strategy based on market timing is entirely dependent on how confident you are about your predictions. The more confidence you have in your market timing abilities, the more leverage you can use in your strategies. Reviewing the empirical evidence on the performance of market timing strategies, it is quite clear that there are very few strategies that yield high success rates in equity markets. In contrast, though, there seem to be strategies that work a high percentage of the time in the currency and commodity markets. It should come as no surprise, therefore, that some of the biggest successes of hedge funds in market timing have come in these markets. Even in these markets, though, as the number of hedge funds increases, the potential for excess returns decreases.

MARKET TIMING INSTRUMENTS

Until a few decades ago, investors intent on timing markets could change the mix of assets in their portfolios, shifting toward stocks if they thought that equities were underpriced and away from stocks if they perceived them to be expensive. In fact, investors who were very bearish on stocks had to sell short on individual stocks, an expensive and risky strategy. In the past three decades, the instruments available for market timing have proliferated, starting with futures on stock market indexes in the early 1980s, expanding to include options on these indexes and other financial assets in later years, and then extending in the past decade to exchange-traded funds and credit default swaps.

Futures

Investors have used futures contracts on commodities and currencies for decades, perhaps even centuries, to make bets on market direction, but futures contracts on financial assets are of more recent vintage. The first widely traded futures contract on a stock index was the futures contract on the S&P 500 introduced by the Chicago Mercantile Exchange (CME). Since then, however, futures have been added not only on other stock market indexes in the United States but also on many foreign equity exchanges and on fixed income securities.

If you are a market timer, especially one who trades across asset classes, futures contracts offer you many advantages. First, there are futures contracts on every asset class—commodities, currencies, fixed income, equities, and even real estate—allowing you to go either long or short on whichever asset classes you choose. Second, since you have to put up only a small percentage of the value of a futures contract, you can leverage your bets, thus making your upside that much more lucrative, assuming that your market timing skills hold up. Third, the futures markets are generally liquid, with heavy trading volume, allowing you to make large bets on market direction without a price impact and at low cost. Fourth, on a related note, the convenience of being able to trade entire indexes at low cost allows you to make short-term market timing bets, ranging from hours down to minutes and even seconds. Finally, access to futures markets has leveled the playing field for bulls and bears, allowing the latter to make their bets with just as much as ease as the former.

There are costs that have come with the growth of futures markets. First, the ease and low cost with which investors can time markets has democratized the process. Put differently, anyone can be a market timer, eliminating the advantages that institutional investors used to have over individual investors, especially when making negative bets on market direction. Second, the leveraged bets that futures markets allow investors to make come with a dark underside, where market movements in the wrong direction can lead to margin calls and forced liquidation of positions earlier than desired. Third, there is evidence that futures markets can affect spot prices, with the feedback sometimes increasing volatility and destabilizing the spot markets. Thus, if stocks start going down and institutional investors collectively try to sell index futures to protect themselves against further falls, the herd effect can cause index futures prices to plummet, which, in turn, can cause the spot index to fall even further.

Options

Shortly after the introduction of futures contracts on the S&P 500, the first options contracts on the index were offered by the Chicago Board Options Exchange (CBOE). As with the futures contracts, you can now buy or sell call and put options on other equity indexes and asset classes.

Options provide many of the same advantages that futures contracts offer, allowing investors to make large positive or negative bets, with liquidity and low costs. They can also sometimes destabilize the underlying asset markets and have feedback effects. There are, however, dimensions on which options and futures are different, and these differences can lead investors to pick one over the other. The most critical difference is on the potential costs of being wrong on market direction. With futures contracts, that cost can be large and unpredictable since you have to cover future price movements in the wrong direction. With options contracts, the cost is limited to the price you paid for the options if you are a call buyer. However, the trade-off is that a futures contract is essentially costless, though you are required to put up a margin to ensure that you honor the contract. Buying a call or a put option will cost you, with the cost increasing as a function of the volatility of the underlying index of asset class.

So, assuming that you are bullish about a market, should you buy futures or call options? Conversely, if you are bearish, should you sell futures or buy put options? To make that decision, you have to consider two factors. The first is the degree of certainty you possess about your market timing abilities: the more certain you feel, the greater the payoff to using futures instead of options. The second factor is the price you are paying for the downside protection on options. If you feel that options are overpriced (i.e., that the implied volatility in the options is much higher than the true volatility), you will be more likely to use futures contracts.

Exchange-Traded Funds (ETFs)

An exchange-traded fund is essentially what it claims to be, a market-traded security that tracks a market. It is generally created by a sponsor, who chooses both the index that the ETF will track and a method for tracking the index. Between 2000 and 2010, the number of ETFs increased from 80 to 923 and the amount invested in ETFs increased from $60 billion to more than a trillion. The first ETF, created in 1993, tracked the S&P 500, but you can now buy and sell ETFs on almost every asset class and subclass: sectors, commodities, global equities, fixed income.

Since ETFs can be used by market timers to make bets on the underlying markets, it is worth examining the trade-off on using ETFs instead of derivatives (futures or options). Like options contracts, ETFs offer you the benefits of knowing your costs with certainty at the time of the investment, though borrowing money to buy ETFs can make these costs uncertain. Like futures contracts, ETFs do not require you to pay a time premium to make a market bet. Unlike options or futures, which have finite lives, you can hold an ETF for any period you choose. Ultimately, the pricing of indexes, options, futures, and ETFs is all linked together by arbitrage, since you can create your own synthetic version of any of them by using the others. Consequently, it is unlikely that any of them is going to offer you an incredible bargain. The choice then has to be made on your comfort level with each alternative, the liquidity in each market, and your time horizon as an investor, with ETFs being more suited for investors who want to make longer-term bets.

CONNECTING MARKET TIMING TO SECURITY SELECTION

Can you be both a market timer and a stock picker? We don't see why not, since they are not mutually exclusive philosophies. In fact, the same beliefs about markets that led you to become a security selector may also lead you to become a market timer. For example, if you believe that markets overreact to new information, you may buy stocks after big negative earnings surprises, but you may also buy the entire market after negative economic or employment reports. In fact, there are many investors who combine asset allocation and security selection in a coherent investment strategy.

There are, however, two caveats to an investment philosophy that includes this combination. First, to the extent that you have differing skills as a market timer and as a security selector, you have to gauge where your differential advantage lies, since you have limited time and resources to direct toward your task of building a portfolio. Second, you may find that your attempts at market timing are undercutting your stock picking and that your overall returns suffer as a consequence. If this is the case, you should abandon market timing and focus exclusively on security selection.

CONCLUSION

Everyone wants to time markets, and it is not difficult to see the reasons for the allure. A successful market timer can deliver very high returns with relatively little effort. The cost of market timing, though, is high in terms of transaction costs (higher turnover ratios and tax bills) and opportunity costs (staying out of the market in years in which the market goes up). In fact, you need to be right about two-thirds of the time for market timing to pay off.

If you do decide to time markets, you have a wide range of market timing tools. Some are nonfinancial and range from the spurious like the Super Bowl indicator (whose correlation with the market is pure chance) to feel-good indicators (that measure the mood of people and thus the level of the market) to hype indicators (such as cocktail party chatter). Some market timing is centered around the macroeconomic variables that affect stock prices—interest rates and economic growth—with the intuitive argument that you buy stocks when interest rates are low and in advance of robust economic growth. While the intuition may be impeccable, markets are tough to time because they are based on predictions of these variables. Thus, high economic growth, by itself, may not lead to higher stock prices if the growth was less than anticipated. One way to incorporate forecasted growth and risk into the analysis is to estimate the intrinsic value of the market; that is, value the market as the present value of the expected cash flows you would get from investing in it. While this may yield good long-term predictions, a better way of getting short-term predictions may be an assessment of the value of the market, relative to its own standing in prior years and to other markets.

While the menu may be varied when it comes market timing strategies, there is little evidence of actual market timing success, even when we focus on those who claim to have the most expertise at it. Collectively, mutual funds seem to exhibit reverse market timing skills at worst, and neutral market timing skills at best, switching out of stocks (and into cash) just before big up movements in the markets and doing the opposite before stock price declines. Even those mutual funds that market themselves as market timers—the tactical asset allocation funds—do not add any value from market timing. The asset allocation advice that comes from investment newsletters and market strategists also seems to suffer from the same problem of no payoffs.

If you believe that you are the exception to this general rule of failure and that you can time markets, you can do it with varying degrees of gusto. The simplest strategy is to alter your asset allocation mix to reflect your market views, but this may require you to be out of stocks for extended periods. If you want to be fully invested in equities, you can try to switch investment styles ahead of market moves, moving from value investing (in periods of high earnings growth) to growth investing (if growth levels off) or shift your money across sectors of the market. Finally, if you have enough faith in your market timing abilities to pull it off, you can buy undervalued and sell overvalued markets, and make significant profits when they converge. The risk, of course, is that they will diverge instead and that you will see your portfolio suffer as a consequence.

EXERCISES

1. Do you think that you can time markets? It not, why not? If yes, why do you think that you can?
2. If you believe that you can time markets, try answering the following questions:
   a. Is your market timing restricted to one market (say, the stock market) or do you use it across markets (commodities, bonds, currencies, etc.)?
   b. What indicator or indicators do you use in determining that a market is mispriced? Why do you think it works?

    c. Are there any potential costs that you see from timing markets? If yes, how do you try to minimize these costs?
3. Assuming that you try to time markets, address the following:
    a. Is your market timing long term or short term? Is it defensive (to protect against losses) or aggressive (to augment profits)?
    b. Which market timing approach (asset allocation, speculation) do you use?
    c. What market timing instruments (ETFs, derivatives) do you employ? Why?
4. Pick a market timer who is in the news right now (usually because the timer got the last market move right). What market timing indicator does he or she use to time markets? What track record does he or she have over the long term?

Lessons for Investors

To be a successful market timer, you have to:

- *Be right about two-thirds of the time:* The payoff to timing markets correctly is high, but the cost of getting it wrong is also high. The payoff comes from staying out of the market in bad years, but the cost is that you may stay out of the market in good years.
- *Find an indicator that works consistently:* There are dozens of indicators that are used to time markets, but few of them seem to work consistently over long periods. Even those that do only give you a sense of direction (up or down) but not of magnitude (how much up or how much down).
- *Recognize that you do not have many successful role models:* Attempts at market timing on the part of professionals—money managers, investment newsletters, and market strategists—have generally failed. Most of them tend to follow markets rather than lead them.

CHAPTER 13

Ready to Give Up?
The Allure of Indexing

Many investors begin life as active investors, convinced that they can beat the market, and end up conceding failure in this quest. For such investors and for those who never believed that they had a chance of beating the market, the most practical alternative is investing in an index fund. An index fund is designed to mimic an index and generate returns that are equal to the index (and not beat it). While we give up the chance of ever beating the market with an index fund, we do gain some significant benefits. First, there are almost no trading costs since there is little portfolio turnover, other than adding new stocks to the index and shedding those that leave. Second, their low turnover makes index funds more tax efficient than other funds.

Index funds were created in the early 1970s and have swiftly caught on as an investment alternative. Ironically, the performance of active investors and money managers provides the best endorsement for index funds. The returns earned by active money managers have trailed the return on the S&P 500 index for much of the past few decades. In addition, the market timing abilities of money managers seem to be limited. Under such circumstances, you can and should ask whether it makes sense to pay active money managers to lose money for you.

THE MECHANICS OF INDEXING

How do you go about creating an index fund, and once created, how do you maintain it? Note than for an index fund to mimic an index, you not only need to hold every stock in the index, but the proportion invested in each stock also has to match up to the weighting of the stock in the index. In this section, we first explore how you would create an index fund that has these characteristics and then look at why some index funds may choose not to fully replicate the index that they purport to follow.

A Fully Indexed Fund

A fully indexed fund is relatively simple to create once the index to be replicated has been identified. There are three steps in the process. The first step is to obtain information on what stocks (or assets) go into the index and their weights in the index. Note that weighting schemes vary widely across indexes. Some indexes weight stocks based on their market capitalizations (S&P 500), some are price weighted index (Dow 30), and some are based on market float (New York Stock Exchange Composite). There are even indexes where the weights are based on trading volume on the exchange. The second step is to invest the fund in each of the stocks in the index, in exactly the same proportions that they are weighted in the index. An index fund has to be fully invested in the index, since cash holdings can cause the fund's returns to deviate from those of the index.

Once the index fund is created, there are two maintenance requirements. First, indexes change over time, as some firms are removed from the index due to acquisitions, due to bankruptcies, or because they no longer meet the criteria for the index, and new firms are added. As the index changes, the index fund will have to change as well—the deleted firms will have to be sold and the added firms will have to be acquired. While changes are relatively rare for well-established and mature indexes such as the S&P 500, they can be much more frequent for indexes that track changing or growing markets (as is the case with technology or emerging market indexes). The second requirement is that the weights in the fund will have to be monitored and adjusted to reflect changes in the weights of the ingredients of the index. One of the advantages of indexing a market-capitalization-weighted fund is that it is self-adjusting. In other words, if one stock doubles and another stock halves, the changes in their weighting in the index fund will mirror changes in the weighting in the index.

A Sampled Index Fund

In some cases, it may not be practical to construct a fully indexed fund. If you are replicating an index that contains thousands of stocks, such as the Wilshire 5000 index or an index of illiquid assets or stocks, the transaction cost of creating and maintaining the index might be very large. One way around this problem is to create a fund that looks very much like the index but does not quite replicate this. You can accomplish this objective by sampling the index and buying some of the stocks listed in the index. Vanguard, which has long been the leader in the index fund business, uses sampling for its Total Market Fund that attempts to replicate the performance of all stocks traded in the United States, as well as its small stock and European index funds.

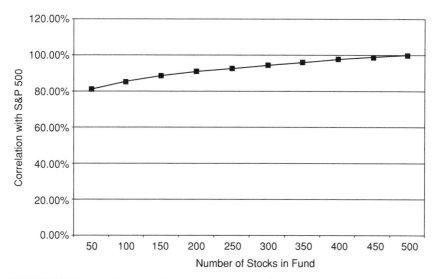

FIGURE 13.1   Correlation with the S&P 500 Index

How close can you get to the index with a sampled index fund? One way to measure the closeness is to measure the correlation between an index fund and the index that it tracks. A fully indexed fund should have a correlation of 100 percent, but a sampled index fund can get very close even with a much smaller number of stocks. Figure 13.1 presents the correlation between a sampled index fund and the S&P 500 as a function of the number of stocks in the index fund.

Note that the correlation is fairly high even with 50 stocks and very quickly converges to 100 percent.

A HISTORY OF INDEXING

In many ways, index funds owe their existence to the early research done on efficient markets by academics. Prior to the 1960s, the conventional wisdom was that you entrusted your savings to money managers on Wall Street and they delivered high returns in exchange for management fees and transaction costs. No individual investor, it was believed, could compete against these professionals. As financial economics came into being as a discipline in the 1950s and 1960s, researchers increasingly found evidence to the contrary. In fact, the efficient market hypothesis, which argued that market prices were the best estimates of value and that all of the time and resources spent by money managers trying to pick stocks was in vain, acquired a strong following. While most practitioners remained resistant to the notion that markets were efficient, there were some who saw opportunities in these academic findings. If diversification was the primary source of portfolio gains and picking stocks was not a fruitful exercise, why not create funds that were centered on diversification and minimize transaction costs? Indexing was initially made available to institutional investors in 1971, and soon individual investors were able to play the indexing game when the Vanguard 500 Index fund made its debut in 1976. Over the past three decades, it has grown to become the second largest equity fund in the world, with about $93 billion in assets in November 2011. Index funds have also widened their reach beyond the S&P 500, with 63 percent of all U.S. index funds invested in non–S&P 500 stocks, including other domestic equities (32 percent), global equities (13 percent), and bonds (19 percent) at the end of 2010.

In the past three decades, index funds have gradually increased their share of the overall market not only for individual investors' savings but for pension and insurance money; the percentage of money invested in index funds, as a percentage of total money invested in mutual funds, has increased from 5.2 percent in 1995 to 14.5 percent in 2010; among just equity funds, index funds now account for almost 25 percent of invested money. This is not to suggest that index funds have not had their ebbs and flows. The initial impetus for index funds came from the abysmal returns delivered by portfolio managers in the 1970s. While many of these portfolio managers cannot be faulted for not seeing the long-running bear market and high inflation of the period, the subpar returns did draw attention to their management fees. Ever since, the growth of index funds seems to slow in boom periods (the early 1980s and the later 1990s), when it looks like active money management can pay off, and picks up again when markets stagnate or decline. Figure 13.2 graphs out the growth of index funds from 1993 to 2010, broken down by category.

The choices in index funds have proliferated, and you now see funds indexed to almost every conceivable index. For instance, Vanguard offered 48 index fund choices for investors in November 2011, with choices across capitalization (small-cap, mid-cap, and large-cap), return objective (dividends versus capital appreciation), style (value versus growth), global (domestic and international), and asset class (equities, bond, and balanced) funds. It even offers a social index fund, composed of mid-cap and large-cap companies that have been screened to meet social, human rights, and environmental criteria. Most of these funds are sampled funds rather than fully indexed funds, and some have restrictions on withdrawals. While we have used the Vanguard funds to illustrate the diversity of choices when it comes to index funds today, there are other fund families that also have started competing for this very large market.

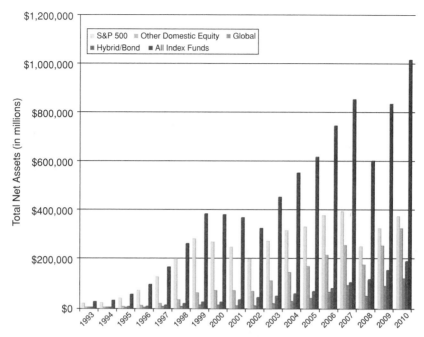

FIGURE 13.2 Total Net Assets—U.S. Index Funds at the End of 2010
Source: Investment Company Institute.

ARE ALL INDEX FUNDS ALIKE?

You would expect index funds that replicate the same index to be perfect substitutes for each other, but they are not. In other words, differences seem to remain, albeit small, between two index funds that replicate the same index. The first difference is in transaction costs, with some funds reporting much lower transaction costs than others. A perusal of all S&P 500 index funds listed on the Morningstar database in November 2011 indicates that annual returns on these funds lag the index by margins ranging from 10 basis points to 30 basis points or more; this is a simple measure of the transaction costs at these funds. The cost differences can be traced to economies of scale (larger index funds should be able to spread their fixed costs across more investors) and to execution efficiencies (Vanguard, with its long experience in the index fund business, has much lower execution costs).

(continued)

The second difference is in how closely the funds track the index. You can measure this by looking at the R-squared of the funds. A perfect index fund should have an R-squared of 100 percent, but some index funds fall short. Some do because they use sampling for larger indexes, and the more inefficient their sampling the system, the lower the R-squared will be. Others that try to replicate the entire index still fail because of execution lags and because remittances and withdrawals prevent them from being fully invested in the index. Using the Morningstar database again, the R-squared for S&P 500 index funds range from a low of 97 percent to a high of 100 percent. As an investor looking at index funds on a specific index, you want to pick the fund with the lowest expenses and an R-squared close to 100 percent.

THE CASE FOR INDEXING

The case for indexing ironically is best made by active investors, who try to beat the market and often fail badly. This seems to be true not just for individual investors but also for the professional money managers. In this section, we consider the depressing evidence that notwithstanding the numerous inefficiencies that academics and practitioners claim to find in markets, usually in paper portfolios in hypothetical studies, converting these paper profits to real profits seems to be very difficult to do.

Individual Investors

There are thousands of individual investors who attempt every day to pick stocks that they believe will do better than the market. The systems they use for stock picking run the gamut from the naive to the sophisticated. Some base their stock picks on tips from friends—insider trading with six degrees of separation—whereas others use rigorous quantitative analysis. Aided by easier access to data, more powerful personal computers, and online (and cheaper) trading, individual investors have narrowed the gap between themselves and those on Wall Street. But is this a good thing? Are investors earning higher returns than they used to?

These questions have been partially answered by researchers who gained access to the brokerage accounts of 78,000 clients of a large discount brokerage service. Barber and Odean examined the trading records of individuals who used this brokerage service in a series of papers and came to several interesting conclusions:

- The average individual investor does not beat the market, after netting out trading costs. Between 1991 and 1996, for instance, the annual net (of transaction costs) return on an S&P 500 index fund was 17.8 percent whereas the average investor trading at the brokerage house had a net return of 16.4 percent.[1]
- The more individual investors trade, the lower their returns tend to be. In fact, the returns before transaction costs are accounted for are lower for more active traders than they are for less active traders. After transaction costs are accounted for, the returns to active trading get even worse.
- Pooling the talents and strengths of individual investors into investment clubs does not result in better returns. Barber and Odean examined the performance of 166 randomly selected investment clubs that used the discount brokerage house. Between 1991 and 1996, these investment clubs had a net annual return of 14.1 percent, underperforming the S&P 500 (17.8 percent) and individual investors (16.4 percent).

There was one hopeful note in the study. The top-performing quartile of individual investors do outperform the market by about 6 percent a month. Building on that theme, other studies of individual investors find that they generate relatively high returns when they invest in companies close to their homes compared to the stocks of distant companies,[2] and that investors with more concentrated portfolios outperform those with more diversified portfolios.[3] Finally, a study of 16,668 individual trader accounts at a large discount brokerage house finds that the top 10 percent of traders in this group outperform the bottom 10 percent by about 8 percent per year over a long period.[4]

---

[1] B. M. Barber and T. Odean, "Too Many Cooks Spoil the Profits," *Financial Analysts Journal* 57 (2000): 17–25.

[2] Zoran Ivkovich and Scott Weisbenner, "Local Does as Local Is: Information Content of the Geography of Individual Investors' Common Stock Investments," *Journal of Finance* 60 (2005): 267–306.

[3] Zoran Ivkovich, Clemens Sialm, and Scott Weisbenner, "Portfolio Concentration and the Performance of Individual Investors" (working paper, University of Illinois at Urbana-Champaign, 2005).

[4] J. D. Coval, D. A. Hirshleifer, and T. Shumway, "Can Individual Investors Beat the Market?" (SSRN Working Paper 364000, 2005).

In summary, while there is a small subset of individual investors who are disciplined enough to beat the market even after incorporating transaction costs, the average individual investor does not beat the market and the degree of underperformance increases with trading activity.

Professional Money Managers

There are many who would view the evidence in the preceding section as predictable. After all, individual investors are amateurs without the access to the information and trading resources available to mutual fund and pension fund managers (i.e., professional money managers). Professional money managers are supposed to be better informed and smarter, have lower transaction costs, and be better investors overall than individual investors. In fact, based on this belief, we trust money managers with our savings, pay large fees for money manager expertise, and tolerate large transaction costs and taxes. In return, we would expect actively run funds to do better than index funds that mimic the market.

Does the Average Mutual Fund Beat the Market?

Until the 1960s, the conventional wisdom that professional money managers did much better than individual investors was widely accepted but not really tested, partly because the data were not available and partly because the tools for testing the proposition were not developed. The development of the capital asset pricing model (CAPM), in conjunction with access to data and statistical packages, allowed Michael Jensen to conduct one of the first studies of mutual funds in 1968.[5] He examined the returns earned by mutual funds from 1955 to 1964 and compared them to what you would have expected them to earn, given their risk exposure. The expected returns for each fund were calculated using the beta that estimated for the fund and the capital asset pricing model. In fact, the difference between the actual return and the expected return from the CAPM is still called Jensen's alpha, reflecting the influence this study had on empirical finance for the next three decades. His findings, summarized in Figure 13.3 as excess returns on mutual funds, were that the average portfolio manager underperformed the market between 1955 and 1964.

Note that an excess return less than 0 indicates that a mutual fund underperformed the market. By this measure, more than 60 percent of the mutual funds underperformed the market and the average fund delivered returns that were about 1 to 2 percent less than expected.

---

[5]M. Jensen, "The Performance of Mutual Funds in the Period 1945–1964," *Journal of Finance* 2 (1968): 389–416.

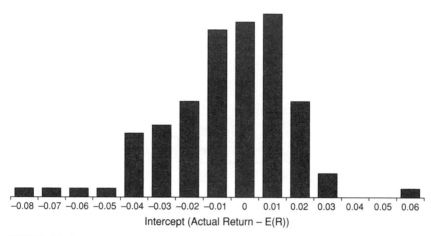

FIGURE 13.3 Mutual Fund Performance, 1955 to 1964: The Jensen Study
Source: M. Jensen, "The Performance of Mutual Funds in the Period 1945–64," *Journal of Finance* 2 (1968): 389–416.

These results when published created a controversy that has never quite died out. On the one hand, you have many academics and some practitioners arguing that there is no value added by active money managers. On the other, active money managers have come up with a number of problems they have with the Jensen study, and argue that fixing these problems will reveal to the world the extent of the excess returns they generate. Burton Malkiel updated this study to look at mutual funds from 1971 to 1991.[6] His conclusion is slightly more positive, in the sense that he finds that prior to management expenses, the average mutual fund matches the market. After expenses, though, the average mutual fund underperforms the market by about 1 percent.[7] In a study that both updates the numbers to today and globalizes the findings, Ferreira, Keswani, Miguel, and Ramox look at mutual funds in 27 countries and find that they collectively underperform market indexes by 0.20 percent; excluding the United States, the underperformance is 0.10 percent.[8]

---

[6]B. G. Malkier, "Returns from Investing in Equity Mutual Funds 1971 to 1991," *Journal of Finance* 40 (1995): 529–572.
[7]This is based on using the Wilshire 5000 as the index. The underperformance is much greater (about 3.20 percent) when the S&P 500 is used as the index.
[8]M. A. Ferreira, A. Keswani, A. F. Miguel, and S. B. Ramos, "The Determinants of Mutual Fund Performance: A Cross-Country Study" (SSRN Working Paper 947098, 2011).

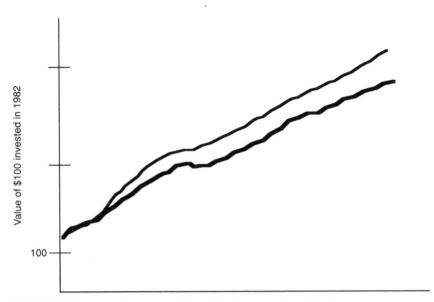

FIGURE 13.4 Actively Managed Bond Funds versus Bond Index
Source: J. C. Bogle, *Bogle on Mutual Funds* (Homewood, IL: Richard D. Irwin, 1994).

Does active money management work better in the bond markets? Figure 13.4 compares the performance of actively managed bond fund to the Lehman Index (a widely used index of bonds that has since been renamed for obvious reasons) between 1983 and 1992.[9]

Over this 10-year period, the average actively managed bond fund underperformed the bond index by about 1.5 percent a year; $100 invested in the bond index would have grown to $303 by the end of the period, whereas it would have an ending value of $263 if managed by the actively run bond funds. This result has been replicated by other studies.

Measurement Issues The Jensen study was revolutionary for introducing the notion of risk-adjusted returns to empirical research but it was also limited on a number of dimensions. First, its focus on betas and the capital asset pricing model allowed money managers to claim that the results reflected failures in the model rather than in their performance. Second, the sample used in the Jensen study was a fairly small one and it did not factor in returns from funds that may have been in existence in 1955 but failed before 1964. This problem is referred to as survivor bias. Note that this is

---

[9]J. C. Bogle, *Bogle on Mutual Funds* (Homewood, IL: Richard D. Irwin, 1994).

likely to make the results more negative rather than less negative since it is the poorest-performing funds that usually fail. In this section, we will look at studies that have tried to use alternative measures of risk and control for survivor bias.

Excess Return Measurement   In the past two decades, evidence has steadily accumulated on the limitations of the capital asset pricing model and its failure to explain the returns of stocks, especially small cap and low P/E ratio stocks. This has provided ammunition for money managers who have wanted to debunk the evidence in Jensen's study. However, there seems to be little evidence that using alternative measures of excess returns generates results that are more positive for money managers. Let us consider a few of these measures:

- *Comparison to the market.* Since any risk and return model is likely to come under assault for one weakness or another, you could revert back to a much simpler comparison of returns on mutual funds to a broad index such as the S&P 500. John Bogle, who pioneered passive investing when he led Vanguard, noted in his book on investing that 166 of 205 mutual funds underperformed the Wilshire 5000 between 1983 and 1992. In Figure 13.5, we report on the percentage of active mutual funds that are outperformed by the S&P 500 each year from 1971 to 2010. Note that more than 50 percent of the active funds beat the S&P 500 in only 13 out of the 40 years. Defenders of mutual fund managers will undoubtedly argue that this measure is biased against mutual funds because they hold cash. Since many of these funds choose to hold cash as a market timing device, we have little sympathy for that point of view.
- *Other risk measures.* The Sharpe ratio, which is computed by dividing the excess return on a portfolio by its standard deviation; the Treynor measure, which divides the excess return by the beta; and the appraisal ratio, which divides the alpha from the regression by the standard deviation, can be considered close relatives of Jensen's alpha and were discussed in Chapter 6. Studies using all three of these alternative measures conclude that mutual funds continue to underperform the market.[10] In a study that examined the sensitivity of the conclusion to alternative risk and return models, Lehmann and Modest computed the abnormal

---

[10]Sharpe used the ratio in 1966 to evaluate 34 mutual funds to conclude that they underperformed the market. Treynor used his index to come to same conclusion a few years later.

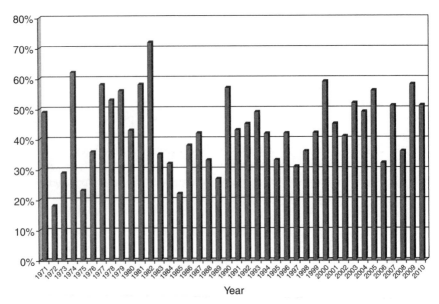

FIGURE 13.5 Percent of Money Managers Who Beat the S&P 500
Source: S&P SPIVA Report.

return earned by mutual funds using the arbitrage pricing model for 130 mutual funds from 1969 to 1982.[11] While the magnitude of the abnormal returns earned is sensitive to alternative specifications of the model, every specification of the model yields negative excess returns.

- *Expanded proxy models.* In Chapter 2, we referenced the study by Fama and French that found that small-capitalization stocks with low price-to-book value ratios earned much higher returns than you would have predicted with the capital asset pricing model. In Chapter 7, we also noted the evidence that has accumulated on price momentum; stocks that have done well recently are more likely to continue to do well, at least in the short term. If you do not control for these well-known empirical irregularities, you are likely to find negative excess returns in mutual funds that invest in large-capitalization stocks with high price-to-book ratios. Carhart used a four-factor model, including beta, market capitalization, price-to-book ratios, and price momentum as factors, and concluded that the average mutual fund still underperformed

---

[11]B. N. Lehmann and D. M. Modest, "Mutual Fund Performance Evaluation: A Comparison of Benchmarks and Benchmark Comparisons," *Journal of Finance* 42 (1987): 233–265.

the market by about 1.80 percent a year. In other words, you cannot blame empirical irregularities for the underperformance of mutual funds.[12]

Given this evidence, it seems safe to conclude that the poor performance attributed to mutual funds cannot be blamed on researchers using the wrong benchmarks for comparison.

Survivor Bias   One of the limitations of many studies of mutual funds is that they use only mutual funds that have data available for a sample period and are in existence at the end of the sample period. Many databases of mutual funds report only on live funds and remove funds that cease operations. Since the funds that fail are likely to be the poorest performers, there is likely to be a bias introduced in the returns that we compute for funds. In particular, we are likely to overestimate the returns earned by mutual funds by focusing only on the survivors. While this topic has been studied by numerous researchers, the first comprehensive study of survivor bias was by Carhart (referenced earlier) who examined all equity mutual funds (including failed funds) from January 1962 to December 1995. Over that period, approximately 3.6 percent of the funds in existence failed each year, and they tended to be smaller and riskier than the average fund in the sample. In addition, and this is important for the survivor bias issue, about 80 percent of the nonsurviving funds underperformed other mutual funds in the five years preceding their failure. Ignoring them, as many studies do when computing the average annual return from holding mutual funds, results in annual returns being overstated by 0.17 percent with a one-year sample period to more than 1 percent with 20-year time horizons. In practical terms, this would mean that if we found mutual funds to have underperformed the market by 1 percent a year over the past 20 years and we ignored the failed funds, the real underperformance would be closer to 2 percent a year.

Performance by Subcategories   It may not surprise some that the average fund does not do much better than the market. After all, you could argue that when institutional investors account for 60 to 65 percent of the overall market, it will be difficult for them to collectively beat the market. In fact, Charles Ellis has a provocative treatise on money management that is titled *Winning the Loser's Game* that makes exactly this point and should be

---

[12]Mark M. Carhart, "On Persistence in Mutual Fund Performance," *Journal of Finance* 52 (1997): 57–82.

TABLE 13.1 Excess Returns by Market Capitalization and Style, 2007 to 2011

	Value	Blend	Growth
Large-cap funds	−2.90%	−1.03%	0.49%
Mid-cap funds	−1.30%	0.25%	2.08%
Small-cap funds	−0.37%	−0.08%	1.08%

required reading for anyone embarking on a money management career.[13] You may still believe that there are subsets of funds or superior fund managers that consistently beat the market. In this section, we consider a number of subsets of funds and examine their performance relative to the market.

By Market Capitalization Do mutual funds that invest in small-cap companies do better than those that invest in large-cap companies? After all, small-cap companies are the ones where active investing should be most likely to pay off, since there is at least the possibility that investors have overlooked key fundamentals about the company. On a raw return basis, the answer seems to be yes. On an excess return basis, the answer depends on how you adjust for risk. Table 13.1 summarizes the excess returns (using the capital asset pricing model) for small-cap, mid-cap, and large-cap funds, categorized by investment style from 2007 to 2011.

Small-cap funds do better than large-cap funds, and growth funds outperform value funds, but the results should not be surprising since the capital asset pricing model consistently yields lower expected returns for small-cap and low-P/E stocks. When a three-factor or four-factor model that corrects for this bias is used to compute excess returns, these differences either narrow or disappear.

We also looked at the simple measure that we introduced in the preceding section—the percentage of actively managed funds that beat the index, as computed by Standard & Poor's (S&P). To make the comparison fair, S&P used different indexes for the three groups: the S&P 500 for large-cap companies, the S&P 400 MidCap Index for mid-cap stocks, and the S&P 600 SmallCap Index for funds that invest in small-cap companies. Figure 13.6 summarizes the results from 2000 to 2010.[14]

Across the entire time period, none of the fund classes outperformed their respective indexes. In fact, large-cap funds did slightly better at beating the index benchmark than mid-cap and small-cap funds.

---

[13]C. D. Ellis, *Winning the Loser's Game* (New York: McGraw-Hill, 1998).
[14]SPIVA reports, Standard & Poor's.

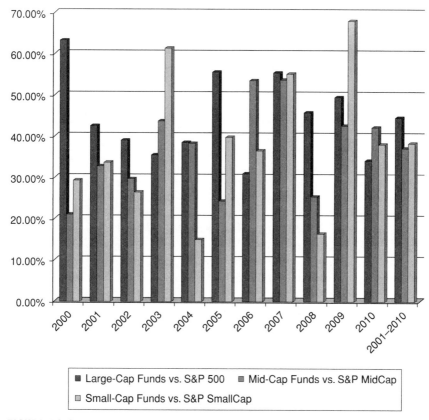

FIGURE 13.6 Active Funds versus Index: Percentage of Large-Cap, Mid-Cap, and Small-Cap Funds That Beat Respective Indexes
Source: S&P SPIVA Report.

By Style Mutual funds vary when it comes to investment styles and objectives. Some funds label themselves as growth funds and invest in stocks with high expected growth rates and P/E ratios. Others are value funds, specializing in stocks trading at low multiples of earnings and book value. There are also yield funds (that concentrate on stocks paying high dividends), diversified funds, and small-cap funds. The managers of funds in each of these style classes will probably claim that their group outperforms passive investors and it is investors in the other groups that are responsible for the overall underperformance. In a paper examining the money management industry, Lakonishok, Shleifer, and Vishny classified pension funds into growth, value, yield, and other and examined the annual return and percentage of

TABLE 13.2 Performance by Fund Style

Fund Style	Annual Return, 1983–1990	% of Managers Beating Respective Index
Growth	17.10%	41%
Yield	18.90%	56%
Value	18.00%	48%
Other	18.20%	46%
All funds	17.70%	46%

Source: J. Lakonishok, A. Shleifer, and R. Vishny, "Contrarian Investment, Extrapolation, and Risk," *Journal of Finance* 49 (1994): 1541–1578.

money managers in each group that beat the S&P 500 between 1983 and 1990.[15] Their results are summarized in Table 13.2.

For every style class, other than yield, more than 50 percent of the managers underperformed the S&P 500. In addition, the returns on the S&P 500 exceeded the annual returns earned by funds in every class.

Growth and value fund investors may take issue with this study because of the comparison to the S&P 500, arguing instead that the comparison should be to a growth index and a value index respectively. While this does seem self-serving (since both groups present themselves to investors as the better overall investment), growth funds emerge looking better from this comparison. The average value fund investor underperforms a value index by about 1.2 percent more than an average growth fund underperforms a growth index.[16] Figure 13.7, drawn from a book by Bernstein on investment styles, presents comparisons of growth and value funds to their respective indexes between 1987 and 1993.[17]

While this comparison was made using only a small sample of value and growth funds, it adds some basis to the notion that growth investors, on average, may have an easier time beating their passive counterparts. As noted earlier in Table 13.1, growth funds continued to outstrip value funds in the 2007–2011 time period.

One of the limitations of categorizing mutual funds based on style is that they often make investments that are at variance with their purported

---

[15] J. Lakonishok, A. Shleifer, and R. Vishny, "Contrarian Investment, Extrapolation, and Risk," *Journal of Finance* 49 (1994): 1541–1578.

[16] L. K. C. Chan, H. L. Chan, and J. Lakonishok, *On Mutual Fund Investment Styles*, *Review of Financial Studies* 5, no. 15 (Winter 2002): 1407–1437.

[17] R. Bernstein, *Style Investing* (New York: John Wiley & Sons, 1995).

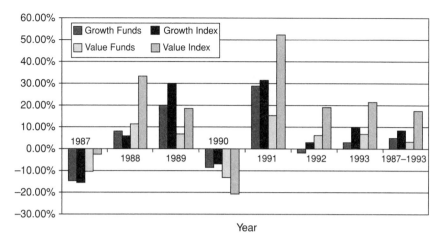

FIGURE 13.7 Returns on Growth and Value Funds
Source: R. Bernstein, *Style Investing* (New York: John Wiley & Sons, 1995).

style. Thus, you often find value funds that buy growth stocks and growth funds investing in mature value companies.

Emerging Market and International Funds   While active investing may not have much of a payoff in a mature market with wide access to information like the United States, intuitively you would expect the payoff to be much larger in emerging markets, where information is still not widely disseminated, or even in some European markets, where information tends to be tightly controlled by companies. You would therefore expect active mutual funds in these markets to do much better than they do in the United States, relative to passive indexes. Ahmed, Gangopadhyay, and Nanda examined 172 emerging market funds listed on Morningstar between 1980 to 2000 and computed the excess returns for these funds. Figure 13.8 summarizes their results.[18]

In each of the groupings, the actively managed funds underperformed the index. These results mirror those found in earlier studies of emerging market funds and suggest that active money management does not necessarily pay off in terms of excess returns, even in markets where money managers have information advantages. While this may seem surprising, transaction

---

[18]P. Ahmed, P. Gangopadhyay, and S. Nanda, "Performance of Emerging Market Mutual Funds and U.S. Monetary Policy" (SSRN Working Paper 289278, 2001).

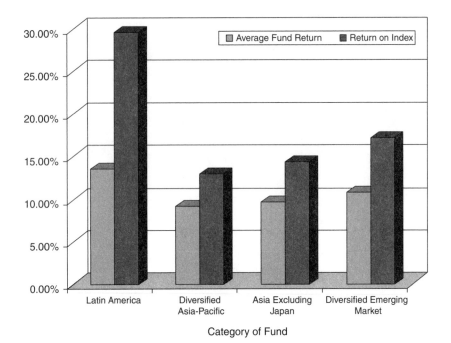

FIGURE 13.8 Emerging Market Funds versus Indexes
Source: P. Ahmed, P. Gangopadhyay, and S. Nanda, "Performance of Emerging Market Mutual Funds and U.S. Monetary Policy" (SSRN Working Paper 289278, 2001).

costs are also higher in these markets and whatever is gained by picking better stocks may very well be lost in trading costs.[19]

What about funds in other developed markets? Actively managed Japanese funds underperform the index by even more than their U.S. counterparts. A study by Cai, Chan, and Yamada concluded that the average rate of return on 800 actively managed Japanese mutual funds between 1981 and 1992 was only 1.74 percent a year whereas the Japanese equity

---

[19]S&P has teamed up with CRISIL to look at how often actively managed mutual funds in India outperform indexes, and their findings mirror their findings in the United States. Over a five-year period ending in June 2011, the equally weighted return across equity mutual funds lagged the returns on the index between 0.5 percent and 1 percent annually, and only 35 percent of large-cap and 44 percent of diversified equity mutual funds in India beat their respective indexes.

market increased by 9.28 percent a year during that same period.[20] In one of few bright spots for active money management, Otten and Bams examine 508 actively managed European funds in 2000 and find some evidence of excess returns, especially in small-cap funds.

Other Categorizations   There are a number of other ways in which mutual funds can be categorized and, while we will not dedicate entire sections to each, we summarize the results here:

- *Load versus no-load funds.* Some mutual funds charge an up-front fee, usually a percentage of the money invested in the fund. These fees are called loads and can range from 2 to 5 percent of the investment. The funds justify these up-front costs by arguing that they will deliver much higher returns than funds that do not charge these fees. Again, the evidence does not back up these claims. Morey compares the performance of load and no-load funds both before and after the adjustment of the loads. Using a sample of 301 load and 334 no-load funds from 1993, he tracks performance in the next five years, incorporating the effects of funds that cease to exist.[21] Figure 13.9 summarizes his findings. The results are clearly not favorable to load funds. Not only do they fall short of no-load funds when we consider the load-adjusted returns, but they fall short even when we look at preload returns.
- *Age and size of fund.* Are funds that have been around longer (more seasoned funds) better or worse investments than newer funds? Morey, in his earlier-quoted study of load and no-load funds, attempted to answer this question as well by categorizing funds into seasoned (more than 10 years old), middle-aged (5 to 10 years), and young funds (less than 5 years) in 1993 and examining returns over the subsequent five-year period. Figure 13.10 presents his conclusions.

---

[20]J. Cai, K. C. Chan, and T. Yamada, "The Performance of Japanese Mutual Funds," *Review of Financial Studies* 10 (1997): 237–273. While this is a truly mind-boggling difference, it should be noted that the net asset values of Japanese mutual funds are adjusted for tax liabilities. In fact, Brown, Goetzmann, Hiraki, Otsuki, and Shirashi (2001) argue that much of these negative excess returns can be explained by tax effects. S. J. Brown, W. N. Goetzmann, T. Hiraki, T. Otsuki, and N. Shirashi, "The Japanese Open-End Fund Puzzle," *Journal of Business* 74 (2001): 59–77.
[21]M. R. Morey, "Should You Carry the Load? A Comprehensive Analysis of Load and No-Load Mutual Fund Out-of-Sample Performance," *Journal of Banking & Finance* 27 (2003): 1245–1271.

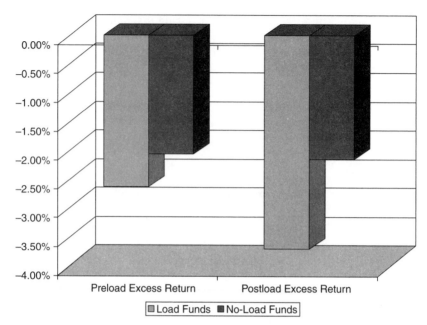

FIGURE 13.9 Jensen's Alpha: Load versus No-Load Funds
Source: M. R. Morey, "Should You Carry the Load? A Comprehensive Analysis of
Load and No-Load Mutual Fund Out-of-Sample Performance," *Journal of Banking
& Finance* 27 (2003): 1245–1271.

> Younger funds seem to do much better than older funds in terms of
> both excess returns and delivering higher returns per unit of risk (Sharpe
> ratio). When funds are categorized by size, you find similar results,
> with smaller funds delivering marginally better performance than larger
> funds, though both lag the indexes. Indro, Jiang, Hu, and Lee examined
> the relationship between fund size and returns by categorizing funds
> into 10 size classes from largest to smallest.[22] Though the funds that
> are in the bottom two deciles (the smallest funds) earn lower returns
> than other funds, largely because of higher costs, the economies of scale
> quickly decline and funds that exceed an optimal size (the top 10 percent
> of funds in terms of size) also have lower returns.
> - *Fund manager characteristics.* Does experience make fund managers
>   better? Are older fund managers more likely to deliver high returns than
>   younger fund managers? When funds are categorized based on the age

---

[22]D. C. Indro, C. X. Jiang, M. Y. Hu, and W. Y. Lee, "Mutual Fund Performance:
Does Size Matter?" *Financial Analysts Journal* 55 (May/June 1999): 74–87.

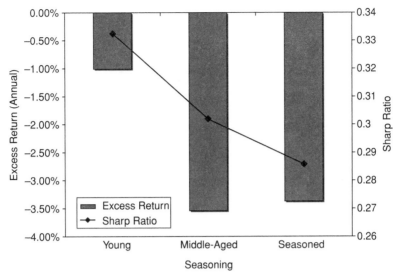

FIGURE 13.10 Excess Returns by Fund Age
Source: M. R. Morey, "Should You Carry the Load? A Comprehensive Analysis of Load and No-Load Mutual Fund Out-of-Sample Performance," *Journal of Banking & Finance* 27 (2003): 1245–1271.

and experience of their managers, younger managers are more likely to generate positive excess returns than older managers. Younger managers are also more likely to exhibit herd behavior than older managers and to be fired after poor years (which may explain why they exhibit herd behavior in the first place).[23] One study even looked for differences between male and female money managers and found no significant differences in returns.[24]

- *Retail versus institutional funds.* There are some funds that cater exclusively to institutional and very wealthy individuals. They have minimum

---

[23]J. Chevalier and G. Ellison, "Are Some Mutual Fund Managers Better Than Others? Cross-Sectional Patterns in Behavior and Performance," *Journal of Finance* 54 (1999): 875–899. They look at funds between 1988 and 1994 and correlate performance to age, SAT scores, and status of undergraduate institution. They find at the managers with higher SAT scores who went to more prestigious undergraduate institutions have slightly more positive returns than other managers.

[24]S. M. Atkinson, S. B. Baird, and M. B. Frye, "Do Female Mutual Fund Managers Manage Differently?" *Journal of Financial Research* 26 (2003): 1–8. They also find that net asset flows into funds managed by females are lower than for males, especially for the manager's initial year managing the fund.

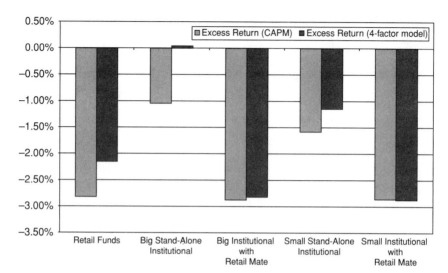

FIGURE 13.11 Institutional versus Retail Funds: Annualized Excess Returns
Source: C. James and J. Karceski, "Captured Money? Differences in the Performance Characteristics of Retail and Institutional Mutual Funds" (SSRN Working Paper 299730, 2002).

investment requirements of $100,000 or greater. Some of these funds are stand-alone offerings and some are offered by fund families that have retail mates. In Figure 13.11 we report the annual excess returns earned by these funds from 1995 to 1999 categorized by whether they cater to retail or institutional investors, and categorize the latter by minimum investment requirements—big if the minimum investment is greater than $500,000; small if the minimum is between $100,000 and $500,000—and by whether they are stand-alone or have retail mates.[25] Note that the only funds that marginally beat the market are big institutional funds that have no retail mates.

- *Socially responsible funds.* In the past decade, a large number of funds have been created to cater to investors who want to avoid companies that they deem socially irresponsible. Though the definition of social responsibility varies from fund to fund, the managers of these funds all argue that investing in ethical companies will generate higher returns in the long term. Arrayed against them are others who believe that

---

[25]C. James and J. Karceski, "Captured Money? Differences in the Performance Characteristics of Retail and Institutional Mutual Funds" (SSRN Working Paper 299730, 2002).

TABLE 13.3 Continuity of Performance for Pension Funds, 1983 to 1990

Quartile Ranking This Period	Quartile Ranking Next Period			
	1	2	3	4
1	26%	24%	23%	27%
2	20%	26%	29%	25%
3	22%	28%	26%	24%
4	32%	22%	22%	24%

Source: J. Lakonishok, A. Shleifer, and R. Vishny, "Contrarian Investment, Extrapolation, and Risk," *Journal of Finance* 49 (1994): 1541–1578.

constraining your investment choices will result in lower returns, not higher. In a finding that is bound to leave both groups dissatisfied, Bauer, Koedijk, and Otten examined 103 ethical funds in the United States, United Kingdom, and Germany from 1990 to 2001 and found no significant differences in excess returns between these funds and conventional funds.[26]

Performance Continuity When confronted with the evidence that the average actively managed fund underperforms the market, the reaction of some active money managers is that the average return is brought down by the laggards at the bottom. A profession, they argue, should be judged based on how those who are best do, rather than by the average. If they are correct, the best money managers should show both consistency and continuity in performance and earn much higher returns than the market.

Transition Likelihood Perhaps the simplest way to check for continuity is to rank money managers, based on performance, in one period and then look at the rankings in the next period. Lakonishok, Shleifer and Vishny, (referenced earlier) categorized pension fund money managers from 1983 to 1989 into quartiles based on performance each year, and looked at the likelihood of repeat performance. Their results are summarized in Table 13.3.

Note that you would have 25 percent in each box if performance rankings were completely random—a manager is the first quartile this year will have an equal chance of being in any of the four quartiles next year. The

---

[26]R. Bauer, K. Koedijk, and R. Otten, "International Evidence on Ethical Mutual Fund Performance and Investment Style," *Journal of Banking and Finance* 29 (2005): 1751–1767.

TABLE 13.4 Continuity of Performance for Mutual Funds, 2008 to 2011

	Quartile 1	Quartile 2	Quartile 3	Quartile 4	Merged/Liquidated
Quartile 1	24%	26%	19%	23%	8%
Quartile 2	16%	21%	27%	24%	12%
Quartile 3	18%	19%	25%	22%	15%
Quartile 4	27%	18%	14%	16%	25%

actual percentages are not significantly different from 25%, with one exception. A manager who is in the lowest quartile this year has a higher chance of being in the highest quartile next year than in any other quartile. This should not be surprising, since this is exactly what you would expect from mutual funds that take considerable risk and make big bets on a few stocks. If the bets pay off, they move to the top of the rankings; and they do not, they drop to the bottom.

Standard & Poor's provides updated versions of these transition matrices for mutual funds, allowing for liquidations and mergers. In its most recent assessment, S&P classifies active mutual funds in March 2008 into four quartiles, based on performance in the prior three years, and looks at the probabilities that they will remain in their respective quartiles based on returns over the next three years (April 2008 to March 2011) in Table 13.4.

As with the pension fund study, the degree of persistence is low, with the worst mutual funds in a three-year period actually being the most likely to transition to being the best ones in the subsequent three-year period. It is also worth noting that funds in the bottom two quartiles are far more likely to cease to exist in the next period.

Third Party Rankings and Ratings The rankings in Table 13.3 were based entirely on returns and can be faulted for not considering other qualitative factors. There are services like Morningstar that rate mutual funds, and rankings of mutual funds are also provided by the financial news media (the *Wall Street Journal*, *Forbes*, and *Bloomberg Businessweek*, for example). These services also tend to have a powerful impact on the mutual fund business, with evidence that funds flow into those funds that have experienced a ratings upgrade from Morningstar and away from those funds that have experienced a ratings downgrade.[27] But do funds that score high on these rankings repeat in future periods? More generally, are these rankings that

---

[27]D. Del Guercio and Paula A. Tkac, "Star Power: The Effect of Morningstar Ratings on Mutual Fund Flows" (SSRN Working Paper 286157, 2007).

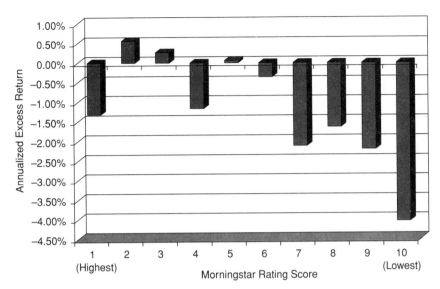

FIGURE 13.12 Annualized Return Based on Morningstar Ratings, 1994 to 1997
Source: C. R. Blake and M. M. Morey, "Morningstar Ratings and Mutual Fund Performance," *Journal of Financial and Quantitative Analysis* 35 (2000): 451–483.

are often used by investors as the basis for picking funds useful at predicting future performance?

Blake and Morey examine these questions, using the Morningstar ratings. Morningstar, which maintains one of the most comprehensive databases on mutual funds, assigns ratings ranging from one star (poor) to five stars (outstanding) to funds, based on both past returns and consistency.[28] The influence of these ratings is illustrated by one study that found that 97 percent of the money flowed into funds with four or five star ratings.[29] To test whether ratings provide any predictive power, Blake and Morey created a weighted score based on the 3-year, 5-year, and 10-year ratings (with 20 percent, 30 percent, and 50 percent weights respectively) for each fund and ranked the funds into 10 deciles based on the weighted score. They then computed the excess returns on funds in each decile between 1994 and 1997, and the results are summarized in Figure 13.12.

---

[28]C. R. Blake and M. M. Morey, "Morningstar Ratings and Mutual Fund Performance," *Journal of Financial and Quantitative Analysis* 35 (2000): 451–483.
[29]This statistic was quoted in a *Wall Street Journal* article by Karen Damato titled "Morningstar Edges Toward One-Year Ratings." *Wall Street Journal*, April 5, 1996.

Morningstar ratings seemed to have little or no predictive power except for those funds in the lowest ratings. These poorly rated funds tended to do much worse than other funds in the following year. The highest-rated funds did worse or no better than the funds in the average ratings.

In response to the criticism that its ratings did not have predictive power, Morningstar did revamp its rating system in 2002, making three changes. First, it broke funds down into 48 smaller subgroups rather than four large groups, as was the convention prior to 2002. Second, it adjusted the risk measures to more completely capture downside risk; prior to 2002, a fund was considered risky only if its returns fell below the Treasury bill rate, even if the returns were extremely volatile. Third, funds with multiple share classes were consolidated into one fund rather than treated as separate funds. A study that classified mutual funds into classes based on these new ratings in June 2002 and looked at returns over the following three years (July 2002 to June 2005) finds that they do have predictive power now, with the higher-rated funds delivering significantly higher returns than the lower-rated funds.[30]

A study of rankings in the financial magazines of 757 funds between 1993 and 1995 by Detzler finds that while the funds that are ranked highly tend to have high preranking performance (which should be no surprise since the rankings are heavily influenced by recent performance), their performance in the postranking period is no different from funds that are ranked lower.[31] About 54 percent of highly ranked funds underperform the market in the postranking period, and about 65 percent of these funds have much poorer postranking returns than preranking returns.

The Hot Hands Phenomenon While much of the evidence that we have presented so far suggests that there is little continuity of performance, there is some contradictory evidence that has accumulated about the very top-ranked mutual funds. A number of studies[32] seem to indicate that mutual

---

[30]M. R. Morey and A. Gottesman, "Morningstar Mutual Fund Redux," *Journal of Investment Consulting* 8, no. 1 (Summer 2006): 25–37.

[31]M. L. Detzler, "The Value of Mutual Fund Rankings to Individual Investors," *Journal of Business and Economic Studies* 8 (2002): 48–72.

[32]M. Grinblatt and S.Titman, "The Persistence of Mutual Fund Performance," *Journal of Finance* 42 (1992): 1977–1984; W. N. Goetzmann and R. Ibbotson, "Do Winners Repeat? Patterns in Mutual Fund Performance," *Journal of Portfolio Management* 20 (1994): 9–18; Hendricks, Patel, and Zeckhauser, "Hot Hands in Mutual Funds: Short Run Persistence in Performance, 1974–1987," *Journal of Finance* 48 (1995): 93–130.

TABLE 13.5 Repeat Winners by Year, 1971 to 1990

Year	Percent of Repeat Winners	Year	Percent of Repeat Winners
1971	64.80%	1980	36.50%
1972	50.00%	1981	62.30%
1973	62.60%	1982	56.60%
1974	52.10%	1983	56.10%
1975	74.40%	1984	53.90%
1976	68.40%	1985	59.50%
1977	70.80%	1986	60.40%
1978	69.70%	1987	39.30%
1979	71.80%	1988	41.00%
1971–1979	65.10%	1989	59.60%
		1990	49.40%
		1980–1990	51.70%

Source: B. G. Malkiel, "Returns from Investing in Equity Mutual Funds 1971 to 1991," *Journal of Finance* 50 (1995): 549–572.

funds that earn above-average returns in one period will continue to earn above-average returns in the next period.

Malkiel tested for this "hot hands" phenomenon by looking at the percentage of winners each year who repeated the next year in the 1970s and 1980s.[33] His results are summarized in Table 13.5.

NUMBER WATCH

Best-performing mutual funds: Take a look at best-performing mutual funds over the past year.

Table 13.5 tells a surprising story. The percentage of repeat winners clearly is much higher than dictated by chance (50 percent) in the 1970s. However, the percentage of repeat winners during the 1980s looks close to random. Is this because mutual fund rankings became more ubiquitous during the 1980s? Maybe. It is also possible that what you are seeing are the

---

[33]B. G. Malkiel, "Returns from Investing in Equity Mutual Funds 1971 to 1991," *Journal of Finance* 50 (1995): 549–572.

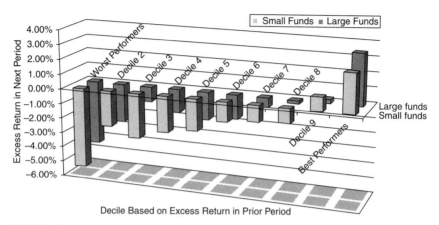

FIGURE 13.13 Persistence in Mutual Fund Performance, 1999 to 2008
Source: E. J. Elton, M. J. Gruber, and C. R. Blake, "Does Size Matter? The Relationship between Size and Peformance" (SSRN Working Paper 1826406, 2011).

effects of overall market performance. In the 1970s, when the equity markets had a string of negative years, mutual funds that held more cash consistently moved to the top of the rankings. Malkiel also compares the returns you would have earned on a strategy of buying the top funds (looking at the top 10, top 20, top 30, and top 40 funds) from each year and holding it for the next year. Again, the contrast is striking. While the top funds outperformed the S&P 500 in the 1973–1977 and 1978–1981 time periods, they matched the index from 1982 to 1986 and underperformed the index from 1987 to 1991.

So, does the hot hands phenomenon continue to hold? If yes, why does it persist? Elton, Gruber, and Blake look at all mutual funds from 1999 to 2009, and document that the funds that have done well in the past continue to do well in the future and those that have done badly continue to do badly, as evidenced in Figure 13.13. This study also finds that the top-performing funds decrease fees (rather than increase them) and the fees increase at the worst-performing funds, and that there is no relationship between fund size and persistence. In other words, persistence in performance is just as strong with large funds as with small ones.[34] As to why it persists, they

---

[34]E. J. Elton, M. J. Gruber, and C. R. Blake, "Does Size Matter? The Relationship between Size and Peformance" (SSRN Working Papers 1826406, 2011).

offer several hypotheses: that large funds may hire the best analysts and that they are able to control a larger share of the resources of the fund family, as well as get first access to the investment opportunities that the fund family discovers.

Luck or Skill?   Even the most pessimistic assessments of mutual funds conclude that some of them have delivered high excess returns over extended periods. The question then becomes whether this performance should be attributed to the skills of the managers of these funds or to luck. To answer this question, Fama and French took a novel tack by running simulations of mutual fund performance using histories of individual fund returns from 1984 to 2006 as the raw data, setting the average excess return to zero, and comparing the distribution of the excess returns generated for the simulated funds with the distribution of actual excess returns across funds. On a net return basis, they could not reject the hypothesis that the excess returns earned by some mutual fund managers can be entirely attributed to luck and that the average mutual fund manager underperforms by the amount of management expenses. On a gross return basis, the average mutual fund manager breaks even with the market.[35]

In Summary

Looking at the evidence on mutual fund performance, we find that the average mutual fund underperforms the market, and this underperformance cannot be explained away by critiquing the risk and return models used by researchers. The underperformance is also pervasive and seems to affect funds in every style category. It also gets worse for funds that have up-front loads and higher expense ratios. In fact, the only mildly positive result is that growth funds do less badly against their indexes than value funds do against their indexes.

   If the argument being mounted by active money managers is that we should focus on the winners, the results reveal a disconnect. While the probability that funds that have been successful in the past will continue to remain so in the future is low, the most successful mutual funds in the past period, on average, deliver much better risk-adjusted returns in the next period than the least successful ones. In fact, there are lots of reasons to avoid the worst-performing funds. Not only are they more likely to continue

---

[35]E. F. Fama and K. R. French, "Luck versus Skill in the Cross Section of Mutual Fund Returns," *Journal of Finance* 65 (2010): 1915–1947.

to perform badly in the future but they are also far more likely to fail (be liquidated) and to have higher expenses and management fees.

FUNDS OR FUND MANAGERS—WHO DELIVERS THE EXCESS RETURNS?

Most of the studies of mutual funds that we have reviewed here look at the funds themselves rather the fund managers. But who really is responsible for the excess returns on a fund? Is it the fund itself, because of competitive advantages it has built up over other funds, or is it the fund manager, because of his or her special skills at picking stocks? Consider the question in the context of Fidelity Magellan. Was its success in the early years of its existence due to the fund family—Fidelity—or was it attributable to Peter Lynch's special skills at picking growth companies? The question is important not only for purposes of attribution but also because it may shed some light on the findings in the previous pages. If success at a fund is due to superstar managers rather than the fund's own qualities and these managers tend to shift from one fund to another or set up their own funds, you would not expect to see excess returns persisting at funds. You should, however, observe continuity in performance if you track individual money managers.

While it is more difficult to track money managers rather than funds, there are some studies that have attempted to do so. There studies indicate that performance continuity is just as difficult to find with money managers as it is with funds. Though there are a few high-profile examples of success (such as Lynch), there are far more examples of managers who have followed successful tenures at one fund with failures at their own funds or at different funds.

WHY DO ACTIVE INVESTORS NOT PERFORM BETTER?

Based on the evidence in the preceding section, we cannot avoid drawing the conclusion that active investors underperform the index (and by extension, index funds). In this section, we consider some of the reasons for the underperformance of active funds. While much of the evidence comes from looking at mutual funds, you could extend it to cover individual investors.

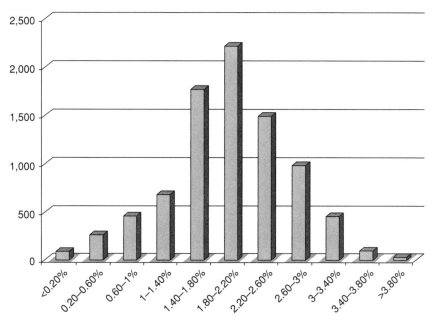

FIGURE 13.14   Total Annual Expenses: U.S. Mutual Funds in 2011
Source: Morningstar.

Transaction Costs

The simplest explanation for the difference in returns between actively managed mutual funds and index funds (or passive investing) is transaction costs. Index funds are inexpensive to create (there are no costs to collecting information and no analyst expenses) and inexpensive to run (minimal transaction costs and management fees). For instance, the Vanguard 500 index fund has transaction costs and management fees that amount to 0.17 percent of the fund. In contrast, the transaction costs and management fees at actively managed funds can easily exceed 2 percent. Figure 13.14 presents the expense ratios in 2011 of all equity mutual funds in the United States.

The average expense ratio in 2011 for these equity funds is about 1.98 percent, composed of net expenses of 1.31 percent and a management fee of 0.68 percent. Since these are annual, recurring costs, an actively managed fund has to generate an excess return of this amount on its stock picks to cover its expenses.

The key variable determining expenses is turnover. Funds that trade more will usually generate higher transaction costs, but the effect of turnover will be much greater if the fund trades smaller and less liquid companies.

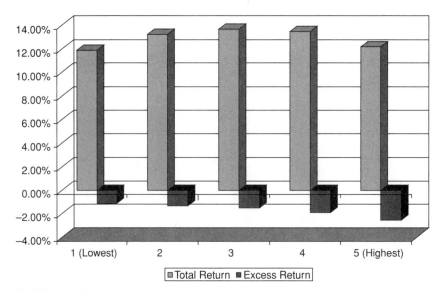

FIGURE 13.15 Turnover Ratios and Returns: Mutual Funds
Source: J. M. R. Chalmers, R. M. Edelen, and G. B. Kadlec, "An Analysis of Mutual Fund Trading Costs" (SSRN Working Paper 195849, 1999).

In fact, Chalmers, Edelen, and Kadlec find that the relationship between turnover and excess returns is fairly weak, as evidenced in Figure 13.15.[36]

Note that while the funds with low turnover have slightly less negative excess returns than funds with high turnover, they also earn lower total returns. When the study looked at the relationship between total costs (including trading costs and other expenses), the results are much stronger (see Figure 13.16).

Funds with higher total costs have much lower total returns and much more negative expense ratios than funds with lower total costs.

High Taxes

In Chapter 6, we considered the interrelationship between taxes and transaction costs. Mutual funds that trade a lot also create much larger tax bills for their investors and this can best seen by contrasting the pretax and after-tax returns at funds. In Figure 13.17, we consider the difference between pretax

---

[36]J. M. R. Chalmers, R. M. Edelen, and G. B. Kadlec, "An Analysis of Mutual Fund Trading Costs" (SSRN Working Paper 195849, 1999).

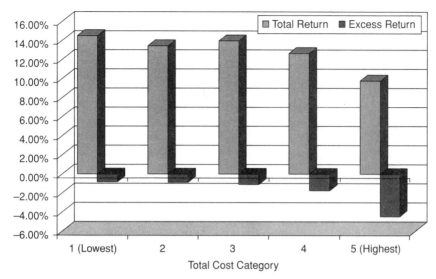

FIGURE 13.16 Trading Costs and Returns: Mutual Funds
Source: J. M. R. Chalmers, R. M. Edelen, and G. B. Kadlec, "An Analysis of Mutual Fund Trading Costs" (SSRN Working Paper 195849, 1999).

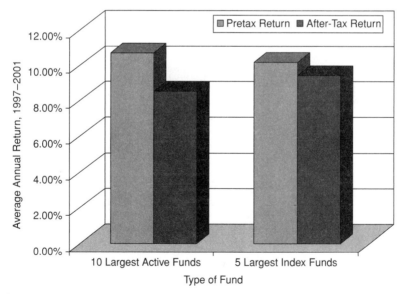

FIGURE 13.17 Tax Effects at Index and Actively Managed Funds
Source: Morningstar.

and after-tax returns at the five largest index funds and contrast them with pretax and after-tax returns at the 10 largest actively managed funds.

Note that the after-tax return at an active fund is almost 20 percent lower than the pretax return. In contrast, the difference between pretax and after-tax returns is much smaller at index funds.

Too Much Activity

We invest in actively managed funds because we want them to be actively seeking out undervalued stocks. But does this activity pay off? In the study by Lakonishok, Shleifer, and Vishny that looked at pension funds, they contrasted the return that funds would have made if they had frozen their portfolios at the beginning of each year with the return that they actually made, after trading through the year. You can consider the difference between the returns as the payoff to active money management and Figure 13.18 presents the results for funds in different style classes.

The results indicate that far from adding value, activity reduces returns by between 0.5 percent (for yield funds) to 1.4 percent (for other funds). In other words, these funds would have done better if they had sent everyone home at the start of the year and not traded over the course of the year.

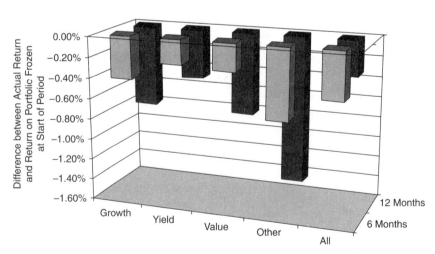

FIGURE 13.18 Payoff to Active Money Management
Source: J. Lakonishok, A. Shleifer, and R. Vishny, "Contrarian Investment, Extrapolation, and Risk," *Journal of Finance* 49 (1994): 1541–1578.

Chen, Jegadeesh, and Wermers paint a more favorable picture of the stock-picking skills of mutual fund managers.[37] While they find no evidence that stocks that are widely held by mutual funds do any better than other stocks, they do find that stocks that are bought by mutual funds earn higher returns in subsequent periods than stocks that are sold. They also conclude that growth-oriented funds have better stock-selection skills than funds in other categories.

Failure to Stay Fully Invested in Equities—Delusions of Market Timing

Actively managed funds often hold far more cash than they need to meet normal needs, and these cash holdings often reflect the market timing views of managers, increasing when managers are bearish and decreasing when they are bullish. As a consequence, mutual funds will tend to underperform the equity index in periods when the equity index increases by more than the riskless rate. Active money managers concede this drain on returns, but argue that their investors are more than compensated by the payoff from market timing. In particular, mutual fund managers contend that they keep investors out of bear markets and thus reduce their downside. In Figure 13.19, we compare the performance of actively managed funds and the S&P 500 in six market downturns.

The results don't indicate much market timing ability, since active funds did even worse than the S&P 500 in four of the six downturns. There is another cost, as well. Active money managers often seem to shift into cash during bear markets and they tend to stay in cash too long. Looking at the returns on active funds and the index in three bear markets in the 1970s and 1980s and in the 12 months after each bear market, we find that whatever additional returns may have been earned by active funds during the bear market are effectively wiped out in the 12 months following. In summary, then, the cash holdings of active money managers seem to cost them more in opportunities lost than any potential gain from market timing.

Behavioral Factors

There are three other aspects of mutual fund behavior that seem to contribute to their poor performance. One is the lack of consistency when it comes

---

[37]J. L. Chen, N. Jegadeesh, and R. Wermers, "The Value of Active Mutual Fund Management: An Examination of the Stockholdings and Trades of Fund Managers," *Journal of Financial and Quantitative Analysis* 35 (2000): 343–368.

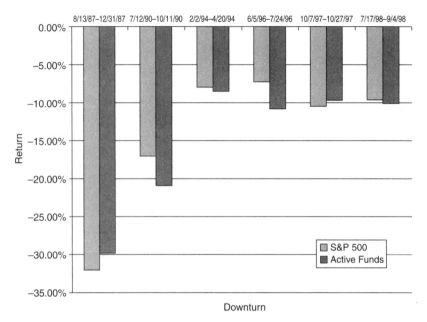

FIGURE 13.19 Index Funds versus Active Funds—Market Downturns
Source: Wall Street Journal.

to investing style/strategy, the second is the tendency to indulge in herd behavior, and the third is the practice of making portfolios look better after the fact (window dressing).

1. *Lack of consistency.* As we noted in an earlier section, funds all too often invest in assets that do not match their stated objectives and philosophy. In fact, explicitly or implicitly, managers switch from one investment style to another. Studies seem to indicate that there is substantial switching of styles from period to period, usually in reaction to market performance in the preceding period. Brown and Van Harlow examined several thousand mutual funds from 1991 to 2000 and categorized them based on style consistency. They noted that funds that switch styles had much higher expense ratios and much lower returns than funds that maintain more consistent styles.[38]

---

[38]K. C. Brown and K. V. Harlow, "Staying the Course: The Impact of Investment Style Consistency on Mutual Fund Performance" (SSRN Working Paper 306999, 2002). The style consistency is measured using the R-squared of a fund with an index that reflects its stated objective. A fund that has a lower R-squared is deviating more from its stated style.

2. *Herd behavior.* One of the striking aspects of institutional investing is the degree to which institutions tend to buy or sell the same investments at the same time. Thus, you find the institutional holdings in a company drop off dramatically after a poor year and increase in sectors that outperform the market. With emerging markets, you often notice the phenomenon of institutional flight from an emerging market after a severe market decline. Borensztein and Gelos examine emerging market funds in Asia, Latin America, Europe, and the Middle East/Africa and report that there is significant herding behavior in each of these regions.[39] There are two negative consequences to funds from herding. The first is that collective selling can make a retreat into a rout, and a small price drop on an investment into a big one; similarly, collective buying can push stock prices up for all buyers. The second is that herd behavior wreaks havoc on investment strategies. A portfolio manager who sells a low price-earnings ratio stock after a price drop may be undercutting her own long-term potential for returns.

3. *Window dressing.* It is a well-documented fact that portfolio managers try to rearrange their portfolios just prior to reporting dates, selling their losers and buying winners (after the fact). This process is called window dressing and it is based on the premise that investors will look at what is in the portfolio on the reporting date and ignore the actual return earned by the portfolio. Whatever the rationale for window dressing, it creates additional transaction costs for portfolios. O'Neal presents evidence that window dressing is most prevalent in December and that it does impose a significant cost on mutual funds.[40]

FINDING THE RIGHT FUND

What are the lessons that individual investors can draw from past studies on mutual funds? These are a few:

- *Pick a fund that best fits your philosophy and needs.* Before you pick a fund, develop a view on markets. In other words, choose

(continued)

---

[39] E. R. Borensztein and R. G. Gelos, "A Panic-Prone Pack? The Behavior of Emerging Market Mutual Funds" (IMF Working Paper No. 00/198, 2001).
[40] E. S. O'Neal, "Window Dressing and Equity Mutual Funds" (SSRN Working Paper 275031, 2001). He estimates that window dressing costs mutual funds about $1 billion each year in transaction costs and price impact.

an investment philosophy first. If you have trouble developing a philosophy, go with an index fund.

- *Do not invest in a load fund.* The up-front load creates a burden that is too large for even a good portfolio manager to overcome.

- *Avoid funds with high turnover ratios.* Funds that trade a lot tend to have high trading costs (which eat into your pretax returns) and create large tax bills (which reduce your after-tax returns).

- *Avoid funds that do not stay style consistent.* A fund manager who keeps shifting styles not only trades more (see preceding item) but also lacks a core philosophy on investing.

- *Avoid equity funds that have large cash holdings.* While funds may claim that they use cash holdings to time markets, there is no evidence that they can. You can make your own decisions on how much cash to hold.

- *Look at the rankings but don't them let them determine your fund choices.* Fund rankings may create some short-term momentum, but in the long term, they tell you nothing unless they are abysmal. (If they are abysmal, avoid the fund since it may not be in existence much longer.)

ALTERNATIVE PATHS TO INDEXING

If you decide to be a passive investor, there are alternatives to buying an index fund. Exchange-traded funds are among the fastest-growing and most liquid securities traded in the United States and represent, in the views of their proponents, a much more efficient way of investing in indexes. In the past few years, we have also seen a variety of derivatives being created on indexes that also allow us to create the equivalent of an index fund at a much lower cost. Finally, we have also seen the development of a class of funds that categorize themselves as enhanced index funds. They claim to provide all of the benefits of indexing—diversification, low transaction costs, and tax efficiency—while delivering the excess returns that are a product of active investing.

Exchange-Traded Funds

In 1993, the American Stock Exchange began trading depositary receipts on the S&P 500 (SPDR, pronounced Spider). As an individual investor, you can buy SPDRs just as you buy other stocks and trade the index with relatively small amounts of money and trivial transaction costs. Not surprisingly, SPDRs have become the most heavily traded instruments on the AMEX. The success of SPDRs has opened the door for a large number of other exchange-traded funds (ETFs)—DIAMONDS (indexed to the Dow Jones Industrial Average), Nasdaq-100 shares, and iFT-SE (indexed to the FTSE Index in the United Kingdom). In the last chapter, we noted that as exchange-traded funds have proliferated not only on equity indexes but also on sectors and other asset classes, they have become a tool for market timing investors.

There are many who argue that exchange-traded funds are a much more efficient and cheaper way of replicating indexes than buying index funds for several reasons:

- They can be bought and sold all through the trading day. In addition, you can put restrictions such as limit orders and stop-loss rules on the trade, just as you would on an individual stock.
- Unlike index funds, you can sell short on exchange-traded funds. This provides you with a way of taking advantage of your market timing skills, and also allows you more flexibility in terms of creating composite positions.
- Index funds sometimes deviate from the index, either because of sampling or because of execution problems. An exchange-traded fund always replicates the index.

Does this mean that exchange-traded funds will drive index funds out of existence? Not necessarily. Elton, Gruber, Comer, and Li take a close look at SPDRs and conclude that there are a few hidden costs.[41] The first is that there is a management fee of about 0.18 percent charged every year for maintaining the securities and the returns are also reduced by the transaction costs incurred in replicating the index. In other words, SPDRs bear the same costs that an index fund bears in replicating the portfolio and have an additional management fee assessed on top of that. The second cost is that dividends received on the underlying stock cannot be reinvested but have to be held in a non-interest-bearing account. As a result of this, the researchers find that SPDRs underperform the S&P 500. Table 13.6 presents the returns on SPDRs and the S&P 500, and measures the shortfall each year from 1993 to 1998.

---

[41] E. J. Elton, M. J. Gruber, G. Comer, and K. Li, "Spiders: Where Are the Bugs?" In *Exchange Traded Funds* (SSRN Working Paper 307136, 2002).

TABLE 13.6   SPDRs versus S&P 500

	1993	1994	1995	1996	1997	1998	1993–1998
SPDR NAV	8.92%	1.15%	37.20%	22.72%	33.06%	28.28%	21.90%
S&P 500	9.19%	1.32%	37.56%	22.97%	33.40%	28.57%	22.17%
Shortfall	–0.27%	–0.17%	–0.36%	–0.25%	–0.34%	–0.29%	–0.28%

Of the 28 basis point shortfall, the researchers estimate that 18.45 basis points comes from the management fee and the balance is caused by the noninvestment of dividends. In contrast, the Vanguard 500 institutional index fund underperformed the index by only 10 basis points a year, and the individual index fund underperformed the index by 17 basis points.[42]

There may be tax advantages associated with investing in an exchange-traded fund. When exchange-traded funds are redeemed, the trustee has the option of distributing the securities that comprise the index rather than cash. If the securities distributed on redemption are those with substantial capital gains, exchange-traded funds may be able to reduce investors' ultimate tax bills, relative to index funds.

In summary, investors get the advantage of immediate liquidity with exchange-traded funds, but they do pay a price for the immediacy both in terms of transaction cost (from buying and selling SPDRs) and slightly lower returns. These costs may decrease over time as management fees come down, but for the moment, index funds still have a cost advantage and may be more efficient investments for investors with no need for liquidity and with long time horizons. A comparison of the trading costs of ETFs and index funds led Guedj and Huang to conclude that investors who value liquidity more are more likely to invest in hedge funds and that ETFs are better suited for narrower and less liquid indexes.[43]

Index Futures and Options

There are both futures and options traded on the S&P and other equity indexes, and they can be used to replicate the index. For instance, a passive investor with $10 million to invest can generate the equivalent of an index fund by buying a futures contract on the index and investing the cash in Treasury bills. If futures contracts are priced at their arbitrage value

---

[42]The Vanguard index fund, which is open to individuals, has slightly higher costs and underperforms the index by about 17 basis points a year.

[43]I. Guedj and J. Huang, "Are ETFs Replacing Index Mutual Funds?" (SSRN Working Paper, 2009).

(as defined in Chapter 11), the return on such a strategy should be equal to the return on the S&P 500 less the transaction cost of buying a futures contract. For a large institutional investor, this cost should be very low and the strategy may yield slightly higher returns than investing in an index fund. Derivatives-based strategies do not make sense for individual investors, since they tend to have much higher transaction costs. For these investors, index funds will continue to dominate and generate higher returns than alternative strategies.

Enhanced Index Funds

Enhanced index funds claim to have all of the advantages of index funds, while delivering the excess returns associated with actively managed funds. There are no free lunches in investing, though, and enhanced index funds are no exception. In fact, enhanced indexing is, in our view, an oxymoron. You are either an index fund or an actively managed fund but you cannot be both. Enhanced indexing is really active money management with self-imposed constraints on activity.

Mechanics The idea behind enhanced indexing is simple. Staying as close as you can to the index, you try to find pockets of mispricing that allow you to deliver slightly higher returns than the index. Broadly speaking, there are four classes of enhanced indexing strategies.

1. In *synthetic enhancement strategies,* you build on the derivatives strategies that we described in the preceding section. Using the whole range of derivatives—futures, options, and swaps—that may be available at any time on an index, you look for mispricing that you can use to replicate the index and generate additional returns. With a futures-based strategy, Elton, Gruber, Comer, and Li note that since the implicit spot price (estimated from the arbitrage relationship) in S&P futures contracts is generally slightly lower than the actual spot price, a strategy of investing in futures may generate returns that exceed the returns on the index.
2. In *stock-based enhancement strategies,* you adopt a more conventional active strategy using either stock selection or allocation to generate the excess returns. To see how the first would work, consider a strategy of holding all but the 20 most overvalued stocks in the S&P 500. If you could correctly identify these 20 stocks, you would have a portfolio that closely mimicked the index while delivering higher returns. In the second approach, you would hold all the stocks in the index but you would overweight those stocks or sectors that you believed to be undervalued and underweight those that you believed to be overvalued.

How would you identify these? You could use any of the strategies described in earlier chapters, ranging from screening to intrinsic valuation, to come up with the valuations.

3. In *quantitative enhancement strategies*, you use the mean-variance framework that is the foundation of modern portfolio theory to determine the optimal portfolio in terms of the trade-off between risk and return. Thus, if you have the expected return and standard deviation of each stock in the S&P 500 index and the correlations between every pair of stocks, you can find the portfolio that generates the best trade-off between return and risk.[44]

4. In *fundamental enhancement strategies*, you tilt the index fund more heavily or only toward stocks that have been shown to generate excess returns in the past: value stocks with price momentum, for instance. Arnott, Hsu, and West argue that "fundamental indexing" yields the best of both worlds: the low transaction costs of index funds and the excess returns of value-based strategies.[45]

Especially with the second and fourth strategies, notice that the only real difference between an enhanced indexing strategy and any other active investment strategy is the constraint that the portfolio you create stay close to the index. In fact, it is misleading to even label these funds as "index" funds, since they are active investing strategies in a different guise. You could argue that investors in these funds would be better served if these funds stripped the index component from their labels and looked for more efficient ways to exploit the inefficiencies that they claim to benefit from.

Tracking Error, Information Ratio, and Closet Indexing   Since enhanced index funds claim that they are index funds that deliver extra returns, their risk is measured by looking at how much the returns on these funds deviate, period by period, from the returns on the index. As we noted in Chapter 6, the measure used for this is tracking error and is computed by taking the squared deviations of the returns on the fund from the returns on the index. A fund that perfectly tracks the index will have zero tracking error. An enhanced indexed fund will always have a tracking error that exceeds zero, but if it delivers on its promise, it will also have a return greater than the

---

[44]This is not a new idea. Harry Markowitz laid the foundations by capital market theory by explaining portfolio optimization in the 1950s.

[45]R. Arnott, J. Hsu, and J. M. West, *The Fundamental Index: A Better Way to Invest* (Hoboken, NJ: John Wiley & Sons, 2008).

index. The performance measure used therefore to evaluate enhanced index funds looks at the ratio of returns in excess of the S&P 500 to the tracking error.

$$\text{Information ratio} = \frac{(\text{Return on enhanced fund} - \text{Returns on index})}{\text{Tracking error}}$$

The nature of the constraint imposed on enhanced index funds becomes clear when we look at the tracking error. Since it is measured as the deviation between the fund's return and the index return in any period, and positive deviations count as much as negative deviations, it operates as a limit on investing outside the index or letting allocations within the fund deviate too much from the index allocations. In other words, if you are a portfolio manager who is judged based on tracking error, and you have to choose between two undervalued stocks, one undervalued by 10 percent and within the index and one undervalued by 25 percent and outside the index, you may very well go with the first because the latter will create a much larger tracking error.

If you define enhanced index funds as funds that have low tracking error and try to deliver excess returns, they are not that different from their mirror image on the active management side: active funds that are closet index funds. These funds preserve the front of active funds, with claims to an investment philosophy, promises of higher returns, and high management fees, but are increasingly passive in their holdings, thus resembling index funds, in a large subset of their holdings. One study of U.S. mutual funds argues that not only is closet indexing common in the mutual fund business, but its prevalence is increasing over time and it results in these funds underperforming the market.[46] Computing the passive portion of the portfolio by comparing the holdings of active funds to an index and using Fidelity Magellan to illustrate the shift over time under different managers, you arrive at the results in Figure 13.20.

While some of the shift toward passive investing can be attributed to the growth in the fund from the small, growth mutual fund that Peter Lynch ran to the behemoth in the later periods, it is clearly also a function of managerial style, with the fund essentially becoming an index fund under Robert Stansky, who ran the fun for an extended period, before reverting back to more activity in recent years. A recent extension of this study to global mutual funds finds that the phenomenon of closet indexing is

---

[46] M. Cremers and A. Petajisto, "How Active Is Your Fund Manager? A New Measure That Predicts Performance" (SSRN Working Paper, 2009).

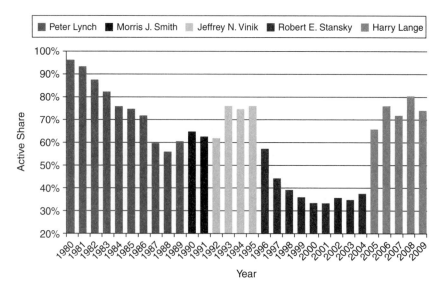

FIGURE 13.20   Fidelity Magellan: Active and Passive Portions
Source: M. Cremers and A. Petajisto, "How Active Is Your Fund Manager? A New Measure That Predicts Performance" (SSRN Working Paper, 2009).

prevalent globally and that closet indexers underpeform the market by roughly 1 percent.[47]

Performance   While the promise of enhanced index funds is index fund risk with enhanced returns, it remains an open question as to whether this combination is delivered. Riepe and Zils examined 10 enhanced index funds, two of which used synthetic enhancement strategies and eight of which used stock-based or quantitative strategies, from 1991 to 1997.[48] They compared the annual returns on each fund to the returns on the S&P 500 index, and their findings are summarized in Figure 13.21.

While the names of the funds were not revealed, the period for which each fund had been in existence was provided and is reported next to the fund. Note that three of the 10 funds delivered returns lower than the S&P 500, which clearly puts the "enhancement" part of the strategy into question. When the standard deviations in returns on the funds were compared

---

[47]M. Cremers, M. A. Ferreira, P. P. Matos, and L. T. Starks, "The Mutual Fund Industry Worldwide: Explicit and Closet Indexing, Fees and Performance" (SSRN Working Paper 891719, 2011).

[48]M. W. Riepe and J. Zils, "Are Enhanced Index Mutual Funds Worthy of Their Name?" (working paper, Ibbotson Associates, 1997).

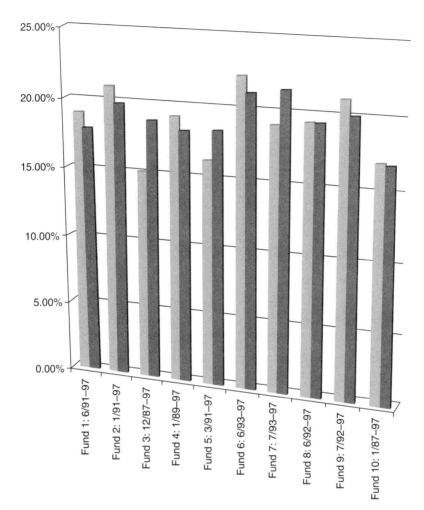

FIGURE 13.21 Enhanced Index Funds versus S&P 500
Source: M. W. Riepe and J. Zils, "Are Enhanced Index Mutual Funds Worthy of
Their Name?" (working paper, Ibbotson Associates, 1997).

to the S&P 500 (in Figure 13.22), seven of the 10 funds reported standard deviations that exceeded that of the index, raising doubts about the
"indexing" part of the strategy.

A study of the behavior and holdings of enhanced index funds finds interesting patterns in their deviations from the index. In particular, enhanced
index funds are overweighted in stocks with higher liquidity, larger capitalization, and higher past performance (price momentum). They are less

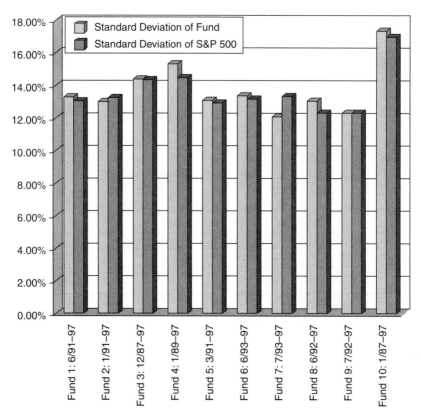

FIGURE 13.22 Enhanced Index Funds: Standard Deviation versus S&P 500
Source: M. W. Riepe and J. Zils, "Are Enhanced Index Mutual Funds Worthy of Their Name?" (working paper, Ibbotson Associates, 1997).

rigid about rebalancing their portfolios and more patient about trading, especially around index rebalancing (where new stocks get added and others get removed from the index).[49]

These findings do not surprise us. The only rationale that can be offered for why a more constrained strategy (like enhanced indexing) may outperform a less constrained strategy (like active money management) is that it protects fund managers from their own excesses. The constraints on staying within the index may reduce the style shifting and resulting turnover that is

---

[49]A. Frino, D. R. Gallagher, and T. N. Oetomo, "The Index Tracking Strategies of Passive and Enhanced Index Equity Funds" (SSRN Working Paper 621462, 2005).

so destructive in conventional mutual funds. If finding bargains in a market is difficult to begin with, handicapping yourself to stay within a specified index and constraining yourself to have returns that also track the index returns will make it doubly difficult to find those bargains.

ACTIVE/PASSIVE ALLOCATION

We have presented the choice between index funds and actively managed funds as an all-or-nothing proposition: you either invest all of your money actively or invest all of your money passively. However, there are some investors who may be more comfortable splitting the funds that they have to invest between passive and active management, depending both on their views of the payoffs to active money management and on where they are in the investment cycle. Thus, you may allocate 60 percent of your funds to actively managed funds and 40 percent to index funds in one year and reverse the allocations in the next.

Another way you can combine passive and active investing is to use specialized index funds to exploit your market timing skills. If you have a good track record on forecasting which style of investing— value or growth—will dominate in the next period, you may switch from value index funds to growth index funds to exploit this skill. Similarly, you can use sector-based index funds to take advantage of sector rotation in the market.

CONCLUSION

In the preceding six chapters, we presented substantial evidence of irregularities in market behavior related to systematic factors such as size, price-earnings ratios, and price-to-book value ratios. We noted that there are individual investment strategies that seem to make excess returns on paper and that there may even be arbitrage opportunities. If you can trade on information in a timely fashion, you may be able to augment these returns. You can consider this chapter to be both a cautionary note and a reality check.

While there may be pockets of inefficiency in the market and substantial evidence that markets make mistakes, there is also the sobering evidence that professional money managers, who are in a position to best exploit these inefficiencies, have a very difficult time consistently beating financial markets. Read together, the persistence of the irregularities and the inability of money managers to beat the market provide testimony to the gap between tests on paper portfolios and real-world money management. It should also remind us of the fact that investors and portfolio managers are human and succumb to some very human frailties—hubris, insecurity, and herd behavior, to name a few. The performance of active money managers provides the best evidence yet that indexing may be the best strategy for many investors.

EXERCISES

1. Pick an actively managed mutual fund at random and evaluate the following:
    a. The pretax returns generated by this fund over the past quarter, year, and five years.
    b. The after-tax returns generated by this fund over the past quarter, year, and five years.
    c. The management fees and other expenses at the fund on an annual basis.
    d. The turnover ratio at the fund over the past year and five years.
2. Look at the Vanguard 500 Index fund over the same periods and estimate the same numbers.
3. Given your fund's categorization (small-cap, mid-cap, or large-cap; value, growth, or blend), find an index fund in the same category. Estimate the numbers for this index fund.
4. Assess whether you as an investor would have beaten the index fund over the past year and the past five years:
    a. On a pretax return basis, with no adjustment for risk.
    b. On an after-tax return basis, with no adjustment for risk.
    c. On a pretax return basis, with an adjustment for risk (Sharpe ratio or Jensen's alpha).
    d. On an after-tax return basis, with an adjustment for risk (Sharpe ratio or Jensen's alpha).
5. Given your performance evaluation numbers in the last part, how would you explain the mutual fund's performance? (If it outperformed, what explains the outperformance? If it underperformed, why?)

Lessons for Investors

To invest successfully in actively managed funds, you need to:

- *Understand that the odds are against you:* The average active mutual fund underperforms the average index fund on a pretax basis. On an after-tax basis, actively run funds underperform index funds by even more. The underperformance shows up in funds in every style class.
- *Recognize why active funds underperform:* The average active mutual fund is much too active, trades too much, and holds too much cash, all of which drag down returns. You need to find funds that stay consistent in their investment styles and keep their expenses (both management and trading) under control.
- *Not rely too heavily on past performance:* While there may be some short-term persistence in fund performance, it is weak and it is very likely to be overwhelmed by the additional fees and expenses that funds add on after a good year.
- *Pick a fund that is close to your investment philosophy:* In other words, if your instincts lead you to be a value investor, you should pick a value fund.
- *Keep open the possibility that an index fund may still be your best choice:* You should measure active funds not against each other but against index funds in their category. If they consistently fail to measure up, notwithstanding your best efforts to pick the right funds, you should switch to index funds.

CHAPTER 14

A Road Map to Choosing an Investment Philosophy

If the purpose of this book is to provide you with the tools to pick an investment philosophy, you may very well feel that it has failed. After all, there seems to be both good and bad in every philosophy and no one philosophy seems to dominate over time and yield consistent winners. What purpose has been served, you may wonder, from this examination of diverse and contradictory views of how markets work and fail to work? In this chapter, we hope to not only wrap up loose ends but also bring the process of picking a philosophy back to you as an investor.

A SELF-ASSESSMENT

As we noted in Chapter 1, there is no one investment philosophy that is best suited for all investors, and much of what we have said in the intervening chapters reinforces this point. A strategy that works for an investor who is patient and has substantial capital to invest may not work for an investor with unpredictable cash needs and a smaller portfolio. In this section, we consider three aspects that will help determine your investment philosophy: your personal characteristics as an individual, your financial standing, and the beliefs you have formed about markets.

Personal Characteristics

Investors who pick investment philosophies that do not fit their personalities are destined to abandon them sooner rather than later, weighed down not just by the fact that they do not work for them but by personal discomfort with the vagaries of their portfolios. While some of the factors in this section may come perilously close to being on a psychiatrist's couch, you cannot be a successful investor if you do not have a clear-eyed view of your own strengths and weaknesses.

- *Patience.* Some investment strategies require a great deal of patience, a virtue that many of us lack. Much as you may plead with the powers that be for more patience, you have to accept the reality that you may not be suited to an investment strategy that requires 10 years of waiting for rewards. If impatient by nature, you should consider adopting an investment philosophy that provides payoffs in the short term.
- *Risk aversion.* Your willingness to bear risk should play a key role in what investment philosophy or strategy you choose for yourself. If you are risk averse, adopting a strategy that entails a great deal of risk—trading on earnings announcements, for instance—will not be a strategy that works for you in the long term.
- *Individual or group thinker?* Some investment strategies require you to go along with the crowd and some against it. Which one will be better suited for you may well depend on whether you are more comfortable going along with the conventional wisdom or you are a loner or an independent thinker. If you are easily subject to peer pressure, the odds are high that you will be uncomfortable with contrarian philosophies. If, however, you are comfortable going against the crowd, the fact that most investors are betting against you may bother you little or not at all.
- *Time you are willing to spend on investing.* Some investment strategies are much more time and resource intensive than others. Generally, short-term strategies that are based on pricing patterns or on trading on information are more time and information intensive than long-term buy-and-hold strategies.
- *Age.* If you are an individual investor, your age clearly will make a difference in your choice of investment philosophy. To begin with, as you age, you may find that your willingness to take risk, especially with your retirement savings, decreases. Investment philosophies that you found attractive when you were younger may no longer be attractive or appropriate vehicles for you. With age, they say, also comes wisdom, though we are not sure that this adage applies to investing. It is true, though, that even as a successful investor, you will have learned lessons from prior investment experiences that will both constrain and guide your choice of investment philosophy.

In summary, your choice of investment philosophy is only partially under your control. Even if you are a patient investor who is willing to go against the crowd, you may find that as you age and become more risk averse, your philosophy and the strategies that go with it have to be modified.

THREE SIGNS OF A MISFIT

1. *You lie awake at night thinking about your portfolio.* Investors who choose investment strategies that expose them to more risk than they are comfortable taking will find themselves facing this plight. It is true that your expected returns will probably be lower with low-risk strategies, but the cost of taking on too much risk is even greater.

2. *Day-to-day movements in your portfolio lead to reassessments of your future.* Though long-term movements of your portfolio should affect your plans on when you will retire and what you will do with your future, day-to-day movements should not. It is common in every market downturn to read about older investors, on the verge or retirement, having to put off retiring because of the damage created to their portfolios. While some of them may have no choice when it comes to where they invest, most investors do have the choice of shifting into low-risk investments (bonds) as they approach retirement.

3. *Second-guessing your investment decisions.* If you find yourself second-guessing your investment choices every time you read a contrary opinion, you should reconsider your strategy.

Financial Characteristics

Your choice of investment philosophy will also be affected by your financial characteristics: your job security, the money you have to invest, your cash needs, and your tax status. Since these characteristics change over time, you may have to modify your investment choices to reflect these changes.

Job Security and Earning Capacity   One of the interesting characteristics that we see with financial markets is that investors become more risk averse as the economy weakens; you see this in the widening of default spreads on bonds and in the increase in equity risk premiums during recessions. While we can present a macroeconomic story for why this happens, we suspect that a great deal of what we see reflects personal insecurity. In the midst of a recession, even those with jobs worry more about their investments and demand larger risk premiums for investing in assets. The flight to quality and, at the limit, to riskless investments is exacerbated by natural and financial crises.

Your investment philosophy will also be heavily influenced by what you perceive your earning capacity to be. If you expect to earn a high income that more than covers your expenses, you have a far greater degree of freedom when it comes to picking an investment philosophy. If, though, your income barely covers your expenses or, worse still, it falls short, your investment portfolio will have to be tailored to meet your cash needs.

How will this affect your choice of investment philosophy? If you are lucky enough to have a high and predictable income, you can adopt an investment strategy that yields little in the short term but has large payoffs in the long term. If the lessons about risk and return that we have drawn in investing apply to human capital, high-income jobs will probably come with less security, and you will have to invest accordingly. Ultimately, your willingness to bear risk and your time horizon will be heavily influenced by both the level and the predictability of your earnings.

Investment Funds Your choices in terms of investment philosophy expand as the funds at your disposal increase. It may be unfair, but if you have a few thousand dollars to invest, you have little choice but to invest in an index fund. If, by contrast, you have several hundred thousand dollars to invest, most of the investment philosophies in this book become viable. When considering the investment funds at your disposal, you should look at not only your savings but also money that you have accumulated in pension funds, individual retirement accounts (IRAs), and insurance savings accounts. While you are sometimes restricted in your investment choices on some of these funds, you have more choice now than you used to and odds are that your choices will continue to increase over time.

Cash Needs One of the perils we face both as individual investors and as portfolio managers is unpredictable demands for cash withdrawals. For individual investors, this may occur as the result of a personal crisis—a sickness that is not covered by health insurance or the unanticipated loss of income. For professional money managers, it arises because clients can change their minds and demand their money back. If this occurs, you may have to liquidate your investments and lose any long-term return potential that you may have in them.

If your cash demands are unpredictable, what can you do? While you may not be able to forecast when cash withdrawals may need to occur, you can still consider the probabilities when you choose your investment philosophy. If you are a salesperson and you make the bulk of your income from commissions, you should expect more volatility in your income and a greater likelihood that you will have cash withdrawals. If you are a portfolio manager of a small technology fund, you should also assume that your investors are much more likely to shift their savings out of your fund, if you have a bad year. In either case, the expected need for cash shortens your time horizon and may ultimately require you to adopt an investment philosophy with a shorter payoff period.

Tax Status Much as you wish otherwise, you have to pay taxes and it would be imprudent to pick an investment strategy without considering your tax status. Investors who face high taxes on income should choose investment strategies that reduce their tax liabilities or at least defer taxes into the future. What makes the interplay between investment philosophy and taxes complicated is the fact that different portions of the same individual's income can be subject to different tax treatment. Thus, an investor, when deciding what to buy with her pension fund where income is tax exempt, may adopt a strategy that generates large amounts of current income, but when investing her personal savings, she has to be more careful about tax liabilities.

Market Beliefs

This is perhaps the most difficult component for investors to wrestle with, for several reasons. The first is that so much of what we believe about markets comes from anecdotal evidence—from friends, relatives. and experts in the field. It is to provide a counterbalance that we have looked at the prevailing empirical evidence and disagreements among researchers on what works and does not work in financial markets. Needless to say, our work is never finished since new research continues to be done and there are new market experiences to chronicle.

The second problem is that your views about market behavior and the performance of investment strategies will undoubtedly change over time, but all you can do is make your choices based on what you know today. In fact, while staying consistent with regard to an investment philosophy and core market beliefs may be central to success in investing, it would be foolhardy to stay consistent as the evidence accumulates against the philosophy.

FINDING AN INVESTMENT PHILOSOPHY

We have looked at a variety of investment philosophies in the course of this book and provided some evidence on when they work best and when they fail. We have also categorized these strategies based on a number of different dimensions: time horizon, funds needed for success, and beliefs about market behavior. We will begin with a summary of these findings and then look at matching an investment philosophy to your financial and personal characteristics.

The Choices

Considering again all of the choices in terms of investment philosophy laid out in this book, we can categorize them based on the three criteria noted earlier. While some of these categorizations are hazy—a strategy may be more medium-term than long-term or more opportunistic than contrarian—they are useful nevertheless.

Time Horizon   The time horizon required to succeed at an investment philosophy and the strategies that flow from it run the gamut. At one extreme are the long-term strategies such as investing in loser stocks (ones that have gone down the most over the past six months or year). These require you to invest for five or more years, and success is by no means guaranteed even then. At the other extreme are strategies where the time horizon is measured in hours or days, which is where we would categorize trading on earnings announcements and pure arbitrage strategies. In the middle lie strategies that need several months to a few years to unfold (buying stocks on relative strength is one example).

Capital Requirements   The funds that you need to invest to be successful at investing also vary across strategies. Some strategies require very large portfolios and the benefits that flow from them: low transaction costs, large positions in individual companies, and diversification. This is true, for instance, with activist value investing and activist growth investing. Other strategies may be feasible even to investors with small portfolios; a style-switching strategy where you switch from value to growth mutual funds and vice versa, depending on your expectations of earnings growth in future periods would be a good example. Finally, there are some strategies where you need to be large enough to be able to have low execution costs and access to debt but not so large that you create a price impact every time you trade. This is the case with several near or pseudo arbitrage strategies.

Market Beliefs   We can categorize all of the investment strategies described in this book into three groups based on the underlying market beliefs that drive them. The first set of strategies can be categorized as momentum strategies; that is, they are based on the assumption that what has happened in the recent past is likely to continue to happen in the future. Here, we would include most of the technical momentum indicators, such as trend lines and relative strength, as well as some passive growth investing strategies that are based on momentum in earnings growth. The second set of strategies are contrarian strategies, where you assume that there is a tendency for all aspects of firm behavior—earnings growth, stock returns, and multiples such as price-earnings (P/E)—to revert back to historical averages over time. Value investing strategies, where you buy stocks whose prices have hit lows or after substantial bad news, are a good example, as are market timing strategies based on normalized P/E ratios and interest rates. The third set of strategies are opportunistic, where you assume that markets make mistakes and that these mistakes can sometimes lead prices to overshoot (which is what contrarians assume) and sometimes to undershoot (which is what momentum investors assume). Most arbitrage strategies and some technical indicators (such as price patterns and cycles) can be categorized in this group. Note that there is a fourth group here that we have not recognized explicitly. If we assume that markets are efficient—mistakes are random, cut both ways, and are unlikely to be uncovered by investors searching for them—the appropriate strategy is indexing.

In Table 14.1, we categorize most of the strategies described in this book, based on time horizon and market beliefs. We also highlight in italics the strategies that we believe are *not* feasible for small investors.

THE RIGHT INVESTMENT PHILOSOPHY

Once you have an inventory of your personal needs and preferences, finding an investment philosophy that is most appropriate for you should be a simple exercise, but you have two choices:

1. *Single best strategy.* You can choose the one strategy that best suits you. Thus, if you are a long-term investor who believes that markets overreact, you may adopt a passive value investing strategy.
2. *Combination of strategies.* You can adopt a combination of strategies to maximize your returns. For instance, you may mix in a basic long-term strategy of passive growth investing with a medium-term strategy of buying stocks with high relative strength. Obviously, you are hoping to augment your returns from the first strategy with your returns on the second. In creating this combined strategy, you should keep in mind the following caveats:
   - You should not mix strategies that make contradictory assumptions about market behavior over the same periods. Thus, a strategy of buying on relative strength would not be compatible with a strategy of buying stocks after very negative earnings announcements. The

TABLE 14.1 Categorizing Investment Philosophies

	Momentum	Contrarian	Opportunistic
Short-term (days to a few weeks)	Technical momentum indicators: Buying stocks based on trend lines and high trading volume. Information trading: Buying after positive news (earnings and dividend announcements, acquisition announcements).	Technical contrarian indicators: Mutual fund holdings, short interest. These can be for individual stocks or for the overall market.	*Pure arbitrage in derivatives and fixed income markets.* Technical demand indicators: Patterns in prices such as head and shoulders.
Medium-term (a few months to a couple of years)	Relative strength: Buying stocks that have gone up in the past few months. Information trading: Buying small-cap stocks with substantial insider buying.	Market timing, based on normal P/E or normal range of interest rates. Information trading: Buying after bad news (buying a week after bad earnings reports and holding for a few months)	Near arbitrage opportunities: Buying discounted closed-end funds. *Speculative arbitrage opportunities: Buying paired stocks and merger arbitrage.*
Long-term (several years)	Passive growth investing: Buying stocks where growth trades at a reasonable price (PEG ratios).	Passive value investing: Buying stocks with low P/E, PBV, or P/S ratios. Contrarian value investing: Buying losers or stocks with lots of bad news.	*Active growth investing: Taking stakes in small growth companies (private equity and venture capital investing).* *Activist value investing: Buying stocks in poorly managed companies and pushing for change.*

Italicized strategies: Strategies that are *not* feasible for small investors.

582

first strategy is based on the assumption that markets learn slowly whereas the latter is conditioned on market overreaction.

- When you mix strategies, you should separate the dominant strategy from the secondary strategies. Thus, if you have to make choices in terms of investments, you know which strategy will dominate.

Review and Introspection

Investing is a continuous process, and you learn (or should learn) all the time from both your successes and your failures. You learn about how other investors in the market behave, and you learn about yourself. Your circumstances in terms of job security (or at least the perception of it) and income also change. As a consequence, you may have to revisit the decision of which investment philosophy is best suited for you repeatedly, and in some cases, change that philosophy to reflect both what you have learned in the recent past and your current status. In making these changes, though, you should fight the temptation to go with the strategy that worked best in the recent past or worked for someone else.

It is worth noting that to succeed with an investment philosophy, you have to bring something to the table that is in scarce supply in markets at that point in time, and it is good to isolate what that competitive edge is. Is it that you are more patient or need liquidity less than most other investors? Is it your tax status? Is it your capacity to collect and process information? Whatever advantage lies at the heart of your success needs to be nurtured and protected.

CONCLUSION

Choosing an investment philosophy is at the heart of successful investing. To make the choice, though, you need to look within before you look outside. The best strategy for you is one that matches both your personality and your needs. If you are patient by nature, have a secure income stream, and have little or no need for cash withdrawals, you can choose a strategy that may be risky in the short term but has a good chance of paying off in the long term. If, by contrast, you cannot wait for extended periods and you have immediate cash needs, you may have to settle for a shorter-term strategy.

Your choice of philosophy will also be affected by what you believe about markets and investors and how they work (or do not). You may come to the conclusion that markets overreact to news (in which case you would migrate toward contrarian strategies), markets learn slowly (leading to momentum strategies), markets make mistakes in both directions (yielding opportunistic strategies), or market mistakes are random. Since your beliefs are likely to be affected by your experiences, they will evolve over time and your investment strategies have to follow suit.

EXERCISES

1. Self-assessment:
   a. Time horizon:
      i. Psychologically, what is your time horizon? (How patient are you?)
      ii. Financially, what is your time horizon? (If you have significant cash flow needs in the near future, your time horizon is shortened.)
   b. Risk aversion:
      i. Are you more or less risk averse than most investors?
      ii. How did you come to this judgment?
         Try this online test to measure your risk aversion: http://hec.osu .edu/people/shanna/risk/invrisk.htm.
         It leads you through a series of simple choices to make a judgment of your risk aversion.
   c. Taxes:
      i. In the most recent year, what did you pay as your effective tax rate (taxes paid/adjusted gross income)?
      ii. What was your marginal tax rate (on your last dollar of income, including state and local taxes)?
      iii. Do you foresee your tax rates changing in the future?
      iv. Is any portion of your portfolio subject to a different tax treatment, such as a 401(k), pension plan, or IRA?
2. Market assessment:
   a. Given that markets make mistakes, do you think that those mistakes are systematic and can be exploited?
   b. If yes, what types of mistakes do you think markets make?
3. Investment philosophy/strategies:
   a. Given your personal characteristics (from exercise 1) and your views on the market (from 2), what investment philosophy or philosophies best fits you?
   b. What strategy or strategies do you plan to employ within this philosophy? Why?
   c. Why do you think you can beat the market with these strategies?

Index